Conceptual Foundations of Business

THE IRWIN SERIES IN MANAGEMENT

CONSULTING EDITOR   JOHN F. MEE   *Indiana University*

AMMER   *Materials Management*   rev. ed.

BRENNAN   *Wage Administration: Plans, Practices, and Principles*   rev. ed.

BROOM   *Production Management*   rev. ed.

CHAMPION & BRIDGES   *Critical Incidents in Management*   rev. ed.

EELLS & WALTON   *Conceptual Foundations of Business*   rev. ed.

FARMER & RICHMAN   *Comparative Management and Economic Progress*

GREENE   *Production Control: Systems and Decisions*

HANEY   *Communication and Organizational Behavior: Text and Cases*   rev. ed.

HOUSTON   *Manager Development: Principles and Perspectives*

JONES   *Executive Decision Making*   rev. ed.

JUCIUS   *Personnel Management*   6th ed.

JUCIUS & SCHLENDER   *Elements of Managerial Action*   rev. ed.

LING   *The Management of Personnel Relations: History and Origins*

MCDONOUGH & GARRETT   *Management Systems: Working Concepts and Practices*

MEGGINSON   *Personnel: A Behavioral Approach to Administration*

MOORE   *Manufacturing Management*   5th ed.

MOORE & KIBBEY   *Manufacturing: Materials and Processes*

MORRIS   *The Analysis of Management Decisions*   rev. ed.

NADLER   *Work Design*

NIEBEL   *Motion and Time Study*   4th ed.

PATTON, LITTLEFIELD, & SELF   *Job Evaluation: Text and Cases*   3d ed.

PRINCE   *Information Systems for Management Planning and Control*

REED   *Plant Layout: Factors, Principles, and Techniques*

RICHARDS & GREENLAW   *Management Decision Making*

ROSCOE   *Organization for Production: An Introduction to Industrial Management*   4th ed.

ROSCOE   *Project Economy*

SCOTT   *Organization Theory: A Behavioral Analysis for Management*

SEIMER   *Cases in Industrial Management*

SIEGEL   *Industrial Psychology*

SIMONDS & GRIMALDI   *Safety Management: Accident Cost and Control*   rev. ed.

SPRIEGEL & MYERS (eds.)   *The Writings of the Gilbreths*

TERRY   *Principles of Management*   5th ed.

THAYER   *Communication and Communication Systems: In Organization Management and Interpersonal Relations*

TIMMS   *The Production Function in Business: Fundamentals and Analysis for Management*   rev. ed.

VORIS   *Production Control: Text and Cases*   3d ed.

WEBBER   *Culture and Management: Text and Readings in Comparative Management*

Conceptual Foundations
of Business

RICHARD EELLS
Director, Studies of the
Modern Corporation, and
Adjunct Professor of Business

CLARENCE WALTON
Dean, School of General Studies, and
Professor of Business Institutions

Both of Columbia University

1969
Revised Edition

Richard D. Irwin, Inc., Homewood, Illinois
Irwin-Dorsey Limited, Georgetown, Ontario

Revised Edition

FIRST PRINTING, MARCH, 1969

Library of Congress Catalog Card No. 69-17162

Printed in the United States of America

Preface

DURING THE last half century, American business has become one of the most complex institutions in a rapidly evolving and equally complex society. This evolution has resulted from rapid growth and structural change, progress in technology, extensive product and market diversification, and most significantly, from a growing recognition of the cultural impact of business. The corporation, initially conceived simply as a convenient means of marshalling capital and transacting business, has become a vigorous influence among the social institutions of our day. Profit is, and will continue to be, the major measure of the effectiveness of any business, but the complete goals of today's large business organization are no longer exclusively economic. If "a great society is a society in which its men of business think greatly of their function," then such men—to be prepared to handle the involved and far-ranging affairs of a modern business—should see their institution as a part of a larger whole.

Today, more than ever before, the survival of business as an independent institution depends not on profit alone, but on the values businessmen perceive in such basic concepts as freedom, ownership, governance, a flexible economy, and progress with reasonable stability, all of which have created and which help to sustain competitive business enterprise in the free world. For those who would manage the corporation, mere capability is not enough. The corporate executive must be broadly grounded in his attitudes and able to make decisions and take actions that are at once profitable and compatible with the accepted values of his society.

Just a decade ago, a Faculty Task Force on curriculum revision of the Graduate School of Business, Columbia University, chaired by Professor Ernest M. Fisher, stated the intent and the broad purposes that lay behind the establishment of a proposed new course on the "legal, philosophical, and historical foundations" of the institution of business in the United States, describing it as:

v

. . . a study of the major ideas and institutions that make up an important part of the environment within which business transactions take place. The ideas would be those philosophical concepts which have helped to shape business and society and which continue to compete for the people's loyalty. The institutions to be covered would include not only business institutions but also those legal and political institutions which have a major bearing on business.

While the total task of curriculum revision was made possible by generous assistance of the Ford Foundation, the course project was financed in part by grants from the General Electric Foundation, and the United States Steel Foundation.

Once the study had produced the course, and the course had been offered at Columbia in four successive academic terms, the course demanded a text. It was to meet this need that the first edition of the present book was prepared. We have approached the study of business as an institution by synthesizing the thinking from a number of disciplines, including economics, but ranging beyond into areas of philosophy, history, and the social sciences.

The present text is designed to enable students of business to broaden their horizons and better prepare themselves for the increasing number and variety of considerations that now enter into the conduct of a business. It should be useful also to businessmen who have come to realize from experience that the "going concern" must frequently take new bearings if it is to keep going, and that only by such reappraisal of its environment can it affirm its course and maintain its progress.

The authors wish to express their gratitude to Professor J. P. Farhi of Hofstra University for his help with Chapter 15, and to Professor Miguel León-Portilla, of the University of Mexico for the Appendix on the business institution in Pre-Columbian Mexico.

February, 1969   RICHARD EELLS
                                                     CLARENCE WALTON

Table of Contents

General Introduction

It is an overworked truism to say that today's business leader needs a breadth of view and depth of perception not demanded of his 19th-century predecessors. Two factors, particularly, operate to make difficult the actual realization of the businessman's stated need. The first is the large corporation whose many-sidedness makes synthesis difficult to achieve. Divided as it often is into a line-and-staff hierarchy designated as Operations and Services, it today employs not only technical specialists, skilled labor, and salesmen, but a wide variety of professionals who have brought into it knowledge from many disciplines. Indeed, professionalization itself is both cause and effect of our division-of-labor concept. The facile way we speak of the human being as "economic man" or "political man," the way we tend to identify people not by what they are but by what they do—accountant, farmer, lawyer—are examples.

The second obstacle to synthesis is related to the modern intellectual tradition. Growth of knowledge has encouraged specialization because inquiry appears more fruitful as one studies parts rather than the whole. Political science has broken from social philosophy even as economics has parted from political science. While the specialization has brought great gains, it must also be noted that certain losses were occasioned as well. One might note, for example, how the intellectual loss (occasioned by the moving away of economics from social philosophy) was compounded by the drift of philosophers and political theorists—especially since the days of Bentham and his fellow philosophic radicals—from the world of economics.

Fragmentary knowledge and fragmentary work have convinced many observers that man himself has been irreparably dissected, that he has been reduced to a shadow by his own Frankenstein.

1

Roderick Seidenberg, reviewing these tendencies in his *Post Historic Man*, concluded that man himself had become like his tools, his workbench, his gadgets—simply a prop on a vast, somber industrial stage. Though we recognize these problems, it is our conviction that affluence need not corrode moral fiber nor organizational bigness dwarf the significance of the individual man. Yet these things surely can occur unless we examine certain concepts which make man, his institutions, and his forms of organization meaningful.

For these reasons we have found it revealing to consider the meaning of today's business in the light of those ideas and concepts which are the foundations upon which our society is constructed: freedom, ownership, the market economy, constitutionalism, and the idea of progress with stability.

In any free and democratic society these foundations are periodically threatened. Under the towering civilization reared by the West, the seismic tremors are so audible that the traditional American optimism appears, to many, more a hideous vice than a heroic virtue; there are, as a current image puts it, cracks in the cornucopia! Perceptive scholars like Emmet Hughes and Robert Heilbroner warn that our abundance and glory are fast fading into a grimmer kind of existence. "Optimism as a philosophy of historic expectations can no longer be considered a national virtue. It has become a dangerous national delusion."[1]

The indictments follow one of two major themes. The first leads to an excoriation of Americans because economic wealth and technological brilliance are dissipated by political impotence. A decade ago Barbara Ward predicted the likely development of the sixties when she wrote the following:

> In short, in the world of the Sixties, we in the West shall form a small, wealthy elite in the vast, poverty-stricken society of mankind—a society shot through with revolutionary prospects and desires. Confronted with this fact, we have only two choices. We can follow the fatal road of other wealthy elites, like the pampered courts of Cnossus or the French nobility at Versailles, play our games and close our hearts until the unfolding of a wider destiny engulfs us all.
>
> Or we can use our wealth to redeem the promise of our free society and extend its work to our fellow men who everywhere labor and look

---

[1] Robert Heilbroner, *The Future As History* (New York: Harper & Bros., 1960). See also Emmet John Hughes, *America the Vincible* (New York: Doubleday and Co., 1959).

for change and growth with minds divided between penury and hope. The Sixties will compel the taking of this decision. On it, in great measure, our future in freedom depends.[2]

The second criticism concerns the alleged failure of American leadership—in government, in labor, and in business—to develop those necessary refinements in our basic ideas which make traditional concepts meaningful to modern conditions, when they have such relevance, and to go on from there toward the formulation of new concepts and new syntheses, when they do not.

There is, for example, a general awareness that both corporate and union management share a basic interest in understanding what "freedom of association" can do to provide a common dynamic and rationale for their respective functions and operations. Furthermore, it is widely recognized that the modern corporation has already run so far beyond the legal and economic rationalizations that seek to legitimize and explain it, that neither the scholar nor the executive can find a satisfactory vocabulary to articulate its essential meaning. There is a general conviction that such concepts as liberty, justice, and authority are principles which have an enduring vitality in every society. But what these concepts mean or how they relate to the current business order has not been systematically evaluated. Yet they are the anterior conditions which foster those conceptual foundations of business without which the American business system, as we know it, could not long endure.

It is precisely in these areas that we wish to push our inquiry. Janus-like, this investigation looks forward to probe into the meaning of a "great society" and backward to the Greeks, recognizing that what was pure gold for one society may be dross to another. For example, Aristotle's apologia for slavery or his *reproof* of the profit motive are unacceptable to American democracy and modern business, even while his insights into the social nature of man continue to have validity.

Clearly, then, two points begin to emerge. In dealing with the two aspects of this study, *concepts* and *institutions,* both history and prophecy have their respective roles to play, and the obvious interplay among various major concepts makes rigorous separation useless. To talk of freedom is to invite immediate scrutiny of freedom's restraints through the application of law; to study the market or

---

[2] *New York Times Magazine,* Dec. 27, 1959.

competition is to sense relationships with and dependence upon freedom; to consider ownership is to become involved in analyses of property, of contract, of justice, and of a man's work and leisure. The circle is ever widening.

What makes execution of the task doubly difficult is the fact that often the terms employed have emotional overtones and subjective meanings. Yet even when these are happily absent, the concepts may still elude precise definition because the historical and empirical data are inadequate, or because the terms themselves have undergone subtle changes of emphasis which scholars have been slow to notice and indicate. Thus we often equate feudalism with the medieval period when in point of fact feudal-vassal institutions had ceased to be an essential characteristic of the political system or social order of Western Europe by the end of the 13th century. A more modern misconstruction is the use of the term capitalism to describe an economic situation which no longer matches what was originally comprehended by this word. There is also the obverse confusion resulting from the tendency to describe old disciplines in terms of their modern function. Beyond titles for the functions of business organization like Government Relations, Labor Relations, Human Relations, Marketing Services, Legal Services, and a variety of other similar headings, lie such traditional academic disciplines as political science, sociology, anthropology, and psychology.

In this work we go beyond these specifically "business" functions to include forays into history, philosophy, and literature because we agree with William Benton who said that "it's not the function of an institution of higher learning to train a student for his first job, the common fault of business colleges. The principal objective should be to equip him with the navigating instruments for what Dr. James B. Conant, former president of Harvard, calls 'the continuous voyage'—the process of self-education."[3] Beyond the more precise economic goals of business institutions, intelligent administration of the large organization of our time demands a managerial point of view that is equally large. And this in turn calls for an awareness that leadership has a long historical and cultural heritage which provides an effective frame of reference for analysis and understanding of contemporary institutions.

One of the purposes of this text is to demonstrate the extent to

---

[3] William Benton, "The Failure of the Business Schools," *Saturday Evening Post,* Vol. 234 (Feb. 18, 1961) , pp. 26 and 73.

which traditional knowledge has contributed to—and been proliferated by—economic organization. We shall also attempt to provide
materials out of which parts may be related meaningfully to other
parts. The various essays are designed primarily, therefore, *to provide background* and, it is hoped, informed opinion for the suggested
readings which have been included under each major heading. In
a real sense, this book is an invitation to return to that kind of liberal study whose fundamental premise relies on a conviction of "the
dignity of man." It is based, as Panofsky eloquently stated, "on
both the insistence on human values (rationality and freedom) and
the acceptance of human limitations (fallibility and frailty) ; from
this two postulates result—responsibility and tolerance."[4]

It is one of the paradoxes of history that, by and large, *humanistic* progress has always been realized through the emergence, by
some means, of an elite—the capable and fortunate few. The Academy of Plato or the medieval cenoby are examples. But in the
modern world a liberal education cannot be confined to the "born
gentleman": it depends upon a generous, even prodigal Nature to
provide an "economy of abundance." The business world, too, must
"work to make the aristocrat, the man of grace, the person, as
numerous as fate allows."[5] In this era, when mass society threatens
dehumanization, we must still affirm that no society can long exist
unless the lowliest are free to become patricians or philosophers to
the fullest extent of their powers.

We can all agree that knowledge of what is at stake in science
and technology should become common knowledge, because such
knowledge has made the 20th century. Science and technology gave
us the compass which enlarged the world through discovery and
exploration; it also gave us the telescope, the microscope, and now
the computer—all tools which have increased our power to perceive,
and thence to conceive.

At the same time, a humanistic education, with its emphasis on
human ideas, human nature, and accumulated human experience,
to say nothing of the skills of communicating this information,
should also be common knowledge. Knowledge, all knowledge, is a
coat without seam. The emphasis of specialization which became
necessary to cope with the emergence of large organization in gov-

---

[4] Erwin Panofsky, "Art as a Humanistic Discipline," *Meaning in the Visual Arts*
(New York: Doubleday and Co., 1957) , p. 2.

[5] Mark Van Doren, *Liberal Education* (Boston: Beacon Press, 1959) , p. 31.

ernment, labor, education, and business, has erected an artificial dichotomy between the scientific and the liberal curriculum.

A decade ago the intellectual world was buzzing with the excitement—and controversy—generated by C. P. Snow. While much of the turbulence has subsided, it is worth recalling his ideas in order to stress a crucial point. At a symposium held at Harvard in May, 1960, on Snow's thesis (that there is a dangerous divorce between scientists and humanists as developed in *The Two Cultures and the Scientific Revolution*) the panelists pointed out that Snow's phrase "two cultures" overlooked an indispensable and extraordinary subculture: the group of organizers, enterprisers, decision and policy makers such as bankers, lawyers, and industrialists. This group who *made* the industrial revolution achieved a stupendous feat of social organization. For it was carried out over several decades within a stolidly traditional political and social framework by adapting, expanding, and accommodating society to industrial and technological change—all within a milieu that was indifferent, or even hostile, socially and aesthetically.

Other speakers at the symposium distinguished between *science,* "the effort to know and understand all aspects of reality," and *technology,* "the application of science." Science is knowing. It is a good that must be accepted and respected by society. But technology involves the necessity for social and political decisions; that is, every application of the technologist means far-reaching social and political decisions. Therefore, we must educate the governors, the administrators, and the businessmen to make these decisions intelligently and humbly. In short, the context of decision in technology implies aims, goals, and the aspirations of society as a whole. These are long term, prudential, and political.

Next, the panelists discriminated between *creating* (the "bringing forth of something new") and production (the "fabrication or multiplication of things already invented or made"). Creativity, it was maintained, should unreservedly be encouraged as a good. Conversely, production inhered in social and political conditions, and thus begot perplexing social and political problems.

We are living, they agreed, in a historical universe, with the ascent of matter through various organic forms culminating in man as a knowing and creating animal. Man, biologically, is a peculiar organization of molecules, but we cannot stop with the "merely material view," a spokesman said, because one such organization of molecules wrote *Hamlet*. In short, from the ultimate particles to the writing of poetry, there is one continuum; that is, when we have man, we have technology *and* poetry. Man is the only biological species with a highly developed capacity for symbolic thought, the use of language, and with the ability to build up a complex body of tradition known as culture.

An eloquent statement of this basic proposition has come from the distinguished French anthropologist, the late Pierre Teilhard de Chardin, who said that "life no sooner started than it swarmed."[6] Indeed, while man was originally only one of the innumerable branches forming the autonomous and psychic ramifications of life, man alone has moved beyond instinct to thought with unique capacities to know and create. He is at once *homo sapiens* and *homo faciens*. If a man's birthright lies in his being a knowing and a creating animal, he cannot sell it for the mess of pottage which is technology.

From the "pavement cipher" to the "halfman of the arts," through the "organization," "biological," or "economic" man this has been an era of fractionated identity. This is seemly because, perversely enough, the second industrial revolution, which reduced men to fractions, also made feasible the idea of man as an integer of work. This is to say that not only social life, but especially industrial life, is founded upon specialization and routine. Each one collaborates according to his talent and to his function. Only such stratification of labor, specialization of task, and stability of routine made modern products possible. The toolmaker was, figuratively, chained to his milling machine. The assembler "put his life on the line," the manager was detained in conference. But today, the time-tested verity of the axioms "every man to his last," "each operator to his lathe," "each professional to his license," no longer obtains in the same way. Although specialization is necessary to modern industry, it is inadequate to citizenship in a republic. To be a citizen, at once contemporaneous, aware, and free, in a free society, demands some acquaintance with history and politics, sociology and economics, religion and philosophy, and, above all, a respect for, and a sense of, responsibility. These same prerequisites compounded with resourcefulness, imagination, a "feel" for the age, plus some prescience, are required in the higher reaches of business management. We have

---

[6] *The Phenomenon of Man* (New York: Harper & Bros., 1959), p. 92.

been insisting that we all must work together in the common cause and the common task of civilization. Each must do it according to his function, according to his place in society. But this cannot be done *en masse.*

The sociologists have been reminding us of late that, although we conceive of ourselves as a mass society, we are not, by any means, an unshapable or ungovernable mass. Lately, ours has been more precisely described as a spearhead society wherein certain creative minorities—social, political, industrial—push forward inquiry, first for reconnaissance, then for direction and propulsion. This does no injustice to our democratic notions because we have conceded from the time of Jefferson that any fertile and lasting democracy must depend on an aristocracy of talent and virtue if it is to survive.

The managerial spearhead must push to recruit and foster a professional cadre. The willing amateur, however devoted and hard-working, will not suffice. We cannot stress too much the fact that the professional manager today—especially in the multinational corporation—has a job increasingly like that of the English public servant or colonial officer. Yet his assignment goes beyond this. The British civil servant, despite his education and dedication, appears to have lost contact with the Parliament and, hence, with the aspirations of the people. The professional manager, however, must strive to maintain his special skills and knowledge and translate them into fruitful actions which accord with the ambitions and values of the vast clientele he always serves and sometimes leads.

Thus the manager, while remaining *homo faber,* the industrious craftsman, must increasingly, in the discharge of his work, become *homo sapiens.* For the manager to remain the maker or shaper of products only is to enclose himself in a cultural vacuum where standards fall into disrespect, communications break down, and the more human considerations degenerate or lapse into a kind of decrepitude.

Gerald Heard[7] paraphrases Taylor's "Managerial Mutation" very neatly. Taylor's equation, he said, is simple, but can be extended throughout the social structure: Whenever you advance the apparatus you must advance, equally, the mind that manages it. Science and technology have been the benefactors of the manager. They have improved his apparatus, bettered his technique, ad-

---

[7] Gerald Heard, "Waiting for the Third Act," *Limits of Control—IV* (Series), The (London) *Times* Literary Supplement (June 3, 1960), p. 355.

vanced his modes of knowing and making and serving—but the gap must be closed because we have, if the equation holds true, to *advance equally* the mind of the manager. This involves, of course, more than machinery, more than production, more than function as such.

It seems safe to infer that the more the organization is engaged in the production and sale of goods and services for profit, the more impact it has on the greater society around it. As government and unions circumscribe its entrepreneurial opportunities by making demands on its wealth and setting limits to the power of that wealth, the manager of economic organization must leave the exclusive profit maximization formulas of pure economic theory behind him and move into the mainstream of human existence. Thus the rise of the large organization and of the need for men to manage it invariably creates demands that the holders of economic power employ it for other than exclusively economic ends.

In the July, 1960, issue of *Réalités,* Danielle Hunebelle, discussing the educational opportunities in France, observed that "in the battle for energy it is not oil nor the atom which will conquer, but human energy. In the battle for raw materials, it will be brains. The disjunction is appallingly simple and stark." She remarked that over the next 50 years France will need "dynamic, educated, and intelligent people with a maximum amount of culture."[8]

In the same article, the English spokesman, Ritchie Calder,[9] described how the six nations of the European economic community, France, Germany, Italy, Belgium, Holland, and Luxemburg, now aim at free exchange of *men,* as well as of money and materials within the Common Market area. It is highly probable that a professional man or technician in one country will sooner or later practice in another. There is thus bound to be some standardization of educational qualifications and some adaptation and assimilation of national educational systems. Under technical and economic pressures we may see some kind of medieval thought exchange being reintroduced in the 20th-century idiom.

Courtney C. Brown, Dean of the Graduate School of Business at Columbia, has remarked that the "rebirth of interest in the humanities in educational programs for business, initiated not so much by

---

[8] Ritchie Calder and Danielle Hunebelle, "Western Education: A School Report to be Ashamed Of?" *Réalités* (July, 1960) (English Edition), p. 57.

[9] *Ibid.*

the business schools, as by businessmen themselves . . . may be the most exciting challenge of all in the years ahead."[10] General education for the businessman is being scrutinized throughout the country. Such terms as "business stateman," "generalist," "humanist executive," and "the well-rounded manager" all attest to industry's interest in fostering men whose capacities are not limited by their function.

Indeed, education throughout the West is faced with a simpler predicament. How can the free peoples of the West adapt their educational system, which matured during the Middle Ages, the Renaissance and the Enlightenment, to the shocks and rigors of the age of automation and the atom? In an address during National Education Week, in November, 1957, President Eisenhower stated that we will need not just engineers and scientists but people who keep their heads—leaders who can meet intricate human problems with wisdom and with courage. We are going to need not only Einsteins and Steinmetzs, but Washingtons and Emersons. And surely we shall also need managers: the men who translate technology into production and people (workforce) into polity.

The early Middle Ages were dark because man lived in ignorance of the civilizations that had preceded them. The Renaissance created an awareness of the fact that long before Christendom was thought of there had grown up, flourished, and decayed a society of men far more civilized than any that had followed it. And the culture reclaimed from this past did much to advance and promote the new, more pragmatic, and much more extensive, scientific civilization of our time.

Like the barbarian hordes of antiquity, however, the march of the new learning, seeing only superfluity and no great utility to its immediate purpose in the so-aptly named liberal cultures, has ignored the humanities. Jacques Barzun can say that all subjects are really interrelated through the single mind of man, and that we shall never be able neatly to carve up the domain of thought along fixed lines. But it is not yet apparent to industry that problems of leadership, anticipation, and self-development are problems of philosophy, history, psychology, political science, and not of any one of these without the other. We need to be reminded that—

---

[10] Courtney C. Brown, "Business in Cap and Gown," *Saturday Review* (January 19, 1957), p. 18.

The humanities are a form of knowledge. Like other knowledge, this deals with man's life in nature and society, but it is acquired through the study of man's spiritual creations—language, history, philosophy, and religion. This filtering of the subject, man, through the medium of mind has the effect of keeping always in the foreground the element of novelty, of uniqueness, of astonishing unpredictability. Whereas the study of nature assumes and finds its uniformities, and whereas the scientific study of society tries also to grasp what is regular and inevitable, the study of nature and man through the humanities dwells on what is individual and unlike and anarchic.[11]

The business situation necessarily concerns itself with the regular and the predictable as it involves the institution *qua* institution. And yet the unique and anarchic has a persistent way of intruding on the affairs of the organization. An individual impoverished by unemployment may accuse the civic community for not providing poor relief, the church for not extending charity, the corporation for discharging him.

Today we often hear demands for an extended social role for the corporation because of its wealth and power. But has the economic organization a legitimate and logical right to add charity or social service to its goals? Or are these the proper functions of the churches, of charitable organizations, or of government? Despite the careful distinctions implicit in the questions, it has been said that "slowly, —or perhaps not so slowly, industrial United States is moving toward a form of economic republic without historical precedent."[12] If this is the case, has this new republic assumed responsibilities commensurate to its resources?

These are important questions. It is hoped that by raising them this book will broaden the interests of business students; that it will serve as provocative reading for those younger men already in business who still have time to examine their environment and its effect on the direction of the enterprises to which they are giving their working lives; and that it will stimulate thought among those random readers who are curious about business as an influence on the shape of tomorrow. For, although it is only in the last section that we

---

[11] Jacques Barzun, "The Misbehavioral Sciences," *Adventures of the Mind* (New York: Alfred A. Knopf, 1959) , p. 31.

[12] Adolf Berle in E. Mason (ed.) , *The Corporation in Modern Society* (Cambridge, Mass.: Harvard University Press, 1959) , Introd. p. x.

have concentrated on change as an aspect of American progress, these discussions tend to emphasize variations in the nature of freedom, ownership, governance, and the economy.

As this text now stands, it consists of introductory chapters on business history and a series of essays grouped around the basic concepts of the liberal American tradition. This arrangement makes it possible for the reader to concentrate on any single idea, and to think about it and read about it as he wishes, since the individual papers in these sections are set up as units, each with content outline and bibliography. The section on the Economy is necessarily less extensive than some of the others because subjects such as competition, profit, money credit and capital formation, and the market are already examined in considerable depth in today's business schools.

The foreword to each section is not a summary of the material contained in it. Rather it is intended as a kind of running introduction, containing reflections on the broader questions relating to the environment of the facts discussed in the essays that follow. The first chapter is largely an environmental study which examines the evolution of Western attitudes toward business in Europe. It sketches the public image of business through ancient, medieval, and modern times as it develops from a despised social necessity through its late 19th-century flowering and apotheosis to its present-day position of ambiguity.

As the study progresses, it begins to suggest that modern business organization is as much the author as the result of many of the innovative changes of our time. The evolution of the American corporation expresses the aims, vitality, and adaptability of a society which science, technology, and organization have raised to a high peak of productive accomplishment. The corporation has become a superb instrument for generating material goods and services but, because of the traditional insistence on accountability for wealth and power, it is now being challenged as to the uses of these. It has arrived at a moment in our national history when it should complement its characteristic and traditional concern for market and investment with an examination of its own significance in relation to the human and societal costs of production. This question cannot be handled from the exclusively economic or technicist point of view. Nor, it would appear, can it be resolved from a strictly humanistic approach.

Though the conclusion is not drawn precisely in these terms, what is implicit here is the view that the business corporation today is a new kind of community. A man who goes into any kind of business usually thinks he can serve himself financially by serving society, which he sees as a market that he believes is there, or that he can create by virtue of his product or service. The child selling lemonade on a hot afternoon by his front step is the pristine example of this kind of human conviction. Moved up a few years into a shop, a plant, or an office skyscraper, this same urge is what drives both the single-product entrepreneur and the organization employee, whether he be a laborer or a manager, an accountant or a financier, a machinist or an engineer, a foreman or a staff sociologist. Under the corporate standard these are men in business who have brought into it not only their drive to earn money by production or service, but their aggregate special training and skills, so that they can better serve their own and one another's economic ends by meeting the larger demands of society.

The focus of this text, therefore, is on corporate business as the all-embracing economic phenomenon of the 20th-century. For though a man's economic endeavor could in a subsistence economy separate itself from the community, this is impossible today. Zoning alone, a product of community living, restricts the old back-yard or front-parlor private economies. Modern packaging, advertising, and marketing make the efforts of many small, family businesses look rather like shoestring affairs. The small businessman, in addition, frequently depends for his market on the prosperity of large industries to whose employees he caters. The large business itself finds that the needs of the greater society dramatically intrude upon its community when it enters the defense business, and some of its own private character is radically altered. Its new components, created to deal with government orders, are quasi-public in character. When a business is called upon to take part in the defense effort, it does not first ask whether this is wasteful of resources, whether there is any real consumer's market, nor whether profit can be maximized consistently in such a field. There are noneconomic considerations that precede the traditional economic ones.

The interdependence in our society fostered by the nature of modern business, makes of the contributor-claimants on the corporation an industrial citizenry without franchise, save for that segment which can invoke collective bargaining to represent it. The others can sell out, exercise what has been referred to as the sacred right to quit, or refrain from consumption as an expression of the will of the people. But in an economic republic, one's assets, skills, or needs can only go from one type of economic organization to another. The individual may be able to survive without investment opportunity, but he cannot exist without income. Nor can he use that income without patronizing some economic organization for food, clothing, and shelter.

Business organization today is not the expression of a charter that can be amended or revoked. It is a fact of life that must constantly be reckoned with. It must be examined, not excoriated, so that it can be influenced by men's principles rather than coerced by their prejudices. And it must be staffed by men prepared with some knowledge of what it is they are identified with, so that they will be able to conduct their dealings with wisdom and foresight.

It is the hope of the authors that this work will provide a further impetus to an understanding of the most interesting manifestation of contemporary enterprise so far conceived—the American business organization. Back in 1913, upon completing his monumental work on the theory of associations, *Das deutsche Genossenschaftsrecht,* Otto von Gierke remarked that he did not believe that any other person would soon tread again the path he had taken. Unlike Gierke, we are persuaded that many scholars and business executives are already walking along parallel pathways toward the same general goal. We share the first result of our inquiry—indeed, of our adventure—with them in the pages that follow.

RICHARD EELLS
CLARENCE WALTON

NEW YORK CITY
January, 1969

I. BUSINESS IN HISTORICAL CONTEXT

1. Business in Western Europe

WERNER SOMBART, the great historian of capitalism, held that "all culture, and consequently all economy, is historical. As there is in the abstract no religion, no language, no state, but merely a certain religion, a certain art, a certain language, a certain state, so there is no economy [or business] in the abstract, but a particularly constituted, historically distinguishable economic life."[1]

By abstracting from selected phases of business history—ancient to modern—those characteristics which give adequate explanation of the meaning of business, we shall attempt here to answer with concrete examples such questions as: How was business actually

---

[1] Werner Sombart, "Capitalism," *Encyclopaedia of the Social Sciences*, Vol. III, p. 196.

17

carried out? What promoted business and what hindered it? What were the relationships of other cultural institutions to business? Perhaps the businessman, so often castigated for a myopic historical sense, can discover from even a limited and cursory examination of the past some valuable clues to these questions. Unlike other ages, ours has been characterized as an era of accelerating change. Even so, twentieth-century business has an ancestry, and its nature is the product of many centuries of evolution and creative adaptation, however unprecedented its pace today.

THE ANCIENT WORLD

THE GREEK IDEAL

The Greek ideal of the self-sufficient household managed by those skilled in animal husbandry and in agriculture had little place for the merchant. But reality has a way of distorting ideals. Mountainous terrain and a scarcity of fertile soil forced Greece to import from other Mediterranean peoples the foodstuffs and raw materials it lacked. These imports were paid for through the export of specialized farm products, like olive oil and wine, and specialized industrial goods, like iron tools, pots, and works of art. Indeed, the Greeks offer testimony to a proposition that has almost universal applicability: trade implies the existence of surplus in one area and of demand for this surplus in another. It also implies the willingness and availability of people to carry the goods. Such carriers are more apt to be found in areas where there are groups of people who cannot find employment either in agriculture or in existing industries.

The growth of commerce in Ancient Greece was painfully uneven, but grow it did, and Greek exchange during the later Hellenic period exhibited remarkable vigor. Improvements in the systems of roads, the increasing use of money as a medium of exchange, the diffusion of a common language and a uniform system of law, and the consequent development of similar forms of business procedure promoted a lively commerce within the various Hellenic city-states. The great lawgiver Solon (c. 639–559 B.C.) even persuaded his fellow Athenians to adopt the Euboic standard of weights and measures so as to facilitate commerce with the prosperous communities of Asia Minor.[2] And there existed a rather sophisticated group of

---

[2] M. L. W. Laistner (ed. and trans.), *Greek Economics* (New York: E. P. Dutton, 1923), pp. xv–xvi.

bankers (the *trapezitae*) who served the business community in an honest and skillful manner.

Yet there were important deterrents to the expansion of Greek trade. Hostility to the trader, political insecurity, lack of progress in nautical sciences, the drive toward self-sufficiency on the part of each city-state, the absence of vigorous mass markets, and a business class that was losing vitality—all combined to plague the business community.

Notwithstanding these limitations, the growth of Greek commerce and banking is indicative of the existence and use of business devices that have become familiar. There is also ample evidence that trade and finance were controlled by a profit motive. One writer noted how "sad it was to see how often Athenian genius was wronged, and Greek love of freedom betrayed by greed and the desire for profit making."[3] M. L. W. Laistner stated that "the enterprising [merchants] made great efforts to keep themselves informed of prices and the state of the markets in different ports, but the absence of modern 'facilities' greatly restricted the possibilities of carrying out a successful 'coup.' "[4] Perhaps the most telling evidence of the existence of the profit motive was Aristotle's condemnation of wealth-getting as an overriding life goal: ". . . some men turn every quality or art into a means of getting wealth; this they conceive to be the end and to the promotion of the end they think all things must contribute."[5]

THE ROMAN VERSION

After the Punic Wars, the economic rationale for Roman trade was identical with that of the Greek city-states. The needs of the Imperial City's great population for food far exceeded what the Italian fields could provide, and her sophisticated classes craved adornments as much as her ruling classes craved conquest. The story of Rome is, in important respects, the tale of a sordid affair between two ruthless self-seekers, each bent on exploiting the other. One, the government, dedicated itself to systematic military expansion and political annexation; the other, business, pledged itself to provide the money for such conquests—always at handsome profits! It might be said in truth that pre-Augustan Rome was ruled by a warrior-aristocratic class that had neither interest in nor ability for the

---

[3] Helen Corke, *Toward Economic Freedom* (London: Methuen & Co., 1937) , p. 28.

[4] Laistner, *op. cit.*, p. xxvi.

[5] Aristotle, *Politics* (Modern Library ed., 1943) , pp. 69–70.

necessary arts of revenue raising, and this goes a long way toward explaining its profligate use of resources. Eagle and vulture shared the same nest!

The Roman state contracted out mining and coinage, road building and tax collecting[6]; it relied on the despised business community to provide moneys for war and for the disposal of loot and captives. Naturally, the businessman took care of himself. If titles were denied, profits were not, and Atticus, the elegant friend of Cicero, provides a striking illustration of the times. Atticus was honored with a statue from grateful debtors of one of the distressed municipalities because he was content with a 48 percent interest rate when he might easily have exacted 73 percent!

For troubled centuries, until the Augustan compromise, the patrician fought the trader. The genius of Augustus was to deny to a rapacious business group some of the time-honored tricks for getting rich at the public expense. Tax collecting was returned to the state, and with this and similar devices in other areas, Augustus turned many businessmen into salaried civil servants. Here the experience of the past has considerable meaning for the present. The price exacted for greater justice and orderliness was uncreativeness and dullness—a moral not missed by Arnold Toynbee and given interesting modern applications by David McCord Wright.[7] In the long duel for control of Rome, the businessman "captured plains and foothills, but, despite his millions, he remained barred from the last high peaks of power, . . ."[8] a history that he was to repeat with singular monotony until modern times.

The attitude of other social classes in Greece and Rome toward the businessman deserves some further elaboration. The most casual sampling of works by the best-known spokesmen for Greek and Roman philosophy reveals a persistent current of mistrust of the merchant. In the fourth century B.C., Plato voiced suspicion of the

---

[6] "Contracting out" has been, historically, a device which created problems and remains so even in our own day. It was a major issue in 1960 behind the first national strike in the history of the Pennsylvania Railroad. See the study by Margaret Chandler and Leonard Sayles, *Contracting Out: A Study of Management Decision Making* (New York: Columbia University Graduate School of Business, 1959).

[7] Arnold Toynbee, "Where are we going—and How did we get this way?" in D. H. Fenn (ed.), *Management's Mission in a New Society* (New York: McGraw-Hill Book Co., 1959), pp. 75–84; David McCord Wright, "Thinking Ahead," *Harvard Business Review*, Vol. XXXVII (May–June, 1959), pp. 23 ff., and "Adventure or Routine," *Harvard Business Review*, Vol. XXXIII (September–October, 1955), pp. 33–40.

[8] Miriam Beard, *A History of the Business Man* (New York: Macmillan Co., 1938), p. 38.

merchant who, although performing certain useful functions, was prone to seek inordinate profits.[9] To Plato the only reasonable solution was to impose severe restrictions, even to the point of prohibiting resident citizens from engaging in business lest they, too, become contaminated. Aristotle, distinguishing between acquisition of goods and management of the household economy, proceeded to make refinements on the former pursuit. If a man's acquisitive instincts led him toward "natural" occupations, such as fishing or hunting, this was all well and good; but once exchange (indirect business) entered into the picture, caveats were in order. If commerce was intended to provide for necessities, it was legitimate, but if the merchant sought simply to amass riches from it, then it became reprehensible.

According to the Greek ideal, the literally "dirty" work of transforming raw materials into goods designed for human needs was to be done by the majority of men, mainly slaves, in order that the elite might engage in pure exercises of the mind—art, philosophy, and politics—the pursuits of leisure. Professor Tilgher summarized the situation in these words:

Deep-rooted in Hellenic thought was the conviction that the external world of material things is an endless recurrence of phenomena which spring up and die down, are born and pass away, are generated and become corrupted, turning continually in a circle on themselves, without beginning or end, in an incessant change, ceaseless and vain. To save oneself from the stormy ocean of the exterior world, to retire into the depths of one's own soul, secure from change, concentrated in an unalterable identity: this was, for the Greeks the goal of life.

Hence any activity which brings the spirit into close contact with the material world seemed to them a painful and humiliating necessity, to be reduced to the lowest possible minimum, if possible to be eliminated altogether. Truth alone is the only worthy concern. . . .[10]

Rome maintained much of the Greek tradition. In the first century B.C., Cicero saw the need of the businessman but distinguished between the wholesale merchant who was performing a praiseworthy function and the small retailer who conducted his operations on the basis of fraud and lies.[11] To these speculations

---

[9] Plato, *Laws*, Book XI, chap. iii.

[10] Adriano Tilgher, *Work*, trans. Dorothy C. Fisher (New York: Harcourt, Brace & Co., 1930), pp. 5–6.

[11] Cicero, *De officiis*, Book I, chap. xlii.

were added, as previously noted, the fierce hatreds of the Roman patrician for the merchant.

THE MEDIEVAL SCENE

When Roman legions no longer struck terror in enemy hearts and when the Empire itself had become obscured in forgotten glory, the lively arts of making, trading, and gaining perished as well. For a century or two the character of Roman trade along the Mediterranean was maintained by Rome's conquerors, the Latinized barbarians, who came in prior to the conquering Teutonic tribes; but in the seventh century, the Islamic Arabs took control and western Europe became virtually landlocked. Although Islam was not intrinsically opposed to commerce, it viewed the foreign trader with contempt, as an importer of the debilitating cultural and religious germs of other lands into the pure body of Moslemism. Trade between East and West, therefore, was not to be countenanced.

From the ninth to the eleventh century, the West was closely bottled up. Commerce stagnated, towns declined, poverty spread, public authority disintegrated. Land became the only real symbol of wealth and the Roman Catholic Church alone retained economic and moral ascendancy. (The influence of feudalism on contemporary European industrial organization should not be underestimated. There is a strong tendency for the modern European businessman to identify himself with the medieval *signore* and adopt a strongly paternalistic attitude toward his employees. In Italy an owner-manager is still commonly referred to by his employees as *padrone*—the "big father"—a phrase dating back to medieval and even Roman times.)

In the early stages of the eleventh century the Italian city-states regained a measure of trade with Byzantium, and when this southern movement was joined to the trade efforts in the north, linking the Low Countries with England, the stage was set for revival. Yet it took centuries, as Henri Pirenne reminds us in his masterful study of this formative period, to fashion practices adapted to the economic revival and to accept as legitimate the notions of commercial profits and interests.[12]

---

[12] Henri Pirenne, *Economic and Social History of Medieval Europe* (New York: Harcourt, Brace & Co., 1937), esp. pp. 1–15 and 162–68. See also Bede Jarrett, *Social Theories of the Middle Ages* (Westminster, Md.: Newman Book Shop, 1942), pp. 154–62.

By the time the Middle Ages reached this apogee in the thirteenth century town life had regained much of its vigor. Yet a distinction has to be made: in one type of town medieval commerce lived off itself whereas in a second the town traded with other parts of the world. Only in this latter type do we find the more developed forms of capitalism, with letters of credit, money exchange, loans at interest, and gold coinage being widely employed.

There are three points worthy of special mention in any assessment of business in the Middle Ages, and these relate respectively to (*a*) attitudes toward business, (*b*) the philosophy of trade, and (*c*) the evolution of the capitalist.

ATTITUDES TOWARD BUSINESS

Since the Church was the dominant medieval institution, its influence on the times was great. As the Church Fathers of Christian antiquity found little systematic treatment of mercantile activity in either the Old or the New Testament, they may have turned, almost instinctively, to the pagans whom they knew most intimately: Plato, Aristotle, and Cicero. Yet this conclusion must be accepted cautiously because the New Testament abounds with Christ's injunctions against the corrupting influences of wealth, and the writings of the Apostle Paul, and of Basil the Great and Jerome (in the Greek and Latin traditions) faithfully mirror these admonitions. Yet these were mainly exhortations against riches per se and the trading function was far less frequently mentioned.

Those Fathers who turned their attention toward commerce invariably reflected the same Platonic and Ciceronian hostility toward the merchant. In the third century A.D., Tertullian asserted that greed was the root of all evil and that greed motivated the merchant; in the following century, St. Ambrose, Bishop of Milan, mirrored this thought by depicting the merchant as one who labored day and night against the principles of justice and honesty. And Ambrose's famous contemporary, St. Augustine, shared these same views, although to a lesser degree. To the early Fathers, as to the Greek and Roman philosophers, farming, mining, and fishing were worthy pursuits, but the exploitative merchant turned the industry of nature into a fraud. These views of the Church Fathers were, in the main, inherited by the medievalists who continued to look at riches—and their acquisition through commerce—with jaundiced eyes. St. Augustine was the best-known figure and his cautious views

of trade were generally well-known and accepted. Yet Augustine
provided some essential distinctions, on which the medievalists built
a more elaborate theoretical structure, which, in turn, provided
the basis for some reorientations of attitudes toward business.

THE PHILOSOPHY OF TRADE

If the prevailing medieval attitude was one of abiding mistrust of
business, there was also a clear recognition that commerce was an
essential feature of the social order. The task of theorists was to
explain with great precision how commerce might be legitimately
carried out. In ancient and medieval times the concern was largely
with the quality of the goods and the price exacted for the product.
Of the two problems, the latter attracted the greater attention
largely because the selling price involved a host of complicated
market factors including supply and demand and changes in goods
caused by interspatial or intertemporal factors.

From the very beginning of Roman law the sovereignty of the
wills of the buyer and seller was recognized as the ultimate arbiter of
price. Buyers and sellers were permitted, therefore, to outwit one
another in bargaining. In the earliest form of sales, such as the
mancipatio of the Law of the Twelve Tables in the fifth century
B.C., the price agreed upon by seller and buyer was valid without
further consideration of the "true" value of the goods. In the Theo-
dosian code there are several imperial rescripts refusing to annul
contracts because the seller had alleged a low selling price. Freedom
of bargaining was as fundamental to Roman law as was the assumption that good faith must prevail.

There was one exception. In the sale of land if a parcel was sold
by the father at less than half the market value the son had the right
under law to repurchase the property at the original sale price or to
exact from the buyer the other half of the market value. This right
was called the *laesio enormis* and since it was a device similar to the
onaah in the *Talmudic Mishnah* there is reason to assume a strong
Jewish influence on Roman trade practices. Yet the basic principle
of free bargaining was retained throughout the Middle Ages—so
much so that efforts were made in certain regions (such as the Lower
Languedoc in France) to remove altogether the remedies traditionally provided under *laesio enormis.*

It is a common error to equate the entire Middle Ages with
feudalism and to ignore the significant evolutions in business prac-

tices during the later medieval period. As business became more active, there was need for refinement and reformulation of some of the cherished tenets of its social philosophy. These refinements were undertaken by St. Thomas Aquinas, who found in Aristotelianism a useful intellectual tool kit. Like his precursor, Aquinas felt there was something degrading in trade and in the haggling over goods and prices; like Aristotle, he justified profits acquired in the effort to make a living. More significantly, Aquinas went beyond Aristotle to introduce the notion of profit for other purposes—notably for charity or for public needs. And his idea that a just price was determined by the public's evaluation of the commodity went far beyond Aristotle.

There is a short tale in the *Summa*[13] that is especially revealing. Here Aquinas tells of a merchant who had been earlier discussed by Cicero in his *De officiis*. The merchant had an opportunity and a problem. He was carrying grain to a famine-stricken town and he knew that other merchants were following him with more grain. Is the merchant obliged to tell the townsmen that more grain is on its way? Or could he maintain silence and sell grain at the higher rate which a desperate and hungry people would pay? Cicero recalled the Stoic philosopher who replied that the merchant was duty-bound to tell the whole story and to sell at a lower price. Aquinas, on the other hand, argued that the merchant was not obliged to tell the story of more grain in the offing, since this was a future event and therefore uncertain. If grain failed to arrive, the merchant lost a just opportunity for reasonable gain. One might argue that the merchant would be more virtuous to tell of the coming caravans, but this virtue exceeded the bounds of simple justice. This tale represents Aquinas' last word on the subject of just price and excludes any explicit theory of cost-of-producing prices.

In his *Commentary on Ethics* Aquinas considered both cost of production and current market price as possible determinants of the just price, but in the *Secunda-secundae,* finished five years later, he definitely favored the latter. Shortly after Aquinas, Duns Scotus (d. 1308) made an explicit connection between market price and cost-

---

[13] Aquinas, *Summa theologica*, II–II, qu. 77.9.3., obj. 4, as quoted by J. W. Baldwin, *The Medieval Theories of the Just Price* (Philadelphia: American Philosophical Society, 1959) , p. 78. Benjamin Nelson shows how the original prohibitions against interest taking yielded to a permissive stage during which lenders were allowed to take interest from strangers. *The Idea of Usury: From Tribal Brotherhood to Universal Brotherhood* (Princeton: Princeton University Press, 1949) .

of-production pricing theory and received credit for an economic solution that approximated the "law of costs" of the 19th century. On the basis of extensive studies Schumpeter, in his classic *History of Economic Analysis,* has concluded that the later medievalists (notably St. Antonine of Florence in the 15th century and Lessius, Molina, and de Lugo, Jesuits of the 16th century) clearly anticipated many of the economic theories elaborated during the 18th and 19th centuries.

One other point must be mentioned. There was a substantial body of medieval social doctrine that took into account the needs and structures of a stratified society subsisting at marginal levels. During the Middle Ages canon law had the universality of an acknowledged public authority. The standard text in all the law centers of Christendom was the *Decretum,* prepared and issued around 1140 by Gratian, a monk of Bologna. But since the *Decretum* drew its descriptive materials from the early centuries of the Christian Era, the canonists were constantly forced to make adaptations to changing conditions. As the lawyers of the medieval world, the canonists drew sharp distinctions between voluntary poverty and idle begging, between holy and accepted asceticism and squalid impoverishment. Yet the attitude was far different from that expressed in the majority report of a 1909 English royal commission— that poverty implied a defect in citizen character. Poverty was no crime in the Middle Ages.

There was, further, a general acceptance of the notion that riches involved obligations to the poor and that the latter had a *right* to charity, even as the former had a duty to extend it. The underprivileged—whether wanting property, health, or education—were presumed to have claims against society, and here again there is a vast difference between, for example, Innocent IV's commentary of 1250 insisting on free schooling for the indigent and the 1847 mandate by the Poor Law Commissioner of England which prohibited the use of public money for the education of poor children.[14]

Finally, the Middle Ages accepted the preeminence of the small group, and it discerned a clear and precise relationship existing between the individual and the group to which he belonged; indeed, one fulfilled oneself only through the group and this meant the Church, the village, and the family. Taxes and fines were often

---

[14] Brian Tierney, *Medieval Poor Law* (Berkeley: University of California Press, 1959).

levied on the group rather than on the individual. In Italian business enterprises, for example, lone-wolf operations were the exception, and the typical operation was the *casa,* a term used to indicate the family business. It was the *casa* that bore the burdens of duties that its members assumed in civic life, paid the initiation fees for admission to the guilds, met charitable obligations, provided the expenses for entertaining visiting dignitaries, sustained the onus of the forced loans or patriotic subscriptions, and passed on bribes for great concessions and the like.[15]

The foregoing discussion takes on great relevance when it is realized that much of our own economic theory has held that its only province was the rather narrow one of the market place. Failure to develop an adequate social philosophy for an industrialized society has been a constant source of tension since the nineteenth century. Working conditions and status are today as relevant to business as is the issue of equitable distribution of profits among various claimants.

THE EVOLUTION OF THE CAPITALIST

Henri Pirenne has argued that there is a distinct and separate class of capitalists for each major period of history.[16] These men arise from the lower strata of society and, having nothing, are prepared to undertake the exciting risk ventures occasioned by changes in the social order. Further, these new businessmen are not related to the previous capitalists but emerge in answer to unmet needs; invariably they enjoy the widest possible freedoms during the early stages of their development. As they entrench themselves, two things happen: they become more regulated by the public authorities, and they become more interested in status and security. Consequently, the "mature" business group fails to maintain contact with changing business conditions and is replaced by the new entrepreneurs, who then repeat the cycle in a sort of Spenglerian rise-and-fall rhythm.

A discontinuous development in business is thus a characteristic of history. A further characteristic, but ancillary to it, is the concept of recurring cycles of freedom and control. The following diagram

---

[15] R. L. Reynolds, "Origins of Modern Business Enterprise: Medieval Italy," *Journal of Economic History,* Vol. XII (Fall, 1952), pp. 350–65.

[16] "The Stages in the Social History of Capitalism," *American Historical Review,* Vol. XIX (April, 1914), pp. 494–515.

suggests the way Pirenne categorizes the great epochs of business evolution:

Freedom (Laissez-Faire)	Public Control (Regulation)
11th and 12th centuries	13th–14th centuries
15th century	16th–18th (mercantilism)
19th century	20th century

This hypothesis—and such it must remain until more definitive evidence has been garnered by historians—has the merit of inviting critical and reflective inquiry into the drifts of our own society. There is need to know much more about technology as a determinant of the business order. There is a necessity to appraise centralizing trends in decision making as facilitated by electronic data processing on one hand and, on the other, by boards of directors which in reality determine policy for companies within companies. It is equally urgent to learn whether risk taking—which Pirenne has posited as the essential element of genuine entrepreneurship—is as understood and as willingly assumed by professional managers today as it was understood and practiced by earlier generations of businessmen. These observations are simply suggestive of some of the things that must be done before we can generate sufficient hypotheses for testing and explaining our modern industrial and business order.[17]

On the basis of the foregoing analysis of the ancient and medieval worlds we might essay certain conclusions and hypotheses which, together, form a basis for fruitful applications to today's problems.

1. Business has always been suspect in the eyes of other value-forming institutions whether we look to the Greek city-state, the Roman Empire, or the Catholic Church.

2. Theories of pricing and markets have been more sophisticated than the attitudes. These theories have reflected the almost uneasy recognition that business was a necessary adjunct to every healthy social order.

3. Political and financial stability are necessary conditions to thriving business activity but when desire for stability has been carried to ex-

---

[17] For an ambitious effort to develop a theory of industrialized societies see Clark Kerr, John T. Dunlop, Frederick Harbison, and Charles A. Myers, *Industrialization and Industrial Man: The Problem of Labor and Management and Economic Growth* (Cambridge, Mass.: Harvard University Press, 1960).

tremes—as evidenced by the Augustan peace in Rome—creativity and innovation have been stifled.

4. Every major historical epoch produces a new class of business leadership. Whether he evolves from previous business leaders or whether he emerges from a totally new class in society (as Pirenne suggests) the need for creative adaptation has been a constant challenge to the business community.

5. There develops, rather persistently, a cycle of "freedom-control–freedom-control" in the history of business enterprise. Clearly, this process has relevance to twentieth-century business.

6. A thriving middle class, living in a vigorous urban atmosphere, appears to be both cause and effect of effective business operation.

THE EARLY MODERN PERIOD: 1500–1750

The shifting focus of trade from the Mediterranean to the Atlantic favored nations like Portugal, Spain, England, France, and Holland. And overseas trade made tremendous demands for new capital which, in turn, made demands on business organization. From medieval practice it was apparent that money men could be brought together as the active participants in the enterprise, or they could be brought together simply as investors, with no policy-making prerogatives. When recourse was had to the first alternative, the resulting organization was the regulated company, such as the English Merchant Company, which exercised monopoly rights over trade in certain regions. As time went on, the other approach (of combining investors' capital) became more common. Entrepreneurs issued stock to the public at a specified price and simply returned dividends if and when success yielded profits. The joint-stock company was one of the major innovations of all time in business organization and the successes of the British East India Company, chartered on the very last day of 1600, brought a train of emulators.

Acceptance of the Profit Principle

These changes—when added to a new spirit of individualism encouraged by humanism and Protestantism—were complemented by advances in the use of coal, in mining, and in manufacturing techniques during the eighteenth century. Luther's emphasis on individual enterprise, on biblical interpretation, and on the importance of work was reinforced and expanded by Calvin, who placed frugality, thrift, and industry—virtues dear to those earlier businessmen—high in his schema of values. Furthermore, by focusing on the notion that worldly success and prosperity might be construed as signs of God's approval for the elect, Calvin provided a religious incentive that harmonized effectively with the spread of the profit motive in Western society. The fusion of these various innovations resulted in analogous changes in the economic system. Under the industrial system, surpluses were built from the performances of machines, creating new wealth through large-scale production at unprecedented rates, and through the acceptance of the profit principle as the legitimate quest and reward for business effort. Money permeated every aspect of economic life and served as a prime regulator for business activity; banks grew and flourished; credit expanded. John A. Hobson, in his book *The Evolution of Modern Capitalism,* enumerates what are to him the essential conditions for a system of industrial capitalism:

First, a production of wealth not required to satisfy the current wants of its owners, and therefore saved.

Second, the existence of a proletariat or laboring class deprived of the means of earning an independent livelihood.

Third, such a development of the industrial arts as enables indirect methods of production to afford profitable employment to organized group-labor using tools or machinery.

Fourth, the existence of large, accessible markets with populations willing and economically able to consume the products of capitalist industry.

Fifth, the capitalist spirit, or the desire and the capacity to apply accumulated wealth to profit making by the organization of industrial enterprise.[18]

These are not, of course, wholly independent conditions; on the contrary, they are closely interrelated. But by comparing these conditions with earlier business ventures, one can discern that this concept of capitalism represents a special case within the broader concept of business. R. H. Tawney summarized the change in this manner:

The rise of a naturalistic science of society, with all its magnificent promise of fruitful action and of intellectual light; the abdication of the Christian Churches from departments of economic conduct and social theory long claimed as their province; the general acceptance by thinkers

---

[18] Hobson, *The Evolution of Modern Capitalism* (New ed.; London: Walter Scott Publishing Co., 1917), p. 2.

of a scale of ethical values, which turned the desire for pecuniary gain from a perilous, if natural, frailty into the idol of philosophers and the mainspring of society—such movements are written large over the history of the tempestuous age which lies between the Reformation and the full light of the eighteenth century.[19]

Economic life is one aspect of a total culture. In previous historical periods—Greek, Roman, medieval—there was a tendency for other aspects of cultural life, such as politics, religion, the arts, and philosophy, to be dominant in the hierarchy of human achievements and satisfactions. Economic life was subordinated to these other arts and sciences as a means of achieving or realizing the purpose of life. Moreover, within the realm of economic activity itself, business was not dominant. So long as people are dependent for their livelihood upon the direct consumption of all they produce, business cannot exist, because there is no place for profit making. Both in antiquity and in the Middle Ages the bulk of mankind was occupied with agriculture, either of a subsistence nature or, where a surplus was obtained, paid to or expropriated by a small minority of large landowners or by the state. Business was an activity of the minority, and it always took a second place to the procurement of food from the soil.

What distinguishes the early modern era from past historical periods is not the existence of business but the emerging dominance of the profit-and-loss calculus in the economic life of society and the acceptance of the pursuit of profit as one of the major and legitimate purposes of life. The unanswered question is whether, by means of continuous and rational business enterprise, profits can be harnessed to larger social purposes.

THE THEORY OF MERCANTILISM

As medievalists had struggled to develop a theory which would accommodate the facts of business life to the values cherished by their society, so too were later economists challenged by trade changes to make a similar effort. The theory was called mercantilism and developed around 1500 in order to make private business interests an arm of the nation-state. Heckscher,[20] among others, has pointed

---

19 R. H. Tawney, *Religion and the Rise of Capitalism* (New York: Harcourt, Brace & Co., 1926) , p. 277.

20 Eli F. Heckscher, *Mercantilism*, trans. Mendel Shapiro (London: Allen and Unwin, 1935) .

out that mercantilism does not describe accurately a compact and consistent system but provides a concept that enables us to assess the period more accurately than might otherwise be the case.

Confronted by the sorry lessons of medieval particularisms (in the form of controls by independent feudal lords, on the one hand, and independent towns, on the other, each of which levied its own taxes and coined its own money), the new nation-state moved logically and determinedly to correct the abuses. Protectionism, bureaucracy, and autarchy were hallmarks of the mercantile state. But if the government subordinated business to its national purposes, the real question of who controlled the governors remained wrapped in enigma. The zenith of French mercantilism was reached during the ministry of Jean Baptiste Colbert (1619–83), son of a Rheims cloth merchant, who was no theorist but a hardheaded businessman interested in a thriving French economy. In England, Thomas Mun was as influential as any man in persuading his countrymen that a protected trade was the nation's greatest asset. Mun himself was a director of the English East India Company and another realistic businessman. The invisible hand of the private entrepreneur was, in short, often the power behind the visible arm of government.

But mercantilism could not survive the onslaughts of the advocates for laissez-faire. David Hume launched attacks against mercantilism in essays published in 1752 and 1753, but it remained for Adam Smith's *Wealth of Nations* to deliver in 1776 what eventually became the *coup de grace*. Smith argued eloquently for business freedom on grounds that with this liberty would come specialization, division of labor, and increased production of goods and services. Smith insisted that the "invisible hand" of the competitive free market would necessarily convert the self-interested actions of individuals into socially beneficial employments. But it was not until the nineteenth century—when England had little to fear from foreign competition—that the nation freely prepared to heed his voice.

THE MODERN PERIOD: 1750 TO THE PRESENT

Events of the last two centuries constitute the most dramatic epoch of material advance in the history of man. To speak of *the* modern period, however, as if it were all of one piece, is to suggest a consistency that is not borne out by history. There are radical differences between the pre-1914 and post-1914 worlds. We must also reckon with a difference in the productive techniques employed at even the most mature stage of the first Industrial Revolution and those new technologies (atomic power, electronics, and automation) that have heralded the second Industrial Revolution. Still in its infancy, this new revolution dates back only to this century's late twenties or early thirties, but, in the opinion of C. P. Snow, "it is in cardinal respects different in kind from anything that has gone before, and will change the world much more."[21]

When emphasis turns to the ways money is secured to sustain expanding production facilities, three other stages in this evolution are discernible. There is initially the period—running primarily throughout the second half of the nineteenth century—dominated by the "industrial" capitalist, that is, the man whose consummate skill at mass production and mass marketing gave him an ascendant role; the second period, covering the years from 1900 to 1930, equated the "finance capitalist" of Wall Street with effective control in American business; finally, there is the current stage, coinciding with the scientific revolution previously noted, wherein dominance is held by the "professional" manager—the man whose skills in organization and administration, broadly conceived, have made him the indispensable figure. Because of his appearance, a conviction has developed that modern business is undergoing specific stresses that are changing its basic *modus operandi*.

Professor N. S. B. Gras of Harvard, in his book, *Business and Capitalism,* developed two theses: (1) that the administrator was the key figure in business history and (2) that his role was changing significantly. James Burnham, following shortly with his book on *The Managerial Revolution,* has argued that these new administrators (required by a society markedly different from anything we have hitherto experienced) will constitute the new ruling class. But our concern here is with how industrial society has worked over the last hundred and fifty years and not with the emerging patterns of contemporary socioeconomic society.

PRACTICES AND ACHIEVEMENTS OF THE FIRST INDUSTRIAL
REVOLUTION

Stripped to its essentials, the Industrial Revolution refers to that historical period starting in the mid-eighteenth century when man

---

[21] C. P. Snow, *The Two Cultures and the Scientific Revolution* (London: Cambridge University Press, 1959), p. 31.

freed himself from primary dependence on animal power. It was the age when old king coal shared regal prerogatives with iron. The earth disgorged coal, iron, and other treasures at stupendous rates and these, in turn, moved to the factory where they were transformed into articles of consumption. The zest of the new age has been caught in the imagery of Paul Mantoux's description:

The characteristic monument containing within its walls the raw material, and embodying in a visible form the very principle of modern production, is the factory. Within are vast workshops through which run belts or transmission wires by which power is distributed. Each workshop is fitted with powerful and delicate machinery, which fills the place with its clatter, aided by the frenzied labour of its disciplined population, which the machines seem to sweep along with them in their panting rhythm.

The one object of all this is the production of commodities as quickly as possible in unlimited quantities. Here are woven goods unrolling themselves in yards and yards of cloth, or piling up in mountains of cylindrical bales; there steel is boiling in gigantic retorts and flinging up showers of dazzling sparks. Continuous production has become the rule for all industrial undertakings, unless it is limited in consequence of a definite agreement between producers. Left entirely to itself, production would rush on to excess, until it became ruinous overproduction; a paradoxical result of the instinctive tendency of capital, which ends in self-destruction.

Once manufactured, these quantities of goods must be sold. Sale, resulting in profit, is the final goal of all industrial production. The immense stimulus given to production by the factory system immediately affects the distribution of commodities. The increased amount of goods on the market lowers prices, lower prices mean increased demand, and more business. Competition becomes more intense. As improvements in transport open an ever wider field to its activities, it extends from individuals to regions and to nations, more eager than ever in the pursuit of their material interests. Conflicts and economic wars are let loose, and the winner is he who succeeds in enlarging, in spite of his competitors, his sphere of operations, and in finding more and ever more new markets. The ambition of producers makes them daring, and the most distant countries, continents hardly get explored, become their prey. The whole world hence-forward is nothing but one immense market, where the great industries of all countries contend as on a battlefield.

A special method of distributing wealth goes with this great productivity, with its enlarged circulation reacting to the confines of the inhabited world. Obviously the consumer is now in a much more favourable position than he was before the Industrial Revolution took place. Goods have greatly increased in quantity, while prices have been, on the whole, considerably reduced. Many things, formerly expensive and hard to come by, are obtainable in localities and in circles where previously they were unknown. Nevertheless the optimistic view with which such a spectacle inspired the classical economist is profoundly changed when the condition of the producers is examined. The whole structure of the factory system is built up on the power furnished by machinery, together with an immense accumulation of human labour, supporting, at the top, the towering and ever-growing force of capital. Producers are divided into two classes. The first gives its labour and possess nothing else, selling the strength of its arms and the hours of its life for a wage. The second commands capital, owns the factories, the raw materials, the machinery, and reaps the profits and dividends. At its head are the great leaders, the captains of industry, as Carlyle called them, organizers, rulers and conquerors.

From this has grown up the social system characteristic of our modern civilization, which forms a whole as complete and as coherent as the feudal system of the tenth century can have been. But whilst the latter was the consequence of military necessity and of the dangers which threatened human life in a Europe given over to anarchical barbarism, the former has been produced by a concatenation of purely economic forces, grouped around the central fact of the factory system.[22]

This kind of industrialism, with its socioeconomic dislocations, continued until man's ingenuity unharnessed the secrets of the atom in practically useful ways and, at the same time, turned electronics into a mighty servant of industry and business. By happy fortune, the development came none too soon since supplies of coal and oil are dwindling; fossil fuels may soon provide inadequate supports for the American economy. Heavy labor is being lifted from man's back and repetitive routine work from man's mind at such a rate that the least skilled may become a new leisure class.

Modern transportation systems have brought most major population centers within half an hour of each other, and probes into outer space suggest that before the end of the century man will be visiting other planets and perhaps planting human colonies. Accomplishments in the half-millennium between 1492 and 1992 promise to stagger the wildest imagination.[23] How man will *relate* his vast ac-

---

[22] Paul J. Mantoux, *The Industrial Revolution in the Eighteenth Century*, trans. Marjorie Vernon (rev. ed.; London: J. Cape, 1928), pp. 26–27.

[23] See, e.g., the report by John Ray Dunning, *Science, Engineering, and the Liberal Arts* (New York: Columbia University, School of Engineering, 1960).

complishments to the universe of other values becomes a major philosophical question for today's theorists.

THE NEW PHILOSOPHY OF BUSINESS

In many respects the refinements and adaptations built into Adam Smith's theories by classical economists represent an achievement in intellectual history. Both as description and prescription, *laissez faire* served eminently well. The theory posited an equation between private interest and public good that seemed in accord with the facts; it trusted to the automatic operation of unrestricted market forces to assure equity, and it rejoiced in the disciplines provided by competition *inter pares*. Indeed, the nineteenth century was an epoch of rising production, rising population, rising living standards, and rising educational levels for the Western world.

Yet the facts began to get out of hand. Invariably, competition between industrial and agricultural countries, between the have and the have-not nation, between the cartel and the small, privately owned firm, between employer and employee, worked to the advantage of the former in each of the cases cited. The result was predictable: reactions set in—and quickly! In point of origin, the first was born of revulsion against an economic order that imposed its costs so brutally on the worker and returned its rewards so handsomely to the owner. Karl Marx and Friedrich Engels issued the *Manifesto* in 1848, and Marx issued the first volume of his monumental *Das Kapital* in 1867.[24] Borrowing his model from the "dialectic" developed at the University of Berlin by Georg Wilhelm Friedrich Hegel, Marx posited a formula of *thesis* (existing capitalist order), *antithesis* (proletarian opposition), and eventual *synthesis* (the classless society). Explicit in the dialectic were three notions: matter as the only reality, necessary class struggle, and inexorable progress leading to victory by the proletariat.

Just a decade after the appearance of the *Manifesto*, Charles Darwin published his classic *Origin of Species* in which he enunciated the theory of evolution of matter from lower to higher forms through a struggle for survival. His caution in restricting the theory to the biological world imposed no similar restraint on social scien-

---

[24] Volumes II and III of the German edition were posthumously printed, edited by Engels (1885–94) ; English translation, 1901–9. Brilliant background sketches of some of Engels' major revolutionaries are given by Edmund Wilson in *To the Finland Station* (New York: Doubleday & Co., 1940) , Part II.

tists who saw in Darwinism both the explanation and the defense of the highly competitive order of the nineteenth century. If England gave Darwin to the world, the United States gave Darwinism its most articulate expression by accepting almost as an article of faith the writings of Herbert Spencer, the English sociologist who extended biological determinism to the social order. Singularly attuned for rationalizing the status quo, this social Darwinism gave to competition the force of a natural law.[25] Thus Marxism and Darwinism arrived at diametrically opposed conclusions and were used for contradictory purposes. One stressed revolution, and the other evolution. Yet interestingly enough—and insufficiently noted—were the similarities in the two doctrines. The common ingredients included emphasis on the universe of matter, acceptance of ruthless conflict as the natural disciplinarian over human affairs, emergence of a "better" class, and the gospel of inevitable progress.

CONCLUSION

In the face of remarkable transformations in today's society, where stands twentieth-century theory? The whole modern period has borne eloquent witness to the influence of certain scientific advances on social philosophy; the Copernican revolution required major revisions in cosmology and adjustment to the fact that this magnificent earth was a puny fraction of a mighty universe; the Newtonian and post-Newtonian eras spawned mechanical models as explanations of society; and Darwinism—as we have seen—provided the basis for lively intellectual reformulations for scholars in the late nineteenth century. There are even now certain signs that Heisenberg's law of indeterminacy, Planck's quantum theory, and the advances outlined by Einstein are being paralleled by economic theory as it turns away from Newtonian molds and into new patterns.

Economic theory in the West is always market oriented. It feeds on theories of supply and demand, competition, and value and exchange theories of supply, for its daily bread. And in this respect it provides sustenance for business institutions. Yet in the still unformulated theory of business, the frontiers go beyond those provided by

---

[25] Darwinism has been studied intensively in its many phases. One of the best inquiries is that of Richard Hofstadter, *Social Darwinism in American Thought* (rev. ed.; Boston: Beacon Press, 1955) , esp. chap. i.

conventional economic theory. The whole world of production involves concern with a philosophy of work, as such, with status for the
laborer, with functions and incentives for the managers. And beyond
that is the *troisième force* represented by the various publics with
which business must deal. Here the dynamic is equity, and in the
present climate a clash between efficiency and equity is likely to result in the emergence of efficiency as the tarnished ideal. Indeed, one
might hazard this speculation: in firms and nations at early stages of
economic development, the drive for efficiency will outrun the drive
for equity, but as productive capacity increases relative to demand,
the pendulum begins a slow and laborious swing until finally, in conditions approximating affluence, the emphasis shifts to justice.

In the contemporary scene, business is no longer the institution
playing a subordinate role in the mighty drama of events. It has
achieved in the secular societies of the West some stature of partnership with other value-forming institutions. Perhaps business has the
potential of becoming for our time a *force civilisatrice*. For, as it
provides the goods and services that make possible the good life for a
greater number of people, it crosses, in peace, those frontiers where
religious differences (Moslemism versus Christianity) or political
differences (communism versus democracy) have hitherto made
amicable exchange impossible.

Whatever the ultimate verdict—whether business has too much
influence or too little, whether it wields its power for good or for evil
—the necessity remains for business to understand itself in terms of
potentialities and restrictions, to discipline itself with restraints
when appropriate and with courage when opportune. Having
achieved both understanding and discipline, business then must
articulate its theory. But understanding must come first.

RECOMMENDED READING

ARISTOTLE. *Politics*, Book I, chaps. ix–xi.

CLOUGH, SHEPARD B. *The Economic Development of Western Civilization*. New York: McGraw-Hill Book Co., 1959.

COCHRAN, THOMAS. C. *Basic History of American Business*. Princeton:
D. Van Nostrand Co., 1959.

GRAS, N. S. B. "Capitalism—Concepts and History," *Bulletin of the
Business Historical Society*, Vol. XVI (April, 1942) , pp. 21–34.

HEILBRONER, ROBERT L. *The Worldly Philosophers: The Lives, Times,* and Ideas of the Great Economic Thinkers. New York: Simon and Schuster, 1953.

HELLEINER, K. F. "Moral Conditions of Economic Growth," *Journal of Economic History*, Vol. XI (Spring, 1951), pp. 97–106.

SCHUMPETER, JOSEPH A. *History of Economic Analysis,* chap. ii. secs. 3–4. New York: Oxford University Press, 1954.

TAWNEY, R. H. *Religion and the Rise of Capitalism,* chap. v. New York: Harcourt, Brace & Co., 1926.

TOYNBEE, ARNOLD, J. "How Did We Get This Way—And Where Are We Going?" in Dan H. Fenn (ed.), *Management's Mission in a New Society,* pp. 3–17. New York: McGraw-Hill Book Co., 1959.

WEBER, MAX. *From Max Weber: Essays in Sociology.* Trans., ed., and with an introduction by H. H. GERTH and C. W. MILLS. London: Routledge and Paul, 1957.

———. *General Economic History,* chaps. xxii and xxx. Trans. FRANK H. KNIGHT. New York: Greenberg Publishers, 1927.

FURTHER READING

ASHTON, T. S. *The Industrial Revolution 1760–1830.* New York: Oxford University Press, 1948.

BEARD, MIRIAM. *A History of the Business Man,* chap. ii, pp. 30–38. New York: Macmillan Co., 1938.

BECK, R. N. *The Meaning of Americanism.* New York: Philosophical Library, 1956.

BECKERATH, HERBERT VON. *Modern Industrial Organization,* pp. 1–79. New York: McGraw-Hill Book Co., 1933.

BRINTON, C. CRANE. *A History of Western Morals,* pp. 215–32 and 293–307. New York: Harcourt, Brace & Co., 1959.

CLAPHAM, SIR JOHN H. *An Economic History of Modern Britain.* 3 vols. Cambridge; University Press, 1930–38.

CLOUGH, SHEPARD B. *The Rise and Fall of Civilization.* New York: McGraw-Hill Book Co., 1951.

CURTI, M. *The Growth of American Thought,* pp. 697–704. New York: Harper & Bros. 1943.

DORFMAN, JOSEPH. *The Economic Mind in American Civilization.* 3 vols. New York: Viking Press, 1946–49.

EVANS, G. H. "Economists, Economic Historians and Business Enterprise," *Business History,* Vol. II (December, 1959), pp. 1–13.

FANFANI, AMINTORE. *Catholicism, Protestantism, and Capitalism,* pp. 1–34. London: Sheed and Ward, 1935.

GREENE, THEODORE M. *Our Cultural Heritage*, pp. 230–51. Houston: Elsevier Press, 1956.

HALSBURY, THE EARL OF. "The Business Leader—Mumi or Momina?" *Journal of Industrial Economics*, Vol. VII (October, 1958), pp. 1–21.

HECKSCHER, ELI F. *Mercantilism*. Trans. MENDEL SHAPIRO. 2 vols. London: G. Allen and Unwin, 1935. 2d ed., revised and edited 1955 by E. F. SÖDERLUND.

HOFSTADER, R. *Social Darwinism in American Thought*. Rev. ed. Boston: Beacon Press, 1955.

HUTCHINS, JOHN G. B. "Recent Contributions to Business History: The United States," *Journal of Economic History*, Vol. XIX (March, 1959), pp. 103–21.

JARRETT, BEDE (FATHER). *Social Theories of the Middle Ages, 1200–1500*. Westminster, Md.: Newman Book Shop, 1942.

LASKI, HAROLD J. *The American Democracy*, chap. i, pp. 1–38. New York: Viking Press, 1948.

PERRY, RALPH. B. *Characteristically American*, pp. 3–33. New York: Alfred A. Knopf, 1949.

PIRENNE, HENRY. *Economic and Social History of Medieval Europe*, chap. v. New York: Harcourt, Brace & Co., 1937.

REYNOLDS, R. L. "Origins of Modern Business Enterprise: Medieval Italy," *Journal of Economic History*, Vol. XII (Fall, 1952), pp. 350–65.

ROSTOVTZEFF, M. I. *The Social and Economic History of the Hellenistic World*, Vol. II, pp. 1200–1304. New York: Oxford University Press, 1941.

2. Business in the United States

IN THE TWO world-famous statements which exploded over the intellectual and political landscape of the Anglo-Saxon world in 1776, one finds that the distinguished authors of each were critical of businessmen. The first, Thomas Jefferson's "Declaration of Independence," heralded the breach between fledgling and mother country. The second, Adam Smith's *Wealth of Nations,* was a declaration of independence for business from dominion by the mercantile state. Jefferson's country-gentleman background made his suspicion of mercantile and financial interests understandable, but the hostility of Smith, hailed so often as the apologist of the free enterprise businessman, is less readily comprehended. Yet the latter was more censorious than the former and Smith's castigation of "the sneaking arts of underling tradesmen" who exhibited "a mean rapacity [and] the monopolizing spirit" was well known among economists.

The difference between Jefferson and Smith may offer an important clue to the history of business in the new world. While the Scottish philosopher opposed an omnipotent state, he was typically European in his distrust of mercantile interests. On the other hand, in America, antibusiness sentiment was less virulent. Historian Thomas Cochran has said that "compared with businessmen of other nations, those of America have always had unusual social prestige."[1] In the struggle for social preeminence American businessmen did not face, as did their European counterparts, intense hostility from the titled nobility, church prelates, or ambitious monarchs. But this should not obscure the fact that American masses remained either indifferent or hostile toward business and toward big business in particular. It was size and fear of monopoly that most easily stirred the wrath of the American people. Even Benjamin Franklin, the "authentic American" and clearly of the business class, early aligned himself with the common people. In 1729, having just turned 23, he wrote a pamphlet entitled *A Modest Inquiry into the Nature and Necessity of Paper Currency* and noted how his ideas were designed to help the *small* businessman. But Franklin also illustrated the success story of the typical new-world entrepreneur. Had he stayed in England, he would most likely have remained among the petty middle class "shut in by a wall of prejudice."[2]

While Smith's hostility to business did not significantly influence the American middle class, his mode of analysis did have substantial repercussions on theory because his formulations helped to precipitate the historic omission in economic theory of the entrepre-

---

[1] Thomas C. Cochran, *The American Business System: A Historical Perspective, 1900–1955* (New York: Harper & Row, 1957), p. 2.

[2] V. L. Parrington, *Main Currents in American Thought* (New York: Harcourt, Brace & Co., 1930), Book II, p. 165. Franklin was acquainted with Adam Smith and had visited the latter before publication of the famous *Wealth of Nations*. He tended to support Smith on the importance of free trade, but it is arguable whether he would have accepted the concept of the "economic man."

neurial role of business. Borrowing heavily from the French Physiocrats and from David Hume, Adam Smith developed such constructs as "capital," "labor," "population," and "land" to explain economic growth, but he gave relatively little attention to the importance of managerial skill and business innovation. These factors of production were assumed to work almost automatically so that there was little room for sociological considerations of businessmen and business institutions.[3]

THE BUSINESSMAN IN THEORY

In taking into account the sociological dimensions one can focus on the businessman as an *individual* or upon the business *organization*. Emphasis on the former means a concern with motivations, the psychology of risk taking, the process of decision making, and the impact of environment on the individual—all areas for interesting speculation but all involving hypotheses quite different from those normally employed by the historian. The latter's concern is mainly with the *business unit* as an economic and social organization.[4] This unit has certain distinguishable features, chief of which are the following:

1. The business enterprise depends on an outside market to which it sells its goods and services.

2. The enterprise requires property which is used as capital for the production of goods and services; on this ground, therefore, persons who merely sell their own labor services are excluded from the category of businessmen because they have no capital investment.

3. Business property is owned by private individuals and government-owned activities would not be considered business enterprises.

4. The element of profit seeking is essential to a business enterprise and, on this basis, hospitals and universities would not be considered business.

5. Required within the business enterprise are fairly sharp distinctions between personal/family obligations and business activities.[5]

How these business enterprises are formed, wither or grow, and are replicated in other surroundings are questions asked and an-

[3] Arthur H. Cole, *Proposal for a Positive Business Economics* (Cambridge: Harvard University Printing Office, 1965) , p. 4.

[4] Louis Galambos, "Business History and the Theory of the Growth of the Firm," *Explorations in Entrepreneurial History*, Vol. IV (Fall, 1966) , pp. 4–5.

[5] Francis X. Sutton, Seymour E. Harris, Carl Kaysen, and James Tobin, *The American Business Creed* (New York: Schocken Books, 1962) , chap. 3.

swered by historians who employ different approaches. Indicating how *space, lateral* development, or *function* specifically operated to explain business expansion constitutes the three most common ways for the business historian to approach his task.

SPACE

Geography has been a crucial factor for businessmen in the United States because the continent represented an area ready for relatively easy exploitation. This exploitation occurred in specific locations through particular instruments which were readily adaptable to other areas. One example was the country store which, moving from Philadelphia to Lancaster and beyond during the colonial period, crossed the Allegheny mountains to occupy new areas on the western plains, there to meet similar institutions emerging from west coast communities.

It was this "filling-up" process, frequently alluded to in general histories of the country, that was the most significant factor for upward leveling of material well-being and for the expansion of business institutions.[6] Spatial expansion was necessary because no community could advance in real income by concentrating only on its domestic markets. Farm families needed salt, medicines, cooking utensils, books, and replacements for equipment. Soon there developed in larger towns so-called specializing merchants who often purchased from general stores and then sold directly to farmers. The spatial characteristics of business were also exhibited by the small communities which became centers where business helped in the outward and inward flow of goods to other businessmen directly concerned with the exploitation of the natural resources of that particular area. The specialized product in a given region might be steel (Pittsburgh), coal (Scranton), or textiles (Lowell), but this product had to be transported to out-of-town markets.

While there is considerable debate over the hypothesis which associates economies of scale with urban size, it is interesting to note how northeastern cities grew as business grew. In the early years the average city size increased without interruption from the first federal census to the eve of the Civil War. In 1790 the average city size was 9,570; by 1820 it had increased to 12,780; by 1840 it had reached 17,650; and by 1860 the figure was approximately 22,400. These

---

[6] Arthur H. Cole, *The Business System and Economic Advance: An Attempt at Historical Generalization* (Cambridge, Mass., 1964), p. 27. Privately printed.

growth patterns occurred in cities where business success depended on the production of one primary good—excepting possibly ship building and shipping itself. While population growth continued to be rapid (55 per thousand in 1800, which reflected the agricultural basis of the society where large families were assets), the generally low level of population meant that relative scarcity of labor would continue to be characteristic of the new country. Therefore business would, of necessity, be innovative if the country was to grow. One form of innovation was spatial expansion which, as has been mentioned, brought in its wake an upward leveling of living standards in all communities and the gradual perfection of a remarkable "producing-assembling-distributing" network.

LATERAL DEVELOPMENTS

Coupled to the spatial factor are lateral or sequential developments where enterprises grew by moving into related fields. One example of a sequential or lateral development would be the spread of one type of activity to a related type: from marine insurance to life and casualty insurance; from the manufacture of cotton cloth to the manufacture of wool fabrics, knit goods, carpets, and related products. Location of new industries in existing cities rather than in rural areas made sense because the former already had good transportation and communication facilities and other complementary services in finance, power, and distribution.[7] The manufacturing operation exercised a multiplier effect to attract other industries and business activities; the increasing size of the market allowed for increasing specialization.

THE FUNCTIONAL BASIS

The expansion of certain market functions performed totally by a single firm may be subject to the law of diminishing returns. It became evident that a cotton textile firm (which initially made its own machinery, constructed its own facilities, retailed its goods, and ran its own crude advertising) might become more profitable by divesting itself of all functions except spinning and weaving. It was this process of specialization-of-function with the growth in market size that was one of the most striking features of industrialization in

---

[7] Simon Kuznets, in *Population Redistribution and Economic Growth, United States, 1870–1950* (Philadelphia: The American Philosophical Society, 1964), Vol. III, p. xxvi.

this country. The success of the market, of course, was related to the success of the export sector and the disposition of income from this sector.[8] This process has led some scholars to hypothesize that the timing and pace of economic growth was effectively determined by the success of the export sector and its specific characteristics, together with the disposition of the incomes received from the export sector.[9]

The foregoing comments indicate in a very simple manner the varieties of ways in which scholars attempt to explain the evolution of the American business system. While the approaches differ, one clear fact emerges and it is this: the business world is not a haphazard intermingling of purely competitive and contentious enterprises. Mutual dependence and mutual understanding are as much a part of the system as the more widely recognized elements of competition and therefore, in a real sense, the business system must be viewed as an integrated and interdependent social organism.[10] The growth of the system reveals competition and cooperation as basic characteristics of the system itself; it also reveals amazing versatility and adaptability. These features are illustrated by the evolutionary process through which American business moved—from colonial to contemporary times.

COLONIAL AMERICA

The American land mass, infinitely varied and infinitely endowed, profoundly influenced living conditions in the new world and was the mold in which American society took form. Farming was the primary occupation and although it is assumed that farmers are always rugged individualists they were frequently found during colonial times working in village communes. From the very beginning, Plymouth was organized somewhat along the communal model and Salem, after an unsuccessful effort at independent holdings, adopted some of the same ideas. In these townships (which were the forms of social organization found in the whole of New England and down along the Jersey coast to Delaware) there early developed a specialization of labor. The swineherd went through

---

[8] Douglass C. North, *The Economic Growth of the United States: 1790–1860* (Englewood Cliffs, N.J.: Prentice-Hall, Inc.) , p. 10.

[9] *Ibid.*, chap. 1.

[10] *Ibid.*, chap. 9.

the small town blowing an early morning horn and the cowherd, goatherd, gooseherd, and shepherd were all to be found in New England towns. There were drummers to call people to meetings and to make announcements, chimney sweeps, corders of wood, bailiffs, and a host of similar specialized occupations. In the common pasture everyone had a right to feed his cows and, not infrequently, small numbers of cattle were kept as common property—sometimes to pay all corporate expenses—as was the case in one Connecticut town where a herd of 2,000 head of sheep produced income used exclusively for the community's public needs.

In the South the parish vestry took the place of the township formed in New England. As Massachusetts provided the model for New England, Virginia provided the model for the South. It was the parish vestry that contracted for the building of the church, employed and dismissed the minister, opened roads and appointed overseers of the roads, levied fines for the disturbances of the peace, selected side-men to collect debts, and the like.

At the outset there were apprentice servants who had been bound for long-term service before leaving England and who were treated as a kind of property in both the North and the South. Englishmen who did not wish to undergo the hardships of the New World often sent servants to take care of estates. There are some accounts of the handling of these apprentices which suggest rather barbarous treatment. (Before 1650 the term of some bondsmen was as high as 10 years, but after the Stuart restoration in 1660 the period of service was permanently reduced to 4 years.) Between 1620 and 1650 the majority of immigrants were bondsmen and, surprisingly, many of them were fairly well educated.[11]

The presence of bondsmen in no way eliminated the harsh necessity for hard work. By the time of the Revolution, 19 out of every 20 soldiers were tillers of the soil and the agrarian setting had important influences on the American character. The ceaseless struggle for survival served to stress work as a great value; the complicated nature of the farmer's job forced him to be a master of many trades so that the nation seemed destined to become peopled by whittlers and tinkerers. As Jack-of-all-trades, the farmer chose to do many things well rather than any one thing superbly. The emphasis on industry, practicality, versatility, and individuality was early im-

---

[11] Edward Eggleston, *The Transit of Civilization* (New York: D. Appleton & Co., 1901), pp. 280–307.

planted in the American character by the very nature of the physical surroundings and the character of the tasks involved in producing a livelihood.[12]

The salient features of the colonial economy, therefore, were clear enough: overwhelmingly the population was engaged in farming or in activities directly related to it. Because there was relatively little increase in efficiency, there was little growth in per capita income resulting from farmers' gains in productivity. The really substantial gains in efficiency occurred in trade and, most paticularly, in international shipping. The colonial businessman was primarily a merchant: in the North, an independent trader, and in the southern colonies, an agent or factor for English or Scottish merchants. There was one other difference between North and South: whereas England could not absorb all of the products produced as surplus by northern colonies, she was able to take almost everything produced for export by the southern plantation economy. Indeed, the colonial period had not gone very far before America demonstrated its abilities in fishing, in whaling, and, most paticularly, in carrying goods all over the world.

Because England took such large quantities of the South's tobacco, indigo, naval stores, furs, and hides, it might be inferred that a favorable trade balance was inevitable for the southerners. Actually, the reverse was true. Terms of trade were much against the Colonials: almost all intangible items (brokerage, commissions, interest) had to be purchased from the English, and prices of English manufactured goods were higher than the prices of goods purchased from the southern colonies. So far as the North was concerned, an interesting paradox developed. Under English mercantilism, American manufacturing was discouraged in order to preclude competition with Britith industry. However, in order to encourage American purchases of English goods, the British had to tolerate colonial competition in foreign trade. Within a relatively short time, therefore, northern businessmen were earning commissions, profits, and brokerage fees on their own accounts by extending trade activities into foreign spheres where English merchants were already functioning. Northern merchants pushed vigorously to develop successful balance-of-payments relationships in their Newfoundland trade, in the

---

[12] Arthur M. Schlesinger, Sr., *Paths to the Present* (New York: Macmillan Co., 1949), pp. 5–22.

island trade, the Southern European trade, and their West Indian–
African trade.

Throughout the 18th century, and up to the very eve of the
Revolution, England and her colonies were also at economic logger-
heads over monetary policy. Fearful that an independent and expanding money supply might furnish additional financial resources
for colonial businessmen to employ in the expansion of their enterprises (meaning greater competition for England), the British imposed tight controls over colonial money. Burdened by debt, ham-
pered by the lack of coins and inadequate commercial banking
facilities, the Colonials were clearly inflationary, whereas the English were as equally deflationary. It was in 1764 that England took
the fatal step. In the midst of a colonial depression which had been
already intensified by the sharp decline in the sugar trade, Parliament passed the Currency Act denying to all colonies the right to
issue and circulate paper money.

Determination to break out of the closed circle of mercantilistic
restraints was, of course, not the only reason for the American
Revolution. Separation by a 3,000-mile stretch of ocean added to the
sense of physical isolation from the mother-country; religious and
political matters were also motivating factors. Reevaluations of the
period by economic criteria indicate that the burden of British mercantile policy was not so great as was sometimes suggested,[13] and export income was probably no higher in the late 1780's than it had
been between 1770 and 1774, suggesting that the new nation was no
better off than it had been during the critical period prior to the war.

THE NEW NATION

THE FIRST STAGE, 1783–90

During the critical years of decision between 1783 and 1790,
contemporaries argued vehemently about the state of the nation.
Was it better or worse as an independent country or as colony under
England? Would it prosper or wither? In 1785, returning to America
after his long absence, Benjamin Franklin felt the country was in
good financial shape. At the same time, Alexander Hamilton wrote

---

[13] Gordon C. Bjork, "The Weaning of the American Economy: Independence,
Market Changes and Economic Development," *Journal of Economic History,* Vol. XXIV
(December, 1964) , pp. 541–60.

his famous "Paper 15" in the *Federalist* and said that the country had "reached almost the last stage of national humiliation." Because America was heavily in debt to foreigners, unable to repel foreign aggression, denied navigation on the Mississippi, treated with contempt by other powers, the country had reached

. . . the lowest point of declension. Is respectability in the eyes of foreign powers a safeguard against foreign encroachments? The imbecility of our government even forbids them to treat with us. Our ambassadors abroad are the mere agents of mimic sovereignty. . . . To shorten an enumeration of particulars which can afford neither pleasure nor instruction, it may in general be demanded, what indication is there of national disorder, poverty and insignificance that could befall a community so peculiarly blessed with natural advantages as we are, which does not form a part of this dark catalogue of our public misfortunes.[14]

If contemporaries differed over the American condition, so have scholars. Fairly representative views are found in works of Curtis P. Nettels, who viewed this period as one predominantly of depression and very slow recovery,[15] and Merrill Jensen, who felt that it was a period of rapid recovery and growing prosperity.[16] Certainly by 1790 the country had passed the economic crisis. With the adoption of the new constitution it passed its severe political crisis and entered a period of prosperity unknown since pre-Revolutionary days. Invention of the cotton gin by Eli Whitney in 1793 assured to the cotton industry a major role in the nation's economic activity. The outbreak of the Napoleonic Wars between England and France tied up shipping and trade in Western Europe and afforded to the new neutral nation an overwhelming advantage in competing for the world's markets.

TRADE AND MANUFACTURING

In summary, it is evident that the most important reason for initial economic growth occurred because of Hamiltonian fiscal policies, particularly the funding of debts and the creation of the first Bank of the United States. The first step established a sound credit basis

---

14 *The Federalist: A Commentary on the Constitution of the United States* (New York: Modern Library, 1937), pp. 87–88.

15 Curtis P. Nettels, *The Emergence of a National Economy, 1775–1850* (New York: Henry Holt Co., 1962), chaps. 3 and 4.

16 Merrill Jensen, *The New Nation*, (New York: Alfred A. Knopf, Inc., 1950), pp. 418–25.

and the second provided the pillar for an expanding capital market. After 1793, however, economic development was tied primarily to international trade and shipping.

Although the typical American businessman was a merchant, by 1812 he began to show increasing interest in cotton manufacturing. People like Nathan Appleton (1779–1861) and Abbott Lawrence (1792–1855) were pacesetters in moving from merchandising into manufacturing. Both had made their early fortunes in shipping and when the two met in Edinburgh in 1811, Lowell was able to get Appleton's assent to cooperate in developing the cotton textile industry. The first attempt was made at Waltham, Massachusetts, shortly after 1814 in an enterprise that was so successful that the company moved from making of plain cloth to the manufacture of printed cloth as well. Expansion in the northeast was so striking that a Loyalist returning to visit Boston in 1808 after an "exile" of 10 years was staggered by the number of new and elegant buildings which had been erected.[17]

Between 1815 and 1860 the growth rate accelerated sharply. The population jumped from approximately 4 million in 1790 to 8.4 million in 1850, with distribution being quite even between North and South—although, by this time, over a million Americans had moved across the Appalachians to settle in the new West. Following the War of 1812 each of the separate regions became more specialized by concentrating on that activity most appropriate to its area. Each region used its own particular staple to engage in a brisk exchange with the others.

Meanwhile, Britain, in the midst of her Industrial Revolution, was hungry for southern cotton to feed her textile industry. The South, in turn, bought England's manufactured goods as well as insurance and shipping services and a fair share of foodstuffs from the West, especially from the farms which were developing along the Mississippi. But southern planters soon discovered that northern commercial shipping and insurance services could be purchased as cheaply, if not more so, than from abroad. Therefore, a pattern of trade developed whereby income from the South flowed outward: to the West for foodstuffs and to the Northeast for services and shipping facilities. As the Northeast intensified its manufacturing activities, it also began to draw southern funds to northern banks. Mean-

[17] Samuel E. Morison, *Maritime History of Massachusetts, 1783–1860* (Boston: Houghton Mifflin Co., 1921), p. 25.

while, the new West not only increased its food shipments to the South but began to provide agricultural products to the Northeast and Europe as well.

The early 19th century was also distinguished by city growth because (during a period of externally oriented commercial development) large cities could provide the advantages of port facilities and foreign trade specialists. By midcentury both New York and Philadelphia had populations of over 100,000 people; Boston and Baltimore numbered over 35,000; and Salem, Albany, and Providence were in excess of 10,000. There was in the growth pattern, however, this interesting paradox: during the four antebellum decades the middle-sized city found it increasingly difficult to compete with either the large or the smaller cities and its rate of population increase lagged.

Presumably the driving force behind this urbanization was expansion in manufacturing employment. The most dramatic and significant development between 1815 and 1860 was the vigorous revival of manufacturing, beginning rather slowly in the 1820's and then accelerating more rapidly during the following decades throughout New England, New York, and Pennsylvania. The iron industry, machinery production, light manufacturing (leather and lumber goods) —all grew substantially to provide a solid base for diversified manufacturing activity. This intensification of manufacturing activity led Professor Walt Rostow (who related economic growth to industrialization) to establish the period for the American "take-off" as having occurred somewhere between 1843 and 1860.[18] However, the take-off theory itself needs considerable qualification.[19]

ADVENT OF THE RAILROADS

A major reason for growth was the railroad, which appeared on the American scene around 1830. Despite sharp opposition from vested interests representing turnpike and bridge companies, stagecoach lines, canal operators, and even tavern keepers, the railroads pushed construction steadily forward. Even after completion, rail-

---

[18] W. W. Rostow, *The Stages of Economic Growth: A Non-Communist Manifesto* (London: Cambridge University Press, 1960).

[19] Simon Kuznets, "Notes on the 'Take-Off,'" in W. W. Rostow (ed.), *Proceedings of the International Economic Association Conference, 1960* (New York: St. Martins Press, 1964).

roads were often forced to pay tolls equal to those of the canals. That local opposition died hard is illustrated by one Ohio school board which declared that railroads were "devices of Satan to lead immortal souls to hell." In Massachusetts, turnpike interests denounced those state legislators who voted to charter the state's first railroad as "cruel turnpike killers and despisers of horse flesh."[20]

Despite the horrendous consequences of the panic of 1837, railroad construction was pushed forward by private investors, mainly in New England where the 1840's saw a fivefold increase in mileage. It was, however, in the following decade that the railroad industry entered its most dynamic period. During the 1850's the country witnessed a series of railroad "firsts." In 1851, three cities (New York, Philadelphia, and Baltimore) achieved their first rail connections with the West when the Erie, the Pennsylvania, and the Baltimore and Ohio, respectively, reached Dunkirk, Pittsburgh, and Wheeling. During the same years the first telegraphic control of trains was introduced, and the first locomotive was used west of the Mississippi. In 1856, California welcomed her first railroad, and in the same year the first railroad bridge was built to span the Mississippi. By 1860 it was clear that Chicago, now served by 11 different systems, was destined to become the railroad capital of the United States.

POST–CIVIL WAR PERSPECTIVES

Wars are often presumed to be major incentives for increased industrialization but because the Civil War was not a "modern" war, it has been alleged that it had relatively little effect on the process of industrialization. The premise for argument is that the struggle did not significantly spur economic development because the small-arms industry exercised little impact on total iron production.[21] If the causes for subsequent changes are in doubt, there is no doubting that important results followed. The jealous particularisms of early America had gone down to defeat; the slave economy could never again frustrate the ambitions of a capitalistic economy;

---

[20] Quoted from John F. Stover, *American Railroads* (Chicago: University of Chicago Press, 1961), p. 17.

[21] Richard F. Wacht, "A Note on the Cochran Thesis and the Small Arms Industry in the Civil War," *Explorations in Entreprenuerial History,* Vol. IV (Fall, 1966), pp. 57–62.

the potentialities of the factory system were now more fully appreciated; and the resources of liquid capital had been substantially augmented. From the smoke of this great conflict emerged an America unlike that any earlier generations had known. "An ambitious industrialism," said Vernon Parrington, "now stood on the threshold of a continental expansion that was to transfer sovereignty in America from mercantile aristocracy to the capable hands of a new race of captains of industry."[22] With this substitution of industrial captains for the plantation masters, the "age of aristocracy" came to an end and the emergence of a middle-class influence wielded mainly by factory owners was assured.

Stated another way, the difference between America before and after the Civil War was the difference between a mercantile and an industrial society. Before the war, New York, Philadelphia, and Baltimore were primarily concerned with trade and finance. The same was true of such mid-America centers as Chicago, St. Louis, and Cincinnati. The men of wealth were merchants, bankers, and urban real estate operators. At the outbreak of the Civil War a fortune of $500,000 was large and even one of $100,000 commanded great respect. There were, of course, millionaires—25 in New York, 18 in Boston, and 9 in Philadelphia. The richest man of his day, John Jacob Astor, left $20 million when he died in 1848. Fifty years later, when Andrew Carnegie disposed of his interests to the United States Steel Corporation, he was worth an estimated $500 million and John D. Rockefeller was probably worth twice that amount when he retired from active management of Standard Oil in 1911.

THE FIRST TYCOONS

The talked-about men of the age were tough-minded, audacious, and inventive. The "Wall Street crowd" (Daniel Drew, Commodore Vanderbilt, Jim Fisk, Jay Gould, Russell Sage) were, in Parrington's colorful phrase, "blackguards for the most part, railway wreckers, cheaters and swindlers, the picturesque and the rascality."[23] It was the period for those swashbuckling captains of industry who built America's first great industrial enterprises—that is, the large private, profit-oriented firms which were involved in the handling of goods through successive industrial processes, from the procurement

---

[22] V. L. Parrington, *Main Currents in American Thought* (New York: Harcourt, Brace & Co., 1930) Book III, pp. 3–4.

[23] Parrington, *op. cit.,* p. 12.

of raw materials to the sale to ultimate customers. Emergence of these industrial enterprises had particular impact on the swift growth of industrial and commercial centers. The urban population, which from 1840 to 1880 had increased approximately 4 percent a decade, rose to a 6 percent average increase per decade between 1880 and 1900.

While the depression of 1873 slowed down both geographical dispersion and the vertical integration of industry, the drive again accelerated after 1880 when great corporate enterprises began to appear in significant numbers on the American scene.[24] The first great wave of industrial empire building which occurred after the high prosperity peak of 1860 posed a challenge to industrialists to create administrative structures appropriate to their newly won domains. With few exceptions, the enterprise could no longer be managed successfully by one man, or by small family groups, and full-time professional managers began to appear increasingly. This era was the seeding time for the development of professionals who managed but did not own the enterprise's property.

ORGANIZATIONAL INNOVATIONS, 1880–1900

The coming of the first integrated enterprises during the 1880's and 1890's met the twin necessities of administrative reform and adaption to change. These integrated forms evolved for reasons related to an increase in output and even more because of the assumption of new functions. In the seventies nearly all American enterprises engaged in manufacturing only. They bought their own supplies and sold finished products through commissioned agents, wholesalers, and other middlemen. By the end of the century, however, great enterprises not only manufactured goods but sold them directly to retailers and consumers, purchased and produced their own essential materials and supplies, and were busily engaged in developing effective management control over each of the operations.

The large multifunction manufacturing enterprise developed essentially along lines provided by two different strategies of growth. In one, a single company began to expand and to integrate by creating its own marketing organizations; in the other, a number of

---

[24] The material is derived substantially from Alfred D. Chandler, Jr., *Strategy and Structure: Chapters in the History of the Individual Enterprise* (Cambridge, Massachusetts: M.I.T. Press, 1962) , pp. 19–51.

manufacturing companies joined together in horizontal combination to consolidate manufacturing activities and then moved quickly either forward into marketing or backward into purchasing. The first strategy was attractive to firms whose products were based on new technology and whose markets were found in the urban centers. Here, the usual distribution channels were unsatisfactory and the company was forced to create its own marketing organization. The second strategy proved attractive to industries which produced more stable commodities and employed less complex technology. In the latter types the expanded output often resulted in overproduction which induced a search for ways to assure markets. But both strategies represented responses to a rapidly growing national market.

The Swift Company is an excellent example of an enterprise growing through vertical integration by the creation of a new marketing organization. Gustavus Swift was a New England wholesale butcher who moved to Chicago in the mid-1870's. After the Civil War he saw that Boston, New York, Philadelphia, and other urban centers needed much more meat than could be supplied locally. He concluded that there existed a great opportunity to bring together the new meat supply of the West and the new urban demands in the East by exploiting the latest technology of refrigeration. In 1878, after his successful experimental shipments of refrigerated meats to the East, he formed a partnership with his younger brother, Edwin, to market fresh western meat to eastern cities.

Once the Swift brothers had decided to use refrigerated cars for shipment they recognized the necessity for refrigerated storage plants and for warehouses in every major city. They also perceived the need for a vigorous marketing organization to oversee local operations and to fight consumer prejudices played upon by local butchers. Butchers, in a defensive mood, had created the National Butchers Protective Association to prevent the sale of fresh western meat in eastern markets. Despite local hostility, Swift's strategy proved successful and by 1885 Swift had encorporated his enterprise and had successful meat-packing establishment in Omaha and St. Louis, and later, in St. Joseph, St. Paul, and Fort Worth. By 1890, Swift had created a huge vertically integrated empire that was so efficient his competitors (Armour, Morris, Cudahy, and Schwarzschild and Sulzberger) were forced to imitate his behavior. It is significant that companies which did not emulate the Swift prototype remained small and local and that the "big five" who did integrate vertically now dominate the meat-packing industry. Each of the so-called big five not only centralized its administration to coordinate its various functional activities, but also developed goods that could further utilize the vast resources it had now assembled. Concerned originally with beef only, the companies now added a full line of meat products to include lamb, pork, and veal; in order to use their branch networks more effectively they began to market eggs, dairy products, and poultry; to secure more profit from their disassembling operations they went into the leather, soap, fertilizer, and glue businesses. Swift's story was paralleled by other agricultural-processing industries whose products were intended for urban consumers. James B. Duke in tobacco, James S. Bell in the flour industry, and Andrew Preston in the banana industry, were among those who followed along the lines initially plotted by Swift.

In the field of consumer durables, innovators found it necessary to create their own marketing and distribution organizations. Cyrus McCormick, the pioneer harvesting equipment manufacturer, and William Clark of the Singer Sewing Machine Company, both sold their products initially through commissioned agents; but both soon discovered that salaried men working out of branch sales offices displayed, demonstrated, and serviced the company's equipment more effectively and cheaply than did agents. Following the Civil War, McCormick and Singer concentrated on building national, and then international, sales departments. Because they purchased raw materials from only a few industrial companies rather than from individual farmers, their purchasing problems were less complex than for firms like Swift and Duke which were engaged in processing agricultural products. Yet the final result was the creation of a very similar organization.

When attention is turned to firms engaged in manufacturing technologically advanced durable products, another pattern of business evolution becomes clear. In the electrical fields particularly (shortly after Thomas Edison had demonstrated the practicality of an incandescent lighting system), General Electric and Westinghouse emerged quickly to dominate the industry. Both firms were developing electrical machinery as a source of power for industrial and transportation business, as well as for the generation of light.

Marketing of electrical goods was so complicated, technologically, that highly trained salesmen, more often than the customer, knew what was really needed. Because salesmen had to be in close contact

with the production department, both General Electric and Westinghouse developed a manufacturing department to administer a
number of scattered factory operations, a sales department to manage the national network of district offices, an engineering department responsible for basic design, and a finance department to keep
track of the intricate flow of capital.

Steel manufacturers also had technically advanced products and
an increasingly growing market; and they, too, began to develop
their own marketing services. In the 1870's steel was produced for
the first time on a large-scale basis, and then primarily for the
railroads. In the next decade, however, demand arose for structural
steel to meet new urban building requirements. Andrew Carnegie's
decision to use steel produced at his Homestead works for structures
other than rails dramatically symbolized the change in both the
market and the technology. Carnegie clearly foresaw the need for a
large sales force when the customers were no longer simply a few
railroad purchasers, but rather increasingly included contractors
and builders, manufacturers of machinery and farm equipment, and
representatives of other industries of many and diverse kinds. Each
order had its own specifications and, like the electrical industry,
close coordination was required between sales and manufacturing.

Since it was more economical to market standardized items in advance of sales, and because this created serious and costly dependence on outsiders, it became necessary to establish warehousing
organizations. By the 1890's, all of the largest steel companies (Carnegie, Illinois Steel, and Jones and Laughlin) had their own marketing organizations. Again the smaller steel manufacturers remained single-function enterprises, buying their raw materials from
outside sources and selling their products to the middlemen. From
the experience of large electrical and steel companies came examples
later used by organizational builders at DuPont: from the pioneers
in harvester equipment manufacturing and sewing machines came
experiences useful to General Motors.

The second basic strategy occurred in enterprises employing less
advanced technologies. Here horizontal combination and consolidation were the more common routes to the formation of the vertically
integrated enterprise. The threat of excess capacity was a primary
stimulus to initial combinations in most American industries because
the domestic market became incapable of keeping pace with the productive capacities of the many small enterprises. Every depression be-

came a stimulus for small entrepreneurs toward greater willingness to combine in order to control or limit competition. From 1875 until 1890 many small producers of leather, sugar, salt, whiskey and other products joined in large horizontal combinations, but these federations were usually short-lived. Production and price schedules were hard to enforce and inefficiencies (created by the duplication of resources) were a constant bother. Sometimes the federation dissolved into its original parts, but more often than not, it consolidated. Every true consolidation involved both new legal and administrative forms.

The necessary legal innovations occurred in 1889 when New Jersey amended her general incorporation laws to permit one corporation to purchase the stock of another. Prior to this action, permission for one corporation to hold another's stock required a special charter or an amendment passed by the state legislature. Moreover, some states penalized out-of-state corporations by prohibiting them from owning real estate within their jurisdictions or by subjecting them to additional special taxes. When other states borrowed the New Jersey pattern (which now permitted a single parent company to hold the majority of stock of locally chartered subsidaries) it meant that businessmen had an inexpensive way to operate over a wide area and still retain legal control over these geographically dispersed entities.

Administrative innovations may have been even more important than the legal ones. A combination was not really an administrative combination unless the executive office could do more than set price and production schedules; it became truly consolidated only when the headquarters could determine nearly all of the enterprise's activities; in short, the loose alliance was fused into a single company. Production could be concentrated in the most favorably located factories, new technology could be rapidly adapted to a larger manufacturing unit, and the relationship of production to marketing facilities could be more effectively achieved.

The heavy fixed cost of these enlarged plants created such a demand for continuing high volume of output that manufacturers found it unsafe to rely on commissioned selling. The agent or wholesaler was interested in obtaining a satisfactory commission and had no particular motive for pushing the product of one client over another. The manufacturer, on the other hand, was interested in spreading *his* market and of insuring its relative stability. Thus, horizontal consolidation and centralization immediately created much greater pressures for vertical integration than did mere combinations. As a result, consolidated firms often began their own wholesaling and even retailing.

The reason for moving from combination or federation to consolidation and integration was stated effectively by the managers of the National Biscuit Company in their 1901 *Annual Report*. The firm noted that a major "first" decision for every company was to control competition by either fighting it or buying it. Because the first meant a price war and the second constantly increasing capitalization, the National Biscuit Company was forced to ask whether it was really necessary to control competition. The answer was historic: *"We soon satisfied ourselves that within the company itself we must look for success."* This meant stress on improving the internal management in order to obtain full benefits from the purchase of raw materials, from economies in manufacturing, and from more effective service by the sales department. What the National Biscuit Company achieved was a transformation from a combination to a consolidated firm and thence to an integrated multidepartmental enterprise similar to what had occurred with Swift, Singer Sewing Machine, General Electric, and Westinghouse.

During this same decade some enterprises went even further to handle not simply their own marketing and manufacturing but even the production and transportation of raw materials. This expanded form of vertical integration was stimulated through enterprises whose raw materials came from the ground where the limited supply of output could be controlled by a few firms. To gain an assured source of supply Standard Oil moved into the production of crude oil during the 1880's. Similar strategies were carried out in the fertilizer industry and in steel. In the latter instance, the initiative was taken by the Carnegie company which was worried over the problem of steady adequate supplies and therefore moved to purchase large holdings in the Mesabi Range. Other companies quickly followed Carnegie's lead and then moved to develop their own railroads and fleets of ore boats to provide transportation of ore from mine to mill. Combinations among producers of semifinished steel and other metal products brought a wave of mergers among the users of steel, copper, and other semifinished materials on the eve of the 1900's.

Whatever reason led to the combination, each combination usually consolidated its constituent companies into one single operating organization. It was this profound concern over price-cutting competition and the threat of unemployed resources that led to the formation of the United States Steel Corporation—a billion dollar merger which included Carnegie, Federal, and National Steel Companies, plus five or six other fabricating enterprises. Originally, United States Steel remained essentially a federation of operating divisions loosely controlled by the holding company and operated under the shrewd eye of Elbert H. Gary. Only after Gary's death did the corporation's general offices in New York begin to assume a structure similar the one developed by Alfred P. Sloan for General Motors many years earlier.

What the country was witnessing—as a result of the expansionist strategies and consolidations of the Rockefellers, Swifts, Dukes, Garys, and Westinghouses—was the application of the principle of "unintended secondary consequence": a change in one strategy demanded other market, structural, and organizational innovations at all levels. Interestingly enough, *the industrialists who met the administrative challenges were rarely the entrepreneurs who created the great industrial domains.*

WALL STREET LEADERSHIP AND MERGERS

While the initiative for mergers and combinations came from industrialists, it is quite clear that on the eve of the 20th century it was Wall Street which saw the important financial advantages in the merger movement. The J. P. Morgan Company, founded in 1837, really began to exercise leadership only a half century later when it entered the field of railroad refinancing. During the short three-year span from 1899 to 1902, the consolidation and integration movement reached its height when 79 integrations were completed through Morgan intervention, with combined capital in excess of $4 billion. The United States Steel Corporation had a capitalization of $1 billion in common and preferred stocks and almost $.5 billion in bonds. The Morgan Company was further instrumental in the creation of the Amalgamated Copper Company, the American Tobacco Company, the American Woolen Company, the General Electric Company, United States Leather Company, and others.

Concerned by these developments, Congress established in 1903 the Bureau of Corporations which, though lacking judicial sanctions, did have investigatory powers so that it could expose many of the more unpalatable practices of monopolies. In 1904, the Supreme

Court used the Sherman Antitrust Law to order the dissolution of the Northern Securities Company, a railroad holding company put together by J. P. Morgan and Kuhn, Loeb & Company. It was less government pressure and more market pressure, however, that effectively braked the merger movement because by 1904 the drive had largely spent itself. All of the significant industries capable of genuine integration had already been organized and the greater part of the companies thus formed were heavily overcapitalized. But prior to this date, investment bankers, and most particularly the Morgan interests, played the significant roles. It was the Morgan Company that rehabilitated the Baltimore and Ohio Railroad in 1887, gave direction to the future of the Chesapeake and Ohio in 1888, and established the Southern Railway Company in 1893. Having achieved a dominant position in the railroad industry, the Morgan firm next turned, in the 1890's, to heavy industry to create the Federal Steel Company as a major rival to Carnegie Steel. It was the contest between the two that led to the merger and the formation of the United States Steel Corporation in 1901.

An alarming trend developed. Morgan's partners not only sat on the boards of directors of railroads, communications systems, and industrial corporations, but were also heavily influential among the largest insurance, trust companies, and commercial banks of America. Morgan representatives were found on the boards of the New York Life Insurance Company, the Equitable Assurance Company, the Manhattan Bankers and Guarantee Trust Companies, the Chase, the Liberty, and the Hanover banks. In all, Morgan and his partners held 77 interlocking directorates in nearly 50 of the largest financial, industrial, and transportation companies of the country, whose total capitalization and resources came to $10 billion.

GOVERNMENTAL REACTIONS

These developments led to predictable reactions. In 1911, the Supreme Court found that the Standard Oil Company of New Jersey and the American Tobacco Company were combinations in restraint of trade under the Sherman Antitrust Law. The following year the subcommittee of the Democratic House's Committee on Banking and Currency, the so-called Pujo Committee, initiated an intensive critique of the business community by focusing on the concentration of credit and money through the merger of competitive banks and trust companies, the purchase of stocks in competitive banks, the existence of interlocking directorates, and the extension of investment and banking influences into the insurance, railroad, and utility fields.

It was inevitable that these developments should become issues for violently partisan debate in the political arena. Along with other factors it hastened the split between the Republicans, who were divided between Taft and Theodore Roosevelt; it provided favorable grist for the Socialist mill so that Eugene Debs increased his vote from 420,000 in 1908 to nearly 1 million in 1912; it helped Woodrow Wilson to move to the White House. In his first inaugural address Wilson pledged support to three major domestic policies: tariff revision, banking and currency reform, and stiffer antitrust legislation.

In less than two years these programs were successfully achieved. The tariff revisions of 1913 which sought to reestablish effective competition between American and foreign manufacturers marked a definite departure from the "protective" principle expounded by Republican legislators who had dominated policy since the Civil War. In December of 1913 Congress passed the Federal Reserve Act which provided for government supervision and coordination of bank-owned regional Federal Reserve banks through the Federal Reserve Board. While there would be no central bank as such, the Board was to act as a central banking agency. Although the "Fed" proved reasonably elastic and responsive to the needs of business, it was unable to prevent serious financial disturbances and it took no action on the Pujo Committee's findings.

Finally, Congress vindicated Wilson's pledge to curtail private monopoly by passing the Federal Trade Commission Act and the Clayton Antitrust Act in the fall of 1914. The Bureau of Corporations, set up in 1904, was abolished and the Federal Trade Commission was given power to scrutinize activities of corporations engaged in interstate commerce and to check on the manner in which industrial corporations carried out court decrees. The Clayton Act could now be summoned to give added strength to provisions in the Sherman Antitrust Act. Price discriminations were now declared illegal if the effect of such discrimination might be a substantial lessening of competition or a tendency to create a monopoly. Exclusive selling or leasing contracts were also declared illegal and intercorporate stock-

holdings were banned. Interlocking directorates in industrial corporations capitalized at one million or over (which were, or had been,
competitors) were also outlawed.

THE TWENTIETH CENTURY

WORLD WAR I AND AFTER

Permeating these statutes (which were designed to give flesh to
the skeleton of Wilson's "New Freedoms" program) was a firm
resolution to preserve business competition. It may well be said that
the death of J. P. Morgan in Rome in the spring of 1913 and the
passage of the Federal Reserve Act in December of that same year
marked the end of a period in which the money trust exercised its
greatest influence in this country. But domestic developments came
under the shadow of international events when war broke out in
Europe in 1914. The war came at a time of deepening depression in
this country and instead of producing a flood of orders, the initial
effects were to curtail further the demand for American goods. It
was not until early 1915 that European orders began to rise to a
point where there was a reversal in the flow of money and a gradual
emergence from the depression.

Morgan interests played a crucial role during the war by undertaking to provide leadership for a $500-million Anglo-French loan.
Despite this aid, by 1917 Allied credit showed signs of tremendous
stress. About $2 billion worth of bonds and $1 billion in theoretically short-term paper had been absorbed by the American market
and the financial houses now expressed concern as to whether they
could market any large additional issues. The country was obviously
involved economically in the success of the Allied cause and recognized that its long-term prosperity depended on sales to Britain and
France. At a crucial moment in February 1917, Germany announced the resumption of unlimited submarine warfare and the
dawn of an international financial crisis between the Allied powers
and the United States was averted by America's entry into the war.

It is impossible to identify precise dates for important points of
departure into new molds. It is certain that from the First World
War to 1932 Americans went through a period of severe questioning. The country witnessed a revolution in morals, the supremacy of
rural and small town America was challenged by the rise of the city,
participation in the war reinforced the traditional American convic-

tion that evil came from alien sources, and the post-war mood of disillusionment further convinced the country that a policy of isolation was a policy of wisdom. By the end of the Harding period the country was absorbed almost totally with the excitement of a boom economy. With slight interruptions the prosperity ran from 1922 until the fall of 1929. One key to material success during this decade was the enormous increase in productive efficiency which was partly the result of the application of Fredrick W. Taylor's theories of scientific management and partly the result of spreading technological innovations.

Henry Ford provides some essential clues toward understanding the new times. Ford helped to revolutionize industrial production by introducing the first moving assembly line with an endless chain conveyor at his Highland Park plant in 1914. In 1913 it had taken 14 hours to assemble a car; now Ford workers assembled an automobile in roughly an hour and a half. Industrial production almost doubled during the decade—soaring from an index figure of 58 in a 1921 depression year to 110 in 1929. When it is realized that this increase was achieved without any expansion of the labor force, the results of industrial management become more impressive.

The differences between 1914 and 1924 alone are striking. Before the war, technology had not really invaded the American home. Only a small percentage of families owned a telephone. However, the number of telephone installations tell a dramatic story: from 1,355,000 in 1900 to 10,525,000 in 1915, to 20,000,000 in 1930! Telephones were one obvious indication that many of the new industries were geared to the American home. Beef packers and farm producers provided Americans with a more varied diet than ever before; when people moved into city apartments with kitchenettes, the canning industry received a special impetus; and new synthetic industries were sparked by the war, resulting in a great expansion in the chemical industry.

The key element in the 1920 prosperity parade, however, was the stimulation of the construction industry, which was due, in part, to the growth of cities. During this decade New York received a new skyline, the Grand Central section of Manhattan was almost entirely rebuilt, and Fifth Avenue had an almost complete face-lifting. Buildings soared upward and upward, and on May 1, 1931, the "race to the skies" ended successfully, with victory for the Empire State Building which climbed above the Bank of Manhattan's 71 stories and the

Chrysler Building's 77 stories. Outside the great cities, construction went on at even faster rates to meet the demands from families moving to suburbs. Grosse Pointe Park near Detroit grew 700 percent, Shaker Heights outside of Cleveland grew 1,000 percent, and tremendous real estate booms occurred in California and Florida.

BUSINESS PREEMINENCE

The ascendency of American industrialism was recognized by Russian and German scholars who talked seriously and reverently of "Fordismus" as the key to national success. A British traveler noted that, just as in Rome a visitor goes to the Vatican to seek an audience with the Pope, a tourist in America sees Detroit as the mecca and seeks an audience with Henry Ford. So impressive was the hold of industrialists, even on the young, that a group of college students voted Ford the third greatest figure of all time—surpassed only by Napoleon and Christ. So great was the confidence of the American people in Ford that when he announced his Model A early in 1928, over a half-million people made down-payments without ever having seen the car and without even knowing the price.

Perhaps never before in the history of the nation was the business class so secure in its preeminence. Calvin Coolidge expressed the common belief when he said that brains are wealth and "wealth is the chief end of man!" On another occasion Coolidge remarked that "the man who builds a factory builds a temple and the man who works there worships there." The highest accolade was to call a professor or a doctor a good businessman. Bruce Barton's *The Man Nobody Knows* (a best seller in 1925) may have been most revealing in this one comment: "He (Jesus) picked up twelve men from the bottom ranks of business and forced them into an organization that conquered the world." To Barton, Jesus was the world's greatest salesman and his parables the most powerful advertisements of all time.[25]

The 1920's were, in real terms, the booming phase of the second great industrial revolution. The electric light and power industry, the chief field for mergers during the twenties, grew fantastically, with the output of electrical power multiplying over 19 times between 1902 and 1929. Giant utilities came to the fore and 3,700 small utility companies vanished between 1919 and 1927. Chief

---

[25] William Leuchtenburg, *The Perils of Prosperity, 1914–1932* (Chicago: University of Chicago Press, 1958), pp. 188–89.

among the giants were the United Light and Power Company, Commonwealth and Southern, and the Niagara-Hudson Company. Despite Woodrow Wilson's efforts, the merger movement accelerated rapidly in American banking. Branch banking grew phenomenally and the entrepreneurial genius in this area was one Amadeo Peter Giannini, who developed a chain of over 500 banks throughout California under a single holding company. His Bank of America National Trust and Savings Association in San Francisco became the major rival to the established banks of Manhattan.

Chain stores spread fantastically during this same period. The Great Atlantic and Pacific Tea Company grew from 400 stores in 1912 to 15,500 in 1932 and had a volume of sales greater than Ford at its peak. By 1929 the 200 largest nonfinancial corporations in America owned nearly half the corporate wealth of the nation and were growing at a rate much faster than the smaller businesses. Four meat packers controlled 75 percent of the production in their industry, four tobacco companies accounted for 94 percent of the cigarette output, and four motor companies dominated the auto industry.

One of the most singular ideologic developments was a shift in personal goals: whereas the 19th-century American sought individual success, his 20th-century successor sought preeminence in the corporate bureaucracy now open to him because of the emergence of professional managers occasioned, in part, by the divorce of ownership from control.[26]

The results of this new found prosperity were mixed. The nation emphasized materialism yet spent twice as much as before the war on libraries, almost three times as much on hospitals, and invested as much in education as all the rest of the world combined. In December, 1928, President Coolidge declared: "No Congress of the United States ever assembled, on surveying the state of the Union, has met with a more pleasing prospect than that which appears at the present time." In the year of 1928, everything had a Midas touch. The volume of sales on the New York Stock Exchange jumped from 236 million shares in 1923 to 1.125 billion in 1928. Spring found the market in a frenzy and from June to August alone, industrials climbed 110 points, increasing within a single summer the value of industrial stocks by almost a quarter. General Motors, which sold at 99 in 1925, was pegged at 212 in 1928.

---

[26] Adolf A. Berle, Jr., and Gardiner C. Means, *The Modern Corporation and Private Property* (New York: Macmillan Co., 1932).

THE GREAT DEPRESSION

Within a year the roseate dream had turned to a nightmare. In early September of 1929 the stock market broke, rallied, and then broke again; in October it performed unevenly and erratically. On Tuesday, October 9, industrial stocks had fallen 43 points and the ticker closed two-and-a-half hours behind schedule. The prosperity of the 1920's, founded on construction and on the automobile industry, could no longer be sustained. A year after the crash 6 million men walked the streets looking for work. In Cleveland, 50 percent were jobless, in Akron 60 percent, and in Toledo 80 percent. In Donora, a Pennsylvania steel town, only 277 of 13,900 workers held regular jobs. During the three years after the crash an average of 100,000 workers were fired every week.

Caught in the maelstrom, President Hoover was flogged by critics as a stooge of Wall Street and a do-nothing President. He was neither. Hoover stepped up federal construction, urged local governments to accelerate spending, and sought promises of increased capital investments from railroads and utilities. Perhaps his one blind spot was his reliance on local initiative. As a matter of fact, the worse the depression became, the less the cities did. Except for New York (and possibly Pennsylvania, New Jersey, and Wisconsin), state governments did almost nothing for the unemployed. A hundred American cities made no relief appropriations whatsoever during 1932. As breadlines lengthened, the mood of the unemployed grew uglier. Farmers banded together to prevent banks and insurance companies from closing mortgages; 15,000 pickets marched in Taylorsville, Illinois, to stop operations of the Christian County mines in 1932; 3,000 Communist hunger marchers paraded in Washington; over 15,000 unemployed veterans moved on Washington to demand full and immediate payment of bonuses only to be dispersed by troops under the Army Chief of Staff, Douglas MacArthur.

THE NEW DEAL

It was abundantly clear that Hoover's days in the White House were numbered. The landslide victory for Franklin D. Roosevelt in 1932 was no surprise. F.D.R. and his New Deal advisers made much of the argument that a mature economy and the closing of the West were factors explaining the decline in economic advance. The task, therefore, was not the discovery or exploitation of natural resources or the production, necessarily, of more goods; rather it was, said Roosevelt, "the soberer, less dramatic business of administering resources and plans, already in hand. . . ."[27]

One explanation for the depression that appealed to some professional economists was provided by John Maynard Keynes. Keynes argued that whereas consumer expenditures depend mainly on the size of the national income and the character of its distribution between the poor and rich, producer-goods expenditures and investment depend mainly on the state of business sentiment. On this point Keynes argued that national income could only increase if investment increased, and vice-versa—a notion with which most businessmen could agree. He concluded finally that the duty of ordering the current volume of investments cannot be left in private hands—that is, to business sentiment—but must include the government which has an important positive role to play.[28] The New Dealers were happy to embrace Keynes' lesson that government spending could create prosperity.

It is not yet clear, however, that a poor income-distribution pattern was the chief cause of the troubles. Figures suggest that the concentration of income in the upper brackets was also increasing during the satisfactory periods of economic growth from 1900 to 1913. Whether the failure to revive quickly after the 1929 crash was due to government regulations, the inflexibility of big business, an inefficient income distribution that caused excessive saving, the war debt problem from World War I, the existence of a mature economy, or the absence of new innovation have been analyzed endlessly. One point is clear: after 1929, business faced years of the most severe criticism in its history. "Fordismus" was followed by a forlorn loss of confidence in business.[29]

WORLD WAR II

The tremendously successful response of business to the challenges of World War II not only helped turn the tide and fortunes of war, but occasioned a renewed confidence in the American business system itself. By 1945 the war effort, consuming 57 percent of

---

[27] Richard Hofstadter, *The American Political Tradition* (New York: Alfred A. Knopf, Inc., 1948), p. 326.

[28] John M. Keynes, *The General Theory of Employment, Interest and Money* (New York: Harcourt Brace & Co., 1936).

[29] Earl Cheit, (ed.), *The Business Establishment* (New York: John Wiley & Sons, 1964).

the national income, had created a situation unprecedented in American history. Civil War costs had barely gone above 25 percent of national income in the North and World War I had approached this mark only in 1918. While business and government seemed to have repeated the errors committed during the previous wars, in retrospect the business achievement was truly remarkable.

The war forced both government and business to cooperate more closely for mutual survival. In the process it also caused businessmen to look backward more realistically to the New Deal and to recognize that the "forced marriages" of that period had led to a kind of partnership which could grow in importance in subsequent years. Examples are the Federal Trade Commission and the Securities and Exchange Commission which found it necessary to seek the advice of business, and government contracts which provided tangible incentives. Between 1940 and 1943, of $18 billion worth of war plants built by private companies, three quarters were units exceeding $10 million and nearly a third were units exceeding $50 million. In short, the government was operating on contracts with relatively few large corporations. Private industries, such as General Electric, were given approval to experiment with atomic equipment and the Duquesne Light Company was one of the first in the construction of pilot atomic plants for industrial use.

By the end of the war, a Roper poll found that a majority of the American people believed that few businessmen had the good of the nation in mind when they made important decisions. Five years later *Look* magazine, in another poll, found 80 percent approval for business. When analyzed, however, reasons for approval hinge on material benefits rather than on respect for responsible leadership. And yet, almost in paradox, it was the postwar period that saw business leadership take a significant turn in its philosophy to consider—possibly more seriously than ever before—the public and social responsibilities that go with great wealth and great power.

CONCLUSION

In this historical development (wherein business leaders have rather regularly asserted that free enterprise is as essential to democracy as free elections) a curious paradox still persists. What was noted at the turn of the century still persisted in 1960, and may be found to persist in 1790. It is this: despite the widely held view that the United States is a business society, the majority of wage earners did not regard themselves as businessmen or probusiness. "Regardless of prosperity, better public relations, and more independent business enterprises in relation to the rest of the population," said Thomas Cochran, "a feeling of unity with the aims of business leadership seems to be lacking. People apparently respected but did not trust business leaders. Corporations might in truth become guardians of the common welfare, but the public was not yet convinced. . . . American businessmen, for all their important position in society, did not epitomize America as did the independent farmers of an earlier era."[30]

Yet those who believe firmly in the values of both cultural, political, and economic pluralism insist that the role of private enterprise is vital, and that the large and mature corporation, in cooperation with government, or in creative competition to government, can help to achieve a new golden age for the nation. The history of American business provides contradicting bases for prophesy. It also provides a clear testament to the practical application of such basic concepts as freedom, "associationalism", contract, and the like to American institutions.

RECOMMENDED READINGS

ANDREANO, RALPH. *New Views on American Economic Development.* Cambridge, Mass.: Schenkman Publishing Co., 1965.

BAUMOL, WILLIAM. *Business Behavior, Value and Growth.* New York: Macmillan, 1959.

CHANDLER, ALFRED D., JR. *Strategy and Structure: Chapters in the History of the Individual Enterprise.* Cambridge: M.I.T. Press, 1962.

COCHRAN, THOMAS C. *The American Business System: A Historical Perspective.* New York: Harper & Row Torchbooks, 1957.

HACKER, LOUIS. *The Triumph of American Capitalism.* New York: Simon & Schuster, 1940.

JONES, PETER D' ALRAY. *The Consumer Society: A History of American Capitalism.* London: Penguin Books, 1965.

MARRIS, ROBIN. *The Economic Theory of Managerial Capitalism.* New York: The Free Press, 1964.

MILLER, WILLIAM, (ed.) . *Men in Business: Essays in the History of Entrepreneurship.* New York: Harper Torchbooks, 1962.

---

[30] Cochran, *op. cit.,* p. 204.

NORTH, DOUGLASS C. *The Economic Growth of the United States: 1790–1860.* Englewood Cliffs, N.J.: Prentice-Hall, Inc., 1966.

———. *Growth and Welfare in the American Past: A New Economic History.* Englewood Cliffs, N.J.: Prentice-Hall, Inc., 1966.

SUGGESTED READINGS

FOGEL, ROBERT W. *Railroads and American Economic Growth: Essays in Econometric History.* Baltimore: The Johns Hopkins Press, 1964.

Fortune magazine. *U.S.A.: The Permanent Revolution.* New York: McGraw-Hill Book Co., 1951.

HARRIS, SEYMOUR (ed.). *American Economic History.* New York: McGraw-Hill Book Co., 1961.

KROOS, HERMAN. *American Economic Development: The Progress of Business Civilization 2d ed.* Englewood Cliffs, N.J.: Prentice-Hall, Inc., 1966.

LEUCHTENBURG, WILLIAM. *The Perils of Prosperity, 1914–1932.* Chicago: University of Chicago Press, 1958.

NATIONAL ASSOCIATION OF MANUFACTURERS. *The American Individual Enterprise System: Its Nature and Future.* 2 vols. New York: McGraw-Hill Book Co., 1946.

ROBERTSON, ROSS. *History of the American Economy.* New York: Harcourt, Brace & Co., 1955.

TEMIN, PETER. *Iron and Steel in Nineteenth Century America: An Economic Inquiry.* Cambridge: M.I.T. Press, 1964.

WILLIAMSON, HAROLD (ed.). *The Growth of the American Economy: An Introduction to the Economic History of the United States.* Englewood Cliffs, N.J.: Prentice-Hall, Inc., 1951.

II. FREEDOM

ACCORDING TO John Adams, liberty is a self-determining power in an intellectual agent. It implies thought, choice, and power. And for Adams and his contemporaries, freedom was the natural atmosphere of the human mind. The idea of freedom for human instincts would have shocked them, had it occurred to them at all. But they would have understood, far better than we do, the modern totalitarian systems which are linked to ideologies that deny the value of reason. They understood, if not from experience then from history, that dictatorship is necessarily associated with irrationality. When the power of thought and individual expression may be exercised by only a few, there is no place for freedom.

Philosophers from Aristotle to Jean-Paul Sartre have generally conceded that freedom is a quality of the human spirit and that man, merely by virtue of being a man, possesses the capacity for exercising and enjoying liberty.[1] It is at this point that a difficulty arises. If freedom of thought is an uncontestable human right, freedom to choose is conditioned by individual value judgments that display some discipline or lack of it. As a consequence, the power to act, once a choice has been made, becomes circumscribed by custom, convention, or law. For, in securing to the individual his freedom to choose, society finds it necessary to prescribe rules that channel or restrain what might otherwise be impulsive or antisocial behavior

---

[1] Mortimer J. Adler, *The Idea of Freedom* (New York: Doubleday & Co., 1958), p. 150.

73

that could endanger the choices, lives, and property of the multitude of human beings who constitute it.

Under our constitution this difficulty is further compounded by the fact that we are explicitly "dedicated to the proposition that all men are created equal." But differences in the nature of human drives, abilities, and even physiques are such that in countries in which economic and social equality are established politically, individual freedom appears to dwindle in proportion as the goals of the state are realized. Whether there can be equality *and* freedom is a subject that has been debated. But what is behind the juxtaposition of the two concepts in our polity is the idea that rights entail duties. In asserting his constitutional right to life, liberty, and the pursuit of happiness, the individual assumes a responsibility for the lives, liberty, and welfare of those around him. They are no less privileged than he, and, should he lose sight of this fact in his dealings with them, the law steps in to arbitrate.

This intrusion of law becomes more, rather than less, as times goes by. There are several reasons advanced to explain why we are having to forego the old proposition that a government governs best which governs least. To begin with, it is probably a fact that the ancient concepts of honor and duty that loomed so large in the minds of the men who wrote the Constitution have somewhat weakened. The 19th-century's enthusiasm, more pronounced here than abroad, for applying the survival theory of the evolutionists to social and economic life may have had something to do with this. Then, the growth of technology and of the massive organization it made possible may have promoted a kind of impersonality that made it possible for the idea of laissez-faire to develop without any countervailing idea of responsibility. "It's just good business" described the functioning of a system assumed to be amoral and therefore not responsible. This was freedom in an ethical vacuum, operating as it cannot operate among men because human choices are invariably conditioned for good or ill by some innate value system.

Of late years, society seems to have been driven to revive the ideas of duty and honor, not merely by the appeal to law, but by fostering group action based on the principle of freedom of association. Groups, large or small, are being formed at every level of our culture, sometimes merely for entertainment but more frequently to represent their membership's ambitions, hopes, and values to the larger society of which they are a part.

The organization man is not the unique product of the corporate world. He exists in trade and professional associations and in the wide variety of leagues and clubs that are so popular in our society. Many of these fraternities tend to demand the protection of their rights by the enforcement of duties, as they see them, on individuals or organizations outside their membership as well as within it. The idea of such associations is not new. Nor has their nature changed much since Adam Smith, with as much cynicism as truth, observed:

People of the same trade seldom meet together, even for merriment and diversion, but the conversation ends in a conspiracy against the public, or in some contrivance to raise prices. It is impossible indeed to prevent such meetings, by any law which either could be executed, or would be consistent with liberty and justice.[2]

These free associations have the power to shape a new America. They may be altering the nature of our freedom, as their drive for the protection of their common heritage of rights demands from their membership a kind of group loyalty that may seriously restrict individual freedom of choice. In view of this speculation, perhaps we should examine the nature of individual freedom as it will exist during the 1970's, to see what rights we have and what duties we may have acquired.

In our society it is presumed that a man may live where he pleases, eat what he likes, marry as he chooses, work where and at what he finds personally rewarding. But too often the presumptions run head-on into taboos and prejudices. Aside from these subtle barriers to the exercises of freedom are regulations which apply to all. Once a man sets up a domicile he must observe fire, health, and building regulations. His children's births must be registered. He may not chastise, exploit, or neglect them beyond certain limits, and the law further compels him to have them vaccinated against small-pox and to send them to school for a prescribed number of years. It prevents them from voting until they have reached a legal and literate age.

As far as his daily living is concerned, he must register the car he drives and qualify for a certificate to drive it. He must then observe speed limits, traffic codes and patterns, parking regulations, inspection regulations, and toll-road regulations and tariffs. Once he has chosen his work, he may be required to join a trade union or a

---

[2] Adam Smith, *The Wealth of Nations*, Book I, chap. x, p. 2.

professional society. State and government then take a part of his wages for the task of sustaining the common good and demand an accounting of him once a year. As far as his recreation is concerned, he may not hunt even during an open season without a license. He may be a spectator at sports as he chooses but may not organize sports activities on a traveled street. It is illegal for him to bet on a horse race, except at the track. It is likewise illegal for him to buy or sell liquor without the approval of the state. He may not deliver papers, shine shoes, or play a musical instrument on a street corner without a license. And, if all these frustrations are too much to bear, the law does not permit him to take his own life, and, should he try and fail, there are penalties. Should he run afoul of the law and be condemned as a result of serious crime, he cannot choose the manner of his dying; he cannot ask for hemlock and depart with dignity and beauty in the grand classic manner. The nature of his demise is prescribed by law, from state to state: gas chamber, rope, or chair, though the choice of these is made in advance, one might argue, over the years, through choice of residence or choice of criminal occupation. Once deceased, the citizen who has departed, whether in the order of nature or according to the sanctions of law, sets in motion a train of civic amenities regulating his interment, and he has now no hope whatever of being interred somewhere in his own yard, however extensive it may be.

It is obvious that even in a free society man lives in the eternal dilemma of being encouraged to think and choose for himself in the midst of civil limits that demand that he get permission to follow choice through to action. If liberty "implies thought, choice, and power," it is the power to act that is restricted. This results, perhaps, from the growing pressure in a society as complex as ours for guarantees of freedom from both fear and want. In an era in which the average man begins to feel that he can act on fewer and fewer decisions of his own, the charm of freedom *from* supplants the original drive for freedom *to*. But the idea that freedom to do something arises out of freedom from inhibiting factors is not a new one. Aristotle insisted that a certain amount of goods was necessary to a man for a good life—a good citizen's life, that is. It is perhaps on this basis that it is argued that security, well-being, and freedom are one and the same. The idea behind state socialism, essentially, is that when basic human needs and wants are met by social plan, a cleaner, better, more wholesome world emerges. But this theory is rejected by those who believe that restrictions on individual initiative, however charitable the aim, will ultimately vitiate the natural ability to choose.

While the first concern of the average man would appear to be economic, since it is on this efficiency that his survival depends, it is frequently on political determinants that his prospects for a life with liberty depend. Political freedom can be divided into two categories: *procedural* (freedom from), which guarantees the citizen exemptions from threats to his liberty (habeas corpus, search warrants), freedom from fear, from want, and so on; and *substantive* (freedom to), which guarantees him fulfillment. Under this latter heading fall what have been described as the fundamental liberties of a free people: freedom of worship, of speech, of the press, and of assembly.

In a republic, government is the people's big organization. Once they have given it authority to represent them, it must act, but authority is vested in men as leaders and these leaders must have the capacity to implement their authority with power. Many citizens, therefore, are concerned over the growth of the power of government. The question that remains to be resolved is whether economic power and political power can be held in balance by individual foresight, reflection, and choice; or whether, if liberty is to remain feasible as a way of life, it will tend to be regarded as a collective rather than an individual prerogative.

If rights entail duties, as we have traditionally maintained, then for the preservation of freedom these duties must be freely undertaken. It appears to be true that, in the past, economic freedom has been exercised without much awareness of social expectations. Society's insistence, through government, that its needs be recognized and met has caused conspicuous changes in the historical attitude of the tycoons of the 19th-century. Further, sheer organization size has moved a broad sector of society within the economic confines of business. One of the most interesting aspects of this evolution is that the dynamic energy of business is redirected, not taken away. The capitalist system, thus altered, has given the lie to Marx. Our people have taken a hand in the ordering of the economic system, not with intent either to destroy or to dominate, but to equalize some of its pressures.

The pristine American drive for a coherent and adaptable public government repeats itself today in the push to improve the functioning of those private economic associations—the corporation and the labor union—which are now larger than many civil states. These two have much to offer society in the way of fostering the ideal of freedom, if only as examples of their potential for developing and bettering the human condition.

It remains for the corporation and the union, as free associations, to develop, independent of external pressures on them, the kind of sound internal government, concerned as much with polity as with profit, that can make decisions based not on unthinking expediency but on the thought, choice, and power of intellectual agents.

For we have reached a point in our political and economic evolution where tradition seems to fail as a referent. In view of the technological and scientific originality of the 20th century, this is not surprising, for neither the direction nor the rate of change can be independent of the nature of the men who foster it. We live in a time when the convictions out of which our free nation was born must be reaffirmed, and individual willingness to meet the responsibilities that Freedom entails must be revived, even in association.

The chapters that follow discuss the concept of freedom of association as a tradition in this country and as it relates to the largest of our private associations, the corporation and the labor union.

3. Freedom of Association

OUTLINE

TRUE FREEDOM of association is possible only in an open society. Business associations, trade unions, and professional groups, if they exist at all in a society that is not free, are merely a part of the administrative machinery of government. They can be eliminated altogether if they do not appear to be necessary to the common good.

Yet associations represent responses to unfilled human needs. When social processes approach a condition analogous to the physicist's concept of equilibrium, society moves with relative serenity, and existing associations are adequate to the demands of organized man; the international order exhibited this phenomenon between the Congress of Vienna in 1815 and the outbreak of World War I. Unhappily, the social machine rarely moves with clockwork regularity, and serious threats to the status quo invariably result in the

jurist's being hastily summoned to resolve matters. Should the judge
fail or somehow evade his responsibility, then the soldier stands
ready to become the final arbiter.

Survival of free associations demands two minimal conditions:
the right of people freely to respond to changes through organizations
that usually are, in their initial stages, extralegal in nature, and the
ability of a judicial system to incorporate new institutions into the
corpus of jurisprudence through careful definition and refinement.
The manner in which the Supreme Court has moved in expanding
the concept of property from claims on corporeal things to include
noncorporeal items is an example frequently touched upon—perhaps never more tellingly than in John Commons' early work in
1904.[1]

The changing interpretations that have been typical of contract,
of property, and of employer liability have also been true of the
concept of association. In the medieval world the formation of a new
religious sect was heresy to the Church, which viewed its mission as
divinely ordained; in the 16th century the formation of private
corporations for the narrow ends of the incorporators was heresy to a
nation-state, which considered its dynastic aims as paramount; in
18th-century England the formation of industrial workers' associations was anathema under the Combination Acts. The point is clear:
when the economic or political order changes significantly, chain
reactions set in that lead to the rise of new associations and the fall
of older ones. Yet there is a time lag before the courts become aware
of the significance of these new social forms. Rarely does the old
order extend a welcome hand to the new social unit. And, in that
important interval, the new associations must demonstrate a tough-
ness, a resiliency, indeed, an essentiality, to enable them to survive
until the mantle of legal protection envelops them.

In this country today both corporations and unions—relative
newcomers to the family of associations—are doing things to enlarge
the nation's conscience in some areas and to offend the community's
sense of values in others. In either event, gains and losses will be
reckoned in terms of our answers to the following questions:

1. Do the individual's responsibilities toward, and claims
against, the associations differ with varying kinds of association?

2. Is there a hierarchy of associations, with those on the lower

---

[1] John Commons, *Legal Foundations of Capitalism* (New York: Macmillan Co.,
1924).

strata deriving rights and privileges from superior ones? Or do men have an intrinsic right to associate freely, thereby imparting to organizations resulting from such decisions the right to exist and operate largely independent of the will of other associations?

3. Are relationships among the various existing associations determined by conflict? Or may an intrinsic harmony be sensed in interassociational functions and purposes?

These questions can most effectively be viewed by distinguishing between two major sets of problems that inhere in (*a*) individual-group relationships and (*b*) intergroup relationships, respectively.

THE INDIVIDUAL AND FREEDOM OF ASSOCIATION

Philosophically, there is an apparent paradox in the Western tradition, which insists on the inviolability of the individual human being even as it asserts man's dependence on other men for the fulfillment of his human potential. This duality in man's nature has led to speculation regarding the appropriate powers and restrictions that human associations have and do not have. The question usually gets down to this issue: since man needs associations, do the associations themselves have a life of their own? Do they, in effect, have claim to existence that effectively transcends the rights of the individuals who compose them?

Democratic and totalitarian societies answer this question differently. The Greco-Roman political traditions and the Judeo-Christian religious creeds have always asserted that society exists for men. The Marxists and Fascists have insisted that—at least in the case of the state—the individuals exist for the political entity. Andrei Vishinsky's *The Soviet Concept of Law* is a classic contemporary statement of this view.

Yet assertion of the prior claims of the individual have not prevented democracies, as Holmes wryly noted, from marching unwilling conscripts off to war at the point of a bayonet—a practice that, among other coercive practices of modern states, led Holmes to conclude that "the sacredness of human life is purely a municipal ideal of no validity outside the jurisdiction. I believe that force . . . is the *ultima ratio*."[2] To Holmes it was clear that this issue was theoretical to the point of absurdity, since the facts clearly indicated

---

[2] Oliver Wendell Holmes, *Holmes-Pollock Letters*, ed. Mark de Wolfe Howe (Cambridge: Harvard University Press, 1941), Vol. II, p. 36.

that every powerful association always moves to preserve its life at the expense of the lives of its citizens. Here is one instance in which the views of a distinguished Soviet jurist and a distinguished American jurist seem remarkably harmonious.

Perhaps the confusion arises from failure to note the important differences between associations that men, because of their needs, are compelled to form and associations where the range of freedom to associate and disassociate is comparatively large. Man's nature involves certain drives that require the support and co-operation of his fellowmen. In the purely biological order, survival of the species demands association. The West is still struggling with the implications of family obligations to the initially contracting partners and to the subsequent offspring. And, when families become involved with other families, the need for a civil society with new kinds of authorities becomes essential for orderly living.

ESSENTIAL AND CIRCUMSTANTIAL ASSOCIATIONS

These considerations lead to distinctions between "natural" associations (those absolutely needed for human existence and hence involving more coercive control over man's will to disassociate) and the forms of human organization that develop out of historically created needs. In a word, family and state appear to be universal and enduring imperatives, whereas modern corporations, modern unions, and modern lodges or other fraternities are generated by the particular circumstances of time, place, and special needs. These latter forms of association are clearly man-made reactions to man-made conditions. Unions were never dreamed of in a pastoral, slave economy; business corporations and trade associations were impossible under the closed economy operations of the so-called "dark ages." This modest distinction between what associations man must accept, simply because he is what he is, and associations he may invent because of his ability to get himself into and out of awkward situations, provides a clue to the dilemma that Holmes never fully came to grips with in terms satisfactory to the conscience and intellect of free men.

In the pursuit of its legitimate ends, one of which clearly is survival, the state, to sustain itself, may avail itself of its monopoly over violence; it may summon unheroic men to meet heroic challenges on the grounds that the death of order would result in such chaos that the individual man himself could not decently survive. Even here, it is difficult to sense the appropriate distinctions between a state (viewed as a condition for human existence) and the particular government that adorns the basic institution with its bureaucracy, symbols, sanctions, and the like.

When, therefore, we now proceed to define freedom of association as the absence of external restraint on a person's desire to associate with others for common purposes, we recognize that such freedom is greater or less as the need for that particular association is greater or less. Man's nature can impose an imperium that he may not particularly like but that he most particularly needs; circumstances may lead to somewhat the same result but, since circumstances change, the associations that base their legitimacy on it invariably face a continuing demand for re-examination of their *raison d'être* and for defense of their continued existence. That man instinctively recognizes these gradations can be illustrated with a few quick examples. In earlier periods of Western society, arranging a marriage was a solemn and protracted affair, and churches and courts set up elaborate safeguards around the marriage contract to prevent easy disassociation. In the case of the state, man's freedom to associate or diassociate is practically nil. With a corporation, we come to a different kind of arrangement; here a stockholder may move in and out almost at will and with more latitude for alternatives than the individual citizen has in moving in or out of a political party. The modern business corporation represents "voluntary man's way of achieving industrial competence" and reflects, therefore, the consequences of that freedom to form associations that is an important element in every humane society.[3] Similarly, the union represents the laboring man's voluntary effort to achieve justice and status in a democratic order.[4]

In discussing associations, therefore, it must be noted that we are speaking of the *freely formed contractual types* represented by corporations and unions and not of those associations that are rooted in human nature itself. Walter Lippmann's comments on this distinction are appropriate:

Though it is clear, I think, that the business corporation is a creature of the state, there are many other forms of human association which are

---

[3] Roger M. Blough, *The Corporate Key to a Greater Society* (New York: McGraw-Hill Book Co., 1959).

[4] "The fight for greater social justice is the *raison d'être* of the trade union movement." *Trade Unionism as an Ethical Force in a Pecuniary Society* (address by Solomon Barkin, Tenth Annual Conference of the International Association of Personnel Women, (New York, April 30, 1960).

born and flourish and yet do not depend for their existence upon a legal
privilege. The family is such an association, and so is a community, a religious fellowship, a learned society, a clan, a guild.

Surely an organization like General Motors Corporation is a wholly
different type of association from a family, a club, a church, a trade-
union, a bar association, a medical society, or a political party.

Though here as in all human phenomena, there are borderline cases
which it would be hard to classify, it would be doctrinaire not to recognize the practical difference between a business organization and a natural association. The one is held together by a cash nexus in a framework
of legal rights; the other is bound together by kinship or fellowship.

The associations into which men group themselves spontaneously,
naturally, instinctively, voluntarily, present a very different problem of
social control from those which are deliberately contrived and organized.
In the case of the business corporation and the public agency the problem is to define the purposes of the legal creature and to see that it conforms to them. This is the problem of regulating business corporations
and government bureaus in the public interest. But in the case of natural
associations, the problem is not how the state shall regulate an organization it has created, but how it shall accommodate the smaller associations
to each other and to the social order as a whole.

This has been a perplexing problem throughout the development of
the modern state. For if the natural associations are let entirely alone, a
chaotic struggle for survival ensues in which certain groups, be they family, clans, or churches, or guilds, or political parties, become dominant
and tyrannical. This was so much the condition of affairs in the seventeenth and eighteenth centuries that from the time of the civil wars in
England to the French Revolution, from Hobbes to the Constituent Assembly of France which made the Declaration of the Rights of Man,
there was a growing disposition to deny all autonomy to any association.
"The Nation is essentially the source of all sovereignty; nor can any individual or any body of men, be entitled to any authority which is not expressly derived from it" *(Declaration of the Rights of Man)*. But it was
soon evident that to deny to any body of men any authority which is not
expressly derived from the nation, that is to say, from the national legislature, was to found what we now call a totalitarian state. It was to bring
the individual, the family, the local community, the church, and the
guild directly under the centralized authority of the officials of the state.
Thus, as Gierke pointed out, the isolated individual was left confronting
the absolute state with no "groups that mediated between the State and
the Individual."[5]

---

[5] Walter Lippmann, *The Good Society* (Boston: Little, Brown & Co., Atlantic
Monthly Press, 1943), pp. 308–11.

While this last condition is actually inherent in the pathology of totalitarianism, one must not lose sight of the fact that when the power of any association grows so large that it can exert irresistible pressure on the others, it becomes an equal threat to freedom.

FREEDOM OF ASSOCIATION IN THE CONTEXT OF HISTORY

As a general proposition, it can be asserted that the more absolute the dominant association is during a given period, the less likelihood there is for voluntary association to come into being and to flourish. Whenever any small group of men becomes dedicated to acquisition of power at the expense of other social and moral authorities, storm signals fly. In modern times it has been the state that has posed the major threat to freedom, but it must not be forgotten that "voluntary" associations can produce results that impose certain kinds of involuntary servitude on others. Toward the close of the nineteenth century, James Bryce confessed his gnawing concern over corporate power when he wrote:

He who considers the irresponsible nature of the power which three or four men, or perhaps one man, can exercise through a great corporation, such as a railroad or telegraph company, the injury they can inflict on the public as well as on their competitors, the cynical audacity with which they have often used their wealth to seduce officials and legislators from the path of virtue will find nothing unreasonable in the desire of the American masses to regulate the management of corporations and narrow the range of their action.[6]

Yet Bryce's concern has a hollow ring to the present-day heirs of those early corporation executives; the new executives insist that the world of the 1890's is separated from 1960 by more than a time dimension involving only four-score years. Edward Hanley, President of Allegheny Ludlum Steel Corporation, declared in an address to the American Iron and Steel Institute on May 28, 1959, that the pendulum has swung too far in the direction of monopoly unionism, which he defined as "the exclusive privilege of certain individuals and/or organizations to carry on a traffic in the organizing and control of unions of working or laboring persons." He added:

That this is truly the situation we find today among the production employees in numerous industries is obvious on its face. Some 99% in the

---

[6] James Bryce, *The American Commonwealth* (New York: Macmillan Co., 1897), p. 856.

automobile industry are members of the UAW; some 96% of the rubber workers are members of the rubber workers union; some 98.7% of the employees in the steel industry belong to the United Steelworkers Union; some 99.4% of the employees in the printing and publishing industry are members of the unions; and so on.

In addition, inter-union agreements are being threatened which, if consummated and exercised, would enable one or two men to wield, ultimately, the greatest power that has ever been concentrated in this country.[7]

The point at issue here is that the more power any association seeks and acquires the more ruthlessly it can behave toward its own larger constituency and the more effectively it can isolate the individual from other kinds of rewarding associations. In the larger perspective of history three factors may be identified as having operated to isolate man from those smaller associations that he can contrive and effectively control: the rise of the nation-state, the religious revolutions, and the emergence of capitalism in its modern guise.

The state has always been viewed as a major threat to freedom of association, since it alone has a monopoly on coercive measures and a control over modern man unequaled by other associations. The net effect of statism has been to destroy the vitality of intervening associations. Between *Leviathan*, the state, and the individual citizen was a wide, insuperable gulf. Technology and the machine process generally contributed to the isolation of the individual. Emile Durkheim in one of his monumental studies declared: "What is factually characteristic of our development is that it has successively destroyed all established social contexts; one after another they have been banished either by the slow usury of time or by violent revolution, and in such fashion that nothing has been developed to replace them."[8] Other scholars, like Le Play and Duguit in France; Gierke in Germany; Maitland and Tawney, Belloc and the Hammonds in England; and Riesman, Kahler, and Herberg in America, have called attention to this same phenomenon.

The second factor that weakened the traditional bonds between man and his own communities occurred during the period of the

[7] Edward Hanley, *The Minutes of the Last Meeting* (Pittsburgh: Allegheny Ludlum Steel Corporation, 1959), pp. 2–3.

[8] Durkheim, *Le Suicide* (Paris: F. Alcan, 1897), p. 446.

Reformation. The rise of Protestantism in the sixteenth century challenged the concept of a corporate church with its hierarchy, its sacraments, and its liturgy. The new man of God relied on *his* interpretation of the Bible, on *his* expression of individual faith, on *his* unmediated personal prayers. This heroic yet lonely man, this solitary voice of the individual conscience, became the hallmark of the new religious order, and the price was again a weakening of a sense of community.

The third factor was modern capitalism. The concept of the economic man (spurred by impulsions toward self-gain and competitive endeavor) was clearly parallel to Calvin's man of God supported by inner conviction and by conscience. Philosophers, from the times of the Physiocrats in France and of Adam Smith in England, have sought to find in the individualistic aspect of capitalism the roots of harmony and progress. Impersonal markets, invisible hands, and machine processes reduced the sense of personal solidarity with others and personal responsibility for others. Here, parenthetically, it may be remarked, lies the essence of the contemporary challenge to business and unions as free associations. It lies within their destiny to make membership creative, responsive, and rewarding or to hasten the drift to what Hilaire Belloc has called the "Servile State."

The need to balance man's drive for individual autonomy and liberty with modifications on his independence and freedom necessarily imposed by associations is obvious.

Since society cannot function without the presence of spirit, men will insist on collectively worshipping idols rather than suffer the agonies of rootlessness and despair. Where subtle and satisfying forms of organic solidarity are unavailable, men will seek to escape chaos by adopting or imposing the yoke of mechanism. To be truly viable, the forms of association must ingeniously pattern the claims of human nature, the expectations of men in society, the underlying functions of social life, and the changing requirements of culture. It is plain that a society founded on sheer egoism, a society which operates on too grand a scale, at too rapid a pace, will undergo atomization, anomic loss of a sense of belongingness. Such under-integration of the moral community and the spatial order may always be expected to generate pendular reactions.

If liberal society recurrently runs the risk of under-integration and absence of compelling loyalties and coherent motivations, totalitarian society offers us no other prospect than that of over-integration, the substi-

tution of mechanism for spirit. The killing yoke of undivided oneness
. . . is thrust at us because we cannot bear the ravages of total absence of
community. . . .[9]

THE AMERICAN EXPERIENCE

The genius of America has been its capacity to sustain and foster
these intermediary associations which restore the sense of community
without reducing man to a cog within the organization. On this
point, no one has been more widely quoted than Alexis de Tocqueville, largely because no one has improved upon the observations he
made over a century ago:

I do not propose to speak of those political associations by the aid of
which men endeavor to defend themselves against the despotic action of a
majority, or against the aggressions of regal power. That subject I have
already treated.

Those associations only which are formed in civil life, without reference to political objects are here adverted to. The political associations
which exist in the United States are only a single feature in the midst of
the immense assemblage of associations in that country. Americans of all
ages, all conditions, and all dispositions constantly form associations.
They have not only commercial and manufacturing companies, in which
all take part, but associations of a thousand other kinds—religious, moral
serious, futile, general or restricted, enormous or diminutive. The Americans make associations to give entertainments, to found seminaries, to
build inns, to construct churches, to diffuse books, to send missionaries to
the antipodes; they found in this manner hospitals, prisons, and schools.
If it be proposed to inculcate some truth, or to foster some feeling, by the
encouragement of a great example, they form a society. Wherever, at the
head of some new undertaking, you see the government in France, or a
man of rank in England, in the United States you will be sure to find an
association.

A government might perform the part of some of the largest American companies; and several states, members of the Union, have already
attempted it; but what political power could every carry on the vast multitude of lesser undertakings which the American citizens perform every
day with the assistance of the principle of association? It is easy to foresee
that the time is drawing near when man will be less and less able to produce, of himself alone, the commonest necessaries of life. The task of the
governing power will therefore perpetually increase, and its very efforts
will extend it every day. The more it stands in the place of associations,

---

[9] Benjamin N. Nelson, "The Future of Illusions," in *Man in Contemporary Society*
(New York: Columbia University Press, 1955), Vol. II, p. 975.

the more will individuals, losing the notion of combining together, require its assistance; these are causes and effects which unceasingly create each other. Will the administration of the country ultimately assume the management of all the manufactures which no single citizen is able to carry on? And if a time at length arrives when, in consequence of the extreme subdivision of landed property, the soil is split into an infinite number of parcels, so that it can only be cultivated by companies of husbandmen, will it be necessary that the head of the government should leave the helm of state to follow the plow? The morals and the intelligence of a democratic people would be as much endangered as its business and manufactures if the government ever wholly usurped the place of private companies. . . .

Nothing, in my opinion, is more deserving of our attention than the intellectual and moral associations of America. The political and industrial associations of that country strike us forcibly; but the others elude our observation, or, if we discover them, we understand them imperfectly, because we have hardly ever seen anything of the kind. It must, however, be acknowledged that they are as necessary to the American people as the former, and perhaps more so. In democratic countries the science of association is the mother of science; the progress of all the rest depends upon the progress it has made.

Amongst the laws which rule human societies, there is one which seems to be more precise and clear than all others. If men are to remain civilized, or to become so, the art of associating together must grow and improve in the same ratio in which the equality of conditions is increased.[10]

Clearly, freedom of association is not an absolute right and may be modified to the degree that man's nature, or special circumstances, make the association necessary for the survival and prosperity of man himself. Beyond these basic needs, however, are the wide range of problems and ambitions that spur men voluntarily to form associations for specific purposes. The essential difference between open and closed societies is the difference in the freedom accorded individuals to form such voluntary associations. Man has a necessary relationship to the state and a circumstantial one to corporations and unions; since the former involves greater compulsion over man, there is the need continuously to view government functions in the light of an easily formulated question: can and will this function be discharged as effectively by voluntary associations? Not to be missed,

---

[10] Alexis de Tocqueville, *Democracy in America* (New York: Alfred A. Knopf, Inc., 1945), Vol. II, chap. V, pp. 106 and 110.

of course, is the recognition that private associations can also transcend their boundaries to assume powers and functions not traditionally theirs. This recognition underlies the dialectic that goes on continuously between the adherents of the welfare state and the metrocorporation, respectively.

When men voluntarily band together for private purposes they inevitably accept certain role functions that a division of labor imposes; they accept in other words, limitations on their individual freedoms to do certain things in certain ways at times of their own choosing because they believe that their individual good is more effectively served through association. But, once society reaches a point where no real option any longer exists to associate or disassociate from an allegedly voluntary association, that association is no longer voluntary in anything but name.

This is what leads us to try to understand how freedoms (and the limits on freedom) are promoted or impeded by "voluntary" associations, such as corporations and unions, in a highly complex and industrialized society. Are right-to-work laws devices to protect real or nominal freedoms of laborers? When corporations are involved in defense contracts, must they accept from governments the police powers involved in security clearance and impose dismissal for disloyalty rather than for inefficiency? These questions illustrate the impact of special circumstances on the operations of free associations and on man's relationships to them.

The ramifications of these questions touch a variety of problems. In terms of constitutional guarantees we know that freedom of association is a civil right, protected by the First Amendment to the Constitution and made applicable to the states by the Fourteenth. Of the four "freedom to" guarantees in Article I, freedom of assembly, which includes the freedom to belong to an organization of one's choice, has perhaps been the most hotly debated in the years since World War II. This controversy resulted from public fear of the growth of Communist-dominated organizations, and the prospect that freedom of association might be a shield for treasonable political activity. At times, the issue of freedom seemed to be overborne altogether by a new philosophy of association. Of this state of affairs Justice William O. Douglas has stated that "association with or membership in an organization found to be 'subversive' weighs heavily against the accused. He is not allowed to prove that the charge against the organization is false. The case is closed; that line of defense is taken away. The technique is one of 'guilt by association'—one of the most odious institutions of history. . . . Guilt under our system of government is personal."[11]

The political argument as such does not concern us here. It is relevant to a discussion of economic association to the extent that it involves a right guaranteed by the Fifth Amendment, the right to work, which Justice Douglas, in another context describes as follows:

The practice of using faceless informers has apparently spread through a vast domain. It is used not only to get rid of employees in the Government, but also employees who work for private firms having contracts with the Government. It has touched countless hundreds of men and women and ruined many. It is an un-American practice which we should condemn. It deprives men of "liberty" within the meaning of the Fifth Amendment, for one of a man's most precious liberties is his right to work.[12]

Clearly, Justice Douglas has rested his conclusions on the assumption that such associations are voluntary; and, since they are voluntary, any credits or losses attached thereto may provoke either personal praise or personal culpability. The emphasis takes a different turn, however, when a worker is forced to join a union and forced to support it with dues. It is different when corporate management is summoned to enforce rules and sanctions imposed upon it by governments. What, then, happens to the equation that balances personal responsibility with organization objectives? Are we moving, in some of our practices, closer to a situation that existed in Hitler's Germany, where soldier and civil servant could excuse themselves from personal responsibility on the ground that the "organization" commanded it?

Clearly, any voluntary association must retain the volitional element that accords to individuals the right to associate with or disassociate from it. Once this fact is recognized, the basis for analysis and appraisal changes completely.

A HIERARCHY OF VOLUNTARY ASSOCIATIONS

Let us now move beyond the individual-organization relationship to the relationships among the organizations themselves. This

---

[11] W. O. Douglas, in "Joint Anti-Fascist Refugee Committee v. McGrath," in Edwin S. Newman (ed.) , *Freedom Reader* (New York: Oceana Publications, 1955) , p. 86.

[12] Douglas in "Peters v. Hobby," *ibid.,* p. 94.

touches the question of business-government relations as revealed in complaints often voiced by the business community against "government intervention." The use of the pejorative suggests that businessmen view various government activities as unnecessary and unwarranted invasions of their rights and freedoms. The question impinges, furthermore, on the relationships that exist among various kinds of business as, for example, the typical complaint by small business against "big business." To ask whose voice should prevail when conflicts arise is not the same as asking whose voice does prevail, but it may turn out that our practices are not too divorced from our principles in this respect.

Turning our attention initially to the appropriate relationships between governments and business, we can again approach the discussion on two levels: analytical and historical. From a purely analytical position, one could develop a syllogism that would assert as a major premise this proposition: The economy is that part of human activity that produces and distributes goods and services required by society. The minor premise involves recognition that society has noneconomic ends, since man, for whom society exists, is a spiritual, intellectual, emotional, esthetic being. Therefore, the economy is subsidiary to society, since the latter must provide for the larger ambitions and needs of man.

This suggests that to the degree that the state is responsible for security, public order, education, the enforcement of contracts, and the protection of patents (and the list may be extended), its mandates must prevail over the narrower objective of profit-making. But this logic, which suggests a hierarchy in which the state overrules the merchant, has been repeatedly challenged by history. Hungry people have surrendered freedom for food and liberty for lodging. For, though the soul is superior to the body in the long run, keeping soul and body together is a man's dominant concern for the short run.

How have we responded traditionally to problems raised by governments and by business? The responses have shown a remarkable convergence in one very important respect. Whether explanations are sought for the state or for the corporation, the argument of analogy has been regularly employed, and the analogy has involved comparing organizations to the *human organism*. The state was viewed as a juristic personality among certain English theorists like Ernest Barker, who urged that, since this is so, the state should hold itself legally responsible for the torts of its agents.[13] The traditional theory of corporations as *personae fictae* was first clearly stated by Innocent IV in 1243 as part of the Papacy's efforts to protect various cathedral chapters against the Emperor's encroachments. These chapters were "persons" with certain rights, conferred by the Church and inalienable so far as the Empire was concerned. These collectivities struck F. W. Maitland as "permanently organized groups of men; they seem to be group units; we seem to attribute acts and intents, rights and wrongs to these groups, to these units."[14] These insights have been refined and given a new currency by Kenneth Boulding in ways that offer exciting prospects for developing new hypotheses to explain the theory of American business organizations.[15]

The question of what kind of "person" a state or a corporation really is becomes relevant to us only as it turns to the question of "who begat whom." Concretely, does the modern corporation (which, unlike unions, must seek a charter from the state) owe its origins and its powers to the modern state? There have been two major theoretical strands in the Western tradition which bear significantly on this issue. The first is the so-called "concession" theory, which grew out of the common law of England; the second, what might be termed the "inherence" theory, which bourgeoned in Germany among scholars like Hugo Krabbe and, most particularly, in *Das deutsches Genossenschaftsrecht* (1868–81) by Otto von Gierke. These Germans argued that there inheres within every group of men who wish to organize the right to form such organizations without reference to the will of the government.[16]

THE CONCESSION THEORY

The common-law tradition always held that the corporation was a creature of the state and, as such, was strictly accountable for

---

[13] Ernest Barker, "The Rule of Law," *Political Quarterly*, Vol. XI (May, 1914), p. 117.

[14] F. W. Maitland in his Introd. to Otto von Gierke, *Political Theories of the Middle Age* (Boston: Beacon Press, 1958), p. xviii.

[15] Kenneth E. Boulding, *The Image: Knowledge in Life and Society* (Ann Arbor: University of Michigan Press, 1956), esp. chaps. ii, iv, and x.

[16] See Hugo Krabbe, *The Modern Idea of the State* (trans. with an introduction by George H. Sabine and Walter J. Shepard) (New York: Appleton & Co., 1922). Otto von Gierke (*op. cit.*, p. xxxi): "Nowhere has the concession theory been proclaimed more loudly, more frequently, more absolutely, than in America" and nowhere with "more lip-service."

performing the limited functions granted it as a public service. The American colonists always feared corporate power, and in Pennsylvania only one business firm was incorporated during the entire colonial period. Jacksonianism, with its emphasis on the common man, reinforced the conviction that the common law was intended to protect and promote individual rights and that individual enterprise meant exactly what it said—the right of an individual to make his own destiny on the basis of equality of opportunity.[17] In this ingrained fear of business organizations the corporation was most suspect. There was general assent to the proposition that what the state could create the state could destroy and that corporations, therefore, existed on the sufferance of the civil authorities.

Marshall's decision in the Dartmouth College case, holding that state legislatures could not violate a contract (and the act of incorporation was considered to constitute a contract) put the state courts in a quandary. Even after this decision some states held with the Pennsylvania Supreme Court in *Ehrenzeller* v. *Union Canal Company* (1829) that a legislature could always step in after incorporation to dissolve the business. But time and events were running against this view and, even before the full force of industrialization was felt here, the Supreme Court of Pennsylvania had reversed itself to hold, in *Brown* v. *Hummel* (1847), that while the State could alter the corporation of a public body, like a town or city, it could not touch a private corporation, since such action constituted an impairment of contract.[18]

Yet the suspicions continued and states invariably imposed on corporations three sharp restrictions. They were permitted a limited aim (corporations were allowed to perform only one service), a limited time (the charters were for fixed periods), and a limited amount of money. Inexorably, the common-law tradition was eroded to a point where old suspicions might linger but where new needs had the benediction of the courts. The evolution provided the perfect illustration of the way law responds to problems by redefining old terms and giving them new dimensions.

------

[17] See Arthur Schlesinger, Jr., *The Age of Jackson* (Boston: Little, Brown & Co., 1945).

[18] See John E. Walsh, "The Abandonment in Pennsylvania of the Common Law Tradition respecting the Chartering of Business Corporations" (unpublished Master's essay, Lehigh University, 1953).

THE INHERENCE THEORY

The Germanic tradition has never been hospitable to Roman or to common-law views insisting on the corporation's dependence on the state for its sanction, and our internal movement appears to be more toward validating the Germanic interpretation. Modern scholarship has taken these factors into account. At the end of World War I, John Neville Figgis, in his *Churches in the Modern State* (1919), argued that churches had a right to autonomous existence, and Harold Laski extended the notion to economic groups.[19] This position has been most effectively stated in the following terms:

Still more typical of the present day is the vast and growing number of associations for economic and social purposes which are not local in their character. Units of capital and of industrial management have grown not only in size but in the effectivenss of their co-operation; they have extended their organization not only through the length and breadth of single states but also across the national boundaries. Organizations of labor have been forced into a parallel extension in order that they might develop the strength to cope with organizations of employers. Nor are these modern associations invariably economic in purpose. They exist for the most diverse aims and on widely different scales. Their fundamental condition is a consciousness of common interest; where such a consciousness exists, an association can arise which is limited only by the breadth of the interest and the degree of loyalty it can evoke. Associations of this sort have always existed but at the present moment their enormous extension is a social fact in our European and American civilization of first-rate importance.

Now collective or corporate units such as these are certainly not mere numbers of individuals standing in quasi-contractual relations to one another. The group itself has ends which it pursues with more or less consistency; it has a settled policy which no individual can modify at will. Its collective character is as fixed as the character of an individual. It can assert collective rights and assume collective obligations. In short, it has the same type of energy and inertia which in the individual we call will or personality. Such groups are real juristic persons, competent to possess legal rights and to perform legal acts. *Moreover, the granting of a franchise by the state neither creates nor fundamentally alters the essential nature of these collective persons.* Whether they happen to be organized as corporations within the restricted and rather artificial legal meaning of

---

[19] Harold J. Laski, *Authority in the Modern State* (New Haven: Yale University Press, 1919) .

the term, or whether they prefer to hold their property under a trusteeship, or to organize themselves as business partnerships is a legal techni-
cality which has little bearing upon their real character. *Their effectiveness depends upon the social bonds that unite their members and upon
the need of human nature for a group-life such as they afford. The state
cannot make them; it cannot always destroy them. It may recognize them,
but in so doing it merely recognizes something which exists as a fact and
which is in no sense produced by recognition.*[20]

OLD CONCEPTS AND NEW PRACTICES

Again it becomes the task to draw inferences from certain important concepts in terms that are relevant to the contemporary world
of business. If American society is moving to reject the common-law
tradition (that corporations are creatures of the state and subject to
dissolution by their sovereign creator for malfeasance), we face, as a
consequence, the necessity of demanding from such voluntary associations certain assurances. Society at large needs to be convinced
that the corporation has clear but limited objectives, with clear but
limited powers. It must not encroach on the domain of other voluntary associations without expecting challenge and restriction. The
corporation must further impose on its members a discipline regarding the common objective, even as it assures means for making
individual wills heard and individual judgments both responsive
and responsible. General Motors and Du Pont may worry about
antitrust suits, but they need not worry about dissolution through
government fiat. Free men have come a long way with their voluntary associations, and, as a corollary to bigger size and power, the
journey has involved greater responsibilities.

One might submit the hypothesis that the modern big business
enterprise is the economic man as interpreted by the classical economist. And, like the economic man of yore, its impulsions to self-
aggrandizement—plus the rationalization that self-seeking is good for
society at large—invite critical reactions. The old Italian *casa* of
medieval times sought to maximize profits and quickly came under
demands by municipal authorities to entertain visiting dignitaries,
support public charities, construct public buildings, and the like.
Have we run the full circle in the evolution of modern business? Are
the claims that society is currently making for corporation support
of education and hospitals, even of community ventures like sym-

---

[20] Krabbe, *op. cit.,* pp. xlii–xliii. (Italics added.)

phonies and museums, part of a long tradition that demands much from those who have much?

Thus far, these matters have been left to the discretion of executive management. But there is another area represented by government regulation where such liberty does not prevail. If a sovereign state loses the right to dissolve a corporation, does it follow that the impulsion to regulate business in public interest becomes more widely felt? Laissez-faire introduced into the American intellectual currents the notion that a dichotomy exists between public and private activities. Historically, public responsibility has been imposed upon all who engaged in common trade, and where there is a failure in performance the call is for state intervention. Any effort by private corporate interests to capture American regulatory commissions must therefore be viewed with apprehension. Walton Hamilton warns that simply creating an ICC or a CAB does not reduce the need for continuous scrutiny and that we have indeed witnessed in these two agencies a conversion of controls to sanctions.[21] The obverse side of the coin offers a reminder that regulatory commissions, being at once administrative and judicial units, represent a breach in our traditional theory of the separation of powers. Therefore, the public agencies themselves need constant surveillance. Furthermore, government hostility to big private business corporations has been a national characteristic ever since the American Revolution, which was, from an economic point of view, a small businessman's revolt against large enterprise as reflected in British mercantilism.[22] Government's skepticism of big business, and business' efforts to capture the very agencies set up for its control, suggest that the problem is far from solved.

RELATIONSHIPS AMONG THE ASSOCIATIONS: CONFLICT OR HARMONY

Are associations necessarily in conflict with others, so that, for example, "big business versus small business" will always represent

---

[21] Walton Hamilton, *The Politics of Industry* (New York: Alfred A. Knopf, 1957), esp. pp. 59–63. There is further evidence that without the actual support of the regulated the independent regulator is doomed to fail. This was the result of Joseph B. Eastman's efforts as Federal Co-ordinator of Transportation under the New Deal to get management and unions to nationalize railroad operations. See Earl Latham, *The Politics of Railroad Co-ordination* (Cambridge: Harvard University Press, 1959).

[22] This point is stressed by Kenneth E. Boulding in his *The Organizational Revolution* (New York: Harper & Bros., 1953), pp. 138–39.

an American phenomenon? Or do various voluntary associations actually complement one another and by so doing create an enduring kind of harmony in society?

THE NEED FOR CONFLICT

The first view springs from a conviction that conflict is the stuff of life and that competition is the word Americans have employed to recognize and to describe this inevitable condition. Each of the associations fashioned by man tends to be competitive, and this is so simply because every association sooner or later lays claim to the whole man. The medieval Church welcomed a child into its domain with baptism, sanctified his marriage, blessed his death, and saw to it that his lifeless body was interred in a cemetery hallowed by the priest. The modern state has largely superseded the Church and even goes beyond the religious organization to insist on school attendance; licensing of doctors, barbers, and beggars; granting of patents and copyrights; and arranging for the proper recording of the death certificates. These pretensions lead irrevocably to competition among them:

Institutional friction and instability are, therefore, the normal state of society, and the hope of peace and quietude is an idle dream. Competition, imbalance, and friction are not merely continuous phenomena in society, but in fact are evidences of vitality and "normality." They reveal a healthy competitive institutional relationship in which no one is permitted completely to dominate the scene; for, in the circumstances, the peace represented by the dominion of one institution over all of the others is unhealthy; it is evidence of lack of resilience of the part of the other institutions and is a sure sign of a spreading tyranny. The formal peace represented by the power of one institution over all of the others is synonymous with death.[23]

To speak of conflict as being essential to a vital society is to invite invidious comparisons with Marx. Yet long before the Hegelian dialectic provided the substructure on which Marx was to build his elaborate edifice of class conflict, the Christians were invited by St. Augustine to consider the nature of the essential struggle between good and evil in the City of God. The necessity of drawing refine-

---

[23] Frank Tannenbaum, "Institutional Rivalry in Society," in Richard C. Snyder and H. Hubert Wilson (eds.), *Roots of Political Behavior* (New York: American Book Co., 1949), pp. 168–69.

ments between class conflict and associational conflict led Frank Tannenbaum to observe:

The very idea of the class struggle is subject to revision; for the concept is a verbal formula derived from older ideas inherent in European theology and has nothing to do with the description of industrial society, though it may have some reference to a more static agricultural community. It is a verbal construct fitting a preconceived notion of the nature of "progress," and has within it the commitment to historical inevitability. It is really a part of European theology translated into mundane terms.

If the idea of a horizontal division of society into classes is an inadequate description of social conflict, this does not deny that conflict exists both between the institutions and within them. Between the institutions the conflict is moral, psychological, and political, for the guidance and governance of the whole man. Internally, within the institutions there is a many-sided contention which might be considered a conflict of numerous interests. But these conflicts are continuous and irreducible.[24]

HARMONY AS A REGULATING PRINCIPLE

There is no question that the distinction just made between class conflict and conflict among associations is a valid one. Yet there is one point of similarity which invariably attracts notice. This similarity is found in the assumption that directors of the dominant class or association move inexorably to maintain and extend this domination, and it is this drive that is the root of conflict. There are other scholars, however, who argue that this assumption is incorrect when applied to such voluntary associations as business corporations and labor unions. Let us take the case of management and workers. It is inconceivable to hold that the goals of the enterprise can be met only through profit maximization, desired by stockholders but achieved at the expense of those working within the firm. Such a position does violence to logic, since neither workers nor managers would continue in roles that reduce them to a kind of serfdom; rather, the corporate goals must be defined in terms that relate the efficiency of the enterprise to the satisfaction of perceived goals—an insight developed early by Chester Barnard. If this proposition is true, then workers and managers complement one another; they

---

[24] *Ibid.*, p. 18. The notion that man is destined to be guided all the more "in proportion as the functions of life undergo division" and that the resultant organization becomes an intrenched bureaucracy that invites attack by "fresh opponents" was developed for the political sphere by Robert Michels in his *Political Parties*, trans. Eden and Cedar Paul (New York: The Free Press, 1949), pp. 404 and 408.

must work cooperatively and harmoniously. It is not the goals, but inappropriate means to these goals, that provoke conflict. Since man can and must correct these faulty techniques, the corrections lead to further improvements and further harmony in the operation.[25]

Thus far, the argument, held to the internal operations of a corporation, may be sustained because stockholders, managers, and workers who share in the enterprise have a common interest in its prosperity and survival. Can the position be extended with respect to relations among associations of various types? Or must big states exploit little ones, big business dominate little business, *ad infinitum?*

Adherents of a theory of harmony insist on the importance of distinguishing between conflict as a social fact and conflict as a determining principle. Clearly, conflict will be in evidence as new associations are born and as men struggle to make adjustments. But have we too long labored under an intellectual legacy from England's experiences during the Napoleonic wars when shortages led to violent clashes between the landed and laboring elements? So long as economic activities were left to impersonal forces, so long were antagonisms allowed to fester. Yet man has learned how to affect, how to direct, how to render more efficient and more equitable the economic order he once left to the blind decision of impersonal markets. Since this fact is now widely recognized and accepted, it is asserted that associations can be directed to complement rather than to war against one another. The growth in knowledge and skills makes this achievement much more likely. Money managers are having to cope with business cycles; "human engineering" has benefited from advances in social psychology that improve work arrangements within the plant; electronic data processing makes more and better data available to the decision makers. In view of the advances in human knowledge, the rational ordering of associations can be more effectively achieved. The logic of the division-of-labor concept can be refined by associations themselves so that a functional integration can be made a reality for society. The argument receives support if it is admitted that much of the social

---

[25] This point of view was developed brilliantly more than a decade ago by Neil Chamberlain in *The Union Challenge to Management Control* (New York: Harper & Bros., 1948), esp. pp. 240–60. See also Solomon Barkin, "A Trade Unionist Appraises Management Personnel Philosophy," *Harvard Business Review*, Vol. XXVIII (September, 1950), pp. 59–64.

conflict in America is unnecessary, that it is a practice we can ill afford when survival depends on industrial efficiency and the satisfaction of human wants and needs through harmoniously evolving social practices.

Although the evidence of modern history suggests that conflict, rather than harmony, has been the typical way of the West in resolving difficulties, the newer model invites sympathetic attention. "The essence of modern thinking is the effort to discover and stress the elements not of conflict but those of cooperation in the enterprise."[26] The growth of profit sharing, pensions, the setting-up of factory committees elected by workers to run recreational, health, and safety programs are concrete examples of the spreading conviction that harmony and cooperation are the logical regulations within associations and that conflict has neither merit nor purpose in the relations among men.

CONCLUSION: POSITIVE AND NEGATIVE ASPECTS

Freedom of association for the purpose of establishing and carrying on a business enterprise in noncorporate form is based on the fundamental principle of freedom of contract. The privilege of incorporation, on the other hand, was viewed traditionally as a "concession" granted by the sovereign; but the trend has been toward acceptance of the "inherence" theory, which asserts an innate right to freedoom of incorporation (under general incorporation statutes), though with important reservations of state "police powers" and expanding federal legislation. Two trends bear watching. The first relates to efforts to capture regulatory bodies and turn them into sanctions for corporation practices. The second relates to governmental policy that has reflected suspicion of large-scale businesses; the internal limitations on the size and character of business associations have been less restrictive than the external limitations.

On the positive side, freedom of association means, in practice, minimal restraint on voluntary association and "the right to organize" for unity of action. The right of disassociation, or the right not to join or to withdraw from an association, is the negative side of freedom of association. With specific reference to the development

---

[26] Barbara Ward, *Faith and Freedom* (New York: W. W. Norton & Co., 1954), p. 224.

of modern business institutions, freedom of association in these two aspects has been important to:

1. Enterprisers who require combinations of capital and human resources in order to establish and maintain large organizations for the profitable production of goods and services, with minimal restraints on the right of association and the right of disassociation (freedom to organize a firm or to incorporate and freedom to shift one's resources from one organization to another).

2. Individual enterprisers (including professionals) who wish to operate their businesses without undue constraints to join combinations or guilds. Freedom to practice a trade or a profession without the authorization of a trade or professional association has been limited in many jurisdictions by licensing laws that devolve upon private (or quasipublic) associations the authority to prescribe conditions of entry into the trade or profession and to set the standards of performance for its practitioners. Should one be free from such external restraints on one's right to remain unassociated, or governed by occupational associations not of one's own choosing?

3. Employees (wage and salary earners) who wish to minimize external restrants on their right to organize for collective bargaining and other purposes or to disassociate themselves from unions not of their own choosing. Earlier governmental restraints on the right of workers to organize for collective bargaining and other purposes were based primarily on common-law doctrines of conspiracy and restraint of trade. The relaxation of these limitations on freedom of association for wage earners was followed by active governmental support of the right to organize and bargain collectively, mainly on the basis of governmental powers over commerce.

More recently, these governmental powers have been increasingly exercised for the purpose of supervising the collective bargaining process, with potentialities of some restrictions on the right of association. The right of an employee not to join a labor union or to withdraw from one with which his employer has a union-shop or a closed-shop collective agreement is currently being debated with respect to "right-to-work" laws. Unlimited freedom of association in both the negative and the positive aspects does not prevail unqualifiedly in any contemporary country. Under totalitarian and authoritarian regimes (Communist, Fascist, National Socialist) freedom of association for enterprisers and workers is the exception rather than the rule. Under liberal and constitutional regimes, while there are varying limitations, the right to associate freely is a major characteristic of such systems.

It is evident that the question of freedom of association is hedged about with social questions involving the general welfare. As a human right, it is limited, even it would seem at times attenuated, by social circumstance and considerations of justice as it relates to that circumscribed level that has been designated as freedom of action, the area beyond the span of free choice. As this century moves away from the concept of Social Darwinism, which sponsored the notion that only the fittest, through ruthless struggle, were entitled to survive economically and socially, it rests the interpretation of the right of freedom to associate on the idea that the common good is best promoted through the interactions of large numbers of functionally integrated associations.

RECOMMENDED READING

BOULDING, KENNETH E. *The Organizational Revolution,* chaps. ii and viii. New York: Harper & Bros., 1953.

CHAMBERLAIN, NEIL W. *Labor,* chap. ii. New York: McGraw-Hill Book Co., 1958.

DAHL, ROBERT A., and LINDBLOM, CHARLES E. *Politics, Economics and Welfare,* p. 15, diagram 4, with explanatory text on pp. 13–16. New York: Harper & Bros., 1953.

GELLHORN, WALTER. *Individual Freedom and Governmental Restraints,* chap. iii. Baton Rouge: Louisiana State University Press, 1956.

GIERKE, OTTO VON. *Political Theories of the Middle Age.* Trans. F. W. MAITLAND. Boston: Beacon Press, 1958.

HALLSWORTH, J. A. "Freedom of Association and Industrial Relations in the Countries of the Near and Middle East," *International Labour Review,* Vol. LXX (November, 1954), pp. 363–84.

————. *Ibid.* December, 1954), pp. 526–41.

INTERNATIONAL LABOR OFFICE. *Freedom of Association and Protection of the Right to Organize* (International Labor Conference, 30th sess.). Geneva, 1947.

————. *Industrial Relations; Application of the Principles of the Right to Organize and Bargain Collectively* (International Labor Conference, 31st sess.). San Francisco, 1948.

KERR, CLARK. *Industrial Relations and the Liberal Pluralist,* pp. ii–xv. (Reprint 80 from *Proceedings of the Seventh Annual Meeting of the*

Industrial Relations Research Association.) Berkeley: Institute of Industrial Relations, University of California, 1955.

LASKI, HAROLD J. "Freedom of Association" *Encyclopaedia of the Social Sciences,* Vol. VI, pp. 447–50.

LIVERMORE, SHAW. *Early American Land Companies: Their Influence on Corporate Development,* pp. vii–xxvi. Ed. with an introduction by JULIUS GOEBEL, JR. New York: The Commonwealth Fund; London: Oxford University Press, 1939.

MILL, JOHN STUART. *On Liberty,* esp. chaps. i, iii, and v.

NISBET, ROBERT A. *The Quest for Community.* New York: Oxford University Press, 1953.

POPPER, KARL R. *The Open Society and Its Enemies.* 2nd rev. ed. London: Routledge and Paul, 1952.

SCHWARTZ, HARRY. *Russia's Soviet Economy,* chap. xv. 2nd ed. New York: Prentice-Hall, 1954.

TANNENBAUM, FRANK. *A Philosophy of Labor,* chap. i. New York: Alfred A. Knopf, Inc., 1951.

TOCQUEVILLE, ALEXIS DE. *Democracy in America* (Henry Reeve text, ed. PHILLIPS BRADLEY), Vol. I, chap. xii, and Vol. II, chaps. v and vii. New York: Alfred A. Knopf, Inc., 1945.

FURTHER READING

BUCHANAN, SCOTT. *The Corporation and the Republic.* New York: Fund for the Republic, 1958.

DAYA, E. "Freedom of Association and Industrial Relations in Asian Countries," *International Labour Review,* Vol. LXXI (April–May, 1955), pp. 364–93, 467–97.

FRANKFURTER, FELIX, and GREENE, NATHAN. *The Labor Injunction,* chap. i, pp. 1–5. New York: Macmillan Co., 1930.

FRIEDMANN, WOLFGANG G. "Corporate Power, Government by Private Groups and the Law," *Columbia Law Review,* Vol. LVII (February, 1957), pp. 169–86.

JENKS, WILFRED. *The International Protection of Trade Union Freedom,* chaps. i–ii. London: Stevens & Sons, 1957.

KATZ, WILBER C. "The Philosophy of Midcentury Corporation Statutes," *Law and Contemporary Problems,* Vol. XXIII (Spring, 1958), pp. 177–92.

MACIVER, ROBERT M. *The Modern State,* pp. 165–82. New York: Oxford University Press, 1926.

SULTAN, PAUL. *Right-To-Work Laws: A Study in Conflict.* Los Angeles: Institute of Industrial Relations, University of California, 1958.

TANNENBAUM, FRANK. "The Balance of Power in Society," *Political Science Quarterly,* Vol. LXIV (December, 1946), pp. 481–504.

VEREKER, CHARLES. *The Development of Political Theory.* London: Hutchinson University Library, 1957.

VERNENGO, ROBERT. "Freedom of Association and Industrial Relations in Latin America," *International Labour Review,* Vol. LXXIII (May–June, 1956).

WATKINS, FREDERICK. *The Political Tradition of the West: A Study in the Development of Modern Liberalism,* chaps. v and ix. Cambridge: Harvard University Press, 1948.

4. Labor in a Business Society

OUTLINE

THE LABOR UNION as a form of free association is not the result of an effort at social camaraderie outside the workplace, though such groupings sometimes grow out of common dissatisfactions as well as common purposes. It is the result of concerted efforts on the part of men whose only property was muscle power or craft skill to survive the type of social atomization that accompanied the industrial and political revolutions of the eighteenth century. In one light, union-ism is a continuing conservative rebuttal to the kind of liberalism that made the American nation—because this liberalism was built on ownership and a self-reliance that laid the burden of survival on the landless masses.

The technological environment that developed almost simultane-ously with the drive for liberty, equality, and fraternity was a partic-

106

ularly unhappy medium for fostering these three ideas. In a predominantly agricultural environment, such as colonial America provided, a man could go it alone if he had confidence and determination, meeting the stresses of nature with the strain of human muscle and human courage. But industrial civilization, though it is also demanding, makes little claim on the "whole man" as this suggests someone with five wits, two arms, two legs, and an intellect, whatever its limitations. Technology asks him for the skill of his hands or the power of his arm and shoulder muscles, and even these it offers to extend with the power of machinery, built initially with hands but markedly more efficient. Technology merely asks enough manpower to make horsepower more efficient and, compared to megaton power, neither of these is today even worth consideration.

It is not surprising that a man asked to think of himself as manpower should find it difficult to refer to himself as *I* with much conviction. It is not necessary to delve into Freud to indicate the loss of self-respect as well as self-identification that results from this predicament. One possible substitute for identity is fraternity. Early in the course of the liberal movement, labor realized that its essential freedom was to survive as best it could, that its only equality was with the rest of the masses scrabbling to keep body and soul together from one day to another. It appears to have settled upon the fraternity of its own kind as its share in a free society.

As an aspect of human association, unionism is the product of that hope for brotherhood that is peculiar to human nature. If, like all manifestations of human hope, it is sometimes short-sighted and self-centered, it should nevertheless be honored for its valor and not condemned for its ambition. Labor's drive is based on desperate need and not upon preconceived dogma. In America it has been instrumental in making the good life available to a great number of people; indeed, it has become the basis of mass consumption and mass production.

THE MEANING OF "LABOR"

The Bible, with its assurance that man was born to labor as the bird to fly, distinguishes labor as not merely a human capacity but a common human responsibility. The ancient world allocated labor, in the sense of a survival type of effort, to slaves and did not even regard these slaves as citizens because of the subhuman nature of their occupation. In this strictest sense, "labor" has always been the term that describes muscular effort employed in the more arduous tasks of keeping body and soul together. The hewers of wood and the drawers of water, and all those engaged in the dirty but necessary tasks involved in keeping a society alive, have been described traditionally as laborers. Hannah Arendt[1] makes an interesting distinction among levels of employment by classifying *labor* as effort of a subsistence character, *work* as less driven, more rewarding economically, and more constructive in character, and *action* as the work of the mind, of the citizen relieved of the burdens of both necessary labor and profitable work and intent upon building and perpetuating a polity. The man of action, therefore, and he alone, has time to be a good citizen and to cultivate the life of reason to the extent that subsistence and income are taken care of for him. To the American society, however, the word "labor" means not a state of life but a formal association whose complicated history reflects its origins. The conceptual nature of work and its meaning in relationship to leisure will be handled analytically in the following section.

LABOR AS UNIONISM

American labor unionism has followed no single path to its present form, and its practices still show the imprint, though often dimly, of a variety of ideological roads that earlier labor traveled. The rhetoric of older union leaders, for example, is filled with fiery phrases of class warfare or with plodding platitudes of an atavistic socialist strain, but it has no meaning. That rhetoric is a decaying signpost, remembered because brave pioneers erected it, but ignored in practice because it points nowhere.[2]

In considering labor problems we delve deeply into the complex reality of the business system. If unions loom large, it is not because of the universality of membership or organization. Only one quarter of the total labor force (or one third of the nonagricultural labor force) is unionized. Since fewer workers belong to unions than do not, one might as easily ask why workers do not join unions as why they do. The answers to this question would differ widely because unionization reveals no simple pattern.

---

[1] *The Human Condition* (Chicago: University of Chicago Press, 1958).

[2] Arthur M. Schlesinger, Jr., *The Age of Jackson* (Boston: Little, Brown & Co., 1950), esp. chaps. xi and xxvi.

In underground coal mines, steel mills, auto plants, truck lines, and garment lofts most production workers have joined unions and have long had the opportunity to do so. Farm workers and white-collar employees in banks, stores, TV repair shops, schools and offices, are apparently little concerned with organizing and have largely remained outside union bounds. Omens of change are, of course, increasingly in evidence when public school teachers bring metropolitan and even statewide operations to a halt. When doctors threaten to strike and public health nurses walk off the job—or when social case workers absent themselves for "sickness" that strikes with remarkable simultaneity—large numbers—one knows that important changes are in the offing but contradictions abound. High-salaried airline pilots support a militant, tightly knit union, while only a very few miserably paid, poorly educated household workers in hospitals are enrolled in unions. Assembly-line workers doing dull routine work in large auto plants have helped to organize the second largest union in America, but file clerks, employed in large offices by the hundreds and even thousands, show indifference to any union. Miners, a breed apart in isolated, backwoods communities, were one of the first groups of workers to fight mightily—and bloodily—for a union, yet farm laborers, as isolated in the community as miners, have only sporadically fought for a union, setting up at best ephemeral organizations too weak to maintain themselves, let alone provide resources for organizing others as the miners did in the thirties.

THE DEVELOPMENT OF UNIONISM: TWO THEORIES

Two able and profound students of American labor, Selig Perlman and Frank Tannenbaum, have proposed theories to explain the causes of unionism, though they do not attempt to explain the causes of *non*unionism, which may be quite different and more difficult to identify. Writing in 1928 before the rise of mass unionism, Perlman concluded that workers joined with each other in stable solidarity as they became conscious of the scarcity of job opportunities.[3] Through unions, workers asserted collective ownership over jobs and strove for job security that would provide individual, meaningful freedom at the place of work. Consciousness of job scarcity arose, according to Perlman, from the workers' economic pessimism, which springs from

---

[3] Selig Perlman, *A Theory of the Labor Movement* (New York: Macmillan Co., 1928).

an awareness of their inability to take advantage of the limited number of economic opportunities that exist in the complex and changing world of business.

Perlman's theory may account for the skilled craft unionists who dominated labor organization at the time that he was conducting his research. Workers pursued job security and job control by insisting upon restrictive work rules, rigid job jurisdiction, and the closed shop. The new union members of the succeeding decades, however, appeared less narrowly concerned with job control and work rules. They admitted all industrial workers to their membership and concerned themselves with industry-wide and even nation-wide programs —minimum wages, social security, pensions, and unemployment pay —as well as plant and job policies.

Professor Tannenbaum has asserted that workers were driven to organize by a more basic need than job control and by a more fundamental force than job scarcity. The heart of the matter, as he sees it, was the workers' need to assert their moral status and restore their dignity as men. Labor leaders did not organize workers; machines, mines, and assembly lines had done that by grouping and then fusing individual workers into collective associations. Once formalized as a union, workers exercised through their functional groupings a necessary moral role in the whole of society, concerning themselves with all the interests of man: economic, political, and social.[4]

What may be more important than the details of either theory is that both take unionism seriously. To Perlman, it is a response of people made insecure by a business system; to Tannenbaum, it provides a moral dignity to men stripped of moral standing by an industrial world. Both see unions as necessary and needed institutions in our society. They arise not from exogenous or alien demands but as the workers' response to the promise of life in America.

THE EARLY STAGES OF AMERICAN UNIONISM

Whether the causes of unionism mentioned by either scholar are necessary for union organization, they certainly are not sufficient to explain the development of unions. The fierce struggle in the bloody Homestead strike of 1889 indicated that steel workers *desired* a union but that they did not have the ability to maintain one in face

---

[4] Frank Tannenbaum, *A Philosophy of Labor* (New York: Alfred A. Knopf, 1951).

of Andrew Carnegie's determined refusal to recognize workers' associations. Nor could the Pullman workers in Chicago successfully organize, whatever their desires, when the federal government enjoined their strike in 1895. Workers cannot form unions until their desire and their ability to do so coincide, and few can doubt that until the mid-thirties many more workers were willing to join unions than did. Our courts and laws imposed a double standard of legality upon business and labor. In the first half of the nineteenth century courts held unions to be conspiracies in restraint of trade, and magistrates condemned workers for trying to escape the "beneficent forces of a competitive market."[5] Later, under the Sherman Antitrust Act judges applied a "rule of reason" to indicted corporations, but when unions appeared before them they enforced far less elastic rules. In pursuit of self interest, the law allowed wide latitude to corporations, even to driving a competitor out of business through "reasonable" practices. But judges enjoined workers if the workers so much as picketed an employer. Picketing clearly impinges upon property rights, and in the legal view of the time it did not serve any compensating or legitimate self-interests of workers.

Workers who did organize were enabled by their strategic jobs or market position to force employer recognition in spite of legal impediments. Mine employers could not easily replace the skilled, tool-owning, contract coal miners who walked off the job. Around this core of indispensable workers, miners were able to build a union at an early date. Skilled weavers and loom fixers in early textile mills formed a strategic group whose strength enabled them to organize themselves and other textile workers. Cutters, whose crucial skill could make the difference between profitable success or indebted failure in the competitive garment industry, used their position first to secure recognition of their demands and then to organize the rest of the garment workers.[6]

But it was strategic position, rather than skill, that was the vital ingredient of union success.[7] Relatively unskilled teamsters, for example, were able to organize in the larger cities before 1900 because

---

[5] Charles O. Gregory, *Labor and the Law* (2nd ed.; New York: W. W. Norton & Co. 1958) .

[6] John T. Dunlop, "The Development of Labor Organization," in Richard A. Lester and Joseph Shister (eds.) , *Insights into Labor Issues* (New York: Macmillan Co., 1948) , pp. 163–93.

[7] Selig Perlman, *A History of Trade Unionism in the United States* (New York: Macmillan Co., 1922) .

they controlled a production bottleneck. Their demands were usually so small compared to the value of the goods they transported that manufacturers and buyers preferred to satisfy rather than to fight them.

Even control of a strategic position, however, did not insure continuing strength. However necessary and valuable workers were to employers when sales were high and efficient productivity was at a premium, a decline in sales and rising unemployment cut deeply into workers' bargaining power. Union strength changed with tides of prosperity and depression—even as it does today. If coal piled high near the pits, miners could not protect their wages or their previously won gains; if clothes were not selling, garment workers were hard put to it to keep their union alive, let alone to bargain for better working conditions. Thus, though unions sprang up in such boom times as 1829–36, 1867–70, and 1879–88, they withered quickly in depressions. Not until skilled craft workers, such as cigar-makers, carpenters, plumbers, and molders became numerous enough to form national unions out of local groups did American unions achieve some stability. By restricting membership to the strategic workers, husbanding their resources, and avoiding strikes whenever possible, unions after 1886 became a permanent though harassed part of the industrial scene.

Workers desiring to join unions had to fight for the opportunity. In the face of open-shop drives, yellow-dog contracts, and implacable employer resistance, strikes became the prerequisites for union growth and survival. Both sides used blunt force and explicit coercion, and the first to surrender or to tire lost. The Wagner Act, enacted by Congress in 1935, radically changed union organizing and made openly coercive tactics illegal or impolitic.

With the federal government encouraging unions and collective bargaining, peaceful voting replaced organizational strikes. Workers had now gained mandatory recognition of their unions from employers by demonstrating majority approval. Electioneering, campaign speeches, posters, and rallies by both sides have largely replaced organizational strikes. The largest number of voters, not the most strategic worker groups, is now the essential basis of unionism.

Peaceful and secret elections, under the auspices of a government agency (the National Labor Relations Board), should—one might think—give all workers desirous of joining unions the freedom to do so. With the power of government on their side, can anyone doubt that workers enjoy full freedom to join or not to join unions as they wish? Many union leaders and employers do still doubt it. Union men charge employers with coercion and threats issued under the hallowed veil of free speech, and employers accuse union organizers of coercion and injury through boycotts and picket lines. Perennially the National Labor Relations Board is asked to distinguish the fine shadings between the "persuasive" powers of speech used by employers, who hold the right to manage and direct workers (in the plant and in mill towns outside the plant as well), and "coercive" powers of pickets used by unions, which may threaten immediate harm while they promise possible future benefits.

So sensitive an issue is union organizing, and so far-reaching the impact of collective bargaining upon managerial authority, that a procedural device, such as an election, does not guarantee freedom of choice for workers. Conflict continues between workers who desire unions and employers who do not want them.[8] The conflict is subtler, quieter, and perhaps less destructive to property and production than before. For that very reason, however, we may be less aware of it and more contentedly ignorant of the power struggles that continue in unorganized sectors of industry. All too often it is assumed that public policy has been decided once and for all while, in fact, autonomous and almost anonymous NLRB officials construct new policies that may be wise or foolish when viewed from the perspective of the greater society.

Representational elections have encouraged large industrial unions to enroll all workers in many plants and in many industries.[9] These unions, conducting their affairs in a businesslike way, deserve to be classed under the heading "business unions." Even their corruptions parallel the kinds of corruption that creep into business practices from time to time; those union leaders most severely criticized by congressional committees have been men who were in the "business of unionism." Regular collective bargaining, peaceful arbitration, conservative investment of welfare funds, systematic if not very fruitful organizing, prudent management of income and expenditure, and stable, professional leadership are characteristics that loom large in the dominant business unionism of recent times.

Workers have joined and found satisfactory for a time many

---

[8] See, e.g., a union viewpoint in the report of the Textile Workers Union of America, *All Rights Denied* (1955).

[9] Neil Chamberlain, "The Structure of Bargaining Units in the United States," *Industrial and Labor Relations Review*, Vol. X (October, 1956), pp. 3–25.

types of unions, discarding them when they no longer served workers' purposes. In the early 1830's unions made a spectacular entrance into local politics. In New York and Philadelphia, the nation's largest cities, their Workingmen's parties held the balance of political power. Active in other cities, too, they were able to induce Democrats to adopt, in party platforms, programs for free public education, universal suffrage, mechanics lien laws, and nondiscriminating militia service, but their political success did not protect them from economic adversity. The severe depression that began in 1837 wiped out all unions and imposed a long famine on union growth and expansion.

Slowly, small new unions grew up in urban areas. Stimulated by labor shortages during the Civil War, they became strong and bold enough to form the National Labor Union in 1867. It included political as well as union organizations and quickly succeeded in securing the eight-hour day for federal employees. Further successes did not follow; the states were less responsive to labor than was the federal government, but constitutional limits restricted federal authority too much to make it worth influencing. By 1872 the National Labor Union was through.

In 1879 one of the most astonishing organizations in American labor history, the Knights of Labor stripped away its secret trappings and began a spectacular rise. The Knights allied themselves with the great agrarian upheaval of the period and followed a policy of uplift and reform for all workers, regardless of job or craft, race, sex, or creed. In this policy the CIO, half a century later, resembled the Knights and succeeded where the earlier organization failed. After a strike for recognition against Jay Gould's sprawling railroad empire in 1886, the Knights' membership soared to 700,000. The Knights collapsed with nearly the speed of their ascent owing to two factors: defeat in a second railroad strike and withdrawal by skilled workers into the American Federation of Labor. By 1893 the Knights claimed only 75,000 members. Their concern for unskilled workers, their interest in producer cooperatives, and their support of political reform has continued as one strain of union thought and policy, but experience has subdued and at times buried the enthusiasm which the undisciplined Knights instilled within their crusading ranks.

The American Federation of Labor under Samuel Gompers' leadership pragmatically rejected uplift, welfare, and reform. The

craft unions that made up the AFL confined themselves to immediate issues of wages and working conditions, bargaining for skilled
workers who could use their strategic position to enforce their narrow demands. Many union leaders had been Socialists or were sympathetic to Socialist aims. While rejecting that party's program and
avoiding partisan political entanglements, they nevertheless left a
Socialist imprint on such unions as the clothing and garment unions, and a few traces remain even today among some teamster
affiliates.

More radical and revolutionary in its anarchistic philosophy
than the Socialists were the Industrial Workers of the World, who
splashed across the headlines of the nation's newspapers between
1897 and 1920 as the organization struck in mine, harvest field,
logging camp, and textile mill. Dedicated to overthrowing the capitalistic system, its strikes and war sabotage left a legacy of violence
which the business unions of the AFL have tried to live down. To
large segments of public opinion one union was like another; if
World War I saw the IWW trying to destroy the business system,
might not the AFL unions seek to do the same at some later date?

After 1918 came schemes of employee representation. This type
of company unionism allowed the form but seldom the substance of
power to workers. Yet its mark upon present-day unionism is still
apparent and lingers on under "sweetheart" agreements between
bought-off union leaders and management. It inadvertently prepared workers and their leaders for more independent union activity.

EUROPEAN AND AMERICAN PATTERNS

This all too brief sample of the rich and varied heritage of American unions should warn against any easy explanation of American
unionism's rise and purpose. Clearly, union concern with and involvement in politics, to pick out one controversial strand, is nothing new, though current debate often gives the impression that the
sight of unions collecting political contributions, engaging in lobbying, supporting office seekers, or endorsing presidential candidates is
some foreign and dangerous aberration of union life.

What is significant is the sharp divergence from European patterns, where workers moved to the creation of political parties and
sought to capture control of the government. Among scholars and
within the unions themselves there has been considerable debate

over the wisdom of the unions' political involvement. One side argues that the more mature (and presumably more learned and wise) political labor movements of Europe should be our models. The other side claims maturity for American unions, since business unionism followed successfully upon the failures of political union-ism.

A more fruitful approach is to see labor's development in each country as a response to its peculiar environment. Comparing the value of American business unions with those of Israel, for example, hardly makes sense. The Israeli labor federation, Histadrut, is deeply involved in business and government as well as in trade-union affairs. It controls factories, employs workers, directs invest-ments, and helps make government policies. Israeli unions often, in effect, bargain with themselves under government policies of their own making.[10] This kind of unionism is not necessarily better or worse than ours. It is simply different, arising from the needs of a new nation whose only managerial and leadership resources existed in trade-unions.

American unions differ from most foreign unions in their rela-tive freedom from political involvement, especially at the national level. One possible reason for this difference is found in the sources of the different business unions. As they emerged in the old AFL, they impressed their pragmatic stamp upon American unionism and could reject a labor party or other entangling political activities because they already enjoyed all the benefits that political efforts at the material level could bring. By the time of Jackson, American workers enjoyed or could soon expect to enjoy all the political rights of a liberal democracy.[11] Full suffrage, direct elections, public schools, and abolition of the few feudal customs that found root here came quickly. American political parties, always eager to adopt the program of any voting group, were considerate of labor's politi-cal grievances, while European unions had to devote their major attention and resources to the struggle for those democratic rights that underlie strong and secure business unionism.

Winning democratic rights by political action was one thing, but achieving economic and union rights in like manner was quite an-other. The limited powers of the federal government, the judiciary's conservative concern for property rights, and the general weakness

---

[10] Margaret Plunkett, "The Histadrut: The General Federation of Jewish Labor in Israel," *Industrial and Labor Relations Review,* Vol XI (January, 1958) , pp. 155–82.

[11] Perlman, *A History of Trade Unionism in the United States, op. cit.,* p. 287.

of unions effectively blocked attempts to seek gains through political action. Under the Constitution the federal government could regulate commerce among the states, but the courts held that most labor problems were clearly of an intrastate character. Within the various states, unions found little support for their labor demands, since rural representatives dominated state legislatures.

Well might Gompers and the AFL enunciate a policy of voluntarism; they had no other sensible choice! For unions in the late nineteenth and the early twentieth century to eschew national political action, to organize only those workers who voluntarily asked to join, and to seek gains and benefits through their own economic strength was a policy of necessity. After a half-century of that policy, many came to believe that voluntarism was an ideological stand against government help and aid, and the pragmatic origin of this attitude was forgotten. Thus, when the New Dealers first proposed social security, the AFL leaders denounced it as a breach of voluntarism. A little reflection easily convinced labor leaders, however, that while denunciation of social security was in keeping with old policy, it was not in accord with modern realities. Labor supported social security and many more of the New Deal's welfare programs.

Of course, unions had always worked when and where they could through politicians to gain favorable legislation, ordinances, and rulings from governmental bodies. The building-trades unions were active at the city level, pushing through housing codes that benefited their members; the railway brotherhoods played politics in the empty western states, where a few strategic votes by railroad workers and their families carried weight. As early as 1898 the railway unions secured congressional passage of the Erdman Act, which penalized employers who discriminated against union activity among railroad workers. The Supreme Court later struck down the Act as unconstitutional, but the railroad brotherhoods lobbied successfully for other aid. In 1916 the Adamson Act guaranteed an eight-hour day for operating crews, and in 1926 the Railway Labor Act included unionism and collective bargaining. As the railway brotherhood has demonstrated, unions had no deep aversion to political activity if such efforts held out any promise for labor.

Unions since 1932

National politics began to promise rewards after the Supreme Court reinterpreted the Constitution in 1935 through a decision that extended federal regulation to all activities *affecting* commerce among the states.[12] This reinterpretation extends the reach of federal regulation so far that in practice only the prudence of Congress and its regulatory agents and the cost of administration limit it. The extension of federal regulation brought great rewards to unions. The setting of minimum wages and maximum hours, the establishment of unemployment insurance, old-age pensions and workmen's compensation, and the guarantee of the right to organize and bargain collectively strengthened unions as never before. Labor leaders took full advantage of their newly won power to assert union demands, forgetting that, while a friendly Congress and administration could now provide formerly undreamed of favors, an unfriendly Congress and administration could penalize and restrict labor as never before. Too many labor leaders had forgotten what the advocates of voluntarism had warned: what government could give, government could also take away. Throughout the thirties and forties American unions played grandstand politics with spasmodic enthusiasm but with little serious attention to political realities.

In 1947 Republicans and Democrats in Congress did what labor leaders had come to believe was both impossible and unthinkable. They imposed restrictive regulations upon unions despite a President's veto. Few of those who voted for restriction against unions wanted repeal of the Wagner Act or a return to laissez-faire in labor affairs. The new Taft-Hartley Act used the powers of the federal government to extend federal regulations still further—but in a direction wholly disliked by unionists. It subjected them to sanctions for unfair labor practices, set up procedures for discouraging such practices as the closed shop, limited the union, and banned compulsory checkoffs. The statute required periodic reports and financial audits, restricted political contributions, and made a feeble attempt to regulate welfare funds. None of the new regulations injured unions as much as the shocked leaders predicted, and many of the regulations reflected a proper public concern over certain union practices.

Taft-Hartley's passage thoroughly alarmed even the most nonpolitical of labor leaders. It demonstrated the value, indeed the necessity, of political action. Thus, ironically, Senator Robert Taft, the personification of conservatism in his day, might bear major responsibility for persuading American unions to build and maintain an effective political force on the national arena.

---

[12] *National Labor Relations Board* v. *Jones & Laughlin Steel Corp.*, 301 U.S. 1 (1937).

As yet, union success has been something less than overwhelming, and it seems that, except for defensive purposes, unions may be unable to unite politically. The immediate interests of one union often run counter to the ambitions of another. The textile and pottery workers want high tariffs, while the auto and aircraft workers want lower tariffs. The teamsters lobby for more highway funds, lower fuel taxes, and more ICC regulation of railroads and fight the determined railroad brotherhoods' attempts to free railroads and to regulate trucks. Sawmill and lumber workers join textile workers to seek higher minimum wages, but the high-paid plumbers and electricians could not be less concerned. Coal miners, in need of area redevelopment to reduce high unemployment, seek wide diffusion of lucrative government contracts, but the machinists and steel workers prefer to push for higher defense spending, with contracts going to their industry's large companies. Diversity of perceived interests makes unions vulnerable to divisive stresses and strains when they attempt to formulate a comprehensive political program. How successfully union leaders can accomplish so difficult and delicate a task remains to be seen. Until labor leaders propose something more dynamic and relevant than their current, warmed-over policies of the thirties, one may be justifiably skeptical of much success.

GOALS: LIMITED OR UNLIMITED

The goals of unionists are as complex as the reasons for which they joined unions and as varied as the kinds of unions they have helped organize. One may be tempted to accept as unionism's goal the one Sam Gompers gave: "more—more—more." It is succinct and selfishly human. To accept it, however, may be to mistake symbol for reality. Is there any more reason to think that union men want only "more" than there is to believe that businessmen want only "profits"? Are not "more" and "profits" shorthand symbols for a whole galaxy of benefits and rewards sought by union and businessmen? Both terms surround themselves with a pecuniary and material value, a value urgently sought after in our society and one easy to accept and to justify in a business economy. Money can buy so much! Material goods carry with them such notions of prestige, status, security, and well-being that they seem, conveniently though cynically, to sum up all our goals.

Unions have bargained for higher wages and shorter hours, better working conditions, pensions, supplemental unemployment ben-

efits, and severance pay; they have insisted upon grievance procedures, an end to arbitrary discrimination in promotions, layoffs,
hiring, and transfers. They have asked to share administration of
collective agreements and work rules. Unions have sought to gain
public recognition as an important community institution, with a
legitimate right to represent worker interests at all levels of social
affairs. Union demands have ranged from those of shop stewards
who want to help set piece wage rates to that of Walter Reuther,
who wants union representation on the Board of Governors of the
Federal Reserve Board.

PLURALISM AT WORK

An analysis of the dynamics of labor suggests that tensions within
the house of labor may set limits to both union demands and union
activities. That the labor movement is not homogenous has become
sufficiently clear from a brief review of the movement's history.
Neither are individual unions solidly united organizations, driving
toward clearly defined, commonly accepted goals. Unions are, first of
all, bodies politic wherein contending leaders vie for approval of
their policies and differing interest groups seek adoption of their
favorite programs.

Not infrequently union leaders have preferred a declining membership to recruitment of new members from a different group or
class of workers. In the early thirties, weak and shrunken craft
unions refused to admit semiskilled and unskilled workers who were
eager to join. The reasoning was simplicity itself: an influx of new
members with different interests and new demands would have
upset old policies favoring skilled workers. Today local union
officers, who serve a declining number of production workers in
aircraft plants, stoutly fight against enrolling the growing number of
clerical and technical employees. They see the rising white-collar
worker as a potential competitor for union office and control. What
chance of election would present leaders have if clerks and technicians gained equal rights to vote and to determine union policy?

Even with production workers alone, an elected union leader
must mediate among a host of competing interest groups. Men with
seniority want layoffs on the basis of last on, first off; junior men
prefer a shortened work week for all. Young men demand a fast pace
when working under piece rates, but older men prefer a slower
tempo. Married men with families seek overtime and want it shared
equally; single men, less in need of income, would like to adopt a

stand against all overtime. Less skilled workers want the opportunity to perform higher skilled work, but the skilled workers fear job encroachment and demand strict observance of job classifications. Semiskilled piece-rate workers seek "loose" rates that allow big earnings—to the chagrin of skilled maintenance men on fixed day rates. Workers near retirement favor pensions, but new employees push for supplemental unemployment benefits. One work group tries to erect bumping walls around itself so that a layoff affects the fewest number of its members; if they are successful, the members of another work group must bear an increased burden of unemployment at the next layoff.

Any union leader who can build a strong and stable coalition of support from such a welter of conflicting and competing interests is a statesman indeed. Not all unions present equally difficult political challenges, but all present a continual challenge that wearies the ablest of leaders. For the sake of continuity within the union and to promote harmonious industrial relations, union leaders may find it expedient to protect themselves from the clamor of shortsighted shop leaders and the irresponsibility of workers on the job who give and withdraw their support and dues according to whims.

Thus to bargain away a five-cent-an-hour wage increase in return for a union shop may make good sense. The union as an organization gains added security and an assured income; perhaps in future negotiations a stronger, richer union can win the five cents for the members as well. To strengthen this position further and to avoid contentious issues that divide his membership, a union leader may be tempted to turn his attention to general benefits that accrue to every worker, such as shorter hours, more vacations, and extra fringe benefits.

Assured of members by the union shop, concentrating on high-level bargaining, and engulfed in the dramatics of negotiations and convention oratory, top officers of national unions may be tempted to forget that the bulk of union work is carried on in the shop and at the work benches. Shop stewards settling grievances, division representatives handling complaints, local grievance committees working out the details of bumping rights, and a host of other local union men performing daily, routine, petty services make a union. For workers, unions are most relevant as they protect them against arbitrary foremen, most meaningful when they win claims for back pay or reinstatement on a job.

Effective unionism needs both local leaders and national leaders and shop negotiations as well as industrywide or companywide bargaining. Responsive union officers will seek overall agreements and grievance settlements; workers expect not only general wage adjustments but also adjustments in piece rates. If top union leaders slight the shop needs of workers, they strike at the very life and meaning of unionism. Yet if these leaders respond to the necessities of shop workers, the public may adjudge them socially irresponsible.[13]

RESPONSIBLE UNIONISM

Asking union members to be responsible in using their organized economic power is an ambiguous request. To whom should they be responsible? As members of the public, we may feel quite strongly that striking railroad workers ought to consider commuter needs, but the strikers, confronted with a contracting-out proposal that threatens their jobs, may place family responsibilities for making a living first. Until each man is willing to adjust his own personal responsibilities, the better to meet public responsibilities, we might hesitate to charge irresponsibility too freely.

How does one judge a union president like John L. Lewis, who encouraged mechanization of coal mines and fought miners' attempts to preserve jobs through work rules and other customary practices? Lewis achieved his aim of getting men out of unhealthy, dangerous mines, and productivity has soared. But unemployment among coal miners has risen to the melancholy levels of the Great Depression, and the misery of the coal towns in West Virginia, Kentucky, and Pennsylvania is a blot upon our complacent prosperity. How judge a union leader like Mike Quill, who led his members in a strike that tied up the Pennsylvania Railroad for nearly two weeks in order to gain restrictive work rules or severance pay for desperate workers who have faced and must still contend with rapid technological displacement? The delineation of union goals and the identification of union demands is not an easy task, but it is easier than passing wise judgment upon the goals that unions *should* pursue.

Whatever the goals of unions may be and whatever demands workers may make, they are but one term in the equation of unionism. Without the exercise of power, goals go unfulfilled. Determining whether union demands point toward desirable goals and re-

---

[13] Clark Kerr, *Unions and Union Leaders of Their Own Choosing* (New York: Fund for the Republic, 1957).

sponsible actions may be less important than analyzing the sources and limits of union power. The legal right of union members to interfere with production by striking, picketing, and conducting boycotts gives unions undoubted economic power. They can close down the nation's coal mines, reduce steel output to a trickle for weeks on end, stall traffic on the vast rail networks, and idle tankers, freighters, and passenger ships along our coasts. Contemplating such power, one may be persuaded that it is great indeed.

But, what criterion of power do we use? Compared to fifty years ago, when few unions dared conduct a plantwide strike, let alone an industrywide strike, today's unions are indeed powerful. But, if we measure power in terms of lost working time, we find that accidents usually lose us an average of ten times as much time as we lose through strikes. If we include losses due to worker illness, or just the common cold, strike losses would appear even smaller in comparison.

Neither of these measures of power is particularly enlightening. A single steel plant may have been more vital to the nation's economy fifty years ago than a whole industry is today, since many more steel substitutes are now available. And the losses from accidents and illness differ from industry to industry and are spread over the whole year, while strike losses are concentrated and specific in their impact.

LABOR POWER AND OTHER POWER CENTERS

One may be able to keep a balanced perspective on union power by remembering that the union's ability to stop production when others wish it to continue is not unique. Whenever market conditions dictate, employers and managers may close plants or reduce output for months on end, despite the readiness, willingness, and ability of workers to work. The resulting unemployment and loss of production may be a lingering, wasting cancer, more destructive to the community than the clear, swift wound of a strike. Managers act as they must under our economic system, responding to its requirements. Acting from necessity, however, does not excuse them from their responsibility for the power they wield any more than it does union leaders.

History suggests that strike losses can be more apparent than real. When coal miners were striking for higher wages and better conditions of work in the forties, they typically were working only a third of the year in any case. More recently, in the steel strike of 1959, workers largely substituted picket-line duty for unemployment. In 1958 the steel industry produced at 60 percent of capacity. Expecting a strike in the last half of 1959, steel management kept production at nearly full capacity during the first six months, while steel users stocked up with supplies to carry them through the strike. After a record 116-day strike, the industry still was able to record a production mark of 63 percent of capacity for the year. After a few months of high production to replenish inventories, steel output again dropped in 1960 and for months remained at about half-capacity. All steel workers shared the loss of wages during the strike, and during the years of low output only younger men paid the costs. Strike or no strike, the nation as a whole is denied steel that is not produced, whether because of walkout or depression.

It may be that the reason why the power to strike appears as large and threatening as it does is that the legitimacy of union rights is not fully accepted. The right of employers to stop production is sanctioned by economic theory and by the ideology of private property. So well accepted is this right that even union leaders and unemployed workers seldom question it. Were we to accept without question the right of unions to stop production as a means of protecting the self-interest and future well-being of their members, as we accept the right of employers to stop production in order to protect profits and stockholders' equity, union power might not loom quite so large in the public mind as it does today.

Draining the emotional content from a discussion of union power does not, however, remove the problem of this power. Whether unions possess greater or less power than employers in general is not the point at issue here. In particular instances, union power to strike is great enough to injure, unduly, private persons and the community. The Teamsters have been known to threaten a complete boycott of a small truck line if the employer did not sign a union-proposed agreement enforcing a union shop. In such a case, plain, unsubtle force or the threat of it suffices to deny any bargaining power to the employer and any choice to the workers. The interests of already organized truckers may be better served by forcefully bringing wages and work standards to a uniform level and by increasing dues revenues, but to those who make public policy the opposing interests of the unorganized may weigh as heavily.

The unions' use of their power to strike poses a serious problem in another situation. Some activities are vital to the health, safety, and defense of the community. For unions to disrupt or interfere with them can inflict grave injury, with little or no compensating gain for anyone. When carpenters and plumbers strike at an atomic products installation, or machinists close down missile sites and testing grounds, they threaten our national defense. When garbage collectors or hospital workers go on strike, they endanger the health of a city. Neither cities, states, nor the federal government can long survive a free exercise of strike power in such situations.

The problem is clear; the remedy is not.[14] The emergency strike provision of the Taft-Hartley Act (with its 80-day cooling-off period, fact-finding board, vote on last employer offer, and final report to Congress) is not fully satisfactory. It has seldom contributed to the settlement of an emergency strike and has frequently made a bad set of circumstances worse.

Labor experts can agree upon the general approach to emergency strikes that promises the most success. In those areas in which the public cannot tolerate strikes, and we must define these thoughtfully, strikes should not be allowed to occur. The government must always apply firm pressure to both sides to bargain in good faith, and penalties should fall upon the intransigent. If collective bargaining fails, the government then must insure continued production while providing an alternative procedure for arriving at a settlement that will not necessarily favor one of the parties. To be effective, the procedure should mobilize public opinion behind the particular settlement proposed. But a general approach to the difficult problem of emergency strikes is much easier than a specific one; in practice, there may be no single satisfactory approach or solution.

INTERNAL GOVERNANCE: ARE UNIONS DEMOCRATIC?

Strikes can create troublesome problems of peace and order for government, greatly inconvenience the public, and deal severe blows to the economy. If workers readily and willingly support such strikes, sacrificing needed wages and risking possible loss of jobs, and if managers prefer the losses and dangers of strikes to settlements, then the rest of us had better assume that serious issues divide the parties. Resolving disputes through strikes may be painful, but it

---

[14] Irving Bernstein *et al.* (eds.), *Emergency Disputes and National Policy* (New York: Harper & Bros., 1955).

may also be useful and even necessary in a democratic society that cannot otherwise reach consensus on such divisive matters as wages, conditions of work, and industrial authority.

Should unions impose strikes to gain demands or to protect rights that do not serve workers' interests, we face a more disturbing problem than the strikes themselves. However challenging the use of economic power by democratic unions may be, the challenge is preferable to that posed by undemocratic unions. The unions' economic power is great, and in an ordered, democratic society one might properly insist that such power be used only with the consent and approval of union members.

Democracy in unions surely is not any simple, direct, town-meeting kind. The tens of thousands of workers represented, the large size of companies bargained with, and the multitudinous activities unions engage in forbid it. For unions to be effective, members must delegate authority to centralized offices, whose incumbents will competently and reliably carry out overall bargaining, research, administration of common funds, and coordination of local union policy. These duties require of officers more than merely democratic leadership; they also require other and contradictory talents, such as military, fraternal, administrative, and business leadership.[15]

Emphasis on any single talent may limit the extent and exercise of union democracy. Strikers may understandably see freely expressed opposition to the leaders of an ongoing strike as treason and subversion. The desire of members to have professional handling of pension and welfare funds may make members reluctant to turn out of office an able but undemocratic administrator. A hard-fisted, experienced bargainer whose shrewdness pays off in high wages may succeed in making his autocratic union management palatable.

Employers may also accept undemocratic union leaders. When businessmen find a responsible, "sensibly business-minded" labor leader, they may not be bothered much if he treats his members in a dictatorial fashion.[16] A "sound and reliable" union leader rarely meets businessmen who object to doing business with him. Employers and managers generally got along well with Dave Beck, and their praise for his "businesslike approach" constituted as devastating a comment on certain shoddy business values as any made by avowed

---

[15] Sylvia Kopald, "Democracy and Leadership," in E. Wright Bakke and Clark Kerr (eds.), *Unions, Management and the Public* (New York: Harcourt, Brace & Co., 1948), pp. 180–84.

[16] Daniel Bell, "Nate Shefferman, Union Buster," *Fortune,* February, 1958, p. 120.

critics of business. Some employers recommended Jimmy Hoffa as a man of his word, however he conducted his union. To deal with him may be preferable to negotiating with Walter Reuther, who is personally incorruptible and a leader of a union far more democratic than the Teamsters.

Instability within unions reinforces the centralizing tendency of national-union control. Workers are constantly organizing and disbanding locals within each national union. New locals need special help and careful watching as their inexperienced, untrained officers assume legal and financial responsibilities for which the parent union is liable. And when locals disband, the central union again must have sufficient powers to guarantee that all union obligations are fulfilled and local funds are dispersed honestly. Centralized national unions surely have a legitimate function in controlling many aspects of local union life. Profligate, inexperienced local leaders could easily drain a union of its strength and substance were there no checks and limits to their authority.

Even in established locals, membership continually fluctuates. Annual losses of 5–20 percent and gains of equal magnitude are probably not at all uncommon.[17] Such changes require the central union to have sufficient powers to introduce and impose union responsibility upon new members and to safeguard locals whose trained and experienced personnel leave.

Despite these pressures toward strong, central control of unions, the nation has every right to expect and require unions to follow reasonably democratic procedures. No one should expect, of course, simon pure or simple democracy, any more than one expects it in any large, complex organization. Nor should anyone expect to enjoy union democracy without paying some cost for the privilege.

Increased democracy does not necessarily promise better industrial relations or more peaceful collective bargaining. The businessman who urges his workers not to allow themselves to be made the pawns of "labor bosses" will invariably complain of his inability to settle matters in a "sensible" way with local leaders. They are too responsive to the shop members. He prefers to deal with the "more understanding" (less responsive?) union leader from the national office.

More frequent elections, freer speech by dissident union members, and stricter, fairer judicial protection of members' union rights

---

[17] Philip Taft, *The Structure and Government of Labor Unions* (Cambridge: Harvard University Press, 1954), pp. 122–23.

invite more open criticism of union policy and encourage more frequent challenges to officeholders in elections. Extremists may thus limit the ability of moderate union leaders to promote reasonable programs. Less experienced men from the shop, unaware of the necessary compromises in collective bargaining and the usefulness of continuity and reliability, may, if given the democratic opportunity, push union officers into upsetting established, workable programs, permitting wildcat strikes, or subverting the regularly established collective agreement.

More democratic procedures may make it easier for those who wish to use the organizations for their own personal gain or for ideological purposes to infiltrate and corrupt the unions. Democracy is no defense against corruption, as any student of American government administration before civil service well knows. And democratic procedures may be more likely to frustrate than realize the desire to eliminate supporters of anti-American ideologies. As in any large organization, most union members display an almost total apathy toward routine union activities. A 1 percent turnout at a local meeting to ratify or reject a collective agreement is normal, and a 10 percent turnout is considered most extraordinary.[18] Even in secret strike votes held at the place of work, a quarter to a third of union members will not vote. Under such circumstances, a determined, dedicated minority can influence union decisions out of all proportion to their numbers.

But the costs and dangers of union democracy do not negate democratic rights to union members and shop workers; they do suggest care in the formulation of public policy guaranteeing those rights. A much debated guarantee has been "right-to-work" laws, which forbid compulsory union membership. These laws, however, do not remove the legal requirement that unions represent all workers, whether members or not. The result is that under a "right-to-work" law, unions must provide bargaining services for all workers but can demand dues support from only voluntary members. The law protects the rights of individuals opposed to unions, of course, but at the expense of union strength and resources and therefore perhaps to the detriment of collective bargaining.

Proponents of "right-to-work" laws argue that if unions must forcibly recruit members, then their program and services stand indicted. The argument embarrasses union leaders, and their replies

18 Leonard Sayles and George Strauss, *The Local Union* (New York: Harper & Bros., 1953), p. 173.

sound more shrill than convincing. If collective bargaining for workers is desirable, and unions can be important instruments of democracy in an industrial society, public policy might more wisely support unions and collective bargaining and protect the rights of individual workers in their role as union members. Rather than fight for "right-to-work" laws that weaken collective bargaining as they strengthen individual rights, why not discuss separately the merits of weakening union strength in collective bargaining and of protecting the worker?

Union members deserve an effective and impartial judicial system to protect the rights, privileges, and immunities of all members. The procedures must be simple, and cases must move quickly, for neither workers nor unions can afford protracted proceedings. If a worker is guilty of undermining the union or of violating union rules, the union needs protection; if a worker is not guilty as charged, he ought to be free to work at his job and to make his voice heard in the union. To guarantee a reasonable degree of impartiality, the accused ought to be able to appeal simply and quickly, with little or no financial penalty, to an impartial judge outside the union.

A fundamental way of protecting the worker's rights and individuality within unionism is to allow workers greater opportunity to participate in decisions that affect their daily working lives. Not only have union leaders centralized power in the national offices, but local leaders (with the aid and approval of industrial-relations managers) have also gathered into their hands much of the authority and control formerly exercised by foremen and shop leaders. The result is that, day by day, workers have little role to play in union or even shop affairs. Yet it is in informal shop groups, not in formal union meetings, that workers can most effectively make known their views, discuss their particular problems, and have a real voice in the decisions made. At smoking breaks and during lunch hours workers are not confused and silenced by the unfamiliar procedures of organized meetings.

If unions could bring the work groups, already present in the shop, more clearly into the unions' orbit by recognizing them as legitimate union bodies, allowing them regular responsibilities and assigning them compensating liberties, workers could better handle many matters now decided and administered by local or national union officers. But for union leaders to decentralize even some control and activities with local unions may be to run the risk of increased instability and divided policy. Again we must weigh carefully the gains for individual rights against the losses to collective bargaining and to our present system of industrial relations. But if unions only remain faithful to their original motivation—freedom and dignity through fraternity—rather than to atavistic patterns for realizing their goal, they can surely bring about industrial democracy.

CONCLUSION

The history of the labor movement in the United States reveals the essentially pragmatic nature of unionism. Unlike their European counterparts, American Labor Leaders have shown little disposition to espouse ideological causes and this reluctance explains, in part, why there is no labor or socialist political party of substance. Union history also demonstrates the restrictive views taken by the courts in their interpretations of the "freedom-of-association" concept. Businessmen won the right to establish corporations roughly a century before workers achieved the legal right to form unions.

Whether unions have exercised their powers responsibly—or irresponsibly—is a question often answered more by one's prejudice than by fact. That unions can and do call crippling strikes (trainmen on railroads, teachers in New York, garbage collectors in Nashville, longshoremen in Seattle) is a fact of life. But the crippling effects turn out often to be less damaging in the long run than is generally supposed. Yet responsible and thoughtful men are asking whether the strike is not inducing hardships on society that outweigh the gains achieved by a particular set of workers. Outlawing the strike seems unlikely as public policy; sharper restrictions on its use seems more likely.

Within the unions the problem is one of "democracy." As an ideal few quarrel with the concept; as a practical matter there are many—in and out of business and in and out of unions—who feel that it can become seriously defective. Referral, for example, of a contract agreed to by management and union negotiators to the rank and file can have the effect of forcing both sides to adopt aggressive and unrealistic postures; it can lead to the politics of "upsmanship" in union elections; it can result in short-term gains and long-term losses.

Yet the same criticisms might well be leveled at the idea of democracy in the political realm and it is, therefore, the function of leadership to discipline the ideal with a sense of reality—even as realism must be ennobled by an appreciation of what the ideal itself represents. In all such endeavors the ultimate test remains: Is the union the living embodiment of man's eternal quest to create and control organizations responsive both to his needs and to his nature?

RECOMMENDED READING

CHAMBERLAIN, NEIL. *Social Responsibility and Strikes.* New York: Harper & Bros., 1953.

DUNLOP, JOHN T. "The Development of Labor Organizations," in *Insights into Labor Issues,* ed. RICHARD LESTER and JOSEPH SHISTER. New York: Macmillan Co., 1948.

HOXIE, ROBERT. *Trade Unionism in the United States.* New York: Appleton-Century-Croft, 1924.

KORNHAUSER, A.; DUBIN, ROBERT; and ROSS, ARTHUR M. *Industrial Conflict.* New York: McGraw-Hill Book Co., 1954.

MILLIS, H. A., and BROWN, E. C. *From the Wagner Act to Taft-Hartley.* Chicago: University of Chicago Press, 1950.

MILLIS, H. A., and MONTGOMERY, R. E. *Organized Labor.* New York: McGraw-Hill Book Co., 1945.

PERLMAN, MARK. *Labor Union Theories in America: Background and Development.* Evanston, Ill.: Row, Peterson & Co., 1958.

PERLMAN, SELIG. *A Theory of the Labor Movement.* New York: Macmillan Co., 1928.

———. *The History of Trade Unionism in the United States.* New York: Augustus M. Kelley, Inc., 1950.

PETRO, S. *The Labor Policy of the Free Society.* New York: Ronald Press Co., 1957.

TAFT, PHILIP. *The AFL from the Death of Gompers to the Merger.* New York: Harper & Bros., 1959.

———. *The Structure and Government of Labor Unions.* Cambridge: Harvard University Press, 1954.

TANNENBAUM, FRANK. *A Philosophy of Labor.* New York: Alfred A. Knopf, 1951.

TYLER, GUS. *The Political Imperative: The Corporate Character of Unions.* New York: Macmillan Co., 1968.

FURTHER READING

BARBASH, JACK. *The Practice of Unionism.* New York: Harper & Row, Publishers, 1956.

BERNSTEIN, I., *et al. Emergency Disputes and National Policy.* New York: Harper & Bros., 1955.

CHINOY, ELY. *Automobile Workers and the American Dream.* Garden City, N.Y.: Doubleday & Co. 1955.

COMMONS, J. R. "The American Shoemakers: A Sketch of Industrial Evolution, 1648–1895," *Quarterly Journal of Economics,* Vol. XXIV (November, 1909), pp. 39–84.

DUNLOP, JOHN T. *Industrial Relations Systems.* New York: Henry Holt & Co., 1958.

GREGORY, CHARLES O. *Labor and the Law.* New York: W. W. Norton & Co., 1958.

GROB, GEROLD. *Workers and Utopia.* Evanston, Ill.: Northwestern University Press, 1961.

HOWE, I., and WIDICK, B. J. *The UAW and Walter Reuther.* New York: Random House, 1949.

KERR, CLARK, and SIEGEL, M. "The Structuring of the Labor Force in Industrial Society: New Dimensions and New Questions," *Industrial and Labor Relations Review,* Vol. 8 (January, 1955), pp. 151–68.

KUHN, J. W. *Democracy in the Grievance Process: The Workers' Challenge to the Union.* New York: Columbia University Press, 1961.

LEISERSON, W. M. *American Trade Union Democracy.* New York: Columbia University Press, 1959.

LIEBERMAN, E. *Unions before the Bar.* New York: Harper & Bros., 1950.

LIPSET, S. M.; TROW, MARTIN A.; and COLEMAN, JAMES S. *Union Democracy: The Internal Politics of the International Typographical Union.* New York: The Free Press, 1956.

SAYLES, L. R. *Behavior of Industrial Work Groups, Prediction and Control.* New York: John Wiley & Sons. 1958.

SEIDMAN, J. *Union Rights and Union Duties.* New York: Harcourt, Brace & Co., 1943.

TAFT, PHILIP. *The Structure and Government of Labor Unions.* Cambridge: Harvard University Press, 1954.

ULMAN, LLOYD. *The Rise of the National Trade Union.* Cambridge: Harvard University Press, 1955.

WALKER, C. R., and GUEST, ROBERT H. *The Man on the Assembly Line.* Cambridge: Harvard University Press, 1952.

WALTON, RICHARD, and McKERSIE, ROBERT. *A Behavioral Theory of Labor Negotiations.* New York: McGraw-Hill Book Co., 1965.

5. The Corporation: Idea and Reality

OUTLINE

FEW CHAPTERS in the history of business are as fascinating as the story of the growth of the modern corporation. The genesis of the corporate idea in the ancient law and the adaptation of this idea to the requirements of modern industrial society has philosophical as well as economic implications that the student of business would do well to contemplate. For there is no aspect of modern business in which misconceptions reign so generally.

From the point of view of the concession theorists, the corporation is nothing but a fictitious person. In Chief Justice Marshall's famous phrase, it is "an artificial being, invisible, intangible, and existing only in contemplation of law."[1] The state presumably commands its birth and death; and it exercises its "powers" as mere privilege and not a matter of right. Yet this ghostly creature may

---

[1] *Dartmouth College* v. *Woodward,* 4 Wheaton 518 (1819).

achieve such real influence in the world of affairs as to arouse both fear and envy, and thus "giant corporations" become the subject of bitter political debate.

In an industrial society, in which "freedom of enterprise" is an article of faith, the corporate form of business organization is the dominant one among the larger units of private enterprise. Yet sober and otherwise realistic businessmen are often quite willing to pay lip service to the notion that legislatures may dangle the corporate puppet on a legalistic string and command it to live or die according to the sovereign will. In practice, the *right* to do business in corporate form is stoutly insisted upon and is, in fact, well established not only under general incorporation statutes but also in rules of law that throw a protective cloak about the corporate "person." The bloodless apparition of a legal form has become in fact a real organism of vital significance to the political economy of a free society.

Unlimited "free enterprise" is a myth; it exists in no contemporary industrial society. This is true even of business in other than corporate form: in individual proprietorships and partnerships. Even in a constitutional democracy, the "police power"[2] of governments is broad enough to sustain restrictive legislation in the form of licensing and numerous types of regulatory acts. The corporate form of business enterprise, because of the concession theory of corporateness and as a result of the vast resources that can be brought under the collective control of the corporate "person," is theoretically even more vulnerable to public regulatory power. Yet in our political economy there is in fact an extraordinarily wide range of freedom for this very corporate form of enterprise, and this freedom is traceable in part to the fiction that the corporation is no ordinary person.

The great advantages of the corporate form to the businessman are not confined to the elementary propositions that the incorporators may sue and be sued as a unit, that the institution can endure beyond the natural lives of the members of the association, and that they can conveniently consign part of their property to it for ven-

---

[2] The "police power" of the states is an indefinite and inherent power to provide for "the public health, safety, morals, and general welfare" or the general "power to govern men and things" (*License Cases*, 5 Howard 504, 583 [1847]) , whereas most of Congress' powers are defined by reference to a specified subject matter like "commerce among the States," etc.

tures of limited liability to themselves. Walton Hamilton put the matter clearly in his discussion of the "corporate veil":

The legal make-believe that the corporation is a person, the ingenuities by which it has been fitted out with a domicile, the elaborate web of "as-ifs" which the courts have woven,—have put corporate affairs pretty largely out of reach of the regulations we decree. Because the person corporate makes its legal appearance in wraps, the judges who give effect to public policy must—note that a fiction must be employed to strip away a fiction—"pierce the corporate veil." And in a bout of many rounds between controller and controllee, the art of veiling has reached such perfection as by comparison to make Salome with her seven veils a somewhat naked lady. As a result the law in its majesty issues its stern command; the person against whom its darts are cast is too cleverly armored to feel the blow.[3]

The corporation, unlike real persons, has "no anatomical parts to be kicked or consigned to calaboose; no conscience to keep it awake all night; no soul for whose salvation the parson may struggle; no body to be roasted in hell or purged for celestial enjoyment." Nor, as Hamilton points out, can anyone lay "bodily hands upon General Motors or, Westinghouse . . . incarcerate the Pennsylvania Railroad or Standard Oil (N.J.) complete with all its works."[4]

Yet more recently it has been said that the corporation does have a soul[5] and should institutionalize the corporate conscience in the form of some modern version of the medieval Lords Spiritual of the Norman kings.[6]

Nowadays there is a strong plea among businessmen themselves for a new sense of "social responsibility" on the part of corporate leaders. From other quarters the critique of the modern corporation becomes increasingly sharp and penetrating; there is said to be a need for checks and balances in the business system and elsewhere in society to keep "corporate power" within legitimate bounds,[7] and

---

[3] Walton H. Hamilton, "On the Composition of the Corporate Veil" (Publications of the Brandeis Lawyers' Society) (Philadelphia, 1946), p. 4.

[4] *Ibid.*

[5] Cf. Carl Kaysen's comment on "the soulful corporation" in "The Social Significance of the Modern Corporation," *American Economic Review*, Vol. XLVII (May, 1957), pp. 311–19.

[6] Adolf A. Berle, Jr., *The Twentieth Century Capitalist Revolution* (New York: Harcourt, Brace & Co., 1954), chap. iii.

[7] See Walton Hamilton, *The Politics of Industry* (New York: Alfred A. Knopf, 1957). See also John Kenneth Galbraith, *American Capitalism: The Concept of Countervailing Power* (Boston: Houghton Mifflin Co., 1952).

arguments are made for more rigorous enforcement of antitrust laws and laws protecting the various interests associated with corporate activity.

For these and other reasons the student of modern business needs to take a careful look at the past, present, and future of corporate enterprise. We shall therefore first review the history of the corporate idea, then have a look at today's corporate reality, and, finally, ask whether this reality is compatible with the public interest.

THE CORPORATE IDEA IN RETROSPECT

GENEALOGY OF THE MODERN CORPORATION

The present-day business corporation has two genealogical lines. One line derives from the crown-chartered companies created by the medieval Church and the sovereign states of western Europe. These were the creatures, clearly and directly, of the Church and of the political sovereigns from the 12th century on. The concept of such bodies was first elaborated by the Italian canon lawyers of the 12th century; their prototypes in Roman law have been only dimly identified by scholars.

But the other line of descent is the more important. In the discussion on "Freedom of Association" the importance of the right to form business organizations was stressed. Men formed such bodies without the sanction of a sovereign as far back as we can trace business activity under modern conditions. They obviously drew on the traditional right to form churches, guilds, local towns or boroughs, libraries, and clubs of all sorts without reference to the political state. These associations were personal and local, the living creations of their organizers, not mere fictitious persons created by the state. In the 18th century in England and the early 19th century in the United States, there flourished many business organizations that possessed all the essential attributes of the corporation but lacked charters or other official sanction.[8] The definition of the corporation as "an artificial being, invisible, intangible, and existing only in contemplation of law" failed to reflect this historical fact.

By the mid-19th century these two roots of the corporation's

---

[8] Armand B. DuBois, *The English Business Company after the Bubble Act, 1720–1800* (New York: Commonwealth Fund, 1938) ; Shaw Livermore, *Early American Land Companies: Their Influence on Corporate Development* (New York: The Commonwealth Fund; London: Oxford University Press, 1939) .

family tree were combined in the business corporation chartered as a freely available privilege under general incorporation statutes. These statutes were the product of two forces. One was the negative reaction against the idea of crown-chartered or legislature-chartered companies, which by 1840 had become suspect as narrow monopoly grants—in foreign trade, banking, insurance, toll roads, canals, and railroads. The other force was the positive assertion and widespread use of men's right to form private voluntary associations in a democracy. The democratic or "antiprivilege" sentiment of the nation was translated into the right of *anyone* to secure a formal state charter with all the legal privileges and status of the old selectively chartered companies.[9]

The theory of the modern business corporation thus traces its genealogy to two contrasting parental lines: the autocratic doctrine that corporateness is conferred by public act and cannot be generated merely by agreements, and the democratic doctrine that corporateness is a right common to all men—a right grounded in the constitutional principle of freedom of association. The current conflict of views about the nature, the powers, and the responsibilities of business corporations arises in part out of this ambivalence of corporation theory in the growth of Western political and juridical thought.

THE CORPORATION AS A STATE-CREATED ENTITY

In his masterly account of the struggle between the two historic modes of thought about the corporation—on the one hand, as a natural group with the inherent qualities of a "warm" organic unity; on the other, as a purely artificial creation of the sovereign—Otto von Gierke wrote of the "combat" of ideas that filled the centuries after the Middle Ages:

A combat it was in which the Sovereign State and the Sovereign Individual contended over the delimitation of the provinces assigned to them by Natural Law, and in the course of that struggle *all intermediate groups*

---

[9] Livermore, *op. cit.*, p. 9. These forces were at work in both England and the United States. The 1862 Companies Act in England was regarded by F. W. Maitland (*Collected Papers*, Vol. 3, p. 389) as one of "capitulation" by parliament. In substance, both the English Companies Acts and general incorporation laws in the United States have said to the business community: "Since you believe that a true entity for business purposes can be created by voluntary agreement, we prefer to have you bring such organizations under our supervision; such small and routine requirements will be laid down upon you that you will be encouraged to secure the specific legal advantages which you have long possessed." Livermore, *loc. cit.*

were first degraded into the position of more or less arbitrarily fashioned
creatures of mere Positive Law [i.e., the command of the Sovereign], and
in the end were obliterated.[10]

The struggle still goes on today, as is evident if we compare the
"solemn inanities of Blackstone"[11] respecting the nature of the corporation—inanities that are as solemnly repeated in many contemporary textbooks—with pluralistic theory.[12]

The growth of industrialism within the framework of a constitutional society would have been impossible had the concession theory
been followed to the letter. Even the last centuries of the Middle
Ages, as Gierke pointed out, were "centuries brimful of vigorous
corporate life" that was in no way the derivative of a centralized
authority in church or state.[13] The triumph of the nation-state with
its claims of sovereignty from the 16th century on did not really
change this situation, though it is certainly true that in more recent
times the authoritarian and totalitarian state, in some contemporary
instances with frightening efficiency, has managed to degrade and
almost obliterate all intermediate voluntary groupings between the
atomized masses and a towering state bureaucracy.[14]

In view of the political dangers inherent in the concession theory
of corporateness, it is remarkable that any businessman would willingly align himself with so authoritarian a concept. Yet the peculiar
attraction that bad theory exerts for those who pretend to abhor all
theory leads corporation officials regularly to repeat the peculiar
doctrine that the corporate "privilege" can be withdrawn by the
state, which alone had "breathed the breath of life" into the corporate entity.

There are, in fact, many competing theories that underlie our

[10] Otto von Gierke, *Political Theories of the Middle Age*. (Trans. F. W. Maitland)
(Cambridge University Press, 1900) (Italics not in the original.) Beacon Paperback,
1958, p. 100.

[11] Julius Goebel's "Editor's Introduction" to DuBois, *op. cit.*, p. ix. John Marshall's
oft-quoted definition of a corporation in the Dartmouth College case (1819) as "an
artificial being, invisible, intangible, and existing only in contemplation of law" goes
back to Blackstone and other English sources, which adopted the concession theory
quite uncritically.

[12] See chapter on "Pluralism."

[13] Gierke, *op. cit.*, p. 98.

[14] Cf. Karl R. Popper, *The Open Society and Its Enemies* (Princeton: Princeton
University Press, 1950); Carl J. Friedrich and Z. K. Brzezinski, *Totalitarian Dictator-
ship and Autocracy* (New York: Frederick A. Praeger, 1965), Part V: "The Directed
Economy"; and Wm. Ebenstein, *Today's Isms, Communism, Fascism, Capitalism,
Socialism* (5th ed., Englewood Cliffs, N.J.: Prentice-Hall, Inc., 1967).

modern corporation statutes, each reflecting a different conception of the role that government should play in this area:

At one extreme, under the so-called "enabling act" theory, the privilege of incorporation would be made freely available, with a minimum of special conditions and limitations. Somewhat more restrictive is another theory whose adherents, although essentially persuaded of the social efficacy of enlightened self-interest, favor the interposition of legislative safeguards at critical junctures where experience has indicated that difficulties may arise. Another theory would, by legislative prescription, even more systematically impinge on freedom to contract, not only to protect investors and creditors, but to create and preserve the atmosphere of public confidence so necessary for business prosperity. And, finally, at the other extreme, the proponents of the so-called "social responsibility" theory urge that corporate power be exercised not primarily for the benefit of investors and creditors, or even customers and employees, but rather for the benefit of the general public.[15]

The competing theories just described are the more or less inarticulate premises that underlie recent corporation statutes, which in many states have been undergoing extensive revision. This diversity of theory, read against the history of corporate growth, indicates that the modern corporation is a hybrid.

Oscar Handlin[16] has shown clearly that the original business corporation in this country was not the pure form erroneously described by Chief Justice Marshall; but he also shows that the states were not forgoing their sovereign right to control the formation of corporations or their prerogative to limit corporate life, to give or withhold limitation of liability, and to permit or exclude nonchartered groups in specific fields of business. These two streams of development of the present corporation—one, the idea of the freely associated group, the other the idea of the chartered "body corporate"—are also shown in confluence in the case of *Warner* v. *Beers* in 1840.[17] There it was decided that certain nonchartered associations, authorized by the New York state legislature to engage in banking in order to provide competition for the "monopolistic" chartered banks, were not automatically to be considered as chart-

---

[15] Melvin G. Shimm, Foreword to "The New Look in Corporation Law," *Law and Contemporary Problems,*" Vol. XXIII (Spring, 1958), p. 175.

[16] O. and M. F. Handlin, "Origins of the American Business Corporation," *Journal of Economic History,* Vol. V (May, 1945), pp. 1–23.

[17] Wendell 103 (N.Y. Court of Errors, April, 1840).

ered corporations. Their legal and tax status turned on the answer to the question as to whether these nonchartered banks were or were not corporations.

In one of the opinions Senator Verplanck, a well-known scholar in his own right, made an exhaustive study of the distinguishing earmarks of a "corporate body," showing that private, nonchartered associations had all the characteristics that legal literature had used to define the chartered corporation.[18] The transferability of shares, for example, and authority of suing in the name of officers, were not to be regarded as a characteristic of "bodies corporate" alone, for he found examples of copartnerships in which these qualities had been specifically conferred in England on associations *not* incorporated by act of parliament. Nor was a common name to be regarded as a corporate criterion. The same was true of limited liability: it could exist in nonincorporated associations and be absent in corporate bodies.

There are several very useful and beneficial necessary powers and attributes, very often accompanying corporate privileges, especially in moneyed
corporations, which, in the existing state of our law, as modified by statutes, are more prominent in the public eye, and perhaps sometimes in the
view of our courts and legislatures, than those which are essential to the
being of a corporation. Such added powers, however valuable, are merely
accessory. They do not in themselves alone confirm a corporate character,
and may be enjoyed by unincorporated individuals.[19]

Thus, in concluding that the nonchartered banks were not subject to corporate taxes, Senator Verplanck was convinced that one "must look to the strict legal meaning of the phrase *body politic or corpo-rate,* and not to those circumstances or adjuncts which amount only to descriptions of the manner in which such bodies are frequently constituted when used for purposes of profit."[20]

The significance of these views is that, despite the concession theory, here was a case in which "corporateness" granted by the sovereign was not the precondition for doing business under a form

---

[18] At that time the Court was composed of members of the New York state senate.

[19] Verplanck's opinion in *Warner* v. *Beers* at pp. 145–46. Among the nonessential powers, he listed "the convenience of holding real estate for the common purposes, exempt from the legal inconvenience of joint tenancy or tenancy in common" and "the continuance of the joint property for the benefit and preservation of the common fund, indissoluble by the death or legal disability of any partner."

[20] *Ibid.,* p. 154.

of organization that would ordinarily have been regarded as nothing but a corporation. The presumed special privileges, in short, of *corporateness* granted by a legislature could be obtained for the most part in the absence of such a grant.

Technically, the legal powers of a corporation are those conferred upon it, expressly or by implication, by its charter and the corporation law of the jurisdiction in which it is "domiciled."[21] The corporation has no other *legal* powers; but, of course, it may enjoy considerable power that is in no way traceable to law alone, and it may also suffer great reverses of power without the slightest change in any rule of law.

The distinction between a corporation's authority to act *intra vires*—that is, within the scope of its legally conferred or permitted powers—and the same company's financial, industrial, or other capabilities is obvious. Yet this distinction would be meaningless if it were not for the organic realities of the "going concern."[22] For an understanding of this aspect of corporate growth one must consider the history of business in its economic and social dimensions as well as its existence as a purely legal entity.

THE CORPORATION AS A FREE ASSOCIATION

The concession theorists' Sovereign Command in granting a charter would "create" no corporation unless there were incorporators ready and willing to establish a company. "The association of human beings, bound together in order to achieve a purpose, is the fundamental and teleological basis for the coming into existence and the continuing in existence of a corporation,"[23] whether it be a town, a college, a hospital, or a business company. The community

---

21 Corporations "choose the most hospitable state for domiciliary purposes," i.e., the state of incorporation, and, "as a requisite to a home, the corpus must maintain an office within a state; but the housing requirements are of monastic austerity. A suite, a desk, even a drawer in a filing cabinet may suffice. A single room in an office building in [one] city is said to house more than a thousand state-made souls; and the building as a whole is said to be the most ghost-infested in the land. A census of souls corporate would turn New York, Pennsylvania, Illinois, Michigan into only moderately populated states. The real congestion is in Florida, Delaware, Nevada; and a few blocks in Wilmington present the greatest density of persons in all the world. For in addition to all the artificial souls which reside there [judicial interpretation has] placed the homes of all their human stockholders in the same vicinage." Walton H. Hamilton, "On the Composition of the Corporate Veil," *op. cit.*, pp. 10–11.

22 Cf. John R. Commons, *Legal Foundations of Capitalism* (New York: Macmillan Co., 1924), chap. v.

23 A. S. Dewing, *The Financial Policy of Corporations* (5th ed.; New York: Ronald Press Co., 1953), Vol. I, p. 4.

of purpose essential to corporate life cannot be supplied and sustained by positive law alone and frequently exists in the absence of any legal action—and in the face of legal opposition.

Nor do we refer here to the corporation as a contract in the legal sense of that word.[24] It takes more than a formal agreement among incorporators, between state and corporation, and between state and stockholders to create and maintain a company like the Union Pacific Railroad or Sears, Roebuck. The "going concern" is, in its essence, not even to be found in the "homogeneity or rather integrity of the property owned by the corporation and dedicated to a single economic purpose."[25]

The going concern is animated by real people, has a common purpose of its own, exhibits a collective behavior unique to it, and is "governed by common rules of its own making."[26] As Commons once observed, it is the combination of a "going plant" ("a technological process of production and consumption of physical things") and a "going business" (a process of buying and selling, borrowing and lending) and is "made up of action and reaction with nature's forces, and transactions between human beings according to accepted rules."

From one point of view the modern business corporation is *imperium in imperio,* a state within the state, which Leviathan jealously regards as a competitor for power and for the loyalty of his subjects. From another standpoint, it is "the most highly developed and useful means of voluntary cooperation," for "by the very nature of the rules which govern it, a corporation provides easy ways for persons to join or leave, as owners or employees," and, "by utilizing the corporate form, the group can acquire a size needed to initiate

---

[24] On the composite series of contracts that form the legal basis of the corporation, according to some authorities, see Dewing, *op. cit.*, pp. 8 *ff*. Thus *Cook on Corporations* (8th ed., 1923), Vol. 2, p. 492: "The charter of a corporation having capital stock is a contract between three parties, and forms the basis of three district contracts. The charter is a contract between the state and the corporation; second, it is a contract between the corporation and the stockholders; third, it is a contract between the stockholders and the state." Some have wondered how the corporate creature can bind its creator, the state, in the act of procreation; but the fiction persists.

[25] Dewing, *op. cit.*, Vol. I, p. 17. It is, as he goes on to say, "an institution, gradually evolved through centuries of changing economic environment, that gives form and substance to [the] need for projecting a purpose beyond the limits of a single human life."

[26] Commons, *op. cit.*, pp. 8 and 144–45. "The transaction is two or more wills giving, taking, persuading, coercing, defrauding, commanding, obeying, competing, governing, in a world of scarcity, mechanism and rules of law." *Ibid.*, p. 7.

and accomplish modern-sized jobs, a task to which no other form of voluntary association lends itself so readily."[27] As a "metrocorporation"[28] it may seem to absorb unduly the private lives of its employees; but in traditional and "well-tempered" forms[29] it serves more benign purposes, and at all events it provides the center of economic life for millions of the productively employed.

The true character of "the corporation" must be seen in perspective. The term refers to big business and small business, with many intermediate sizes, and with numbers of employees that range from a few to a half-million or more. It refers to industrial firms, commercial banks, insurance companies, merchandising firms, transportation companies, and utilities. Some are closely held by a few stockholders; in others there are over a half-million. In the very large corporation, measured in numbers of shareholders, who may dispose of their equities with comparative ease, one may speak of the business as a voluntary association of its shareowners. But this does not adequately describe the association. For it is also an association of managers and other employees, who, in fact, constitute, together with the directors, the "animated body" of the going concern; and few of these may own any substantial part of the company's voting stock.

Only in the relatively small incorporated business and in sole proprietorships and partnerships are owners actively engaged in the affairs of the firm. In the large corporation the "managerial revolution" has led to considerable freedom of action for corporate managements, whose objective may be not solely profits for stockholders but service and the equitable distribution of corporate gains among shareowners, workers, suppliers, and customers. As managements become increasingly professionalized, moreover, the canons of their profession may dictate other objectives than monetary gain, even for the purposes of equitable distribution.

Growth and continuity of the firm, its prestige in the business community and in the public esteem, its reputation as a "good corporate citizen"—these may be competing goals that will greatly influence the purpose of the association. Add to these considerations

---

[27] Roger M. Blough, *Free Man and the Corporation* (New York: McGraw-Hill Book Co., 1959) , p. 7.

[28] Richard Eells, *The Meaning of Modern Business* (New York: Columbia University Press, 1960) , chap. iii.

[29] *Ibid.,* chaps. ii and xv.

the forces inherent in the multiplicity of "interest groups" in a corporate constellation, as discussed later, and it will be seen that the true picture of the modern corporation emerges in terms of neither the state-created entity (the *persona ficta*) nor the freely associated "owners," but rather in terms of a complex social institution with many facets.

It is, of course, a "free association," but it is far more than that. In the case of many of the larger corporations—and even of some of the smaller ones in certain localities—the going concern is a vital element in the whole social structure of the community. It becomes a part of the total organization of "public service,"[30] as Leon Duguit used that term, although the services are performed by associations having a corporate personality independent of the state.[31] From this point of view, the corporation has a right to an autonomous existence and to a kind of "collective personality" that emerges in response to the need for such services.

The fundamental condition for the emergence of such autonomous associations as churches, labor unions, universities, and business corporations can thus be interpreted as a consciousness of common interest, and "where such a consciousness exists an association can arise which is limited only by the breadth of the interest and the degree of loyalty it can evoke."[32] Corporate units of this kind are not mere numbers of individuals standing in quasi-contractual relations to one another:

The group itself has ends which it pursues with more or less consistency; it has a settled policy which no individual can modify at will. Its collective character is as fixed as the character of an individual. It can assert collective rights and assume collective obligations. In short, it has the same type of energy and inertia which in the individual we call will or personality.[33]

The modern business corporation is thus derived historically from the confluence of legal doctrine of the *persona ficta* as a state-created entity and the historic practice of men in a free society to organize voluntarily for the pursuit of common purposes—quite

---

[30] See Hugo Krabbe, *The Modern Idea of the State* (Trans. George H. Sabine and Walter J. Shepard) (New York: Appleton, 1922), pp. lii ff.

[31] *Ibid.*, p. xliv, referring to the pluralistic theories of John Neville Figgis and Harold J. Laski.

[32] *Ibid.*, p. xlii.

[33] *Ibid.*

independent of state action. The corporate idea, as it crystallizes in modern incorporated businesses, can be seen as one species of a genus that embraces all kinds of "real" groups that arise from commonly recognized needs and purposes.

THE CORPORATION TODAY

EXTENT OF CORPORATE BUSINESS

The corporation has become in many respects the dominant form of business organization in the United States. As distinguished from proprietorships and partnerships, the corporation provides a vehicle by which men can combine some of their capital as a "sideline" to their other economic activities and assign its management to professionals.

The role of the corporation in the total structure of business in the United States can best be seen in the following statistics. Of the 11 to 12 million business units, from the smallest proprietorships to the largest companies, there are about a million—largely corporations—that do something like five times the business of the 10 million proprietorships.[34] But most of these are small corporations. Probably 98 percent of the corporate business is done by half a million companies; but here the large clearly overshadow the small, since one tenth of 1 percent of the bigger industrial corporations—a mere 500 firms at the top of the list—account by themselves for about one third of all the activity in the corporate industrial field.[35] To focus the picture more finely, the aggregate sales of the top 50 industrials about equal those of the bottom 450. The total of profits for the top 10 industrials is equal to almost half of total profits for the remaining 490.

If we now take into the picture not only the industrials but all corporations, each with assets or sales of at least a billion dollars, the list runs to about 150 companies in all: about 50 industrial firms, the top 40 banks, the top 20 insurance companies, the top 10 merchandisers, the top 10 transportation companies, and the top 20 utilities. These "supercorporations" are not properly describable

---

[34] Robert L. Heilbroner, *The Limits of American Capitalism* (New York: Harper & Row, 1966), p. 10. He estimated that well over half of the million or so companies did less than $100,000 a year in sales and that this half accounted for only 2 percent of the business of the corporations as a whole.

[35] *Ibid.*

simply as "big business." Their vital role in the structure of American society is well stated by Heilbroner in describing what would happen were they suddenly to disappear:

To begin with, the nation would come to a standstill. Not only would the Union and the Southern Pacific, the Pennsylvania, the New York Central, and a half dozen of the other main railroads of the nation vanish, leaving the cities to starve, but the possibilities of supplying the urban population by truck would also disappear as the main gasoline companies and the tire companies—not to mention the makers of cars and trucks— would also cease to exist. Meanwhile, within the nine largest concentrations of urban population all activity would have stopped with the termination of light and power, as the utilities in these areas vanished. In addition, communication in all areas would break down with the disappearance of the telephone company.

If we make the heroic assumption that the cities would survive, the problem would be to reconstitute the productive capacity of the remaining firms. This would have to be done without the steel capacity of the United States, Bethlehem, and Republic steel companies, the chemical output of Du Pont, Monsanto, Union Carbide, and Dow Chemical, the electrical machinery of General Electric and Westinghouse, or the transportation equipment made by Caterpillar Tractor, General Motors, and Ford. Meanwhile the farm sector would have to readjust to the disappearance of the agricultural machinery of International Harvester, the processing equipment of Swift, Armour, General Foods, Procter and Gamble, National Dairy, and Borden, and the indispensable containers provided by the big can companies.

Distribution patterns would have collapsed with the disappearance of the A & P, First National, Safeway, Food Fair, Kroger, Penney, Woolworth, Sears, and Montgomery Ward. Defense would have crumbled with the removal of General Electric, I. B. M., Sperry Rand, and the makers of virtually all planes and missiles. A national credit debacle would have followed the closing of the Chase Manhattan, First National, Bankers Trust, Manufacturers Hanover, Chemical, Morgan Guaranty, and Irving Trust banks in New York, and their counterparts in San Francisco, Chicago, Los Angeles, Pittsburgh, Detroit, Boston, Cleveland, Philadelphia, Dallas, Seattle, Portland, and Milwaukee, not to mention Buffalo, Winston-Salem, Mineola, and Houston. With these top forty banks would also go the twenty biggest insurance companies, taking with them $500 billion in life insurance, and effectively bankrupting a majority of American families.[36]

The corporation, despite its marvelous advantages in conducting modern business, has not crowded out the single proprietor or the

---

[36] *Ibid.*, pp. 11–13.

partnership. The opportunity to enter many lines of business as a proprietor or partner still exists and is very much used. This is all the more remarkable when the ease, low costs, lack of hampering legal restraints, and permission by most states to form "one-man" or family corporations are remembered.

Yet the "big business" of the country, which is almost always business in corporate form, sets the tone for the private sector of our economy, and it is the relatively small number of executive leaders in these large corporate units whose decisions are watched with the greatest interest. For "we live not only in a corporate society but a society of large corporations" and their control "is in the hands of, at most, a few thousand men."[37] The problems posed by the emergence of these large organizations are so different in degree, as compared with those of an economy of small enterprises, as to present wholly new issues of business and public policy. Before considering these issues, however, we should take a realistic look at corporate enterprise as it appears to security analysts who must watch this sector of the world of business constantly and with the greatest care.

"The General Staff" of American Capitalism

In the financial investment community of the United States there are some dozen thousand security analysts who have been called appropriately the "General Staff of American Capitalism."[38] They keep several thousand companies under critical review, comparing their results, criticizing the results, and on occasion applauding achievements. These security analysts do not stand aloof from the corporate scene. They are active participants who conduct continuous studies of companies with the best analytical tools they can muster. These studies, based in part on interviews with company managements, often in great depth, strongly influence the climate of investment and the direction which financing and corporate moves may take in the arrangement and rearrangement of industry and company structures.

This development in the relations of the public to corporate management is not spelled out in any charter or constitutional document. It has arisen in practice and is a force of no mean consequence. Management and directors are sensitive to the security

---

[37] E. S. Mason (ed.), *The Corporation in Modern Society* (Cambridge: Harvard University Press, 1959), p. 5.

[38] This is the title of an article in *The Times* (London) of July 17, 1967, by Armand G. Erpf, general partner in Loeb, Rhoades & Co., New York City.

analyst's judgments and in turn his recommendations to the trust companies, pension funds, investment trusts, insurance companies, foundations, universities and other nonprofit corporations, as well as to the vast body of individual investors through the members of the stock exchanges, the investment bankers, and the security dealers.

In advising this array of clients security analysts have devised some typological descriptions of American corporate enterprise that seldom appear in the textbooks. The analyst's view of companies helps to point up the dynamic elements in the economy. The typologies reflect to some extent the interests and hopes of the investing public as well as sober financial analysis. The grades and kinds of equities that interest this large and influential public indicate significant expectations about the immediate and long-term future of American capitalism. There is a sharp distinction, for example, between companies that are well established and serving conventional markets, whose growth may be moderately ahead of or merely in pace with the growth of the economy as a whole or even lag behind it, as against the industries and companies that are carving out new markets because of new sociological needs and urgencies or new technologies, with markets unsaturated and promising sustained forward momentum at several times the annual growth of the economy. Investors (including institutional investors in the nonbusiness private sector) have at times shown an avid demand for this innovative, creative segment of America's corporate capitalism and have been willing to pay up to 45 times earnings for the common stock of such companies, while 12 times earnings was at the same time cautiously bid on some valid investment opportunities in the first category.

A sharp distinction is also drawn by investors between slowly and rapidly growing companies. Those which grow slowly, when they require financing to meet capital expenditures over and above their cash flows, must resort to fixed high-interest obligations or an equity issue at a moderate earnings multiple that benefits existing shareholders very little since there is not much premium ingredient in the new money. Rapidly growing companies, on the other hand, if they enjoy high multiple valuations, can use in one way or another a high value currency to finance facilities or to acquire other companies. The preponderance of factors operative in security markets favors the growth of growth companies, and these factors include the investors' emphasis on the rate of growth and the analytical, intellectual justification, whether right or wrong, of the views influencing the investment climate. Among the growth stocks the security analyst will draw a distinction between "sociological trends" and "technological trends." While companies in both areas enjoy the advantages of high multiples and the willingness and capacity of Wall Street to finance them for their current and long-term needs, "cognizance should be taken that the sociological stocks such as publishing, medicare, recreation, travel and credit, are partly beneficiaries of government and consumer expenditure propensities, whatever the innovative accomplishments of the respective companies, while the technological groups, to a degree, create their own revolutions through the genius of real invention."[39] This, too, is qualified. "The cold war, with the vast expenditures of the government over the past decade and a half, and the increasing stimulus of grants and contracts for research and development," are said to be "partly responsible for the fallout of the rise in invention and technological changes which have been so enormous in the hundreds of companies formed to administer to the defense, space, communications and other endeavors associated with national need." Yet "the ability of Wall Street to finance all sorts of ventures, whether large or small, perilous or soundly conceived," is said to have "stimulated greatly the growth of this whole segment of corporate activity which has no, or but little, counterpart in many of the other economies of the world."[40]

Another way of convassing the investment scene, aside from the growth and nongrowth distinction, is to regard the companies as run by merchants, by industrialists, by scientists, or by managers. Merchants are attuned to sales appeal and to improving the attractiveness of the products they distribute and, by and large, this is done extremely well and not without an occasional significant innovation. They provide stimulation to the propensity to spend in an increasingly affluent society, and to no small extent have contributed to the degree of satisfaction and material well-being which distinguishes the American mass market and standard of living. In this, as well as in the field of multiplying human effort by harnessing various resources, is the contribution of the industrialist, who focuses on efficiency, costs, production, product improvement, productivity, and methods of distribution.

Here, too, the operation is skillfully attuned and there is, more or

---

[39] Erpf, *op. cit.*
[40] *Ibid.*

less, a continuous innovative trend. The science-oriented companies, however, outflank the whole business of more, and better, and cheaper through applications of the host of modern technologies which has blossomed out of the scientific revolution and which continues apace. This is the new, where imagination can be let run loose, the fields of the exotic, the undreamed of, or only dreamed of, being thrust into the commonplace. Finally, the professional manager, through the so-called conglomerates, is attempting to apply under his aegis professional standards of management over a variety of enterprises, and hopes through the heightening competence and the ability to plan and budget and finance to raise the order of achievement. The theory here is that professional talent, excellent professional talent, is widely available in marketing, production, and science, but that a peculiar catalytic agent, financial management, is a missing element. When this is provided to the individual specialties, accelerated progress results, and under its umbrella there need not be any commonage or mutuality among the parts.

A SPECTRUM OF COMPANIES

A useful typology for the corporate scene is Erpf's "spectrum of companies."[41] Roughly a half-dozen layers of companies in the American corporate enterprise system are discernible. They fall into two categories: "public corporate capitalism" and "democratic capitalism" as distinguished from 19th-century bourgeois family-owned personal capitalism. Within each of these two categories there are several gradations.

In *public corporate capitalism,* characterized by separation of ownership and control as among stockholders, the management, and the directors, the latter must go before the stockholders at least once annually to justify their stewardship. In this general category one finds the very large institutional companies. The question of social responsibility weighs heavily in executive decision making. The criterion of profitability is not the sole test of good business performance in such companies. And because there are other criteria than profit, it is in these companies that one is more likely to find attention given to such issues as the corporate-arts nexus, not only as a matter of social responsibility, but more broadly as a facet of the institutional company's "fit" into a society moving toward higher

---

[41] Armand G. Erpf, "The New American Capitalism," an address before the Financial Mail Investment Conference, Johannesburg, South Africa, November, 1964.

cultural goals. Yet this broad category of publicly owned companies contains some that are not so institutionally and socially oriented.

1. The great multibillion-dollar corporations have become institutions of the land. These are the old-line, long-established companies, many having had their origins in the activity and burst following the Civil War, and then again around the time of World War I. We all know these companies. They encompass the railroads, steels, automobiles, mass retailers, oils, communications, copper, and many manufacturers. These are the huge companies characterized by a large number of stockholders, in many cases more stockholders than employees; professional management teams, many echelons deep; boards of directors, usually culled from outstanding names and increasingly owning minor or negligible percentages of total share outstanding. Such directors tend to think of themselves as trustees and conservors, and are no longer doers or creators.

These companies, because of their size, must operate under bureaucratic procedure, and to the extent that they are big, they are subject to the threat of antitrustism. Social pressures are upon them to stabilize employment, and they proceed cautiously in the development and unfolding of their long-term plans. Perhaps because of their gigantic size and the dominance of their position in their respective markets, perhaps because many phases of their operations are mature, their growth rate is more consistent with the growth of the country as a whole than superior thereto. The upsurge of business from 1946 to 1958, during a period of shortages the world over, engulfed them in an atmosphere of dynamism that in many cases was temporary. In any event, whatever the bold and aggressive developments in one or another of their many activities, the impact has to be related to a multibillion-dollar base. The shares of these companies, with important exceptions and leaving out the revaluation of the postwar decade, move in price occasionally, gradually, and in general not as dynamically as newer segments of the economy.

2. Next, there are large-sized companies, many of which moved out of the private sphere in the last few decades and represent the corporate organization outside the heavy segment of our industrial structure. It is perhaps possible to characterize them as more aggressive, not yet the full target of government antipathy. A number are growing faster than the economy as a whole.

3. In a third layer, there are companies largely of the service

type, many of which represent new industries as far as the market place is concerned but old in their activity or history; some are new institutions in their particular fields and are not infrequently dominant in their respective markets.

These three types or layers constitute our public corporate capitalism. At these strata of the capitalistic structure of our economy one would expect to find characteristic tendencies and tensions of management concerning external relationships. There is concern about social responsibilities, insofar as these responsibilities seem to call for support of the arts, but at the same time concern about what the stockholders think of new departures in external relationships, and especially in fields that may seem to some quite unrelated to business. Next, there is the development among professional managers, especially younger men with widened cultural horizons, of keener interest in a "great society" and their companies' part in the "cultural boom," but at the same time the pull of their economic interests in other directions.

Finally, there is a willingness in the larger companies to push out the frontiers of managerial discretionary authority into unexplored terrain—whether for social-responsibility reasons or out of sheer venturous and "business statesmanship" notable in the new breed of big business executives who find this outlet for a place in the sun.

Turning now to the second broad category of *private capitalism*, three subtypes are discernible: (1) enterprises in the more traditional sense of the term; (2) ventures; and (3) wildcatters.[42] All three of these types of companies fit more clearly into the older genre of capitalism than the public-capitalistic companies we have just described.

The characteristics of these private-capitalistic companies can be put briefly: The enterprises do have public stockholders, professional managers and directors, but there is no such separation of ownership and "control" as one sees in the first general category of companies. The ownership, the direction, and the management are all much more coincident. The driving hand of a management-ownership is much more evident. Tension between managerial concern

---

[42] Wildcatting, in the oil industry, means sinking a well in unproven acreage and either finding the oil or losing the money, all of this taking place usually in a brief period of time, though the business may be a wildcat even when the experimental period is prolonged. Wildcatting occurs in other fields than minerals. In such ventures, the investor takes a calculated risk on a breakthrough not only in the security markets but also in technological supremacy that will yield a large return.

about social responsibility and stockholder reluctance (real or imagined) to move into new areas of corporate activity is absent. The ventures are a group of companies in which capital and management combine to explore or exploit a business concept or concession. Here, again, there is not the separation of ownership and "control" that one finds in the general areas of public corporate capitalism. Public stockholding is not so widespread. Finally, there are the wildcatters who engage in radical speculation and have little or no interest in those external corporate relationships that characterize the great institutional companies.

In the enterprises, ventures, and wildcatters one sees the ferment of private capitalism. Here is the field for bold exercise of intuition, for adventuresomeness, and for agility. Risks are recognized and undertaken with the aim of becoming bigger, stronger, and finding a firm position in the industrial structure either through growth or combination. Ultimately, many of these companies find safe harbor as divisions of the great institutional organizations who, for one reason or another, have not moved into their areas.

These three subtypes of companies in the category of private capitalism engage in activities that are distinctive, but they blend into each other and their borderlines are blurred. A mark of distinction might be their relative degree of fragility. In all three, however, the private stockholders, to a large extent, ride along on the coattails of the dominant managerial ownership who determine the policy, contsitute the decisive force, and have no qualms as to the predatory pursuit of their profit objectives. For this reason many investors prefer such managements if their objective is speculation, while other investors, of a more conservative bent, may lean toward the companies in the general category of public corporate capitalism.

CORPORATIONS AND THE PUBLIC INTEREST

The interplay of social forces reflected in the types of corporate enterprise described above leads to many issues of business and public policy. If society secures great advantages from the rise of large corporate business, it also faces new problems that are not easily resolved. Should courts and legislatures go slow in placing onerous restraints on corporate "life" in any private sector out of respect for the impetus that corporate bodies provide for our economic, educational, religious, and cultural advancement?

ISSUES OF POLICY AND POLITY

The chartered bodies of the Church (abbeys, monasteries, orders) and of the sovereigns of the early modern period were designed to assist socially useful projects and to give incentives and powers to the men who managed their affairs. But, by the same token, the corporations (whether we think of cities, universities, foundations, welfare agencies, churches, artistic and cultural groupings, or business enterprises) become power structures; if they did not, they could hardly become effective organs of the social and economic structure.

The student of modern business should, therefore, approach the study of corporations with due regard for their wider social implications. The defensiveness of many businessmen in the face of current attacks on "big business" is often too negative in neglecting the role of the large industrial unit in the historical process that Boulding has called the "organizational revolution" of our time.[43] We are living in an age of Big Labor and Big Government as well as Big Business. In all big organizations there are characteristic problems of efficiency, of power, of legitimacy. All, in one way or another, present challenges to the traditional ways of doing things and to established conceptions of authority and property.

The emergence of large concentrations of capital and human resources under the corporate rubric has raised some major issues both of corporate policy and corporate polity. For those engaged in the formulation of business policy within the corporation itself there are not only problems of "scientific management" involving the efficient operation of a vast organization; there are also problems of corporate governance in the larger sense: the relationships between stockholders and executive managers and the nature and locus of authority in the total constellation of interests that comprise the going concern. We return to this question in the next chapter.

For the public policy-maker, the large corporation raises the general problem of harmonizing the goals of the "lesser commonwealths" with the goals of the greater society. Ever since the Civil War there has been a rising protest against and a vigorous defense of large organizations in all three areas of business, labor, and government. Those who nostalgically yearn for the status quo ante insist

---

[43] Kenneth E. Boulding, *The Organizational Revolution* (New York: Harper & Bros., 1953).

that these concentrations of power must all be broken up. In business, this would mean atomization into a competitive economy on the classical model—an improbable outcome. The alternatives are better controls of the organizations we have and are likely to have for the indefinite future. Such controls can be exerted through (*a*) governmental regulation, (*b*) the establishment and maintenance of competition and of a free, pluralistic society, and (*c*) the internal constitutionalizing mechanisms of the power concentrations themselves.

THE AMERICAN ECONOMIC REPUBLIC

The corporate system in the political economy of the United States is an "American Economic Republic," to use Adolf Berle's apt term.[44] "Despite classical economic theory," he writes, "American society is not being used by, but, rather, uses the profit-seeking market-enterprise system, and certainly is not governed by it. Private enterprise in the United States is thus essentially an instrument of the State—not, as was formerly believed (perhaps accurately), an end for which the state exists."[45] But corporations do not thereby become part of a totalitarian structure. The actual system has "left both classic capitalism and classic Communism in their nineteenth-century historical museum" and reflects, perhaps more than any other system, a "twentieth-century revolution" in American capitalism. The change came after the economic crisis of 1933 and is most clearly shown in the Employment Act of 1946. There it is declared to be the policy and responsibility of the federal government to use all practical means

to coordinate and utilize all its plans, functions and resources for the purpose of creating and maintaining, in a manner calculated to foster and promote free competitive enterprise and the general welfare, conditions under which there will be offered useful employment opportunities, including self-employment, for those able, willing and seeking to work and to promote maximum employment, production and purchasing power.

This declaration of policy, according to Berle, has become a basic provision in the constitutional law of the American Economic Re-

---

[44] Adolf A. Berle, *The American Economic Republic*, Harvest Edition (New York: Harcourt, Brace & World, Inc., 1963).

[45] *Ibid.*, p. x.

public. While he concedes that concentration is the major phenomenon in industry and commerce, neither atomization into small units
nor a complete statist takeover is practical or possible. Industry by
industry, plans are more likely to be made, either by special state
dispensation as exceptions to antitrust laws or by clear state or
federal intervention to stabilize certain economic sectors in the
public interest. "A degree of concentration and of oligopoly and of
administered price, responsibly handled, seems to have provided a
more or less acceptable balance" between the desire for market
freedom, on the one hand, and freedom from the free markets' less
desirable results for all parties on the other.[46] Concentration is in
fact subject to a variety of disciplines which the state may in the end
use by intervention to satisfy the demands of consumers, labor, and
producers.

The American Economic Republic, Berle concludes, is "a guided
and managed economy, loosely organized and flexibly administered"
resulting from "state-directed planning," though at the same time a
substantially free market is maintained by the state. It is maintained
artificially, through antitrust laws, as "an instrument to prevent
unacceptable aggregations of economic power," such as monopolies,
and to preserve "a system in which any individual may enter the
free-market sector with a new enterprise or a new idea." There is
heavy reliance on the state in this economic republic to expand
productivity by the noncommercial route, yet "nonstate institutions
of all kinds can be and are used for administration, and to a limited
extent for financing."[47]

The noncommercial route is one in which the services rendered
and the results produced are distributed not merely to paying users
or consumers, and in which the motivation is not the search for
profit. Thus purely profit-seeking avenues of expansion are far from
being the only way to increase economic activity; the esthetic and
knowledge-seeking values promise to become even more powerful
forces in this respect than they are today. Universities, foundations,
philanthropic and cultural institutions, untrammeled by state bureaucracy and current politics though to a limited extent state-fi-
nanced, are among the productive forces, particularly in an age
when advancement of science and the arts measures growth and

---

[46] *Ibid.*, p. 161.
[47] *Ibid.*, pp. 213–15.

power as much as capital growth in the more traditional and restricted sense.

THE PUBLIC INTEREST

How can the state protect the public interest in the American political economy, with its considerable corporate structure? A stipulated definition of "public interest" is a basic requirement here. Public interest is a *comprehensive* interest that does not serve exclusively or dominantly any particular class, party, or any special economic or other group within the community in question. The scope of that *community* requires specification in any given account of public interest. It is assumed that we are here discussing national rather than provincial communities, and that the public interest of the world community is not what we have in mind, unfortunately, for we speak here of contemporary nation-states and not a still unrealized world order.

There are two broad aspects of governance in the public interest that need to be distinguished. Pursuit of the public interest necessitates not only the exercise of community (including national) power on behalf of the public but also the use of private-sector substantive powers to govern on a wide scale, including important decisional powers in the productive and distributive processes of the economy. In a free society, considerable power to govern human affairs must be left with or conceded to many kinds of private-sector organizations. They must be free, and even obligated, to act on behalf of community interests that are clearly public, as well as for their own private purposes. Aside from economic matters, religion, the advancement of science, education, and the arts are examples of substantive areas of public interest that cannot safely be monopolized by public bureaucracies. And the public interest requires specific recognition of the rights that these private-sector organizations serve through a pluralistic pattern of mixed public and private authority.[48]

Private rights, on the other hand, have to be protected against the undue exercise of both types of authority. Most of these private rights are universally recognized. The Universal Declaration of

---

[48] The relations of "public interest" to other political concepts such as "rights" and "authority" are well analyzed in Richard E. Flathman's *The Public Interest: An Essay Concerning the Normative Discourse of Politics* (New York: John Wiley & Sons, Inc., 1966).

Human Rights specifies, for example, among the fundamental prerogatives of the peoples of the world certain *political* rights ("to
take part in the government . . . directly or through freely chosen
representatives"), rights to *information* ("to seek, receive, and im-
part information and ideas through any media and regardless of
frontiers"), rights to *health* ("to a standard of living adequate for
the health and well-being of a man and his family, including . . .
medical care"), rights to *learning* ("education shall be free, at least
in the elementary and fundamental stages"), rights to *family and
personal relations* ("to marry and found a family" and "to leave any
country, including [one's] own, and to return to [one's] country"),
religious rights ("to freedom of thought, conscience, and religion
. . . to manifest [one's] religion or belief in teaching, practice,
worship, and observance"), and *economic* rights ("to own property," "to protection against unemployment" and "to just and favorable remuneration insuring for [one's] self and [one's] family an
existence worthy of human dignity"). In connection with these
latter economic rights there is a further specification of rights to
respect and dignity: "the economic, social, and cultural rights indispensable for [a man's] dignity and the free development of his
personality."

Whether all of these rights are essential to the substance of
public interest is, under present conditions of world politics, determined by every sovereign nation itself. Yet it is possible to measure,
with some degree of precision, the public-interest achievement and
performance goals of any collectivity, public or private, in terms of
the human rights one accepts as fundamental.[49] Public interest necessarily implies "a commonwealth of free men" in which there is
"widespread rather than narrow participation in value shaping and
sharing."[50] A common interest in a wide range of values that assure
high respect for human dignity may very well be essential to the
public interest, and this requirement may lead to social structures
and procedures that transcend private-interest structures and procedures.

---

[49] As demonstrated in *Comparing Nations: The Use of Quantitative Data in
Cross-National Research,* Richard L. Merritt and Stein Rokkan, (eds.) (New Haven
and London: Yale University Press, 1966) ; and the *World Handbook of Political and
Social Indicators,* by Bruce M. Russett, Hayward R. Alker, Jr., Karl W. Deutsch, and
Harold D. Lasswell (New Haven and London: Yale University Press, 1964) .

[50] H. D. Lasswell, "The Public Interest: Proposing Principles of Content and
Procedure," in Carl J. Friedrich (ed.), *NOMOS V: The Public Interest* (New York:
Atherton Press, 1962) , pp. 57–59.

Here again, some distinctions must be drawn in order to point up the public-interest obligations of vitally necessary private-sector organs such as business corporations. The "public order interest" covers relatively important common interests that require enforcement by some legal order—notably a nation-state with the ultimate sanctions available to sovereign power. The "public civic interest," by contrast, can often best be advanced and protected by less drastic means, while some common interests can best be conceived in parochial terms and upheld with only the mildest of sanctions. "What is labeled public or private in a given context depends upon what is warrantably left to inclusive or exclusive judgment," to the judgment, that is to say, of relatively large and widespread groups or relatively small and local ones.[51]

Corporations thus have a role in protecting the public interest. Like other private-sector entities in the United States, they cannot pursue exclusively private interests but are called upon to advance as well a number of "public civic interests." The interplay of private and public interests is indeed so marked in the American social structure, and in its constitutional processes, that there can be no realistic conception of "public interest" in that particular nonsocialist economy without due attention to both points. Constitutionalism, as we have shown in another chapter, requires a whole complex of restraint devices for the containment of power, and among these is the diffusion of power centers not only within public government (as in the "separation of powers" and other methods of dividing power such as federalism and electoral processes based on limited tenure for representative officials) but in society generally through a pluralistic structure.

The corporation is only one of many elements in this pluralistic structure, which is basic to American constitutionalism and to the prevailing conception of what the public interest requires. It requires, among other things, a respect for the autonomy of many respectable private-sector organizations and even a tolerance for the suspect. Foundations, universities, churches, the press, hospitals, museums, research laboratories and "think factories" (nonprofit and profit), societies for arts and letters, mutual-benefit ethnic groups, as well as labor unions and other societies—even some at the fringe with "beatniks" and "hippies"—are all elements in this highly variegated structure. In its entirety this pluralistic complex reflects the

---

[51] *Ibid.*, pp. 66–67.

diverse interests of a moving, changing, developing, unfolding people and society that is driven by conscience and aspirations as well as the propelling energy of profitable enterprise.

The corporation's economic role in this complex is explainable only when one sees the joint pursuit of the public interest by public and private sectors in true perspective. Expenditures by national, state and local governments now approach a fourth of a trillion dollars, or 30 percent of the Gross National Product. Here the state obviously pursues the public interest which includes expenditures for services, supervision, research, analysis, medicare, etc. Public income maintenance payments now come to between $30 and $40 billion, the most numerous beneficiaries of this cash flow being recipients of social security benefits.[52] Government workers number 11.5 million compared to a total of 74 million civilian workers, including those in the "concentrated corporations"; the percentage of government workers has been rising. There is no corporate impediment to governmental activities for the public interest in taking care of the poor, educating people on an unprecedented scale, medicare for the ill, social security payments for pensioners, research for health and other purposes, control of standards and quality of product in the business system, the maintenance of minimum wages, maximum hours of work, and standards of the working environment. These and other public measures reflect a rising conscience in both the public and private sectors, for the private, and especially the corporate, business sectors have generally either supported the trend or have been politically unable to forestall it. Corporate taxes to a large extent support the trend, for corporations account for more than half the national income.[53]

"Corporate concentration," however, is no longer generally regarded as a threat to the pluralistic structure which is essential to

---

[52] The Social Security Administration reported that almost 23 million persons were receiving monthly cash benefits under the old-age, survivors, disability, and health insurance programs at the end of February, 1968. People on welfare aid formed a sizable and growing group. They numbered more than 8 million, about half of these being children of indigent parents. These payments were rising.

[53] The corporate share of the national income, however, seems to be declining due, among other things, to the very rapid growth of the services sector of the economy. See Robert L. Heilbroner, *The Limits of American Capitalism* (New York: Harper & Row, 1966), p. 16, citing an analysis by V. Fuchs in *The Public Interest*, No. 2, Winter, 1966, pp. 9–10. On recent concentration of economic power, see Gardiner C. Means, "Statistical Appendix to Revised Edition" in Adolf A. Berle and Gardiner C. Means, *The Modern Corporation and Private Property* (rev. ed.; New York: Harcourt, Brace & World, Inc., 1968), pp. 343–59.

public interest, as it once was by critics of the American business system. Careful students find unmistakable evidence of the decline in power of big business, not only because of the slowdown in growth among the largest companies, but also due to the counter-vailing power of labor, the operation of federal antitrust and fair labor legislation, the resurgent political and economic forces in the "small business" sector, consumer movements, and perhaps most of all the rise of new nonbusiness elites. notably those based on science and technology.[54] According to Galbraith, the new power centers are in the "technostructure" of scientists and technologists. But what-ever the direction of this shift of power within the corporate struc-ture itself, there is always an adequate scope of public authority to protect the public interest.

It is a mistake to assume that there are insuperable legal and constitutional barriers to federal and state action in the public interest on corporate matters. Despite the "fragmentation of public authority" that one foreign observer finds in our governmental structure, he also sees there "the capacity of American society for profound political change in pursuit of a shifting consensus" [55] and an indication of national capability to move decisively when an overwhelming national interest demands it. While it may be true, as he says, that "in America the active political interest in government planning has derived chiefly from social rather than economic problems," [56] the fact is that the "Constitutional Revolution, Ltd.," noted by E. S. Corwin as having begun in the thirties, has greatly widened national powers to deal with national problems, while the powers of the "American Economic Republic" over commerce and industry have been further extended by both domestic and interna-tional crises since then on a whole range of issues that affect corpo-rate enterprise.

---

[54] See the sources cited in Heilbroner, *op. cit.*, esp. at pp. 43 *et seq.* He concludes that "business has experienced a considerable diminution in its ability to influence the immediate course of events, comparing the pre-Depression era with our own." He notes the rise of new elites "in American society whose importance in and competence for the direction of national affairs is clearly on the increase, compared with that of the business elite." On the other hand, he sees the possibility of a more liberal-minded business elite now on the rise, committed to "a reasonably free use of government's economic powers to promote growth and stability, a substantial widening of the welfare structure, [and] a generally open attitude toward social problems at home and abroad."

[55] Andrew Shonfield, *Modern Capitalism* (New York: Oxford University Press, 1965) , pp. 336 and 352, note 55.

[56] *Ibid.*, p. 356.

6. The Business Corporation: A Constellation of Interests

OUTLINE

THE GREAT INTEREST shown by scholars and businessmen in the role of the modern corporation in society has stimulated a general reevaluation of the *constellation of interests* at the core and on the periphery of the organization.

The traditional view was that a corporation is a merging of only one kind of interest: the property interests of its stockholders. But when the executive managers of the large industrial corporation today face the problem of "corporate responsibilities," the answer does not seem as simple as that. When they are confronted with the issue of "legitimacy"—the right to exercise the authority they must have to run a complex organization—certain problems arise:

Who selected these men, if not to rule over us, at least to exercise vast authority, and to whom are they responsible? The answer to the first question is quite clearly: they selected themselves. The answer to the second is, at best, nebulous.[1]

Responsibility in the case of individual proprietorships is clear: it runs directly to the owner. Nor was it difficult to assign responsibility in the early stages of manufacturing development, when the corporation was just another form of enterprise. "The owner, if not the manager himself, selected the management, and the management was responsible to the owners"; and "the traditional justification not only of private enterprise but of private property rested on that assumption." [2]

Today it is different. We not only have the familiar separation of ownership and managerial control in large corporations with widely dispersed stockownership; we also have the "paraproprietal society," in which property itself becomes so tenuously defined that the thread that connects the actual users of "property" with those who hold pieces of paper such as trust indentures is impossible to trace in terms of the old concepts of property rights.[3] In large organizations it is always easy to identify the body of persons who, day in and day out, stand at the *physical* controls, who keep the concern going, who constitute the "bureaucracy," in Weber's use of that term. The bureaucracy is the core of any organization, whether in government or in business; but to whom are the bureaucrats—or the officers-in-charge, if one prefers—ultimately responsible for their acts?

Chester I. Barnard distinguishes between two kinds of corporate responsibilities aside from legal obligations: " (1) those which may be called internal, relating to the equitable interests of stockholders, creditors, directors, officers, and employees; and (2) those relating to the interests of competitors, communities, government, and society in general."[4] It seems doubtful, however, that the most meaningful divison is in terms of the internal and external relations of the

---

[1] E. S. Mason (ed.), *The Corporation in Modern Society* (Cambridge: Harvard University Press, 1959) , p. 5.

[2] *Ibid.*

[3] Paul P. Harbrecht, S. J., *Pension Funds and Economic Power* (New York: Twentieth Century Fund, 1959) , chap. x.

[4] C. I. Barnard, "Elementary Conditions of Business Morals," *California Management Review,* Vol. I (Fall, 1958) , p. 7.

corporation. The boundaries of "the corporation" are not easy to define. In practice, stockholders and creditors are *external* to the organization operated by directors, officers, and employees. Barnard's distinction makes it difficult to analyze realistically the kinds of "corporate responsibilities" that executive managers must keep in mind as they consider the claims made upon them and the decisions they must reach in meeting and disposing of these claims.

The varieties of claimants on the corporation—and hence upon the recources controlled by managerial decision makers—can best be understood in another way: through a study of the art of governance[5] within the corporate constellation and through a consideration of the roles of *direct* and *indirect* claimants and contributors to the wealth and welfare of the organization.

DIRECT CLAIMANTS ON THE CORPORATION

SECURITY HOLDERS

Those who supply the capital represented by the capital stock, the corporate bonds, and the notes with maturites in excess of a year are potent contributors to the corporate enterprise. The contributors of capital thus fall into several categories of senior and junior security holders. Their respective "stakes" in the venture are variously defined by law and custom, and their claims on the corporate usufruct vary accordingly.

In the traditional corporation the common stockholders are the "share owners" of the company, and it is the aim of the proponents of the "people's capitalism" to distribute this ownership as widely as possible so that the public, as a whole, will have a direct and concrete stake in private enterprise. But a distinction must be made between this kind of ownership in business and the property owned by a sole proprietor or a partner i.1 an unincorporated business.

The property of a corporation is owned by the *personal ficta* and not, either in law or in fact, by the "share owners." The corporate "person" acts through its board of directors, as a collective body, and it is they alone who may determine how the property is used, how

---

[5] In corporate affairs, the art of governance must be distinguished from the "science of management." The latter term ordinarily refers to the business of running an organization efficiently and not the running of the business as a whole successfully. Management is a problem in tactics; corporate governance involves strategy. The stategic decision areas command the attention of "top management" (including boards of directors), stockholders, and even some of the "indirect claimants" as described here.

earnings are calculated, and how net earnings are distributed. Although they must act within the boundaries of legally set norms, their discretionary area for decision making is wide. In exercising its powers as established by charter and corporation law, the business corporation functions like a representative government rather than a direct democracy, for the shareholders elect the board, which in turn has broad powers of business management.[6]

Delegation of the power to manage the business is expressly authorized by many statutes. In practice, corporate enterprise cannot be carried on except through executive committees and officers such as president, treasurer, and corporate secretary. Broad powers may be delegated by the board to a chief executive officer under either the express or implied powers of the board. But this officer's authority is not necessarily so limited. It may arise through tacit acquiescence by the board in the executive officer's actual exercise of authority. E. Merrick Dodd, Jr., a distinguished authority on corporation law, has observed[7] that, although authority by acquiescence is well settled in law, "it seems somewhat difficult to reconcile that result with another well-established principle, that directors cannot properly act except by formal resolution at a board meeting."

The nexus between the shareholders, as the ultimate source of authority, and those who actually manage the day-to-day affairs of the company is thus considerably attentuated even as a matter of law. In practice it has become more so through "devices," such as have been described by Berle and Means,[8] which widen the divergence of interest between ownership and "control," and through the growth of pension and trust funds, which own large blocs of voting stock but do not exercise their voting rights to control the management of corporate affairs.[9]

---

[6] In typical corporation statutes the only powers expressly given to shareholders are the powers to elect directors, to enact bylaws (charters sometimes confer this power on the directors), and to approve or disapprove directors' resolutions proposing amendments to the charter, reduction of capital, merger, consolidation, sale or lease of all the corporate property, or dissolution. See E. M. Dodd, Jr., "Company and Corporation Law," *Encyclopaedia Britannica* (1958 ed.), Vol. VI, p. 149.

[7] *Ibid.*

[8] A. A. Berle, Jr., and Gardiner C. Means, *The Modern Corporation and Private Property* (New York: Macmillan Co., 1932), Book II. See the critique of this book by David McCord Wright, "The Modern Corporation—Twenty Years After," *University of Chicago Law Review*, Vol. XIX (Summer, 1952), pp. 662–67, and the authors' reply to their critics in the 1968 revised edition of their work.

[9] See A. A. Berle, Jr., *Power without Property: A New Development in American Political Economy* (New York: Harcourt, Brace & Co., 1959), esp. pp. 49–56.

If, as the more adamant traditionalists[10] argue, the common stockholders alone have a legitimate claim on the earnings of a company, it is obvious that the structure of authority in most corporations does not guarantee such a result. On the contrary, what we have is a business institution in which the directors tend to act as "trustees for the institution and not merely as attorneys for the stockholder" and in which "the management of large corporations is largely unaccountable to the stockholders."[11] This is not to say that management bears no responsibility to stockholders, but that the line of accountability does not run to the "ultimate owners" directly. And it is often said that managerial responsibility ought not to run either directly *or* indirectly to the share owners *alone*. In the early thirties, Berle and Means wrote that

the passive property right [of stockholders] today must yield before the larger interests of society. . . . [It] seems almost essential if the corporate system is to survive, that the 'control' of the great corporations should develop into a purely neutral technocracy, balancing a variety of claims by various groups in the community and assigning to each a portion of the income stream on the basis of public policy rather than private cupidity.[12]

The contrary view is that this amounts to establishing an authoritarian status for a managerial elite "who from their *own* ethical standards will 'assign' income shares." [13] It is one thing to say that the risk-bearing stockholder has little function; it is quite another to say that he deserves little respect. When the demands of other claimants are given equal weight, it is argued, the nature of corporate enterprise is radically altered and the foundations of capitalism are threatened.

The issue thus joined is certain to become one of the most

---

[10] Louis O. Kelso and Mortimer J. Adler, *The Capitalist Manifesto* (New York: Random House, 1958) . See Eells, *The Meaning of Modern Business*, pp. 77–94.

[11] George B. Hurff, *Social Aspects of Enterprise in the Large Corporation* (Philadelphia: University of Pennsylvania Press, 1950) , pp. 96 ff. "Management has come to wield a kind of floating power. . . ."

[12] Berle and Means, *op. cit.*, p. 356.

[13] Wright, *op. cit.*, p. 663. ". . . the mere paramountcy of the social interest," he protested—conceding that to all reputable economists property rights have always been considered subordinate even by the most orthodox, "is not *ipso facto* a self-evident reason for establishing the rule of an authoritarian group of managers to dole out income payments to this or that group as suits or seems fair to them—no matter how high-minded such managers may be." *Ibid.*, p. 664.

difficult for strategic decision makers of the future, in the fields both of business and of public policy.

EMPLOYEES

Employees as a group are clearly direct claimants on the corporate enterprise because they are direct contributors to it and are contractually related to the firm. Like the contributors of risk capital, they invest something they own. Their investment is comparable in that they expect a return on it from the fruits of the venture.

Dividends have been called "the wages of capital." The earnings on some "blue chip" common stocks are almost as certain as the guaranteed return on some preferred stocks or bonds. The holders of common stock of this grade anticipate equity appreciation, which, for tax and other reasons, is more valuable to them than a high annual dividend. In much the same way, people invest the best part of their lives in some established and promising companies at a rate of return—in the form of wages and salaries—that may seem modest enough at the start but is acceptable in anticipation of other benefits.

Nor are these benefits only the expected wage and salary advances over the years; the anticipated income includes those "fringe benefits" that increasingly go along with the job, plus some benefits that nowhere appear in the formal employment contracts. Association with certain companies yields "psychic income." Prestige, a sense of security, the feeling that one works for a "good corporate citizen" in a laudable field of endeavor, satisfaction in work that contributes to one's skills and enlightenment about some aspect of nature or society—these are some of the considerations that attract the necessary human resources to the organization, just as the anticipated growth and earnings prospects of a company attract capital resources.

Both kinds of contributor-claimants—employees and security holders—occupy positions near the center of the corporate constellation. This is obvious if one thinks of the corporation, not in terms of the fictitious entity of the lawyers or the *alter ego* of property owners, but rather as a real organic unity with a "life" of its own. The corporation as an organization merging human and material resources for creative common purposes thus comprises two indispensable contributor-claimant groups.

The "employee group" so conceived embraces, however, two clearly distinguishable categories: managers and nonmanagerial contributors. The status of an employee depends upon the category in which he is placed by the organizational theory of the society in which a firm is established.

In Sir Henry Maine's familiar thesis concerning the progress of society "from status to contract" lies one key to the organizational theory of any society and the roles, in that society, of the various categories of human resources. Maine thought that progressive societies show a development from status-bound roles to those based more and more on freedom to contract. It may be, as Maitland and Pound have argued, that civilization is not so mysteriously dependent on freedom of contract as Maine seems to have thought and that it may be more dependent on contract's being limited in its scope. Systems of status,[14] however, tend to become ossified in a way that bars industrialization and, in general, bars the emergence of new types of organizations in response to changing social values.

In an age and a culture in which business enterprise is downgraded, human resources tend to be siphoned off into such activities as warfare, religious contemplation, or the political arena. In industrial societies, bent on mastering the forces of nature for the improvement of man's physical and social environment for utilitarian ends, the status of people engaged in scientific and industrial activity is attractive enough to draw the more able and the more active. When that society is a free and "open" one, imbued with democratic ideals, there is a high degree of social mobility, both horizontal and vertical, and freedom to associate in response to current social needs.

Western industrial societies, as they have developed under the influence of the Industrial Revolution and democratic constitutionalism,[15] illustrate Maine's thesis. There, with the breakdown of the guilds, the human resources become more freely accessible to the great innovators and the great organizers[16] in business and scientific

---

[14] Rushton Coulborn (ed.), *Feudalism in History* (Princeton: Princeton University Press, 1956), provides a rich source of historical and comparative studies of societies based on status. On the rise and fall of the market economy, as one aspect of the transition from status to contract and a possible reversal of the trend today, see Karl Polanyi, *The Great Transformation* (Beacon paperback ed.; Boston: Beacon Press, 1957). See also the comment by K. Smellie on the validity of Maine's thesis in *Encyclopaedia of Social Sciences,* under "Maine, Sir Henry James Sumner," Vol. X, pp. 49–50.

[15] See Chapter 19 below on "Constitutionalism."

[16] Cf. Ernest Dale, *The Great Organizers* (New York: McGraw-Hill Book Co., 1960).

enterprise, for men are no longer bound to castes, guilds, "estates," social classes, and cultures. They break through the "cake of custom" and migrate upward (or downward) and from place to place in search of work befitting their abilities and ambitions.

Freedom of movement, freedom of contract, freedom of inquiry, access to property and protection of property rights for all—these are characteristics of the free and open societies in which the epoch of "contract" has replaced that of "status." Competing enterprises and innovating organizers bid for the best talent available, and with the concomitant freedom of association prevalent in an age of "contract" it is possible to build large organizations with minimal interference by the established institutions of church and state.

Had it not been for this comparative freedom to bargain for appropriate human as well as "capital" resources, the modern corporation in its present form would not have been possible. The significance of the managerial competence in recruiting this factor of production was recognized by Alfred Marshall when he added management to the traditional three factors of production—land, labor, and capital—of earlier economic thought. "Labor" and "management" thus became separate elements of human resources in an enterprise. In the modern corporation, as distinguished from proprietor-managed enterprise, both "labor" and "management" fall logically in the category of employees, and the services of both are bargained for, though under increasingly different conditions.

A revision of Maine's thesis may now be in order as we move from conditions of individual bargaining for the services of "labor" to conditions of collective bargaining between "management" and labor unions. Labor unions, like other vocational and professional groupings born of the freedom to associate, tend to become modern versions of the old guilds.[17] They provide for more than a stronger bargaining power; they also answer a need for a feeling of community, security, even exclusivity, in a society in which people "escape from freedom" and are drawn by competing forces into safer camps of the social arena.

As a result, the corporation and its labor force cannot in fact

---

[17] There is no direct historical tie between the medieval guilds and modern labor unions. The reference here is rather to the resurgence of private associations of all kinds as quasi-public vocational groups authorized or permitted by law to regulate entry into trades and professions, thus reintroducing "status" in modern dress. Cf. Walter Gellhorn, *Individual Freedom and Government Restraints* (Baton Rouge: Louisiana University Press, 1956), pp. 105–51, and literature there cited.

become an undivided community, a cohesive "grouping of men about their tools,"[18] so long as employees as a group are drawn in opposite directions, with one subgroup polarized toward the institution of the firm and the other toward the institution of the labor union.

The fact of the matter is that employees, as a contributor-claimant group, today fall into two divergent subgroups: employees of the firm who manage its affairs at the top level, just below the board, and other employees. Just how far down into the organization the former subgroup reaches is a debatable issue. Some would have it include all those who are identifiable with management's interests in some way, including foremen and white-collar workers, who enjoy the confidence of executive managers to some degree. Unions, on the other hand, seek to push the boundaries of this subgroup upward toward the strictly managerial line.

There is, in short, a competition for the loyalty and solidarity of employees between firm and union. Insofar as an employee's loyalties are polarized toward the outside organization, his place in the constellation of corporate interests moves toward the periphery of that constellation.

The corporate executive of the future will have to recast the theory of the firm to account for this trend. The implications are many. One, of course, has to do with the whole area of "human relations," or the restoration of organic unity in the enterprise as a human association, and not merely an aggregation of capital in the accounting sense of that term. Another implication is that the distribution of corporate income among contributor-claimant groups will require formulas consistent with a viable theory of the firm and the controlling norms of social theory in the corporate environment.

The first of these implications has led to a remarkable growth of literature in the field of organization theory that covers the problems of unity of effort under democratic conditions in all large organizations.[19]

The modern business corporation governs much of the lives of many people as to not only their strictly economic activities but their other interests as well. The role of unions in bargaining for

---

[18] See Frank Tannenbaum, *A Philosophy of Labor* (New York: Alfred A. Knopf, 1952), chap. v.

[19] See Rensis Likert, *Human Organization: Its Management and Value* (New York: McGraw-Hill Book Co., 1967); James G. March and Herbert A. Simon, *Organizations* (New York: John Wiley & Sons, 1958); and R. S. Edwards and H. Townsend, *Business Enterprise* (New York: St. Martin's Press, Inc., 1958).

better wages, for example, may not be so significant as are other kinds of concessions they get from management: seniority for layoffs and promotions; protection against arbitrary managerial action with respect to changes in payrates, prior notice in layoffs and dismissals, and grievance procedures;[20] and equality of treatment without reference to race, sex, or color. The success of a firm is often attributable not so much to skills in finance, engineering, and marketing as to the wisdom reflected in the art of governance (and not just the science of administration) on the part of its managers.[21]

The other implication as to claims on the corporate usufruct has led to a resurgence of debate among economists and social scientists generally about the essential nature of the business corporation and its role in the political economy as a whole. When "management" and labor unions vie for larger cuts of the corporate-earnings pie, what is left for the stockholders? What is the cost to others—to customers, who in the end pay for the product of the enterprise, and to the general public, which is also a contributor indirectly through taxes and other means that maintain the necessary "business climate" for profitable production?

The place of the employee group as a contributor claimant in the corporate constellation of interests is an unsettled issue—or rather bundle of issues—the outcome of which will depend on both business and public policy. Up until now, the union-management struggle for power has been confined mainly to the arena of the corporate constellation; the struggle tends increasingly to be fought out in the larger arena of state and national politics.[22] Both labor leaders and corporate managers must accordingly prepare themselves for the strategies required in both arenas. In this field of business policy, as in so many others, the corporate decision maker is drawn into larger issues of public policy as well.

CUSTOMERS

According to Peter F. Drucker, "there is only one valid definition of business purpose: to create a customer." It follows that "any busi-

---

[20] On the major significance of the "grievance function" of unions see Neil Chamberlain, "The Corporation and the Trade Union," in E. S. Mason (ed.) , *op. cit.*, p. 134.

[21] See Chapter 19 below on "Constitutionalism" with reference to the movement for "constitutionalizing the corporation." It should be noted that the employee subgroup of wage-earners is not the only contributor-claimant group that may in future demand "due process" in corporate governments. All the other direct claimant groups here discussed enter the picture.

[22] See Neil Chamberlain, *ibid.*, pp. 139–40.

ness enterprise has two—and only two—basic functions: marketing and innovation."[23] This is in line with the doctrine of customer sovereignty: "King Customer" must be pleased above all.

Here some distinctions are in order. Does one mean that the general public is the legitimate determiner of corporate policy? Or is something else meant—for example, the meeting and creating of "demands" for salable products and services, regardless of the "public interest" as expressed by representatives of the general public? Obviously not all products of profitable enterprise are "good" products, and some salable services are proscribed by law and morals. Customers and consumers are not necessarily identical groups, nor can either be designated, without careful qualification, as a direct contributor-claimant group in any corporate constellation of interests.

A corporation's customers are the main source of its business income; but it is one thing to center the goals of the business on supplying demand and quite anther to proliferate corporate objectives so as to meet all the ideal requirements of a hypothetical consumer public.

The corporation, as a business device, will serve equally well to "create a customer" or to advance society to its highest goals. The two purposes are not mutually exclusive, to be sure, but business policy is more nearly identified with the former. To go on with truisms about the dependence of business success upon business ethics does not add anything. The customer group, then, as the group of actual and potential buyers of what a corporation has to sell at a profit, is correctly designated as a direct contributor claimant in the corporate constellation.

Customers of the large industrial company ordinarily include other large companies, government agencies, wholesalers, and dealers, which are hardly to be caricatured as a gullible "consumer public." Their relationship to the vendor company—our focus of attention in discussing the corporate constellation—is a contractual one, presumably with none of the overtones of solidarity and "community" that exist in the exployee-management relationship. Yet there is a "business community," of which customers are an important part, and in this community the relations between corporate management as vendor and other managements as customers are decisive for the success of the vendor enterprise.

---

[23] Drucker, *The Practice of Management* (New York: Harper & Bros., 1954), p. 37.

The nature of these relations, the customs of trade that regulate behavior, are not widely understood by the general public; nor do these patterns of business practice bear much resemblance to popular stereotypes of "competitive capitalism." The conduct of customer relations in the large corporation and among large units resembles diplomacy: in the strategies of offer and counteroffer are to be observed one, but only one, of the instruments of corporate policy.[24] Negotiation of sales has to be accompanied, in other quarters of the organization, by negotiation for supplies of material and human resources, by the more or less direct uses of economic and other forms of power to protect corporate interests, and by the instruments of internal and external communication.

Customer relationships, then, in the large business corporation, have to be seen in perspective as but one type of many kinds of relationships, all carried on simultaneously, and often not with the commonly hypothesized "individual consumer" at all, but with other large organizations in an atmosphere remote from the "higgling" of noisy and bustling markets. When one talks of customers as a contributor-claimant group in the modern corporation, one must call to mind more than a source of income, a buyer at the counter, or the user of a small gadget in the home. The customer relationship is often one of relative intimacy, conducted among a comparatively small group of buyers and sellers who are well known to each other and to their competing counterparts in the industry.

This kind of relationship is far more frequent and intimate than are the relations between managers and stockholders, for example, or between managers and union leaders. Yet the traditional stereotype of the corporation would certainly place the security holder much nearer the center of the corporate constellation. In a legal sense, he is. But legal fiction and business fact have often to be separated for clear analysis, and, when one comes to the question of "corporate responsibilities to the public," it is undeniable that management does think first of the source of remittances.

These sources are changing. The trend toward self-financing of capital improvements in the very large organizations is giving increasing importance to transactions in this area. Large organizations may choose to expand their plants from earnings and may only rarely need to seek remittances from the sale of stocks and bonds. Nor do the stockholders necessarily object to lowered dividends on

---

[24] Eells, *op. cit.*, note 10 above, pp. 185–88.

this account. The long-run gains to them from capital appreciation can be more attractive than immediate returns that are more highly taxed. This means that while the security-holding group is not necessarily more remote from the center of the interest constellation, it is more removed from the center of corporate *activity* than is the customer group.

SUPPLIERS

The sources of supply for the large corporation as a going concern are extremely diverse. In the widest sense, suppliers include all contributors of material, financial, and human resources. Supply refers also to certain social costs that are not accounted for in the entrepreneurial outlays but instead are shifted to and borne by third persons and the community as a whole.[25]

Here we are concerned with those direct contributor-claimant suppliers outside the firm whose goods and services are reflected directly in entrepreneurial outlays, except for taxes. Logically, tax payments might be considered as a part of these outlays to governments as suppliers; but governments as vendors and customers fall more clearly into the category of direct contributor-claimant interests in the corporate constellation alongside other external units that buy from and sell to the firm.

A distinction can also be made between satellite and nonsatellite vendors as sources of a firm's supply. The former depend heavily on the firm as their principal, or even their sole, customer, so that special relationships arise. This is particularly true of dealers and distributors of the firm's product. A large firm has to be concerned about the life of its vendor companies, large and small, so that the interest of the firm in sustaining a "free enterprise system" in the abstract boils down to a quite concrete concern for the health of the economy as it affects specific entities in the categories of "small enterprise" as well as Big Business.[26]

---

[25] K. William Kapp, *The Social Costs of Private Enterprise* (Cambridge: Harvard University Press, 1950). He includes costs resulting from the impairment of the human factor of production; depletion and destruction of animal resources; depletion of energy resources; soil erosion, soil depletion, and deforestation; and social costs of air and water pollution, of technological change, of unemployment and idle resources, and of distribution and transportation.

[26] Cf. Eells, *op. cit.*, pp. 244–47, and sources there cited; Joseph D. Phillips, *Little Business in the American Economy* (Urbana: University of Illinois Press, 1958); and Melville J. Ulmer, "Industrial Patterns of the Business Population," *Survey of Current Business,* Vol. 28 (May, 1948), pp. 10–15.

The sources of direct supply are of such vital importance to a firm that in some of the larger organizations a deliberate effort is made to see that the scientific and technological knowledge that the company generates in the course of its operational and staff work is passed on so far as possible to its vendor firms. Such knowledge—of science, engineering, finance, manufacturing, marketing, and public relations work—thus becomes a "plus value," which the company makes available to others over and above its payments for supplies.

The ethical and legal norms that apply to a firm's relations with its suppliers are undergoing change all the time, partly as a result of a deeper understanding of the interdependence of units in the economy, and partly because of pressures that originate outside the firm. Some of these pressures take the form of legislation. A major objective in business policy is to forestall the intervention of public policy in the corporation-supplier relationship.

INDIRECT CLAIMANTS ON THE CORPORATION

The foregoing groups of contributor claimants stand in a more direct relationship to the firm than do others. From one point of view, the others have no *claim* on the firm at all. Where there is no express or implied contractual relationship, it may be argued that obligation is nonexistent and that, as one moves out from the firm's center to the periphery of interests in the corporate constellation, the most tenuous bonds tie the outlying interest groups to the firm itself.

But the rapid growth during the past few decades of "public relations" (more properly, simply *relations*) work of large companies casts serious doubt on this thesis. There is increasing emphasis on the "social responsibilities" of the businessman in general and of large corporations in particular. Nor is this growing concern observable only among the critics of Big Business; many business executives have been among the leaders in the movement, as can be seen in the rapid growth of corporate giving for educational, scientific, and charitable purposes. The trend is observable also in the development of such organizations as the Committee for Economic Development[27] and the National Bureau of Economic Research, to whose studies of the American economy many corporations contribute, and

---

[27] See Karl Schriftgiesser, *Business Comes of Age* (New York: Harper & Bros., 1960), for the history of this interesting organization.

the intensive efforts within large corporations to study and improve the "business climate" and to make their relations with local communities and governments more effective.

We turn here for a brief discussion of the three most important categories of indirect claimants on the corporation: competitors, local communities, and the general public as it is represented by public governments.

COMPETITORS

A competitive firm has no obligation, strictly speaking, toward competitors; its obligation, if any, is to the competitive system and to the norms that organized society establishes for competitive conduct. All responsible business executives recognize that, quite aside from their legal obligation to obey antitrust laws, there is a moral obligation to competitors that arises independently of the rules of law. Some of this nonlegal obligation has its roots in "enlightened self-interest" to the extent that competition is regarded as "the life of trade," or as a stimulant to innovation and *esprit de corps* in the organization, and so on. Nor can one safely discount ethical and religious motivation in this area of decision making.[28]

In some large firms "market power" is deliberately kept below the level at which the antitrust laws might be regarded as applicable. This is an instance of enlightened self-interest as a guide to business policy. But, in a larger sense, the observant executive will know that "power" in any large organization has many implications for the outsider that have little relevance to antitrust policy. The real "competitors" of the large corporation include, in the minds of the layman, many groups of interests with which a firm does not compete at all in the antitrust sense. As the debate over "Big Business" moves from the technical realm of antitrust to the wider sphere of the "struggle for power" in society, the problem of business policy becomes more political than economic.

This is where the knowledge required for business statesmanship enters into the decision process of any large business organization. The firm must be seen as an integral element in a pluralistic society

---

[28] ". . . we can hope . . . that whether or not there is a 'corporate conscience,' there may at least be 'corporations of conscientious men.' We can base that hope on the vigor and tenacity of the moral principles that underlie our civilization." W. T. Gossett, "Corporate Citizenship," *The John Randolph Tucker Lectures, 1953–1956* (Lexington, Va.: Washington and Lee University, 1957) , Vol. II, p. 189.

in which "balance of power" engages the attention of social scientists, legislators, public administrators, and judges.

LOCAL COMMUNITIES

The most immediate peripheral group of interests that vitally concern a corporation is the local community—or rather the numerous local communities—in which it operates as a going concern. The contributions of these communities are many, and so are their claims on the businesses located there.

Schools that provide well-educated employees and attract their families; churches that contribute to moral tone and character formation; social service organizations that contribute to health and safety; public utilities that provide the supply of water, energy, transportation, and other indispensable services; sound local governments that furnish police, fire, and sanitary protection; highway facilities—all these are elementary requirements of the immediate business climate.

The claimant community specifies its own requirements: regular employment, good working conditions, fair play, satisfying work, local purchase of a reasonable part of the firm's supply of goods and services, the maintenance of a plant worthy of a good neighbor, and interest in and support of the local government and of local charitable and cultural projects.

THE GENERAL PUBLIC AND GOVERNMENTS

The contributions of the general public have been alluded to earlier with reference to the "social costs of private enterprise." As a taxpayer, the corporation is clearly a direct contributor[29] to public governments as claimants on the fruits of enterprise. The tax burden of corporate enterprise is indeed so heavy that there is strong protest against it as inequitable. It probably is inequitable, but the rule of the tax gatherer is to produce "the most feathers with the least squawks," and the corporate squawk has not yet been loud

---

[29] In a survey of the 120 largest firms representing 20.6 percent of all corporate sales in the United States it was reported that in 1958 they paid out 7.8 percent in taxes, 50.8 percent for supplies and materials, 28.4 percent to employees, 5.6 percent for depreciation and amortization, 4.13 percent to stockholders; 2.23 percent was retained by the firms. Lloyd J. Buckwell, Jr., *The Big Corporation: Where Its Money Goes* (St. Paul, Minn.: Macalaster College, 1960). Taxes paid by these corporations were in excess of $10 billion—nearly 9 percent of all the funds governments received—and do not include income taxes paid by stockholders on dividends.

enough to reduce the pull. The question arises whether, if corporate enterprise were to allocate to "Society, Inc.," the correct portion of its earnings to cover the "social costs," the present level of corporate taxation would be lowered or raised.

That "correct portion" is probably incalculable. To calculate it, one would also have to balance off on the other side the unaccounted-for contributions now made and likely to be made in future by a given firm to "Society, Inc."—also an unquantifiable amount. The net value of the contributor-claimant relationship to corporation and public government, respectively, will never be calculated in terms of taxation or immunities therefrom. On the contrary, a corporation, like every other interest nucleus, must participate in "the great game of politics"—or, in more academic terms, the governmental process of society as a whole. More and more this fact is being realized in corporate managements, although the present state of the law with respect to corporate engagement in politics is one that gives limited recognition to this fact.

But the coordinate political functions of the modern corporation are still little understood today, either in the business community or on the part of legislators.[30] The beginnings of an understanding of it can be seen in the establishment, in some large firms, of "government relations" components that go beyond the limited techniques of lobbying to more creative kinds of communication between business and public government. A true basis for such a relationship, however, depends upon more widespread understanding of the pervasive nature of government itself, of which *public* government is but one element. The corporation, because of its organizational character—a collectivity with unique legal and other characteristics —has to bear its fair share of the burden of government, just as do all other legitimate voluntary associations.

One of the major problems for the corporate executive of the future will be to determine the nature and scope of "proper participation" in this process. This problem touches, not only the *external* relations of corporations with public governmental agencies at local, state, national, and international levels, but also the *internal* relations between management and the direct claimants in the corporate constellation. The external relations are now being slowly developed by many companies, with some promise of a maturing

---

[30] Eells, *op. cit.*, pp. 319–26.

philosophy to guide them.[31] But almost everything remains to be done by way of developing a sound theory as to the governmental process within the corporation.

THE CORPORATE IMAGE AND "SOCIAL RESPONSIBILITIES"

We may conclude this analysis by brief comment on two important aspects of the role of corporate enterprise in society: (1) the corporate image in public relations and (2) the much-debated problem of "social responsibilities."

THE CORPORATE IMAGE

The "image"[32] of a corporation, as held both by its members and by outsiders, is a crucial determinant of its success. Public relations work is often conceived as the task of projecting a favorable "image" to the public, although the relations work of any company in fact involves much more than that. Corporate executives have, first, to construct an image in the minds of those who act on behalf of the company and, then, to effectuate through all the instruments of corporate policy a system of external communication that will assure a wide public sharing of this image.

The goal of relations work is often said to be public acceptance of the company, but this is only part of the task, if by public acceptance is meant only the conversion of external receivers of the company's outgoing messages to a favorable attitude. Communication works both ways. There are many incoming messages, too, and the receptors of these messages need to be so sensitive and so organized as to channel what is received to the "central agents" of the organization.

By "messages" we mean not only the content of what is sent out and received through the usual media of verbal and written communication. Acts are symbolic, and everything anyone associated with a company does may speak volumes to observers both within and without. In its bargaining actions through many markets, and in the use of the economic and legal powers at its disposal, a company

---

[31] See Chapters 20, 21, and 22 below. The role of American business corporations in underdeveloped areas raises the issue of relations with foreign governments and international agencies to a prominent position of business policy.

[32] Kenneth E. Boulding, *The Image* (Ann Arbor: University of Michigan Press, 1956), discusses the subject at length.

communicates to all receptors messages of all kinds having more or less impact. That is why all the instruments of company policy are significant when one wants to coordinate external communications for favorable results.

An especially heavy responsibility therefore rests upon those who are expected to keep "the public" well informed and at least non-hostile. Obviously, much more has to be done in this area, for the company's objectives will always require positive action in the company's favor by outsiders, to say nothing of the need for unity of effort within the organization itself. The job of "public relations," therefore, is not merely a minor aspect of management but a major kind of functional work in the organization.

The executive head has to construct a tenable image of the company and its place in society. As Boulding remarks, "he is a receiver of messages from the receptors of the organization, and his job is to transform these messages into instructions or orders which go out to the effectors."[33] His own value system, or "operational code"[34] intervenes between the incoming and outgoing messages, and the latter—regarded as actions as well as words—are the result of his *image.* He does not function merely as "a sausage machine grinding out instructions from the messages received."[35]

Rather, the process is one that requires two steps: (1) identifying the objectives of the company in their order of priority, so that they can be translated into working principles applicable to all the major kinds of work of the organization, and (2) the formulation of specific policies and programs that will guide the discretionary actions of the "effectors"—those who carry out any "relational" kind of work, whether it be with customers, suppliers, stockholders, labor unions, competitors, local communities, or public governmental agencies.[36]

These requirements are exacting. Few companies state their *real* objectives in writing—in such a way that meaningful policies and programs can be derived from them. And the second stage seldom follows, either as the logical outcome of the stated goals or in clear

---

[33] *Ibid.,* pp. 27–28.

[34] See Eells, *op. cit.,* pp. 150 ff.

[35] Boulding, *op. cit.,* p. 28.

[36] See Richard Eells, "The Corporate Image in Public Relations," *California Management Review,* Vol. I (Summer, 1959) , pp. 15–23, and *The Meaning of Modern Business, op. cit.,* chap. xiv.

enough terms to provide guidance to the "effectors" of communication in its many forms.

All this has a direct bearing on the unity of effort within the organization and on the role that a company plays in society. Boulding observes that from one point of view an organization might be defined as "a structure of roles tied together by lines of communication"[37]—emphasizing thereby that there must be a "stock of images" of the several roles of the members of the organization that is at least consistent with the over-all image of the organization itself. Well-stated objectives, policies, and programs that have been developed by a participative process involving many members are the means of getting this consistency.

But the same principle applies to the relational work of a company in establishing its role in society. The participation of the company's "effectors"—those who interact with external persons and groups as communicators on behalf of the organization—in the life of the larger community is a necessary part of the creation of a widely shared "image" of that society. The role of the particular corporation, as perceived by its "effectors," has to be at least consistent with this over-all image.

"SOCIAL RESPONSIBILITIES"

Thus we come to the question, now much debated, of the "social responsibilities" of the businessman and, more especially, of the dominant form of business organization—the large corporation. For, while few will doubt the vital importance of this kind of organization to a viable industrial nation, there are wide disagreements as to its proper role, its optimum size, its powers (both as a structure of authority within the organization and as an influential unit in the structure of social authority), its capabilities and potentialities, and its conduct as an ethical "person." These questions will soon confront everyone who pursues a business career leading to executive responsibilities.

To a certain extent, corporate executives have been thrown on the defensive in this debate. This is partly because they have conceded their critics' emphasis on the duty-and-liability side of "social responsibilities" to the exclusion of the other side—the necessary conditions for eliciting responsible behavior. But let us take the first

---

[37] Boulding, *op. cit.*, p. 57.

and more common usage of the term, and ask: who is responsible to whom and for what in the conduct of corporate enterprise in our free society?

These are usually defined as the direct and indirect claimants we discussed earlier. The order of priority in the listing of these claimants is debatable. Some would put the general public, as represented in public governments, at the top. But this conflicts with the traditional view that security holders—the ultimate owners—have prior claims if the concept of private property has any meaning. Others say that the shareholders are only "passive owners," with limited liability and therefore properly limited authority and only the most modest claims on the enterprise. Employees, and especially the executive managers, are said to be in actual control, with varying implications as to the nature of their claim on the fruits of the enterprise. In the opinion of some, this control amounts to usurpation; in the opinion of others, executive managers bear the brunt of responsibility for a company's success or failure and must therefore be accorded correlative authority, even to the extent of acting as arbiters of the claims of all other groups (including the managerial group itself) on the corporate yield. To still others, the "customer is king," and "consumer sovereignty" acts to displace the prior claim of any other group.

Who is the responsible actor in this drama? The corporation acts only through its board as a matter of law, but in fact the "effectors" we discussed earlier are under the actual direction of the executive managers. In no practical or legal sense are the directors as a body the "representatives" or agents of the shareholders, so it cannot be said that the "social responsibilities" of a company are those of its ultimate owners. In a loose sense, there is a trust reposed in the board, with wide scope for discretion, and a delegation of wide discretionary authority by board to managers to conduct the affairs of the going concern. In practice, then, everyone looks to "management" to assume these "social responsibilities" or at least to formulate them for board approval with respect to the major types of responsibility.

But what are the major or minor types of responsibility? As to the ultimate owners, is it a "fair return" on their investment or all the net profits in any year? As to customers, is it a "fair" price for products or all that the traffic will bear? (Or is it a "good" product and constant innovation to provide more and better new products?)

As to employees, is it a "fair" wage and good working conditions or status, with all the overtones of security and the dimensions of the good life? As to others in the business community—competitors, suppliers—is it the minimal standard of conduct in a hard and competitive drive for profits or behavior in accordance with some ideal code? As to the public and governments, is it a shrewd avoidance of infractions of the law and the building of stout barriers against any encroachment of government on business, or a common pursuit of the general welfare through some form of mixed economy?

The question of the "social responsibilities" of the modern corporation thus turns out to be no simple issue but a large bundle of issues. It cannot be reduced to the single relationship between corporation and society, for the referents in these ambiguous terms are unclear. But that is not all. The term "responsibility" is also ambiguous.[38] Does it mean duty or dutifulness, accountability, liability, answerability, or what? Does it refer to the quality of fictitious as well as real persons—in other words, can one speak of an *organization's* responsibilities or only of those who act on its behalf. And if only the latter, then how can one be held responsible for acts that one is not free either to commit or to omit—a consideration that obviously raises some unresolved issues about the scope of managerial authority. And if one is properly held responsible, is there a definable "situation of responsibility"?[39] What sanctions can properly be imposed to hold a "responsible" person, real or fictitious, accountable for his actions, and whose business is it to apply the sanctions?

Confronted with questions of this kind the ready proponents of social responsibilities for the modern corporation may well be given pause. When the subject is pursued logically, it leads to questions more nearly comparable with the problem of political and administrative responsibility in modern constitutional governments. For the modern corporation is in one sense a kind of private polity, quasi-public in many of its organizational characteristics.

But the corporation is also a competitor among nonstate groups:

In the free economy, the "entrepreneur" is the agent at once of consumers and of those who furnish the labor and property-services employed.

---

[38] For the variety of meanings assignable to the term see Carl J. Friedrich (ed.), *Responsibility* (New York: Liberal Arts Press, 1960).

[39] Herbert J. Spiro, "Responsibility and the Goal of Survival," in *ibid.*, p. 299.

He must have considerable power, but this he gets and keeps by satisfying all parties "better," in their judgment, than competitors for the role. Their freedom is that of dealing with one or another of the latter. In a special sense the entrepreneur is "responsible" to his consumers, whose wants he must not only satisfy but anticipate in advance, at great cost and with great risk of loss. . . . he partly "makes" the wants as to details—but all in open competition. . . .[40]

One cannot fairly expect too much, from either the political or the economic order, in remedying the real and supposed defects in either order; there is no revealed road to absolute freedom or absolute responsibility.

On the other hand, there can be constructive moves toward better "situations of responsibility" in both the political and the economic orders and in the corporation in particular. This means effort to meet three conditions so that one *can* become responsible: (1) discretion as to courses of action, (2) the availability of resources to implement the plan of action chosen, (3) the availability of knowledge about the probable consequences of the decision.[41]

The first two conditions, involving as they do the adequacy of authority, the necessary structure of authority, and the necessary sanctions available to corporate management, are problems that many shy away from. The third condition deserves a further comment. A responsible person is, in an important sense, one who is capable of rational conduct. But the norm of rationality in decision making for corporate managers poses hard problems. Abstract authority is hollow without the knowledge required to put it into effective use. What an executive ought to know about the consequences of his decision is knowledge that is now available to him only to a very limited extent. He needs to know more than his "intelligence services" can possibly provide in such areas as marketing, labor relations, and "public relations." But it is not too much to ask of him that he gather all the intelligence that *is* available and that he stimulate the growth of those sciences that can help him move toward a sound situation of responsibility.

The emphasis on "social responsibility" as legal or moral liability and accountability with threat of sanctions could well be shifted to "responsibility in the sense of 'capacity to cause,' that is, to choose

---

[40] Frank H. Knight, "Political Responsibility in a Democracy," in *ibid.,* p. 186.

[41] Spiro, *op. cit.,* p. 299.

in the light of knowledge about consequences and with resources for implementation."[42] This may not satisfy the more astringent critics of Big Business. It could enable business leaders, however, to evolve a more constructive approach to their own solution of a problem of first importance to them and to society.

The corporation as an institution is so much a fact of American life that it is difficult to imagine what the world of work and action was like without it. Many will argue that it has not completely fulfilled the expectations aroused by its performance in time of stress. But there is no doubt that the "American way," if we are referring to material comforts, is made possible by its organization and its use of resources. Further, as Edward Mason has said: "We look to the corporation for the technical improvements that spark our economic growth. The corporation recruits our youth from college and provides them with pensions in their old age. It is the present support of community chests and other local charities and the future hope of institutions of higher learning. All this is not to suggest that the corporation cannot be touched, but that to touch the corporation is to touch much else."[43]

If we question its power and its motives, we perhaps fear its failure more. It would have an impact on too many lives. For, if the public is people, one by one, so is the corporation. The legal concept of *persona ficta* has obscured its true identity because it may be said —and with considerable truth—that the corporation is always in the process of growth and change and this process is no more visible than in the arena of its responses to external forces. Whether it is moving from a "soulless" to a "soulful" entity is an intriguing question, the answer to which carries important practical implications.

RECOMMENDED READING

BERLE, ADOLF A. "Modern Functions of the Corporate System," *Columbia Law Review,* Vol. LXII (March, 1962), pp. 433–49.

BERLE, ADOLF A. *et al.* "The Modern Corporation: A Symposium," *University of Chicago Law Review,* Vol. XIX (Summer, 1952), pp. 639–835.

---

[42] *Ibid.,* p. 298.

[43] Mason, *op. cit.,* pp. 1–2.

BERLE, ADOLF A., and MEANS, GARDINER C. *The Modern Corporation and Private Property.* Rev. ed. New York: Harcourt, Brace & World, Inc., 1968. Especially the authors' new prefaces, pp. vii–xxxviii.

EELLS, RICHARD. *The Government of Corporations.* New York: The Free Press, 1962.

GALBRAITH, JOHN KENNETH. *The New Industrial State,* chaps. 6, 7, 25, and 26. Boston: Houghton Mifflin Co., 1967.

HARBRECHT, PAUL P., S.J. "The Modern Corporation Revisited," *Columbia Law Review,* Vol. LXIV (December, 1964), pp. 1410–26.

KATZ, WILBER G. *et al.* "The New Look in Corporations Law," *Law and Contemporary Problems,* Vol. XXIII (Spring, 1958), pp. 175–398.

KRABBE, HUGO H. *The Modern Idea of the State,* pp. xl–lxx. Trans. G. H. SABINE and W. J. SHEPARD. New York: Appleton, 1922.

LANIER, R. J. "Ownership and Control in the 200 Largest Nonfinancial Corporations," *American Economic Review,* Vol. LVI (September, 1966), pp. 777–87.

MASON, EDWARD S. (ed.). *The Corporation in Modern Society.* Cambridge: Harvard University Press, 1959.

WALTON, CLARENCE C. "Big Government, Big Business, and the Public Interest" in IVAR BERG (ed.), *The Business of America.* New York: Harcourt, Brace & World, Inc., 1968.

WIENER, JOSEPH L. "The Berle-Dodd Dialogue on the Concept of the Corporation," *Columbia Law Review,* Vol. LXIV (December, 1964), pp. 1458–67.

People v. *North River Sugar Refining Company,* 121 New York 582 (New York Court of Appeals).

Venner v. *Southern Pacific Company,* 279 Federal 832 (U.S. Circuit Court of Appeals, 1922).

Warner v. *Beers,* 23 Wendell 103 (New York Court of Appeals, 1838). Bottom p. 145 to end 4th par., p. 154.

Dodge v. *Ford Motor Company,* 204 Michigan 459 (Supreme Court of Michigan, 1919).

FURTHER READING

BERLE, ADOLF A., JR. *The 20th Century Capitalist Revolution,* chaps. i–ii. New York: Harcourt, Brace & Co., 1954.

BERLE, ADOLF A. *et al.* "Symposium on the Impact of the Corporation on Classical Economic Theory," *Quarterly Journal of Economics,* Vol. LXXIX (February, 1965), pp. 1–51.

DILL, WILLIAM R. "Business Organizations" in JAMES G. MARCH (ed.), *Handbook of Organizations,* pp. 1071–91. Chicago: Rand McNally Co., 1965.

HACKER, ANDREW (ed.). *The Corporation Take-Over.* New York: Harper & Row, 1964. Also, Garden City, N.Y.: Doubleday & Co., Inc., Anchor Books, 1965.

HARBRECHT, PAUL P., S.J. *et al.* "Company Law Revision: A Synthesis of Opinion," *University of Detroit Law Journal,* Vol. XL (April, 1963), pp. 439–509.

HAYEK, FRIEDRICH A. "The Corporation in a Democratic Society: In Whose Interest Ought It and Will It Be Run?" in MELVIN ANSHEN and G. L. BACH (eds.), *Management and Corporations 1985,* pp. 99–117. New York: McGraw-Hill Book Co., 1960.

LIKERT, RENSIS. *Human Organization: Its Management and Value.* New York: McGraw-Hill Book Co., 1967.

MANNE, HENRY G. "The 'Higher Criticism' of the Modern Corporation," *Columbia Law Review,* Vol. LXII (March, 1962), pp. 399–432.

MILLER, WILLIAM (ed.). *Men in Business,* chap. xi. Cambridge: Harvard University Press, 1952.

RIPLEY, WILLIAM Z. *Main Street and Wall Street,* pp. 3–54. Boston: Little, Brown & Co., 1927.

WALTON, CLARENCE C. *Corporate Social Responsibilities.* Belmont, Cal.: Wadsworth Publishing Co., Inc., 1967.

WALTON, CLARENCE, and EELLS, RICHARD (eds.). *The Business System: Readings in Ideas and Concepts,* Vol. 2, pp. 1365–1491. New York: Macmillan Co., 1967.

WARREN, WILLIAM C. *et al.* "In Honor of Adolf A. Berle," *Columbia Law Review,* Vol. LXIV (December, 1964), pp. 1377–1467.

WEAVER, DAVID B. "The Corporation and the Shareholder," *The Annals* of the American Academy of Political and Social Science, September, 1962, pp. 84–94.

7. Recent Trends in Corporate Social Responsibilities

A CENTURY-OLD immersion in legalistic waters flowing from Chief Justice Marshall's historic definition of a corporation as an "artificial being, invisible, intangible, and existing only in a contemplation of the law,"[1] makes any theoretical journey against the traditional current an extraordinarily difficult one. Yet postwar events indicate that a new kind of corporate philosophy is in the making—one that would move the corporation from a soulless to a soulful form of being.

Exactly 15 years ago two events occurred which heralded the possible coming of significant philosophical changes. The first was the drafting by the Committee on Corporate Laws of the American

---

* Gratitude is due the editors of the *Review of Social Economy* for permission to use material that appears in Clarence Walton's article "Speculations on the 'Soulful' Corporation" (March, 1968), pp. 1–25.

[1] *Dartmouth College* v. *Woodward* (1819). Long before Marshall, Pope Innocent IV had spoken of other forms of corporations in similar language. To Innocent IV, the corporation as a fictitious person could neither sin nor commit crime; incapable of evil, this soulless being was also incapable of virtue. See F. W. Maitland's introduction to Otto Gierke's work, *Political Theories of the Middle Age* (Cambridge, Mass.: Cambridge University Press, 1900).

Bar Association of the so-called "model business corporation act" in 1953 and the subsequent enactment into statutes by many states of its basic recommendations. Underpinning the statutory changes was the "enabling act" theory which revealed a major concern lest unduly restrictive applications of common law doctrines be applied against corporate management.[2] Although enabling theory was not to be identified with public responsibility, it did seek to enlarge—or, at least, safeguard—the discretionary area for business decision making. The second also took place in 1953 when, through the now famous *A. P. Smith* case, business successfully challenged the doctrine (recognized as well-nigh inviolable since the 1883 British case of *Hutton* v. *West Cork Railway Corporation*) that a corporation existed only as a profit-making enterprise and for the equitable distribution of income to owners.[3]

The perceptive student of business might have perceived even earlier a fundamental ideological split within the private sector itself in the 1944 decision of the Committee on Economic Development to continue work. The CED had initially worked out a gentleman's agreement with the U.S. Chamber of Commerce and with the National Association of Manufacturers to dissolve itself after peace had been achieved; however, the infant organization had begun to develop a philosophy that rejected much of the classical ideology then espoused by the NAM and the Chamber.[4]

Since the war—by preachment and in practice—the private business community has demonstrated a growing willingness to accept an enlarged sense of social obligation—but not without serious misgivings in some quarters. In a scathing speech to the National Security Industrial Association (NSIA) (which includes some 400 members from the aircraft, electronics, motors, oil, chemical, food, and other major corporations), Columbia's Paul Goodman declared that responsibility for sharing in the determination and implementation of the nation's goals could not be placed in business hands.

These goals indeed require research and experimentation of the highest sophistication, but not by you. You people are unfitted by your commitments, your experience, your customary methods, your recruitment,

---

2 Wilber G. Katz, "The Philosophy of Mid-Century Corporation Statutes," *Law and Contemporary Problems*, Vol. XXIII (Spring, 1958), pp. 177–92.

3 *A. P. Smith Manufacturing Company* v. *Barlow, et al.* (May 19, 1953). New Jersey Supreme Court (Chancery Division). *Atlantic Reporter*, pp. 186–196.

4 See Karl Schriftgiesser, *Business Comes of Age* (New York: Harper & Bros., 1960), and *Business and Public Policy* (Englewood Cliffs, N.J.: Prentice-Hall, Inc., 1967).

and your moral disposition. You are the military industrial of the United States, the most dangerous body of men at present in the world, for you not only implement our disastrous policies but are an overwhelming lobby for them, and you expand and rigidify the wrong use of brains, resources, and labor so that change becomes difficult. Most likely the trends you represent will be interrupted by a shambles of riots, alienation, ecological catastrophes, wars, and revolutions, so that current long-range planning, including this conference, is irrelevant. But if we ask what *are* the technological needs and what ought to be researched in this coming period . . . the best service that you people could perform is rather rapidly to phase yourselves out, passing on your relevant knowledge to people better qualified, or reorganizing yourselves with entirely different sponsors and commitments, so that you learn to think and feel in a different way.[5]

Yet an equally passionate social crusader and scholar, Kenneth Clark, in a speech to another professional business group, expressed the conviction that business was the only powerful institution which really cared about the social evils eating away at the heart and soul of American life. To Clark it was significant that it was the large corporation, not the White House, which pressed Congress to retain the Peace Corps, and not entirely because the program was a source of revenue. In a sense the "last refuge of the social conscience, turns out to be those institutions which official liberalism has instructed us for 50 years were the most antisocial we had."[6]

Clearly both Goodman and Clark were putting economic policy to a moral judgment; both were demonstrably concerned with developing practical programs designed to civilize and humanize contemporary society; both had some vision of a "good" society.[7] And, in a sense, both represented the different shades of contemporary opinion which either jeer or cheer the birth of a seemingly "more benign

---

[5] Paul Goodman, "A Causerie at the Military-Industrial," *New York Review of Books* (November 23, 1967) , pp. 14–19. Goodman's assessment invites uneasy comparison with philosopher Karl Jasper's recent dissection of contemporary Germany as a country morally adrift in a 1967 prosperity as it was morally adrift in the 1931 depression, *The Future of Germany* (Chicago: University of Chicago Press, 1967) .

[6] Murray Kempton, "The Saddest Story," *The New York Post* (October 26, 1967) .

[7] It is not inappropriate to note that an articulate member of the Catholic Economic Association had castigated the C.E.A. for default on its obligation to provide dialogue which would employ the criteria used by Professors Goodman and Clark. Cornelius A. Eller, S.J., "Is the C.E.A. Achieving Its Purpose?," *Review of Social Economy*, Vol. XI (March, 1958) , pp. 69–73. The debate continues. See the "Report of the 1960 Committee on Aims and Objectives," *loc. cit.*, Vol. XXI (September, 1963) , pp. 172–75.

stage in the evolution of capitalism." But as Eugene V. Rostow has pointed out, this "fascinating sociology of the modern endocratic corporation, with its divorce of ownership and management, and its hierarchical features . . . does not provide a substitute for the competitive norm in defining an acceptable social goal for the process of price-making."[8]

It might be asked in rejoinder whether the "competitive norm" is itself totally adequate for the purpose noted and whether price making alone exhausts the content of "acceptable social goals." Perhaps the need is less met by "substitution" of other norms for competition and more through enlargement of the enterprise's range of social goals. The purpose of reexamining new trends in policy formation by the large corporations is not to justify to stockholders and other claimants these modifications of established practices but to explain them. Specifically the analysis attempts the following:

1. To specify the different versions or models of corporate responsibility and to indicate how each relates, more or less directly, to primary concern for one of the corporation's many claimants: from individuals *within* the firm to the general public *without.*

2. To indicate the point where, in the above models, corporations view their responsibilities, as *enforced* by external agents (law, unions, or other countervailing forces) and those *voluntarily* assumed.

3. To provide examples of some recent theories which, holding that the traditional economic model of the firm is inadequate, seek to fill the vacuum through an essentially positivistic approach.

4. To speculate briefly on recent developments within the normative sciences which may suggest possibilities for added theoretical contributions toward our understanding business responsibility.

THE SOCIAL RESPONSIBILITY MOVEMENT: FICTION OR FACT?

No one pretends that the current impetus toward greater acceptance of responsibilities by business has reached the proportions of other social movements in American history. The antitrust crusade of the progressives trumpeted by William Jennings Bryan and the "dry" movement by the prohibitionists both led to historic changes in the law—though it must be added quickly that the latter was a

---

[8] Eugene V. Rostow, "To Whom and For What Ends Is Corporate Management Responsible?" in Edward S. Mason, *The Corporation in Modern Society* (Cambridge, Mass.: Harvard University Press, 1959), p. 67.

total failure and the former's popular support has steadily diminished, even as the Justice Department is busier than ever with prosecutions.

Is the whole idea of business responsibility new? Of course not. The *casa* philosophy of the middle ages created expectations that wealthy merchants would support orphanages and hospitals and the expenses of certain public ceremonial occasions. In the United States, businessmen have given money for charitable purposes; they have participated in public affairs; they have been patrons of the arts. What then makes the new version so hard to understand and to accept? It is the fact that salaried professionals (better educated than their predecessors) who are today's corporate managers not only seem ready to challenge the profit-maximizing ethos of hallowed history but are willing to undertake ventures not readily identified with the strictly business purposes for which they are presumably paid by stockholders. There is, of course, the usual and convenient rationale that the corporation is interested in long-term profits and in survival. But hard-headed realists wonder whether some of the current activities by corporations really contribute to these goals; whether businessmen fall back on the handy justification by self-interest because no other reasoned apologetic has been developed.

How do business executives themselves justify their new posture? The rhetoric is loud and fairly clear. One typical expression came from Alexander N. McFarlane, president of Corn Products Company, who noted that the real purpose of business is never a product but a process. It is a process that seeks to organize the corporation "to serve the needs of its own people, as well as meet the aspirations of others in society."

The concept of the role of the large business corporation is changing materially, and corporate managers must venture into areas seemingly far-removed from the corporation's original profit-pursuing purpose. Because the business corporation has become a very influential factor in society, people are beginning to expect not only economic but social responsibility.[9]

Alcoa president, John Harper, argued that the obligation to accept broader social responsibilities had to be accepted because no

---

[9] Alexander N. McFarlane, "The Search for Purpose," *The National Industrial Conference Board Record* (February, 1965), pp. 29–32.

other real option existed. To him public responsibility goes far beyond living up to the letter or spirit of the law. Yet his was scarcely a quixotic approach because Harper cautioned business against galloping off in all directions, "performing all kinds of good work at the expense of its primary function—which is to produce and sell at profit goods of quality and quantity required by the consumers."[10] Quite obviously business did not exist to compete with the Salvation Army and in Harper's version of corporate responsibility charity had a minimal role. It was a virtue more properly related to an individual's personal values rather than to the organization's goals or values.

That one can perceive modest shades of differing emphasis between these two executives is possible. That differences might be quite substantial in some cases is apparent because of the novelty of the idea itself, and because of the vastly differing conditions facing officers in different situations: small versus large companies, industrial versus food companies, domestically-oriented firms versus multinational enterprises, etc. Robert Heilbroner, for example, has discerned "an enormous distance separating the idea of business prerogatives implicit in the tone of a Blough or a Cordiner and that expressed by a Houser or a Watson."[11] And there is obviously a reluctance to break patterns, well established by early social movements and ideologies, which legitimize privilege and differential rewards. The real rupture, therefore, is in the challenge posed clearly to the preeminence of property claims over all others.

Is the somewhat ambivalent rhetoric found in public statements by executives the only source of understanding? Possibly the oracular ambiguity can be dispelled by looking at performance. Large corporations are being challenged from many quarters. Speaking to the American Paper Institute on June 22, 1967, Edward Booher, president of the McGraw-Hill Book Company, posed the issues quite realistically when he said that the major challenge is to improve the quality of life. "In 1967 our major domestic concerns are poverty and education. In 1977 these will still be major concerns, but we will have comparable programs to improve cities; to create new transportation systems; to control air pollution, water pollution, and noise;

---

[10] John Harper, "Private Enterprise's Public Responsibility," *Social Service Outlook,* Vol. II (November, 1967), p. 1.

[11] Robert Heilbroner, "The View from the Top," in Earl Cheit (ed.), *The Business Establishment* (New York: John Wiley & Sons, 1964), p. 31.

and to increase the country's cultural wealth."[12] And in all efforts the big city ghettos with their teeming Negro, Puerto Rican and Mexican minorities will provide the major challenges.[13]

Corporate responses to the various ills catalogued above are sometimes bold and imaginative and, at others, timid and tentative. When, however, chief executives themselves begin to tell stockholders, directly at share-owner meetings or through annual reports, of their commitment to social responsibilities, the boundary between posturing and performance starts to vanish. Only the barest sampling can give a sense of the direction that business has taken. Walter Wheeler, Jr., and John Nicklis, chairman and president respectively of Pitney-Bowes, wrote in the company's 1963 report of their acceptance of responsibilities in efforts "to find constructive solutions to major problems of American life—employment, education, race relations, housing and urban renewal."

At the 1967 Annual Shareholders Meeting, Xerox chairman, Joseph C. Wilson, responded to a question telegraphed by Minister Franklin Florence, president of the FIGHT organization which, at that time, was engaged in a bitter controversy with Kodak, a corporate neighbor of Xerox in Rochester. The setting and the timing made Wilson's remarks worth noting.

We have worked closely for a couple of years with FIGHT in a very experimental, small effort to improve the employment situation for those who are not qualified—particularly Negroes, but not confined to Negroes —by our usual standards. This relationship has been an extraordinarily good one. We have had the same kind of relationship with other organizations in Rochester—the Urban League . . . , the New York State Department of Labor, etc. I think, though, that we have had more credit than we deserve. . . . It has been a minor effort, and an experimental one. We are doing it again next year with what we call the *Step-Up program*. . . . But other people, and particularly the Eastman Kodak Company, have been doing the same thing.[14]

The examples could be multiplied indefinitely. Pacific Telephone and Telegraph worked closely with the Urban League of

[12] "The Decades Ahead from a Publisher's View," *Science*, Vol. CLVIII (November 17, 1967) , p. 882.

[13] *Ibid.*, p. 883.

[14] *Xerox Corporation 1967 Annual Meeting of Shareholders*, p. 7. For a sharp criticism of Kodak's position see Wayne Cowan, "High Noon at Flemington," *Christianity and Crisis* (May 29, 1967) , and the subsequent exchange of views between him and Reverend James Rockwell, a Rochester minister, in the same journal (August 7, 1967) , pp. 195–96.

California and local churches to begin a vigorous recruiting and training program. The company raised the number of minority workers on its payroll from approximately 4,300 in 1962 to over 8,000 in 1967. The Polaroid Corporation in Cambridge is hiring Negroes who have no high school diplomas and permitting them to earn the certificate on company time and at company expense. Western Electric Company, which in 1937 had a ratio of 80 percent white to 20 percent black among its machine shop operators, has reversed that ratio through a new program launched only a few years ago. Metropolitan Life and Equitable Life Assurance Company have worked constructively with Harlem groups.[15] Like Xerox, many of these programs are modest and experimental but the practical first steps have been taken.

Nor are corporate concerns and involvements restricted to the domestic scene. Jersey Standard told its shareholders in 1966 that the company had cooperated fully during the previous two years—and would continue to cooperate in 1967—with the federal government in efforts to meet the balance-of-payments gap.[16] IBM has operated along the same lines. Such "noble experiments" could grind to an abrupt halt because the life cycles of new social movements and ideologies are not consistently enduring. Mounting stockholder protests,[17] adverse public opinion against a benevolent despotism,[18] restrictive legislation, or negative results are among the factors that could lead executives to withdraw to more conventional ground. Certain questions, therefore, become exceedingly timely. If it is not

---

[15] "More Jobs for Negroes," *Nation's Business* (September, 1967), pp. 574–77.

[16] *The Standard Oil Company of New Jersey: Annual Report 1966*, p. 6.

[17] Jersey Standard itself has not been without "explosions" of this sort. At its annual meeting on May 23, 1962, Mr. Watson Washburn declared, "You directors are giving away millions of dollars of your corporation's money for charity. This seems wrong. Your company is supposedly run solely for stockholders' benefit. It is not an eleemosynary institution. . . . The current practice is especially reprehensible when, as here, nearly $10,000,000 has been given away since 1955 to educational institutions, many of which teach socialism and ridicule businessmen, savers, and investors, as recently explained in the well-documented best-seller, *Keynes at Harvard.*" *The Standard Oil Company of New Jersey: Annual Report 1962.* The right to speak is not the only stockholders' right, and for a convenient listing of them, see Jacob Weissman, *Law in a Business Society* (Englewood Cliffs, N.J.: Prentice-Hall, Inc., 1964), pp. 38–44.

[18] William Ghent's ideas, *Our Benevolent Feudalism* (New York: Macmillan Co., 1902), have been echoed in important respects by Theodore Levitt, "The Dangers of Social Responsibility," *Harvard Business Review*, Vol. XXXVI (September-October, 1958), pp. 41–60. This is, curiously enough, the same largely unresolved question posed by President Hoover's Committee on Social Trends back in 1933. "Shall businessmen become actual rulers; or shall rulers become industrialists; or shall labor and science rule the older rulers?" *Recent Social Trends* (New York: Report of the President's Research Committee on Social Trends, 1933).

to remain a vogue and, hence a vulnerable movement, how is this new concept of responsibility to be incorporated by scholars into theory? Will economics continue to provide the most satisfactory theoretical formulations for accommodation? Or is a more catholic and interdisciplinary approach inevitable?

CONCEPT "INVASION"

In every field new concepts emerge from older and established ones. The emergence occurs when traditional notions are seen in new ways to meet a new situation or where they serve as projective models of a new situation. Donald Schon has demonstrated how concepts are often expressed in metaphors which last indefinitely—such as the Greek theory of scale, the Greek notion of vision, Solon's theory of justice, the atomism of Lucretius.[19] In quite another context Schon has spoken of scientific "invasions" to indicate the process whereby technological changes have invariably come to established industries from outside sources. We know, for example, that all major transformations in textiles have come from the chemical industry.[20] In somewhat analogous ways this idea of "corporate responsibility" has invaded traditional theory. And economists have been particularly wary against efforts to try to theorize about it meaningfully. Many see in recent theoretical formulations what Professor Ben Lewis has called a "creeping admonitionism" wholly foreign to our way of life. He declared flatly: "Economizing by conscience is a symptom of, and not a cure for, organic disabilities which are beginning to be plainly discernible in our economic body."[21]

Lewis' well-reasoned skepticism releases old ghosts from the closet: Is economics value-free? Clearly economists admit involvement with value judgments regarding the choice of their problems and their epistemological criteria. Beyond these value issues is the well-known fact that economic theory has been enlivened by debates between "little" inflationists and "little" deflationists, between free-traders and protectionists, between planners and price-mechanists. The often unarticulated assumptions, so frequently charged with

---

[19] Donald A. Schon, *Invention and the Evolution of Ideas* (London, England: Tavistock Publications, Ltd., 1963), esp. chap. IV.

[20] Donald A. Schon, *Technology and Change* (New York: Dell Publishing Company, 1967).

[21] "Economics by Admonition," *American Economic Review: Proceedings*, Vol. XLIX (May, 1959), p. 385.

normative implications,[22] has led an English scholar to say that "the economist coming with a more or less extreme belief in individual enterprise and the price mechanism, on one hand, and the economist believing in more or less an extreme way in socialist planning on the other hand, tend to assert as empirically valid widely different and contradictory pictures of the economic world and of economic behavior and its motivations."[23] And we are told that even the simple mechanic of recording financial data touches on value judgments. "Every decision made by the accountant," said V. E. Odmar, "is a valuation decision fraught with possibilities of justice or injustice in some economic interests."[24]

Economic theory claims to be neutral regarding ends but the market itself is not a passive instrument but a social institution which, in John Maurice Clark's words, "acts as if it had a life and purpose of its own, independent of those of the people who operate it and doing things to them that none of them planned or desired. It will be our master, not our servant, subjecting us to its purposes, not serving us, unless we are very clear what these purposes are. . . ."[25] Clark's point is simply that every society has a teleology whose full purposes go beyond what the market alone provides. *Policy* inevitably involves the establishment of goals and priorities and of means-ends relationships; social responsibility is a policy decision. The arena of debate is, therefore, moved inexorably beyond traditional economic parameters so that other disciplines are now expected to make contributions.

Adolf Berle, Jr. probably reflected the new trends, with their obvious rejections of the more conservative approaches represented by Lewis and Rostow, when he asserted that modern business concentrates are not really private and that it "is indefensibly disingenuous to assert that these operations are primarily following economic laws more or less accurately outlined by classical economists a century ago when the fact appears to be that they are following a slowly *emerging pattern of sociological and political laws, relevant to the*

---

[22] Gunnar Myrdal, *The Political Element in the Development of Economic Theory* (Cambridge, Mass.: Harvard University Press, 1965), esp. pp. 11–15; 191–95.

[23] T. W. Hutchinson, *"Positive" Economics and Policy Objectives* (Cambridge, Mass.: Harvard University Press, 1964), p. 63.

[24] "Some Aspects of the Evolution of Accounting Functions," *The Accounting Review* (October, 1954), p. 638.

[25] *Economic Institutions and Human Welfare* (New York: Alfred A. Knopf, Inc., 1957), p. 33.

rather different community demands of our time."[26] The patterns suggest sharp dislocations in traditional theories and attitudes toward profit and toward competition and not a few business executives have pilloried economists for not accommodating their models to current realities.[27]

These realities often determine the reasons for corporations assuming a social responsibility posture and the tenet itself can be better understood if effort is made to clarify the different strands woven into the doctrine. This undertaking leads to the first major objective of this analysis.

MODELS OF CORPORATE SOCIAL RESPONSIBILITY

Some writers, influenced by the study dealing with the "American business creed,"[28] have tended to establish the meaning of corporate social responsibility within two major segments. The first, termed the "classical tradition" of business responsibility, restates the traditional theory of the firm: an enterprise exists to maximize profits for its owners; all other claimants are really *outside* the enterprise's purview. Against this is posed the new version which, under the rubric of "managerial ideology," claims that the corporation has an obligation to *balance* the various needs of the many claimants on the corporation's resources. Between the two polarities are various subsets which merit some recognition. In all, six "models" might be briefly identified:[29]

1. *The austere model*

The *austere* model holds that a firm comes into existence when owners commit the capital resources they possess to the enterprise. The

---

[26] *The Twentieth Century Capitalist Revolution* (New York: Harcourt, Brace & Co., 1954), p. 12. Benjamin M. Selekman declared that the need was for a new economics which would draw more heavily from the insights of John Commons. See Selekman's, *Moral Philosophy for Management* (New York: McGraw-Hill Book Co., 1959), pp. 122–33.

[27] An articulation of one thoughtful businessman's view on these concepts may be found in a talk given by Leon Hickman, executive vice president of Alcoa, "Prices, Competition and Morality," in Courtney Brown (ed.), *The Ethics of Business: Corporate Behavior in the Market Place* (New York: Columbia Graduate School of Business, 1963), pp. 15–35. See also, C. West Churchman, *Predictions and Optimal Decisions* (Englewood Cliffs, N.J.: Prentice-Hall, Inc., 1961).

[28] F. X. Sutton, *et al., The American Business Creed* (New York: Shocken Books, 1962).

[29] These "models" were first developed in Clarence C. Walton's *Corporate Social Responsibilities* (Belmont, Cal.: Wadsworth Publishing Company, 1967), chap. 5. For the historical background, see Morrel Heald, "Management's Responsibility to Society: The Growth of an Idea," *The Business History Review*, Vol. XXXI (Winter, 1957), pp. 377–91.

firm exists because of the owners and owes its gains primarily to those responsible for its existence.[30] This is what has been termed the "classical" version by Sutton and his colleagues.

2. *The household model*

The *household* model, suggested by Aristotle's early notion that all involved within economic undertaking are "companions of the cupboard," extends the reach of corporate obligations directly to the workers within the firm. It clearly rejects the Ricardian assertion that labor is simply a factor of production. Recently a distinguished financier, Armand Erpf, expressed this philosophy when he said that "the exciting thing about modern capitalism, American modern capitalism, is that it is moving into other areas than the mere production of commodities. And in those areas, more and more the human being is not a commodity, but must become an independent, vital entity. And you can't have a creative corporation where you continue to treat people as though they were organization men or a commodity."[31]

3. *The vendor model*

The *vendor* model asserts that an enterprise exists "for the production of goods and services at the lowest possible cost, and at prices which measure the comparative pressure of consumers' choices."[32] In this version of social responsibility a firm discharges its tasks by making the consumer the primary object of its attention; quite obviously the nexus between the production-consumption-profit equation is so close that the concern for consumers can appear to be self-serving. On the other hand, some industries, such as pharmaceuticals, claim a special commitment to the vendor model.

4. *The investment model*

The *investment* model has been described (in an earlier book) in these words: "In summary if corporation-giving is guided by policies which aim toward the balanced best interests of the share owners, customers, employees, suppliers, and the public, the proper test of the validity of any particular gift is not whether it advances the interests of any of these groups to the exclusion of the interests of the others. The justification . . . is not what it achieves for the community alone, but rather what it does to protect the wider corporate environment that sustains the share

---

[30] For a closely reasoned defense of the austere model, see F. A. Hayek, "The Corporation in a Democratic Society," in Melvin Anchen and George Bach (eds.), *Management and Corporations 1985* (New York: McGraw-Hill Book Co., 1960).

[31] Armand Erpf, *New York Times*, December 15, 1967.

[32] Rostow, *loc. cit.*, p. 67.

owners' profitable investments."[33] The investment model is a refinement of the early Smith notion that what prompts rational men to act is enlightened self-interest.

5. The civic model

The *civic* model theorizes that an enterprise, like a citizen, holds special rights and incurs special obligations commensurate with those privileges in a democratic society. Whereas the investment model looks first to survival of the system because it is essential to the good of the "self," the civic model tends not to be self-serving. Companies may undertake a wide variety of assignments even when the undertaking promises no return on investment to itself and may, in some cases, cause even an added cost burden.

6. The artistic model

The *artistic* model, the latest and newest version of corporate social responsibility, maintains that executives who are themselves creative and dynamic have a positive role to play in partnership with other creative segments of society. The goal is less a material one and more the intangible one of enhancing the aesthetic and moral qualities of life.[34]

THE CRITICAL POINT

If one looks carefully at each of the foregoing models it becomes clear that the essential element in corporate social responsibility currently inviting attention is the point where the firm moves from *obligations imposed* to *responsibilities assumed.* The search for profits is hallowed by tradition and established in law; similarly workers' rights since the Wagner Act (household model) are increasingly protected by law through decisions of the National Labor Relations Board and, when these fail, there is always the possibility of a test of strength through the strike. Although to a less marked degree, the consumer in the vendor model is also protected by a wide variety of federal and state statutes and by his capacity to discipline the unruly seller by withholding his purchases. Yet in important respects the consumer is poorly organized to exert his power and in the presence of administered pricing in many areas his chance to enforce his "withholding" sanction is weakened.

On balance, however, there appears reason to support the generalization that the *austere, household* and *vendor* models respectively

---

[33] Richard Eells, *Corporation Giving in a Free Society* (New York: Harper & Bros., 1956), p. 29.

[34] Richard Eells, *The Corporation and The Arts* (New York: Macmillan Co., 1967. An Arkville Press Book), especially Chapter 21.

fall substantially within the "obligatory" areas. Thus the critical point is reached between the *vendor* and the *investment* models because the rationale for the latter (long-range profit and survival) is harder to articulate and to defend. In the *A. P. Smith* case the court reasoned that support by business of higher education was clearly in the interest of a free society and a free enterprise system, thus sustaining the logic of the investment model. But it is not at all clear that many actions, taken with the investment motive in mind, really add appreciably to the stated objective.

There seems little doubt that the *civic* and *artistic* models provide the greatest freedom for voluntary action on the part of a corporation in furthering its external social obligations. Companies can and do take different routes. In the balance-of-payments problem International Business Machines sought to cooperate fully but the Ford Motor Company took another route. And sponsorship of art centers, ballet groups, symphonies and museums appeals to Jersey Standard yet is spurned by Rayonier.

A convenient exercise in seeking to distinguish kinds of social responsibility a company undertakes was provided recently by Jersey Standard which defined its responsibilities to the public in these terms:

Jersey recognized that its freedom to do business in a community or a country depends ultimately on public sanction. Accordingly, in pursuing its objectives of long-term growth and increasing amounts of current income for shareholders, it seeks to conduct its business in a manner that contributes to the social health and economic progress of the societies of which it is a part. Among its most fundamental policies are (*a*) the provision of good products and services at fair prices; (*b*) efficient development of oil and gas deposits to achieve maximum utilization; (*c*) the conservation of natural resources, including air, water, forests, and wildlife, as well as energy resources; (*d*) cooperation with governments in economic and social development projects; (*e*) *ethical behavior;* (*f*) recognition and support of the cultural traditions and interests of host countries and the aspirations of their people; (*g*) *initiative in helping* solve community problems; (*h*) acceptance of its responsibilities affecting the rights, dignity, health, safety, and opportunities of employees; and (*i*) fostering better communication—and better understanding—among people locally, nationally, and internationally.[35]

If one looks at the creed, the opening statement appears to fall within the investment model; (*a*) and (*b*) suggest the vendor

---

[35] *This Is Standard Oil Company of New Jersey* (1967), p. 5.

model; (*c*), (*d*), (*g*) and (*i*) impinge on the civic model; (*e*) and (*f*) range near the artistic model; and (*h*) is directly related to the household model. Distinguished by its absence is a clear and explicit avowal of goals held preeminent in the austere model—although it might be argued that this appears in the opening phrases. One could easily accept the qualification and not be hindered from drawing the inference that the historic or classical model of business responsibility is a casualty in modern business practice.[36] Profit maximizing will never die—it has been maimed, and for reasons not unrelated to the fact that the share owners today are less *investors* in the sense of risk taking and are more *depositors*.[37] The matter of survival will always be critical and the importance of nexus between the enterprise and the nation cannot be underestimated.[38]

On the other hand, there seems little doubt that the productive machinery of America is sufficiently well organized to meet the material needs of the American people—despite the poverty pockets and high unemployment rates among minorities. There is consequently a willingness to move into new ventures which transcend but do not replace the making of goods and services, and this new high adventure is the making of a good society. The fact that many of the commitments are implicit makes the analysis more difficult.[39] The logic of the inquiry now leads to the last two of the four stated objectives; namely, (*a*) an examination of the latest theoretical formulations developed to explicate the concept of corporate social responsibility and, (*b*) the possible role that normative sciences might play in this enterprise.

SOME RECENT THEORIZING

While publication of the Berle-Means study in 1933[40] represents a benchmark to date the incipient stage when ideas such as "mana-

---

[36] Theodore Levitt, *The Twilight of the Profit Motive* (Washington, D.C.: Public Affairs Press, 1955), esp. pp. 1–5.

[37] Dow Votaw, "The Mythology of Corporations," *California Management Review*, Vol. IV (Spring, 1962), pp. 58–73.

[38] Peter Drucker, "Business Objective and Survival Needs: Notes on a Discipline of Business Enterprise," *Journal of Business*, Vol. XXXI (April, 1958), pp. 87–88.

[39] Alexander Sesonske, *Value and Obligation: The Foundations of an Empiricist Ethical Theory* (New York: Oxford University Press, 1964), p. 3.

[40] Adolph A. Berle, Jr., and Gardiner C. Means, *The Modern Corporation and Private Property* (New York: Macmillan Co., 1932). For a serious criticism of the Berle-Means thesis see Clive S. Beed, "The Separation of Ownership from Control," *Journal of Economic Studies*, Vol. I (Summer, 1966), pp. 3–29.

gerialism," "legitimacy," and "corporate responsibility" were thrust to the forefront of discussion, it was not until the postwar period that the inquiries assumed the contours of a full-fledged debate. Because much of the early literature on these topics has become fairly well-known the present inquiry focuses only on selected examples which have appeared very recently.[41]

A most intriguing effort was undertaken by Harold Johnson who sought to incorporate a theory of social responsibility within the sphere of positive economics. Johnson holds that the "responsibility" concept may be viewed theoretically (1) in terms of utility maximization by the entrepreneur and (2) in terms of those social variables revealed by the preference function of inputs and of customers. He personally feels that the second approach is more congenial to traditional theory and in this context he concludes that business social responsibility really "exists if the general preference function of the manager includes variables that coincide with what the American community regards as desirable."[42] One must note in passing that a certain homogeneity is presumed to exist among the various groups which constitute the "American Community," but this assumption is often tested when local community values differ from the larger consensus—as U.S. Steel's 1963 experiences in Birmingham dramatically illustrated. In that year the philosophy of management threatened the "separatism" doctrine of Alabama's Governor Wallace and other segregationists.

Meanwhile, the behavioral scientists—culling relevant ideas from psychology, anthropology, sociology and the other social-science

---

[41] This decision means the unfortunate omission of contributions from A. A. Berle, Herrymon Maurer, Howard Bowen, Kenneth Boulding, and other pioneers. Unnoted, too, will be the older but perennially intriguing studies by C. J. Hitch and R. L. Hall, who demonstrated that English business managers did not employ marginal analysis in arriving at decisions, "Price Theory and Business Behavior," *Oxford Economic Papers* (May, 1939), pp. 12–45, and the refinements made thereto by Armen A. Alchian, "Uncertainty, Evolution and Economic Theory," *Journal of Political Economy*, Vol. LVIII, no. 3 (June, 1950), pp. 211–21. The authors apologize for not including notes on the contributions of many other economists.

[42] Harold L. Johnson, *Graphic Analysis of Multiple-Goal Firms: Development, Current Status, and Critique* (University Park: Penn State University Center for Business Research, 1966), p. 30. Further insight into Professor Johnson's position may be obtained through his article, "Socially Responsible Firms: An Empty Box or a Universal Set?," *Journal of Business*, Vol. XXIX (July, 1966), pp. 394–401. It is interesting to compare Johnson's views with the pioneering article which raised some of the same questions by Benjamin Higgins, "Elements of Indeterminacy in the Theory of Non-Perfect Competition," *American Economic Review*, Vol. XXIX (September, 1939), pp. 468–79.

disciplines—have not been idle. Again, reliance is on the positivistic approach in variegated efforts designed to expand the theory of the firm to include the interplay of social forces between internal and external factors. Within this purview, the enterprise emerges not as a profit-maximizer but as an optimal "satisficer."[43] There is little question that startling advances are in the offing for the behavioral sciences. Recollection of how theoretical gains in mathematics and physics over the past three decades have influenced the development of new quantitative tools such as linear programming, queuing theory, and the like reinforces the conviction that the behavioral sciences also will be enormously stimulated by gains now being recorded in the biological sciences.

The layman, for example, senses the importance of recent announcements by Professor Arthur Kornberg and his research associates at Stanford regarding further understanding of DNA. The New York *Times* (December 17, 1967) said that some experts were hailing the Kornberg discovery enthusiastically, feeling that it may now be possible to "make an exact duplicate of a genius, such as an Einstein, with DNA." The mind is staggered by the claim.

On reflection, however, it becomes apparent that today's theories in economics and in the behavioral sciences do not seek to explain *why* an executive would want to be socially responsible in the first place, how he would be expected to resolve conflicts between his utility and contrary community demands, or how the corporation's non-economic functions can be fully encompassed within economic or behavioral theory.

As a result, theorists have recently turned to sociology and anthropology. Talcott Parson's view of role theory[44] has encouraged Thomas Petit to suggest that role-fulfillment by the manager offers the most satisfying interpretation of social responsibility for analytical purposes; it is realistic because if a manager runs contrary to social change he will eventually "lose his position, power, prestige

---

[43] Contributions in this area continue to mount and one can only give illustrative examples of the literature. Helpful guides would include Leonard Sayle's *Management Behavior* (New York: McGraw-Hill Book Co., 1964); A. H. Maslow, *Motivation and Personality* (New York: Harper & Row, 1954); Douglas McGregor, *The Human Side of Enterprise* (New York: McGraw-Hill Book Co., 1960); Richard Cyert and James March, *A Behavioral Theory of the Firm* (Englewood Cliffs, N.J.: Prentice-Hall, Inc., 1963).

[44] Talcott Parsons, *Structure and Process in Modern Society* (New York: The Free Press, 1960), Chapters I and II.

and income."[45] Further only through the manager can an impersonal organization receive direction, be infused with an esprit, behave responsibly, and thereby become "soulful." Managers seek therefore to control the environment.

Of the four major avenues open for exerting social control (spontaneous field control, manipulated field control, command, and reciprocity) the first is more congenial to the American value systems. The key to Petit's reasoning is captured in this statement:

> This study has taken the position that when competition became less effective as a spontaneous field control, it was natural that some other form of spontaneous field control developed to supplement it *because of American value orientations.* To be sure, many other control techniques have been employed. Antitrust and public utility regulation have had some success as forms of command control. Public planning schemes have operated as manipulated field controls. But because of our opposition to authoritarian means of control and our dedication to control processes that are so ubiquitous and invisible that they form part of the landscape, it was highly likely that another form of spontaneous field control would develop to supplement competition.[46]

It is interesting to observe how this sociologically oriented theory allows explicitly for the retention of values. Yet the methodologies employed here recall the efforts made in welfare economics and organization theory to find an analytically convenient place to install values—without defining precisely the types involved.[47] The installation has been made with relative ease by Petit because he holds that a "business ethic, to be acceptable to society, must be compatible with the prevailing economic ideology and theory."[48] The tautology is evident. But is the function of ethics to conform? Or to set perspectives by which ideology is judged? One notes that the definition makes the "is" the "ought" and, in the process, re-

---

[45] Thomas Petit, *The Moral Crisis in Management* (New York: McGraw-Hill Book Co., 1967), chap. V and pp. 122, 123. Petit has done an excellent job of reviewing the literature and of developing his theory as an extension and advance over previous ideas of social responsibility.

[46] *Ibid.,* p. 122. Italics mine.

[47] How "welfare economics" assumed the existence of certain values is developed by Paul Samuelson, *Foundations of Economic Analysis* (Cambridge: Harvard University Press, 1947), chap. VIII. Two scholars who argue that values must be explicitly recognized in the behavioral sciences are Ija Korner, "Values—A Stepchild of Psychology," *International Journal of Social Psychology,* Vol. IX (Summer, 1963), pp. 224–29, and M. Brewster Smith, "Research Strategies Toward a Conception of Positive Mental Health," *American Psychologist,* Vol. XIV (Fall, 1959), pp. 673–81.

[48] Petit, *op. cit.,* pp. 11, 108.

duces ethics to a formulation where consensus becomes the determinant of an ethical system.

Another attempt to give sustained attention to value problems in business was undertaken by Professors Alvar and Carol Elbing.[49] Convinced that business has always been a social system and that it could not, therefore, be explained exclusively by economic criteria, the Elbings seek to analyze the social criteria that affect preference systems. Cultural anthropology provides critical linkages in tracing these values. From Kluckhorn is derived the definition of value as "the concept of the desirable."[50] Because the "desirable" changes from time to time and from culture to culture, every moral maxim must be put to a test by critical methods which yield no fixed or absolute answers. Social responsibility flows, therefore, less from the individual manager's conscience or moral precepts and more from an interplay by various social groupings engaged in reciprocal relationships within the social system. Values are revealed in the operations of the market place, in precepts of law, and in the ideology of a democratic society.[51] Yet one wonders whether these operations reveal only the character of social institutions. Is not a further step required to determine how a social institution *ought* to be organized and how it *ought* to behave.

THE NORMATIVE SCIENCES

The course of theoretical developments related to corporate social responsibilities demonstrates quite clearly an inexorable movement toward value analysis—thereby lending credence to claims recently made that a general theory of management will be stated only when value theory makes its overall contributions.[52] There is

---

[49] Alvar O. Elbing, Jr., and Carol J. Elbing, *The Value Issue of Business* (New York: McGraw-Hill Book Co., 1967).

[50] Clyde Kluckhohn, *et al.*, "Values and Value-Orientations in the Theory of Action," in Talcott Parsons and Edward Shils (eds.), *Toward a General Theory of Action* (Cambridge: Harvard University Press, 1951), p. 395. This accords with the definition of value given by Professor Vogt after his studies into the Navajo culture; Evan Z. Vogt, "Navajo Veterans: A Study of Changing Values," *Museum of American Archaeology and Ethnology*, Vol. XIV (1951), pp. 6–7. See also Elbing, *op. cit.*, pp. 7–10.

[51] Elbing, *op. cit.*, 178–79.

[52] William C. Frederick, "The Next Development in Management Science: A General Theory," *Journal of the Academy of Management*, Vol. VI (September, 1963), pp. 212–19. Relevant, too, is R. Tagiuri, "Value Orientations and the Relationships of Managers and Scientists." *Administrative Science Quarterly*, Vol. X (1965), pp. 39–51.

now a greater willingness to concede that corporate social responsibility is a "concept as worthy of rigorous scientific analysis as competition." The explicit premise of Petit[53] is that scientific rigor will come only from a positive approach; it was, as well, the strongly implied position for the Elbings.[54] We are possibly witnessing a reassertion of Feuerbach's old maxim that theology is anthropology—and nothing more: "to speak of God is to speak of man himself!"[55]

Much of the current theorizing suggests agreement with E. A. Havelock who reexamined the Greek liberal tradition and concluded that mankind has labored much too long under the dead weight of Plato and Aristotle—philosophers who allegedly never really understood economic theory. The need is to revive interest in the anthropologies of the pre-Socratics like Sophocles and Euripides.[56] It is true, however, that challenges are being developed—despite the general favor accorded the positive method in contemporary social science. Taking issue with the concept of social responsibility as defined by Drucker a decade ago (and, one might infer, with definitions by Johnson, Petit, and others more recently) that "social responsibility is management behavior in conformity with prevailing mores," Samuel Gluck has insisted that these methodologies "totally ignore the classical content of social philosophy and the methods of ethical analysis."[57] Gluck, the philosopher, finds support from S. P. Asch, the psychologist, who has also insisted that ethical judgments cannot be reduced to more elementary functions.

---

[53] Petit, *op. cit.*, pp. v, 11.

[54] Elbing, *op. cit.*, pp. 210–11. "The life stream of our age is empirical investigation. Value inquiry must come into this life stream; [there exists] a sound case for the behavioral science methods as the most critical methods available for the objective value inquiry."

[55] Larry Shiner, *The Secularization of History: An Introduction to the Theology of Friedrich Gogarten* (Nashville: Abingdon Press, 1966) .

[56] E. A. Havelock, *The Liberal Temper in Greek Politics* (London: Jonathan Cape, 1957) , esp. pp. 380–90. It is this secularization of life, with its reliance on reason and its exclusion of faith, that disturbed Lev Shestov, who insisted that mankind must make a critical choice: God or man. See *Athens and Jerusalem* (Athens: Ohio University Press, 1967) . Trans. by Bernard Martin.

[57] Samuel F. Gluck, "Philosophies of Management in Historical Perspective," *Annals of the American Academy of Political and Social Science*, Vol. CCCXLIII (September, 1962) , pp. 10–19. Gluck sharply criticizes scholars like Neil Chamberlain, *Social Responsibility and Strikes* (New York: Harper & Bros., 1953) ; Peter Drucker, *The Practice of Management* (New York: Harper & Bros., 1954) ; Elton Mayo, *The Social Problems of an Industrial Civilization* (London: Routledge and Kegan Paul, 1949) ; and, inferentially, others who allegedly operate exclusively within the positivistic methodologies to derive values.

"Phenomenally, right and wrong are not wholly identical with the generic experience of desire or aversion, or with anticipation of reward and punishment. . . . We all feel we value a thing because it has value, and not that it has value because we value it."[58]

How may ethical analysis run? Gluck speaks of three levels: (1) *morality* which reflects the codes of a given culture, (2) *ethics* which ask whether the codes ought to say what they do, and (3) *meta-ethics* which probes into the meaning of basic ethical terms such as right and wrong, good and evil. To illustrate his conviction that much of current theorizing is faulty, Gluck poses these questions:

Are stock options to executives and directors unethical, even though in our society they are not immoral? If so, is the disclosure of broker-age-house holdings in the securities they promote merely the causal acknowledgment of unethical practices? . . . What separates the statisticians who work for the Tobacco Industry Research Committee from their colleagues at the American Cancer Society? Is one group in error? Or dishonest? To answer "neither," but that they start with different logical and mathematical postulates, shows only that, though philosophers may argue as to whether science in itself is neutral or value free, it always operates in a normatively moral and critically ethical context.[59]

Some philosophers might even fault this very question by arguing that ethical principles do not render specific answers to practical moral dilemmas but provide, rather, only the standards by which lower-order rules might be measured.[60] Yet even within these limited ranges the uses of critical ethical inquiry bear reconsideration. When, for example, Schumpeter remarked that all "analytical work begins with material provided by our vision of things, and this vision is ideological almost by definition,"[61] two of his Harvard colleagues proceeded to give specificity to that vision by pointing out that in every view *"ethical oughts* are as intrinsic in human enter-

---

[58] S. E. Asch, *Social Psychology* (Englewood Cliffs, N.J.: Prentice-Hall, Inc., 1952), as quoted by Theodore V. Purcell, "Work Psychology and Business Values: A Triad Theory of Work Motivation," *Personnel Psychology*, Vol. XX (Autumn, 1963), pp. 241–42.

[59] Gluck, *loc. cit.*, p. 19.

[60] Henry David Aiken, "The Levels of Moral Discourse," *Ethics* (July, 1952), p. 244. See also William K. Frankena, "The Concept of Morality," *The Journal of Philosophy*, Vol. LXIII (November 10, 1966), pp. 688–96.

[61] *History of Economic Analysis* (London: Oxford University Press, 1954), pp. 41–42.

prises as the *technical musts.*" These "oughts" are not precisely measurable like the technical requirements but exist clearly enough in the "Judeo-Christian tradition, the Greco-Roman tradition, and the ideas of equalitarian democracy."[62]

But are these traditions to be assessed only within the American setting? Or is there another standard whereby American value structures can be judged?[63] We have become perfectly aware that the old moral tradition in America was overly-simplistic: good was good because God commended it and evil was evil because God forbade it. John Courtney Murray, for one, noted that the "American morality" of the nineteenth and early twentieth century had rejected the older intellectual traditions of ethics which equated morality with right reason. It presumed there existed the possibility for direct transference of personal values to the social structure, and this led to the formation of facile absolutes which were "ill-suited to cope with the growing complexity of an industrial age, domestically and in foreign relations."[64] The role of reason and the existence of two distinct spheres for value analysis, personal and social, become important.

It is precisely at this point that contributions from the normative sciences are of potential value. Granted that profit maximization is inadequate, is a larger view of "self-interest" (disciplined by a new kind of competition through Parsonian spontaneous field control) the final answer? Theodore Purcell, for one, would answer negatively. In his view "an adequate philosophy of management is needed, not to play down the profit motive, but to balance it with other dynamic motives that exist realistically, regardless of managerial strategies."[65] And these motivations, insists Purcell, cannot exclude religious elements because man is a social and religious being. Therefore, theory remains incomplete unless, and until, it receives insights from industrial theology where theology is defined as "faith seeking understanding."[66] But where will ethical and/or theological insights come from? Petit himself makes explicit reference to "the

---

[62] Sylvia Kopald Selekman and Benjamin H. Selekman, *Power and Morality in a Business Society* (New York: McGraw-Hill Book Co., 1956), pp. 86 *et seq.*

[63] Petit, *infra*, fn. 53.

[64] John Courtney Murray, "Morality and Foreign Policy," *Worldview*, Vol. III (May, 1960), pp. 2, 3.

[65] Purcell, *loc. cit.*, p. 245.

[66] *Ibid.*, p. 249.

situation ethics" of Joseph Fletcher[67] although others, too, have made important contributions to its formulations.[68] The moral imperative of "love" is the key to the "new morality." But corporations are asked by society to seek justice (more than love) as the pillar of a sound social system.

But beyond this casual relationship are many problems which substantially separate the approaches represented by the new morality and the more traditional one. These differences go well beyond the criticisms hurled at the "new morality" by Dean Robert Fitch of the Pacific School of Religion that it employs too many fetish phrases such as mature, adult, responsible, responsive, in ways that offer the "water of life, but drown (us) under a cascade of cliches."[69] Needed, presumably, is a form of hard ethical inquiry that provides sharper definitions and insights for the executive.

Efforts to redefine the ethical nature of moral judgments—"decisions through compromise" may clarify theorizing on conflict situations which are fairly normal in executive decision-making.[70] The distinction between an obligatory course of action and one involving prudential judgment is difficult to achieve but is also desirable. Further, the old hostilities toward empiricism may become less intense as probings indicate the relevance of empirical data (bearing on the consequences of an action or policy) as possible justifications of moral decision.[71] This represents a new willingness to take ethics and apply canons of judgment which are more persuasive to social scientists.

What is needed is an enlargement of ethical speculation to the point where it, too, can construct intellectual perspectives within which the American "business creed," the religious and secular traditions, the concept of egalitarian democracy (noted by Selekman

---

[67] Petit, *op. cit.*, pp. 163–64.

[68] Joseph Fletcher, *Situation Ethics* (Philadelphia: Westminster Press, 1966) ; John A. T. Robinson, *Christian Morals Today* (Philadelphia: Westminster Press, 1964) ; and Douglas A. Rhymes, *No New Morality* (Indianapolis: Bobbs-Merrill, 1965) .

[69] Robert E. Fitch, *Religion in Life*, Vol. XXV (1966) , p. 86. Another sharp critic is E. L. Mascall, *The Secularization of Christianity* (New York: Holt, Rinehart, & Winston, 1966) . One should not miss the lively debate between Professor Fletcher and Dr. Herbert McCabe on the "new morality" as covered in *Commonweal*, Vol. LXXXIII (Jan. 14, 1966) , pp. 427–40.

[70] Charles E. Curran, "Dialogue with Joseph Fletcher," *Homiletic and Pastoral Review*, Vol. LXVII (1967) , pp. 821–29.

[71] John G. Millhaven, S.J., "Toward an Epistemology of Ethics," *Theological Studies*, Vol. XXVII (1966) , pp. 228–41.

as constituting the warp and woof of American values) may all be critically reviewed.[72]

A final note should be appended. Contemporary society shows symptoms of deep divisions which threaten the stability of the system. It may be true that conflict situations are overplayed because of the hunger by the communications media for exciting news; but the dangers implicit in white-versus-black tensions, in student-versus-faculty confrontations, in labor-management flare-ups in critically needed public services, cannot be brushed away. The social order desperately seeks new mechanisms to achieve integration. This integrative system relates to such things as status, honor, dignity, personal security and the like.

What provided for integration in the past were such basic social institutions as the family, the church, and the school. But these institutions are themselves in deep trouble and their weaknesses literally force men to look elsewhere. Businessmen always assumed that their contributions to the public welfare were completely fulfilled through the exchange system—a system built on *quid pro quo* relationships. Today, however, the exchange calculus, if rigorously applied, could not meet the needs of the hard-core unemployed for jobs, the needs of ghetto residents for decent housing, the needs of functional illiterates for training.

Quite unconsciously and often as a last resort has society turned to business for help on problems that are as much social as economic in nature. This "turning-to" philosophy has permeated the thinking of the Urban League and, more recently, of the Urban Coalition. It is implicit in the statement attributed earlier to Professor Kenneth Clark. As corporations respond to these new imperatives they are driven to go beyond the profit motive to defend their actions. In summary, it may be suggested that the mature enterprises, having established their capacities for efficient production and acceptable earnings, are going beyond their exchange functions to share in the forging of an integrative system.

SUMMARY AND CONCLUSION

Voluntary moves by corporate executives to use organizational resources to help satisfy expectations from a wide range of claimants

---

[72] See James Gustafson, "Christian Ethics" in Paul Ramsey's (ed.), *Religion* (Englewood Cliffs, N.J.: Prentice-Hall, Inc., 1965), pp. 287–354, and Helmut Thielicke, *Theological Ethics*, I (Philadelphia: Fortress Publishers, 1966), edited and translated by William H. Lazareth.

has resulted in a new version of business responsibility which has caught theoreticians off guard. Scholars noted the change early enough but traditional economic theory was somewhat reluctant to respond to the needs for theoretical refinements. Naturally enough, the emphasis has been heavily on the positivistic approach on grounds that the economic order has its own autonomy and its own rationale; where attempts have occurred to expand the theorizing to include non-economic criteria the same methodology has been employed and, predictably, with the same results:—emphasis on utility maximization by the executive, and on spontaneous field-control as a replacement for an outmoded theory of market competition.

While normative approaches to the theory of corporate social responsibility have been limited, there are small signs that efforts are being made to fill the vacuum. After all, the concept of the just price became more congenial to scholars only when it was recognized that the term was used to describe critically the nature of a *social* judgment formed by the body of buyers in the market place—and not an *individual* judgment formed by the conscience of each man. Ethical criteria have also been applied critically to concepts in modern welfare economics.[73]

Once the presumed separation between economic life and social life was breached by the emergence of the powerful corporation, it became clear that the social fabric—as Alexander von Humboldt observed a century ago—provides that "other interests, beside the material wants of life, occupy the minds of men."[74] To the question: "do executives meet their full social responsibilities by exclusive concern with having their corporations produce goods and services to the fullest possible degree?" company policies and practices are producing more and more negatives. Corporations are themselves claiming a role in trying to influence the American "style of life" in nonmaterial ways by seeking to help shape and influence the evolution of the culture itself. These "other interests" do indeed occupy the minds of executives, as Humboldt has averred.

---

[73] Edward J. Kane, "Justice and Welfare Economics: A Slightly Mathematical Approach," *Review of Social Economy*, Vol. XXI (September, 1963), pp. 103–116. Compare Professor Kane's critique to the position taken by Stephen Worland, "Justice and Welfare Economics," also in the *Review*, Vol. XVII (September, 1959), pp. 97–111. An earlier and uneven attempt to relate ethics and the social sciences was undertaken at a conference held at Notre Dame in 1957, the results of which were incorporated into a volume edited by Leo R. Ward, C.S.C., *Ethics of the Social Sciences* (South Bend: Notre Dame Press, 1958).

[74] *Cosmos: A Sketch of a Physical Description of the Universe* (London: Bohn, 1849), translated by E. C. Otté.

Questions remain. Is corporate social responsibility a current cult that will be gone with the first chill winds of economic adversity? Or does it have a more durable base so that scholars must provide critical assessments of the theories which underpin it? Indications are that the latter is, more likely, a true reflection of reality. And that being the case, normative science can take the "corporation-responsibility" tenet and join in the intellectual search for answers to illumine Hobbes' commentary: "If men acknowledge an obligation to others because of a long view of self interest it is said to be a prudential obligation. If, however, obligation is based on something other than self-interest, is it a moral one."[75] Will an adequate theory of corporate social responsibility include one or, perhaps, two of the models noted previously? Or all? In the interim the practised executive continues to take positions. Arnold Maremont, who runs his own business, exemplified one view when he said:

Let's not confuse the company managers in their role as managers with their role as individuals. A company man, in a social responsibility sense, is not a man at all. He is just two dimensions and he is not human. Since a corporation has no conscience and is not a person, it cannot be charitable. It cannot take shareholders' profits to help mankind, womankind, or even the animal world.[76]

Yet from David Rockefeller, respected president of Chase Manhattan Bank, came this public pronouncement:

A creative management philosophy must be one which not only seeks through efficient operation to maximize profit but which also recognizes its responsibility to render economic service—service by private enterprise to the public interest. The British statesman, Lord Halifax, liked to define service as "the rent we pay for our room on earth." In the case of business enterprises, this rent comes due not once a month but every day of the year. We can pay it by contributing through creative management to making this a better and more prosperous world for all mankind.[77]

While the debate still stirs stormy rhetorical waters, the business "facts of life" are indicating an almost inexorable trend toward the directions espoused by men like David Rockefeller.

---

[75] Thomas Nagel, "Hobbes on Obligation," *Philosophical Review,* Vol. LXVIII (1959), pp. 68–83.

[76] *The National Conference Board Record* (April, 1964), p. 9.

[77] From the address by David Rockefeller, "Creative Banking and the Changing City," Columbia-McKinsey Foundation Lecture (April 16, 1964).

RECOMMENDED READING

BERG, IVAR (ed.). *The Business of America,* Part V. New York: Harcourt, Brace & World, Inc., 1968.

CHEIT, EARL F. (ed.). *The Business Establishment.* New York: John Wiley & Sons, Inc., 1964.

EELLS, RICHARD. *The Corporation and the Arts.* New York: Macmillan Co., 1967. An Arkville Press Book.

ELBING, ALVAR O., and ELBING, CAROL J. *The Value Issue of Business.* New York: McGraw-Hill Book Co., 1967.

McGUIRE, JOSEPH. *Business and Society.* New York: McGraw-Hill Book Co., 1963.

PETIT, THOMAS. *The Moral Crisis in Management.* New York: McGraw-Hill Book Co., 1967.

WALTON, CLARENCE C. *Corporate Social Responsibilities.* Belmont, Calif.: Wadsworth Publishing Co., 1967.

FURTHER READING

Annals of the American Academy of Political and Social Science. Vol. 343 (September, 1962).

BROWN, COURTNEY (ed.). *Plain Talk on Business and the Public Interest.* New York: Columbia University Graduate School of Business, 1963. Especially Chapters 3, 7–9.

CLARK, JOHN MAURICE. *Economic Institutions and Human Welfare.* New York: Alfred A. Knopf, Inc., 1957.

JOHNSON, HAROLD J. *Graphic Analysis of Multi-Goal Firms: Development, Current Status and Techniques.* University Park, Pa.: Penn State University Center for Business Research, 1966.

SCHRIFTGIESSER, KARL. *Business and Public Policy: The Role of the C.E.D., 1942–1967.* Englewood Cliffs, N.J.: Prentice-Hall, Inc., 1967.

WALTON, CLARENCE C. (ed.). *Today's Changing Society: A Challenge to Individual Identity.* New York: Institute of Life Insurance, 1967. Especially Chapters 5, 7, and 9.

III. OWNERSHIP

THE QUESTION raised in Part II of this inquiry—whether freedom is really compatible with equality—can be answered by resolving the apparent dilemma in terms of ownership. For equality, as we understand it, means equality of opportunity and, like freedom of action after natural freedom of choice, it is fostered by law.

The idea of equality thus has two aspects: one is legal or constitutional while the other is proprietal. Of the two, the proprietal aspect of equality—ownership—is probably the older. This assumes that the will to own property precedes lawmaking for its protection. In primitive societies, the grouping-together of people and property comes before any consciousness of the need of a polity that will control and protect both. It is therefore possible to infer that the concept of "freedom under law" develops out of the instinct for acquiring property for self-preservation and the necessity for safeguarding its possession.

The institution of private property is based on a natural human tendency to survive. From the moment that the command to labor was laid upon man, it was inevitable that some would work harder, some would have better land or better hunting grounds, and some would have better luck. The lot of the sons of Adam was therefore uneven from the very beginning.

When we move to the concept of contract or covenant, it is interesting to observe that the Mosaic law represents a type of contract between man and God, which defines the duties of man toward God and of man toward man. The covenant assumes the ultimate authority of God and an enlightened human responsibility. The right to possess property is underlined at least twice in the commandments —thou shalt not steal, and thou shalt not covet thy neighbor's goods. And the last six commandments all hinge upon the protection of property rights to the extent that one regards life, domestic tranquillity, and a good name as part of ownership. Implicit in these directives is

. . . the radical equality of all human beings in their passion-born right to seek their preservation. But their right to seek the means of life is meaningless unless they are confirmed in possession of those things which they have lawfully acquired; or, in other words, natural equality is outraged by insecurity in possession. It is alike outraged by an impediment upon the fullest exercise by individuals of their self-preservative powers, within the limits set by the requirements of others. The absence of any such impediment upon the self-preservative powers is, however, an aspect of freedom as we now commonly understand it, which aspect is called freedom of contract.[1]

The complicated body of law that has developed to protect ownership is thus based on the simple assumption that every rational man knows his own interests best and should be permitted to serve them. What distinguishes our society from those preceding it is that in this country the drive for freedom came before the hope of extensive ownership. By the time the Pilgrims landed, the concept of private property had been well established in the Old World. But long and painful experience had demonstrated that ownership was precarious without a liberal polity. Small wonder that the first concern of the Founding Fathers was to establish a religious and political atmosphere in which life and liberty, as well as the equal right to ownership of real property, would be consistently secure.

The undertaking was well conceived. Great fortunes were carved out of a wilderness by plain men with little more to build on than equality of opportunity under law. Their heirs are today's aristocracy, created not so much by royal grant as by the energy of their forebears, who used their rough frontier equality to create first a political freedom and then a commercial commonwealth.

This commonwealth, as it developed, could be described as more

---

[1] Joseph Cropsey, *Policy and Economy* (The Hague: Martinus Nijhoff, 1957) , p. 64.

free than the polity that fostered it. In a democracy, in which majority vote ultimately prevails, the political preferences of the minority necessarily tend to be set aside. In economic life this imbalance is avoided by a principle of contract which requires the assent of all individuals involved. Freedom of action was similarly less inhibited in the economic sector until its astounding growth and power had to be restricted by law in the same way that the acts of the individual citizen are restricted.

For the untrammeled pursuit of economic opportunity has brought about a curious change, both in the nature of ownership and in the nature of equality. As Andrew Hacker has put it: "To paraphrase George Orwell, the possession of property makes some men more equal than others."[2] The rise of huge organizations, profit or nonprofit, as a result of improved technology and the response of enterprise to the demands of consumers for a better and easier way of life, has changed both the nature of individual property ownership and the scope of opportunity. This change has been subtle but radical. Paul P. Harbrecht describes these changes as follows:

Today's man has neither shop nor field, nor the satisfaction of work that puts his personal stamp on a product. He depends upon others to fix the time of his labor and his leisure. Protection for his old age comes from the government, the insurance company or the pension fund, and the inheritance he will leave his children is largely dependent upon the same institutions. As a result of his ties to these external sources of the good life he finds himself no longer independent. Where he was once master of a domain—small perhaps, but his own and tangible—he now looks to a complex of contracts, equities and expectancies over which he has very little control. Though he enjoys comforts of which his forebears did not even dream, by their standards he would be considered poor. His tangible wealth is small, though his security may be great.[3]

We have moved, in short, from the idea of property as real assets, such as land, gold, or cattle, to the idea of property as promises: securities, mortgages, bonds, bankbooks, and paper money. All these are symbols of ownership; they do not connote actual possession. They are law-born entities, and their ability to command "real" wealth depends ultimately on the survival of the political system

---

[2] Andrew Hacker, *Politics and the Corporation* (New York: Fund for the Republic, 1958) , p. 7.

[3] Paul P. Harbrecht and Adolf A. Berle, Jr., *Toward the Paraproprietal Society* (New York: Twentieth Century Fund, 1959–60) , pp. 37–38.

behind them. Under the present system the hoarding of assets ceases to be a facet of the thrift once regarded as a virtue and becomes a socially dangerous pathology. For these assets are the lifeblood of our proprietary economic system.

But the consequence of this change in the nature of property is that not every man who holds it is qualified to manage it in his own best interests. Ownership of this new kind of property demands a specialized knowledge such as belongs to bankers, brokers, accountants, or managers. The control of property, therefore, is no longer in the hands of its owners but in the books of those better able to manage it.

This development has also given rise to a new type of property right that is based not upon the ownership of things but on specialized knowledge of how to handle them. In fact, such knowledge has itself become a form of property:

> In our century, the place of property is taken by knowledge, because our political and economic well-being depend to an ever-increasing degree on science, technology, and administrative technique. Large-scale organization, characteristic of modern activity, further reduces the importance of private ownership. More and more, it is not the possession of material property, decisive in landed and commercial economies, but the possession of scientific insight, technical skill, and experience that determines one's place in society.[4]

Those persons engaged in professions for which long and advanced education is a prerequisite are the possessors of knowledge and skills highly prized by a society that needs them for survival and that can afford to buy them. Having invested time and intelligence in a special kind of property, knowledge, for which there is such effective demand, they become thus owners of a property that may be said to legitimize their professional use of it. Peter Drucker observed:

> Power can be legitimate only in relation to a basic social belief. What constitutes "legitimacy" is a question that must be answered in terms of a given society and its given political beliefs. Power is legitimate when it is justified by an ethical or metaphysical principle that has been accepted by society.[5]

---

[4] "Foreword" to the issue: "The Russian Intelligentsia," *Daedalus,* Vol. 89 (Summer, 1960) , p. 438.

[5] Peter Drucker, *The Future of Industrial Man* (New York: John Day Co., 1942) , pp. 34–35.

If power follows property, then the power of the manager of enterprise is vested in part in his stake in the knowledge of how an enterprise is managed. This is his special kind of ownership, and it provides his authority for managing. The frequent criticisms of the lack of entrepreneurship in contemporary business have ignored the emergence of a new kind of entrepreneurship that places a premium on the ingenuity, creativity, and imagination necessary to keep a complex organization in a state of continuing and effective operation. The art of administration is not new, but the dimensions in which it is being exercised is. The old entrepreneur of the Carnegie-Rockefeller variety saw the fruit of his knowledge realized in the burgeoning of new plants and the amassing of large personal fortunes. The new entrepreneur, represented by the knowledgeable manager, sees his proprietary claim not in the amount of stock he holds in the corporation over which he may preside but in that knowledge which makes him—and men like him—the possessors of a particularly valuable asset in 20th century society.

Without this property of knowledge, the manager would not be asked to consider his responsibility to society for the control of a wealth he does not own; today, however, traditional individual accountability for wealth is vitiated by the fact that it must be handled by groups of men with the authority of knowledge. As a result, its actual owners tend to see their shares as personal assets rather than as a share in responsibility for the conduct of the business in which they have invested. "The average stockholder doesn't think of his stockholdings as ownership—any more than he thinks of himself as the part owner of the bank where he has a savings account—or a part owner of the government because he has some Defense bonds."[6]

Nor can this be described as a postwar development. W. Z. Ripley commented on it in the twenties in *Main Street and Wall Street* in a chapter called "Giving Up Control." The story, in brief, is that James Doe, having been given his father's investment in the Boothbay Harbor Electric Light Company, is also given a lecture on accountability for wealth in which is quoted Justice Brandeis' statement: "There is no such thing, to my mind . . . as an innocent stockholder. He may be innocent in fact, but socially he cannot be held innocent. He accepts the benefits of the system. It is his business

---

[6] Cameron Hawley, *Executive Suite* (Boston: Houghton Mifflin, 1952), p. 324.

and his obligation to see that those who represent him carry out a policy which is consistent with the public welfare." James's father concludes with the remark: "This accountability for wealth underlies and justifies the whole institution of private property upon which the government of our country is founded."[7]

However, as a result of mergers, by the end of 1923 James's little company was bound up with 22 other companies in some 10 other states from Maine to Texas. And in conclusion Ripley exclaims:

> What an amazing tangle all this makes of the theory that ownership of property and the responsibility for its efficient, far-sighted and public-spirited management shall be linked to one another. Even the whole theory of business profits, so painstakingly evolved through years of academic ratiocination, goes by the board. All the managers, that is to say, operating men, are working on salary, their returns, except on the side, being largely independent of the net result of company operation year by year.[8]

While the word "independent" used in this context is something of a paradox, the idea that management's salary orientation puts it at a remove from company profit making is worth examining. It implies that the old idea of individual entrepreneurship has somehow become enclosed by job description; that, in short, opportunity in economic organization has become standardized, limited not merely in terms of salary but by the nature of the task assigned. Are we to infer that this situation illustrates a diminishing opportunity for ownership in our time? Certainly a number of terms like "egalitarianism," "collectivism," or "conformity" have been evoked to describe the situation. "Conformity" is the word that describes one aspect of the trend in which an element of choice figures. "Egalitarianism," an older word, has a connotation of heavier pressures, political as well as socioeconomic. Call it what one will, the tendency is apparently worldwide and is not confined to those societies in which everyone is equal and no one is free.

A decade ago Charles de Gaulle, in his book *Le fil de l'épée,* saw in this trend an opportunity for the military spirit to come into its own once again. It is probably a platitude to observe that in societies dedicated to freedom and equality the army tends to lack

---

[7] W. Z. Ripley, *Main Street and Wall Street* (Boston: Little, Brown & Co., 1927), p. 79.

[8] *Ibid.,* p. 83.

both prestige and popularity. De Gaulle saw in the gradual waning of the cult of individualism a new hope for the military life. He reasserts its potential for leadership in an environment that he describes as follows:

Individualism is out of favor, and everywhere the claims of collectivism are being pushed to the forefront. Not a trade but has been unionized. Political parties make a great play with their rules and their exclusions. Sport is highly organized. At the same time, the hustle and bustle of modern life has enforced the application of strong discipline in factories, offices and streets against which our fathers would, most certainly, have rebelled. Increasing mechanism and the division of labor have forced eclecticism and eccentricity onto the defensive. No matter what the nature and conditions of work may be, forces of circumstance have led to an equalization of labor and leisure. Education is becoming standardized, and housing conditions are more and more identical. From Sydney to San Francisco, taking in Paris on the way, clothes are being cut to the same pattern. Even faces are beginning to have an uncanny resemblance to one another. Without, perhaps, going so far as to agree with M. Maeterlinck that humanity is reverting to the conditions of the ant heap, we cannot help but realize that it is up in arms against individualism and independence. It remains for the army to turn this trend in evolution to account. Already, in such matters as organization, distribution of duties, training, and uniform, it is certainly not moving against the current of this age of trade unionism, the highway code, Taylorism, and the chain stores.[9]

The statement is at once challenging and surprising because of its inference that something good will come from some group out of standardization. The counterargument is stated by Andrew Hacker as follows:

Independence of mind, freedom of action, can only result from possessing a source of income which is securely one's own. This is why Jefferson called for an America in which everyone would be a property owner. It is idle to call on propertyless men to be heroes or martyrs. One in ten thousand will answer such a call, and he will do it for reasons which are both unpredictable and highly personal in their origin.[10]

Looking about, may we conclude that the rise of the welfare state indicates that constitutional guarantees to the individual with re-

---

[9] Charles de Gaulle, *The Edge of the Sword* (trans. Gerard Hopkins) (New York: Criterion Books, 1960), p. 70.

[10] Andrew Hacker, *op. cit.,* p. 7.

gard to both property and equality have proved insufficient to cope with the complex economic and social conditions of the mid-20th-century? Is the opportunity to own, to control, to excel, on the wane?

There is a further disquieting sign for those who see in the labor movement today the beginnings of a move from contract to status. The thesis is not well documented, and its principal argument seems to be based on labor's insistence of late years less on higher wages than on fringe benefits that will give some permanence to present prosperity. Granted that these benefits are status oriented, they are still secured through contract, and it is difficult to see how they could be come by any other way.

If India's caste system can be considered to be a good example of what status means to opportunity, then there is no need to pursue this question. Lack of control over his assets or his work skills appears to make a man a pawn in some larger game that he cannot play alone. To seek status rather than freedom of opportunity would be to destroy the potential of the future for both the worker and his heirs—in the name of a limited kind of security.

There is little doubt that the legal recognition of property rights, which is at the heart of our system of government, encourages a man to make the effort to produce. Nor is there much doubt that equal opportunity makes it possible for a man to produce more than he needs, so that his earnings can work for his future security.

What is in doubt is whether or not the complexity of our society is reducing plurality of ownership, whether of property or of work skills, to a few vast centralities that will substitute promises of security in exchange for routinized opportunity to which many are called but only a few are chosen for freedom and equality as we now know it.

The following chapters on "Property," "Contract," "Work," and "Leisure and Free Time" treat some of these problems with more precise attention and detail.

8. Private Property

OUTLINE

THE INSTITUTION of private property has been with us for so long that many persons regard it as part of the "natural order of things," like the position of the stars in the sky or the orderly succession of night and day. But in point of fact this institution is no more a

223

physical natural law than any other of the social mechanisms that man has devised. Consider, for example, the ages of prehistory, when nomadic existence was the rule and man roamed over vast areas of the earth in constant search for the means to preserve a precarious existence. Or consider the state of the North American continent at the time of the early European discoverers and explorers. In those days private property, if it existed at all, was something quite different from what it is now. And today we are faced with an evolving process that may produce yet a different concept of property tomorrow.

To face the fact that private property is a man-made institution is not to deny its value or the fact that it is "natural" to man in the sense that it conforms to his needs. True, some thinkers have ascribed much evil to the system and have called for its abolition. At one time, Bertrand Russell, for example, maintained that there was no justification for private property in land and that the institution of private property is a creature of the sword, an outgrowth of man's instinctual impulse to violence. A century earlier Joseph Proudhon (1809–65) asked what is property and answered: "It is robbery!" Proudhon insisted that private property was a device whereby one man's thoughts, will, personality, and energies are taken from him and put under the control of another. Proudhon's premises have been like intellectual lightning rods to many radical theorists who have influenced the French syndicalist movement.

And when discussions turn on the relative values of communal versus private property the contributions of Karl Marx become an essential part of the literature. For it was Marx who most carefully distinguished between two very different kinds of property: one based upon the producer's own labor and the other based upon the exploitation of the labor of others. And since the latter method of building and obtaining property constituted the basis of capitalism, orthodox Marxism demanded the abolition of this system which rewarded the owners of this kind of private property.

The debate over private property has a long history. Aristotle (384–322 B.C.), taking issue with Socrates, pointed out the psychological difficulty for men living together and having all things in common and especially "in their having common property." To Aristotle it was manifestly better that property should be private but its use common, and by this apparent contradiction the ancient Greek was suggesting that private property had social obligations. It remained for John Locke (1632–1708) to give the formulations that had the greatest impact on American theory. Starting with the Biblical notion of property coming to mankind in common from God, Locke was able to demonstrate that private property could emerge without the expressed compact of all of the commoners. And this would occur, said Locke, if one carefully considered the following argument:

> Though the earth, and all inferior creatures, be common to all men, yet every man has a property in his own person: this nobody has any right to but himself. The labour of his body, and the work of his hands, we may say, are properly his. Whatsoever then he removes out of the state that nature hath provided, and left it in, he hath mixed his labour with, and joined to it something that is his own, and thereby makes it his property. It being by him removed from the common state nature hath placed it in, it hath by this labour something annexed to it that excludes the common right of other men. For this labour being the unquestionable property of the labourer, no man but he can have a right to what that is once joined to, at least where there is enough, and as good, left in common for others.[1]

It is interesting to consider this paragraph. It is out of a curious blending of an individual's art with God's nature that produces private property; this private property exists, morally and philosophically, because something has been added by individual efforts to the common property. And yet there is this qualification: there must remain enough property in common, and in as good a condition as that held by the private property-holder, so that none is denied the right to sustenance and livelihood.

What has impressed some critics is the fact that Locke, having alledgedly produced a magnificent apologia for private property on the basis of natural rights and natural law, then proceeded to remove all natural law limitations on the property right. For it was Locke's view, as noted, that land should remain and be maintained in as good condition for the use of others, and that the land appropriated for private use should be only as great as could be made use of by the private user-owner. This latter limitation was designed to prevent spoilage. But when money was introduced into society the "spoilage limitation" was effectively removed and, in the process, the natural law limitations were also disrupted. This view (plus the fact that in

---

[1] John Locke, *Two Treatises of Civil Government* (1690), Book II, par. 26 in Everyman's Library, Vol. 751 (London: J. M. Dent & Sons, Ltd., 1947).

his *Considerations* Locke seemed to believe that a wage laborer had no other property except his labor) has inspired some critics to attack the premises of liberal representative government. Of these premises the most salient was Locke's view that pursuit of private good in a legitimate way resulted inevitably in the public good. Locke, in short, based his conclusions regarding the right of private property ownership on nature but then moved to eliminate any "natural restrictions" on capitalistic appropriation. He seems to have provided a natural class differential and a positive moral basis for a capitalist society.

It is this highly individualistic content of liberal capitalism that disturbed moralists like Popes Leo XIII and Pius XI. Both agreed with Locke on the importance of the right of private property arising out of nature itself. Indeed in his early encyclical, "The Condition of Labour," Leo XIII noted that "men always work harder and more readily when they work on that which is their own; nay, they learn to love the very soil which yields, in response to the labour of their hands, not only food to eat, but an abundance of the good things for themselves and those that are dear to them. It is evident that such a spirit of willing labour would add to the produce of the earth and to the wealth of the community."[2]

But these Popes were deeply concerned lest "the individual character of ownership blind the property holder to its social character." Pius XI stated the position in these terms:

There is, therefore, a double danger to be avoided. On the one hand, if the social and public aspect of ownership be denied or minimized, the logical consequence is Individualism, as it is called; on the other hand, the rejection or diminution of its private and individual character necessarily leads to some form of Collectivism. To disregard these dangers would be to rush headlong into the quicksands of Modernism.[3]

While theories concerning the origin, appropriateness, and "rightness" of private property furnish the basis for valuable speculation and provide, indeed, the perspectives within which moral judgments may be made, there is also needed substantially new kinds of analysis to demonstrate how the institution of private

---

[2] Pope Leo XIII, "The Condition of Labour," in *Five Great Encyclicals*, Rev. Gerald C. Treacy, S.J. (ed.) (New York: The Paulist Press, 1956), pp. 1–30.

[3] Pope Pius XI, "Reconstructing the Social Order," *loc. cit.*, p. 137.

property works today. What are its advantages and disadvantages? What is the future of private property? In the following comments, less than exhaustive attention will be given to the philosophical issues. Rather the effort is to suggest a sound analytic base for practical judgment about the concept of private property in contemporary industrial society. To assert this as the primary objective is not to deny, in the slightest, the importance of legacies that have come from philosophy. For the roots of property are often seen as much in customs rationalized in philosophy as in the need for economic productivity. But the theory of natural rights has largely remained expressed in terms of negations against power; it has failed to develop a doctrine of positive contents of rights based on a realistic understanding of what the function of property is in a complex society. In short, if we turn from the metaphysical idea of freedom, as realized through property, as being too abstruse and too ambiguous to meet present exigencies, we sense, nevertheless, the historic Lockean legacy which continues to influence our responses to the age-old issue of private v. communal property.

THE CONCEPT OF PROPERTY

The emphasis on "things" which suggests that property rights are simply person-thing relationships can be very misleading. In the modern world real property is usually absentee-owned and a substantial part of what is understood as property may have value that is quite intangible and not related to a specific thing at all. Therefore property becomes a relationship between person and person because it is a power possessed by one to exclude others from present or future use of a given resource. Property, therefore, can be conceived as (a) a power to prevent others from using a tangible thing; (b) power to keep others from bringing things into existence (patent rights), or (c) power to insist that a future share in some kind of economic utility, whose value is at that point quite uncertain, must be recognized. Perhaps it is fair to say that ownership is best expressed in terms of the number of persons, the period of time, and the extent of control whereby an owner can assure his own right or of use of a given thing. A wrongful possessor is not an "owner." One of the great law teachers of the early part of this century defined property as follows: "A true property may, therefore, be shortly defined as possession coupled with the unlimited right of possession. If these two elements are vested in different persons there is a divided ownership."[4]

Thus the concept of property may be compared to a bundle of sticks, each stick representing one of the legal rights attached to the concept. Often the complete bundle of legal rights is fragmented, with certain rights in a particular piece of property owned by one person or group and with other rights in the same property owned by other persons or groups. This fragmentation may be physical or temporal or both. For example, the owner of a building leases it to a tenant for a period of five years. We have little difficulty in identifying the "owner" of the property, yet the tenant has one of the legally enforceable rights in the property, that is, the right of complete possession and control—even to the exclusion of the owner in many instances—for a limited period of time. Another example: An owner gives his piece of land to one person for the duration of the life of that person, and thereafter to another. Each of the donees is, in a sense, an owner. The first in point of time is called the "life tenant"; the second, the "remainderman." A final example: An owner of land sells the right to any oil that may underlie the property, retaining for himself the ownership of the surface.

KINDS OF PROPERTY

While it seems prudent to employ specific categories to define different kinds of property for different kinds of legal purposes it ought to be noted forthrightly that the blending of legal and nonlegal conceptions often leads to ambiguity. Frequently there can be a rapid and fallacious shift from one meaning to another. Lawyers traditionally insist that property denotes a *right* over a determinate thing and Blackstone and Austin are summoned from the past as great exponents of early English jurisprudence to sustain this view. But even in the law these categories shade into one another with the result that distinctions are sometimes difficult to draw.

But there are also other differences. Property-in-a-thing and property-in-an-obligation are differentiated sharply by the manner in which the owner enjoys his property. The owner of a garden or of a horse enjoys his ownership without the aid of any other persons

---

[4] James Barr Ames, "The Disseisin of Chattels," in *Select Essays in Anglo-American Legal History* (Boston: Little, Brown & Co., 1909), Vol. III, p. 563.

and may be said to have a right *in rem;* in contrast, the only way the owner of an obligation can realize the fruits of his ownership is to compel performance by the obligor and the right is *in persona* and, consequently, less absolute or, at least, less individualistic.

Yet the categories into which property falls are useful guides to analysis despite the clear recognition that these categories shade into one another and, in some instances, the classifications are historical accidents. In countries with legal traditions deriving from Roman law (sometimes called "civil law"), which include most of the nations of Western Europe, property is divided into the categories of "movable" and "immovable." In "common-law" countries, which include most of the English-speaking community, a similar but not exactly analogous, distinction is drawn between "real property" and "personal property." It will be useful to consider these latter concepts more precisely.

REAL PROPERTY

Real property consists of ownership interests in land, in things under the surface of land, in things attached to the surface of land, and in the air space above land up to a usable height. The coming of the airplane did not mean that a jet flying over private land was an act of trespass. But it might have meant trespass if the ideas of property had not changed to adjust to newer realities. For it is known that Accursius, an Italian jurist living in the 13th century, stressed that the validity of one of the maxims in the Justinian code of Roman law was this: "whose is the soil, his is also to the sky." This principle may have been translated into English law because King Edward I invited Accursius' son to become a lecturer on law at Oxford University. But the Justinian reference was actually to the preservation of open sky over burial places and probably reflected the medieval faith in the resurrection of the body and its transfer to heaven.

It has frequently been asked what logic should be applied to property represented by air space. For mankind generally it may have been a long cherished hope that the upper air would be as free as the high seas and for the same reason, namely, that no one could control the sky or air effectively. Yet it is worth noting that when England was mistress of the seas she actually considered making a claim to the oceans, including the North and South Poles, during the 17th century. And even while American jurists admit freely that the old Accursian view that ownership "to the sky" could not be taken literally, they have been hard put to determine where "effective possession" begins and ends. Generally speaking the rule is that effective possession depends on such factors as location, surface use, and the nature of the surrounding area. One lawyer drew this distinction: Possession by a rancher whose animals could be alarmed by passing airplanes may be said to reach higher than that of a farmer or the owner of unimproved land. High buildings, or the presence of many persons, can make a difference, and as land use changes, possession may be found to move up and make trespass of previously harmless passage.[5]

What might be termed "subsurface" ownership has had an even more fascinating history than ownership rights over the terrain. Mining law has wrestled with two contradictory propositions. The first holds that minerals are an integral part of real property and are therefore controlled by the landowner; a second proposition insists that the public community always reserves a basic right to mineral resources and can, as a consequence, regulate exploitation. After the Glorious Revolution of 1688 in England, the power of the King was substantially curtailed and the power of the rising middle class who held property meant that the landowners were given great leeway in exploiting the country's coal resources, especially when dwindling forest reserves meant a necessity to find coke to replace charcoal for smelting.

The American tradition has been profoundly influenced by the British experiences. But the rush for profits can also lead to important changes in the law of property. Mine owners, when driving shafts below the surface, need not necessarily disturb their neighbors' property as they extract the coal. When pumping for oil, owners can drain a pool under another man's land—again without direct harm to the neighboring property. Here the concern is for the private owner. But whereas North America has been rather generous in allowing private owners to exploit subsurface resources, Latin American countries have tended to insist that subsoil resources are reserved to the state for the good of the general public.

Despite these areas where lawyers dispute on technical grounds over issues of national significance the average person worries more about such everyday property issues as those problems created by

---

[5] Jacob Weissman, *Law in a Business Society* (Englewood Cliffs, N.J.: Prentice-Hall, Inc., 1964), p. 54.

overhanging trees from a neighbor's yard or by eaves which obstruct the light and air of the owner. The generic terms for such rights is "easement," but to make the right meaningful, the aggrieved owner must show that a hurt is involved; and a hurt, to be actual, must be serious and justifiably upsetting to persons of normal sensitivities.

PERSONAL PROPERTY

Personal property includes all property not classified as real property. For convenience, it is divided into tangible and intangible personal property.

Tangible personal property. This consists of physical objects not affixed to real property. Thus, a lighting fixture is personal property until it is installed in a house; thereafter it is part of the real property. On the other hand, growing crops are real property until severed; thereafter they are personal property. Jewels, furniture, and *objets d'art* are examples of tangible personal property.

Intangible personal property. This consists of legal rights or claims, often evidenced by possession of a document or certificate of some sort. The most important form of personal property today is the corporate security, to be described more fully below. (It should be noted that not all intangible claims are treated as personal property. The claim to an interest in real property—that is, the claim of a remainderman to complete ownership of real estate following the death of a life tenant—is classified as real property, even though it is intangible.) The right to the exclusive use, for a limited time, of certain products of the human brain—patents, copyrights, and trademarks—is also an important form of intangible personal property.

Because intangible property is typically the form in which modern property is found, the law tends to stress in unique ways a definition of property *as that which society will allow as legitimate power over others.* An illustration serves effectively at this point. During the World War I, International News Service began to copy items from early editions of the Associated Press for telegraphic transmission to its own members across the country. When the Associated Press sought an injunction, the courts had to determine how to phrase the question of what constitutes private property.

The question might have been phrased in these terms: did the Associated Press develop an absolute property on uncopyrighted news because it had labored to get access to the information first and, as a consequence, had full control over its transmission? Or were newsworthy items part of the public domain and hence, public property? The Court argued that if the Associated Press had acquired, at a fairly substantial cost, something that might be sold fairly at a substantial profit, then a "competitor who is misappropriating it for the purpose of disposing of it to his own profit and to the disadvantage of the complainant cannot be heard to say that it is too fugitive or evanescent to be regarded as property. It has all the attributes of property necessary for determining that a misappropriation of it by a competitor is unfair competition because contrary to good conscience."[6] Yet two Justices, Holmes and Brandeis, entered strong dissents. Brandeis insisted that the product of the mind should not become private property simply because it cost the producer some money and labor. Granting property in news would, in his judgment, work against the public interest and against the free press.

On the basis of this case, however, newspapers later challenged radio stations which took items from early editions of the newspapers for radio news broadcast. The fact that the challenge was not pressed (because the Supreme Court dismissed the matter on jurisdictional grounds) means that the definition of property in this instance has not been sharpened but it may be presumed to follow the general outlines developed in the 1918 International News Service case.

Finally, there is one special form of intangible personal property that is almost peculiar to business operations. This asset, known as "goodwill," is defined as a value of business over and above the recorded costs of tangible and other intangible assets. Thorstein Veblen was one of the first to enlarge the definition of property and capital respectively from that of corporeal property to that of "expected earning" capacity. To him, goodwill comprised "such things as established customary business relations, reputation for upright dealing, franchises and privileges, trademarks, brands, patent rights, copyrights, exclusive use of special processes guarded by law and by secrecy, exclusive control of particular sources of materials. All of these items give a differential advantage to their owners but they are of no aggregate advantage to the community. They are wealth to the individuals concerned—differential wealth; but they make no part

---

6 Weissman, *op. cit.*, pp. 56–61.

of the wealth of nations."[7] It was this concept that led Irving Fischer to suggest that the businessman, in a sense, "owns his customers" because of this intangible property represented by good will.[8]

In 1896 the Supreme Court followed Veblen's suggestions (in the Adams Express Company case) to stress the role of goodwill and the concept of "expected earnings"; it is the buying and selling of this earning capacity which constitutes property that has little direct relationship to physical capital. John R. Commons declared that goodwill, though an intangible asset, is the most important property of modern business. Competition which breaks goodwill is "predatory" competition; hence the "live-and-let-live" policies, which look to the future security of the "going concern," become all important.

The concept of goodwill, as constructed by the courts, is grounded on the principle of scarcity, for its assumption is that opportunities are limited, margins are close, and therefore each competitor should endeavor to retain his present customers and his present portion of the trade. This has become one part of "business ethics" which holds that cut-rate prices are not even good for customers because the pricing priorities are ultimately disfunctional. And on another point Commons noted that although the future income of goodwill may be highly speculative, yet, in a transaction, its ownership as a present economic quantity "may be transferred at a pecuniary valuation involving expected sales, prices, interest, and a high degree of risk, and therefore a higher rate of discount. It may be deemed worth more by one party than by another yet, objectively, it is the same economic quantity, the modern meaning of capital as assets."[9]

PUBLIC ENCROACHMENTS ON THE PRIVATE CHARACTER OF OWNERSHIP

Just how private is private property? It is easy to demonstrate that property, especially that which is productive, has rarely if ever in our Western civilization been entirely free from the claims of the polity.

---

[7] John R. Commons, *Legal Foundations of Capitalism* (Madison: University of Wisconsin Press, 1957) , p. 168.

[8] *Ibid.*

[9] John Commons, *Institutional Economics* (Madison: University of Wisconsin Press, 1959) , Vol. I, p. 442. See also pp. 788–90.

HISTORICAL

In history the feudal period furnishes the clearest example. During the medieval period, the haphazard nature of ownership went through a metamorphosis. Gradually the theory developed that all land was ultimately owned by the sovereign, all possessors being merely tenants owing fealty and military or other service as a condition of their tenure. Lords who held land as a grant direct from the king were called "tenants-in-chief," and they, in turn, had power, for a time at least, to grant portions of their lands to subtenants on conditions of fealty and service to them. (The process was known as subinfeudation and was terminated by statute when it began to get out of hand.) The Norman conquest served as the basis for the imposition of this system of landownership over all England. The requisites of landholding—rendering personal military service, furnishing conscripts, paying rents, furnishing agricultural labor, and the like—can be compared to our modern taxes, since these things furnished the economic and military basis of the feudal polity. As such, they constituted a definite encroachment on the full freedom of private ownership: landholding without attendant duties.

Indeed one of the persistent characteristics of the entire medieval period (from the collapse of the Roman Empire in 476 A.D. to the 11th century) was an almost "communistic" tradition among the Fathers of the Church toward property. The one thing that had impressed the doctors, from Ambrose and Augustine to Peter Lombard, was the sharp inequality of property holding and its resultant moral consequences. Thus it came about that the theologians and the Romanists were often of the same opinion in seeing ownership as crucial to a just society. It is worth noting, however, that while the theologians stressed the communitarian aspects of property ownership the decretalists (those who dealt with Canon law as the primary law of the medieval world) practically ignored the traditional view.

In general the decretalists held that private ownership was not limited by any law of nature except clearly in case of famine when goods were to be put to the disposal of the entire community; otherwise private ownership could be allowed. Gradually, however, it became clear in the writings of masters like Alexander of Hales and Albert the Great that distinctions might be drawn between the law of nature and the implications of original sin for a fallen humanity. Experience dictates that private property must be established for the good of peace, order, and prosperity because sinful man would not be motivated by other forms of ownership. In this view private property became justified by the common law of nature and by, in a loose sense, a secondary natural law inspired by the requirements of an imperfect world.[10]

One clear example where Church teachings profoundly influenced the nature of ownership may be seen in its religious tenets on marriage. For centuries the formal act of marriage had been determined by local laws and customs, but toward the end of the 12th century the Papacy imposed the rule that simple consent created the marriage bond. Being insoluble and monogamous, the Christian marriage meant, for society, a series of stable and unified units for the economy. By favoring joint ownership for man and wife, and by its insistence on the dowry, the Church literally determined the economic basis of the household. It was family needs that became the norm for prices and the criteria for wage patterns. And in certain countries like Poland, large families meant a hastening of the division of property and thus contributed quite directly to a breaking up of the family group and even to a degree of individualism that seemed, in practice, to run counter to the ideal of family solidarity.

The rise of commerce and the consequent decay of the feudal system had already occurred by the time America was colonized. This explains why the complicated system of feudal land tenures was never incorporated into the American law of property. But the concepts and terminology of a system that lasted for some 600 years are not so lightly thrown off. They still influence property law today, as the reading of a modern real estate deed clearly demonstrates. It is interesting to note that the feudal system was based on the notion of separation of ownership from control and use of property. As pointed out by Harbrecht and Berle in *Toward the Paraproprietal Society*,[11] some striking parallels exist between the property concepts of the feudal era and those of today.

A further example of public encroachment on private ownership is represented by the sovereign power of eminent domain: the power of the state to take over the ownership of property for public pur-

---

[10] N. N. Postan, *et al.* (eds.), *The Cambridge Economic History of Europe* (Cambridge: Cambridge University Press, 1963), Vol. III, chap. 8.

[11] Paul P. Harbrecht, S.J., and Adolf A. Berle, Jr., *Toward the Paroproprietal Society* (New York: Twentieth Century Fund, 1959–60).

poses where necessary, a power happily coupled, at least since Magna Carta, with the concomitant duty to pay just and reasonable compensation for such taking. Another example of public encroachment on private ownership is represented by the ancient common law of "nuisance." Since early times a man's neighbors have had legal redress against antisocial uses of property. Our modern law of zoning is an outgrowth of this early concept.

CONTEMPORARY

While the landowner today no longer owes knight service to a lord and is under no obligation to plow the fields of his grantor, this does not mean that his ownership is freer than that of his feudal ancestor. Most people would agree that the "private" character of property is even more restricted today than in periods when the rendering of personal service was a condition of ownership. The most important restriction on full freedom of property rights today is, of course, the compulsion to pay taxes on both real and personal property or face eventual loss of ownership. In the United States the *ad valorem* tax on real property, and to a lesser extent on personal property, forms the primary basis for support of municipal government and its attendant social services.

But taxes are not the only encroachment on private property today. Governments impose restrictions on the use of property in order to realize the common aims of the polity. Thus municipal zoning regulations and building codes restrict the exercise of complete ownership rights. If property is used for economic gain, additional duties are imposed relating to occupancy, facilities, rents, and the like. In some areas desirable social policies, such as nondiscrimination against racial minorities, are tacked on to some types of residential property use. The same policy finds expression in the refusal of the polity to give effect to racial restrictions in deeds transferring property. Much of the property used in industrial production and in trade in the United States today is subject, by state or federal law, to the requirement of a nondiscriminatory hiring policy.

One of the major developments in this country during the past decade has been the emergence of government as a major source of property and wealth. This development has resulted in a dependence of more and more Americans on their relationship to the government. The nature of the government's largesse consists of income and benefits derived from the government under social security arrangements, unemployment compensation, aid to dependent children, veterans' benefits, and welfare systems. When it is recognized that, at the turn of this decade, total federal, state, and local social welfare expenditures were almost $58 billion, then inferences may be drawn on the great effect this form of public wealth has on individual property. When it is further realized that almost 10 million people now hold government jobs (and jobs represent the most substantial form of property which most individuals possess), it is again realized how important the transformations of the last decade have become. To these may be added the power of franchises, subsidies to industry, government ownership of public lands, and the nature of the services that governments provide. Charles Reich has made the following observations:

> The significance of government largesse is increased by certain underlying changes in the form of private wealth in the United States. Changes in the form of wealth are not remarkable in themselves; the forms are constantly changing and differ in every culture. But today more and more of our wealth takes the form of rights or status rather than of tangible goods. An individual's profession or occupation is a prime example. To many others, a job with a particular employer is the principal form of wealth. A profession or a job is frequently far more valuable than a house or a bank account, for a new house can be bought and a new bank account created, once a profession or job is secure.[12]

It becomes perfectly clear that the recipient of government largesse always feels the power of government and this is just as sure for the large university receiving research grants as it is for the individual receiving an unemployment check. The liberal who harkens back to the economic and philosophical tenets of nineteenth century liberalism finds these developments disheartening. There are others who hold that the coming of the "public interest state" is a necessary and inevitable development, and because property is not a natural right, but a deliberate construction by society, it is the function of the public-interest state to construct the necessary restraints over licensing boards, welfare workers, public health aides, insurance experts and the like, to the end that essential private ownership, as a bulwark of individual liberty, is preserved.

---

[12] Charles A. Reich, "The New Property," *Yale Law Journal*, Vol. LXXIII (April, 1964), p. 374.

PRIVATE PROPERTY AND THE OWNERSHIP OF THE MEANS OF PRODUCTION IN AN INDUSTRIAL SOCIETY

In ancient times the primary source of wealth was land. The needs of society for food, clothing, and shelter were directly satisfied by the production of the soil. Clothing and shelter were directly supplied by vegetable and animal products, timber, minerals, stone, and clay. Very little processing and an equally rudimentary system of distribution were sufficient to nourish man and beast.

With the growth of commerce and industry, however, there evolved a more complicated system of supplying needs of an organized society. The factory system, and the consequent need for a complicated distribution system, brought in its train the need for large aggregations of capital. The tools of production could no longer be supplied by the ownership of land or by ownership or control over human labor through slavery or serfdom.

Thus it came about that the owners of surplus wealth began to pool their funds in order to establish and maintain the more complicated ventures that an evolving society demanded. The legal means adopted for this end was the corporation, an artificial entity endowed with legal "life" by virtue of its capacity to sue and be sued in its corporate name and to take and hold ownership of real and personal property. Other forms of common ownership and management of capital aggregations were also devised, and some of these persist as partnership, limited partnership, and business trust, but none are so well adapted to the needs of an expanding capitalist industrial society as the business corporation.

At first, the suppliers of capital exercised management and control individually or jointly over the property acquired with pooled capital, and this, of course, is still characteristic of a very substantial number of small enterprises employing the partnership or the corporate form of organization. But as greater and greater capital aggregations became necessary, the supplier of capital gradually became less and less of an "owner" in the traditional sense of the term. More and more frequently he relinquished active management and control in return for a claim against the capital aggregation, a claim for a portion of its future fruits. Ownership interests were necessarily fragmented by the very size of the capital aggregation and the number of capital-suppliers. Owner management is obviously impossible when there are 2 million "owners" (as in the case of the American Telephone and Telegraph Company). Thus it came about that one of the most important items in the bundle of legal rights we call property—the right to manage and control the property—was lost, not through the fault of any person or group but through the practical exigencies of the evolving social mechanism. Professor Berle has stated that this change has rendered the concept of "property" meaningless; we now live, according to his view, under a system of power rather than a system of property, and in capitalist societies the holders of power are the managerial class.

This development has stimulated observers to remind us that in the economic sphere rights are now more clearly attached to men and not to things—something that has always been true in the political sphere. The result is that, from an economic point of view, society has passed from a private property system to a corporate power system. Again very significant social implications may be discerned. Historically private property meant the dispersion of power because it attached rights to material things which themselves are quantifiable and divisible. But the emergence of the financial corporation has brought control of wealth in concentrated large blocks.

There is a certain validity in comparing the current corporate system to the landed estates of medieval times because, quite clearly, the domain was the center of economic and political life in an agrarian society. Those who resided within the domain found no advantage in going outside the lands of their lords; trade was nonexistent and there was therefore, no such thing as profit since a man could not sell his produce even if his greater efficiency resulted in surplus production.

If there was, in the great domain, no such thing as production-for-profit it may be argued that the vast majority of Americans are also not engaged in production-for-profit; they are wage earners in a corporate domain. Even the managers regard themselves more as executives than proprietors and their personal interests are tied to corporate success and corporate survival—and far less to private profit as part of private property. Quite clearly the enterprise is measured increasingly by its capacity to meet the material needs of men. And this capacity depends heavily on the executives whose property, in a real sense, is his power. Therefore power attaches itself not to property but to the manager who controls property. And the manager can retain control over this property and, therefore, control in power relationships only so long as he performs his function effectively.[13]

PRIVATE PROPERTY AND THE CONCEPT OF OWNERSHIP AS APPLIED TO THE MODERN CORPORATION

As pointed out above, the modern industrial corporation presents a picture of fragmented ownership—some of the legal rights inherent in the ancient concept of private property are held by one group, and others of those rights are held by other groups. It will be helpful to examine the "ownership" of a corporation by looking at the various categories of capital-suppliers. Since the corporation owns the physical assets, the question must be faced: who owns the corporation?

COMMON STOCK

The capital-supplier who becomes a common stockholder has an interest that is closest to the older concepts of private property. This stems particularly from the fact that on liquidation common stockholders own all the assets left after paying off senior claims, as described below. More importantly, the common stockholder still has, at least technically, a voice in the control of the property through his right to vote in the election of the real managers, the board of directors. (While the possibility of nonvoting common stock exists, only a very small proportion of industrial assets is held by corporations with such stock.) In small corporations, the voting power of the common stockholder may be significant. Even in large corporations it can be important if the shareowner has a substantial proportion of the common stock.

But in most of today's large corporations one shareowner, although his investment may be substantial in number of dollars, cannot exercise much control through his own voting power alone. In such corporations, the board of directors is generally a self-perpetuating body. Occasionally, it is true, dissatisfaction with management can grow to such proportions that a successful grouping of dissident stockholders with sufficient voting power to oust the existing board of directors is possible. Despite newspaper publicity, how-

---

[13] Harbrecht and Berle, *op. cit.*, pp. 17–25.

ever, proxy contests are a rare occurrence and the efforts of the "corporate democrats" to induce share owners to exercise real power in the directing of corporate policy have resulted in more publicity than real accomplishment.

The common stockholder today is, by and large, a claim holder, having legal right to some of the fruits of the enterprise when, as, and if the directors agree that the tree is ripe for shaking. Instead of capital hiring management, as was originally the case, it is often said that today corporate management "hires" its equity capital as represented by its preferred and common stock. In the case of the common stockholders the consideration for hiring is a tacit understanding that a certain dividend rate will be maintained, assuming reasonable business prosperity, and a tacit assumption that the company will be so managed that the value of the stock will appreciate over the years.

PREFERRED STOCK

The capital supplier who becomes a preferred stockholder is likewise a "fragmentary" owner. His rights are set forth in that portion of the corporation's basic constitutional document—its charter or articles of incorporation—that creates and describes the preferred stock terms. Usually, the preferred stockholder relinquishes the right to vote so long as his dividends, the amount of which is prescribed, are paid. Thus, he is even less an owner in the traditional sense of that term than is the common stockholder. True, his dividends are paid before any dividends can be paid on the common stock, but in return for this "preference" he usually gives up his right to profits over and above his fixed dividend rate. On liquidation, his claim to the assets of the corporation has priority over that of the common stockholder, but when he has been returned his initial capital contribution, plus any "premium" specified in the charter, he has no further ownership interest. Furthermore, his capital may be returned by the corporation, whenever it is no longer necessary, by the simple "redemption" of his shares, unless the charter specifically provides that the preferred stock is "noncallable."

OTHER FORMS OF CAPITAL CONTRIBUTION

All other forms of capital contribution are generally classed together as loans. Traditionally, the lender has not been considered an owner in any sense; yet, when his claim is compared with that of the preferred stockholder, the differences, though legally significant, do not seem too great economically. The lender, like the stockholder, commits capital to an enterprise in return for some of its fruits and the future return of his capital. The fruits are called "interest" rather than "dividends," and the return of the capital is due on a fixed date instead of at the termination of the enterprise or at some indefinite time.

Loans may be secured or unsecured. In the case of secured loans, lenders have a legal claim, in case of default, against all those assets mortgaged to secure their loans. Unsecured loans, however, are not protected by a mortgage on all or any particular corporate property. Nevertheless, such a creditor may obtain a legal judgment for moneys due and then require that the corporate assets be sold to satisfy such judgment. Or he may push the corporation into a bankruptcy proceeding, in which all assets are sold and the proceeds paid to the various claim holders in order of the priority of their claims. Unsecured creditors, of course, receive nothing from specifically mortgaged assets unless there is something left over after the claim that those assets secure has been paid in full. But they do receive payment in full before anything is distributed to preferred of common stockholders in liquidation.

By such techniques the creditor group may become "owners" of the corporate assets. More important, their economic power in many cases enables them to obtain, by contract, a voice in the direction of the enterprise. To the extent that creditors obtain such a voice— commonly by having one of their number placed on the board of directors—they are exercising an ownership interest in the property.

FURTHER FRAGMENTATION OF OWNERSHIP: CLAIMS UPON CLAIMS

Fragmentation of ownership is carried even further when the formal owner, or claim holder, finds himself owning not a claim against a pooled aggregation of capital but merely a claim against a financial institution, which, in turn, owns claims against working capital aggregations. Such is the case of the "owner" who has an interest in a pension or profit-sharing trust, or has shares in an investment company or investment trust ("mutual fund"), or is an owner of an insurance policy, or is a beneficiary of a private trust. These modern forms of ownership must be briefly examined because of the large number of individuals who hold such claims and the very substantial capital aggregations that are managed by such entities.

TRUST

One of the earliest forms devised by the English common law for divorcing beneficial ownership from the management and control of property is the trust. It is still in wide use today. The device is simple, easy to comprehend, and easy to effectuate. The owner of property may, either during his life or by will, transfer legal or nominal ownership ("title") of real or personal property to one, called a trustee, with instructions to hold it for the benefit of another, called the beneficiary. The trustee is referred to as the legal owner; the beneficiary as the equitable owner, "equitable" because his rights were not recognized by the old law courts and relief had to be sought in the courts of equity or chancery, which had been created to adapt the rigors of old common-law rules as justice or "the king's conscience" demanded. The trustee's powers and duties are set forth in the deed or will that creates the trust. Generally, these documents authorize him to manage and control the property and often to sell all or any part of it and reinvest the proceeds. Instructions as to the termination of the trust and the delivery of the property, with legal ownership, to a beneficiary or back to the creator ("settlor") must also be set forth, for the law does not permit perpetual trusts (except in certain cases involving eleemosynary activities). Originally, trustees were individuals, but in modern times this fiduciary function has also been assumed by banks and other financial institutions. If the trust property consists of corporate securities, the beneficiary has merely a claim upon a claim upon physical assets. This mirror-like aspect of capital management can be multiplied if the trust property includes insurance policies or securities issued by financial institutions or investment companies.

Since the trust was the first device invented for the separation of control from beneficial ownership, it is not unusual to find legal writers and thinkers attempting to apply analogies from the well-defined principles of trust law to other situations involving the separation of ownership from control. Thus it is frequently said that a corporation's directors are "trustees" of its fund for the benefit of the shareholders. In a sense this is correct; yet it would be misleading to assume that judicial control over directors' acts is as strict as judicial control over trustees' acts.

PENSION AND PROFIT-SHARING TRUSTS

The convenience of the trust form has led to its use for a wide variety of purposes for which it was not originally intended. Chief among these is the use of the trust form (with a corporation rather than an individual as trustee) as a device for accumulating capital for the benefit of corporate employees until the termination of their employment. At the present time, the income tax laws of the United States and of many other capitalist countries tend to favor the creation of such trusts. Contributions to such trusts may be made by employers and employees. The employer's share is deductible on its corporate income tax return if the trust meets certain standards, the most important of which is that it must not discriminate in favor of the officer-director-shareholder group. Further, the income earned on the investments of such a trust escapes income tax. The widespread growth of pension trusts since the early 1940's has led to very substantial capital accumulations in this form. Thus, once again, the real owners are removed from the physical assets that their capital indirectly purchases by the interposition of trustees, usually financial institutions, which have the power of management. True, in some trusts some control powers are retained by a committee of beneficiaries, but this is more often a formality than a reality.

MUTUAL FUNDS

The divorce of management from beneficial ownership is dramatically illustrated by the rise and growth of mutual funds over the past generation. Whether the mutual fund takes the form of a special type of trust (the so-called Massachusetts trust) or the form of a corporation with activities limited to the holding of the securities of other companies (an "investment company") makes little difference. The end result is the same. An investor buys the securities of an institution that offers the service of pooling his funds with those of others and uses the aggregated capital for the purpose of buying and selling the securities of corporations according to some general plan. For this service the investor usually pays an "initiation fee" based on the amount of capital he contributes. In addition, the fund usually employs an outside proprietary company to manage it, in return for a salary or fee based on income earned by the fund or the value of assets managed. In the United States, mutual funds come under special tax rules, and investor protection is enhanced by state and federal regulation.

INSURANCE

Many persons find it hard to think of an insurance contract as property, largely because they think of it in its original connotation —a purchase of protection against a defined risk. While much insurance is still written on this basis, the more significant portion of the capital devoted to insurance contracts today represents an investment as well as a purchase of risk protection. Even pure risk-protection contracts represent investment to some extent if they are written by mutual insurance companies, since the profits of such companies belong to the policyholders who have voting rights (which, however, are rarely exercised). Except in the case of term insurance, the customary form of life-insurance contract today involves substantial investment features. Dividends are paid on policies, and the investor may borrow against the policy or even cash it in and receive back all or a portion of his capital investment. The accumulated capital representing investment in insurance contracts is another example of a significant breakdown in the older concept of property. Beneficial ownership is divorced from the management and control of the funds, which, in turn, are invested in claims against other capital aggregations.

CONCLUSION

What will happen to the concept of private property in the future? Great possibilities for interesting speculation are opened up by man's exploration of space. Who will own the moon and the planets when these celestial bodies are brought under the control of earth men? And who will own the pathways of space? It is safe to say that man will, in his usual fashion, attempt to adapt the old concepts of property to the new spheres of man's domain. Thus we may expect the law of space to use analogies from our law of terrestrial oceans, and the law of planets to be adapted from the law for newly discovered and hitherto unoccupied lands. But these interesting questions lie beyond the scope of this study.

A question of more immediate concern relates to the future of private property in Western society under present conditions of fragmented ownership. Will the large group of "passive recipient" shareholders (to use the Berle phrase) continue to grow, as more and more individuals accumulate income beyond their immediate needs and become investors? Will the managerial class continue to increase in prestige as it becomes clear that power to control property is more significant than the right to enjoy its fruits? Will access to this select group become restricted as more persons, freed from the burden of labor, seek substitute activity? And will the managers act with wisdom in apportioning the fruits of enterprise among the various groups having claims on those fruits—labor, customers, security holders, the managers themselves, and the general community? Must new methods for social control be devised to guide the managers? Or is it sufficient to suggest that those who are going to control property study to know themselves—that they may, by becoming good men, do good works with the power they will increasingly possess?

Varied answers may be given to the question, How shall management be controlled in the use of the enormous power inherent in the giant and growing capital aggregations of today? Some, viewing all power as dangerous, would employ decisive methods to curb it, to fragment it, or to balance it. Others would substitute state power for private power. The student should consider whether the situation now requires or may be expected to require new or different institutions and, if so, how these are to be achieved.

RECOMMENDED READING

BERLE, ADOLF A., JR. *Power without Property*. New York: Harcourt, Brace & Co., 1959.

——. *The Twentieth Century Capitalist Revolution*, pp. 29–32. New York: Harcourt, Brace & Co., 1954.

FREMANTLE, ANNE (ed.). *The Papal Encyclicals in Their Historical Context*, pp. 166–72. New York: New American Library, 1956.

HARBRECHT, PAUL P., S.J., and BERLE, ADOLF A., JR. *Toward the Paraproprietal Society*. New York: Twentieth Century Fund, 1959–60.

LABOUR PARTY (GREAT BRITAIN). *Industry and Society* (Labour Party Policy Pamphlet). London, 1957.

LOCKE, JOHN. *The Second Treatise of Civil Government*, chap. v. Reprint. Oxford: Basil Blackwell, 1946.

Pound, Roscoe. *Jurisprudence,* Vol. V, chap. xxx, esp., pp. 126–27 and 139–48. St. Paul: West Publishing Co., 1959.

Reich, Charles A. "The New Property," *Yale Law Journal,* Vol. LXXIII (April, 1964), pp. 733–87.

Russell, Bertrand R. *Why Men Fight,* chap. iv. New York: Century Co., 1917.

Titmuss, R. H. *The Irresponsible Society.* London: Fabian Society, 1960.

FURTHER READING

Arnold, Thurman. *The Folklore of Capitalism.* New Haven: Yale University Press, 1937. Reprinted in 1959 as a Yale Paperback.

Berle, Adolf A., and Means, Gardiner C. *The Modern Corporation and Private Property.* Rev. ed. New York: Harcourt, Brace & World, Inc., 1968.

Commons, John R. *Legal Foundations of Capitalism.* Madison: University of Wisconsin Press, 1957.

Goyder, George. *The Future of Private Enterprise.* Oxford: Basil Blackwell, 1951.

Lerner, Max (ed.). *The Portable Veblen.* New York: Viking Press, 1948.

Maine, Sir Henry. *Ancient Law.* Reprint. London: Everyman's Library, 1954. Originally published in London in 1861.

Tawney, R. H. *The Acquisitive Society.* New York: Harcourt, Brace & Co., 1948. Originally published in 1920.

Weissman, Jacob. *Law in a Business Society.* Englewood Cliffs, N.J.: Prentice-Hall, Inc., 1964.

9. Contract

"CONTRACT" is the term used to describe an agreement that has legal consequences. Clearly, trade and commerce could not flourish if freely made bargains were not generally carried out. One of the functions of the state, acting primarily through the judicial process, is to enforce such performance by ordering the promisor to fulfill his bargain on penalty of fine or imprisonment or by granting judgment against him for money damages when, without legal justification, he fails to perform. The compulsion of the state replaces the private use of force, which characterized less civilized times. A great writer on the law of contract, Sir Frederick Pollock, puts it as follows:

Enforcement of good faith in matters of bargain and promise is among the most important functions of legal justice. It might not be too much to say that, next after keeping the peace and securing property against violence and fraud so that business may be possible, it is the most important.[1]

---

[1] Sir Frederick Pollock, "Contract," in *Encyclopaedia Britannica* (1958 ed.), Vol. VI, p. 342.

It is perfectly evident when society accepts and abides by the "specialization of labor" concept it must create an exchange mechanism whereby a man who produces something efficiently can exchange it for a necessity that he himself would produce less efficiently than another. He gives in order to get—and in the "giving-getting" arrangement he enters into bargaining relationships with other producers and vendors. Normally these bargaining procedures occur with little or no formality, but when the object of the bargaining commands a high price or when the bargaining has long-range consequences, it is frequently protected by a formal contract.

There were hard and pragmatic reasons to encourage the refinement of the law of contract—perhaps the most important part of the law during the 19th century. The predominance of contract law occasioned two famous remarks—the first by Sir Henry Mane, who declared that the most distinctive feature of modern society was a movement from *status* to *contract,* and a second by the great legal historian, F. W. Maitland, who branded contract as the "greediest" of legal categories because it consumed so much time and energy of jurists and barristers. What was said of England may have been said of every major Western industrial nation because everywhere contract came to occupy the core of private law. Even public law was made to depend, as far as possible, on hypothetical agreement by parties to the political arrangement under the Social Contract theory.

It is not surprising that the very pragmatic English businessman encouraged his country to take the lead in the law of contract. The fact that English businessmen enjoyed a worldwide reputation for honesty led other European businessmen to respect the English code and to demonstrate a willingness to have contracts construed according to English law—often by arbitrators in the City of London. Perhaps the greatest tribute to the British system of contract law is the fact that Scotland (despite the Act of Union which insisted on the perpetuation of the traditional Scottish system of private law) never allowed national pride to keep it from sharing in the full fruits of English contract arrangements.

But the pragmatic basis for a law of contract—encouraging business and preventing violence—does not tell the whole story, as a glance at history will show. There is a moral basis for compelling a man to keep his promise. The value concepts of most people have from earliest times included two related norms: (*a*) deceit is wrongful and ought not to be practiced; (*b*) a man ought to do what he undertakes to do, especially when his given word induces another to take action or give a promise in reliance thereon. Yet these ideas have never achieved universal acceptance, nor have they ever become absolutes. Thus, it has often been accepted that deceit is justifiable when practiced upon an enemy in wartime, and there are numerous circumstances in which the fulfilment of promises gives way before other concepts of overall fairness.

The development of our ideas on contract thus reflects an interweaving of two strains—one purely practical and pragmatic in flavor; the other essentially moral or ethical.

HISTORICAL BACKGROUND OF CONTRACT

The use of the power of the state to enforce bargains was not easily realized. Despite advances in Roman law the early Romans hardly developed any general law of contract. They tended to think in terms of particular contract such as a partnership, a sale, or a hiring, and these contracts were limited in number. As a matter of fact, Roman law in the ancient world never accepted the tenet that any seriously intended pledge, however lacking in form, was binding.

It is not surprising that the Church—with its deepseated suspicions of the trader and with its profound concern for truth—should have taken a stricter view of contracts. For the Roman maxim of the *nudum pactum* (a simple understanding between parties is not a basis for claims) the medieval canonist substituted the opposite maxim. In canon law, therefore, it was argued that a man who does not carry out his promise is guilty of falsehood because a Christian's word must be kept whether he is under oath or not. And since the simple transfer of a commodity, unimproved by work, was viewed with suspicion by the moralist, who feared speculation, it followed that the Church sought to make certain that the contract was properly drawn up with due regard for the rights of others, and then rather strictly enforced. This is not to suggest that there were not basic principles in Greek and Roman traditions. The Nichomachean Ethics emphasized that parties to a contract must possess equal consideration under it and an equal desire to benefit from the exchange. One of the earlier rules of Diocletian declared that a sale could be cancelled if the agreed price turned out to be less than half the just or market price. Underlying the Aristotelian idea of fair contract was the concept of reciprocal services, and Albertus Magnus took this idea to mean that a builder should, for example, accept from a shoemaker a stock of footwear equivalent in value to the house he had built for that craftsman—rather than to establish some arbitrary price for his services which might enrich, without justification, one or other of the two parties. This affirmation of the equivalence of service leaves the problem of the *computation of values* unresolved.

The concept of *value* bothered the medievalist a great deal because fluctuations in the value of money made it difficult to determine the true justice of a contract and induced further difficulties to repair the consequences of wrongs. A decretal of Pope Alexander III allowed a vendor who received less than a just price the choice between cancelling the contract or receiving a supplement which would then reestablish the legality of the transaction.

The ecclesiastical courts, regarding broken pledges as sinful, could enforce fulfillment on penalty of excommunication. One exception must be stated: from earliest times the civil authority provided a remedy for unpaid debts. This exception, however, was not based on the theory of enforcing a good-faith promise but rather on an analogy to the unlawful detention of another's specific property.

Contract law, the younger discipline, takes its earliest analogies from its older sister, the law of property. In the same historical chain we find early the development of the obligation created by deed, recorded on parchment and sealed, which was given recognition in lay and religious courts alike. The promisor has, by deed, "conveyed" to the promisee a thing of value—the promise—of which the promisee has become owner; the courts must give recognition to that ownership by providing sanctions against its abuse.

As the secular political system grew in power and complexity, the secular courts began to consider matters formerly within the exclusive jurisdiction of the ecclesiastical courts. The concurrent growth of trade and industry soon made it clear that an important source of business, and resultant lucrative court fees, was being overlooked by the king's judges. It was in this context that the common law began to adapt its curious and seemingly rigid forms to provide access to litigations in commercial cases.

In making the extension, the judges turned for analogies to the law of torts, that is, private wrongs. The law already gave redress for deceit and for trespass. If a man undertakes to perform some act for another and does it incompetently or fraudulently, elements analogous to deceit and trespass appear. Later, the larger step was taken of admitting to the class of judicially cognizable wrongs the complete failure to perform what one had agreed to do. It seems clear that the new type of action, called "assumpsit," was based on analogy to tort rather than property law. The bargains sought to be enforced were simple, frequently oral, rather than written on parchment. They were sealed and couched in the scholarly phrases of conveyance, which betokened expensive clerical preparation. By slow extensions and modifications the common law eventually developed an entire scheme of contractual principles, stemming in large measure from tort analogies and, to a lesser extent, from property analogies.

Concerning the legal sanctions employed to enforce a promise, it should be pointed out that the judgment for money damages against the defaulter came first; it was only later that the more drastic remedy of a judicial decree requiring specific performance on pain of contempt of court was devised. The former remedy was granted by the law courts; the latter was the invention of equity—a supplementary judicial system, peculiar to common-law countries, growing out of the semireligious notion of the king's conscience.

CLASSICAL MODEL OF A CONTRACT—BASIC PRINCIPLES

The classic legal model of a contract presupposes two persons, reasonably equal in economic power, bargaining with each other. The initiator of the transaction proposes an *offer,* to which the other manifests acceptance. Acceptance must be complete and unqualified; any variance of the terms of the offer constitutes in effect a counteroffer, which the original offerer may accept or reject. This tennis-court procedure continues until there is mutual assent to the terms, and at that instant the legal rights and duties are fixed. Contrary to popular belief, not all contracts have to be in writing to be enforced, though, by statutory enactment of ancient lineage, certain types—for example, contracts for the purchase and sale of real estate—must be in writing bearing at least the signature of the person against whom enforcement is sought. Many unwritten but enforceable contracts are made without even an oral expression by one party. Thus, the purchaser at an auction is bound by the raising of his hand or any other agreed-upon or understood signal if the auctioneer closes the bids.

Each party to the bargain makes some commitment. In common-law countries, promises that are wholly gratuitous—that is, those not matched by some counterpromise (bilateral) or bargained-for act immediately performed (unilateral) have not historically been thought worthy of society's compulsive sanctions, except for promises embodied in formal sealed writings, as discussed above. In modern times a tendency to do away with this requirement of "valuable consideration" appears in contracts that contain a formal recitation that the party whose undertakings are recited acknowledges receipt of a token consideration in money, usually $1 or $10. The formal recital is like the seal in older form instruments—it merely means that the promisor really intends to subject himself to legal sanctions. Even in such situations, however, one generally does not have to look very far to find the essence of a truly two-sided bargain—each side assuming some commitment or other. The technical requirement of "consideration" for validation of contracts, and the numerous exceptions that courts have created to that general rule, have been the subject of much learned discourse, disclosing an interesting facet of "is" and "ought" in the law.

It is difficult to conclude from any survey of legal definitions of the term that one is more authoritative than another. Probably the most popular definition is the one offered by the American Law Institute which declares that a contract "is a promise or set of promises for the breach of which the law gives a remedy or for the performance of which the law in some way recognizes a duty." Whatever the definition, there are at least five fundamental notions involved in the making of a contract. These include: (1) *A mutual assent* of two or more (2) *competent parties,* in a (3) *form* required by law, supported by (4) a *valid consideration* and having a (5) a *valid purpose* and a *valid subject matter.*

LAISSEZ-FAIRE AND PATERNALISM IN CONTRACT ENFORCEMENT

This notion of two equally strong persons or entities exchanging promises that society, with even-handed justice, will enforce rigorously against either who defaults may have fit most cases in an earlier age. Indeed, contract law is often thought of as an essential pillar of the laissez-faire polity. The fact is that in this, no less than in other branches of law, laissez-faire has given way to paternalism, a term employed here generically to mean a public concern with certain values considered to be above tampering by contract. In a real sense, paternalism represents a return to a value judgment of long historic lineage, namely, that in a free society each individual must get his due and that contract provisions that improperly affect personal security, personal liberty, civil rights, or fair return on risk investment, or constitute an undue invasion of property, or a denial of just wages are not to be countenanced. Medieval scholars, like Bernardine of Siena and Antoninus, called this *commutative* justice, a notion that is at the basis of the law of quasi contracts. In 1862 Mark Hopkins expressed an American version of this view when he said that there were certain things a man cannot divest himself of by contract.

The state will grant or deny protection to contract only within certain limits—these being defined for each age in accordance with value judgments as to what is fair and right, as well as to what is the proper role of the state. A few examples will suffice to illustrate this point. To start with some simple cases: a man's promise exacted by force or the threat of force is voidable at his option; further, where fraud, deceit, or misrepresentation induce the undertaking, it will not be enforced. Contracts made by persons mentally incompetent or under a certain age are likewise generally voidable.

Voiding a contract becomes extremely technical at times. For example, it has been said that misrepresentation constitutes grounds for voiding a contract. But misrepresentation must be one of fact and not simply a statement of opinion or belief, or a prediction or a promise. If a seller declared that a buyer will make a certain profit, or that the land will produce a certain quantity of wheat, and these statements prove to be untrue the buyer has no recourse because the courts have traditionally held that this is simply a "sales pitch." But if the seller declares that he paid a certain amount of money for the property or that a third person had made a certain offer and these are untrue, then misrepresentation has occured.

Probably even more difficult is the problem of innocent misrepresentation. All societies admit that a party can sometimes make a mistake and therefore claim not to be bound, but it seems that only English law interpolates between fraud and mistake a third feature which is known as "innocent" misrepresentation. This is presumed to occur when one party has induced another party to enter into a contract by representing to him as true something which was false but which he did not know to be false at the time he made the statement. If the contract is voided, it does not give damages to the other party who is also innocent as it would have done had the representation been fraudulent. The doctrine of rescission for innocent misrepresentation is unknown in continental systems of law. The result tends to be that continental law is more lenient than English law to a party who says: "I am entitled to be released from an obligation because I acted under a mistake." English law is typically not very hospitable to such a plea because the law dislikes dealing with mistakes as such. Therefore the English, quite pragmatically, look at the results of the mistake rather than the mistake itself.

Problems relating to a "meeting of the minds," which is at the heart of the contractual arrangement, are invariably difficult for the courts to handle. It means that when differences reach the court the tendency will be to examine the objective evidence and not to give primary attention to subjective impressions of one or more of the contracting parties. Therefore a mistake in one's expression of assent may not lead to a binding contract if the other party should have known it was a mistake. But if the objective references are rather explicit and clear, the law will hold that the contract can bind both parties even when both acted on the basis of mistaken private judgments. This will occur even if both can prove, on the basis of third-party testimony, that their true subjective impressions were different than those recorded in the contract.

Lest these be thought too obvious even to merit mention in a civilized society, we proceed a step further. Contracts that offend against established norms of business behavior, prescribed by judges or legislatures, cannot come under the state's protection. Thus, many business promises that violate governmentally prescribed trade policy are voided under the antitrust laws. Interest on loans above the permissible rate may not be collected. Other contracts may be denied legal protection for contravening even less well-defined norms of the polity. In many states betting contracts may not be enforced, on grounds that they contravene "public policy." Likewise, bargains in violation of public or fiduciary duty, such as those involving bribes, are unenforceable.

Yet the foregoing examples do not set the limits of paternalism.

Bargained-for promises are frequently denied legal sanction on the vague ground of "impossibility" or "frustration of the adventure." These technical terms merely mean that the circumstances contemplated by the parties or the premises on which their agreement was based did not exist or did not ensue. Thus the intervention of war, natural calamity, or "act of God" often excuses nonperformance despite the failure of the parties to provide appropriate escape clauses. In most such instances the refusal of society to enforce performance is cloaked in language that seeks to convey the impression that the court's interpretations are filling the gaps that imperfect foresight omitted. Actually, what is being prescribed is a social judgment of fairness, though this will generally yield to express language in the contract providing for the rights of the parties in case the unexpected event occurs.

There is another phenomenon that requires comment. It has been assumed that the contract is really the law tool of the businessman, yet when there are violations of contract, the businessmen themselves behave rather differently than might be presumed. In ordinary business life, contract remedies are not pursued when a breach occurs; more frequently the claims are settled outside of court. Why businessmen are somewhat loathe to engage in lawsuits may be due to the fact that lawsuits are expensive. But there is a more subtle reason. Under the ideal conditions of a market (where one is a price-taker and not a price-maker) it should be presumed that a businessman would sue when a promise is broken on the theory that his competitor would not refuse to do business with him in the future if the price were right. But actually there is a feeling of "relationships" and that one's place in the market system may mean something much more than a formal agreement which is breached.

One theorist has suggested that instead of relationships in the market one should forthrightly consider using the word "status" when dealing with oligopolistic firms. The sense of status resides in "the mutual awareness of the few who are on one side that their actions affect each other and this awareness need not have resulted in any way from intent of the parties. . . ." If the firm's status vis à vis its fellow oligopolists determines its business personality, with behavior and expression of awareness of mutual relationships rather than individual will, it is difficult to avoid feeling that position rather than private intention is on trial.[2] In essence we are being

---

[2] Jacob Weissman, "Is Oligopoly Illegal?" *The Journal of Economics*, Vol. LXXIV (1960) , pp. 437–63.

summoned to consider whether society has reversed Sir Henry Maine's maxim so that we are moving from contract back to status. The elements of property relationships (described in the previous chapter as characteristic of a paraproprietal society), and the transformation of the business world from bargaining arrangements between individuals to bargaining arrangements among collectivities, suggests that the invitation is not too far-fetched.

Finally, we come to the most thoroughgoing breach in the wall of laissez-faire. In cases in which bargaining power is customarily and seriously disproportionate, positive rules of conduct may be prescribed legislatively or administratively with legislative authority. One example is the insurance contract—where inequality of bargaining power is manifest. The contract is printed on the insurance company's form, and there is obviously no chance to bargain about its terms. Such printed-form contracts—sometimes called "contracts of adhesion"—must often be approved by an administrative agency of the government as a precondition of business use. Another example is the contract of a public utility with a consumer. Here the consumer often does not even know all the terms of the contract, since the document he signs may merely refer to terms, rates, or tariffs filed with the administrative body. Even in situations for which the legislature has not provided specific regulation, contracts of adhesion may find tough sledding in the courts, which may interpret them strictly, insofar as intelligent semantics will permit, against the stronger party who prescribes the form. The standard forms of leases of real estate, usually prescribed by local associations of landlords or their agents, are examples of such contracts.

LATTER-DAY EXTENSIONS OF THE CONTRACT IDEA

Two very special types of contract deserve mention because of their importance in business life today—the contract between a corporation and the government and the contract between a corporation and a labor union. These two types of contractual instruments are chosen because they illustrate an extension of the ancient principles of contract law to a point where we may be witnessing the birth of an entirely new concept of business relationships. The government can and does make contracts that fit the classical model. But of far greater importance are large-scale and long-term contracts involving defense matters. Frequently these are cost-reimbursement contracts, in which the government agrees to pay the contractor his cost of performing the contract plus a fixed fee representing profits. Because of the extreme complexity of many of these contracts and the difficulty of determining allowable costs and proper performance, the contracts themselves might better be considered as compacts establishing a form of *continuing* government-business relationship limited to the particular transaction. Such compacts require skillful negotiation right through the period of performance.

Government contract officers are usually on the job throughout the period to make the countless administrative determinations necessary to the fixing of the reimbursable items and standards of performance. And after it is all over, government frequently gets one more look at the contractor's results and (through what is called "renegotiation" but may be in fact confiscation) can take away what is thought to exceed fair profit. True, renegotiation proceeds according to statutorily and administratively prescribed standards which are intended to protect, albeit imperfectly, against arbitrary judgments. The point, however, is that one of the contracting parties has the advantage of hindsight. Surely this is far removed from the old notions of laissez-faire.

The evolution of the contemporary contract from a single exchange of promise and performance, subject to judicial enforcement, into a prescription of norms of conduct in a continuous business relationship is nowhere more striking than in the field of labor relations. It may be appropriate to point up here the strange history of freedom of contract in the labor field. The real growth of this concept began in 1877. For over 30 years the established legal principle had followed an earlier 1842 case, *Commonwealth* v. *Hunt,* which held that groups of workers could do lawfully what one man could do lawfully, even if the objective was a closed shop. This position was abandoned during the first American nationwide strike by railway workers in 1877, when Justice Thomas Drummond of the United States Circuit Court declared that strikers could not legally prevent other workers from laboring at any wage they were willing to accept. Drummond's logic was impeccable if we grant his premise that social welfare depends upon free competition among individuals. Once this is admitted, then it follows that, if a union prevents a man from making a contract to work, such restraints deny the worker a natural and inalienable right.

Out of this embattled period came the use of injunctions in dealing with labor crises, with illustrations of its dramatic effectiveness coming during the Pullman strike of 1894. Perhaps the most grandiloquent statement of the then prevailing legal theory came from Justice David J. Brewer, who, in an address to the New York Bar Association in 1893, declared that freedom of contract was a right as essential as life, liberty, and pursuit of happiness. The Court "simply nails the Declaration of Independence, like Luther's theses against indulgences, on the doors of the Wittenberg church of human rights and dares the anarchist, the socialist and every other assassin of liberty to blot out a single word."

It took time and tears and suffering to effect a transformation of a theory that—so conformable with the idea of rugged individualism and so translucent in overly simplified logic—used freedom of contract to deny workers a place in the economic sun. Today, labor compacts are negotiated by employer and union representatives, frequently in the full glare of national publicity. These documents, generally called contracts and couched in traditional contractual terms, in fact bear little resemblance to the classical model described above. The traditional public sanctions, injunction or judgment for money damages, are rarely invoked; indeed, the former is considerably limited by statute. Further, traditional freedom of contract is carefully circumscribed by laws preventing the exploitation of the workingman by dominant economic power.

More recently, with the growth of the economic power of labor unions, the government's role has shifted. Rather than holding the scales more equal for the benefit of labor and to prevent exploitation, government is viewed as asserting a third interest standing between, and above, two equally powerful disputants—management and labor. Government's role is to assert the claims of the general public for protection from unnecessary and irresponsible work stoppages, the degree of interference usually bearing close relation to the degree of incipient harm to the public. The legislative, administrative, and judicial tools fashioned to help insure industrial peace, imperfect as they are, furnish a notable example of the practical functioning of a pluralistic and essentially democratic order.

CONTRACT AND FUTURE BUSINESS THEORY

The analysis of contract from the classical models (conceived mainly in terms of rights by private persons) to current extensions as understood primarily in terms of resolving intergroup relations (government, corporations, union) suggests trends that invite interesting speculation. Present economic theory is largely concerned with models and mathematical formulas to measure efficiency of production; this task, by no means easy, is nonetheless more easily susceptible to objective statement than are observations regarding contract or equity, which involve ethical norms and one's own sense of values.[3] Yet contract does involve a history of values. Democratic society traditionally has held contract in higher regard than status. Good brains and willing brawn are more necessary to it than are noble birth and blue blood!

Yet we forget that the price for freedom of contract for western Europe had been the loss of group solidarity. In the sixteenth century the independent movement of detached laborers, cut off from feudal rights and duties and independent of even the nation-state, constituted a visible sign of the growing sense of the "separability" of the individual in carving his destiny. This worker was the first manifestation of the displaced person, the stateless man—but he was *voluntarily* displaced. He roamed where he would to seek gain and fortune. Since it was an act of his own will, it was obvious that the individual man felt that there were greater gains and greater values in mobility, in a right to bargain freely in the competitive market, than under the fixed prescriptions of feudal law. Yet often enough he sold his liberty and ability on such hard terms that his final lot was little better than the serf's.

The gains obviously carried enormous risks. Even under a natural-rights philosophy of contract as an essential element of freedom, court interpretations were used in 19th-century America, as we have seen, to deny workers an effective voice in their own destinies. Conversely, on the eve of the Civil War, the implications for contract in the Dartmouth College case (1819) were being used to protect the private corporation from intervention by the states.

The lesson seems reasonably clear from the record. In an industrial milieu where the factory system imposes both a discipline and an interdependence on goods and men, and in a work society characterized by functional specialization and division of labor, the effective use of contract in an individual person's sense is soon frustrated. Freedom to contract can become more illusory than real. When this situation develops, contract becomes largely the technique of group manipulation and use. Professional managements speak for the

---

[3] Tibor Scitovsky, *Welfare and Competition* (London: G. Allen and Unwin, 1952), p. 69.

large corporation, and professional labor leaders speak for workers; the contract thus arrived at becomes a contribution to a code of administrative behavior by which the individual's personal right to contract is considerably diminished. As a working proposition, then, it may be safely asserted that contract is meaningful today more in terms of its use by organizations and less in terms of its use by individuals. Contract law must therefore be analyzed in terms of large associations.

If the foregoing hypothesis has validity, it follows that a more sophisticated theory of bargaining is needed in social science. Existing models of economic theory tell us precious little about the bargaining process that goes on among business firms like Du Pont and General Motors, or between United States Steel and the United Steel Workers. In economic theory the traditional dependence has been on Edgeworth's model of bilateral monopoly in which only a single trading area is delimited, with no further restrictions of the outcome; there is little said in traditional theory about "pure" bargaining situations in which the outcome depends completely on interactions among only a few individuals. And even in the Edgeworth model, the solution is said to depend upon the bargaining abilities of individuals which is a vague concept more amenable to study by the psychologist than by the economist.

Some time ago an imaginative beginning on this problem was undertaken by J. F. Nash. But what he believed to be a positive theory—that is, the description of *actual* bargaining outcomes—has more recently been given a normative interpretation so that the solution has been taken as the *desirable* outcome of a bargaining process.[4] Subsequent efforts have attempted to provide analysis of the actual process involved in bargaining (disagreement-concession-agreement) and there is no doubt that the lack of interest in the theory of bargaining is being offset.[5]

Because ours is a bargaining society it might appear that the political scientist would have more careful formulations to offer. Yet Robert Dahl has argued that "political scientists have never produced a general theory of bargaining"; if this is true—and we would put some strictures on the generalization—it can be only because the manner in which contracts are arrived at have not been systemati-

---

[4] J. F. Nash, "The Bargaining Problem," *Econometrica*, Vol. XVII (April, 1950), pp. 155–62.

[5] John G. Kross, "A Theory of the Bargaining Process," *The American Economic Review*, Vol. LV (March, 1965), pp. 67–94.

cally explored.[6] Since diplomacy and treaty making are little more than contract development at the international level out of which a theory of group bargaining might be constructed, diplomatic history should have much to teach. Certainly many of the variables can be identified. Bargaining involves weighing alternative opportunities, calculation of risks, ability to extract some gains from the negotiations, and rough balance in powers. In the business setting, this area of freedom to contract is constricted by monopoly and oligopoly, which upset the balance of power postulated in the classical model. The second hypothesis, then, flows naturally from the first: contract is meaningful only as a theory of bargaining is developed to explain adequately maneuverings among groups to regularize their market positions and their positions in industry and in economy.[7]

Finally, there is need for systematic investigation of the use of contracting-out devices by industry itself in America. This involves the burgeoning practice of farming out work, normally done by workers within a given industry, to outside groups in order to cut costs. The 1960 Pennsylvania Railway strike dramatized the seriousness of this issue. Again the issue of contract becomes enmeshed in the decision-making and bargaining techniques of representatives of property for entering into contracts that affect large groups of individuals, in this instance, stockholders and workers. There have been some sketchy explorations, but the field is only now beginning to reveal its potential.[8]

CONCLUSION

The extension of the contract idea and the broadening of the concept, as exemplified above, must be thought of as a part of free society's attempt to devise new institutions and methods for the harmonious adjustment of competing claims in an economic order

---

[6] Robert Dahl, Mason Haire, and Paul Lazarsfeld, *Social Science Research on Business: Product and Potential* (New York: Columbia University Press, 1959) , p. 15.

[7] The neoliberal movement in Germany today is much concerned with this theory of constitutionally guaranteed freedom of private property, opportunity for enterprises and labor, and freedom for contract freed of monopoly. See Henry Oliver's revealing studies, "German Neoliberalism," *Quarterly Journal of Economics*, Vol. LXXIV (February, 1960) , pp. 117–49, and "Order and Coercion: A Logical Critique" *Southern Economic Journal*, Vol. XXVII (October, 1960) , pp. 81–92. Oliver is highly critical of neoliberal theory as currently expounded by men like Walter Eucken and Franz Boehm, of the Freiburg School, and Wilhelm Roepke and Gunther Schmoelders, among the non-German groups.

[8] Margaret Chandler and Leonard Sayles, *Contracting Out* (New York: Columbia University Graduate School of Business, 1959) .

entirely different from that of preceding centuries. Older models may furnish a starting point, but the creative imagination must be prepared to build new structures on traditional foundations. This task, thrust upon mankind near the beginning of the current century, presents to contemporary thinkers in the field of business a continuing intellectual challenge of exciting proportions. The development of appropriate responses affects not merely business profits but the entire economic and political structure of democratic society.

Contract now involves large groups which arrange contracts through bargaining processes that result in open covenants openly arrived at; at other times the agreements are rarely made known to the public at large and are announced even to stockholder constituents after the contract has been signed. Impersonality, gigantic size, and impact on others not privy to the bargainings are some of the characteristics of contract in modern business society. Students of contract today face what theorists long ago wrestled with in terms of ruler and citizen relationships. Molina and Suarez, for example, considered this political bond to be "in the nature of a quasi contract," in which the common interest was the determining factor.[9] Hobbes, Locke, and Rousseau struggled with the same problem in their different versions of the social-contract theory. Practically, then, scholars are being driven to reexamine political theory to seek relevance for contract in a modern business order.

Yet the construction of new theory must take into account the symbols by which a free society lives. As Walter Bagehot reminded us a century ago, an effective social order has two parts: the efficient part, which makes policy and administers and governs under that policy, and the ritualistic or theatrical part, which symbolizes common ideals and values. The new approach to contract will necessarily be more impersonal than the old, and it is likely that conservative tradition in America (with its abiding concern for personal and individual freedom of contract) will be affronted by the newer guises under which it operates. It means that contract and liberty will be looked at more and more in a business setting; that government itself will be viewed as a business operation. Historically, we may be witnessing a shift in emphasis, by which contract is used less to buttress commutative justice and more to underpin social justice and industrial efficiency.

---

[9] John Laures, *The Political Economy of Juan de Mariana* (New York: Fordham University Press, 1928), p. 185.

RECOMMENDED READING

COPPOLA, ANDREW and KATZ, HARRY. *The Law of Business Contracts.* (New York: John Wiley & Sons, 1963.

DICKINSON, JOHN. "New Conceptions of Contract in Labor Relations," *Columbia Law Review,* Vol. XLIII (July, 1943) , pp. 688–704.

KESSLER, FRIEDRICH. "Contracts of Adhesion: Some Thoughts about Freedom of Contract," *Columbia Law Review,* Vol. XLIII (July, 1943) , pp. 629–42.

LENHOFF, ARTHUR. "The Scope of Compulsory Contracts Proper," *Columbia Law Review,* Vol. XLIII (July, 1943) , pp. 586–602.

LLEWELLYN, K. N. "On the Complexity of Consideration: A Foreword," *Columbia Law Review,* Vol. XLI (May, 1941) , pp. 779–82.

————. "Common-Law Reform of Consideration: Are There Measures?" *ibid.,* pp. 863–76.

POLLOCK, SIR FREDERICK. "Contract" (supplemented as to U.S. law by K. N. LLEWELLYN) , *Encyclopaedia Britannica* (1959 ed.) , Vol. VI, pp. 339–45.

POUND, ROSCOE. "Promised Advantages," *Jurisprudence,* Vol. III, pp. 162–64. St. Paul: West Publishing Co., 1959.

————. "Obligation," *ibid.,* Vol. V, p. 199.

RADIN, MAX. "Contract Obligation and Human Will," *Columbia Law Review,* Vol. XLIII (July, 1943) , pp. 575–85.

FURTHER READING

ANSON, SIR WILLIAM. *Principles of the English Law of Contract.* (Oxford: Clarendon Press, 1964) .

FULLER, L. L. "Consideration and Form," *Columbia Law Review,* Vol. XLI (May, 1941) , pp. 799–824.

HALE, R. L. "Bargaining, Duress, and Economic Liberty," *Columbia Law Review,* Vol. XLIII (July, 1943) , pp. 603–28.

HAMILTON, WALTON. "Property According to Locke," *Yale Law Journal,* Vol. XLI (April, 1932) , pp. 872–80.

LAWSON, F. H. *The Rational Strength of English Law.* London: Stevens & Sons, Ltd., 1951.

LLEWELLYN, K. N. "What Price Contract? Essay in Perspective," *Yale Law Journal,* Vol. XL (March, 1931) , pp. 704–51.

SHARP, M. P. "Pacta sunt servanda," *Columbia Law Review,* Vol. XLI (May, 1941) , pp. 783–98.

10. Work

EXPLICIT in Locke's formulation of private property is the notion that man owns himself. But a homelier maxim also reminds man that he operates on "borrowed time," and that each moment consumed is gone forever. Of the many characteristics of "time" probably none more impresses the average person than the elements of "loan" and of "destructiveness." Lucretius spoke of the first quality when he said that "no single thing survives, but all things flow," so that even the greatest objects—planets and stars, sands and seas—are ephemeral. And Leonardo da Vinci spoke to the destructive force of time when he said, "Oh time, thou that consumest all things!"

How society *views* and how individuals *use* time tell much about the quality of a given culture. We are reminded of Thoreau's observation in his *Journal*. He wrote:

What are three-score years and ten hurriedly and coarsely lived to moments of divine leisure, in which your life is concomitant with the life of the universe. We live too fast and too coarsely, just as we eat too fast and do not know the divine flavor of our food. We consult our will and our

265

expectation of men, not our genius. I can impose upon myself tasks which will crush me for life and prevent all expansion.

If the man who does not betake himself at once to sawing is called a loafer, though he may be knocking at the doors of heaven all the while, which shall surely be open to him . . . what infinite leisure requires, as of a life time, to appreciate a single phenomenon!

We know that roughly one third of an individual's life is given to sleeping, another third to working and eating, and another third to leisure. And it may well be the final third that distinguishes man most precisely from all other living things and inspires Thoreau to his preferences. But in a work-oriented culture like that of the United States, the importance of the time spent in laboring is often viewed as of primary importance, and the nature of an individual's work is intimately related to his career which, in turn, indicates what he intends to do with his life. Jacques Barzun noted that a career used to be "a single continuous curve, shaped largely by the performer himself in answering to some ambition, which was said and felt to be overmastering. A clerk plodding along from birth to death was not simply having a career." But he observes further that now, by virtue of the democratic process and with the collectivization of our activities, it is commonly thought that everybody can have a career, should have a career, and that the career ought to be planned.[1]

If we agree with Professor Barzun's definition of work as something that "engages the heart and the mind as well as the hand, something that involves the surmounting of difficulties for results that are deemed important by the worker," then we note the presence of multiple careers and the possible absence of work in modern life.

This sense of mastery over the condition of one's work activities has always been in tension with the imperative of survival. And it was the second quality of work that led Adam Smith to observe that in the kingdom of the living it is only man who, "grown to maturity, still has deep needs for the assistance of other living creatures. That help comes not from the benevolence of others only, but from their desires to secure what others produce." In a well-remembered statement, Adam Smith further declared:

Give me that which I want, and you shall have this which you shall want, is the meaning of every such [bargain] or offer; and it is in this

[1] Jacques Barzun, "Address to 39th Annual Conference of Eastern College Personnel Officers" October 4, 1965. Mimeographed.

manner that we obtain from one another the far greater part of those good offices which we stand in need of. It is not from the benevolence of the butcher, the brewer, or the baker, that we expect our dinner, but from their regard to their own interest. We address ourselves, not to their humanity, but to their self-love and never talk to them of our own necessities but of their advantages. Nobody but a beggar chooses to depend chiefly upon the benevolence of his fellow citizens.[2]

It might be noted that Smith, by employing the word "labor" in preference to the term "work," was speaking in a contemporary idiom. The evolution of the terms tells a great deal about the evolution of society. The Greeks distinguished between servile (manual) labor and the pursuit of liberal arts, so that only the former was considered to be "labor." Medievalists expanded this idea, and St. Thomas urges readers to remember that the human hand is an organ *par excellence* and that ordinary labor is done with the hands. In our time almost every activity is called labor because it has been brought into the job market.

But questions remain: Is a work of necessity different than a labor of love? Is the latter a form of work or leisure? Quite obviously people speak of work in diverse tongues: to some it is debasing and to others ennobling; for some it is a prized endeavor, to others it is to be avoided at all costs; to some work is what you are paid for, while still others insist it is the stuff of life. Despite differences, it is nevertheless true that work holds a high place in the value system of Western industrialized societies; the United States, through the Full Employment Act of 1946, affirmed as national policy the individual's right to work.

THE IDEA OF WORK

Work involves time and energy. So far as time is concerned, preoccupation with it as a concept worthy of serious study is relatively new to philosophy. Medievalists wrote rarely about the concept of history, whereas modern philosophers continually discuss it. Hegel's philosophy is one of dialectical materialism. Heidegger's masterpiece is called *Being and Time,* and in Sartre's *Being and Nothingness,* one of the crucial chapters concerns temporality. Why this new interest is a legitimate question. One theory holds that the

---

[2] Adam Smith, *The Wealth of Nations* (ed. Edwin Cannan) (New York: The Modern Library, 1937), p. 14.

contemporary attitude toward history and time is due to the fact that man's own labor has induced such rapid change that one must be constantly concerned with the implications thereof. The average man today experiences more within a single life time than was ever before possible. In the 13th century when a man reached three-score and ten he could look back at a world that was basically the same as the world of his childhood. The point need not be belabored that an analogous situation no longer prevails. Modern philosophy sees man as a being who actualizes himself and this process of actualization means the use of energy in time for productive purposes.

The distinctions once made between labor and leisure are becoming increasingly blurred. One philosopher, Merleau-Ponty, said that today we call almost everything labor because labor is itself an essential part of the creative process. There is, in fact, a substantial change in the reality within which we deal and this has brought—and is continuing to bring—a change of attitudes and of definitions. For example, Plato found the idea of teachers accepting money thoroughly distasteful and indicted those who would sell science; in our world it is normal for the professor to be paid. In times past charitable activities were motivated by love of man and performed without compensation. Caring for the sick and the insane, the nursing of orphans and the aged, the teaching of poor children, were forms of charitable work that led to the formation of many religious societies. Today these functions are often performed within the world of labor. The very term, "social worker," indicates the distance we have travelled!

Ideas of work have had, therefore, a peculiar history of their own. In the ancient world the Greeks accepted Aristotle's maxim that "no man can practice virtue while living the life of a mechanic or laborer."[3] Work attracted the *specialist* whereas the good life was the ideal of the *amateur,* the all-around man with gentlemanly taste and catholic interests. Indeed, as one examines the ideals of the *agon* it is quite obvious that fifth-century Athens catered to a world dominated by an aristocratic minority. The blacksmith who developed his muscles offended the Appolian ideals; the farmer, bent over his crop, had no chance to contemplate the glories of the heavens; and the merchant, vending his wares, engaged in haggling with his neighbor that made participation in activities related to the public good impossible. But this was more the Greek ideal than the Greek reality

---

[3] *Politics*, Book III, chap. 5.

and even then the ideal was possible only on the basis of a slave economy.

It is worth noting, however, that the Greeks attached as much importance to competition as we do, but they ruled it out as an ideal for the world of business. The Homeric ideal glorified only the winner: in the championship games there were no second or third prizes and no team scores. Thus it came about that there was almost a frenetic competitiveness in all activities that constituted the life of the Greek country gentleman—in arts and letters as well as sports. The Greeks word for work was "ponos" which connoted the sorrows and burdens that fell upon man because of, according to Homer, the hatred borne by the pagan gods towards mankind.

This notion of work as curse and burden was also reflected in the early Hebrew tradition and found its rationale in the doctrine of original sin. According to this view, man was required to undergo the pain of work to expiate for his sins and in order to regain his lost spirituality. But the Hebrews also introduced a positive element because they insisted that work was a means of establishing the kingdom of God on earth. No labor, however lowly, was as reprehensible as sloth, and even the rabbis themselves were supposed to follow some trade or work.

Christians shared the Hebrew view that idleness was far more deplorable than even the most demeaning work. While the early Fathers were concerned lest men use work as a means toward unnecessary wealth, work as an instrument for charity was highly praised. It was in this context that St. Augustus approved farming, handicraft, and small-scale commerce. Because of the diversity of economic needs within different countries it is difficult to speak with certainty on how important theory was to active practice. Certainly in the medieval economy the teachings of the Church played a very considerable role in the way society was ordered.

The Medieval Work Ethic

Up to the 11th century, social differentiation within the ecclesiastical order was a powerful factor on work attitudes because the Church had been divided sharply into clergy and laymen, with monks and nuns belonging to a special category. The clergy controlled a growing proportion of the wealth of medieval society and, according to strict doctrine, were expected to abstain from all worldly business—not merely from menial labor but also from anything which would take them from the service of God. On the other hand, the clergy were also required to manage their benefices in ways that would return a profit to the particular religious unit. Within the clergy, however, were gradations running from the extremely rich to the extremely poor, so that, as an illustration, while the Bishop of Lincoln owned a very large estate, many chaplains in his diocese were on short rations.

Occupying another key role in the social structure were the nobles. In the specification of forbidden occupations the most vehemently condemned were the manual arts, followed quickly by the notarial profession. Indeed, the attitude toward notaries invites critical attention to the theories of "professions." In medieval times some of them were very honorable, some tolerated, and some suspect. But there were often sharp differences between the canonist and the civil lawyers regarding the repute and value that should be attached the various professions. In one of the statutes of the diocese of Arras around 1275, fullers, weavers, dyers, tanners, and shoemakers were considered to be engaged in a dishonest activity; around the same time, in Liege, perfumers were added to the list of prohibited professions already outlawed in Arras. Indeed one might look at these various synodal statutes and discover that somewhere along the line almost every profession reached the labor index—including the brewer, carpenter, baker, blacksmith, and tanner.

But in all categories no profession was more suspect than that of the merchant. Because he was essential, he was tolerated. The moralist sought generally to prohibit the merchant from engaging in speculative trade and from practicing price-fixing that would gouge the innocent buyer. Yet, by the early Renaissance, all forms of work became so sufficiently valued that families took family names from the kind of work they performed. Names like Cooper, Wright, Miner, Shoemaker, Miller, and, of course, Smith, slipped readily into our language. Clearly by the 13th century—the time of Aquinas —the Church had defined work as both a natural right and a duty and the exclusively legitimate basis of a just society.[4] Indeed it is in labor that one finds the foundation of profit and property, of labor associations and of corporations— and all justifiable in terms of the perfection of the human being and the realization of eternal salvation.

---

[4] Adriano Tilgher, *Work: What It Has Meant to Men through the Ages* (London: George C. Harrap and Co., 1931) , pp. 25–38.

By way of summary we can note that throughout the Greco-Roman and Judeo-Christian eras are found constant reiterations of the importance of the contemplative life and, at best, a grudging toleration of manual labor. Quite clearly, work, as such, was accorded a more honorable role by both Hebrew and Christian social theorists. It was, however, during the Renaissance and the Reformation that the *active* life was praised over the contemplative life. Work was beginning to be defined as the major way to serve God; the life of contemplation was often vigorously denounced. Because this activist view coincided with rapid developments in science and exploration, it was only natural that some observers would discover a relationship between work attitudes and economic growth.

THE PURITAN WORK ETHIC

The name most associated with the new ethic of work and with its alleged relationship to the rise of capitalism is Max Weber, whose *Protestant Ethic and the Spirit of Capitalism* is a reference point for all discussions on these related subjects.[5] Much controversy swirls over what Weber really intended to say and whether what he said did, in fact, actually represent a logical explanation for the rise of modern capitalism. Critics of Weber concentrate insistently on the problem of the *causal* relationship of the Protestant ethic to capitalism. But Weber himself had made it very clear that his purpose was *not* to explain the origin or expansion of capitalism; he was definitely interested in the interplay between religious ideas and economic behavior and was drawn to the notion that economic conduct generated an ethical content of its own. In words suggestive of what Professor Barzun declared, Weber held that a man works well not because of compulsion but because of desire, and this commitment to work was a sign of virtue and a source of satisfaction.

An oft-quoted Weber maxim holds that work itself is an obligation so intrinsically important that an individual feels this as a matter of course. In this sense, the ethic of work reflects the spirit of capitalism because work per se becomes important and independent of any relationship to a higher spiritual or transcendental purpose.[6] Part of Weber's idea and ideal of work may have been derived from

---

[5] Max Weber, *The Protestant Ethic and the Rise of Capitalism* (New York: Charles Scribner's Sons, 1930).

[6] Ephraim Fischoff, "The Protestant Ethic and the Spirit of Capitalism," *Social Research,* Vol. XI (1944), esp. pp. 62–68.

observations of his uncle, Karl David Weber, who founded a local enterprise and who lived a life marked by frugality, benevolence, and hard work—characteristics which seem to mark the great entrepreneurs during the early stages of modern capitalism.[7] Weber contrasted this capitalist work ethic with the work ethic of medieval "traditionalism." According to Weber, traditionalism exists when a worker prefers less work for more pay, greater comfort than maximum effort, commitment to old, rather than to new, methods.

What made Weber's approach fascinating was his ability to see as a major problem what everyone else took for granted, namely, the paradox created by the fact that intense religious conviction and intense economic activity are mutually incompatible. It seemed, therefore, to Weber that the medieval Church should have encouraged commercial growth because its control over daily economic life was lax. Yet in point of fact the middle classes rallied to Protestantism despite the more severe regulation of public and private life found in many Protestant countries and, most particularly, in Calvin's Geneva.

How then could one explain the paradox? Weber answered that the Protestant reformers, even though they may not have fully intended it, provided incentives which favored the rational pursuit of economic gain. This was most true of John Calvin (1509–64), whose followers not only glorified work as a defense against such temptations as sexual desire or religious doubts, but stressed also the importance of unremitting labor as a way of life ordained by God whereby man proved himself. Pursuing this line of inquiry, Weber saw the products of reformers as offering a rationale for middle-class living standards which approved, in ethical terms, expenditure only when they were necessary and practical. Perhaps even more important was the fact that in a secularized Puritanism an ethos of planning and self control pervaded all economic activities, and thereby encouraged a worldly success which militated against the ascetic way of life.

Weber found confirming evidence for his view in his 1904 tour of the United States. At one point he recorded this observation:

The view that the gods bless with riches the man who pleases them, through sacrifice or through his kind of conduct, was indeed suffused all over the world. However, the Protestant sects consciously brought this

---

[7] Richard Bendix, *Max Weber—An Intellectual Portrait* (New York: Doubleday Anchor Book, 1962) , pp. 50–64.

idea into connection with this *kind* of conduct according to the principle of early capitalism: honesty is the best policy. This connection is found, although not quite exclusively, among the Protestant sects, but with characteristic continuity and consistency it is found *only* among them. The wholly typical bourgeois ethic was, from the beginning, common to all ascetic sects and conventicles and it is identical with the ethic practiced by sects in America up to the very present.[8]

At this point it is worth noting that Protestant successes came most spectacularly not in countries where the reformers were born but in countries which adopted the reformers' views. It was Sweden, Denmark, England, Scotland, and Holland which moved vigorously to take ecclesiastical land from the Church; around mid-17th century Great Britain was enjoying a high degree of prosperity even as the Anglican Church was slipping into deepest poverty. Power, in a sense, had passed in England from the Church to the monarchy and thence to the business community. These controlling elements had ideas sharply different from the medieval churchmen. Now emphasis was on work to secure property and to increase output, not—as was true of the medievalist—to produce works of beauty or permanence.

This development possibly encouraged or induced the ethic of work as much as religion. Therefore, whereas Weber saw a connection between Protestantism and industrial capitalism because of Protestant preachments, these relationships are more properly related to the industrial revolution rather than to the rise of modern capitalism. Indeed the change in religious thinking to support frugality and hard work (which Weber attached to Calvinistic Protestantism) could not have explained the tremendous increase in the rate of economic growth found in England because this occured roughly between 1540 and 1560—*before* Calvin's disciples had exercised any important influences on conduct in England or in Scotland. Against the Weber view, therefore, are the views of people like R. H. Tawney and John Nef who argued that economic developments modified Christian ethical doctrines of work, rather than the other way around.[9]

Despite the differences of interpretation there seems little doubt that the Protestant ethic had substantial influence on the attitude of

---

[8] H. H. Gerth and C. Wright Mills, *From Max Weber: Essays in Sociology* (New York: Oxford University Press—Galaxy Books, 1958), p. 313.

[9] R. H. Tawney, *Religion and the Rise of Capitalism* (London: 1926); John U. Nef, *Western Civilization since the Renaissance* (New York: Harper Torch books, 1963), pp. 6–14.

the American businessman. Work as a value in and of itself was stressed by Charles E. Wilson who articulated a fairly typical view when he said to a Senate committee, "Now actually it sounds a little funny, maybe, but I have been a great believer in our American system. I have figured that if I worked on my job, the system would take care of me, I sort of neglected my own family affairs, really, in a certain way, but they did pretty well because I worked at the things I was supposed to be working on."[10] One group of analysts of the American creed put the issue in these terms:

> The special achievement of the Puritan tradition was to give a religious sanction to individualism and occupational efforts as values. At the heart of the Calvinistic Puritan tradition as it worked itself out in social life were the linked values of *austerity, individualism,* and devotion to occupations as *callings.* . . . Devotion to an occupation, not merely as a means to earthly reward, but for its strength as a "calling," fitted admirably the pattern set by the religious postulates. This view of occupations as callings gave to the work of the world a special dignity as a path to salvation.

> The importance of this tradition in giving a distinctive cast to American values has certainly been very great. Seeking to define the most characteristic qualities of the American temper Parrington has put Puritanism on a very exclusive list of two (the other was optimism). Taking a wider perspective Troeltsh has argued for a more important place for Puritanism in the Anglo-American tradition than elsewhere in the western world. Within this tradition the American businessman need make no apologies for a narrow, specialized existence filled with the cares of producing and distributing material goods. The dignity of work, the wealth from material gains, and the propriety of a strong individualism, are solidly grounded in the heritage.[11]

SOME SOCIALISTS' WORK ETHICS

One cannot help noting that socialism of the 19th century variety was in close rapport with ascetic Protestantism and free enterprise Capitalism in its stress on work as an end in itself and as a central activity of human existence. Physical labor was given a new importance by some socialist utopians and Charles Fourier is illustrative of one trend. He urged that the social arrangements be adapted to the various stages of life so that the dirty work might well be

---

[10] Quoted from Francis X. Sutton *et al., The American Business Creed* (New York: Schocken Books, 1962), p. 276.

[11] *Ibid.,* p. 277.

performed by those who have a "natural attraction" to it. Lest one be put off by Fourier's comment, it is well to remember his advice: "There is a natural penchant of children for filth, suggesting that God gave children these strange tastes to provide for the execution of various repulsive tasks. If manure has to spread over a field, youths will find it a repugnant job, but groups of children will devote themselves to it with greater zeal than to clean work."[12]

There is another interesting quality in socialist thinking of the 19th century. Writers often compare Marx to the original utopian, St. Thomas More, because both depicted a world where no man was idle and every man took his turn at all kinds of work. But there was one fundamental difference. In the earlier utopian emphasis, tranquillity was stressed as the highest good whereas the socialists introduced a very dynamic element. Impressed by theories borrowed from physiology (and popularized by writers like Bichat), theorists like St. Simon and Comte dwelt not on the equal natures of men but on the fundamental differences.[13] When, therefore, French socialists stressed individualism, self-expression, and self-fulfillment, they always asserted that work played a crucial role in the achieving of all of these necessary goals. St. Simon, for one, had people in his "utopia" continually working on railroads, highways, and canals.

Fourier's imagination was even more inexhaustible. In constructing his "phalanstery" he gave great attention to what was called the "passionate" series (professional-social categories) built around differences in psychology. Into the phalanstery would come some 800 different identifiable psychological types and through this interplay would emerge a natural environment for individual fulfillment. Because work without love was a psychological burden, Fourier developed techniques to make labor attractive by relating it to the individual's erotic inclinations. Man worked only with those whom he loved and he could have as many work patterns as were consistent with the network of his love relationships. As Frank Manuel noted, "This pathetic little bourgeois salesman may have preserved the idea of unequal returns on investment in the shares of the phalanstery, but the poorest man there led a highly stimulated oral and genital existence."[14]

---

[12] Kurt Samuelson, *Religion and Economic Action* (New York: Basic Books, 1961).

[13] Frank E. Manuel, *The Prophets of Paris* (Cambridge: Harvard University Press, 1962), p. 233.

[14] Frank E. Manuel, "Toward a Psychological History of Utopias," *Daedalus*, Vol. XCIV (Spring, 1965), p. 307.

CONTEMPORARY WORK: STULTIFYING OR SATISFYING?

The transition from the handicraft to the factory system meant the dominance of the machine over the tool. And the domination was not without serious psychological implications for the individual. In the preindustrial order a tool was an instrument made to the measure of man, whether it be a shovel, a spear, or a carbine. Tools were built to the specifications of the user. The factory system, on the other hand, depended on the machine, where man, in a sense, became the human slave for an inhuman mechanism. The new significance was expressed in the way society spoke of "hired hands."

Both Engels and de Toqueville observed the life styles emerging from the factory systems of the 19th century and both reached dismal conclusions. Engels expressed his contempt in these words: "The division of labor has multiplied the brutalizing of influence of forced work. In most branches the worker's activity is reduced to some paltry, purely mechanical manipulation, repeated minute after minute, unchanged year after year."[15]

If Engels worried about the possibility of machines "killing men," de Toqueville worried over the likelihood of men "killing time." He reasoned that because the machine had made human labor superfluous, men, as a consequence, were driven to an undesired and undesirable leisure, to become pawns of a welfare state which regulates their property, subdivides their inheritance, and spares tham all the care of thinking and all the trouble of living.

The question persists: is industrial work deadening and demeaning? Does it rob man of one of life's great needs? Or does it free him from drudgery and servility? A century of concern over this issue has led to refinements in techniques for measuring worker satisfaction and dissatisfaction; despite theoretical advances the empirical findings are less than consistent.

On the basis of his study of Pittsburgh engineers and accountants, Frederick Herzberg was eventually able to construct a two-factor theory identified as the "Adam" and "Abraham" theory of man and of the worker respectively. Adam represents the animalistic level where the overriding goal is to avoid the pain inevitable in relating to the environment; above and beyond the Adam level is the desire to achieve and actualize one's own nature—the Abraham

---

[15] Friedrich Engels, *The Condition of the Working-Class in England in 1844* (London: Allen and Unwin. 1892), pp. 118–19.

concept of man.[16] Related to these two different types are the "hygiene" factors—supervision, interpersonal relations, salary, benefits, and job security which are more related to the "Adam" man and the "motivating factors"—sense of achievement, recognition, status, and the like which go with the "Abraham" model.

When hygiene factors deteriorate, a man immediately becomes dissatisfied with his work; yet even when the hygiene factors are met completely the individual does not relate them to his experiences of deep personal satisfaction with the work. The findings reinforce the conclusion that man is a restless and demanding being who must obviously satisfy his basic animal needs but who cannot be content only with this level of satisfactions. Whatever theories are employed, the majority of attitude surveys of workers (starting with the Roper poll in 1947 and continuing to the present) suggest that a relatively small number of workers (less than 20 percent) report genuine dissatisfaction with their work.

By the same token it is difficult to relate the overall findings with research into specific industries. For example, a majority of packinghouse workers indicated that they did not want their children to follow them into similar factory jobs, which is certainly a measure of substantial discontent.[17] And Harvey Swados, who actually worked on an assembly line in the automotive industry, declared that it came as something of a shock to him "to discover that the one unifying force among all those men, so different from one another in ethnic background, educational attainments, and personal ambition, was *hatred of their work*."[18]

Swados' experiences in America are paralleled by the experiences of George Navol in France. Navol, an author of peasant background, in 1946 published recollections of his days as a factory worker in a book called *Travaux*. He reported the endless monotony of the job, the hunger of the peasant hands tending the machines for the earth, the lack of any sense of satisfaction, the wild rush to exit at

---

[16] See F. Herzberg, *Work and the Nature of Man* (New York: The World Publishing Company, 1966), as well as his earlier work, *Job Attitudes: Review of Research and Opinion* (Pittsburgh: Pittsburgh Psychological Research Service, 1957). This idea of multilevel needs and behavior has been expressed by many authors. For one valuable short essay which illustrates the range, see Clare W. Graves, "Deterioration of Work Standards," *Harvard Business Review* (September–October, 1966), pp. 117–26.

[17] Theodore V. Purcell, *The Blue Collar* (Cambridge: Harvard University Press, 1959).

[18] Harvey Swados, "Work as a Public Issue," *Saturday Review* (December 12, 1959), p. 13.

the end of the work day.[19] On the basis of his reading of Navol, one French theorist said that at least the Americans, unlike the French, prefer group-machine work over individual-artisan work and are consequently better adapted to an industrial society.[20]

Why work satisfactions fluctuate is a matter for considerable debate and various theories have been criticized for serious omissions. Robert Dubin, for one, declared that investigators must treat as coordinates the technological behavior system (technical acts related to equipment and its use, or to processes and operations) and other behavior systems, including (a) informal organization, (b) nonformal behavior systems which represent the way in which a job really gets done, and (c) the informal behavior system which involves the direct interpersonal relationships of a voluntary character which are necessary to get a job done.[21] Another investigator, Harold Wilensky, argues that no matter how one analyzes the problem of job satisfactions, the *meaning of work must be sought in a social context, in the identity of the person, and in the individual's life cycle.* On the basis of his studies of factory workers and professional workers, Wilensky concluded that "only one in four men of the upper working class in the Detroit area would try to get anything like their present work; well over half of the lower middle class (clerks, salesmen, technicians, office supervisors, small proprietors, etc.), would try something else. The range of "satisfied" is about 9 in 10 of the professors and mathematicians to 16 percent of the unskilled adult auto workers." Wilensky adds this important note:

> Supplementing these more sophisticated surveys are close observational studies of men at work; they confirm that less skilled factory work, especially in an old-fashioned assembly line, is wholly ungratifying, devoid of every value the doctrines of work have emphasized, whatever its function as a means of livelihood. The incidence of this type of work situation is now small and may be declining. The new technology will free

---

[19] Georges Friedmann, *Ou Va le Travail Humain* (Paris: Gallimard, 1950), pp. 14–52. The same phenomena are reported for many British workers by Constance Reaveley and John Winnington, *Industry and Democracy* (London: Chatto and Windus, 1947).

[20] Friedmann, *op. cit.,* pp. 103–9. The French theorist has been influenced at this point by the research findings of Professor H. Wunderlich, who pointed out that a man's ability to separate his "thinking" from his "doing" was essential to satisfaction in factory work. *Zeitschrift für Angewandte, Psychologie,* Vol. XXV (1948), pp. 321–73.

[21] Robert Dubin, *The World of Work* (Englewood Cliffs, N.J.: Prentice-Hall, Inc., 1958), chap. 61. Dubin feels that since the famous studies of the Mayo School, we have neglected the significance of the technological behavior system (p. 75, fn. 1).

men on the assembly line for something better; others, obsolete, will join the new poor.[22]

There seems little question that a primary challenge to managers is to make work dignified, meaningful, and exciting. Some concerns, like Texas Instruments, are devoting considerable time and energy in trying to devise new work arrangements which seek to restore to workers a sense of achievement and of pleasure. To do this, personnel men seek to glean insights from such simple sports as bowling. The question is asked: Why is bowling so much fun and work so painful? Part of the answer, of course, is found by analyzing the bowler's behavior. The minute the bowler throws the ball he is instinctively aware of the results of his efforts: there is immediate psychological feedback on his performance because he is part of a team; a good performance is reinforced by social approval. Suppose, however, a screen were placed before the pins so that the bowler could not know his effectiveness; immediately the element of spontaneous pleasure is removed. Imagine further then that the bowler is made to depend on a score-keeper who signals the results. One can begin to sense the tension that could develop between player and scorer, respectively. The conclusion seems clear from analysis-by-analogy: executives must eliminate barriers ("screens" such as job fragmentation) and scorekeepers (foremen) so that the worker can have prompt feedback (rewards for work well done and punishment for poor performance), with sanctions and approvals coming from colleagues engaged in similar work.

Perhaps it is still a minority view that would claim that contemporary work is a satisfying experience. One such voice is Remy Kwant, a European-born social philosopher now lecturing in the United States. Kwant holds that during the early days of industrialization, smoke-ridden industrial towns defaced the landscape as ugly factories debased man. Early in the technical age man was cut off from nature, but this was an accidental, not necessary, development; as technology matures it returns to nature. And Kwant added:

If we think of the street cleaners of the past, and if we compare their toil with the easy job of the man who is sitting in a mechanized street-cleaning machine, we become aware of the modern improvement of

---

[22] Harold Wilensky, "Work as a Social Problem," in Howard S. Becker (ed.), *Social Problems: A Modern Approach* (New York: John Wiley & Sons, 1967), pp. 133–34; 136. See also C. R. Walker and R. H. Guest, *The Man on the Assembly Line* (Cambridge: Harvard University Press, 1952).

labor. It is pleasant, therefore, to take organized tours through factories and offices. When painters of the past chose labor as the object of their expression, they painted the tension of muscles and the fatigue of faces. Modern painters express the victory of man over the forces of nature. . . . It may be true that we are living in a period of transition, and that the imperfections we have just indicated are only transitory. As a matter of fact, the monotony of labor proved, in some cases, to be an intermediate phase which made possible the transfer of labor to the machine. Labor had to become inhuman, because only in this way could man learn to perform it in a new, more human way. Almost all the important improvements in every possible field in the course of human history have been realized in this way. We never find a simple and continuous progress which manifests its progressive character at its very beginning. At first, all the innovations are ambiguous. They announce new values, but values of the past seem to be lost. Eventually, however, the values of the past reappear in the new ones. Every renewal seems to be nihilistic at the beginning, because it seems to deny the past. We should, however, believe in the progressive character of history and we should not be alarmed by apparent regressions. Consequently, the unilateral and monotonous character of modern labor may only be a transitory imperfection which will be eliminated by a new integration.

This optimism is more than a mere belief. There are many functions which are attractive to young people. They want to be pilots and stewardesses on planes. It is attractive to them to drive a car on the highways or to operate a crane in the port. They are fascinated by machines and they like to work with them. There seems to be a kind of connaturality between them and the machines, and even primitive people learn how to handle machines after brief instruction.[23]

The foregoing observations may strike many as more expressions of hope than descriptions of current reality and it may well be that certain of the world's work simply cannot be made as satisfying as philosophers would wish and as laborers themselves desire. But implicit in the assessment is the idea that technology does relieve man from back-breaking toil and that the consequent release for more rewarding activity is a net gain. Because the country is moving toward a postindustrial society where services in the health, educational, and leisure-oriented fields are coming into prominence, it could develop that the country will see the emergence of new professions or, at least, paraprofessions. To illustrate: health services rank

---

[23] Remy C. Kwant, *The Philosophy of Labor* (Pittsburgh: Duquesne University Press, 1960), pp. 9–11.

as the third largest employer in the country (only after agriculture and construction), and the need for workers trained in paramedical fields grows daily. The 180,000 practicing physicians depend on some 3,000,000 other workers in auxiliary services.

As paraprofessional fields grow, so do opportunities in the traditional and more recognized professions. In the United States the professionals per 100,000 of the population have increased from 859 in 1870 to 3,310 in 1950, which suggests strongly that as a society industrializes it also professionalizes.

PROFESSIONAL WORK

The identification of reward systems for professionals, therefore, becomes important. The professional seeks to promote his own self-interest and, at the same time, the community's general interest, with recognitions and rewards from each. Money represents achievement; prestige and honors represent awards accorded by society. There is clearly a demand for sufficient monetary income to accord with a style of life appropriate to a professional's needs; there is especially a demand for the esteem accorded the professional in society. And the two imperatives recall the "Adam-Abraham" categories developed by Herzberg.

That different professions yield different incomes and different satisfactions is a well-known fact. Historically, preachers and teachers were low on the income ladder and high on the social esteem scale. But it is even more important to determine what satisfactions the professionals themselves derive from their callings. In one recent study, an investigator rephrased the old question of reliving one's life in this way: "Now, what would you do if you had more time than you actually have? If you had two more hours in the day—a 26-hour day—what would you most like to do with the extra time?" The answers are interesting:

Two in 3 professors, 1 in 4 lawyers, 1 in 5 engineers, and only 1 in 20 of the middle-mass mentioned work or work-related activity. A factor analysis suggest that these responses, together with the "do-it-over-again" response, measure general job satisfaction as part of the respondents' views of their total life time.[24]

Our special interests lead us to inquire into the job satisfactions

---

[24] Wilensky, *loc. cit.*, p. 135, fn. 23.

of professional managers—even though there is still some question regarding the maturity of business management as a genuine profession. Some hold that it is an emerging, or marginal, profession—like library work, pharmacy, and accountancy. But one measure of maturity is the presence of, and respect for, the professional school. And in this context the advances of the schools of business since the war attest to the growing maturity of the executive profession.[25]

Are the business professionals satisfied? Informal samplings of opinion suggest this to be the case and tend to reinforce Arnold Maremont's view. Revealing strands of the Calvinist ethic, Maremont said that the mature executive is one who sees his job "as an end in itself, worthy of complete dedication and preoccupation."[26] But this very dedication to work has been denounced as pathological and detrimental to the individual himself, to his family and associates, to his organization, and to the larger society.[27] The pathology has been identified as the "Hopkins Syndrome" because of the abnormal behavior patterns of Ralph Hopkins in Sloan Wilson's *The Man in the Gray Flannel Suit*. In this context the modern business executive is seen as part of the industrial rat race; he is the "organization man," the economic "automaton," the ulcer-prone individual who, in the process of getting everything done, gets himself undone. It is hard to prove these conclusions as definite evidence of the dissatisfactions of executives. One traditional defense was to point to the number of young people going into business careers. But this refutation is no longer as persuasive as it once was.

YOUTH AND WORK

If this is, in fact, the age of the professions, then it is interesting to explore the professions that are attracting the young. A few years ago one survey indicated that over 83 percent of the graduating class at Harvard planned to do graduate work, 74 percent of Yale's class had similar ambitions, and well over 60 percent of the seniors at Dartmouth, Columbia, Cornell and Pennsylvania were profession-

---

[25] On problems related to the professions, see *Daedalus* (Fall, 1963) , pp. 647–856. More directly related to business management as a profession is the essay by Clarence C. Walton, "Education for Professionalism," *Proceedings*, Association of American Collegiate Schools of Business (April, 1964) , pp. 26–39.

[26] Arnold H. Maremont, "Public Relations—the Tail that Wags the Dog," *Michigan Business Review* (May, 1966) .

[27] Albert Porter, "The Hopkins Syndrome," a paper presented to the 1968 meeting of the Research Society of America and the Institute of Management Sciences (May 1–3, 1968) , San Francisco.

bound. When we begin to dissect the professional preferences into their component parts, an important discovery emerges. A 1966 Lewis Harris poll of 800 college seniors revealed that only 31 percent were seriously considering business as a career and only 12 percent made it a first choice. Roger Rickless wrote in *The Wall Street Journal* (November 10, 1964) that college students were generally turning away from work in the corporate realm. If the typical maxim was: work hard, save, and then enjoy, modern youth seemed determined to reverse the pattern. One Harvard dean put the reversal in these terms: "gratification while young, work when older."[28]

There is no question that in an affluent society the young know full well they will survive, whether working or not working, and that they will live at a level that is not harsh, even if not comfortable by traditional terms. Youths feel that they can drop in and drop out of society almost at will; as a consequence their attitudes toward work are changing perceptibly. Alan Center, vice president of Motorola, warned a business audience that industry was not getting enough of the brighter students and Philip Abelson, editor of *Science* (who attended a Washington University interfraternity council), found few of the young men at that symposium inclined toward a business career. More often than not the young seem to ignore business rather than criticize it.

To argue that the young are uninterested in business because the affluent society provides them with more options is not to speak to the question of job satisfaction. More fundamental is the shift in values toward work itself and toward wealth-getting as the measure of success. As executives seek to make industrial labor more satisfying they move simultaneously to make labor in the executive suites more satisfying. And to achieve this in any full measure means a deliberate involvement by the corporation in activities that the youth deem important, such as slum clearance, racial justice, international prosperity, and peace.

CONCLUSION

Recently a Jesuit, Father Theodore Purcell, completed a survey of the problem of work in American society and added to the social science dimensions a theological imperative. Purcell argues

---

[28] Anthony G. Athos, "The Young and I," *Harvard Business School Bulletin*, Vol. XLIII (Sept.–Oct., 1967), p. 13.

that the old Aristotelean notion of man as a "political" animal, or Adam Smith's notion of man as an "economic" animal needs to be extended. The human person is not simply *homo sapiens* or *homo economicus;* he is also *homo faber.* Through work, challenging or unexciting, easy or difficult, clean or dirty, man finds a method of fulfilling his own being.[29]

Quite clearly in this formulation, no one should be subordinated to the will of another, or forced to perform in activities more properly done by machine or animal. There is, however, the clear point that fulfillment of one's humanity requires work and that a proper perception of the role of work in daily living will mean personal growth and individual spiritual enrichment. So far, then, as work is conceived conceptually, it would appear that earlier ideas of work as fulfillment are being resurrected and given redefinitions appropriate to the contemporary scene. The provenance of work's value becomes not wholly worldly!

RECOMMENDED READING

ARENDT, HANNAH. *The Human Condition.* Chicago: University of Chicago Press, 1958.

DUBIN, ROBERT. *The World of Work.* Englewood Cliffs, N.J.: Prentice-Hall, Inc., 1958.

HERZBERG, FREDERICK. *Work and the Nature of Man.* New York: The World Publishing Co., 1966.

MANUEL, FRANK E. *The Prophets of Paris.* Cambridge: Harvard University Press, 1962.

TILGHER, ADRIANO. *Work: What It Has Meant to Men through the Ages.* London: George C. Harrap and Co., 1931.

WEBER, MAX. *The Protestant Ethic and the Rise of Capitalism.* New York: Charles Scribner's Sons, 1930.

WILENSKY, HAROLD. "Work as a Social Problem." In HOWARD S. BECKER (ed.) *Social Problems: A Modern Approach.* New York: John Wiley & Sons, 1967.

FURTHER READING

BENDIX, RICHARD. *Max Weber—An Intellectual Portrait.* New York: Doubleday Anchor Book, 1962.

---

[29] Theodore Purcell, "Work Psychology and Business Values: A Triad Theory of Work Motivation," *Personnel Psychology,* Vol. XX (Autumn, 1963) , pp. 240–49.

FISCHOFF, EPHRAIM. *"The Protestant Ethic and the Spirit of Capitalism," Social Research,* Vol. XI, (1944).

GERTH, H. H. and MILLS, C. WRIGHT (eds.). *From Max Weber: Essays in Sociology.* New York: Oxford University Press—Galaxy Books, 1958.

PURCELL, THEODORE V. *The Blue Collar.* Cambridge: Harvard University Press, 1959.

11. Leisure and Free Time

TO THE POPULAR MIND, the idea of leisure is identical with the idea of free time and with the style of life freed from the normal burdens of work and worry. The elements of a style of life can be divided into thee major groupings: (*a*) *occupational* characteristics, (*b*) *individual-familial* elements, and (*c*) *social* or *collective* elements. This division relates very closely to the three principle roles that individuals take. Clearly, the occupational element profoundly influences the life style and there is a very substantial difference between the life of a West Virginia miner or a Detroit assembly-line worker, and a Hollywood script writer. Important as these are in determining the life style, it may well be the individual and familial elements are even more crucial because they include housing and the household amenities that go into the making of a home. These elements include cultural activities and therefore are closely related to the use of leisure. The social and collective elements form the final group and relate to education, health, and recreational activities. What is being suggested is that, from the point of view of a healthy adult, all three components of the life style must be in harmony.

The *notion* of leisure is not unrelated to the *problem* of leisure, and the latter, in turn, is uniquely the product of a contemporary society gripped by the revolution of rising expectations. This revolution, when related to an advanced industrialized society, is deeply embedded in the widespread demands for psychological as well as for material benefits. Labor unions urge a shorter work week, with no decrease in weekly wages, as the way to keep technological progress from becoming technological unemployment, while business leaders worry about rising cost and declining production in the face of a work week that is becoming shorter and shorter. Business strategists give greater and greater attention to the kinds of goods that should be produced for a leisure society; park and recreation officials are making careful estimates on the amount of free space and equipment that will be necessary in the leisure-oriented society of the future; and educators ponderously discuss the place of leisure in child, adolescent, and adult education.

In a society where work has been routinized and simplified, where purchasing power of the masses has been increased, where entertainment media can easily reach the masses it is evident that leisure is both an *opportunity* and a *problem*. But the problem of leisure cannot be understood unless it is directly related to the aspirations and the position of those groups in society who allegedly *have* the problem, and to the nature of the socioeconomic changes which create the problem. Not everyone is profoundly disturbed by the same kinds of leisure problems and various efforts are undertaken which sometimes have the effect of disguising the problem. For example, when the need for child labor was banished from contemporary American society, schools moved to take up the slack; but it is a real question whether the youngsters feel that their leisure has been intensified or minimized by the development.

THE IDEA OF LEISURE

If the ancients considered work a sentence and a curse, they regarded leisure as its exact opposite. For the Greeks, the life of leisure was the only life worth living and the capacity to use leisure rightly was, in Aristotle's analysis, the basis of freedom and responsibility. Leisure therefore stands in a class by itself. Aristotle reminded us of this uniqueness in *The Politics* when he said that leisure affords an intrinsic pleasure, intrinsic happiness, intrinsic felicity, and that happiness of this order belongs to no occupation—but only to those who have leisure.

Because leisure is so closely related to the life of contemplation, it is easy to see why the idea of "school" is so closely identified with it. It is interesting, in reviewing Aristotle's position, to note how quickly he disposes of reading and writing as crucial elements in education for the reason that they were primarily useful for money-making, for housekeeping, and for some elemental political activities. Gymnastics also occupied a rather low position in the Aristotelian philosophy of education because it fostered only the single virtue of courage. It is precisely the fact that because these studies are useful they became defective. The higher branches of learning therefore were to be studied with the view toward cultivating the mind for its own sake through the proper use of leisure.

It is further interesting to observe that Plato shared Aristotle's emphasis on the importance of music as a fundamental part of a liberal education. Plato asserted in *The Laws* that any Greek who could not hold his rightful place in the chorus was not really an educated man. Above all else, the Greeks wished to be musicians and music was for them almost synonomous with culture. Sparta, which has always been identified with the martial spirit, was also the musical capital of Greece. One of the classic stories of the ancient world deals with Themistocles, the distinguished Athenian general and statesman, who was shamed at a public banquet when the lyre was passed around and he did not know how to play it.

Toward the end of the Middle Ages this concept of contemplation for its own sake slowly began to lose its hold on the minds of educated men, but not before it had become part of the liberal arts curriculum. The humanists called upon men who did not have to earn their daily bread in the sweat of their brows to put their minds to work (reading, thinking, writing, and calculating), both for their own greater good and for that of the sweating masses who supported them. The hereditary security of the gentleman obliged him to use his leisure to pursue the life of the mind or, at the very least, to see that his estate was carefully administered.

What is sometimes called the "Protestant," or industrial, view of leisure is something quite different from the early Greek and Medieval views. When Calvin raised work to a primary position in human activities, and when industrialization ennobled work, society began to emphasize economically productive functions as the most worthwhile and most significant aspects of life. It was at this time that leisure was relegated to the status of spare time and it was this "idle time" that became the "devil's workshop." Thus it was that society introduced ingenious contrivances for keeping people busy during their free time: Bible reading, required exercises for children and adults, hymns and prayers, and the like, were some of the techniques widely employed. A life of contemplation (which to the Greeks was a supreme virtue) represented the sin of idleness to Protestant divines.

But the view of leisure so clearly expressed in the Calvinist doctrine or in the ideology of industrialism had earlier roots in the Renaissance. In Florence, where the Renaissance flowered, the prevailing philosophy asserted that the world existed to be transformed. Man's greatness and the spark of his divinity were found not in the individual's capacity for contemplation but in his ability to subdue nature and subjugate it to his will. It is, however, interesting to note that the clever Florentines praised a particular kind of work: work that was at once both highly individualistic and highly artistic. Thus it was that the sculptor, painter, architect, and scientist came to occupy a prestigious role in Renaissance society and to represent the ideal of the leisure class.

It is curious to observe how this classical side of the Renaissance gradually lost favor as the modern period of commerce began to flower. It was Adam Smith in *The Wealth of Nations* who advanced the thesis that a human act is truly productive if it takes raw material and turns it into something useful. And in Smith's vision was a kind of work—factory work—that had never been anticipated by the men of the early Renaissance. With the rise of the factory system, work began to be organized mechanically according to clocks and machines; it began to be thought of not as a total occupation for survival but in terms of so many pieces of time or product. The idea of free time, as the time left over from those hours specified in the job contract, began to replace the old idea of leisure. But unlike leisure, free time is discontinuous. It is not conceived of as time to pursue one's major interests after survival needs have been met, but rather, as time to recuperate and renew so that an individual can return to the job refurbished and refreshed. The result is that while other civilizations have had their leisure classes, contemporary society is the first to attempt to bestow free time on all classes primarily to have men return to the work force as more efficient producers.

THE STATE OF FREE TIME TODAY

Amount of Free Time

In 1850 the average work week in this country was 70 hours, and as late as Andrew Carnegie's day, steel workers worked on 12-hour shifts, seven days a week. A century later, on-the-job time was just under 40 hours. But, oddly enough, the life of the 1850's as pictured in books and the accounts of ancestors seems to have been far more leisurely than ours, though we earn more money per week and have 30 more hours off the job than they had. One of the earliest slogans of the shorter hours movement in the United States ran: "Eight hours for work, eight hours for sleep, eight hours for all the rest." Today we have realized this objective. Since the early 1950's the statistical figure for the average working week in this country has been 39 to 40 hours. The gain in free time would thus appear to be enormous. And yet anyone who works, and in our society it is hardly respectable not to, knows that there is something wrong with this arithmetic.

First, the statisticians have included a factor that confuses the addition—the part-time workers. The old lady who sits 10 hours a week with babies, the young lady who makes her Christmas money clerking over the holidays, or the student who works 3 hours a day checking out library books—these also are included in statistics on the declining work week. If we exclude them, we find that the full-time worker's job adds up to 46 or 47 (regular and overtime) hours a week. In other words, the American worker puts in an average of nearly eight hours a day, six days a week.

This means that the rate of the decline of the work week has been slower than has been assumed. The decline from 1948 to 1967 was 6–8 percent if we include part-time workers; on the basis of full-time workers alone it was only about 3 percent. Today nearly 95 percent of all males between the ages of 25 and 55 and about 35 percent of all females work. Labor-force participation rates for these ages have never been so high. Indeed, it might well be said in paraphrase: "Never before have so many had so little time to call their own."

But there is endless difficulty in calculating free time in terms of the decline in the work week. Such measurements tend to assume that a job is a job, that any hour in 1970 is the equivalent of any hour in 1870—although we know how assembly lines can increase the nervous "duration" of modern employment and how the machine is accelerating the use of time.

Of course, the impact of machines on the duration of time differs. The automobile, or even the lathe, gives the man in command of it a sense of power and possibility. He is stronger when he is operating it, and, when he is tired of it or is done with it, he can turn off this same power with a flip of the switch. But there are also pacing machines, to whose tempo a man must maintain a corresponding pace. These he cannot turn off at his own will because they are operated by a clock or at someone else's discretion. It is these last that have given the industrial age its character. After eight hours of such synchronization of human nature to the mindless regularity of the machine, a man may be more tired than after a similar length of time in a nonmechanized age. This is why he needs free time, even though he may have no energy left for the pursuits of leisure.

There are other reasons why a mechanical acceptance of work-week statistics could prove misleading. The trek away from the city to the suburbs has greatly increased the time consumed by the journey to and from the work place for almost all classes of workers. Suburban living, moreover, presupposes home owning, and home owning demands maintenance. Though the cost of labor and services fluctuates, it is now at an all -time high. As a result, the working man cannot really afford to hire skilled labor but must undertake it himself, in his so-called free time. Plumbing, wiring, painting, roofing, carpentry, brickwork, even landscaping become part of the free-time responsibility of the commuter-worker.

As if this were not enough, do-it-yourself extends to every aspect of the worker's life. Labor-saving devices are to some extent labor adding. Families that could in the past have afforded a laundress, a seamstress, and perhaps a yard man now supply themselves with electric washers and dryers, sewing machines and power mowers. All these may contribute a sense of self-reliance and speed, but their operation inevitably consumes time that would otherwise be free.

Shopping is another time devourer. The supermarket customer, eager to prove that he is a canny shopper, forgets that he must first learn the location of products in the market, then consider amounts and prices. The time he feels that he has saved picking up his own wares may be lost in line as he waits for the clerk, whose work he has done for him, to add up purchases and pack them for the customer to deliver to his home himself.

The greatly increased mobility of the work force also steals away time on a scale unimagined in 1860. The average car owner drives 6,000 to 7,000 miles a year. Each year one in every four families moves to a new area, usually to start a new job. Since this has become common experience, there is no need to dwell on the heavy investment of time that goes into moving and getting settled in a new locale. Finally, there is another factor to confuse figures on the length of the work week. According to the Bureau of Labor Statistics, one out of every three American women is in the work force. She works an average of 35 hours a week. Does her husband have more free time as a result of this increase in family income? Hardly, when one considers that with no one at home all day it becomes his lot to share in the shopping, the cooking, and the child-tending through the week. If we add all factors of contemporary life that take away free time—commuting, mobility, do-it-yourself, "moonlighting" (the after-hours job), and working mothers—the increase in real free time between 1860 and today dwindles enormously.

EMPLOYMENT OF TIME

The debate on the amount of free time available to modern man rages intensely. There is little question, however, that for the average industrial worker the job no longer commands the loyalties and provides the moral values that were presumed to exist under the Calvinist ethic. With this process society itself loses an important source for normative integration. Thus it is coming about that the functions formerly performed by the institutions of work are being transferred to so-called "leisure institutions." This is occurring in much the same way that functions formerly performed by the family or by the Church have increasingly been shifted to the schools. Now we are concerned that "free time" provide the same moral functions or moral values that were previously provided by the institutions of work. Therefore experts who talk about the problems of leisure or who decry "mass" culture are speaking more to the symptoms than to the root problem, namely, a profound concern with the sources of moral solidarity. The problem of leisure therefore becomes one of finding values for the use of free time which command a consensus and provide a moral identity.

It is perhaps not surprising that educators should be most deeply concerned with the appropriate uses of leisure. But much that passes for liberal education, especially for adults, is offered as a device for meeting the problem of free time badly spent, not liberal education in the traditional sense of the word. Businessmen are also prone to speak of problems created by an affluent, leisure-oriented society. Their motivations are mixed.

It may be certainly true that business leaders are concerned about the declining work week and its implications for productivity or for payrolls. In certain parts of the world efforts are made by the employer to develop programs that will involve the employee in the effective use of free time or, more properly put, in the "effective use" as the businessman would define effectiveness. Not infrequently, business firms provide inducements to employees to continue with education or to engage in similar pursuits. Tuitions are met through company resources but often the inducement is to make the worker a more effective agent of the firm, rather than an effective human being.

Quite clearly, the foregoing is a generalization open to challenge. Generally speaking, business tends to take a laissez-faire stance regarding the way employees spend their free time. Labor leaders too, take a laissez-faire attitude and tend to act as though the employee knows perfectly well how to spend his free time. To put the problem of free time and leisure in its simplest terms, it can be noted that so long as Americans want costly things they cannot have much free time to enjoy them. What free time does exist will be spent exploiting the goods and services the time and money have brought. And only for the fortunate few are work and leisure reasonably identical; thus creative artists share with business executives a common dedication to work and the 56- or 60-hour work week is not uncommon for either. "Time off" is often spent on work-related activities.

Perhaps there is an important clue to the meaning of leisure in early American history through remembering that while the First Continental Congress had resolved in Lockean terms in 1774 that the colonists were entitled to the rights of "life, liberty, and property," the great Declaration of July 4, 1776, asserted as "unalienable" the rights of "life, liberty, and the pursuit of happiness." These words, already used by George Mason the month before in the Virginia Declaration of Rights, reflected more than the thought of that classical scholar in contemplative retirement near Alexandria; they expressed a purpose of human freedom that was later written into the bills of rights of many states.

It is relevant, therefore, to relate the problem of leisure in its American setting to the philosophy of life and of society espoused by the Founding Fathers. To be free of necessity and to have an opportunity to pursue excellence in and of itself was a colonial ideal. And in this vision the Colonials could not have been more "classical." It was not casual insight therefore that led James Bryce to declare that the Founding Fathers had gone back 2,000 years for the source of their ideas.

NEW PROBLEMS FOR THE NEW LEISURED

AGE

However devoted he may be to his work, the executive, like other employees beyond age 65, faces the prospect of retirement. Statistics show that thanks to medical advances we have a rapidly growing group of retired "senior citizens." The rise of Golden Age clubs in every large city demonstrates that free time, in the form of retirement, is not as happy a state as might have appeared. A man whose work has been his one real interest in life, may not, in the course of it, have employed his free time consistently at anything long enough to be able to turn it into an occupation for his new leisure.

Nor can retirement be regarded as the advent of leisure when inflation has reduced the value of pension, insurance, or social security benefits to a level at which they are inadequate for survival, let alone for the maintenance of previous living standards. Retirement is a period when one has time at last for cultivating hobbies, for socializing, or, as the blood becomes thin, for moving in one final migration to a warm climate. But all this requires money. Retirement is also a time when medical expenses may be higher than they were in the less worn-out days. Thus what should have been leisure often turns into free time to look for part-time work to help the budget.

YOUTH

At the other end of the spectrum we have youth—the gum-chewing, Coke-drinking, pop-record-buying crowd that is kept out of the work force until age 16, regardless of its drives or ambitions. Advertisers of late have waxed lyrical over the consumer potential of this group. Unlike the aged, their cost of living needs are provided for. The money they pick up at odd jobs is therefore not for necessities but for luxuries, and these are pushed their way with both energy and ingenuity. Youth constitutes a new market, not only for the traditional child luxuries, sweets, soft drinks, bicycles, and baseball bats, but also for the more complex and expensive marvels of electronics and machinery, radios, phonographs, cars, and boat motors. Many of these more expensive items are provided for them by their indulgent or socially ambitious elders.

But there are clear evidences of a reaction to this kind of free time. The rebellion of youth against the business rat race is being equalled in intensity by a rebellion against an alleged hedonistic culture of the middle class. The notion of service—in Peace Corps or in ghetto schools—has taken hold of modern youth in a way that suggests the beginning of a new crusade. What is interesting in the phenomenon is the fact that youth sees in these activities not an imperative to work but an opportunity for self-fulfillment. In this sense their pursuit of happiness is following a route substantially different from the one taken by their forebears. The more optimistic of the analysts of the leisure problem see in youth's dedication to service a return to an ideal where the activity is viewed as good in and of itself. Its utility occupies a secondary role.

THE HOUSEWIFE

How much free time does the housewife actually have? What with washing and cleaning mechanized or commercialized, the preparation of meals simplified by prepared, frozen, and canned foods, and most clothing store bought, women appear to have been dispossessed as housekeepers in the traditional sense. Except for child-rearing, which the school partly takes over after the first six years of the child's life, they too have become consumers rather than producers.

As a result, their mature lives may be divided roughly into three periods. During the first, when the girl is employed but unmarried, her free time may be said to correspond with that of the similarly situated male employee. Actually, it probably does not, since she puts much of it into the maintenance and improvement of her wardrobe and appearance. If, as some sociologists believe, her object both in work time and free time is matrimony, then the ancient ideal of leisure is not dead in her case because leisure, it may be recalled, means that one's time is spent pursuing a course of one's own choosing, and for its own sake.

For the employed married woman, with or without children, free time is domestic time. She is actually holding down two jobs, with little respite save change, as she moves from one to the other. Once she starts to raise a family, free time disappears almost altogether.

The third period, when the children are grown, is when a woman tends to reenter the work force. For the first time in many years she has a disconcerting surplus of free time. While it could be put to volunteer work and the development of a leisure interest, the high cost of higher education for children, or the desire to provide a few luxuries for a struggling new generation of families, often prompts her to offer her skills for hire. This in itself can consume more time and require more adjustment than she had bargained for. Fifteen or 20 years away from the office, the classroom, the hospital ward, and the laboratory leave a wide gap in information and technique that must be filled, and catching up frequently consumes what would have been free time off the job.

THE ETHICS OF ENTERTAINMENT AND THE USE OF FREE TIME

There are many who question the modern emphasis on free time. There are those who say that the concept of work has hit a new level, as most Americans strain toward a better level of life. People who grumble over the shoddiness of modern workmanship are not prepared to say whether this results from union cynicism, poor training as the older craftsmen die off, the sheer complexity of modern equipment and installations, or bad will or indifference on the part of the individual workman. In an extreme emergency the doctor or the plumber will come to the home after hours, but he usually indicates that this is an exception to his rule. You have intruded workaday matters into that sacred free time, which no amount of overtime pay can compensate.

But what happens to this precious free time? At the consumer or spectator level, we find that people watch TV, listen to the radio or to records, and read newspapers, magazines, and some books. Some of the magazines may be trade journals, but are these better as free-time reading than the weeklies or the picture magazines just because they are job-rated—or are they a kind of cheating on free time? Some people will attend any movies playing in the neighborhood, others insist on foreign films, Academy-award pictures, or revivals of old cinema masterpieces. Add opera-going, concerts, the theater, and you still have consumption, but have you added experience or educational value?

Perhaps the weekend evenings are taken up with cocktail or dinner parties. Socializing is good, we are all agreed, and it is active to the extent that it makes more demands on human nature than a sitting, watching pastime. One can either watch or indulge in bowling, swimming, golf, tennis, and most of the team sports, even if for these last only at a picnic or out in a field with small boys. Dancing, whether folk or formal, choral singing, instrumental music, card playing, or just drinking beer with the crowd are other rewarding participating activities. Gardening, stamp collecting, photography, and cooking or sewing are active but solitary pastimes.

Is it more rewarding to pursue one's diversions alone, or is group activity more relaxing? Answers to each question are unquestionably relative to the needs and natures of the men and women who make them. Perhaps it is better to be a producer than a consumer, but without consumers producers would soon reach a stalemate. Perhaps it is better to have good taste than bad taste. The counterpoise of good and bad as adjectives in this context would certainly seem so to indicate. But is there an absolute in such matters?

Leisure has its standards. And those standards cannot be separated from the cultivation of the mind. Free time, time off the job, has no such standards or tradition. The choice of what to do during free time is thus open to the winds. The prevailing winds are those of advertising. Only education is in a position to bring countervailing pressure. Free time can be had in the future, and in large quantities, but it is doubtful that man will come to prefer time to money in the next decades. Even if more time were thrust upon him, would he do better with it than he is doing now? Probably not, unless man can be made aware of the essential difference between the nature of leisure, as time to pursue a consistent life interest, and the nature of free time, as time off from an all-too-consistent effort for survival.

RECOMMENDED READING

ARISTOTLE. *Ethics.*

————. *Politics.*

DE GRAZIA, SEBASTIAN. *The Political Community,* chap. iii. (Chicago: University of Chicago Press, 1948.

————. *Of Work, Time, and Leisure.* New York: Twentieth Century Fund, 1963.

DEWHURST, J. FREDERICK, *et al. America's Needs and Resources,* Parts II and V. New York: Twentieth Century Fund, 1955.

DONAHUE, WILMA (ed.). *Free Time.* Ann Arbor: University of Michigan Press, 1958.

GOLDWIN, R. A. (ed.). *Toward the Liberally Educated Executive.* New York: Fund for Adult Education, 1957.

HUIZINGA, JOHAN. *Homo ludens.* Trans. R. F. C. HULL. London: Routledge and Paul, 1949.

LARRABEE, ERIC, and MEYERSON, ROLF (eds.). *Mass Leisure.* New York: The Free Press, 1958.

PIEPER, JOSEF. *Leisure: The Basis of Culture.* Trans. ALEXANDER DRU, with an introduction by T. S. Eliot. New York: Pantheon Books, 1952.

STALEY, EUGENE (ed.). *Creating an Industrial Civilization.* New York: Harper & Bros., 1952.

VEBLEN, THORSTEIN. *Theory of the Leisure Class.* New York: B. W. Huebsch, 1918.

FURTHER READING

ARENDT, HANNAH. *The Human Condition.* Chicago: University of Chicago Press, 1958.

BERNERT, ELEANOR H. *America's Children.* New York: John Wiley & Sons, 1958.

BOGART, LEO. *The Age of Television: A Study of Viewing Habits and the Impact of Television on American Life.* New York: F. Ungar Publishing Co., 1956.

GALBRAITH, JOHN K. *The Affluent Society.* Boston: Houghton Mifflin Co., 1958.

HOGGART, RICHARD. *The Uses of Literacy.* London: Penguin Books, 1958.

KELSO, LOUIS O., and ADLER, MORTIMER S. *The Capitalist Manifesto.* New York: Random House, 1958.

LYND, HELEN M. and ROBERT S. *Middletown*. New York: Harcourt, Brace & Co., 1929.

MARITAIN, JACQUES. *Reflections on America,* chap. xviii. New York: Charles Scribner's Sons, 1958.

MYRDAL, ALVA, and KLEIN, VIOLA. *Women's Two Roles: Home and Work*. London: Routledge and Paul, 1956.

RIESMAN, DAVID, *et al. The Lonely Crowd*. New Haven: Yale University Press, 1950.

ROSENBERG, BERNARD, and WHITE, DAVID (eds.) . *Mass Culture: The Popular Arts in America*. New York: Free Press, 1957.

SMUTS, R. W. *Women and Work in America*. New York: Columbia University Press, 1959.

TILGHER, ADRIANO. *Work*. Trans. DOROTHY CANFIELD FISHER. New York: Harcourt, Brace & Co., 1930.

WEBER, MAX. *The Protestant Ethic and the Spirit of Capitalism*. Trans. TALCOTT PARSONS. London: Allen and Unwin, 1930.

WOLFE, KURT. *The Biological, Sociological and Psychological Aspects of Aging*. Springfield, Ill.: Charles C Thomas Publishers, 1959.

IV. THE ECONOMY

FREEDOM to earn a living and to accumulate property—equality of opportunity and government protection for one's legitimate endeavors—are the foundations of the American economy. The commercial, industrial, and financial system built on this base has traditionally been described as "capitalism," but of late years, partly because of the pejorative connotations attached to this word since Marx and partly because of changes within the system itself, it has been called "free enterprise." Yet even this description fails to capture the full dimensions of a vastly complex system that generates private and sometimes public corporations in what is essentially a mixed economy.

The argument that large-scale ownership warps the shape of freedom, that by making some men more free and equal than others it thus defeats the pristine ideals of liberty and equality, has already been discussed. Because capitalism is the economic system that appears to characterize a free society, one may infer that sweeping denunciations of it are perhaps an indirect way of impugning the merits of freedom. But one essayist has said that

. . . to argue that capitalism is freedom would put one in the position of affirming that the chief blessing of liberalism is that it leaves everyone free to become prosperous, however he sees fit. Now capitalism doubtless does leave everyone free in his way, but it is a freedom that by its nature must have ambiguous results for the majority of mankind. . . . Such a

301

misconception (that capitalism is freedom) . . . has prepared the way for the idea that freedom is a mockery because, for multitudes, opulence does not come of it. Related to that misconstruction is the absurdity that a man constrained by circumstances and a man restrained by law are unfree in the same sense.[1]

To argue at the other extreme that there is no relationship between free enterprise and freedom itself leads to equally absurd misconceptions.[2] Behind free enterprise, however unequal its distribution of rewards, lies the indisputable fact of freedom for the individual to choose to associate with or to disassociate himself from particular economic pursuits. The law-protected right to choose an occupation, a profession, or a type of business is the freedom behind the American enterprise system.

Unhappily, our historic ideal of freedom is marred, not only by a tendency toward unequal distribution of the fruits of effort and enterprise, but also by human weakness. Though we are for the most part a law-abiding people, the individualism of the Anglo-American tradition sometimes reveals itself in a certain disregard of the laws governing probity in business dealings and in a tendency to evade civic duties. Thus, freedom under law, even when that law exists only as a regulator, has not invariably produced only good in business and society. This is true even if we leave out of consideration those well-organized and extremely profitable activities of the underworld syndicates that may be the only completely untrammeled free enterprise eixsting in this country. Such organizations have been omitted from our discussion of business because they are antisocial in nature and extralegal in character, and free enterprise, as we understand the concept, can exist only within the framework of law. When one considers that outside the United States there exist cartels, syndicates, and other collusive arrangements which interpose themselves in the free market as accepted, legitimate, and even perhaps progressive business practices, one may assume that the rule of free enterprise under law in the United States is possibly the most conspicuous difference between our economic system and that of other countries.

As was pointed out in our discussion of the concept of freedom

---

[1] Joseph Cropsey, *Polity and Economy* (The Hague: Martinus Nijhoff, 1957), pp. x–xi.

[2] A restatement of the position of classical economists that property rights are human rights is given, albeit too uncritically, by John Chamberlain, *The Roots of Capitalism* (New York: D. Van Nostrand Co., 1959), esp. pp. 25–28.

and ownership, we are living through a period of adaptation to basic changes in our economy, variously described as the Second Industrial Revolution or the Scientific Revolution. These changes are as much organizational as they are industrial or scientific. In the late 19th-century the wealth amassed by ruthless individualism in business enterprise, joined with the inventive skills of a few inquiring minds, set itself the task of speeding up production to meet new needs. Business enterprise had to adjust itself to a vanishing geographical frontier just when new laws were circumscribing its activities. At the same time, the opening of the West had created a vast new market for goods, and there was a railroad system to transport these goods. By the turn of the century, the accumulation of capital in a wide variety of hands and the evolution of new techniques of production and organization had begun to shape a new kind of economy, which has brought with it profound changes in our thinking as well as in our living habits.

The first conspicuous alteration in our economy was the change from a predominantly agricultural society to a predominantly industrial nation. This resulted from the new mass-production technology, which, in turn, gave rise to massive economic organizations in corporate form designed to cater to a mass market. They are so much an integral part of the American scenery that we tend to forget that large-scale industrial enterprise is barely a hundred years old. Even so, the resulting changes in economic mentality, as well as the radically new conditions of production and marketing, have led to the rise of a new type of entrepreneur, the manager. At the same time, the idea of "business" itself has changed. For, with the growth of huge corporations, less attention is paid to entrepreneurship in the old sense of risk venture with capital or with profits, and more to organizational problems and policies. In our recent past, "enterprise" suggested the imaginative entrepreneur who rose up to satisfy unmet demands in the market. It certainly did not mean gigantic concerns governed often by a small anonymous group able to generate demand, influence markets, and determine prices in ways undreamed of by their prototypes.

What, then, is left of the concept of free enterprise? Are current criticisms of big economic organization and thus effect on individuals and on society at large based on past facts or current realities? Is big business the despair or the hope of our people? Is it typical of the free-enterprise system? If so, to what extent does this system remain entrepreneurial? Shortly after World War II, Oswald Knauth, a writer with long experience as a corporate executive, decried the tenacity with which people cling to the philosophy of free competitive enterprise in the face of the new managerial enterprise fashioned to meet the exigencies of the modern world. But this newer form of economy has not yet been broadly recognized in traditional economic or legal theory.

At the time Knauth wrote—and for the most part this is still true —managerial enterprise under the aegis of the large corporation was evolving so fast that its methods were not understood. Codes for its operation were lacking and adequate laws had yet to be worked out. If managerial enterprise continued to be regarded as a variant of free enterprise or of monopoly, Knauth reasoned, little progress would be made in realistic assessments of its true nature.[3]

Thus we may agree with Walton Hamilton that a glib term such as "capitalism" or "free enterprise" belies the variety of the phenomena it professes to comprehend.[4] The activities of the modern multifunction and multiproduct type of business impinge on the economic interests of a wide variety of groups, including professional, skilled and unskilled workers, a broad base of stockholders, and a host of supporting supplier and distributor industries. Such large enterprises can have a profound effect on the economic prosperity of whole communities and sometimes of whole regions. Clearly, the possible area of unchallenged autonomy in enterprise has shrunk.

The corporation today is asked to consider its social responsibility along with its economic interest. Similarly, the union has to think of how far it can push its claim for more wages, if this may ultimately force the business to close or move out of the area. The stockholder has to consider whether foundation grants and pension plans will help to improve personnel and stabilize consumption, even though they take away from dividends. The small local businessman must consider how consumption may be reduced if he insists on so-called fair trade protection. The distributor, if he is dissatisfied, must evaluate the extent to which his business is fostered by the kind of advertising he cannot himself afford. Everyone has a

---

[3] Oswald Knauth, *Managerial Enterprise: Its Growth and Methods of Operation* (New York: W. W. Norton & Co., 1948).

[4] Walton Hamilton, *The Pattern of Competition* (New York: Columbia University Press, 1940), p. 22.

stake in managerial enterprise, and it is perhaps for this reason especially—although there are others—that one must distinguish its nature from that of the traditional free enterprise.

Of course, problems remain. The plight of the individual in modern industrial society, whether it is characterized as managerial, collective, or free, is a matter that still needs to be fairly evaluated. Though some of the postwar "organization man" fixation may be written off as sociological hysteria, there is still a fundamental kernel of truth in it. Mass-production techniques have tended to separate men from the total work effort—and this partitioning of human skills to handle only fragments of the work effort applies from the workbench up to the front office.

Apparently, it is in the nature of man to feel the need of completing the task he undertakes to earn his daily bread. As organization developed, this became less and less possible except for a few. The typical organization man today is the white-collar worker who often lacks the sense of fraternity that unionism seeks to supply to workers, or the sense of mission provided by a responsible executive post. As a result, he is more frustrated than stimulated by his work. Perhaps he has ceased to feel that what he brings to his employment could be had only from him. He feels expendable and consequently less of an individual, identifying, rather, with some bitterness, with the card that the machine processes to pay him—so like all other men that only the machine can recognize him.

His dismay does not go unregarded. The question of such human costs torments modern economic organization, as it does the state and society at large. For a long time, unionism was the main defender of the economically weak. Now the state and the business enterprise itself have taken up their case. The state-sponsored social security system and private pension funds are a concrete result of the current concern for at least the material welfare of human beings as men rather than as "hands."

This concern goes beyond the individual; it has spread to the community of nations. The effort to sustain and foster the economic life first of conquered or war-ravaged countries and more recently of the underdeveloped countries is unique to our time. As the French economist Perroux has remarked:

The mercantile exchange economies and the aggressive economy of fear which have for so long characterized relations between peoples have been subjected to a process of erosion which makes it possible to lay down the unshakeable bases of an economics of Service. The capitalist market and national states are stripped of artificial prestige; they are taken for what they are: instruments of man's adaptation to his environment. Also the world-wide economy which is taking form and which we must make a reality is trying out *territorial, institutional, and procedural frameworks* which definitely remove us from the accomplishments of the nineteenth century.[5]

Another factor creating change in the economy is the defense business, which has been built into the very fabric of peacetime industry. The missiles industry, of course, is largely a government creation. But many of the other defense industries that also have important civilian applications, such as electronic communications, aircraft, and chemicals, have developed quite differently as a result of government participation.

Thus the atomic energy industry is ruled neither by competition, public regulation nor outright government operation—the three traditional forms of industrial organization. As David Lilienthal, the Atomic Energy Commission's first chairman put it to members of the Joint Congressional Committee on Atomic Energy when the program was first initiated, the government was trying to develop a new kind of setup in American industrial affairs which is a hybrid of public and private. . . .[6]

Awards for defense contracts have not always been competitive, and to work on a cost-plus-one-dollar basis, as has happened, is hardly to put profit first as a goal. Is a business which derives the bulk of its earnings from government—and whose product design is set by government contract—a "pure" private enterprise? Indeed, is a firm really in business when it has only one customer, the government, which hopes there will never be any consumers for the wares it orders? There are other unsettled questions. Are defense items a waste of both resources and effort because they are frequently outmoded before they are assembled? Or, to the extent that it maintains employment and its corollary, purchasing power, is defense the only transfusion available in what might otherwise be an anemic economy?

The $80 billion spent annually in this country on armaments doubtless has valuable by-products. Perhaps one fourth of it is devoted to valuable applications of scientific principles that no one

---

[5] François Perroux, "From the Avarice of Nations to an Economy for Mankind," *Cross Currents*, Vol. III (Spring, 1953), p. 203.

[6] Charles E. Lindblom, "A New Device for Government Control?" *Challenge*, Vol. VIII (July, 1960), pp. 14–15.

in business would have either the money or the incentive to cope with were it not for the stimulus of defense contracts. Is it enough that they provide our business system with the acceleration and stimulation of a war emergency without its destruction and loss of life?

But will this defense stimulus suffice? After years of rehabilitation, we have finally left the postwar period behind us. We no longer have shortages. Some of our natural-resource needs are being met by the research and development laboratories of scientifically oriented businesses and by government. Capital expenditure is already going into such long-range research, though the prospect of money profit from it is, to say the least, uncertain. Are the real innovators of the 20th century the scientists? If they do not yet so think of themselves, perhaps they should. The market is waiting for them. Consider the people who have booked passage, or tried to, on that still hypothetical first passenger-carrying rocket. Reflect on the transactions involving real-estate lots on the moon. If they are not merely a whimsey of the tabloids, will there have to be a new phase of law to untangle claims to their possession?

Clearly, another kind of economy is growing up around us. Perhaps conventional businesses will be flexible enough to adapt to its final form. Certainly, they are managing to grow and sustain themselves through the transition period. Despite the increasingly institutional responsibilities that accrue to the economic organization and the growing dependence of all upon relatively few, as long as our society remains free, the foundations on which our economy has been built stand firm.

This is not to say that the foundations are not destined to be severely challenged during the 1970's; indeed, it need only be recalled how the present decade was ushered into existence with exuberant hosannas to the "soaring sixties," only to spend its waning days pondering the many failures of the success story. Within four or five years this country will achieve a trillion-dollar gross national product but the components of the GNP bear careful watching. We know, for example, that if the present figure is compared to the GNP of 1929, two major changes are noted. In the first place the war industry has risen from 1 to 10 percent of the GNP while household consumption has actually declined from 73 to 63 percent.

It is also evident that the problem of unemployment is still a plague. No longer are we fearful that the jobless rate will climb to 7 percent of the labor force, so that unemployment as a problem is not a quantitative one of *how many*, but *who*. And the "who" are obviously those between 17 and 21 in age and, most particularly, the minority workers in our population. The issue, then, changes from worry over the aggregate level of unemployment to the structure of joblessness.

Inflation still haunts the American people. It was once fashionable to speak of inflation as being the consequence of too much money chasing too few goods; but now we face the contradiction of inflation occurring when consumer prices increase annually at 4 percent or higher—even in the face of industry operating at rates substantially below its optimum capacity. Another scar on the national image is the existence of 6 million deteriorating housing units and the presence of another cruel irony, namely, the fact that the number of inadequate housing units has actually increased during the four-war period of the war on poverty.

It is also apparent that other contradictions press upon the nation. In our so-called "grants" economy, subsidies have gone to rich farmers and not to poor farmers who were alleged to be the reasons for national policy. Yet the rich farmer—freed from certain pressures and unfrightened by prospects of a stagnant farm economy—was the one whose innovations have provided the foundation for subsequent riches. Some economists now ask whether there is any point in continuing subsidies to farmers who constitute roughly 8 percent of the labor force and 5 percent of the GNP. Education is another area where the grants economy has failed to operate effectively.

In the presence of these problems it can easily be imagined that critics of business will lay down new barrages on the "establishment." Typically of the new breed of critics is Michael Harrington, whose book, *Toward a Democratic Left* (1968) has had a very substantial impact. Harrington pointed out that private business is so governed by the profit motive that it cannot be expected to divert resources to areas most in need of investment; rather business will go—at home and abroad—into areas where costs are low and potential for sales high. The result is already discernible: big enterprise will grow bigger and richer! Harrington notes for example, that General Motors now has a private GNP of over $20 billion and places ahead of Argentina, Belgium, and Czechoslovakia.

If the problem of efficiency in production is no longer the major one, the problems of equitable distribution and the problem of sharing in economic power will be the ones clamoring for solution in the decade ahead.

12. Money, Credit, Profit, and Capital Formation

No ASPECT of economics is so trying for the student—and often for the specialist as well—as monetary theory. The economy may be viewed from two different vantage points, which yield strikingly different images of its workings even though both images reflect the same underlying reality. The economy may be visualized as a monetary organism or, alternatively, in what has been called "real" terms.

In the first instance we may look at business solely as a complex network of financial transactions, with little or no reference to the actual goods and services that are in fact being manufactured and traded. The balance in one's checkbook, the income account of a

309

corporation, and stock-market quotations are all examples of financial data that have been detached from the actual flow of goods and the human effort upon which this flow depends.

But we may also picture the economy as a system in which commodities are created and sold and men exchange their labor skills for a living. The number of TV sets sold, the number of houses built, and the number of workers hired are examples of business statistics from which money price and cost are absent. These are the "real" economic forces mentioned above.

Each of these viewpoints is valid and necessary. Just because one is less tangible and concrete does not mean that it is therefore less significant. Certainly one could not think of an economy running on money alone with no real activity taking place in the background: no manufacture of products and no rendering of services. To be sure, a preoccupation with monetary factors sometimes leads to dangerous neglect of the real side of economic life. This is especially true during periods of runaway financial speculation. During the great stock market boom of 1929, brokers often had little or no idea of what products were being made by the companies they were warmly touting. This division of the unified economic reality into separate compartments, shut off from all that is not of immediate concern, accounts for much of the strange, often fantastic enthusiasm that appears in times of speculative boom. The social cost of such perceptual failures is heavy.

However, an opposite mistake would be made if the financial nexus of the economy was dismissed as somehow inessential or parasitic. Money is not simply a veil that hides the real operations of commerce and industry; it is also a functional part of the machine. It has been called "the language of economic communication." Once the economy has risen above the primitive subsistence level, a division of labor begins and barter becomes an increasingly clumsy mode of exchange; further, as economic life becomes more complicated, saving and investment tend to divide into separate functions. Then an entire complex of financial institutions comes into being. Finance is inescapable, no matter what economic or political form the social system takes. The need for monetary regulations and allocations exists in capitalist and collectivist societies, in free nations and in dictatorships.

The financial nexus is a triumph of man's talent for abstract reasoning which means, in effect, his capacity to understand rather clearly what instruments are most effective for accomplishing specific tasks. In a real sense money is "natural" to society because it permits man to see the reality underlying exchange relationships; it links material things into a web of economic connections more susceptible to control by the human intellect. A money economy eliminates, or at the very least, subordinates the *subjective* considerations of feelings to the *objective* considerations of true value. Money makes no distinctions between friend and foe, black or white, manager or worker, educated or illiterate. A money economy is, therefore, complex, impersonal, rational, calculating, and objective; as such money becomes a means and an instrument and cannot of itself provide goals or values to a society.

If money itself does not provide the values it remains, nevertheless, the most reliable measure of material values; it flows through the modern economic system much as blood flows through the body, and without it, the vast amount of capital required by advanced technology and the fantastic specialization of labor—two other major qualities of a modern economy—would be impossible to sustain. The need for capital and the degree of specialization combine to make the modern economy an extraordinarily interdependent one so that a disturbance in either part has repercussions on the whole.

Everyone knows that money is useful—few know what it really is. More often than not its significance is appreciated only when something goes awry with the monetary system. Then, as D. H. Robertson observes, a monetary system is like a liver. It does not take up very much of our thoughts when it goes right, but it attracts a great deal of attention when it goes wrong."[1] Thus, we had a practical illustration of the crucial role of financial institutions during the Great Depression. All the material factors of production stood ready for use, and in real terms there was no excuse for anything short of abundance, yet millions were out of work and many thousands were hungry. To a large extent this paradox of poverty in the midst of potential plenty occurred because the economic liver had stopped working properly. The system of money and credit had collapsed, and confidence was lost in the institutions created to regulate the economy. As a result, the whole pattern of financial expectations was shattered.

---

[1] Dennis H. Robertson, *Money* (Cambridge Economic Handbooks, No. 2). (London: Nisbet & Co., 1922), pp. 1–2.

MONEY

FUNCTIONS OF MONEY

Textbooks usually list three functions of money: (1) a medium of exchange, (2) a unit of value, and (3) a store of value. In what is probably its most basic role, money is the "great wheel of circulation." Hence, it has been variously described as "a circulating medium," "a medium of payments," and "an exchange medium." As suggested above, the barter system of exchange is inherently ill-suited to the demands of a complex economy. If the goatherd had no alternative but to trade his milk output for the many articles he needs, neither he nor his suppliers would prosper. The shoemaker, who wants to sell the goatherd shoes, may not like goat's milk. To consummate a transaction that both wish to make, an intermediary (who likes goat's milk and also has something the shoemaker wants) must be found.

But, with increased productive complexity, such arrangements are increasingly difficult to organize. To solve these problems, people soon start looking for one commodity that they can agree to exchange for all other commodities at fixed rates. It is usually something that is useful in its own right or else desirable for its beauty or scarcity. This is how "quasi money" comes into being. The list of items that have been used for exchange in the economic stage lying between simple barter and a fully developed money system is long and odd. Cattle, bronze, and wampum are familiar enough. But how many of us know that porpoise teeth, playing cards, woodpecker scalps, boar tusks, and slaves have also served as money? Today a commodity type of quasi money is still the main circulating medium in many primitive areas.

In spite of its advantages over simple barter, quasi money was not the perfect solution to the circulation problem. For one thing, different peoples had different commodity media and this made intergroup exchange difficult. Much quasi money, moreover, is awkward to carry—it is a nuisance to have to drive a herd of cows to the market whenever one wants to go shopping. For these and other reasons, one valuable commodity, gold, tended increasingly to drive the others from the circulation system. More recently still, monetary reforms have largely removed currency from its traditional form of metallic coin. But no matter what form true money takes, whether it is made of precious metal or chits of paper, its distinguishing features are convenience and universal acceptability. It is both the great stimulant and *sine qua non* of a modern economy.

Money has also been called "a unit of account," "a common denominator of value," and "a unit of value." Behind these descriptive phrases lies the idea of a yardstick against which the relative values or prices of a vast multitude of commodities may be measured. Money supplies this yardstick, playing a role closely connected with that of circulating medium. Thus buyer or seller does not have to remember the values of every conceivable good in terms of all others, as they might well have to in a barter-exchange economy. Instead of having to remember that a cartwheel is worth ten bales of hay or two sheep or six iron bars, the purchaser need only know that it costs $7.50. This simplification of the commercial process gives an important lift to economic activity.

Of the roles of money, "storage of value" has been traditionally considered the most important, but today it is undoubtedly the least important. True money has no ordinary use value; one cannot eat it or pave a street with it. Money's function as a store of value is therefore essentially asocial and private. And many experts believe that in this role it is actually antisocial.

The reasons for the public's declining preference for money as a store of value are threefold: (1) money held in the form of cash or in checking accounts earns no interest or dividends, (2) it can undergo no real appreciation in capital value, and (3) in inflationary times (as during the last three decades) it steadily loses purchasing power. A combination of these factors has driven most stored capital into investment channels that yield an income return or are susceptible to an increase in asset value. Bonds, stocks, realty, and life insurance have largely replaced the old sock in the family mattress. In a growing economy, with its large requirements for new capital, the investment of savings is very desirable from both the social and the individual points of view.

Of course, the investment propensity is reversible. In bad times, or during periods of political turmoil, capital tends to move back into forms believed to be inherently valuable. Liquidity is sought through the hoarding of movable and concealable assets, such as gold. The pickup in the international gold market that normally occurs whenever economic or social conditions appear threatening is an illustration of this response.

KINDS OF MONEY

In developed countries money usually exists in the form of paper currency, checking deposits, and coins. There are other forms, and the specialist will tell us that many subtypes exist within these three general categories. These qualifications are important, but we can hardly enter into much detail here.

Currency printed on paper is a fairly recent innovation, but paper money has gained general acceptance in stable countries. It may be divided into two types: *representative* and *nonrepresentative* tender. The former is "backed" by silver or gold held in the treasury of the state issuing the notes. In some instances the issuing treasury will exchange the notes for a given quantity of the supporting metallic reserve, but representative money is usually nonconvertible.

Nonrepresentative notes, also called rather contemptuously "fiat money," have no backing in bullion. Their sole backing is the credit of the issuing state. Orthodox economists generally oppose granting government the right to issue nonrepresentative bills. They fear that in times of difficulty the government will try to solve its problems (that is, pay its bills) by resorting to the printing press. Uninhibited creation of currency will certainly lead to inflation, but the flexibility of the unbacked issue, which does not bind a treasury to an arbitrary and otherwise useless stock of bullion, perhaps makes up for the potential dangers—that is, assuming a responsible political administration. During the Civil War the United States was forced to print several hundred million dollars in fiat money, popularly called "greenbacks." Up until 1968 a compromise solution had been reached as the law required a certain ratio (a minimum of 25 percent) between the currency issue and the support reserve in gold.

International pressures, however, forced the United States to drop this requirement—thus placing the burden for maintaining a stable currency on the government's capacity to maintain confidence in the economy. By far the most important form of money in the modern economy is the bank check. In fact, the money supply nowadays consists largely of bank deposits, which may be transferred to pay debts. Most large financial transactions and many small ones are completed with the aid of checks. From an economic viewpoint a bank check for $50 *is* money; it does not merely *represent* an equal number of actual dollar bills that are kept elsewhere. Many people seem to have trouble grasping this point, perhaps because of the traditional identification of money with the circulating medium. Convenience, more than any other factor, has served to make checking accounts the most important element in the money flow of the modern economy, so that nine tenths of all transactions, by value if not by number, are handled through checks.

In summary, then, it may be noted that although the government theoretically has the sole authority to create money, most of it is, in fact, created by commercial banks, through checks, subject to general regulation by the government. Money supply depends for the most part on the supply and demand relationship between bankers and borrowers. The Treasury and the Federal Reserve have considerable power over how much money the banks will be allowed to lend. But the money stock, or what the Federal Reserve calls the money supply, consists of these major elements: coins, paper currency, and demand deposits. It is the last which accounts for most of the money in the American economy. When the Federal Reserve System was established in 1914 it meant something to say that a Federal Reserve note was redeemable in gold coin or gold certificate. When the word "redeemable" appears today it is practically meaningless and the statement "this note is legal tender for all debts, public and private" is more accurate and indicates the crucial nature of "acceptability" in a money system.

CREDIT

Credit, no simple concept, plays many public and private roles and has many subtle influences. We shall not attempt here a morphologically complete description of the credit machinery but shall instead try to point out the significant functions that credit performs in the economy.

For many centuries debt had a bad name in Christian societies. To be in debt was morally undesirable, but to place others in debt was deemed especially reprehensible. Perhaps some of the traditional Christian horror of debt was inherited as a reaction against the old Roman practice. In pagan Rome, usury was common and accepted. Many of the most famous families of antiquity made and held fortunes through money lending, often at exorbitant rates of interest. The great *latifundia* of the later Empire were to a large extent built on the basis of expropriation of land for nonpayment of debt. The more unscrupulous lenders came to lend money more with the idea of foreclosure than with intent to earn a fair return on capital. Roman law was largely class law and heavily favored the interests of the creditors.

The Church's traditional opinion of usury was particularly low, though modern scholars have perhaps exaggerated the clerical objection to credit when granted on reasonable terms. One must separate the theological objection to money increasing itself from the practical working-out of the anti-usury injunction, which was primarily employed to prevent the exploitation of the weak and destitute. A survival of this social regulation of credit may be found in the many existing statutes—all too often circumvented—that place ceilings on the legal rate of interest. In the Middle Ages, the Church and not the state was the bane of the loan shark. As Pope Innocent IV opined, correctly for an age of low capital formation, "he who borrows is always under stress of necessity."[2]

FUNCTIONS OF CREDIT

Much of what we have said about the necessity of money to economic activity applies also to debt. The credit system is probably just as crucial to our industrial way of life as money itself, although the relationship is undoubtedly less obvious. And again, as with money, the utility of credit is both personal and public. A few examples will readily demonstrate the truth of these statements.

An engineer working for a large firm has an idea for a new product, which he thinks he would like to develop himself. However, the cost of going into business for himself is too high. Unless outside credit is available, supplied by others who share his enthusiasm for the new idea, the innovator might have to wait many years to bring his product to the market. Perhaps he could never save enough from his salary to begin the undertaking. In that case, both he and society would be the losers. Along with the benefits that the public might gain from the product itself, there is a negative side to consider. Jobs, dividends, taxes, and careers could be lost; hence, to start new industry, debt is often very necessary. Even large, well-established firms often have to enter the debt-capital market to finance their expansion plans.

---

[2] R. H. Tawney, *Religion and the Rise of Capitalism* (New York: Harcourt, Brace & Co., 1952) , p. 44. See chap. ii for the Church's attitude toward money.

But it is not only the establishment of new businesses or the expansion of old ones that requires borrowing; thousands of enterprises need credit as a regular part of their year-to-year operations. Consider the predicament of a distributor of a seasonal commodity —say girls' swim suits. A fairly large sum of money must be tied up each spring in inventory, and often the capital needed is beyond the resources of the retailer. He must therefore borrow to "finance his line." Even large corporations find it convenient to incur short-term debt to meet certain recurring temporary demands for cash.

But while there is little debate over the need for business debt, there is argument aplenty over *personal* or *consumer* debt. The growth of individual debt in the United States during the last few years has been truly astonishing, especially when one considers that it has accompanied times of prosperity rather than of recession. Modern consumer credit has far outpaced the old-fashioned charge account, which only the well-to-do could once afford to maintain at their favorite department stores. Perhaps the majority of consumer durable goods sales today are made partly on credit, with repayment terms often extending over several years. Many thoughtful observers feel strongly that the United States is on a "buy now, pay later" binge. What are we to expect if poor business conditions cause a sharp drop in personal incomes? Will a large and damaging number of credit defaults follow?

Further, the opponents of easy consumer debt believe that it has overstimulated the economy in the postwar period. The post–World War II prosperity, they assert, has been distorted by the vast increase in sales that could not have been made without credit. The eventual result of this consumer goods boom, as they see it, can only be a catastrophic bust.

Champions of high consumer credit arrive at nearly the opposite conclusions. They assure us that the prosperity of the last few decades has been founded in considerable part on time sales; without this credit innovation we would already have seen bad times of recession or depression. According to them, easy consumer credit is a permanent change in the American economy. Though it violates certain traditional views concerning thrift, its overall social effect is beneficial. To the objection that excessive consumer debt encourages cyclical instability, they reply that the best way to avoid recession is to increase the purchasing power of the consumer. Credit, they maintain, is an excellent if unorthodox means to achieve this end.

It is impossible to determine at this moment which of the two viewpoints is correct or even which has the more truth in it. Perhaps both will be found to have some validity. Certainly consumer credit has become an integral part of our economy and much of the postwar prosperity is related to it. However, the conservative insight can not be summarily rejected because very high levels of personal debt do have inflationary effects that exaggerate the swings of the business cycle.

From a consumer point of view it is worth noting that an historic event is occurring in consumer credit, "one that eventually may touch practically everyone who needs to borrow, or who buys on the installment plan," acording to H. E. Heinemann of *The New York Times* (November 24, 1968). That event is due to the work of the National Conference on Uniform State Laws, which had completed a four-year project to draft a uniform consumer credit code; states are expected to enact legislation built on principles enunciated by the National Conference. The major recommendations (attributed to Professor Robert Johnson of Purdue) would open the lending market to all responsible sellers, in sharp contrast to the present restrictive licensing requirements found in most state personal loan laws; it would replace the hodgepodge of different ceilings on interest rates with one fairly high uniform ceiling; it would eliminate many devices used by creditors to collect overdue debts such as wage assignments and confusions of judgment.

What is encouraging is the fact that, despite expected opposition, most large finance companies (the Commercial Credit Company, the Household Finance Company, the C.I.T), and many large retailers (Sears and Montgomery Ward) are soldily behind the code.

THE BANKING SYSTEM

The key to the national credit picture is the individual bank. Originally banks developed from the practice of individuals leaving their gold with goldsmiths for safekeeping. These men, in turn, lent it to others in return for interest and gradually began to replace the actual metal with promises to pay on demand. After a period of time, these "promises-to-pay" began to exceed the actual amount of gold on hand. Thus developed the need for what are called *fractional reserves*. The only danger was that the banker had to determine what percentage of his total loans he must be able to back up with metal, and he had to be careful to insure that he did not have too many debts. Today it is far easier for a bank to operate with fractional reserves because of the laws which govern what percentage should be kept in reserve, the laws which state what kind of loans may be negotiated, and because of the experience gained by bankers throughout the years.

There are about 13,500 commercial banks, 517 mutual savings banks, and over 6,200 savings and loan associations in the United States today. These range in size from multibillion-dollar institutions down to the small country bank with assets of a million dollars or less. In this discussion, the focus will be on the role of the commercial banks.

Individual banks create money largely by making loans and buying securities. How this creative process occurs can be simply illustrated by reference to the handling of checking accounts. When money is deposited in an individual's checking account it becomes an asset for the individual, but both an asset and a liability for the bank. It is an asset in the sense that it becomes part of its cash on hand, but a liability in the sense that the bank must pay it to the depositor on demand. However, the deposit does not earn interest. Moreover, the bank is not required by law to keep the entire amount on hand for possible payment to the depositor—only about 20 percent. The balance can be used for other transactions. In addition, since the bank is obligated, again by law, to keep its required reserves in the Federal Reserve Bank, the individual's original amount is worth five times this in deposited reserves. The balance of the amount of the individual's deposit is lent to others. Naturally, this draws interest to the lending bank, which is making the assumption that the individual will leave his deposit in the bank for some period of time. Often, the loan gravitates to another bank in the form of a deposit and the process is repeated. As the available or "loanable" portion of the original deposit moves from bank to bank it keeps creating more money in the form of loans.

The fact that there are many banks in the banking system makes the operation in a sense self-contained. An increase in the deposits of one bank usually means an increase in the deposits of another. Since the flow is generally two ways, and the number of individuals large, the banks can usually count on smooth expansion operations. As a safety precaution as well as for operating ease, most banks keep some part of their deposits in cash, which averages about 2 percent and is called "till money." If follows that as banks expand their deposits they also increase their assets, not only in notes for loans but also in other securities and governmental obligations. To perform these operations, they must, of course, first have reserves. Conversely, the banking system contracts the money supply by decreasing the size of its loan and securities portfolios. Hence, the operations of the individual banks affect and partly control the general level of business activity. When there is an increase in lending activity, business tends to expand. When lending activity slackens, so does commercial activity.

The reasons for these tendencies are not far to seek. Loans are used to hire workers, buy materials, build or rent additional business space, and so forth. All such individual acts mean business for others. More cash in the worker's pocket means more sales for the retailer and hence more orders for the wholesaler. More trade for the wholesaler means more orders for the manufacturer. More rent for the landlord and more business for the producers of raw materials follow. And the wages and profits of these industries return to the retailer in payment for still more sales. But, when bank lending falters, the opposite chain of events is set in motion. All along the line there is less: less trade, fewer orders to fill, fewer men to hire, less income to spend, and fewer goods to produce.

However, we must stress that the aggregate of commercial-bank activities does not by itself determine the level of business activity. Many other factors are involved. The operations of the banks are as much determined by the economy as they determine it. There is a two-way relationship of cause and effect that works out in very complex ways in the economic world. A bank loan to a retailer to expand his business leads directly to more jobs and income and indirectly, through the ramifications of this new income, to a minute upturn in the entire economy. But if the retailer's trade is already poor, he may never dream of coming to the bank to finance an expansion. What would be the point of going into debt for a bigger shop with fewer customers? In this case, the general condition of demand sets a limit to the possible influence of the banks in creating more money and prosperity. Perhaps the best way to grasp this situation is to think of the volume of new credit as an accelerating factor in the business cycle, one that can reinforce business trends in either direction but that cannot to any substantial degree itself initiate an upturn or a downswing.

The United States was one of the last major nations to establish a central bank. When legislation was finally enacted in 1913, it was long overdue. As Carter Glass of Virginia told the House in that year:

> The failure of the system in acute exigencies has caused widespread business demoralization and almost universal distress. Five times within the last thirty years financial catastrophe has overtaken the country under this system; and it would be difficult to compute the enormous losses sustained by all classes of society. . . . The system has literally no reserve force. The currency based upon the nation's debt is absolutely unrelated to the nation's business needs. The lack of cooperation and coordination among the more than 7,300 national banks produces a curtailment of facilities at all periods of exceptional demand for credit.[3]

Because of the tremendous demand for loans, local bankers often took unwise risks which resulted in failure of the bank. This problem was not confined to one community but often spread to others, either through commercial obligations of the failed bank or to the famous "run" on the bank for capital that it did not have. The "local" nature of these banks worked both to their benefit and their loss. The banker knew the local conditions and the local individuals, but was often an amateur or a promoter. Moreover, strictly local conditions often created a tight financial position that was not typical of the country at large. Obviously a growing nation needed facilities for more widespread pooling of funds. In the midst of the Civil War, Congress created the National Banking system to discipline the banking community through tightened reserve requirements and original capital funds. Nevertheless, the tradition of local banking remained strong.

The money panics of 1873, 1884, and 1907 were caused by currency contractions and by seasonal withdrawals of reserves by Western banks from their New York correspondents. The contraction was due to the fact that "Northern" currency had to supply the whole country when the Civil War ended. Because tax collections were greater than expenses, the government began to redeem "greenbacks" and the Treasury was later able to retire much of the debt that provided backing for the national bank notes, with the result that the supply of these notes contracted. An expanding economy facing a contracting currency was destined for trouble.

---

[3] U.S. Congress (House), *Congressional Record* (63d Cong., 1st sess.), Vol. 50 (1913), Part 5, p. 4642.

Within this context, any substantial withdrawal of funds could easily precipitate a crisis and this occured when Western farmers, at harvesting time, often needed to withdraw savings from the local banks or negotiate loans to move their crops to market. The Western bankers, on the other hand, normally held part of their reserves as deposits in the larger New York commercial banks. When these were suddenly called for en masse, the New York banks were often embarrassed; they in turn recalled loans, which usually could not be renegotiated by the debtor elsewhere, since all the big city institutions were temporarily short of loan funds. A brief but damaging credit panic would typically occur. A depression in miniature was induced: jobs, income, and capital were lost.

To end these panics, the Federal Reserve System was, in effect, empowered to create money for the commercial banks in times of credit stringency. It also undertook many other fiscal housekeeping chores, such as national check clearance and member-bank examination. The "Fed" is not, however, a true central bank. Rather it is a decentralized central bank, if such a concept is possible. At the time the Federal Reserve Act was enacted, it was feared that a true central bank on the European model would become an organ of centralized political power; a compromise was therefore reached. The Act established 12 regional banks, each having a considerable degree of autonomy but with a higher Federal Reserve Board sitting in Washington to oversee the whole system.

Two major functions of the Federal Reserve Board are, first, to hold the legally required fractional reserve deposits of member banks, and second, to fix the amount of required reserves. Actually, only an insignificant fraction of a member bank's reserve deposits are in the form of real currency. Reserves normally consist of gold certificates plus loans to other banks or assets like government bonds purchased by payments made in the form of additions to the accounts of member banks. Gold certificates originate when the Treasury Department purchases gold for member banks which accumulate the gold through foreign exchange. The gold certificate is issued by the Treasury to replace the deposits that it has shifted from its own account to the account of the member bank from which the gold was purchased.

There are other ways to increase its deposits. Through "rediscounting," for example, the Fed can lend money to a member bank which needs to increase its reserve deposits. As collateral, the member bank turns over to the Federal Reserve Board some of the notes it holds from its borrowers. In return for this service, the Fed takes a percentage of the face amount as its own profit by discounting the note—that is, by not paying the full face value. Sometimes, the Fed goes into the open market in order to increase its reserves and thus create deposits on its own initiative by buying government securities.

These various operations enable the Fed to play a role in the economy far more substantial than that performed simply by serving as a reserve depository. This new role is closely related to the business cycle. Since the 1930's the Fed has become a leading instrument of government countercyclical policy. The reserve banks, through appropriate policies, indirectly create or destroy money and expand or contract the money supply. During periods of inflationary boom the System ups the percentage reserve requirements that the member banks must maintain with the central bank. Thus, the commercial banks have less money to lend out and the boom tends to slow down. During periods of business slack the Fed lowers its reserve requirements on deposits, and additional funds flow out into the economy. A similar effect is achieved by the System's open-market operations in government securities. When the Board wishes to contract the lending base of the commercial banks, it offers securities at prices that may prove relatively attractive as bank investments. When it wishes to pump money into the economy, it offers to purchase securities at relatively favorable prices and thus releases funds for business loans.

There is little doubt that, within a limited range of commercial fluctuation, the monetary policies of the Federal Reserve System are highly effective. But they seem inherently better suited to control the rising phase of the cycle than the downward reaction, especially if the reaction is sharp and prolonged.

A further check to the effectiveness of the Federal Reserve's countercyclical policies arises from the fact that much credit originates with lending institutions outside the commerical banking system. In addition to savings banks and savings and loan associations, insurance companies, credit companies (such as CIT and GMAC), and many factoring firms are constantly suppyling individuals and businesses with loans. Except through very indirect means, the Fed is unable to counteract the legitimate activities of these and other sources of credit.

PROFIT

It may fairly be said of profit that some people are apologetic about it, that most Americans regard too much of it with suspicion, that everybody wants it, and that no one has ever given a satisfactory definition of it. John Chamberlain said of profits:

To the business man a profit is what is left when he has paid his costs; it is the difference between red ink and black. To the economist who believes that an economic system strains toward equilibrium, profit is a temporary thing which is destined to disappear whenever competition in a given field of endeavor has reached the point of saturation. To a Marxist, profit is wrung from the poor by taking from the worker the "surplus value" he creates over and above the cost of his subsistence. And to believers in an illusory "perfect competition" profit is a monopolistic charge which the proprietor of a patent or the possessor of some temporary secret piles on top of the "natural" price which is compounded of costs, plus the "wage" of management and the interest paid out for the loan of capital.[4]

This quotation sums up neatly some of the more familiar opinions. It is also interesting for its use of such terms as "temporary," "monopolistic," and "wrung from," for these reflect a rather general feeling that unless profit is transitory it tends to become somehow destructive. But short-run profits also arouse suspicions. The word "profiteer," used to describe men who make large profits in war time, for example, evokes that older word, "buccaneer," the sea predator of the past, or that more modern predator, the "racketeer." These three terms describe men who make profits by preying upon their weaker and less ruthless fellow men.

This tendency to associate the idea of profit with the idea of lawless exploitation has led to the ingenious invention of all sorts of euphemisms. Businesses speak of "maximizing" profit, not of "increasing" it, and more recently the term "profitability" has been substituted for the bald word "profit," perhaps because its associations are more moral and hopeful. And yet, to modern man, profit is so essential a condition of business that it appears as natural as breathing, and the ability to make a profit, under ordinary economic conditions and in a manner approved by law, probably denotes a very special kind of ability. Considered in this context, profit is not the result of dubious dealing but of a special kind of creativity,

---

[4] John Chamberlain, *The Roots of Capitalism* (Princeton: D. Van Nostrand Co., 1959), p. 125.

an instinct for meeting or creating a demand and an ability to deploy human and natural resources in an advantageous manner.

Profits are not the same as profit systems because the former always carries a positive connotation whereas the latter is really a profit-and-loss system. Companies continuously reassess their position to determine how next to move to assure adequate profit margins, and in these movements calculated risks must be taken. Some years ago, for example, the General Electric Company faced the possibility that some of its traditional operations would cease to be profitable. A decision was taken to form an entirely new organization within the company to take advantage of and to facilitate technological advances. While the strategy was designed to produce profit, there were, obviously, serious risks involved. But the search for profits means that an enterprise must be conscious of consumer demands and this consciousness leads to more effective utilization of company resources. The profit system therefore can lead to improvements in production which cut costs, can provide incentives for technological and social innovations, and can induce the most efficient allocation of resources.

THEORIES OF PROFIT

Profits are defined in many different ways. In speaking of the income flow of enterprise, economists treat wages, interest, rent, and profits. Very simply, wages, interest, and rent are the returns, respectively, on labor, capital, and land. Economists, without reaching complete agreement, have for a long time discussed precisely what factor profit rewards. The most common dictionary definition describes profits as the excess of a firm's income over its expenditures or costs. What to include as costs, however, becomes a matter of controversy as soon as we try to arrive at a specific definition.

A very brief glance at some of the major theories of profits will show how very far apart economists (as distinct from accountants) still are from agreeing on basic definitions.

Four alternatives are common:

1. In the classical view "the lowest ordinary rate of profit must always be something more than what is sufficient to compensate occasional losses to which every employment of stock is exposed. It is this surplus only which is net or clear profit."[5]

2. Another theory holds that profit is a differential accruing to

_____
[5] Adam Smith, *An Inquiry into the Nature and Causes of the Wealth of Nations* (Edinburgh: Oliphant, Wauch and Innes, 1814), Vol. I, Book 1, chap. ix, p. 157.

the more efficient producer. In this view, prices are always high enough to cover the costs of the least efficient producer in the market. The ability of enterprises of higher efficiency to produce at costs lower than those of the marginal variety yields them a differential return that is considered profit.

3. Another view is that profits accrue to the enterpriser because of his innovations in developing new products, recombining resources, and opening up new product demands. In this case, profits are the "wages" of competent management which, it must be noted, is to be distinguished from routine or bureaucratic management. All managers earn wages—only enterprisers and innovators reap profits. Many persons, for example, were early involved with inventions in the automobile industry; but it remained for Henry Ford to walk off with the great profit windfalls because he knew how to make a car, how to advertise and market it, how to hold customers by providing efficient servicing for it. Usually the profits going to the innovator are temporary because competitors come along rapidly to imitate the innovator and to cut into his returns. This interpretation is associated with Professor Schumpeter.

4. If Joseph Schumpeter's name is associated with the "profit-for-the-innovator" theory, it is Frank Knight of the University of Chicago who is most clearly identified with a definition which links profits to uncertainty. A broker who gambled that the price of wheat would rise sharply and who made a million dollars over a weekend would represent the kind of a man who really deserved and received a profit. The same man might also "lose his shirt." It is the uncertainty between what a man expects to happen and what actually happens that provides the discrepancy or profit. This theory of profit stresses the dynamism of the economy and the necessity for a businessman to undergo risks. If profit is viewed as the return caused by uncertainty then profits are not simply a fourth factor return like wages, rents, or interests. *Profit is part of these factor returns.*

THE MEASUREMENT OF PROFIT

Quantification of the various economic concepts of profits raises serious problems. Yet it is important to calculate profits not only for the individual enterprise but for the aggregate of all enterprises in the economy.

Accountants, faced with the practical necessity for measuring profits in a single enterprise, have developed standard techniques for preparing the balance sheet and income statement. But economic concepts of profit and how it should be measured do not always agree with accounting calculations. In particular, the two approaches differ on what costs must be deducted from enterprise income to reach a profit figure. Among costs, depreciation and the impact of price on valuation of assets generate the greatest controversy. Then, too, economists consider future events as bases for present economic values of an enterprise, while accounting is concerned with past events. This also raises conflict in measuring and interpreting profit figures.

The statistics on corporate profits are voluminous. But, in spite of availability of profit figures for the whole economy, the difficulty of preparing consistent, uniform, and comprehensive profit data should not be underestimated. Profits are an extremely volatile element in national income, rising steeply during boom periods and dropping to low or deficit levels during periods of slow economic activity. For individual enterprises, of course, the fluctuations are even more radical than the national average. Public investigations into the level of profits are common, especially in periods of prosperity. But the same investigative fervor is not often on display, except in business circles, in periods of loss.

PROFIT AND BUSINESS BEHAVIOR

Traditional literature on profits makes the assumption, and sticks with it, that the individual business firm seeks to maximize profit. Frequently this is assumed to be the only goal. Empirical as well as theoretical work in the recent past casts strong doubt on this as a single purpose. There is no doubt that profit is still a dominant goal of individual enterprises. But today many businessmen seek other goals, and they do not necessarily seek a "maximum" profit.

Profit maximization as the goal of the firm has been replaced in some circumstances by the long-range goal of general stability and enhanced reputation, and in others by the simulation of game psychology in which profits become "scores."[6]

The increasing emphasis placed on the corporation as an institution has given it a sense of longer time span. Much of its planning is

---

[6] Lois Shepherd Headings (ed.) , "Sanctity or Sanction: Explorations of Power," *Business Horizons,* Vol. II (Winter, 1959) , pp. 97–110. See also Neil W. Chamberlain, *A General Theory of Economic Process* (New York: Harper & Bros., 1955) , *passim.*

done in terms of long-range effort and means deferring rewards for a long-range future. One of the functions of profits is to provide "lead time" to experiment with new products, services, and markets from which no immediate return can be realized. Moreover, it is today commonplace for established firms to set standards of "reasonable" profit rather than profit in terms of a surplus over marginal costs, since they may be in a more favorable position for the manufacture of certain products than are other companies.

Ours is a profit-and-loss economy. Profit is an incentive for efficiency, loss is the penalty for inefficiency. The solution of the incalculably complex allocation problem of an economic system—in determining what shall be produced, how it shall be produced, who shall produce it, and when—centers on the profit motive. For, in a relatively competitive economy, profits are the reward for resource allocations that serve a manifest economic demand.

CAPITAL FORMATION

NATIONAL GROWTH AND ALLOCATION

In recent years the problem of sustained national economic growth has come to the forefront of both popular and expert discussion. During the 19th century and the first decades of our own century, the continued rapid development of the American economy was a fact that was also taken for granted. This is no longer the case. Perhaps because of the ever-increasing competition of the communist world, farsighted observers have turned their attention to the question of our rate of material advance and that of the other free nations with which we are associated. While some have decried the trend toward "growthmanship," there are others who warn us that, unless the United States keeps expanding its economic capacity at a goodly rate, the international balance of power will shortly shift against us. Over the last decade the average rate of increase in America's gross national product (GNP) has been about 3.2 percent per annum, but since 1953 this average growth rate has declined to only about 2.5 percent per annum. To many minds this is not high enough. To others it is a natural rate of expansion, which cannot be substantially improved without upsetting the structure of the economy.

If, however, we assume that a higher level of growth is needed, the argument over how such growth is to be achieved, or whether it can be achieved at all, is far from ended. Among the many authorities who are optimistic over the prospects for inducing a substantial increase in our rate of growth is David Rockefeller, president of the Chase Manhattan Bank:

. . . if a national effort to accelerate growth were to be adopted, there is reason to hope we could lift our annual rate of economic advance to perhaps 5 percent, or possibly even 6 percent, assuming policies which emphasized economic growth were pursued with sufficient vigor.

This is an exciting prospect. A mere continuation of the post-war growth trend would yield a gross national product in 1970 of more than $750 billion in today's dollars, a real advance of almost 50 percent. If a concerted national effort towards growth yielded a 6 percent per annum advance, the 1970 gross national product would reach $900 billion, or 75 percent above the figure for this year.[7]

A sharply contrasting viewpoint was presented by Professor Arthur Smithies of Harvard University. According to him, the achievement of a high rate of industrial expansion is not so easy a matter and, if possible, can be attained only at a considerable cost:

If the United States, as is frequently urged, is to maintain a 5 percent rate of growth, it seems highly likely that this will mean continued pressure on the labor supply and consequent increases in real wages that are rapid in relation to past experience. Unless some corresponding increase in the productivity trend can also be achieved, the rate of increase of the capital stock may have to be doubled or tripled—a formidable task. A more feasible policy may be to aim at improved allocation of resources in the context of a somewhat lower rate of growth rather than at a total rate of growth that will accommodate everything.[8]

There is also much debate on the question of allocation of the nation's capital wealth. Some critics have claimed that the United States is suffering from a condition of private affluence and public poverty. Edwin L. Dale, correspondent of *The New York Times* has concisely put this side of the issue in these words:

Our society has reached a level of private wealth never before seen on this earth. Yet at the same time there is poverty in the public sector of the economy. Education is underfinanced. Streams are polluted. There re-

---

[7] *How Fast Can We Grow?* (address given by David Rockefeller before the Western Association of Food Chains Convention, Las Vegas, Nevada, April 11, 1960) (printed by the bank, New York, 1960) , pp. 9–10.

[8] Arthur Smithies, "Productivity, Real Wages and Economic Growth," *Quarterly Journal of Economics,* Vol. LXXIV (May, 1960) , p. 197.

mains a shortage of hospital beds. Slums proliferate, and there is a gap in middle-income housing. We could use more and better parks, streets, detention facilities, water supply. The very quality of American life is suffering from these lacks—much more than from any lack of purely private goods and services. The share of government in the total economy has been stable or even declining, while private affluence grows.[9]

The issue of private riches and public poverty comes down to conflicting claims about which it is hard finally to conclude anything. Defenders of the way the nation's capital resources are currently being apportioned will point to statistics showing a steady expansion of public spending for such forms of public overhead capital as schools, hospitals, highways, or parks. The critic will answer that despite the figures of growth in the public sector, still more public spending is needed. However, what does emerge from the debate on national capital formation is an interesting fact. The American mind, 35 years after the New Deal, is still deeply divided on this question: How shall the National Income be allocated between the public and private sectors? For this is what really is at stake in the debate over the adequacy of our stock of public overhead capital. In the years ahead may we expect the rift to close or to widen?

INTERNATIONAL CAPITAL FORMATION

The export of capital is a comparatively recent development in history. Prior to the 19th century it probably would have been thought absurd for one country voluntarily to transfer its substance to another part of the world in the hope of gaining a return. The traditional view would have been that there was a overwhelming chance that the return would fail to materialize and that the capital stake itself would probably be lost. The empires of Greece, Rome, Portugal, and Spain were largely capital importers—or, rather, they extorted capital from their victims.

It remained for the British to discover how the national wealth might be enhanced by the unorthodox method of exporting capital. During the 19th century, English capital, spurred by a highly successful speculation in the Erie Canal, was invested heavily in both North and South America. Some of it was lost, but a generous overall return was earned. The speedy construction of the American

---

[9] Cited in the *Monthly Letter* of the First National City Bank, June, 1960 (New York, 1960).

railroad system and of other public utility facilities was made possible largely through British investment. Of course, the United States could eventually have built them unaided, just as the Soviet Union is today industrializing without substantial foreign help, but the process of construction would have been longer and more expensive. The import of capital is an excellent way to speed and facilitate basic industrialization, while the export of capital may well provide many economic benefits to the exporter. For a capital-rich country, anxious to find markets for its manufactured products, the export of capital is, paradoxically enough, a workable solution. At the beginning the importing country is actually buying from the exporter on credit. Thus, a wide variety of heavy producers' goods may be sold, to be paid for eventually out of manufactured production or from raw-material surpluses.

Even at a lager stage, when the importing country has reached some degree of industrial maturity, the benefits to the capital exporter do not end. In all probability they will increase. Advanced national economies are always one another's best customers. In view of this tendency for international trade to grow in step with industrialization, some students have advocated a policy of extending "untied" international development loans, whereby the borrowing country may purchase from anyone it wishes, even direct competitors of the creditor.

The private foreign investment of the United States has traditionally been small and confined to a few well-defined categories; our businessmen have generally been willing to invest only in *extractive industries*, mining, oil, and specialized agricultural products. Very recently, the high cost of American labor has caused some of our companies to build plants in Europe and import their output into the United States. But this type of capital export is dependent upon the level of specific American tariffs and on the political influence exerted by unions. Its future remains something of a question.

The problem of capital formation outside the United States and Western Europe is to find areas comparable to what in the last century were called the "Regions of Recent Settlement." In some countries, such as Canada, Australia, and Argentina, the prospects for successful diversified foreign investment were then excellent. To some degree such outlets are still available, but the scope of very attractive overseas investment opportunities has since narrowed appreciably. But both Communist powers have chosen to follow a solitary way in industrial development. In the balance of the under-developed or low-income world, prospects for strictly private inter-national investment are dimmer, though certainly not entirely ab-sent.

Because of what one distinguished economist has called "the vicious cycle of poverty," the inducements to invest in many of the backward countries are minimal. The inducement to invest is re-stricted by the size of the market.

The limited size of the domestic market in a low-income country can . . . constitute an obstacle to the application of capital by the individual firm or industry working for the market. In this sense the small domestic market is an obstacle to development generally. We perceive a constella-tion of circumstances tending to preserve any backward economy in a stationary condition. . . .[10]

But if the United States hopes to meet its ambitious growth expectations and if the underdeveloped countries hope to rise in the economic scale, much serious thought will have to be given to the problem of making investment in these areas attractive to private foreign capital.

MONEY AND MORALITY

In a novel at one time on the best-seller list a protagonist makes this remarkable speech—remarkable for its extreme rejection of the moralist's view that the love of money is the root of all evil.

To trade by means of money is the code of the men of good will. Money rests on the axiom that every man is the owner of his mind and his effort. Money allows no power to prescribe the value of your effort ex-cept the voluntary choice of the man who is willing to trade you his effort in return. Money permits you to obtain for your goods and your labor that which they are worth to the men who buy them, but no more. Money permits no deals except those to mutual benefit by the unforced judgment of the traders. Money demands of you the recognition that men must work for their own benefit, not for their own injury, for their gain, not their loss—the recognition that they are not beasts of burden, born to

---

10 Ragnar Nurkse, *Problems of Capital Formation in Underdeveloped Countries* (New York: Oxford University Press, 1953), pp. 6–11. See also Nathan Rosenberg, "Capital Formation in Underdeveloped Countries," *American Economic Review*, Vol. L (September, 1960), pp. 706–14; and Clarence Walton, "A Basic Review of the Foreign Aid Programs," *Review of Social Economy*, Vol. XV (Fall, 1957), pp. 1–20.

carry the weight of your misery—that you must offer them values, not wounds—that the common bond among men is not the exchange of suffering, but the exchange of *goods*. Money demands that you sell, not your weakness to men's stupidity, but your talent to their reason; it demands that you buy, not the shoddiest they offer, but the best that your money can find. And when men live by trade—with reason, not force, as their final arbiter—it is the best product that wins, the best performance, the man of best judgment and highest ability—and the degree of a man's productiveness is the degree of his reward. This is the code of existence whose tool and symbol is money. Is this what you consider evil?[11]

The author's philosophy is phrased less in terms of traditional religious concepts of avarice or selflessness than in terms of the social consequences of man's impulse to make money. Here, the seeking after money is presented as an individual virtue, which also uplifts the community.

But there is another, older view of money. Long ago Aristotle observed that the "most hated sort of trade is usury, which makes a gain out of money itself . . . and this term 'interest,' which means the birth of money from money, is applied to the breeding of money because the offspring resembles the parent. Wherefore of all modes of getting wealth, this is the most unnatural."[12] This same view of money has prompted James Truslow Adams to observe that

. . . dealing inevitably with material things and with satisfying of the world's material wants, the businessman tends to locate happiness in *them* rather than in the intellectual and spiritual, unless he constantly refreshes his spirit away from business during his leisure. When the pressure of business becomes so great as to preclude his reasonable use of leisure for the development of his whole human personality, he is apt to become a complete materialist even if, as is now frequently not the case, he ever had it in him to become anything else. He may live in a palace, ride in the most luxurious cars and fill his rooms with old masters and the costliest manuscripts which his wealth can draw from under the hammer at Christie's, but if he cares more for luxury, and power than for a humanely rounded life he is not civilized, but what the Greeks properly called a "barbarian."[13]

The proper attitude toward money is a subject referred to many times daily, even in the least intellectual circles. But whether one

---

[11] Ayn Rand, *Atlas Shrugged* (New York: Random House, 1957), pp. 410–15.

[12] Aristotle, *Politics*, Book I, chap. x.

[13] James Truslow Adams, *Our Business Civilization* (New York: Albert & Charles Boni, Inc., 1929), p. 19.

regards this preoccupation as good or bad, it should be easy to accept as true what realists—or cynics—assert; in a society like ours almost everyone would rather have money than know how to define it.

CONCLUSION

Observers who watch carefully the strategies adopted by "money-managers" to brake inflationary trends—or to halt ominous deflationary forces—must sometimes feel they are viewing alchemists at work. Ideally these alchemists (whether working for the Federal Reserve in the United States or the Central Bank of London) seek always to convert dross metals into gold; when they convert "good money" to cheap money they are accused of practicing alchemy in reverse.

The nexus between the monetary system and the "real" world of production and commerce was initially noted in this necessarily truncated review; its practical implications were dramatically revealed during the European currency crisis of late 1968 when experts were somewhat unsure whether the proper question to raise was this: Had Europe experienced a French franc—or Deutsche mark—crisis? But there was growing assent to the proposition that Western Europe could not continue indefinitely to practice free trade within the Common Market without a common currency. The relationships between the world of money and the world of commerce was thus openly admitted.

Events at home and abroad demonstrate over and over again the truth of an observation made at the opening of this chapter: "Money is not simply a veil that hides the real operations of commerce and industry; it is also a functional part of the machine."

RECOMMENDED READING

ADAMS, JAMES TRUSLOW. *Our Business Civilization.* New York: Albert & Charles Boni, Inc., 1929.

AMERICAN BANKERS ASSOCIATION, ECONOMIC POLICY COMMISSION. *Our Financial System at Work.* New York: A.B.A.

BACH, G. L. "The Economics and Politics of Money," *Harvard Business Review,* Vol. XXXI (March–April, 1953) , pp. 84–86.

CHANDLER, L. *The Economics of Money and Banking.* 4th ed. New York: Harper & Bros., 1964.

COMMISSION ON MONEY AND CREDIT. *Money and Credit: Their Influence on Jobs, Prices, and Growth.* Englewood Cliffs, N.J.: Prentice-Hall, Inc., 1961.

GRAS, N. S. B. *Business and Capitalism.* New York: F. S. Crofts & Co., 1939.

GRIFFIN, CLARE E. *Enterprise in a Free Society.* Homewood, Ill.: Richard D. Irwin, Inc., 1949.

KNIGHT, FRANK. *Risk, Uncertainty and Profit.* Boston: Houghton Mifflin Co., 1921.

KNOSS, KLAUS, and BAUMOL, WILLIAM (eds.). *What Price Economic Growth?* Englewood Cliffs, N.J.: Prentice-Hall, Inc., 1961.

LAUGHLIN, J. LAURENCE. *A New Exposition of Money, Credit and Prices,* Vol. I. Chicago: University of Chicago Press, 1931.

NURKSE, RAGNAR. *Problems of Capital Formation in Underdeveloped Countries.* London: Basil Blackwell, 1953.

PIRENNE, HENRI. *Economic and Social History of Medieval Europe.* New York: Harcourt, Brace & Co., 1937.

RITTER, LAWRENCE S. (ed.). "Money, Income and Economic Activity" in *Money and Economic Activity.* Boston: Houghton Mifflin Co., 1952.

ROBERTSON, D. H. *Money.* Cambridge Economic Handbooks, No. 2. London: Nisbet & Co., 1922.

FURTHER READING

BAYKOV, ALEXANDER. *The Development of the Soviet Economic System.* London: Cambridge University Press, 1946.

CONDOIDE, MIKHAIL V. *The Soviet Financial System.* Columbus: Ohio State University, 1951.

FEDERAL RESERVE SYSTEM. *Money: Master or Servant.* Washington, May, 1955.

FRIEDMAN, MILTON. "Why the American Economy Is Depression Proof," *Nationalekonomiska Föreningens Förhandlingar 1954,* pp. 57–77 (Stockholm, 1955).

GILMAN, STEPHEN. *Accounting Concepts of Profits.* New York: Ronald Press Co., 1939.

GRAHAM, FRANK. "German Inflation," in *Exchange, Prices and Production in Hyper-Inflation Germany, 1920–23,* chap. iii. Princeton: Princeton University Press, 1930.

O'LEARY, JAMES J. "An Introduction to Interest Rates," *Our National Debt and Interest Rates.* New York: Committee on Public Debt Policy, 1947.

RADFORD, R. A. "The Price System in Microcosm: A P.O.W. Camp," *Economica,* Vol. XII (November, 1945), pp. 198–201.

RAND, AYN. *Atlas Shrugged.* New York: Random House, 1957.

SIMONS, H. C. "Rules vs. Authorities in Monetary Policy," *Journal of Political Economy,* Vol. XLIV (February, 1936), pp. 1–30.

Statements of Sumner Slichter and Neil Jacoby before Joint Economic Committee of the Congress. Part I. *Employment, Growth and Price Levels.* U.S. Government Printing Office, March, 1959.

"Usury" in *Encyclopaedia of the Social Sciences,* Vol. XV, pp. 193–97. New York: Macmillan Co., 1933.

WARD, A. DUDLEY, et al. *Goals of Economic Life.* New York: Harper & Bros., 1953.

13. Competition

BECAUSE the urge to compete is a normal facet of human nature, one might reasonably suppose that it is no more in need of stimulation or restraint in its economic aspects than it might be, for example, in sports or even in the classroom. Implicit in competition is the idea of winning, of coming out on top. But, as is true of freedom, competition imposes duties on the individuals engaged in it. The justice of the outcome is guaranteed by rules for what we call fair play. In competitive sports there are, after all, rules; and even in warfare, which is competition at its bloodiest, there have been, until recently at least, certain conventions observed.

Because of a common fallacy which holds that competition must necessarily lead to loss, suffering, and even destruction of one of the competitors, it is essential to distinguish between the human urge toward competition and the animal urge (shared by man) toward

337

aggression. Studies of animal behavior suggest that aggression in animals is probably best perceived in terms of territorial behavior.[1] Members of territorial species divide the available living space among themselves and, once having settled, attack all intruders. Animals seeking living space usually withdraw when they meet with an already established owner, and hence the seeker's strategy is to avoid a fight. Clashes are controlled by an "attack-avoidance system."[2]

It has recently been suggested by one ethnologist that man, too, was a social-hunting primate who was organized originally on the principle of group territories. It is an essential aspect of group territorialism that group members unite when a foreign group approaches. Because there is always an interplay between haves and have-nots and because, further, our cultural evolution has resulted in the parceling-out of living space on lines of tribal or national areas the aggressive instincts have been intensified. It is the *territorial* more than the *individual* imperative that leads to mass killing and mass aggression among men. In such cases victory over the adversary is itself the prize: often the conflict involves total war premised on unconditional surrender of the enemy.

Competition, on the other hand, rests formally on the principle of individualism. Each competitor pursues his own interests and employs his own resources to enhance those individual interests. Yet the results of the competition are not essentially related to destruction of a competitor, with gains going exclusively to one of the participants. Competition occurs under group interests and the results usually produce values to a third party—often the community itself.

The fact that the competitor's private interest cannot transcend the group's interest, and the further fact that the goal or prize is not in the possession of one of the competitors but lies beyond both, combine to make competition different from other forms of conflict. Professor Georg Simmel stated the difference in these terms:

> Victory in the fight is not really the success of the fight itself but, precisely, of the realization of values outside of it.

Here lies the immense value of competition for the social circles of

---

[1] Konrad Lorenz, *On Aggression* (London: Methuen, 1966) , and Desmond Morris, *The Naked Ape* (London: Jonathan Cape, 1967) .

[2] N. Tinbergen, "On War and Peace in Animals and Man," *Science* (June 24, 1968) , pp. 1411–18.

which the competitors are members. The other types of conflict where the prize is originally in the hands of one of the parties, or where an initial hostility, rather than the attainment of a prize, motivates the fight make for mutual annihilation of the combatants, and to society as a whole leave only the difference obtained by subtracting the weaker from the stronger force. Competition, on the other hand, insofar as it remains free from admixtures of these other forms, usually increases values through its incomparable social constellation. The reason is that from the standpoint of society, it offers subjective motives as the means of producing objective social values; and from the standpoint of the competing parties, it uses the production of objective values as means for attaining subjective satisfaction.[3]

Independent of economic considerations is the fact that competition is presumed to afford opportunities for the expression of freedom, initiative, and opportunity as ends in themselves. Presumably, the individual picks the arena in which he will seek to compete and the choice will, in turn, be influenced by the goals the individual sets for himself. Certainly in the American colonial tradition, competition, like work, was expected to induce a climate wherein a man's moral qualities were tested and strengthened.[4]

It has been said that the social function of competition in economic life is to afford the buyer protection against exploitation by the seller. The theory behind public control over business competition centers, first, on the conflict of interests between the buyer and the seller and, second, on the struggle between individual sellers for a greater share of the market. So far as the seller-buyer relationship is concerned, it is only when the purchaser watches for differentials and takes advantage of them that competition works well. The essential role of the customer cannot be overemphasized. But the buyer's role is significantly influenced by the cultural setting in which competition occurs.

The prevailing temper of 19th-century America has been characterized as rugged individualism, and in a pioneer country such a spirit has certain advantages. The historic roots of the kind of individualism found in Western civilization are hard to identify. It is fairly commonplace to find its locus in the Italian Renaissance of the 13th century when the ethic of individual reasoning, as a source

---

[3] Georg Simmel, *Conflict* (trans. Kurt H. Wolff) (New York: The Free Press, 1955), pp. 57–58.

[4] John Maurice Clark, "Competition: Static Models and Dynamic Aspects," *American Economic Review*, Vol. XLV (May, 1955), pp. 543–57.

of truth, and individual creativity, as the core of society, were manifest. At this period the world witnessed a remarkable accommodation between free individual choice with the social needs of the larger society. The rise of science and the scientific method strengthened the prestige of the individual. Nevertheless, unrestrained individualism also has a socially negative side. In the absence of a corpus of law to anticipate and control it, ruthless individualism will result in the exploitation of the powerless by the powerful. One American scholar perceived in this unrestrained egoism the chief pillar of laissez-faire liberalism and proceeds to indict it in these terms:

There remain those who regard the uncontrolled bargaining by individuals in the marketplace as the ultimate in human relationships and consider government (like Satan in the medieval cosmology) as a perpetual enemy, a necessary evil against which good must be forever on guard. Laisse-faire liberalism has not vanished. Old philosophies never die, and this one is firmly fossilized in higher pedagogy. It reverberates in the sanctums of the University of Chicago, and is impatiently proclaimed by the addicts of Ayn Rand. It echoes in the naïveté of Eisenhower and in the nostalgia and bombast of Barry Goldwater. But it is no longer at the center. It is no longer characteristic. It no longer dominates either the point of view of the Supreme Court or the attitudes of the intellectual community at large.[5]

The first "official" sign of incipient changes in the philosophy of individualism came with the Sherman Antitrust Act in 1890 whereby a legal limit was imposed upon excessive individualism in business, a limit based on the conviction that the public is entitled to a market place in which there is a choice of rival goods and services. Since then, we have laboriously constructed a whole corpus of regulatory legislation and jurisprudence designed to check "antisocial" excesses of business practice.

In the meantime, developments in the nature of business competition have occurred even faster than the developments in law. When trade was limited to such staples as wheat, wool, sugar, and coal, competition was solely a matter of availability, quantity, and price. These alone were the touchstones of profit or loss. Today, the balance of economic power is maintained by a relatively small number of very large corporations and a very large number of small

---

Robert A. Solo, *Economic Organizations and Social Systems* (New York: Bobbs-Merrill, 1967), p. 27.

businesses. Research and development, with its consequent innovation, may be regarded as the modern form of competition. As a result, consumer choice is increasingly influenced by the quality, style, and advertising of competing products. Strict price competition, while still important, is today only one among many ways in which firms compete. A new kind of competition is emerging, although economists are by no means agreed on precisely how it operates and what its long-run economic and social consequences will be.

John Bates Clark, writing almost 50 years ago, sums up the case for competition as follows:

. . . only from a strife with the right kind of rules can the right kind of fitness emerge. Competition . . . is a game played under rules fixed by the state to the end that, so far as possible, the prize of victory shall be earned, not by trickery or mere self-seeking adroitness, but by value rendered. It is not the mere play of unrestrained self-interest; it is a method of harnessing the wild beast of self-interest to serve the common good—a thing of ideals and not of sordidness. It is not a natural state, but like any other form of liberty, it is a social achievement, and eternal vigilance is the price of it.[6]

Competition is thus not only an economic matter but also embraces philosophical and cultural questions. It follows, therefore, that competition may be effectively regulated by norms not tied to social utility and not dependent on statutes. An ascetic, fatalistic, or altruistic ethic may place effective brakes on the practical way in which the competitive urge is expressed. At the same time an ethic of competition not only permits, but may actually encourage, an individual to compete with someone with whom he would avoid personal controversy at all costs. Thus, competition shares with logic, law, and a money-economy an indifference to the subjective element and can result in a form of cruelty where he who is responsible for it is often unaware of the implications of his competitive act.

In this vein, Robert Solo concluded that the Industrial Revolution itself must be looked upon as a general assault on the traditional society by the individual in pursuit of self-interest. The "sealed-in" system of feudal economy, which protected the individual, was fragmented, so that the more callous consequences of industrialization were inevitable. Professor Solo declared:

---

[6] John Bates Clark, *The Control of Trusts* (New York: Macmillan Co., 1901), p. 201.

The values of self-seeking individualism came to be expressed in the forms of functional organization. The economy was organized in an infinite number of discrete operations. Each was the instrument of the will and self-interest of a single individual. Each was subject to that individual's free, rational, self-interested inquiry. Each operation, and consequently the whole economy, was driven by the open-ended desire of the single individual for more for himself, more to consume, more to possess, more to display, more as a mark of worth and success. The "craft economy" of artisan and peasant became the "shop economy" of the technician-inventor and the free-wheeling entrepreneur: "shop economy" in the sense that the individual ran his own business or "shop" in his own way for his own purposes, under the imperative of market competition.[7]

THE MEANING OF COMPETITION

In any analysis of the "capitalistic" market, the concept of competition is inextricably linked to its opposite, monopoly. Unlike the classicists, whose thought tended to assume perfectly competitive markets, modern economic thought increasingly takes cognizance of the fact that neither perfect competition, nor, in a dynamic society, perfect monopoly, really exists. Studies of the market usually reveal a picture of mixed competitive and monopolistic elements. And yet a too easy acceptance of existing monopolistic elements as a norm may contribute to laxity in the implementation of public policy appropriate to stimulating competition. The continuing role of competition as a stimulant to growth is graphically illustrated by the West German experience, where a policy of "prosperity through competition" has led to a period of remarkable economic expansion.[8]

A voluminous literature describes the social values of competition and contrasts it with the alleged evils of monopoly power. Monopoly produces, it is said, an inefficient allocation of resources and therefore leads to a "bad" or the "wrong" composition and distribution of the national income. It results in a lowering of the standard of living for the population as a whole, and it contributes to maladjustments within the economy that may make for instability, unemployment, and inflation. Finally, it slows the rate of economic and technological progress.

---

[7] Solo, *op. cit.*, p. 379.

[8] For a good brief discussion see Carlo Mötteli, "West Germany's Social Free-Market Economy: An Interim Balance Sheet," *Swiss Review of World Affairs*, Vol. VIII (March, 1959), pp. 3–5.

At the same time, monopoly runs contrary to the institutional requirements of a democracy, for it confers powers upon individuals that only the public should possess. Such power may lead to the expropriation and exploitation of the many by the few and may facilitate political and economic trends away from capitalism toward socialism or even communism. In this connection, it is of some interest to note that the Marxist critique of capitalism assigns special significance to the twin concepts of competition and monopoly.[9]

FOUR CATEGORIES OF COMPETITION

While there is much truth in the charges leveled against monopoly, not all the benefits claimed on behalf of competition will stand the test of scientific investigation. The requirement that "there must be competition"—supported as it is by statutes, court decisions, and administrative orders—is very vague, for there are many different definitions and types of competition. For the purposes of this chapter we shall distinguish four kinds of competition: the *general concept* of competition, the *businessman's concept,* the *economist's concept,* and the *legal concept.*

The *general* concept of competition stresses rivalry or conflict. Conflict arises whenever two or more persons have identical or closely similar goals. To try to surpass others is a common feature of competition. In some sports and games, in some types of examinations, in bidding situations, competition ceases only when all but one of the competitors have been eliminated. In business, such bitter rivalry has been called "cutthroat competition" and, pushed to its logical conclusion, results in monopoly. One of the newer approaches to the study of competition in general is through the development of game theory and other mathematical techniques such as linear and dynamic programming. These are being used in attempts to formulate a mathematical theory of conflict.

Closely related to the general formulation just mentioned is the *businessman's* concept of competition, which is often so vaguely defined that almost anything a firm does in the market is called at one time or another a "competitive practice." More than the other concepts of competition mentioned here, the businessman's concept of competition bears the marks of cultural and social evolution. It was the strong desire of American business to break the restraints of

---

[9] George Halm, *Economic Systems: A Comparative Analysis* (New York: Holt, Rinehart, and Winston, 1951), pp. 11–14.

British mercantilism that helped to precipitate the War of Independence, and the history of the following century is the history of the extension of the idea that freedom through competition should be fostered by a policy of unrestricted enterprise. It was this idea that justified the 19th-century transformation, by the courts, of the corporate form of organization, from a grant of monopoly for a quasi-public purpose requiring governmental surveillance, to an institutional form considered to have personal individuality and one that ought to be freely available to any group seeking it and largely immune to interference of government.[10]

The decision by Lemuel Shaw, Chief Justice of the Supreme Judicial Court, in *Commonwealth* v. *Hunt* (1842) is perhaps typical of 19th-century thinking on the subject of competition. The Justice concluded:

Through competition . . . interests of trade and industry are promoted. It is scarcely necessary to allude to the familiar instances of opposition lines of conveyance, rival hotels, and the thousand other instances, where each strives to gain customers to himself, by ingenious improvements, by increased industry, and by all the means by which he may lessen the price of commodities, and thereby diminish the profits of others.

We think, therefore, that associations may be entered into, the object of which is to adopt measures that may have a tendency to impoverish another, that is, to diminish his gains and profits, and yet so far from being criminal or unlawful, the object may be highly meritorious and public spirited. The legality of such an association will therefore depend upon the means to be used for its accomplishment. If it is to be carried into effect by fair or honorable and lawful means, it is, to say the least, innocent; if by falsehood or force, it may be stamped with the character of conspiracy.[11]

While competition had always characterized the American economy, the introduction of a legal definition of it through antitrust legislation at the turn of the century led to a more self-conscious acceptance of it in the business community. The Sherman Act, especially, has become a sort of emotional focus in the value nexus of the enterprise system. Some of the lessons taught by the economic concept of competition have become part of the popular and busi-

---

[10] Paul McNulty, "The Consumer, the Producer, and the History of American Competitive Policy" (to appear in a forthcoming issue of *Yale Review*).

[11] Chief Justice Shaw, in *Commonwealth* v. *Hunt (1842)*, *Massachusetts Reports*, Metcalf, 111, At., 121–135.

ness folklore—for example, the capacity ascribed to competition for fostering dynamic economic growth and technological development. While there are probably few businessmen who would seriously ask for the repeal of antitrust legislation, it is ultimately to business practice, and not to business pronouncements, that the public will look for a statement of the businessman's concept of competition.

The fact that the American businessman is brought up to believe in the utility of competition has not prevented him from continuously inventing new practices that are somehow in restraint of trade. It is the area of highly competitive "small business" that produces the most persistent noncompetitive abuses and cartel-like arrangements. The big businessman can often afford to view competition as a luxury, in view of the market power that he already enjoys, although he, too, must always contend with the competition of other big business firms.[12] The conspicuous growth and enhanced social role of large modern corporations in the last two decades has produced a rationalization of bigness. This raises the question of whether big and small businesses have the same image of competition.

CONCEPTUAL LANDMARKS

The *economist's* concept of competition is usually restricted to the selling and buying of economic goods and services. Sellers' competition, which has attracted most of the attention, exists whenever two or more sellers appear in the same market. Because of the complexity and the diversity of possible constellations of sellers, it can take many forms.

"Perfect competition" refers to a certain type of *price competition* with *homogenous products* and perfectly *free access* of all forms to the market. Such a rigorous definition serves mainly as a model for economic analysis and as a standard for comparison with other models and real market situations. Although it is true that so-called perfect competition is a fiction created for analytical purposes which can never be found in reality, it is also true that this perfect competition is in reality the absence of competition. An economy or industry that had reached this state would be saturated with producers, no longer competing but responding automatically to the dictates of the

---

[12] Albert A. Carretta, "Some Competitive Practices with Which Small Business Must Contend," *Law and Contemporary Problems*, Vol. XXIV (Winter, 1959), pp. 169–182.

market. It appears that it is impossible for a business to compete without attempting to monopolize the market. To understand the problem it is necessary to understand the historical evolution of the term.[13]

Competition has been conceived of in two different ways: as a procedure which relates price and costs with the allocation of resources, and as an idealized situation to be used as a tool for analysis. Classical economics concerned itself almost exclusively with the operational aspects of competition. To the classical economists it was an "ordering force" but this conception is so ambiguous that it has led to some confusion, especially in the differentiation between "force" and "market" and in the number of competing firms necessary to a true competitive market. The next development was the refinement of the concept through the emergence of the idea of competition as itself a market structure which was held by the neoclassical economists. This development was brought about through an examination of competition by Cournot, Jevons, Edgeworth, Clark, and Knight; in this merger of the concepts of competition and of the market, respectively, it is important to note that competition was thought of as being subservient to the market. Perhaps even more important was the fact that competition was never related systematically to the technique of production or to the organizational form of the business firm itself.

Whereas competition to improve production and organizational efficiency affects both the quality and price of goods, only price and market have been correctly examined by economists—to the neglect of quality and, more importantly, of the firm that produces them. The fact that only price and market were thought suitable aspects in the study of competition determined the manner in which competition came to be viewed. Even Adam Smith, whose great contribution was to make competition a general organizing principle of economic society and economic analysis, was touched by these misconceptions.

In one sense then, although Smith played a major role in making the principle of competition the essence of economic analysis, he contributed little to its economic meaning. Indeed it may be suggested that if Adam Smith had really made the resounding contributions to the theory of competition for which he is credited it would

---

[13] Paul McNulty, "Economic Theory and the Meaning of Competition" (unpublished essay) ; see also Herbert A. Simon, "Theories of Decision-Making in Economics," *American Economic Review*, Vol. XLIX (June, 1959) pp. 253–83.

have been along the lines of Schumpeter's insight into the meaning of technological and operational change. The essence of the Industrial Revolution, which came because of the changing mode of production, was untouched; rather the mercantilists' overriding concern with price continued to be the central theme of economic analysis. Meanwhile, neoclassical economists disrupted this possibly productive line of reasoning by introducing into their concept of competition the idea of individuals dominating the economy of competition. But the concept of perfect competition squeezed out the concept of behavioral content so that, using perfect competition as a standard, even price competition (the essence of the competitive process for Adam Smith) is imperfect. If, therefore, price is determined by "costs" of production, little work has been done to understand what determined these costs. It was the manager concerned with operating efficiency who caused, in part, the reorganization of American industry around the turn of the century. Although theory had always assumed that firms would operate in the most efficient manner, fact and theory did not harmonize.

The three remaining concepts of competition can be rather summarily indicated. "Workable competition" is a concept less rigorously defined than is "perfect competition." It is useful for the courts especially because it helps them to apply a more realistic standard of public policy.

"Imperfect competition" is frequently used as a catchall description for any semimonopolistic situation. It is not synonymous with monopolistic competition which refers, among other things, to the tendency of business firms to differentiate products through distinctive trade names, labels, and packaging, thus seeking to compete by means other than price.

"Oligopoly," or *competition among the few,* is a relatively new concept in economic theory. Except for Cournot's path-breaking contribution in 1838, oligopoly theory is quite young. Its practical significance derives from the fact that many markets today (especially in certain basic industries and in the consumers' durable-goods field) are characterized by fewness of sellers.

In view of traditional notions on the subject, and also because of the strong case made in favor of competition by contemporary welfare economics, it may seem somewhat disconcerting to emphasize another strand in economics that asserts that imperfections in the market need not be an obstacle to efficient resource allocation. The theory of monopoly that economists have developed is crucial to the public policy proposals that demand the enforcement of competition. A strong plea for competition comes also from those economists who wish to see the economy managed by means of indirect monetary and fiscal controls for the purpose of maintaining a stable dollar.

THE LEGAL CONCEPT AND THE ENFORCEMENT OF COMPETITION

By and large, the legal concept of competition that has evolved over the years reflects economic theory only in the most general manner. Economists are themselves partly to blame for this unfortunate situation because they often ignore the political and business realities that underlie the enforcement of competition. In the traditions of the law, change comes slowly. As a result, new economic insights have found slow acceptance by the courts. This may be due, in part at least, to lack of communication between economists and lawyers, which contributes to the latters' ignorance of much pertinent work in economic theory.

All antitrust law uses competition, or its lack, as the criterion for determining the legality of business conduct. But, from the point of view of the law, competition is not easily defined. Although a plurality of sellers has been made a conspicuous feature of the legal concept of competition, there remains the difficult task of establishing a precise meaning. Some of the factors that contribute to the difficulty are worth mentioning for an understanding of the legal viewpoint.

The law of competition (statutes, court decisions, administrative regulations) tries to delineate permissible actions by setting negative limits to behavior rather than by stipulating positively what is lawful. Precedent plays an important role in determining what is lawful and what is not. This often results in decisions that show a greater interest in legal precedents than in economic soundness. It probably prevents the formulation of a precise legal concept of competition in favor of a case-by-case approach to the problems involved.

The law of competition—especially as declared by the courts and administrative agencies—is subject to evolution and reflects the changing mores, ethics, and philosophy of the times. Economic facts are, to a large extent, legal fictions, and this is true with respect to competition, as well as to such other institutions as private property and contract. However, there is more ambiguity in the legal interpretation of competition than in other economic concepts.

MAJOR LAWS

The *enforcement of competition* is primarily based upon three rules of law that have their origin in the common-law tradition of our Anglo-Saxon legal heritage. They are the rules against restraints of trade, against monopolies, and against conspiracies. These have been incorporated into the Sherman Act of 1890, the basic antitrust statute. Contrary to some opinion, the original goal of antitrust legislation was to preserve self-policing markets and protect individuals from oppression and denial of opportunities by economically powerful interests. Included among the law's objectives were noneconomic factors, therefore, which the search for economic efficiency was felt to encourage.

Because the objectives of the Sherman Act are not always compatible the Courts have had to accommodate them to achieve an effective operating policy; in rendering decisions, the judiciary seems to have acted on four major principles:

1. If a company attains monopoly power through its own efficiency and without resort to the formation of cartels, the firm's position is respected. In practice there are few actual monopolies in the American economy.
2. In cases of competitor collaboration the justification must be established through evidence that the collaborative effort improves economic efficiency—not increased market power.
3. The absence of economic efficiency is a key consideration in condemning practices which offend *any* of the objectives of antitrust.
4. Equality of opportunity for all businessmen is essential without, however, protecting them from the consequences of their own inefficiencies.[14]

It has been said by one competent social historian that the whole antitrust movement "is characteristically and uniquely American." The idea of competition as a means of social regulation—as an economic, political, and moral force—has grown stronger roots in the United States than elsewhere, partly because it has had little to

---

[14] Harlan Blake and William Jones, "Toward a Three-Dimensional Antitrust Policy," *Columbia Law Review*, Vol. LXV (January-April, 1965) , pp. 437–40.

compete with in the way of aristocratic, militaristic, or labor-social-
ist theories."[15] It also seems true that the law is almost more solicit-
ous of producer interests than it is of consumer interests. And the
small producer was the most cherished of all. In the Senate debate
on the bill its sponsor, Senator Sherman, told his colleagues that the
heart of industrial liberty was the right of every man to *work and
produce* in any lawful occupation.

Other basic antitrust statutes are the Clayton Act, which
amended the law of 1890, and the Federal Trade Commission Act,
both enacted in 1914. The Clayton Act, as amended, prohibits
certain specific types of restraints of trade (price discrimination,
interlocking directorates, intercorporate stockholdings, and, most
important, certain forms of mergers), and it exempts labor organizations and their lawful activities from antitrust prosecution. The
Federal Trade Act established the Federal Trade Commission in
order to help maintain conditions of fair competition. Since this is a
flexible concept under the law, one for which it is difficult to give
specific legislative guidance, the administrative rulings of the FTC
have become a major influence in the enforcement of antitrust
legislation.

Two important amendments to the existing antitrust legislation
were introduced during the late 1930's. The Sherman Act was again
amended by the Miller-Tydings Act to permit certain types of resale
price maintenance. This innovation has been looked on as substantially weakening the original law. The Clayton Act was amended by
the Robinson-Patman Act which was intended to strengthen the
former's price discrimination clauses. In practice the amendment led
to legal actions against pricing on a basing-point system and thus
brought about substantial changes in geographical pricing practices.
A large number of other laws also contain antitrust provisions. The
rule against restraint of trade has been modified to some extent and,
in the opinion of some authorities, has been obscured and weakened
by a too generous application of the "rule of reason" to it.

The law of competition has found expression in cases involving a
great diversity of activities, combinations, and forms of collusion.
Among the most important are collusive trade associations and
other cartel-like combinations in restraint of trade, horizontal and
vertical price-fixing agreements, geographical price discrimination,

---

[15] Richard Hofstadter, "What Happened to the Antitrust Movement?" in Earl
Cheit (ed.), *The Business Establishment* (New York: John Wiley & Sons, 1964), p. 116.

mergers and consolidations, patents and patent pools, and international cartel arrangements.

The Problem of Size

Probably the most controversial issue raised by modern antitrust policy is "bigness," and defining size is a difficult assignment.[16] Here the law seems to have neglected the economist's traditional views more completely than it has in connection with some other antitrust issues. Although the disadvantages of great size are not as evident as classical economics contended, strictly economic arguments in defense of bigness are not especially convincing. In particular, the defenders of bigness do not seem to face up squarely to the monopoly problem.

While many of the efficiencies claimed for bigness can be demonstrated, the general economic superiority of large enterprise is by no means certain. And while decreasing costs generate increases in the size of enterprise, these economies of scale could seldom if ever, in and of themselves, produce the giant members of today's oligopoly markets. One of the major objections to bigness is directed not at the economic power of giant companies but at their potential capacity for social control and at the pressures they exert upon the countless individuals and smaller institutions dependent on them. Be that as it may, the large corporation remains a fact of modern economic, social, and political life, even though antitrust policy has not yet defined appropriate limits for its many roles and functions.

Related to the problem of bigness in business is that of bigness in labor. Big business has its counterpart in today's mammoth labor organizations. It is now labor's turn to encounter necessary legislative regulation. For the question of abuse of power and influence raised by mere size is virtually identical wherever it arises—whether in the realm of business, government, or labor.

COMPETITION, BUSINESS POLICY, AND THE FUTURE OF FREE ENTERPRISE

The enforcement of competition has been largely a matter of public policy. But one important issue here concerns the role that

---

[16] Still very useful on this point is the book by Corwin Edwards, *Big Business and the Policy of Competition* (Cleveland: Western Reserve University Press, 1956), especially chaps. ii and iii.

private business firms themselves might play in the maintenance of a competitive climate. Business spokesmen speak in favor of "competitive" enterprise, but as a rule, their notion of it has little in common with what either economists or lawyers understand by the term. To the businessman, "competition" or "free enterprise" more often than not stood traditionally for a somewhat old-fashioned concept of laissez-faire, meaning "private" as opposed to "public" control of business.

The history of free enterprise, in this country and elsewhere, discloses a marked trend away from unrestricted markets and free competition, especially in the atomistic sense. In countries in which antitrust-type legislation is unknown, cartels, syndicates, and other forms of overt collusion tend to replace the free, competitive market environment. Ever since Adam Smith, experts have pointed to the natural tendency of competitors to form some sort of collusion, overt or otherwise. Although there have been numerous criticisms of the way in which the antitrust laws have been enforced, there is, nevertheless, widespread agreement that they still represent a fairly effective deterrent to business collusion and monopolization in this country.

ROLE OF PRIVATE BUSINESS MAINTENANCE OF COMPETITION

The workings of "fair competition," as conceived by the business community is itself one of the best arguments why business cannot be expected to self-enforce an acceptable standard of workable competition. As some critics have pointed out, "fair competition" is really a form of weakened competition. Most of the trade practices that the FTC is called upon to police disclose such a widespread variety of dubious trade practices that it is difficult to conceive of a really competitive enterprise system that relies exclusively upon private business firms themselves for a major or substantial enforcement effort.

The first step in the enforcement of competition through business firms might be thought to be strict adherence to the existing law, but a major obstacle to obedience lies, as has been noted, in the natural desire of industry to form cartels or to enter into cartel-like arrangements. In many areas, moreover, the law itself is so obscure that a businessman with even the best intentions would have difficulty in knowing exactly what interpretation to put upon it. This legal uncertainty is especially noticeable with respect to oligopoly markets.

A second alternative open to business is the application of principles of scientific management in the determination of size or scope of market control. The use of linear and dynamic programming through *operations research* may prove to be especially useful in large enterprises that desire to acquire additional capacity, either by expansion from within or through mergers, or both. Management science may also benefit smaller enterprises by guiding them into profitable markets.

GOVERNMENT AND COMPETITION

For the foreseeable future, however, antitrust policy seems destined to remain *public policy*. The effort to enforce competition, in other words, will have to be shared by the Congress, by the courts, and by existing, and perhaps new, administrative agencies. Competition is important to the consumer if it will give him what he wants at reasonable prices. This means, among other things, a variety of products available through a variety of suppliers; it is also assumed that competition will foster the development and use of new techniques and ideas. But to attain these objectives will require a more diligent policing of certain markets than has hitherto been the case.

The adequate policing depends, in turn, on asking the right questions; and there is doubt in some quarters that the right queries have been raised. Are resources used efficiently so that the marginal value of an industry's output equals its long-run marginal costs? Does a given action by a firm which comes under government scrutiny contribute to the public interests as these are affected by inflation, growth, and employment? Have we been enamoured with the regulatory process and callous toward the results produced by regulatory agencies? Are the agencies too passive and backward-looking? If so why?[17] Competition in both business and labor is important to the citizen in that it checks the growth of *economic power* which, in turn, could lead to concentrations of political power inimical to democracy.

---

[17] Richard E. Caves, "Direct Regulation and Market Performance in the American Economy," *American Economic Review* (1964), pp. 172–80; and Roger C. Cramton, "The Effectiveness of Economic Regulation: A Legal View," *loc. cit.*, pp. 182–91.

CONCLUSION

The most eloquent affirmation of the values that flow from competition was made by the late John Maurice Clark, Columbia University's distinguished economist, when he declared:

What do we want competition to do for us? What benefits do we expect from it? The main economic benefits may be listed under four heads:

We expect competition to furnish incentives to increased productive efficiency that are more compelling than the interest a monopoly has in improving its processes. To get the benefit of this incentive, where progressive increase in efficiency depends on expensive research and experimentation, requires that business units of large size shall still feel this competitive incentive.

We expect the rivalry of independent producers to give us an ample variety of types and qualities of products to choose from, including new varieties. This competition in quality implies that the offerings of different producers shall be distinctive; that is, they shall be in some respect unique. And I would contend that this uniqueness is a competitive fact, not a monopolistic one, so long as others are free to imitate or not, whichever seems to them more advantageous.

We want the gains from all this to be diffused as widely as possible and as rapidly as consistent with business enterprise having the incentives to the necessary pioneering.

As fast as the state of the arts, or the knowledge of what kinds of products consumers want, become common property, no one can make a special profit by merely equaling this standard. But if he excels it, in productive efficiency or in the quality of attractiveness of his product, he can still make a special profit—for a time, until others catch up and his achievement is in turn absorbed into the state of the arts. If instead of excelling he falls behind, he will make losses; and unless he can better his position, he may end by being forced out of business.[18]

An Alcoa executive, Leon Hickman, expressed the businessman's view that throughout all discussions on competition there have been misconceptions by economists and by regulators and a rather wholesale neglect of factors that have tended in the aggregate to intensify competition.[19] Among these factors are the following: dynamically improved communications and transportation systems; dramatic in-

---

[18] John Maurice Clark, *Economic Institutions and Human Welfare* (New York: Alfred A. Knopf, 1957), pp. 158–60.

[19] "Prices, Competition, and Morality" in Courtney Brown (ed.), *The Ethics of Business* (New York: Columbia Graduate School of Business, 1963), pp. 575–86.

creases in populations who have greater expectations; innovations in business methods and business organizations; the rising level of discretionary income among buyers; expansion of technological research which brings new products to the fore; and pressures from foreign producers.

But beyond the economic advantages of competition, there are certain other important values that flourish in a competitive environment. Competition is the practical way that an individual exercises his right to equal opportunity; it is the incentive to greater human effort and thus complements our concepts of freedom and responsibility; it fulfills admirably the role as catalyst for progress. As such, it can still fulfill an essential role in 20th-century America.

RECOMMENDED READING

BOULDING, KENNETH E. *Economic Analysis*. New York: Harper & Row, 1955.

DEWEY, DONALD. *Monopoly in Economics and Law*. Chicago: Rand McNally & Co., 1959.

HEILBRONER, ROBERT. *The Making of Economic Society*. Englewood Cliffs. Prentice-Hall, 1962.

LEVIN, HARVEY J. *Business Organization and Public Policy: A Book of Readings*. New York: Holt, Rinehart & Winston, 1958.

LEWIS, BEN W. "Open Season on Bigness," *Harvard Business Review*, Vol. XXXVIII (May–June, 1959), pp. 105–13.

MARCUS, SUMNER. *Competition and the Law*. Belmont, Calif.: Wadsworth Publishing Co., Inc., 1967.

MILLIKAN, MAX (ed.). *Income Stabilization for a Developing Democracy: A Symposium*. New Haven: Yale University Press, 1953.

SAMUELSON, PAUL A. *Economics: An Introductory Analysis*. 4th rev. ed. New York: McGraw-Hill Book Co., 1958.

SPROUL, A. "Economic Power Centers and Credit Policy," *California Management Review*, Vol. I (Fall, 1958), pp. 68–73.

WILCOX, CLAIR. *Public Policies toward Business*. Homewood, Ill.: Richard D. Irwin, Inc., 1955.

FURTHER READING

ABBOTT, LAWRENCE. *Quality and Competition: An Essay in Economic Theory*. New York: Columbia University Press, 1955.

BAIN, JOE S. *Barriers to New Competition.* Cambridge: Harvard Business Press, 1956.

BERGE, WENDELL. "Problems of Enforcement and Interpretation of the Sherman Act," *American Economic Review,* Vol. XXXVIII (May, 1948), pp. 173–81.

BERLE, A. A., JR. *The Twentieth Century Capitalist Revolution,* esp. chap. v. New York: Harcourt, Brace & Co., 1954.

BRANDEIS, LOUIS D. *The Curse of Bigness,* pp. 104–8. New York: Viking Press, 1934.

BURNS, ARTHUR ROBERT. *The Decline of Competition.* New York: McGraw-Hill Book Co., 1936.

CHAMBERLIN, E. H. *The Theory of Monopolistic Competition.* 7th ed. Cambridge: Harvard University Press, 1956.

Congress and the Monopoly Problem: Fifty Years of Antitrust Development, 1900–1950: A History of Congressional Action in the Antitrust Field during the Past Fifty Years. H. R. 22, Select Committee on Small Business, House of Representatives, 81st Cong. Washington, D.C.: U.S. Govt. Printing Office, 1950.

COURNOT, A. A. *Researches into the Mathematical Principles of the Theory of Wealth.* New York: Macmillan Co., 1897.

DEWEY, DONALD. *Monopoly in Economics and Law,* pp. 7–69, 82–108, 196–212, 302–10. Chicago: Rand McNally & Co., 1959.

FELLNER, WILLIAM. *Competition among the Few,* pp. 3–54. New York: Alfred A. Knopf, 1949.

GALBRAITH, JOHN K. *American Capitalism, the Concept of Countervailing Power.* Boston: Houghton Mifflin Co., 1952.

GASS, S. I. *Linear Programming: Methods and Applications.* New York: McGraw-Hill Book Co., 1958.

HEXNER, ERVIN. *International Cartels.* Chapel Hill: University of North Carolina Press, 1945.

KAPLAN, A. D. H. *Big Enterprise in the Competitive System.* Washington, D.C.: The Brookings Institution, 1953.

———. *Small Business: Its Place and Problems,* esp. chap. viii. New York: McGraw-Hill Book Co., 1948.

KAPLAN, A. D. H. *et al. Pricing in Big Business: A Case Approach.* Washington, D.C.: The Brookings Institution, 1958.

KNIGHT, FRANK H. *Risk, Uncertainty, and Profit.* Boston: Houghton Mifflin Co., 1921.

———. *The Ethics of Competition.* New York: Harper & Bros., 1935.

LINDBLOM, CHARLES E. "The Union as a Monopoly," *Quarterly Journal of Economics,* Vol. LXII (November, 1948), pp. 671–97.

MACHLUP, FRITZ. *The Economics of Sellers' Competition.* Baltimore: Johns Hopkins Press, 1952.

MASON, EDWARD S. "Monopoly in Law and Economics," in *Economic Concentration and the Monopoly Problem,* pp. 332–50. Cambridge: Harvard University Press, 1957.

NEUMANN, JOHN VON, and MORGENSTERN, OSKAR. *Theory of Games and Economic Behavior.* Princeton: Princeton University Press, 1947.

NUTTER, G. W. *The Extent of Enterprise Monopoly in the U.S., 1899–1939.* Chicago: University of Chicago Press, 1951.

PAPANDREOU, A. G., and WHEELER, J. T. *Competition and Its Regulations.* New York: Prentice-Hall, Inc., 1954.

PIGOU, A. C. *The Economics of Welfare,* chaps. ix–xi. London: Macmillan & Co., 1920.

ROBINSON, JOAN. *The Economics of Imperfect Competition.* London: Macmillan & Co., 1933.

SCITOVSKY, T. *Welfare and Competition.* Homewood, Ill.: Richard D. Irwin, Inc., 1951.

STIGLER, G. J. (ed.). *Business Concentration and Price Policy.* Princeton: Princeton University Press, 1955.

STOCKING, GEORGE W., and WATKINS, M. W. *Monopoly and Free Enterprise.* New York: Twentieth Century Fund, 1951.

TRIFFIN, ROBERT. *Monopolistic Competition and General Equilibrium Theory.* Cambridge: Harvard University Press, 1940.

WILCOX, CLAIR. *Public Policies toward Business,* chaps. ii–iii, pp. 265–89. Homewood, Ill.: Richard D. Irwin, Inc., 1955.

14. The Market

WHY IS IT that a man, when dining out, prefers a restaurant with a wide variety on its menu to one featuring a single dish? Why does the housewife, in her search for so simple an item as a bar of soap, expect to look at a varied selection? The answer, one suspects, is simple: human beings like to have a choice!

Choice involves appraisal, deliberation, and decision—the three elements that underlie every theory of exchange. Appraisal allows a man to employ his values on a proffered good or service so that he willingly gives up something he considers of less value for something he considers of more value. Deliberation, a faculty unique to man, flows from his rationality, and decision relates to his freedom and to his responsibility. This is why students of the market so often go beyond the sheerly economic aspects of exchange and consider the relevance of free markets to such seemingly unrelated things as freedom, human rationality, and personal responsibility; to political forms of government like democracies and republics.[1]

Within the more limited sphere of economics itself it can be shown that the objectives of the market process work to satisfy human wants and therefore the well-being of society as a whole. (This statement is true in general, even though certain markets seek to stimulate artificial wants or to exploit human weakness.) Mobility of productive resources provides the customer with the right commodity, at the right time and place and at the right price. Finally, sales provide the ultimate source of profits for the individual firm. Perhaps the most telling argument of all in favor of a market economy is the historical and anthropological one: whenever a trading and a nontrading people meet, the latter always adopt the practices of the former.[2]

Perhaps at the outset it is only fair to indicate two biases on our part against traditional economic theory as applied to the market process. The first relates to the traditional view that marketing should be viewed primarily in terms of cost. For years the value-added concept has been used for production, but rarely has it been applied to modern marketing. This neglect may be due to the fact that manufacturing results in changes in physical form that can readily be seen, appreciated, and measured. In marketing, the value added is more subtle, but it occurs nonetheless—when wholesalers store goods that would be prohibitively costly for the ultimate consumer to store, when they move the goods or services literally to his doorstep, or even when they make the consumer aware of the existence of a new product or service.[3]

Our second criticism is directed at the tendency to regard a market as "good" or "bad" depending on the speed with which price adjustments are made rather than on the efficiency with which the market facilitates appraisal. One of the most perceptive observations on this point was made by the late Howard Nixon of Columbia University when he declared:

---

[1] See Anthony Downs, *An Economic Theory of Democracy* (New York: Harper & Bros., 1957), for an intriguing effort to answer the question: How can democratic government be conceptualized as an essential part of the market place?

[2] Elizabeth Hoyt, *Primitive Trade: Its Psychology and Economics* (London: Kegan Paul, Trench, Trubner & Co., 1926).

[3] See U.S. Chamber of Commerce, the Domestic Distribution Committee and the Business Statistics Committee. *Value Added by Distribution* (Washington, D.C., 1956), esp. pp. 5–8.

Some modern economists, struggling to reconcile present-day facts with ancient theory, have advanced the suggestion that various non price activities such as product differentiation, branding and advertising, are to be considered as forms of imperfect or monopolistic competition. This is essentially a gloomy approach, for it makes imperfection seem widespread and growing. It constitutes an appeal to prejudice rather than to reason, in that deviations from a preconceived pattern are arbitrarily labeled impure or imperfect. It does, however, have the merit of permitting a somewhat realistic description of exchange motivation. Edward H. Chamberlin, for example, notes that to the buyer a purchased article is really a bundle of utilities, of which such things as personality, reputation, convenience of location or the tone of the seller's shop may be a part. There is in this some recognition of the only basis upon which a defensible analysis of modern market behavior is to be made.

Such an analysis must start with the observed fact that buyers characteristically make some appraisal, however hasty and perfunctory, of the want-satisfying attributes of the things they buy. A product, as Chamberlin suggests, may afford a variety of utilities. These are perceived with varying degrees of clarity by different individuals and by the same individuals at different times. These utilities also vary in the force of their appeal to individuals, and with numerous attendant circumstances, including advertising.

A market is an appraisal center. It is a meeting place or a medium whereby buyers pass judgment on sellers' offerings. If means of communication exist it may be nation-wide or international. Efficient markets are those in which buyers have an opportunity to make their selections from among a wide variety of products that have been designed and presented in such a way as to achieve the maximum appeal to all legitimate wants, needs, desires and impulses. The decision as to which motives are legitimate is a matter for society. The decisions as to which motives shall be satisfied and the selection of appropriate means of satisfaction are matters for the individual.[4]

However, in the modern monetary exchange economy, the market still allocates resources predominantly through some sort of pricing process. But this process is extremely complex. Abstractly, it is possible to conceive of a pricing system without *any* social or governmental restraints. *Ideal* capitalism, a completely frictionless system, is the "pure" economic model of an unplanned market economy. Since ideal capitalism has never existed in reality, it should not be mistaken for 19th-century laissez-faire capitalism and

---

[4] Howard Nixon, "Advertising in Today's Economy" (unpublished essay, Columbia University, Graduate School of Business, 1960).

especially not for the *mixed* capitalistic system functioning in the United States today. Nevertheless, the essential requirements of the free exchange economy are present to a greater or less degree in our modern capitalistic system. Among these requirements, the following are of prime importance:

1. The market performs the essential functions of resource and income allocation without the benefit of deliberate central direction.

2. The factors of production are privately owned by individuals and business firms, who perform the bulk of society's productive tasks for private gain. Thus individual self-interest, represented by the profit motive, is the driving force in the markets. For such a system to function, society must protect and foster freedom of occupation and of investment.

3. The free exchange economy also demands that the individual be free to choose how to spend and save his income. These two freedoms are basic individual rights, not only in the ideal capitalistic system, but also in our working modification of it. For the consumer's "dollar vote" is ultimately the guiding element in the ebb and flow of a market system in which changing prices act as the equilibrating forces.

THE MEANING OF THE MARKET

DEFINITION AND HISTORY

The term "market" is normally used to describe specific exchange relationships between buyers and sellers of given economic goods and services. In the primitive stages of economic development, goods and services were exchanged by barter without the intermediary of money. Normally, this required the simultaneous presence of the parties to the exchange transaction. With the advent of money as a generally accepted medium of exchange, the market took on even greater importance and became one of the truly characteristic economic institutions.

In Ancient Greece and Rome, physical markets were well known. The creation and regulation of markets in both came to be a function and prerogative of the state. The same was true during the Middle Ages, when European markets were generally tightly controlled by the sovereign. However, as more and more shops came into being, some of the importance of the markets was lost. This development was hastened further by the advent of the first Industrial Revolution.

Specialized markets, in which only one type or a limited number of commodities was regularly traded, also sprang up early. As time went on, these exchanges moved into buildings, sometimes into stables, often into taverns. After informal beginnings most of the exchanges eventually adopted the trimmings of formal organization —and, in the process, began to limit the number of direct participants. The modern stock and commodity exchanges, the Chicago Board of Trade, the Furniture Mart, and many others are modern descendants of these early exchanges.

THE ECONOMIST'S CONCEPT OF "MARKET"

The constantly changing, many-faceted nature of marketing is immediately encountered in the plethora of definitions that has been offered to explain the activity. Certainly it is not a concept that can be identified with the act of selling. Not long ago the marketing department of Ohio State University attempted to provide a general definition in these terms: "Marketing is the process in a society by which the demand structure for economic goods and services is anticipated or enlarged and satisfied through the conception, promotion, exchange, and physical distribution of such goods and services. When so viewed as a composite process, marketing is clearly a subject of much broader scope than the compilation of functions or managed activities commonly identified as marketing responsibilities in individual companies. It includes the continuous interaction of original producers, middle-men, facilitation agencies, governments and consumers. As such, marketing possesses a dynamic quality and a sense of purpose."

Economists often speak of the market as if it were a vast aggregate of exchange relationships encompassing the entire economic system. While such a generalization can be extremely useful (it has certainly served the economist well in his formulation of the theory of general economic equilibrium), the concept needs considerably more refinement. Basically, there are two broad categories of markets in every economic system: the markets for the *productive factors;* and the markets for *finished goods and services.* Traditionally, economists have divided the former into at least three classes: markets for land and natural resources, markets for labor (sometimes including management), and markets for capital (largely in the monetary sense). It is in connection with these markets that the theories of rent, wages, interest, and profit have been developed. The markets for finished goods and services can be subdivided into two broad classifications: markets for producer (or capital) goods and markets for consumer goods.

These market classifications can be broken down further according to segments of the economy—broad industrial categories (metals, mining, transportation) or specific industries (steel, aluminum, copper) or types of products (automobiles, air conditioners), products by brands (Ford cars, Westinghouse appliances), and so on.

Definitions however, are sterile and inadequate when compared to the actual decisions that marketers face. To understand the dynamics of the marketing process scholars and businessmen often speak of a "marketing mix." Incorporated in the concept of marketing mix are the following three steps:

1. The selection of realistic objectives which will serve as a criterion against which alternative courses of action are to be measured. In almost all instances the criterion relates to maximum expected long-term profit; somewhat less satisfactory criteria are share-of-market, absolute sales volume, or maintenance of the status quo.
2. The design of the controllable elements of the market—which includes a generation of alternative courses of action, feasibility studies, and market tests. The controllable elements in marketing include product, price, promotion strategies, and distribution.
3. The combination and integration of the two foregoing elements into a unified whole which becomes the basis for appraisal of uncontrollable market forces.

Quite obviously the success of the marketing mix depends upon the care with which objectives are chosen, the depth of understanding of the uncontrollable market forces, the skill with which the elements have been combined to conform, and the effectiveness of implementation.

The difficulties of adopting an adequate marketing strategy are revealed in a variety of examples. Everyone is familiar with the now legendary Edsel car fiasco, but few seem to remember Philco's "Predicta" television set which was superbly designed but was forced to leave the market because of poor consumer response. The General Foods Corporation had a spectacular failure when it tried to introduce a high-priced gourmet foods line during the summer of 1957. Indeed, a New York industrial design firm reported that its research indicated that 23 of every 26 new products introduced by industry were failures, and McCann-Erickson, a large advertising agency, reported only one success for every 25 products put into test markets.

POLITICAL AND GEOGRAPHIC LIMITATIONS

Markets also have their political and/or geographic limitations. International trade, for example, is fraught with controls, both private and public. Where nationalist thinking is prevalent, the free exchange area, if any, is largely confined to the national political sphere. In this respect, the rather popular theories of autarchy (or economic self-sufficiency) that appeared during the 1930's, especially in the totalitarian political settings of pre–World War II Germany, are of considerable interest.

But the limiting of market areas to certain geographic or political zones also exists within national economic boundaries. Many local market areas are the result not so much of regional division of labor as of political influences. Some of these arrangements may also be the result of an identifiable cultural differentiation. But, in an intricate industrial exchange economy, such cultural market pockets are constantly threatened and tend to disappear.

There is no question, therefore, that the foremost market force bearing on the market mix is the state of consumer demand, including the demographic variables which define income and living standards and affect the consumer's buying habits, motivations, and attitudes. In developing a marketing mix the businessman seeks to answer six very basic questions: *Who* is the consumer? *Why* does he buy the products? *What* does he buy? *Where* is the purchase made? *When* is it made? And, finally, *how* is the purchase made? To get some clue into the appropriate answer for these questions the businessman may turn to a variety of sources to develop a "consumer profile." For example, it is well known that in the United States the average household spends about 30 percent of its income for food, beverages, and tobacco and approximately 20 percent of its income for home operations and home improvement. Surprisingly enough, approximately 14 percent out of the total family budget goes for an automobile and its upkeep. On the basis of analysis of these "profiles," certain firms dealing in specialized products can make rather sophisticated guesses on the kind of market that their products will meet.

Crucial to the seller is what, in economic terms, might be called the discretionary income—or, the portion of the income not devoted to meeting basic food, shelter, and clothing needs. *Time Magazine* reported (January 8, 1965) that the United States had clearly become the first society on earth in which people spend less for needs than for wants; and the long-term increase in disposable income will undoubtedly have profound impact on the market for appliances, luxury goods, recreation, and culture.

FREE EXCHANGE ECONOMY SUBJECT TO CONTROL

In times of war the free exchange economy suffers numerous restraints and controls from government agencies that are deemed necessary for "national security." Apart from various wartime controls which temporarily interfere with the rights and freedoms normally enjoyed in a free exchange economy, government also gets directly involved in other kinds of enterprises. The government's operation of synthetic rubber plants during World War II is a good example. Finally, the perfectly free exchange economy requires rigorous sacrifices that are socially unacceptable in a democratic society. The mixed capitalist economy in which we live is subject to a great variety of controls, both direct and indirect, all of which tend to affect the performance of the market.

There is little question that among operating executives the actions of government are crucial. Some government activities are designed to allow the executive to do things which he might otherwise not be able to do in a free market economy. In this category would be patents and copyrights which prevent competitors from duplicating the company's products throughout a fixed period of time. Other government actions are designed to prevent businessmen from doing things they might be able to do in a theoretically free market. In this area it may be recalled, the historic acts include the Sherman Anti-Trust Act of 1890, the Clayton Act and the Robinson-Patman Act of 1914, and the Federal Trade Commissions Act of 1914. The limitations of the last act are illustrative of what national public policy seeks to achieve and are primarily felt in the following areas: control of the quality of the product and information about the quality of the product, including misbranding; standards regarding the acceptability of advertising; and unlawful pricing policies.

STRENGTHS AND SHORTCOMINGS OF THE MARKET ECONOMY

THE ATTACK ON CAPITALISM

Every economic system is a compromise and the modern market or exchange economy, intertwined as it is with government, is no exception. It would be strange if this were otherwise. But the charges that have been brought against the free exchange economy are serious, because they accuse the business community of what amounts to a breach of its public promises. Thus the attack on the free exchange economy or the market is really an attack on capitalism proper. This attack makes at least four charges: (1) The capitalistic market economy encourages an unequal distribution of income and wealth. (2) It sets profits before productivity and thus puts producer interests before those of consumers. (3) It does not naturally bring about full employment; on the contrary, the business cycle, with severe, recurring depressions, seems to be a permanent feature of it. (4) Its system is faced with a basic contradiction of monopoly versus competition—unless checked by law, monopoly is certain to appear, and thus the very essence of capitalism will be violated. The first three points will be analyzed separately here: the last has been rather fully treated in the previous chapter on Competition.

Under capitalism, as under other known economic systems, personal-income distribution is unequal. Though this is less so today because of the progressive income tax and other factors, it is still noticeably true.

The economist attacks inequality of income distribution on several grounds. When incomes are very unevenly distributed, needs are not satisfied according to their importance, which means that luxuries may be produced before the entire population is well fed, housed, and clothed. It may also mean that the individual will be tempted to spend beyond his means in order to achieve a standard of living more nearly equal to that of his richer neighbor.

To the extent that inequality of income distribution is generally regarded as unfair, the economist's criticisms have apparently been accepted by the public. The prevalence of progressive income-tax systems implies a criticism of income distribution in the private sector. The same holds true for systems of rationing and price control, usually associated with wartime shortages. Unemployment compensation, old age benefits, and other social welfare payments also seem to be based on the principle that income inequalities should be reduced rather than accentuated.

One of the most serious objections to income inequality arises from the unequal distribution of educational and professional opportunities that attend it. Related to this are the monopolistic practices encountered in certain highly paid professions where the obvious intent is to keep newcomers as few as possible. To provide free education on a large scale might help overcome some of the disadvantages of income inequality. A similar argument is often made in support of enlarged health programs.

Yet it must be recognized that unequal income distribution has a rationale in every capitalistic economy. At the higher levels of personal income, a volume of saving takes place that is indispensable to capitalism's technological and productive expansion. If economic growth through the free market is to be achieved with a minimum of government interference, a certain degree of inequality is unavoidable. Because abilities differ, rewards for productive efforts are bound to be unequal. Unequal rewards are necessary because monetary incentives are at the root of the capitalistic market system and represent one of the mainsprings of dynamic resource allocation. The disappearance of income inequality would signify that capitalism was being replaced by some other form of social economy.

Closely related to this first charge is the one that states that the profit motive relegates productivity to a secondary role and thus acts counter to the public interest. While capitalist writers point to the superior productivity and higher standards of living prevailing in societies subject to the profit incentive, socialist writers claim that a more equal income distribution would enhance still further the economy's productivity.

Inequality of income distribution, it is argued, reduces aggregate demand below what it would be if incomes were more equally distributed and the government assumed the savings or investment function. Under a profit system, it is not the public need for ever-increased productivity but the hope of further private gain that governs production decisions. These criticisms lean heavily upon an assumption of chronic *under consumption* whose validity has been seriously questioned.

While there is some truth to these allegations, the fact remains that, under certain circumstances, the free market economy sometimes performs magnificently. The profit incentive has proved extremely efficient in guiding resources and in enhancing productivity, and for an instance one need but look at the recent industrial revolution in automation. Whether capitalism or socialism is capable of greater total output is an open question, but the burden of proof seems to lie with the latter.

The business cycle, with its periodically recurring waves of unemployment and inflation, is the most serious problem raised by the free exchange mechanism. Those who attack capitalism on this ground charge that economic instability is the inevitable by-product of the anarchy that, they believe, is an inherent part of the free market mechanism. The mixed enterprise system may provide the answer to this problem. Some unemployment, especially of the frictional variety, will always be present in a market economy. At the same time, it may prove politically impossible to halt inflation altogether and this becomes a particularly nettlesome vexation when industry is operating well under optimal productivity levels.

It is generally agreed that business-cycle control must be achieved by means of appropriate public policy. A conscious policy is required because certain basic, self-accelerating forces are at work in the market economy. George N. Halm suggests that the "policies which, superficially, seem to be the most congenial to the capitalist system, may not be the best for the system."[5] If rational social action is desired, a choice will have to be made with respect to appropriate policies.

Indirect monetary and fiscal policies are currently in favor, with the accent on the former. In addition, we seem to rely heavily on the so-called "built-in stabilizers," such as unemployment compensation and the progressive income tax. Sometimes, especially where the control of inflation is concerned, more drastic measures are advocated, such as wage and price controls or even rationing. This type of direct interference is, however, believed to run counter to basic capitalist principles. Efforts to enforce competition by means of antitrust laws must be looked at as part of the attempt to control inflation, while at the same time providing an economic environment in which flexibility is not eliminated.

---

[5] George N. Halm, *Economic Systems: A Comparative Analysis* (New York: Rinehart & Co., 1951), p. 129.

The subject of monopoly must be mentioned briefly. Monopolistic trade practices tend to frustrate the application and hence any beneficial results of indirect monetary and fiscal policies, and they prevent our realizing the full countercyclical effect of the built-in stabilizers. Certain types of monopoly situations bring about a complete breakdown in the market mechanism. This is especially well demonstrated by the recurring steel strikes, during which the free market for a whole sector of the economy ceases to operate.

The market mechanism has proved to be socially or politically inadequate in a number of private enterprise sectors. In agriculture, for instance, subsidies and acreage control are used to provide a "reasonable" income for farmers. If the market mechanism were allowed to operate unrestricted, the farm population would decline even faster and lead to developments presumed to be undesirable for various sociological and political reasons. Similarly, the rates for a number of public services, such as transportation, are established in a manner more consistent with a socialist economic practice than with the tradition of a free enterprise system.

THE "NEW" ATTACK ON PRIVATE MARKET ECONOMY

Recently, the offensive against the free exchange or private market economy has been renewed in the United States, but this time by liberals rather than by socialists. The new criticism, while it largely covers old ground, should nevertheless be taken seriously. It raises problems that the modern American enterprise system must sooner or later solve. The most comprehensive modern criticism of the American economy comes from Professor John K. Galbraith, who points out that our market economy allocates its monetary and physical resources too unevenly between the private and the public sectors.[6] He paints a rather extreme picture of a private production system that indulges in an excess of planned obsolescence, the result of which is not so much the expansion of the consumer's standard of living as the constant renewal of his past level. Galbraith emphasizes the need for social balance and advocates that a greater share of our national income be devoted to such vital matters as education, health, social security, and unemployment compensation. Of special interest are Professor Galbraith's suggestions for the expansion of

---

[6] John Kenneth Galbraith, *The Affluent Society* (Boston: Houghton Mifflin Co., 1958) , and *The New Industrial State* (Boston: Houghton Mifflin Co., 1967) .

public services that, as in the case of our National Parks, are becoming inadequate to meet the needs of our rapidly expanding population.

Another indictment of the market economy comes from those who believe that free enterprise is encouraging an unduly materialistic outlook. Still others are concerned about the growing role of "hidden persuaders" in advertising and in public relations. Finally, there are those who fear the predominance of big organization, both business and labor, against which the consumer appears to be less and less effective.

No doubt some of this new criticism is as justified today as was Marxist criticism of the far from perfect old-style capitalism. The market economy will always find it hard to satisfy everybody. As a trial and error economy it will experience bad moments which specific public policies will hopefully be able to mitigate. In our society the private business world, moved by the profit motive, must bear the burden of key decision making. However crude its operations may be at times, as a system for supple recovery and economic reconstruction, there has never been anything quite so effective as the free market system. The West German experience during the 1950's clearly attests to this. And if further proof is needed, the various imitations of the private market economy by Communist countries represent a striking vindication.

The free exchange economy can function well only if certain institutional prerequisites exist. Among the legal or constitutional prerequisites, those of the right to private property and to freedom of contract are essential to the smooth functioning of the free exchange economy. Even more important, these institutions must ultimately rest upon a system of shared values and beliefs. To the extent that democratic human relationships are associated with the free enterprise system, the principal of equality or of shared value is a prerequisite. Its counterpart in the market is competition, preferably of an atomistic type, whereby overwhelming economic power aggregations are kept to a minimum. Other prerequisites or values of this type are the need for rational decision making, the desire for security, and the expectation of progress.

Finally, there are certain cultural traditions and customs that circumscribe the field of permissible activities and generally accepted or tolerated procedures. All these, at any given moment, tend to define—for the practitioner—the meaning of "consumer sovereignty" and of "individual self-interest," both of which are key concepts in the free exchange economy.

A NOTE ON ADVERTISING

The concept of a market economy remains the basic postulate of the economic system of our country. It would be inappropriate to omit some mention of advertising as one aspect of the marketing strategies in the contemporary society. The word itself is enough to arouse emotions and to recall the rather lurid attacks on the advertising industry by *McClure's Magazine* at the turn of the century. If one accepts the results of certain opinion research polls then approximately 80 percent of the American public still believes that advertising causes people to buy things that they do not want.

Much of the criticism is aimed at the allegedly dishonest quality of the advertising process and, even more frequently, at advertising's esthetic shortcomings. But the basic purpose of advertising is to implement the selling process by bridging the communications gap between producers and consumers. In the economic model of perfect competition it was assumed that producers and consumers were already in contact and that no problem of communications existed. In the real world, however, this simplified assumption simply does not hold. In a large mass market, advertising has been found to be one of the most inexpensive methods for reaching the widest audience. While no accurate account had ever been made of the number of people engaged in advertising it has been estimated that over 65,000 people are employed by some 4,240 agencies. The cost of this fantastic communication process represented by the advertising industry is staggering. Concealed in the multibillion-dollar bill is, however, the fact that large parts of the expenditure go toward the operating expenses of nearly 500 television stations and over 3,000 radio stations in the United States.

To the consumer, what are the costs of advertising? Again figures are difficult to justify, but it has been estimated that advertising added $20 to the cost of a Chevrolet, some 10 cents to a case of Budweiser, and 3 or 4 cents to a carton of cigarettes. Procter and Gamble, the nation's largest advertisers, spent well over $100 million to reach customers through advertising. It must be noted that the P and G investment seems worthwhile: The company sells well over $1.5 billion worth of goods. Whether advertising necessarily means a higher price in the market depends on a variety of factors. The market price is related to the cost of production. In a decreasing-cost industry, a higher marketing cost can bring about lower production costs by making possible the savings of mass production techniques. The great economist, Alfred Marshall, was of the opinion that such off-setting forces do occur in business but clearly more empirical study is required before precise judgments can be made regarding the relationship of advertising cost to the sale of specific products.

RECOMMENDED READING

BAIN, JOE S. *Social Economy and the Price System,* pp. 48–76. New York: Macmillan Co., 1950.

BURK, GILBERT, and PARKER, SANFORD S. "Detroit's Next Decade," from "The Markets of the 1960's," *Fortune,* Vol. LX (October, 1959), 112–15, 245–56.

DAHL, ROBERT A., and LINDBLOM, CHARLES E. *Politics, Economics, and Welfare,* pp. 173–77; also pp. 177–226. New York: Harper & Bros., 1953.

GALBRAITH, JOHN KENNETH. *The Affluent Society,* pp. 251–69. Boston: Houghton Mifflin Co., 1958.

HOWARD, JOHN A. *Marketing Management: Analysis and Planning.* Rev. ed. Homewood, Ill.: Richard D. Irwin, Inc., 1963.

LYON, LEVERETT S. "Marketing" in *Encyclopaedia of the Social Sciences,* Vol. X, pp. 131–44. New York: Macmillan Co., 1933.

MILLIKAN, MAX (ed.). *Income Stabilization for a Developing Democracy,* pp. 13–24. New Haven: Yale University Press, 1953.

MOULTON, HAROLD G. *Economic Systems,* pp. 22–40. Washington, D.C.: The Brookings Institution, 1948.

MUND, VERNON A. *Open Markets,* pp. 3–31. New York: Harper & Bros., 1948.

———. *Government and Business,* pp. 73–74. 2d ed. New York: Harper & Brothers, 1955.

OXENFELDT, ALFRED. *Executive Action in Marketing.* Belmont, Calif.: Wadsworth Publishing Co., Inc., 1966.

POLANYI, KARL. *The Great Transformation,* pp. 68–76; also chaps. iii–v, xii–xix, xxi. New York: Farrar and Rinehart, 1944.

SUTTON, F. X.; HARRIS, S. E.; KAYSEN, C.; and TOBIN, J. *The American*

Business Creed, pp. 138–60. Cambridge: Harvard University Press, 1956.

WALLICH, HENRY C. *Mainsprings of the German Revival,* pp. 147–52. New Haven: Yale University Press, 1955.

FURTHER READING

BOWEN, HOWARD R. *The Social Responsibilities of the Businessman.* New York: Harper & Bros., 1954.

DAHL, ROBERT A., and LINDBLOM, CHARLES E. *Politics, Economics, and Welfare,* pp. 25–54. New York: Harper & Bros., 1953.

DRUCKER, PETER F. *America's Next Twenty Years,* pp. 52–70. New York: Harper & Bros., 1957.

EINAUDI, MARIO; BYE, MAURICE; and ROSSI, ERNESTO. *Nationalization in France and Italy.* Ithaca: Cornell University Press, 1955.

GRANICK, DAVID. *Management of the Industrial Firm in the USSR.* New York: Columbia University Press, 1954.

HALM, GEORGE N. *Economic Systems: A Comparative Analysis,* pp. 3–87; 89–131. New York: Rinehart & Co., 1951.

JEWKES, JOHN. *Ordeal by Planning.* New York: Macmillan Co., 1948.

KATONA, GEORGE. *The Powerful Consumer.* New York: McGraw-Hill Book Co., 1960.

LANGE, OSCAR, and TAYLOR, FRED M. *On the Economic Theory of Socialism.* Minneapolis: University of Minneapolis Press, 1938.

LEFTWICH, RICHARD H. *The Price System and Resource Allocation,* chap. ii. New York: Rinehart & Co., 1955.

LEONTIEF, WASSILY. *Studies in the Structure of the American Economy.* New York: Oxford University Press, 1953.

LEWIS, BEN W. *British Planning and Nationalization.* New York: Twentieth Century Fund, 1952.

MARSHALL, ALFRED. *Principles of Political Economy.* 8th ed. New York: Macmillan Co., 1948.

MEADE, J. E. *Planning and the Price Mechanism.* London: Allen and Unwin, 1948.

MILLIKAN, MAX F. (ed.). *Income Stabilization for a Developing Democracy,* Part II; also chap. iii. New Haven: Yale University Press, 1953.

OXENFELDT, ALFRED R. *Industrial Pricing and Market Practices,* esp. the two cases studies. New York: Prentice-Hall, Inc., 1951.

PACKARD, VANCE. *The Hidden Persuaders.* New York: David McKay Co., 1957.

SIMONS, HENRY. *Economic Policy for a Free Society,* esp. chaps. i, ii, iii, and iv. Chicago: University of Chicago Press, 1948.

SMITH, ADAM. *An Inquiry into the Nature and Causes of the Wealth of Nations,* p. 423. Modern Library ed.

STEINER, PETER O. "Markets and Industries," *International Encyclopedia of the Social Sciences,* Vol. IX, pp. 575–81.

STEINER, PETER O., and DORFMAN, ROBERT. *The Economic Status of the Aged.* Berkeley: University of California Press, 1957.

SWEEZEY, PAUL M. *The Theory of Capitalist Development.* New York: Oxford University Press, 1942.

WEBB, SIDNEY and BEATRICE. *The Decay of Capitalist Civilization.* New York: Harcourt, Brace & Co., 1923.

WENDZEL, JULIUS T. *The Dynamics of Capitalism.* New York: Harper & Bros., 1956.

WILCOX, CLAIR. *Public Policies toward Business.* Homewood, Ill.: Richard D. Irwin, Inc., 1955.

15. *Invention and Innovation*

THROUGHOUT the long history of human institutions the traditional viewpoint has always been that a state of equilibrium was the most desirable condition. Alexis de Tocqueville, to whom scholars are turning rather frequently these days, clearly and accurately traced the constancy of institutions, despite radical changes in political and ideological affairs. One historian recently remarked that "institutions, the structural foundations of historic societies, have shown a fantastic capacity to resist innovation and the ravages of time."[1] Change occurred, of course, but it was regarded as an occasional

---

[1] A. William Solomone, "The Freedom of History," *Colloquium*, Vol. III (April, 1965), p. 3.

disturbing challenge. The main objective, therefore, was to anticipate and prevent change or, failing that, to organize in such a way as
to make it possible to adapt quickly and painlessly to those changes
that did occur. This "fearful" attitude was based on a simple recognition of the fact that change was often catastrophic—"acts of God"
such as floods, fire, famine, or earthquakes. Viewed in this way, it is
small wonder that change was resisted.

The businessman was also judged on the basis of how well he
adapted to his environment: if he adapted perfectly, he was "right,"
but if he adjusted less than perfectly, he created tensions for himself
and for the economy. It must be noted, however, that these evalua-
tions were based on standards set by forces outside the businessman
himself. Under normal conditions his actions were controlled by the
actions of his customers, his dealers, the government, or banks, and
all he could possibly do was to adapt to changes forced upon him by
outside groups. Within limits he could exercise choice in the location of his plants or in the internal allocation of his resources but
the range of his decision-making power was limited to this *internal*
domain.

This, in essence, was the view of the business enterprise under a
system of "perfect" competition. Simply stated, it was the job of the
plant to produce the product and the job of the salesman to sell it.
This simplistic view could be supported as long as business remained relatively small and uncomplex. When the economic system
became increasingly large and interdependent, a different viewpoint
had to be introduced. This new outlook welcomed change and
recognized the need of living with innovation.

It takes no special recitation of dramatic facts to underscore the
accelerating pace of change in the contemporary world, or to indicate, with examples, the areas in which innovation has produced
spectacular results. The shrinking time lag between basic discoveries
and the application of these discoveries to commercial products is
one excellent indicator of the accelerating rate of change. For example, it took over a century of applied research and engineering in
photography to develop the basic discovery into a saleable product.
In the case of the telephone the time lag was over a half-century;
radio took about 35 years as contrasted to radar which took 15.
Television moved from research to the commercial stage within 12
years, and the atomic bomb in 6.

Technological change obviously affects the economy, and the late

Sumner Slichter declared that technological research had developed sufficiently by 1937 to make Keynes' theory of employment obsolete on the day of its publication despite the invaluable concepts and tools of analysis contained in his work. The Keynesian theory rested upon a theory of consumption and a theory of investment that were seriously in error in the light of technological advances; he was led to the mistaken practical conclusion that economic progress inevitably created chronic deficiency in demand and, in some respects, he repeated the errors of Malthus by failing to sense the impact of technical improvement on demand.

How seriously technical change affects the economy can be seen from two selected examples. Less than a quarter-century ago the "Queen Mary" sailed on her maiden voyage. Carrying 2,000 passengers and a crew of 1,400 she could cross the Atlantic in five days; today jet planes cover the same distance in about six hours. The ship had cost, on today's prices, about $200 million, whereas the typical B-707 costs about $5.5 million. With a crew of nine, the plane carries between 120 and 150 passengers per trip, but its annual carrying capacity equals that of the "Queen Mary." Because of the invention and innovation the death of the Cunard "Queens" was a foregone conclusion. In another case, the Cincinnati Milling Machine Company brought out a new machine costing $40,000 in 1949; six machines, costing $240,000, could bore 108 cylinder heads hourly at a direct cost of 20 cents per piece—half the labor costs of the machines they replaced. In 1954, only five years later, the company built a new machine costing $30,000 which alone could turn out the same volume of production as the six machines, and at a direct labor cost of four cents per piece.[2] In this country there is a $10 billion "industry of discovery" to push technological change at ever-advancing rates.

The whole climate of behavior and of thinking about change has undergone as remarkable a transformation as industry itself. Contrast the fanfare of the annual new car models with the automobile manufacturer of 1912 who advertised a "farewell car" on the theory that no better car would ever be built! It would be a grievous error, however, to conclude that established firms, run by competent man-

---

[2] These ideas were presented by Robert C. Turner in "Progress, Productivity, and Professors," *Proceedings: Middle Atlantic Association of Colleges of Business, October 8–10, 1959* (Pittsburgh: Duquesne University, 1959) , pp. 1–17. Contrasts between this and earlier centuries of the modern period may be observed by reading background material in A. Wolf, *A History of Science, Technology and Philosophy in the 16th and 17th Centuries* (New York: Torchbooks [paperback], 1959) .

agers, are invariably "innovation-prone." The "official" attitude is composed of a number of tenets, chief of which are the following: (1) since a product can hold the market only a given period of time, every enterprise must innovate or perish; (2) invention and technical innovation are essential to growth; and (3) American consumers, conditioned to new products, need only be persuaded to accept change at a rate satisfactory to corporate needs for market expansion.[3]

Contrary to the official company dogma, however, an "underground" view may be found which sees in innovation generally, and in technical innovation particularly, dangerously disruptive and uncertain qualities. There are reported cases of companies speaking boldly of change and acting with calculated timidity in order to prevent it. One such company, beleaguered by competition, called for diversification yet gave its new products coordinator a series of norms which emphasized a minimum of technical innovation, insisted on no additions to the sales force, and demanded a high gross income. The result was that over 25 new products went unproduced.

But in general it is clear that the "tinker mentality" and the willingness to try something new—to be inventive—are part of the American character. It is therefore imperative to ask what the concepts of invention or innovation involve, what forms they take, and what "climate" promotes it.

THE NATURE OF INNOVATION

INNOVATION AS CHANGE

An innovation has been defined broadly as "any thought, behavior or thing that is new because it is qualitatively different from existing forms."[4] But this definition is so comprehensive that it could include both planned and unplanned change. In a much narrower sense, innovation can be construed as connoting purposeful change of the status quo in hope of reward; consequently purposeful change through innovation carries with it the risk of failure. It must be emphasized that innovation is never an abstraction, but occurs always in a particular field and with particular materials, so that by

---

[3] Donald Schon, *The Technology of Change* (New York: Delacorte Press, 1967), pp. 42–45.

[4] H. G. Barnett, *Innovation: The Basis of Cultural Change* (New York: McGraw-Hill Book Co., 1953), p. 7.

organizing reality into relationships having novel esthetic or intellectual concepts, the purposes of the creator are better served.[5] The essential difference, therefore, between innovation and adaptation is one of objectives. In a system of adaptation, the purpose is to maintain stability and to change only when forced to do so. In a system of innovation, it is recognized that profit and growth come only as a result of effort to bring about *purposeful* change. There is, in fact, a long-standing recognition of this concept in our proverbs ("build a better mousetrap") and in our folklore ("the inventive genius inborn in all Americans"). This philosophy assumes that customers' wants are unlimited and that the economic challenge consists in discovering these wants and fulfilling them. But every change from the status quo, where people tend to be comfortable, entails a degree of risk. It is this risk that defines innovation. *Thus innovation is risk-taking change introduced for the purpose of satisfying economic wants and resulting in increased profitability.*[6]

Since innovation in business implies a purpose, the risks of failure are risks inherent not only in the technical aspects of the innovation but in the business aspects as well. Though failures may come from technical sources (either in the laboratory, or in the steps from *laboratory to pilot plant* or *pilot plant to full scale production*), they may come equally, or perhaps even more frequently, from business failures occasioned by inability to obtain adequate financing, deficiencies in marketing techniques, miscalculations in timing or because the public may simply be uninterested or unmoved by the innovation.

INVENTION AND INNOVATION

Innovation is frequently thought of as product development, invention, or simply research. Each of these activities may, in fact, lead to innovation but they must not be defined as innovation. Product and process development, invention, and research are general business tools; innovation is a major area of management decision and activity. This does not mean, however, that the old concept of invention (a "flash of genius") has been abandoned. Indeed, it might be noted parenthetically that in 1891 the court observed, in

---

[5] Everett E. Hagen, *On The Theory of Social Change* (Homewood, Ill.: The Dorsey Press, 1962), p. 87.

[6] W. Paul Strassman, *Risk and Technological Innovation: American Manufacturing Methods During the Nineteenth Century* (Ithaca, N.Y.: Cornell University Press, 1959).

McLain v. *Ortmayer,* that the word "invention" cannot be defined with substantial precision, an observation that was to be repeated 63 years later in *Kwikset Blocks* v. *Hillgren* (1954) ; any attempt to fix precise meaning to the newer concept of innovation will undoubtedly go through ordeals somewhat similar to the concept of invention.[7]

The courts have differentiated invention from routine experimentation. In *General Motors Corp.* v. *Preferred Electric and Wire Corp.,* the court noted that those petitioning for a patent had made and tried a great many different forms before coming at last to that which seemed best. To the judges, at least, there was no evidence that any higher abilities were demanded than intelligent, well-trained, and persistent experimentation, acting in the light of the defects which past experience had developed. Perhaps such qualities are as valuable as sudden flashes of genius; indeed, in the long run, they may be more deserving but the prize in invention does not go to success so achieved. Something more out of the common is demanded. What is needed was stated by the court in *Less Car Load Lots Co. et al.* v. *Pennsylvania R.R. Co.* in these terms:

> Invention is the antithesis of evolution and connotes necessarily the achievement of the unexpectable. It may properly be said to occur only when a demand for an advance in an art has built up a sufficient potential to cause the spark of some man's thought, by jumping an uncrossed gap between an outpost of that art and one of its desiderata to give the world something new in process, product, or device.[8]

Invention, when used to indicate an idea protected or protectable by a patent issued by the U.S. Patent Office, is a very restricted concept. While related to innovation, invention is not coextensive with that term because it deals with *technical* ideas or ideas about things or processes, and clearly does not touch on broad areas represented by social or even technological innovations. Social innovations include basic changes in habits, tastes, organization, marketing, and advertising.

In politics, the idea of judicial review was a major social innovation and, in economics, the idea of a European Common Market

---

[7] Thomas L. Flattery and N. J. Gardner, "Essays Dealing With Today's Concept of Invention," U.C.L.A. *Law Review* (February, 1956) , pp. 173–83 and 184–91.

[8] Chester Biesterfeld, *Patent Law* (New York: John Wiley & Sons, Inc., 1949) , chap. 2.

was equally innovative. Originating ideas basic to business innovations are, to some extent, protected by the law of unfair competition. But even technological innovations may not be based on ideas protected by patent, because a patent is "hedged in" by rather precise technical requirements. An idea may not be patentable if it has been anticipated by a description in a foreign publication, if an application is not filed within one year of publication, or if the invention has been in public use for more than one year prior to the patent application. Thus, an inventor who has used, or published, or has been anticipated in any publication anywhere in the world, or who has sold some early prototypes and failed to file within a year, loses his rights to patent coverage. These ideas, nevertheless, may be the basis for far-reaching technological innovations. *The invention, therefore, is merely a starting point for a technological innovation.* Many contemporary inventors are actually heirs to Edison because they are technological innovators, who perceive a need and apply systematic logic, not a flash of genius, to meet that need. There is a logical inference from analysis of a market, anticipation of the consequences of change, and then action to effectuate the desired outcome.

The patent differs from an innovative idea not covered by patent also in terms of the protection a patent offers. What the inventor seeks through a patent is to obtain time within which a technological innovation may be accomplished by the group undertaking it. Patent protection may be the deciding factor in determining whether to undertake the innovation; an affirmative decision may be accomplished in several ways: i.e., by protecting the market for a period long enough to recover the investment in research and development; by royalties from other business firms to help defray these costs if it is decided to share the market; by permitting the business to obtain financing of necessary research and development to be repaid by royalties; by permitting a business to acquire an idea from outside of its own organization which it wishes to acquire, without paying for it until it brings in profits.

The importance of the patent system in giving protection and time for the development of technological innovations is well illustrated by Xerox and Polaroid. In 1964 Xerox had a total operating revenue of $268,027,165 for an increase in one year of 53 percent over the already high $176,036,387 figure. The Carlson patents tell the basic story. The number of large firms uninterested in the Carlson patents is well known; however, it was patent protection which permitted Carlson to obtain the backing of the Battelle Institute which, in turn, interested Haloid (now Xerox) in him. Even in light of the patents, the financial risk was very high because much development work was needed. This work would not have been undertaken at all if patent protection had not given the company at least a chance to recover its development costs (by providing time to develop the product, to set up a marketing program, and to establish a brand name) before competitors could enter the market.[9]

Polaroid is another famous success story of a business based on patents. Again there is the familiar pattern of lack of interest in Dr. Land's inventions in photography by firms which could logically have launched the innovation. The Polaroid Corporation grew from a $6 million enterprise in 1949 to $139,350,582 in 1964. By March of 1965, Polaroid had received 886 patents of which 654 were still in force. The prospectus issued in June of 1965 noted that important patents will not expire for 15 years and adds that "in the judgement of the company, its patent structure as a whole is important to its business."[10]

While the validity of a patent may not be challenged in a court action, there are limitations. Any use which violates the antitrust laws (such as pooling patents to control a market or tie-in sales of materials for use on a patented machine) are forbidden. Fundamentally, the law forbids the extension of the patent monopoly by use of the patent to control auxiliary markets or processes. Despite problems, patents are still a very vital force in technological innovations. They are the negotiable instrument of the outside inventor who may sell it to an on-going company. Or, if an existing business is not interested, the patent still functions as a negotiable instrument against which funds can be raised to start a business to undertake the technological innovation. W. R. MacLaurin in discussing the radio industry notes a number of examples:

> After 1900, the possible rewards to be obtained from radio patents provided a direct stimulus to inventors and those who financed them. Fessenden, for example, obtained two backers, Walker and Given, who advanced large sums of money to finance his experiments. They did so with the definite hope that this would prove a profitable speculative invest-

[9] See Xerox Corporation, *Annual Report 1964* and "High Hopes at Xerox," *New York Times* (May 31, 1965), p. 20.

[10] See Polaroid Corporation, *Prospectus* (May 25, 1965).

ment. . . . DeForest raised his funds by stock promotion and his patents were played up in the stock appeal. Edwin Armstrong, as a struggling inventor, had no means or sources of capital to tap and for a number of years was able to finance himself only by what he received from patents. And later, in television, a group of California bankers supported Farnsworth in the expectation that his patents would be basic to the new television industry and more than compensate for the initial investment. Without the patent system, it is difficult to see how many of these inventors could have obtained adequate financial support except by joining established companies; and in the critical years, when these men were beginning their experiments, none of the existing firms were interested in their inventions. The patent system, therefore provided an important stimulus.[11]

But Charles Kettering noted that "progress will not come through research, science, and invention alone. These are merely the loose strands of progress. They must be joined by cross-strands."[12] The cross-strands are many and different. By exercising control through patents the scientist, and every other creative talent can better assure himself that his invention will do what he wants it to do in the world. He can license it freely to all worthy comers as though there were no patent at all, and he can refuse to license those whose competence or aims he distrusts. The creative man is, in some respects, the most richly endowed man.

"Every new invention," said Myron Coler, "or bit of technological improvement had its origin in some individual's brain—the product of creativity."[13] No organization or group of organizations control, or begin to control, the available creativity. Land and Carlson were not employees of Eastman Kodak or IBM. Curiously enough, the ratio of discoveries and patents from the independent inventor or small organization has remained relatively constant in the face of vast expenditures on research by large corporations and government. Maurice A. Crews, then Assistant Commissioner of Patents, noted in 1961 that 60 percent of the most important discoveries came from independent persons or from small organizations.[14]

---

[11] Quoted by James W. Falk in "The Changing Patent Climate," *Transactions of the New York Academy of Science* (March, 1964), p. 1053.

[12] Arthur R. Whale, "Letter to *Science*," *Science*, Vol. CXLIII (March 13, 1964), p. 1123.

[13] Myron A. Coler (ed.), *Essays on Creativity in the Sciences* (New York: New York University Press, 1963), p. 74.

[14] "Right to Your Ideas in Danger," *Nation's Business* (January, 1961), pp. 64–65.

In summation it might be noted that invention and innovation shade, often almost imperceptably, into one another so effectively that they may be looked upon as a part of a unified process and not different phases or steps which follow one another in time. The invention involves a tool or technique, or any physical equipment, or a way of doing something which extends the human capacity. Innovation is more related to the process whereby the invention is introduced and diffused throughout a society. The innovator sees a goal, whereas the inventor, as often as not, "discovers" a goal along the way. Often the inventive process works backward—that is, one may discover a phenomenon and then seek a use for it. This occurred in Becquerel's discovery of some applications of radiation from his observation of the fogging of a photographic plate.

Nor may the "surprise" element be discounted, and basic research has provided a dramatic example. During World War II physicists working in the electronics field had made valuable forays into microwave spectroscopy (the study of the interaction between microwaves and gaseous molecules). The first work in basic research was carried out mainly in industrial laboratories by independent groups of scientists. Bell Telephone Laboratories, the RCA Laboratories and Westinghouse were joined by only one university team at Columbia. Of this story, Charles H. Townes of the University of California, Berkeley, gave this fascinating account:

No doubt in the industrial laboratories there was some hope that the new field of physics would have a worthwhile contact with commercial applications. In the case of the Bell Telephone Laboratories, I had myself written a memorandum with some care to convince research management that this could be the case. However, after several years this type of work died out in the four industrial laboratories where it had an early start and moved to the universities entirely. There it attracted a good number of excellent students, as well as experienced professors, because of the insight it afforded into molecular and atomic behavior. Reasons for growth of the field in universities may seem natural enough. Reasons for its decay in industry are equally important, and illustrate rather clearly our dilemma in the planning of research.

Evidently the four large industrial laboratories, although deeply involved with electronics, did not feel at the time that research on the microwave spectroscopy of gases had much importance for their work. I do not know the detailed reasoning of management at Westinghouse and RCA, but after the small teams of research workers which had been quite successful at these laboratories left or lost interest, research in the field was not rebuilt. At the General Electric Company, the research scientist in this field was transferred by management decision to another field considered more pertinent to the company's business. In the case of the Bell Telephone Laboratories, there was a management decision that, while one senior scientist could be appropriately supported, the work was not important enough to the electronics and communications industry to warrant adding a second one. Yet it was out of just this field that two or three years later a completely new technique of amplification was born which now occupies hundreds of scientist and engineers in the same laboratories. Clearly, misjudgment of its potential was not a simple human fault of any one company or individual; it was a pervasive characteristic of the system.[15]

The story lends weight to a conclusion reached by Donald Schon who found that "each step in the process of invention . . . is itself a complex process, a series of related inventions rather than a single act."[16]

TYPES AND PURPOSES OF INNOVATION

Technological. There are two fundamental types of innovation: *technological* and *social.* Technological innovations are most generally related to *products:* frozen foods, transistor radios, photostatic equipment, and the like, which are involved in ways people use or consume products or services. These innovations normally require carefully coordinated teamwork. A research director at Monsanto Chemical put the problem in these terms:

Lack of well-considered company management participation in setting research goals is one of the principal sources of discord and dissatisfaction between research workers and management. The fruits of successful exploratory research can be gathered only if the company can carry the product through the developmental pilot plant, and market testing stages to commercial sale. . . . Research is not an end in itself, and the ultimate payoff depends upon many other functions—finance, marketing, engineering, production.[17]

In very broad terms the idea of technological innovation may be said to include most of the following: the idea or invention; the business decision to employ the tools of an enterprise to implement

---

[15] Charles H. Townes, "Quantum Electronics and Surprise in Developments of Technology," *Science*, Vol. CLIX (February 16, 1968), p. 700.

[16] Schon, *op. cit.*, p. 11.

[17] Coler, *op. cit.*, pp. 78–79.

the idea or invention; the research and development required at all stages of development; financing, including, if necessary, acquisition of the idea or invention, research support, development and production facilities; and distribution of the resulting innovation to assure as much acceptance and use as the potential market can afford.

Innovation may be undertaken for a variety of business purposes. It may seek to meet economic wants, to keep or obtain a position of leadership in a particular industry, to benefit one or more of the various groups that are part of that corporation's constellation of special interests, it may also seek to lessen the impact of technological innovation or, conversely, to widen the impact of technological innovation.

Both the risks of failure and the rewards to be gained by successful innovation are clearly illustrated in innovations undertaken to fulfill economic wants. New product development is the major goal, either for known wants or for new wants which must themselves be created. Two quite different products illustrate contrasting patterns of risk-taking through technological innovations—Xerox copying machines and frozen foods. In the case of Xerox, much costly development work was needed on copying machines before they were marketed; the financial risk was high for a relatively small company and this was known before the decision was made to acquire rights to the patents. But, as *Fortune* noted, "the Xerox Corporation of Rochester is an interesting example that the big rewards in business go to those who take the big risks."[18]

The big risk in frozen foods was not really of a technological character. As early as 1925, Clarence Birdseye had discovered a quick-freezing technique which threatened to revolutionize the food industry. In 1928, the well-known banking house of Goldman Sachs estimated sales potential as high as a billion dollars and took a major financial interest in the Birdseye process. When returns lagged, Goldman Sachs sold out to General Foods at a price of nearly $12 million—a fraction of what was originally paid. Yet 10 years later—on the eve of World War II—frozen foods had paid back less than $8 million to General Foods on an investment that had now reached some $30 million.[19] Worries persisted.

The problem was not the technology, not the costs, not even the

---

[18] *Fortune* (July, 1962) .

[19] "Frosted Foods," *Fortune* (October, 1934) , p. 135.

potential market. Eugene Gibson, who had been put in charge of the innovation by General Foods, noted that his company had taken a significant turn when it hit upon the idea of renting frozen food cases in 1934. But the public refused to change its eating habits. The war provided the incentive because frozen foods were not rationed. The problem, in Mr. Gibson's words, was "to get people to eat peas in the middle of winter—as well as peaches and strawberries."[20] By 1955, frozen foods were estimated to have accounted for approximately 12 percent of an $800 million business. In a decade a new industry had been born!

Social. Related to technological innovations are social ones which reflect a further revolution in the concept of business. According to the revised concept, business must think not only of the customer's product wants but also of his broader demands as they relate to the role of business in the total society. Thus, when it became necessary for business to justify its place in the economy (through its employee, community, and social relations), a social innovation was introduced into the older practice of public relations. According to the new view, the competitive edge which might be gained by the company creating the most advantageous "image" in the mind of the customer could result in the widest acceptance of the company's products and services.

As a result, the concept of social innovation in the broadest sense is becoming more widely accepted. Now, admittedly, social change is influenced by technological invention as has been pointed out.[21] Space ships may alter the whole notion of national sovereignty and of property; even the simple coin-in-the-slot device has affected the range and nature of selling and has generated unemployment in some sectors. But not all social change emerges from or depends upon technical revolutions. When consideration is given to such devices as balance-of-power in international affairs, to judicial review and separation of powers in the national government, to the legal concept of limited liability in the corporation, to devices like the League of Nations and the United Nations, we begin to understand the broad areas in which social innovation has been developed

---

[20] Edwin T. Gibson, *Corporation Executive,* in the Oral History Collection of Columbia University, Butler Library, New York, 1956, pp. 25–30.

[21] A. MacLaurin, "Sequence from Invention to Innovation and Economic Growth," *Quarterly Journal of Economics,* Vol. LXVII (February, 1953), p. 41.

and made useful to mankind.[22] The same consciousness impels management to think of innovation in the broadest sense.

In the aggregate, the basically nontechnological innovations may have had a greater impact on the American economy and may have contributed more to the increase in productivity in this country than have all the technological innovations of the last 10 or 15 years. In the long view of history, it is for social inventions, not technical ones, that Americans will best be remembered.

During the period ahead, in any event, the greater need for innovation seems to lie more in the social than the technological area. Indeed, the technological revolution itself will be totally unproductive unless accompanied by major innovations in the nontechnological field. Innovation in marketing is critically important. Equally needed are innovations in the methods, tools, and measurements for doing the managerial job, in the management of workers, and in the organization of work. Despite progress in this latter area, organization of work may well be the most backward sphere and the one with the greatest potential for increased productivity. Pursuing the problem of organizational innovations one might ask: What are the key ideas about current organizations? Two clearly identifiable innovations relate (a) to the idea of developing *temporary systems* within an organization and (b) to the development of *open systems*. Illustrations serve to indicate wherein social innovations may come.

Temporary Systems. While there is full awareness of the fact that 80 percent of the present products were not on the market 15 years ago we seem unaware that 80 percent of the managers in top slots today were not in these positions 5 or 10 years ago. There is, therefore, much movement at the top and in some companies, top management were found to be in their present jobs less than nine months. This is a far cry from the old view that time was needed to build a stable organization. We must learn, therefore, to develop temporary systems while keeping the basic entity or firm with its value structures operative. How may temporary systems be set up? One way is to set up project management. Project managements challenge the myth of one "boss" only and the need for long seasoning. The project, when completed, can be quickly disbanded and new ones formed.

---

22 William F. Ogburn, "Technology and Governmental Change," in R. C. Snyder and H. H. Wilson (eds.), *Roots of Political Behavior* (New York: American Book Co., 1949), Sec. VI.

Open Systems. The next question for speculation into social innovation is this: How may we organize an open system? To understand the concept requires appreciation of the so-called "closed system" built on engineering and accounting concepts. In the engineering concept work is broken into its various segments and then input-output is measured; the accounting system introduced the notion of double-entry bookkeeping where authority is made commensurate to responsibility.

In contrast to the closed system (which is input-output oriented and stresses detection and correction of error), the open system stresses the *transactional* nature of business. Transaction draws on the environment; it draws energy from its contacts. It leads to new questions: What do we need to know of the environment? Where should such information go? How should it be used? What data do we need regularly? Put concretely, an open systems manager asks questions about the nature of the labor market, and the changed values of workers; he looks to changes in youth and asks what these changes mean to the corporation in the future.

It has been suggested, therefore, that we escape from the notion of the closed system, with its emphasis on a single "best solution," and live with an open system where deviations become diagnostic signs whereby managers can improve the organization. It means toleration of a variety of activities under the principle of equifinality, and it means further challenge to the closed system's ignorance of the environment. For example, Ford Motor Company was once interested in advertising the safety of its cars, but the market did not respond; yet Ford seemed completely caught off guard by recent revelations before Congress on safety problems in automobiles.

Compared to technological innovations in electronics, rocket engines, or synthetic chemistry, social innovations are rather unglamorous. Potential social innovations are rarely discussed except by professional managers; yet success in these areas may well decide whether the population revolution (which has already occurred) will be an opportunity for further growth and strength, or whether it will prove a strain, a burden, and perhaps even a threat to social and economic stability.[23]

It should be pointed out, however, that one school of thought exists which holds that social innovation does not and, in fact,

---

[23] Peter F. Drucker, *America's Next Twenty Years* (New York: Harper & Bros., 1955), as quoted in *Toward the Liberally Educated Executive* (New York: Fund for Adult Education, 1957), pp. 85–86.

cannot exist. It is said that change (or new knowledge) has always existed but that it has never been susceptible to systematic purposeful management. This is, of course, an old argument premised historically on "plan or no plan" and always presented in "either-or" terms: (*a*) survival is impossible without central planning and (*b*) decentralization is anarchy.

CLIMATE FOR INNOVATION

If the innovative attitude is to continue we must consider a number of problems that affect the general "climate" within which business operates. Clearly, one cannot neglect the gospel of progress and success that swept the entire American society during the last half of the 19th-century. From its inception, the American nation has had an almost messianic impulsion to try to make things bigger and better and to pass on the fruits to the rest of the world. From the French (particularly from men like Condorcet and Saint-Simon), Americans secured a readymade philosophical formula for their belief that somehow, in some way, things were getting better all the time.[24] To resist change was to frustrate success.[25] Indeed, a remark attributed by Eric Goldman to George Humphreys, former Secretary of the Treasury, fairly well summarizes any facile generalization one could make of the American cult of progress and success. Speaking of Hemingway's *The Old Man and the Sea,* Mr. Humphreys was alleged to have said, "Why should anyone be interested in some old man who was a failure?"[26]

The cult of progress encouraged belief in innovation. Anthropologists are providing new insights into how positive attitudes toward innovation are built into the social system. Recent studies of the Indonesian villages of Tabanan and Modjokuto provide some interesting clues. Industrialism does not necessarily involve free-enterprise capitalism, but it does involve the decline of magic, the construction of a universal legal and moral code, increased social mobility, the bureaucracy of government, and the isolation of the elementary family from strong, extended kinship ties. The total,

---

[24] Walter M. Simon, "Saint Simon and the Ideas of Progress," *Journal of the History of Ideas,* Vol. XVII (June, 1956) , p. 387.

[25] Rush Welter, "The Idea of Progress in America," *Journal of the History of Ideas,* Vol. XVI (June, 1955) , pp. 401–15.

[26] *Saturday Review Reader* (New York: Bantam Books, 1954) , pp. 132–40.

system-wide conception of change involved in this sort of analysis invokes certain typologies: the *Gemeinschaft* versus *Gesellschaft,* traditional versus modern, folk versus urban, universalistic-specific versus particularistic-diffuse, and so on.

Some of the major findings from the studies of the two Indonesian villages, Tabanan and Modjokuto, are especially worth noting. Innovative economic leadership (entrepreneurship) occurred in a fairly well-defined and socially homogeneous group. In Modjokuto, entrepreneurship came from the ruling family; in Tabanan, from the pious Islamic traders. A second finding suggested that the innovative group had crystallized out of a larger traditional group which has a very long history of "extra" village status. Usually, the entrepreneurial groups stood outside the immediate purview of the village social structure. The entrepreneurs were sons and grandsons of men who came originally as itinerant, market-circuit traders, mostly from the polyglot north coastal areas where the bazaar culture first flourished in the string of harbor towns lining the Java Sea. These mobile and worldly-wise merchants had commercial ties extending over a great part of Java and their successors maintain a similar pattern today.

Tensions are evident in these villages. The larger group (out of which the innovative group emerged) was experiencing a thoroughly radical change in its relationship with the wider society of which it is a part. In Tabanan, the entrepreneurial aristocrats were challenged by the growth of civil bureaucracy. On the ideological level, the innovative group perceived itself as the main vehicle of religious and moral excellence in a generally backward, unenlightened, or heedless community. In Modjokuto, a sort of Muslim puritanism is the doctrine of the overwhelming majority of the entrepreneurs. This group is critical of traditional ethics and worship. There is a sense of representing the "proper" against the prevailing and a conviction that there is a decline of vigor and morals.

From these studies is learned an important fact, namely, that the major problems faced by entrepreneurs are organizational rather than technical. An Indonesian entrepreneur does not have to invent a sugar press, an ice machine, or a tire recapper. He has only to purchase them. There are few "Henry Ford" types—the self-taught inventors and engineers. It is not the technically skilled carpenter or tailor who becomes the manager of the saw-mill or of a garment factory, but the skilled handler of men; indeed, none of the important entrepreneurs seems to have any particular mechanical flair whatever in Tabanan.

The function of the entrepreneur in such transitional (or pretransitional) societies is to adapt customarily established means to novel ends, to take the "bazaar" economy and try to create economic institutions more complex and more efficient, to build larger markets instead of local ones, to introduce specialization of labor rather than traditional forms.

If these rather primitive experiences tell us something of the innovator's role and problems, they cannot provide the full range of insights necessary to understand a highly complex industrial society. In the United States there are certain situations within business itself which contain both assets and liabilities for the innovative manager. First there is the effect of massive organization on the utilization and motivation of the individual and on his creative abilities. The widespread attention given to "conformity" in the large organization, the effort devoted to understanding organization theory, the popularity of any idea that falls into the category of "human relations," all point to the need in large organizations to create an atmosphere in which the creativity of the individual can be encouraged and fostered while, at the same time, control (over the people, the capital, and the facilities necessary for the efficient functioning of the large enterprise) is maintained.

Another area of concern is the degree of government participation in the financing, controlling, and regulating of business. The problem is crystallized in those instances in which new knowledge is gained through research and development carried out partly with public funds. Is new knowledge proprietary or is it public? Businessmen insist that the main incentive behind research and development lies in the fact that the fruits of innovation are open to all, but there is a real danger that the job of undertaking necessary research into new areas will fall upon the government. This has been most noticeable in the defense-technology area but it is happening in other areas as well. Thus, the businessman questions a system that forces him, in the name of public need, to devote the firms' people and facilities to the development of new knowledge over which he has no proprietary protection for products that may be developed as a result.

There is also the widely discussed question of the social and political limits placed upon business-enterprise action. The migration of some industries from the Northeast to the Southeast, for example, can be viewed as moves to reduce costs, increase worker productivity, seek freedom from the restraints of collective bargaining, improve plant, or get close to raw material resources. Many of the communities so deserted, however, view such moves as leading to economic disaster for them. Are efforts to block the "economic" decisions of businessmen a social innovation or an effort to retard progress? In such cases, can the businessman bring forward innovations that satisfy both community pressures and profitability requirements?

Finally, there is the question of business participation in the political process. In today's climate, pervasive political activity by trade unions is condoned, while political activity by business and industry is often condemned. Attempts by companies to move directly into the political propaganda arena, if not into the political action field, have provoked boycotts and other economic sanctions against the companies involved. In this setting, it is reasonable to ask whether an innovative attitude in businesses might not have succeeded in finding ways to pursue legitimate political goals without provoking such reaction.

SOURCES OF INNOVATION

The sources for innovative action are found, then, not only in technologies or laboratory developments but in the ability to understand social trends, to foresee future markets, and to anticipate the probable outcome of action. To appreciate where innovation does *not* originate, one has only to ask the following questions: How many inventions have appeared "before their time"? Why is it that 80 percent of the new products introduced into U.S. markets today fail to achieve a profitable record? Is new-product development more successfully handled by large or by small business? In other words, is the availability of capital alone sufficient, when coupled with new concepts, to insure innovative success in the market? May not innovation, as defined above, be more difficult to carry out in the large corporation than in small and flexible establishments? If the answer is yes, then one of the most important challenges faced by the large corporation is to make sure that the weight of its bureaucracy, traditions, customs, and style does not consistently block off the initiation of innovation by its employees—again a reaffirmation of the need for social innovation to keep pace with technological change.

GUIDES TO INNOVATION

THE MARKET AS A GUIDE

The needs of a country's defense system bring about many risk-taking changes which do not involve the traditional market. For present purposes, however, the term "market" will be used to indicate the influence of the effective potential demand for goods and services in the private sector of the economy; in this sense, the market provides basic knowledge regarding needs and opportunities to innovate. Since the enterprise exists only as long as the society is willing to support it, there can be greater purpose for a business than the creation of customers. In a strictly economic sense, the creation of customers means an understanding of customer wants and needs and the matching of these needs with satisfying products or services. For example, there was a need for a form of aspirin that children could use; since children balk at taking the bitter pill, business produced a flavored, sugar-coated aspirin to make the flavor more palatable. The creation of customers also means the placing of product or service in the market when and where it is wanted. Sears Roebuck, for example, saw automobile insurance as an automobile "accessory" and used the opportunity to merchandise insurance through their stores, thereby taking advantage of a valuable distribution resource. Appropriate "images" of the product need to be created at the point of sale and the image given substance by follow-up services, product improvements, and continued publicity so that a buyer will become "brand loyal."

Politically, the creation of customers calls for an understanding of the individual's needs to participate in the policy formulation activity of society; hence business is continually involved in innovative efforts to insure the widest possible choices in political and economic decisions. When businessmen formulate and abide by standards of responsible political activity, they may earn the right to act as freely as trade unions.[27] Finally, creating customers means a deep appreciation of the imperatives of man's moral conscience and his continual striving to better his lot. It means recognition of the

---

[27] Richard Eells, *Corporation Giving in a Free Society* (New York: Harper & Bros., 1956), p. 119.

fact that, in general, economic transactions must result in gain for both buyer and seller; it means support of education to develop leadership for business, government, education and, indeed, all key institutions of modern society.

ANTICIPATION AS A GUIDE

To translate an innovative idea into practice, it is not enough to satisfy customers by meeting today's demands. The business that anticipates demands, instead of waiting for them to be formulated by others, will be the most successful in the long run. Thus, while the nature and direction of any business is, in the final analysis, determined by the customer, the executive has the assignment of living constantly with the challenge and opportunity to produce those innovations that assure favorable customer reaction.

Creating new wants presents still more complex problems. There is, first of all, the problem of deciding whether a want really exists. And apposite to this is the story of Dr. Zworykin of RCA who approached Dr. Warren Weaver of the Rockefeller Foundation to tell of difficulties in getting RCA to build a prototype of the electron microscope. It was believed that not more than four or five such microscopes, selling at $10,000 to $12,000 each, could be disposed of in the entire world. The Rockefeller Foundation financed purchases of one for each of several universities; today, every good department has two or three.

In some industries new wants are created by introducing products for which it is hoped uses will develop *after* the product is marketed. This has worked successfully in the organic chemical industry. A recent example is Dow Chemical Co.'s large-scale commercial production of a basic chemical building block, ethylenimine. Through this $10 million investment Dow hopes that it may well be on the way to making contributions to dozens of industries. Like other basic chemical building blocks, ethylenimine's main uses will probably develop after it has been marketed. Dow's strategy was explained in these terms:

The revolution wrought by organic chemistry in the last few decades has been based on the chemist's ability to take apart molecules as they exist in nature and to rearrange these molecules so that they perform the kind of functions that man wants them to perform. Plastics, pharmaceuticals, synthetic fibers, agricultural chemicals, and many other fields have stemmed from rearranging or adding to the molecular structure of natural materials. Generally, these changes are made by reacting one material with another. Depending on structure, some chemicals react slowly and stubbornly, or not at all; others react easily and quickly. . . . Ethylenimine is not only highly reactive but also it reacts in unusual ways. These two factors make it a versatile tool to combine with other materials to produce a near-infinite variety of molecular structures, each with its own particular characteristics and functionality.

Consumer wants are discovered simply by looking over any catalogue of consumer goods. As an illustration, one can note the constant striving to add more favorable characteristics to textile and plastic materials. Nylon stockings are the target of a current competitive struggle. Nylon, which has dominated the stocking industry since World War II, is now challenged by new fibers such as polypropylene. Polypropylene stockings are being currently introduced under such trade names as Vectra and Gerfil, but their acceptance is not yet known because fashion may decree heavy patterned hosiery for which neither nylon nor polypropylene is suitable.

The meaning of innovation is clear: Willing to accept and understand what the customer considers to be value, management must *continually* define and redefine the nature of the company's products, services, policies, and practices in the light of market demands and in anticipation of changes in the *total* demands made by society on the business.

PROFIT AS A GUIDE

At the end of the 19th century the American economist J. B. Clark related profit to dynamic changes and the dynamic changes were held to be inventions. Said Clark:

An invention makes it possible to produce something more cheaply. It first gives a profit to entrepreneurs and then . . . adds something to wages and interest. . . . Let another invention be made . . . it also creates a profit; and this profit, like the first, is an elusive sum which entrepreneurs grasp but cannot hold. It slips through their fingers and bestows itself on members of society.[28]

But in 1912, Joseph Schumpeter, in his *Theory of Economic Development,* introduced the concept of innovation as the explanation of profit.[29] In this theory, the primary role is played by the

---

[28] J. B. Clark, *The Distribution of Wealth* (New York: A. M. Kelley, 1899) , p. 405.

[29] Joseph Schumpeter, *Theory of Economic Development* (Cambridge, Mass.: Harvard University Press, 1934) .

entrepreneur (innovator), who recognizes the value of a new idea and is able to convert it into profit. He organizes the resources and carries out the job. The entrepreneur then gets the surplus (profit) that is left after all costs have been paid. According to the "pure" theory of innovation, however, there is no necessary connection with capital risk-taking by the owner. Profit is the reward for upsetting the balance of a stationary economy. But it is the action of the entrepreneur, who may not be the owner, that makes for innovation. Thus, there is no necessary connection with ownership of invested capital. In the present day economy, of course, the risk-taking function is largely in the hands of the manager, who most frequently is not the owner. The key test for innovational activity resides in *profitability*.

In general, then, the principle can be stated that business innovation, designed to create customers, is a necessary management concern. The test of profitability may be deferred over a considerable time span or may be indirectly applied, but, without clear focus upon such anticipated advantage, business innovation may degenerate into aimless and possibly harmful social, political, or economic experimentation. The goal of innovational activity by business is to strengthen the private sectors of the economy and to widen opportunities for individual choices among economic goods—and to do these things in such a way as to earn advantages for enterprise. In a free society, profitability is the ultimate test of performance of private economic enterprise.

When we turn to social or technological innovations not covered by patent, we approach an area far more complex than property protected by patent. The law of unfair competition acknowledges the property of a man in his idea. In *Belt* v. *Hamilton National Bank,* the court said that a person has such a *"property right in his own idea* as enables him to recover damages for its appropriation or use by another when the idea is original, concrete, useful, and is disclosed in circumstances which, reasonably construed, clearly indicate that compensation is contemplated if it is accepted and used."

Theoretically, this statement of rights is reasonable but the standard does not supply the clear negotiable instrument as does a patent. Once the Patent Office speaks, there is an issue of fact if a dispute arises; but it is quite another matter when innovations are said to be the property of one over another claimant. Lawsuits are often based on unsolicited letters to companies and can be for very large amounts. Fear of the vagaries of a jury trial has led most companies to return all unsolicited ideas and to set up protective devices. Almost all of them will refuse to consider any idea unless the person proposing it signs a release or waiver and, in effect, puts his idea entirely in the hands of the organization for any hope of reward. These steps are considered highly necessary by corporate lawyers under the present state of the law.

OBSTACLES TO INNOVATION

It is impossible to set an innovation objective without examining all the "survival" areas of the business: markets, profitability, people and organization, finance, physical resources, and public standing. For example, any change in the market or in market opportunities tends to force change in the areas of manufacturing, design, finance, and personnel. Thus, the central problem is the development of the innovating attitude which induces people to identify and analyze, on a continuing basis, the areas of the business in which change is needed.

In order to survive and prosper in a dynamic economy, business has found it necessary to bring to bear upon the economy and its market the tools and disciplines from many areas of activity once considered foreign to the enterprise—business psychologists, sociologists, chemists, physicists, personnel experts, mathematicians, and many others. Indeed, it has been said that the modern business enterprise is fast taking a place among the central storehouses of knowledge about our society. But coordinating the work from different disciplines can slow down the innovator. Further, with this knowledge has come added responsibility. A simple example is the original experiment with DDT. For a long time great effort had been concentrated on finding an effective means for ridding farms and other areas of harmful insects. When DDT was first brought to the market, it was discovered that it not only destroyed harmful insects but useful ones as well. In one specific case, its use caused the destruction of honey bees and threatened the productivity of fruit orchards. Faced with these legal responsibilities and negative customer reactions, business laboratories quickly effected adjustment in the product formulation.

Business must accept the responsibility for making certain that knowledge available to it is used in ways that will not harm society.

In its eagerness to be first with something new or profitable, no business can afford to endanger people who are involved, directly or indirectly, in a product's use or effects. When a company defaults in this responsibility, not only the irresponsible company but all businesses suffer.

RESISTANCE TO CHANGE

On the other hand, what appears to be good for one segment of society may be interpreted as harmful by another. Change, of itself, is frequently resisted and laws and customs often impede change. Turnpike and canal interests fought the railroads; local butchers opposed Armour's marketing of refrigerated meats. Such attitudes reflect a desire to avoid external challenge.

But perhaps the greatest obstacle to the successful practice of innovation (purposeful, systematic change, as distinct from change induced from outside) is found within its own confines. Functional managers, those who believe themselves to be expert in historical practice but who have given up all experimentation, will argue against the "untried." "Retired" managers—those content to leave things as they are—resent the impositions that the novel places upon them. The egocentrically ambitious, those who calculate and maneuver for personal advantage, test suggested changes solely against the impact they might have upon their personal careers. The staff planner who spins Parkinsonian webs on organization charts and ignores the concept that business organizations can be justified only in terms of serving or creating customers—often opposes innovation.

Finally, there is the person whose focus is only upon the product. Concerned over technical advances in the product, or in processes for its production, he loses touch with the larger dynamics of the economy. For example, it is often said that major aircraft companies, and all their attendant suppliers, have suffered one reverse after another since 1945 because their production and engineering-oriented managements showed a lack of understanding of the customer's (in this case, the government's) stated needs.

Many forces in society impede innovation. The businessman himself has often actively sought, for diverse reasons, to pursue interests and needs other than those of his customers. An attitude that rejects innovative practice and resists change, or an attitude that permits careless novelties to be brought to the market, are marks of irresponsible management.

COSTS

Innovation often comes at a high price. During the so-called "craft stage," costs were relatively low because the innovation was mainly the private property of an individual who belonged to a guild. In advanced stages (where reliance is on scientific analysis and on technology), the costs increase at a rate consistent with the growth in risk. The development of one adhesive reportedly involved $30,000 solely for investigation of the patent literature, followed by an outlay of some $2 million over a two-year period before the adhesive was brought to the market. Complex processes may run into astronomical figures and once an enterprise commits itself to technological or social innovation it becomes extraordinarily difficult to turn back. The problem of innovation within the corporation is one of decision making in the face of continuing uncertainty.

Certainly, the enthusiasm for research, so clearly visible during the 1940's, has been increasingly challenged by management during the following decades; indeed it has been suggested that research seemed to be producing more technical papers than marketable products.

THE CORPORATE SOCIETY

One subtle obstacle to innovation is the organization itself. Historically, most great enterprises were founded by an entrepreneur who took a novel idea and built an organization based upon it into a nationwide operation. Eventually the entrepreneur found himself incapable of managing, single-handedly, a complex entity and the process of dividing and subdividing functions began. Unlike the entrepreneur who instinctively responded to the challenge of risk, and who carried the burden of uncertainty on his own shoulders, the management team not infrequently *sought* to banish uncertainty from work. Entrepreneurs within the enterprise, and especially those holding subordinate roles, have often discovered the utility of floating trial balloons to the top before moving forward with any new idea. If the "boss" is secure and comfortable with the present patterns of production, marketing or financing, he may display an instinctive and built-in reaction against new ideas.

There is a further problem. The contemporary corporation seeks to attract good scientists and engineers imbued with a value system that stresses commitments to theoretical refinements and practical improvements. Scientists and engineers find it difficult to adjust to business values when the politics of finance must be balanced against the requirements of quality. The result can be a sense of alienation within the cadre of men on whom the enterprise most heavily relies for innovative approaches. If the scientist or engineer fails to appreciate reasons why management hesitates to push a new product or process on the market he may become so disenchanted that he leaves the company. Turnover in this type of personnel can severly hamper innovation. On the other hand, if he does remain, he may become such a constant source of friction that the pace of innovation is slowed very perceptibly.

CONCLUSION

A dynamic society imposes heavy responsibility on the business enterprise. The skill, ability, and vision needed to manage the innovative enterprise today call for the most careful selection and preparation of people to manage the business tomorrow. In fact, the entire concept of management development itself is an innovation in management thinking. When a business is mismanaged, the loss to society, as well as the loss to shareowners, workers, or customers, is considerable. But the measurements of "good" performance that applied to yesterday's business can no longer be accepted as adequate. The need is to find and develop new measures of performance.[30]

Innovation also imposes on management the responsibility to accept increased risks. In a rapidly changing and innovating society, the danger of being overtaken is considerably increased. Today's communication and distribution networks, and the varieties of marketing systems that can be devised and put into practical operation, permit very rapid changes which can exert major and immediate impacts upon competitors. More fundamentally, it is possible to change the economic structure of an industry in a short period of time. A company innovates or risks failure.

But there is also the serious risk of failure in another direction. The innovative process implies a "leap into the future." It suggests that man can control the future, even when he does not know what future conditions will be. Such risks are very high. In fact, the use of

---

[30] Yale Brozen, "Business Leadership and Technological Change," *American Journal of Economics and Sociology*, Vol. XIV (October, 1954), pp. 13–30.

the term "planning" conceals how high risks are. For when we plan, we generally believe in our ability to control. But the promise of plans is often different from realized experience.

Each innovation, in turn, forces other innovations, thus increasing the risk of failure. This suggests the need for systematizing the innovative effort and for providing built-in safeguards against failure. It is often thought that centralized planning is preferable to decentralized planning because centralized planning is better able to control the system. In a business enterprise, however, the odds are heavily on the side of the greatest number of attempts to find better ways to achieve business objectives. The single massive attempt to find the *best way* is balked by the terrible risk of total failure.

In anticipating the unknown, no one is assured of success. The best that can be done in business is to seek knowledge of the likely impact of change on a specific situation remembering always that the probabilities of useful prediction are on the side of many events rather than a single one. And the flexibility of the business that accepts innovative practice, and continually reviews its posture toward its customers, gives it a strategic advantage in the face of endless "unknowns."

RECOMMENDED READING

BARNETT, H. B. *Innovation: The Basis of Cultural Change.* New York: McGraw-Hill Book Co., 1953.

BOULDING, KENNETH. "General Systems Theory: The Skeleton of Science," *Management Science,* Vol. II (April, 1956), pp. 197–208.

BRIGHT, JAMES. *Research, Development and Technological Change.* Homewood, Ill.: The Dorsey Press, 1964.

DRUCKER, PETER F. *Landmarks of Tomorrow.* New York: Harper & Bros., 1959.

GABOR, DENNIS. "Inventing the Future," *Encounter,* Vol. XIV (May, 1960), pp. 3–16.

GILFILLAN, S. *The Sociology of Invention.* Chicago: Follett Publishing Co., 1935.

HAGEN, E. E. *On The Theory of Social Change.* Homewood, Ill.: The Dorsey Press, 1962.

KNIGHT, FRANK H. *Risk, Uncertainty and Profit.* New York: Kelley and Millman, 1921.

MOONEY, JAMES D.   *The New Capitalism.* New York: Macmillan Co., 1934.

MORISON, ELTING.   *Men, Machines and Modern Times.* Cambridge, Mass.: M.I.T. Press, 1966.

SCHUMPETER, JOSEPH A.   *The Theory of Economic Development.* Cambridge, Mass.: Harvard University Press, 1934.

SCHON, DONALD.   *Technology and Change.* New York: Delacorte Press, 1967.

WOOLF, HARRY.   *Science as a Cultural Force.* Baltimore: Johns Hopkins Press, 1965, chap. 3.

FURTHER READING

BOEHM, G.   "Research Management: The New Executive Job," *Fortune,* Vol. LVI (October, 1957) , pp. 16 ff.

CARTER, CHARLES F., and WILLIAMS, B. R.   *Investment in Innovation.* New York: Oxford University Press, 1958.

CLARK, JOHN B.   *The Distribution of Wealth.* New York: The Macmillan Co., 1899.

DRUCKER, PETER F.   *The Practice of Management.* New York: Harper & Bros., 1954.

GHISELIN, BREWSTER.   *The Creative Process.* Berkeley, Cal.: University of California Press, 1952.

GINZBERG, ELI, and REILLEY, E. W.   *Effecting Change in Large Organizations.* New York: Columbia University Press, 1957.

HAWLEY, FREDERICK B.   *Enterprise and the Productive Process.* New York: G. P. Putnam, 1907.

KRANZBERG, MELVIN, and PURSELL, CARROLL W., JR.   *Technology in Western Civilization.* New York: Oxford University Press, 1967.

KUZNETS, SIMON.   *Modern Economic Growth.* New Haven, Conn.: Yale University Press, 1964.

MCLAURIN, WILLIAM R.   *Invention and Innovation in the Radio Industry.* New York: The Macmillan Co., 1949.

V. GOVERNANCE

GOVERNANCE is the exercise of an authority that seeks not merely the right to direct and to lead but to control. The problem of government has always been the same in all forms of human association: how to muster both the power and the authority required by the purpose of association to achieve its end in a practical, fair, and orderly way; and how to limit that power and authority to specified areas rather than to permit it to overflow into matters that are not its basic concern.

The reasons for the necessity of government to human associations have been characterized in a variety of ways. A lineage drawing uncertain inspiration from Machiavelli, and articulated by Nietzsche and Treitschke, would assert that governments arise because of man's lust for power over other men. The social contract theorists (despite differences among the adherents of Rousseau, Locke, and Hobbes) would argue that men voluntarily surrendered full autonomy over the self to the group; governments were, therefore, man-made, as the union or the corporation is man-made. Others hold what amounts to a deficiency theory, which sees government as a necessary and natural adjunct complementing man's nature and his need for society. The list of theories rationalizing force into legitimized authority could be extended substantially.

Government means power, and power excites ambitions and fears. The founders of the American form of government seem, in certain ways, to have regarded government as a necessary evil, if one reads rightly their efforts to hedge it about with limits. The long history of Western constitutionalism demonstrates how much intellectual power men have directed to the problem of limiting the authority of those who govern their lives.

In the United States the machinery of government was erected on the idea of constitutionalism, which authorized official power while it circumscribed it within stated limits. Such an idea of restriction on government power was not foreign to the Greeks; nor was the idea of justice. Roman jurisprudence extended this idea by making the consent of the governed a proper source of all legislative authority. The principle of representative government developed to a high degree in late medieval parliaments and in the conciliar movement of the 14th and 15th centuries, which failed to take root in the Church but provided incentive to parliamentary government by urging the supremacy of representative bodies over the Pope. The practice of representative government in churches reappeared as a working doctrine only much later in Presbyterianism, which in turn influenced civil polities in the American colonies in New England.

The idea of a charter as a basic compact establishing the fundamental order was not new when the American colonists drafted their constitution. Both the Virginia and the Massachusetts Bay companies had held charters, and there was precedent, of course, in the Mayflower Compact, in which the colonists promised submission and obedience not to any person among their number but only to laws, duly constituted, to which they were agreed. The systematic use of written constitutions as fundamental and paramount law, enforceable in courts on behalf of citizens whose rights were encroached upon by their rulers, did not emerge until the end of the 18th-century.

Today the various constitutional solutions to the problem of restraints on government are not uniform even among the states of our federal system. But, though their means are not identical, the constitutional tradition of free societies has for centuries urged the principle of justice for the individual man against arbitrary uses of government power.

Though the impetus behind constitutional government was toward justice, what has developed out of it is a science of politics that discusses the central-local distribution of power, the distribution of powers among agencies with functionally defined realms of authority, the chronological distribution of power through periodic elections, and the mature considerations of written constitutions enforceable by courts.

All these problems imply pluralism, with its multiplicity of power centers. Through the principle of freedom of association these have grown and multiplied through the years since the Declaration of Independence, though most of them do not exercise the power of public government and hold authority over only their own sectors. More than anything else, perhaps, this distribution of private power may be said to characterize a nontotalitarian, pluralistic, and constitutional society.

But, quite apart from the initial reasons behind the establishment of government—and that discussion still appears unsettled—its essential objective is the establishment of order in society through responsible leadership. The assumption in a liberal polity, republic or monarchy, is that the governing body represents the manifested choice of individuals who are free to show their satisfaction or dissatisfaction with the status quo at specified times.

The major alteration in the life of our time is the existence of unprecedentedly large private groups, not private individuals (though they are composed of these), who are moving to represent what they construe to be the greatest good for their particular sector of society. As is inevitable, in a highly industrialized society there is also a danger that the importance of the individual will decline, since he has become increasingly dependent on group membership for his living and for his education. We encounter, as a result, interest groups rather than group interests.

The growth of large private associations, with their own problems of government, makes it imperative to ask whether the tradition of constitutionalism, hitherto a principle of public government, is pertinent to such private polities as business corporations. Today, over and above the question of collectivism, the fear has been voiced that the tradition of freedom, without the application of constitutional restraints, might lead to industrial absolutism in the economic sector. According to some critics, the concentration of the control of property in the hands of a few, however dispersed its actual ownership, threatens the concept of pluralism in subtle but inevitable ways. If power follows the control of property, then there is visible in our time a move toward centralization of power among a few large business firms that runs quite counter to the intention of the Founding Fathers.

The need for protection against such concentrations of power manifests itself in the growing tendency to refer to the federal government for arbitration and settlement all the social and economic problems that must arise in a thoroughly technologized society. As a result, government has grown accustomed to assuming a paternalistic role—not merely in this country but abroad. What we appear to have lost sight of in the United States in the 20th century in these circumstances was summed up as follows by His Holiness, Pope Pius XII, in some comments on the general state of the world.

Every citizen ought to be aware that the State, for whose intervention he is asking, in the concrete and in the last analysis, is always the sum total of the citizens themselves; and that, consequently no one can claim that the State impose obligations and burdens, to the fulfillment of which he is not himself determined to contribute, to the extent of his knowledge of his responsibility when using the rights accorded to him by law.

In reality, the questions of economy and social reforms depend only very extrinsically on the sound development of those laws—supposing that they are not contrary to the Natural Law; but they necessarily and intimately depend on man considered as a person, on his moral strength and good will to bear responsibility, and to understand and treat with sufficient knowledge and skill the things which he undertakes and to which he is bound. No recourse to the State can create men like this. They have to rise up in the midst of the people in such a way as to prevent the election ballot,—in which irresponsibility, ignorance and passions also come together,—from producing a decision ruinous for the true and genuine State.[1]

But it must be conceded that another formidable entity has intervened between the individual and his government—*the organized group.*

While orthodox theory and constitutional doctrine pre-supposed only two entities—the State and the individual person—it is now widely believed that the isolated individual does not exist as such and that he is significant only as a member of a group. In addition to the large corporate enterprise which includes both the managerial class and the labor

---

[1] Address to the National Congress of the Christian Union of Managers and Directors, March 7, 1957. (English version by the Vatican Press Office.)

union, the new group includes farm organizations, veterans' associations, and charitable foundations, among others.[2]

Thus a government, conceived on the premise that it is "of the people, by the people, and for the people," must be extremely flexible if it is to meet successfully a situation in which individuals have, through necessity or circumstance, aligned themselves in large, single, self-seeking groups. For if power resides in the control of property, it also resides in the control of large numbers of people. And the theory of governance implicit in Lincoln's classic statement runs contrary to the realities of a complex, vast, and highly industrialized society, in which the individual is seemingly lost in the anonymous mass. Rather than demand that public government consider the plight of the individual citizen, the private governments of those groups into which individual citizens have banded will have to take stock of their nature and ask themselves how closely they must align themselves with the constitutional tradition of the polity at large in order to maintain liberty and justice within their limits. For the individual "cannot cope independently with all the social forces generated within a dynamic industrial economy . . . [where] industrial progress itself creates social problems like housing, community services, technological unemployment, and business cycles."[3]

The nature of government, public or private, appears to alter in proportion to alterations in the nature of the group it was set up to represent and to administer. If one function of public government is to *represent* the mood and opinion of its people and to adjust its policies and procedures accordingly, then another, and perhaps higher function, is to *lead* the people along the path of wise and mature political behavior.

Obviously, the position of a private government in this instance differs from that of public government in several respects. First, it represents, not all the people, but the collective will of a segment of the population. Further, in their private group affiliations, citizens can attach themselves to several private associations, depending upon how the aims of these meet their needs, and some of these associations may actually entertain ambitions that collide with the aims of some of their private units. Moreover, the government of

---

[2] Arthur Miller, *Private Governments and the Constitution* (New York: Fund for the Republic, 1959) , p. 4.

[3] O. A. Ohmann, "Search for a Managerial Philosophy " *Harvard Business Review,* Vol. XXXV (September–October, 1957) , p. 49.

private associations, if it is small, need concern itself only with the needs of its membership. Of course, if it represents as large an association as a big corporation or a national union, its responsibilities are correspondingly larger. There is, in fact, some question as to whether the private corporation, at some point in the course of its growth, ceases to be a private government and becomes an agent of public government. Yet, even if this query were answered affirmatively, the private corporations exhibit marked dissimilarities from each other. Consider the following observation by Arthur Miller.

The Lockheed Aircraft Company has only one true customer (the United States government) and no franchise dealers, while the Bell Telephone Companies have millions of customers, but few suppliers other than Western Electric, and no dealers, and the Ford Motor Company has thousands of customers, numerous suppliers, and many dealers.[4]

There is a further question, which arises in the case of a large firm with a defense business: To what extent does a firm holding government contracts become an agent of the government and hence subject to the same constitutional limitations?

But, even if this question could be given a clear-cut answer, the basic problem of pluralism in contemporary society would not be resolved. As pluralism is represented by large concentrations— whether of money or of people who give rise to a power unrestrained by any specific authority—we align ourselves with Big Government, Big Business, or Big Unionism without stopping to consider that the marked difference among these three is the existence, in the case of the first, of constitutional limitations that reveal themselves in guarantees to citizens and in prescribed organizational patterns that disperse power. But the private governments of large corporations and large unions have attempted to solve the problem of order, solvency, and security, within their own bounds (the natural duties of public government from its initiation), not with written constitutions but with organization charts. The novelty and rapid growth of these two huge associations made it necessary for those at the helm to look about for models of order without division of power, and they appear to have settled—probably unconsciously—upon the patterns of the Roman Catholic Church or of the army. Hence we have, from the latter, the idea of line and staff in the private government of

---

[4] Arthur Miller, "A Modernized View of Due Process" (mimeographed paper), p. 5. See Miller, *op. cit.,* note 2 supra.

corporations and, from the former, the notion of as few levels of command as possible.

But, in the process of transferring the organizational machinery of the Church and the army to the economic system, two important and indeed basic features of these established systems for organizing large and scattered numbers of people were lost sight of. First, both the Church and the army are essentially autocratic. The problem of authority, therefore, is secondary rather than primary, since unquestioning obedience to common goals and common means is implicit in it. In the second place, both Church and army base their appeal as well as their authority on idealism—faith in the one case, patriotism in the other, with their imponderable rewards: salvation and freedom. They have, thus, behind their organization, two conspicuous advantages singularly lacking in economic organization.

The private government of the large modern economic organization, so influential in the lives of the citizens of the republic in which it flourishes, is hence neither fish nor fowl. It is decidedly not a democracy, and yet it is no longer possible for a really big business to be an autocracy. It has been described as an oligarchy or a republic—the latter perhaps in recognition of the fact that unionism has introduced into it a two-party system.

These enterprises, which Peter F. Drucker has called the only meaningful units of local government, exist today in approximately the same relationship vis-à-vis the national government as did the states under the Articles of Confederation. The important constitutional problem of this era, accordingly, is the development of feasible means by which the power of these private governments can be moderated, both with respect to individuals within and without an enterprise and also to the public at large.[5]

This is one way to bring the ethos of the private governments of economic organizations into line with the concepts and institutions of our republic. In a group-oriented society, each group represents its own interests, and, if it is unable to impose them on the others, it bargains for a dilution of the general aims so that its own interest will not be too materially affected. Bargaining has always been a tool in power conflicts.

But private economic governments could themselves take a hand in adjusting their polities to better fit the aims of the republic. It has

---

[5] *Ibid.*, p. 3.

been said that the problem of preserving American society is the problem of preserving the processes of decision making. The forms that this process takes are thus less important than its preservation through a wide variety of pluralities as a basic manifestation of freedom.

To preserve its own decision-making power, economic organization should therefore look to determine whether its values—expressed in product, service, or method of managing—are really in harmony with the American way of life. The assumption of the economic organization that, with the help of technology, it is furthering the pristine American vision of the good life may be mistaken. The American way of life is a way not of status but of equal opportunity, not of media persuasion but of free choice, not of organization but of individualism. Any private government in the United States that fails to take into consideration this aspect of its history may find its private character altered to fit the simple, uncompromising, and still perennial demands of the men who drew up the Mayflower Compact.

The chapters that follow examine more thoroughly the concepts that we have touched upon here: "Freedom, Justice and Law," "Authority and Power," "Pluralism," and "Constitutionalism." The analyses provide a basis for reassessment of such practical issues as the relationships that prevail among the three major associations of our time (government, labor, and corporation), the check and balance systems appropriate to each, and the manner in which ideals of justice and equity can be translated into meaningful realities.

16. Freedom, Justice, and Law

OUTLINE

DESPITE the labors of outstanding minds to give explicit meaning to the dynamic ideals of civilized man as symbolized by freedom, justice, and law, have the results been strikingly fruitful? The philosophers' quest has resulted in substantial contributions to the framing and ordering of democratic societies. From Pericles' *Funeral Oration* down through the English Petition of Right in 1628, the American and French declarations of independence and liberties of the following century, to the United Nations Charter and the postwar constitutions of all major countries, "freedom" and "justice" are the ringing words for rallying men to noble causes and heroic sacrifices.

Among the many expressions of these ideals, the following two illustrate effectively the manner in which appeals for defense of freedom and justice are rooted in theological and in political classics:

> He hath shewed thee, O man, what is good; and what doth the Lord require of thee, but to do justly and to love mercy and to walk humbly with thy God [Micah, 6:8].

> We hold these truths to be self-evident, that all men are created equal, that they are endowed by their Creator with certain unalienable Rights, that among these are Life, Liberty, and the pursuit of Happiness. That to secure these rights, Governments are instituted among Men . . . [*The Declaration of Independence*].

These are moving statements. They do not furnish us with much concrete detail as to what is meant by the terms. Contemporary man labors to translate them. He asks questions of liberty and justice in terms of their relevance to foreign aid programs, government financial assistance to private schools, compulsory health insurance, company programs of nontransferable investment plans, or techniques for deferring income benefits through stock options. He asks questions regarding tax policy generally and depreciation policy specifically. The catalog of problems tinged with implications for justice and liberty would scarcely be begun by this list.

Business executives must seek understanding of these basic but elusive ideals in relation to the problem of survival for the organizations they direct. But freedom, justice, and law for man may not always be easily reconciled to man's business organizations. The political environment of the past century was highly favorable to private enterprise. From the Left it was urged that the law, the accepted doctrine of liberty, and the unformulated substratum of prevailing opinion that we call the idea of justice were all in concert and playing a bourgeois tune; the fundamentals were so favorable to business interests that the practical executive had more concrete things to worry about.

Whatever the merits of that argument, today the world situation is changed; it is less safe for the business interest. We have seen the growth of what might be termed the "bureaucratic–collectivist" ideal, which dominates Communist countries and which, almost everywhere, contests for power with the older, more open forms of policy. Even in the United States, statism is on the move. How this idea came into being and ultimately into power is beyond our scope, except to suggest that the collectivist ideal is partly a response to the unfulfilled demand by men and women everywhere that their expectations for a meaningful human life be met by human institutions designed to the purpose. The struggle for mastery of society is today conducted largely in terms of competing ideas of what is fair or just. Economic issues are widely discussed in this context. Subsidies to the farmer, the removal of tariff and nontariff barriers to world trade, the discount rate, and regulatory legislation have become matters of decency and right as well as matters of dollars and cents.

If, therefore, the articulate spokesmen of private enterprise do not turn their attention to the issue of justice and its relation to law and freedom, the grand struggle for power may eventually go to the collectivists, who appreciate the significance of proselytizing elite groups. Moreover, the collectivists see deeper into the political reality of our times. They know that in the last analysis men are moved by ideas and faiths more than by strictly material considerations.

Thus 40 years of collectivist power in Russia have failed to produce an economic utopia. Yet collectivism remains firmly entrenched, not merely because of vigilant control over the means of power but because of the strength of claims made in the name of justice and freedom. If these terms, as used in the totalitarian's jargon do not contain the values the businessman would assign to them, it is up to him to state his own value preferences analytically and persuasively. This requires efforts in the philosophical area similar to those that businessmen over the past century have devoted to the creation of the greatest wealth-producing mechanism the world has ever seen.

FREEDOM

Of all the hallowed words in the lexicon of Western man, none has a more revered place than "freedom." Yet, as Lord Acton has reminded us, freedom has been used by tyrants as pretext for aggrandizement and by martyrs as impassioned reasons for sacrifice. It has provided in modern Hungary a test case; both the Hungarian revolutionary and the Soviet commissar have rationalized their respective actions under its rubric. What then does freedom mean?

FREEDOM, RESTRAINT, AND LIMITED POSSIBILITY

It is tempting to say that freedom is simply the absence of restraint. In Hobbes's words, "A 'freeman' is he that in those things which by his strength and wit is able to do, is not hindered to do what he has a will to do." Freedom has been defined by Bertrand Russell as "the absence of obstacles to the realization of desires." A basic doctrine of constitutionalism is that government itself must be restrained from encroaching the rights of persons in their life, liberty, and property. Yet constitutional governments also must have powers to restrain some persons and groups that would otherwise infringe or extinguish the liberties of others. Obviously, then, freedom and power are closely interrelated. Freedom in the abstract as a free-floating ideal or independent value has little operational meaning. One must get down to cases, to specific types of actions that identifiable persons and groups of persons are free or unfree to carry on with respect to other persons and groups of persons.[1]

Interpersonal and intergroup relationships are therefore at the heart of realistic accounts of human freedom. This is not to say that inabilities internal and external to man but not due to interpersonal relationships are irrelevant to the problem of liberty. In the nature of things man is limited in what he can do. Natural limitations, when properly understood, will redirect the dialogue about freedom into new channels, and indeed is doing so now. Human ecology, in both its earthbound and its more cosmic aspects, increasingly points to futilities as well as opportunities for man in his search for freedom to realize his desires. The earth's precious envelope of air cannot be endlessly polluted with impunity, for example, and this fact imposes certain limitation on free enterprise; on the other hand, astronautics and other sciences of the space age open up hitherto undreamed-of realms of human action.

There is another dimension of inability to be noted here in passing, for it is highly relevant to the search for human freedom and does touch, if indirectly, our immediate topic of interpersonal and intergroup relationships of interest to the student of conceptual foundations of business: those internal bars to human freedom imposed by distortions of the psyche. Perhaps there is no greater or more promising road to freedom than the release of man's creative potentialities through an attack on the causes of these distortions. The attack must be multiphased; not only the advanced methods of psychiatry,[2] but other ways have to be pursued to free men for living

---

[1] For an empirical interpretation of freedom in these terms see Felix E. Oppenheim, *Dimensions of Freedom* (New York: St. Martin's Press, 1961).

[2] See, e.g., *Mental Health and Mental Disorder: A Sociological Approach,* Arnold M. Rose (ed.) (New York: W. W. Norton & Co., Inc., 1955); and *Personality and Political Crisis,* A. H. Stanton and S. E. Perry (eds.) (New York: The Free Press, 1951).

humanely according to the normative postulates of freedom—the way of enlightenment, the way of art, the bonds of charity in the Biblical sense of that term and applied to community broadly conceived. Participants in the business system, and especially corporate participants, have to be aware of these and other ways to overcome bars to freedom, for they will be called upon to share the burden of lowering the bars and they must be in a position to assess alternative methods.

Let us not ask: Is man free, and can he be free? Let us rather assert that man is qualifiedly free. John Courtney Murray finds the source and authorization of man's freedom ultimately in God's beneficence, in the very act of creation.[3] Herbert J. Muller denies the need for religious authorization and asserts that empirical fact argues for freedom's need, since freedom alone provides the climate for the individual to realize himself.[4] Biologists like Julian Huxley use a sort of "biological ethics" to assert that man is free only as his evolutionary development permits and that this is a very limited kind of liberty. Yet an eminent biologist, Theodosius Dobzhansky, has declared that "natural selection has not propagated genes for ethics, or genes for inventing Euclidean geometry, propounding evolutionary theories, composing musical symphonies, painting landscapes, making a million on Wall Street, loving the soil, or becoming a military leader. . . . Freedom is perhaps the most important of all the specifically human attributes."[5]

Freedom has to be considered a "limited possibility," as Arnold Brecht has said, for there are logical, physical, biological, psychological, and legal impossibilities in infinite number.[6] One function of science is to point up these impossibilities and thereby to contribute objectively to the selection of plans in which governments, public and private, can usefully engage. The task is especially difficult for the social sciences which have to deal with alleged but questionable impossibilities in various types of regimes and economic systems.

---

[3] John Courtney Murray, S. J., *Religion and Freedom* (New York: Fund for the Republic, 1958). For a fuller elaboration of these views, see *We Hold These Truths* (New York: Sheed and Ward, 1960), esp. Part I.

[4] H. J. Muller, *Issues of Freedom: Paradoxes and Promises* (New York: Harper & Bros., 1960).

[5] T. Dobzhansky, *The Biological Basis of Human Freedom* (New York: Columbia University Press, 1956), pp. 132 and 134.

[6] Arnold Brecht, *Political Theory: The Foundations of Twentieth-Century Political Thought* (Princeton: Princeton University Press, 1959), p. 425.

The history of freedom in action and concept throws some light on the nature of the problem.

FREEDOM IN HISTORICAL PERSPECTIVE

"It is the function of freedom to make a dent in the sullenness of man's nature. . . . Civilization has been made by people who wormed their way through the resistance of physical or human nature and who of the secrets they conquered made the experience of the race."[7] It is possible to consider "the whole tumultuous history of Western man as the involved story of embodied freedom."[8] Undoubtedly it is a global story, too. As to the West, however, there are marked periods of conceptual and institutional development to be noted in assessing the place of the business system in that long history.

From the beginning of the 16th century, freedom became a continuing rather than an occasional issue in Western history, a dynamic rather than a stabilizing force directed toward the extension rather than the preservation of control, an institutional framework that moved from the local to the regional level of organization, a distinct and institutionalized value visible in autonomous bodies and temporal agents of liberty. But freedom did not blossom out suddenly and completely during the Renaissance and the Reformation; from then until the middle of the 17th century the freedom of men emerged "to the limited extent that they could choose among the alternative authorities to whom they would owe their primary obedience."[9] It was an age of pluralistic authoritarianism that came to an end with the revolutionary period beginning in the middle of the 18th century. From then on, to the close of the 19th, genuine attempts were made to organize within certain countries of Europe and America orderly cases of general freedom. Freedom became not only a dominant value where authoritarian order had previously taken priority; freedom's banner led revolutions for a new order to replace the dismantled absolutisms.

For those in commerce and industry 19th-century liberalism meant restricting governmental control of business because they thought legislation would hamper rather than help them. But the

---

[7] Max Ascoli, *The Power of Freedom* (New York: Farrar, Straus & Co., 1949) , p. 56.

[8] L. Krieger, "Stages in the History of Political Freedom," *NOMOS IV: Liberty,* Carl J. Friedrich (ed.) (New York: Atherton Press, 1962) , p. 1.

[9] *Ibid.,* pp. 4–5.

liberalism of that era cannot correctly be identified with laissez-faire or merely the social philosophy of the middle class. The freedoms of liberalism were then and are now more inclusive, as Professor Sabine has pointed out.[10] In a narrow sense "liberalism" means "a political position midway between conservatism and socialism, and one that is favorable to reform but opposed to radicalism,"[11] a meaning somewhat more characteristic of Continental than of recent Anglo-American usage. A more extended meaning of the term implies, on the political level, "the preservation of popular institutions of government" and "more generally political institutions that acknowledge certain broad principles of social philosophy or of political morality."[12]

Because the concepts of freedom advanced under the banner of liberalism have been attacked frontally by its avowed and even blatant enemies—communism, fascism, and national socialism—Sabine's statement of the major liberal axioms or postulates is useful. First, its individualism stands opposed to any form of collectivism of the Right or the Left. Secondly, it insists that "the relationships between individuals in a community are irreducibly moral relations."[13] Liberal philosophies tend to revert to natural rights theory in postulating the human individual as uniquely the source of value. It opposes the Hegelian and Marxian tendency to think of societies and institutions as personified abstractions that tower above and absorb human personality. "A crucial characteristic and perhaps the most important characteristic of a liberal government is the negative quality of not being totalitarian," but the right of voluntary association has at the same time been held to be a very important aspect of individual freedom.

That voluntary associations may become as oppressive and illiberal as the state, whose power liberals had sought to tame, now presented a problem of freedom in other forms. Here a further liberal axiom asserts both the necessity of limiting the objectives of all associations (including the state) and the means used to reach those objectives. Finally, there is a postulate about the specific con-

[10] George H. Sabine, *A History of Political Theory* (3d ed.; New York: Holt, Rinehart & Winston, Inc., 1961), chap. 31; "Liberalism: Philosophical Radicalism," and chap. 32, "Liberalism Modernized."

[11] *Ibid.*, p. 741.

[12] *Ibid.*, p. 741.

[13] *Ibid.*, p. 745.

sultative, negotiatory, and reflective methods that must be emphasized in setting and reaching common objectives. It is not that reason reigns, but only that "power exerted after a rational weighing of moral claims is morally different from naked force, and it may well be more intelligent," writes Sabine, "for wisdom consists less in certainty than a built-in corrigibility."[14]

FREEDOM IN INDUSTRY

The contemporary problem of freedom is said to be twofold: "to determine whether there is, through the varieties of historical experience, a common core of freedom; and to redefine for our own generation the valid forms it may take in the myriad of relations into which we must now enter,"[15] as time passes and institutions change. Freedom of enterprise has been one of the forms by the business community. Is it valid today, and under what conditions? Does freedom in this sense mean that all business firms are free to compete with each other, and that this freedom must be preserved by public governmental action that renders firms unfree to restrain or impede competition? Or does freedom of enterprise mean laissez-faire with but minor modifications?

These questions lead to the broader issue faced in the history of liberalism: corporations, like all collectivities, are capable of exercising power that may endanger individual freedom. This power needs more thorough analysis than it has received by social scientists. At times it is exaggerated and misconstrued; at other times it goes unchallenged and is properly the concern of defenders of freedom. In all business relationships freedom for some persons and some kinds of actions carries with it the necessary concomitant that there must be unfreedom for some other persons and activities. There are, in other words, both mutual power and mutual dependence relationships that are unavoidable. But one consequence may be the necessary guarantee of freedom as a right by the governments.

The guarantors of freedom, both for individuals and for business units, will continue to be mainly national governments, given the present organization of political power in the world arena. The freedom of enterprisers, investors, and corporations to move out into that arena does not lie under any guarantee of world law. Their

---

[14] *Ibid.*, p. 753.
[15] Krieger, *op. cit.*, p. 28.

freedom within nations is more limited than it used to be because of enhanced liberties of others.

Since freedom changes with time and with differing organizations, the meaning of the ideal must be found in social fact. "We cannot conceive of liberty," said Croce, "without some social and economic organization," and this means freedom under the canopy of the corporation for millions of Americans.[16] How shall freedom be viewed in this context? The answer must be conditioned by our view of the constituency. Industry needs four parties: workers, stockholders, consumers, and the general community. Industry involves co-operation and mutual aid. Prince Kropotkin, over a century ago, argued, on the basis of his intensive observations of animal, insect, and primitive human life in Central Asia, that the principle of mutual aid is universal in nature within a species. If this concept can be applied as a model to American industry, then liberty is served as mutuality is respected and fostered.[17]

No longer do we tolerate the older practices of New England financiers, who mixed shrewd business with morals by requiring employees to live in company houses and attend church under company supervision and by fixing fines for profanity and other misbehavior. No longer do employees face arbitrary firing (as happened in one Pennsylvania mill when two workers asked for a 10-hour day) or layoff or blacklisting. One need recall only the political power of United States Steel right up to the mid-thirties in such corporation towns as McKeesport, Homestead, and Duquesne. In all these steel communities every town official had to be a mill official, and it was not uncommon for town officeholders to go to the plant for instructions on possible issues. There is the oft-repeated story that a corporation man, who was also mayor of Duquesne during the thirties, refused to permit the wife of the American President to speak in the town, announcing that he "wouldn't let God Himself speak there if he talked in favor of the union." Today, less than a quarter-century later, mayors of these towns are frequently union officials and are often given leaves of absence to hold political office. To serve as a legislator in Harrisburg and to work in a steel mill between sessions is not an uncommon experience. What

---

[16] Benedetto Croce, *History as the Story of Liberty* (New York: W. W. Norton & Co., 1941), pp. 243–44.

[17] George Goyder, *The Future of Private Enterprise: A Study in Responsibility* (Oxford: Basil Blackwell, 1951), chap. vii.

this means, practically, is that corporations now are acting so as to respect the range of worker freedom within the political arena.

Perhaps the sagest advice on the implications of freedom for our society has been penned by a member of the Council of Economic Advisers, who observed that "the ultimate value of a free economy is not production, but freedom, and freedom comes not at a profit but at a cost." It is not to be measured in terms of economic man. Indeed, "economic man responding purely to the dictates of the market may help our thinking as an abstraction. Interpreted as a reality he becomes a menace. The center of the good society is not a bazaar.[18] In terms of modern freedom the challenge consists of balancing the over-all goals of a free society with the need to maintain a dynamic area of initiative in the private sector. And the private sector includes free management, free worker, and free consumer.

Practically, then, freedom is important in providing the drive necessary for the creation of various devices to protect the producer, the worker, and the consumer from arbitrary interferences. These devices must provide adequate property and income, adequate time for leisure, and adequate education to make that leisure productive.[19] The classical model of economic freedom is inappropriate to mid-twentieth-century business society, even as it is inappropriate to our handling of underdeveloped areas. If the "flight from freedom"—to use Colgate President Everett Case's words—is to be arrested, it will be because men construct institutions that satisfy the imperium of both the ideal and the conditions of human freedom.[20]

JUSTICE

It is commonplace to hear that justice is an elusive idea for modern man to comprehend. The implication that older societies understood it more perfectly or applied it more rigorously is open to substantial debate. The Greek notions, with which we shall presently be engaged, were translated to Christendom less through philosophy and more through exhortations to follow the example of Jesus. It was easier and more rewarding for the early Christians to

---

18 Henry C. Wallich, *The Cost of Freedom* (New York: Harper & Bros., 1960), pp. x, 13, and 15.

19 Louis Kelso and Mortimer J. Adler, *The Capitalist Manifesto* (New York: Random House, 1958), p. 29.

20 Everett Case, "The Idea of Freedom," *Saturday Review*, July 4, 1959.

understand what the just Christ did than to comprehend why He did it. The tendency to personify abstractions has always been maintained. English morality plays of the 15th and 16th centuries, such as *The Castle of Perseverance* and *A Warning to Faire Women,* regularly included Justice as a major character; as a matter of fact, the evolution of justice from a theological abstraction to a civil servant achieves its fullest development in 16th-century English drama.

Corporate executives and union chiefs do not fancy themselves to be either philosopher-kings or distinguished jurists. Yet, even as they shy away from abstractions that have involved philosophers in furious debate, they are forced to search the past for meaning. Their inquiry is directed not toward precise dogma but toward general guidelines; they still prefer examples of just men to theories of justice itself.

Historically, the American tradition of justice is found to reside in the Judeo-Christian and Greco-Roman contributions and cannot be summed up in any brief delineation, but a stimulating start can be made by setting forth (1) a working definition of justice, (2) an example of its interpretation in ancient Greece and Rome, and (3) a simplified model to explain its evolution.

DEFINITION

The definition of justice would take into account the fact that *justice is always concerned with something owed* either to oneself or to another. Since, normally, men are quick to care for self-interest, questions of justice usually relate to what is owed to another. At the most elementary level one can appreciate the fact that determining justice in the acts of two individuals is much simpler than determining justice for many. Numbers invariably complicate the game. And rendering what is *strictly* owed is more precisely articulated than is rendering what is owed *indirectly*.

Since ours is a corporate kind of society, justice is handled and thought of largely in terms of group relationships. What a business executive owes in justice to the unknown workers far down the production line—workers he never sees or meets or thinks of in their individual creative capacities—becomes the problem for business leadership. Conversely, the individual worker has less direct knowledge of what he owes to an impersonalized organization when he is part of an assembly line, when the nature of *his* efforts is lost in a vast complex of varying kinds of simultaneous piece productions that ultimately appear in final assemblage. It is not surprising that just men are more relaxed in paying taxes to an impersonal government or in handling machinery owned by an impersonal corporation than they would be in paying bills to the corner groceryman or in using a power mower borrowed from a neighbor. Yet these are precisely the areas of social justice in which theory and knowledge need to be most effectively applied.

Justice, then, is concerned with according to each man his due. The issue involves making determinations of what is, and is not, due; who makes such judgments; and how the decisions are to be carried out.

JUSTICE IN THE ANCIENT TRADITION: REPRESENTATIVE VIEWS

Greece. To the Athenian of the golden fifth century, justice was derivative from the order of society. The good society fostered justice, and justice fostered a good society. It was a social fact, not primarily a personal or individual responsibility. One ancient theory of justice, finding its finest expression in the *Republic* of Plato led an eminent scholar to comment as follows:

> The theory of the state in the *Republic* culminates in the conception of justice. Justice is the bond which holds a society together, a harmonious union of individuals each of whom has found his life-work in accordance with his natural fitness and his training. It is both a public and a private virtue because the highest good, both of the state and its members, is thereby conserved. There is nothing better for a man than to have his work and to be fitted to do it; there is nothing better for other men and for the whole society than that each should thus be filling the station to which he is entitled. This is Plato's elaboration of the *prima facie* definition of justice as "giving every man his due." For what is due to him is that he should be treated as what he is, in the light of his capacity and his training, while what is due *from* him is the honest performance of those tasks which the place accorded him requires.[21]

Five distinct elements in the Platonic conception of justice may be observed in the *Republic*. First, justice is an inseparable aspect of the good society. Individualism has little to do with Plato's concept of justice. In a day when we are turning away from traditional individualism to various types of collectivism, his emphasis on the social context of justice exerts unconscious appeal. Second, Plato

---

[21] George H. Sabine, *op. cit.*, pp. 54–55.

placed little or no emphasis on personal "rights," protected by law and the state. "It is true that in such a social life there are rights, just as there are duties, but they hardly can be said to belong in any particular sense to individuals. They are inherent rather in the services or functions that individuals perform."[22] Third, the concept of legal coercive power is largely absent. The state is seen as a provider of the needed conditions of sociopolitical life (protection against foreign enemies and so on) rather than as a Hobbesian agent terrifying the citizens into respect for one another's persons and property. Plato regarded society as fundamentally complementary and harmonious, not as a "jungle" fostering all against all. Fourth, Plato's philosophy of justice strongly suggests later economic theories of the division of labor. Perhaps it is this quality that gives to it a certain sense of relevance to the flesh-and-blood world, a relevance that seems lacking in more modern, purely legal formulations. Finally, the *Republic* was historically significant as the first utopian work. Since then, every thinker who has despaired of setting the world aright through reform has fled to an ideal polity of his own creation. In our day we have seen a variation on the utopian theme by such writers as Huxley and Orwell, who present an *inverse utopia*. Here the morbid trends and injustices of the present are taken to their logical conclusion in the future, usually a future not too far distant.

Rome. The Roman contribution to the understanding of justice was the concept of law as an aggregation of personal rights. As the *Digest* of the Emperor Justinian affirms: "Justice is a fixed and abiding disposition to give every man his right. The precepts of the law are as follows: to live honorably, to injure no one, to give to every man his own. Jurisprudence is a knowledge of things human and divine, the science of the just and the unjust."[23] Note the pervasive shift in outlook. Justice moved away from sociology towards legality; it became a specialized institutional function rather than the concern of all citizens.

Historians account for this metamorphosis in at least two ways. First, even the most optimistic found it difficult to believe that the vast polyglot empire of Rome could be converted into a perfectly just society. Within any great community, whether it be the New York City of today or the Roman Empire of yesteryear, the forces of

---

[22] *Ibid.*, p. 55.
[23] Digest 1. 1. 10.

wrong and disorder are much more visible. A rough-and-ready system of justice was needed to supplement the police power provided by the imperial legions. The more complicated and heterogeneous a society becomes, the greater the need for defining rules of conduct. With their genius for practical government, the Romans elaborated a code that covered the day-to-day needs of the courts. Justice thus became synonymous with law. The emphasis on personal rights, in place of social function, as the focus of justice was probably the result of a deep shift in the values of the ancient world.

Of course, revolution in political and social outlook began long before the advent of the Roman Empire or the triumph of Christianity, although it undoubtedly reached fulfillment under them. As early as the fourth century B.C. an isolation of the person and an internalization of the human personality became evident. People began to think of themselves as unrelated social atoms. At the same time, religion turned inward, partly as a result of the importation of the oriental mystery cults. The same tendency was felt in the realm of public life, and the obligations of citizenship were less and less recognized. As far as the prevailing idea of justice was concerned, people came to think in terms of what was owed them as individuals, not in terms of what they owed the community or one another.

We should not hastily conclude that all these developments were unfortunate. The mature Roman Law was a remarkable growth, which had much to recommend it. While the game of high politics during the late Empire was deadly and arbitrary for many of those who practiced it, on the level of ordinary life the courts and lawyers inaugurated strikingly liberal and human legal innovations. However, it is certainly true that this individualistic, private-right conception of justice tended to weaken the customary obligation of obedience—at least in practice if not in theory. The sanction of custom, which supplied its own grounds for obedience, and fear of group ostracism became less powerful.

The question of dedication to justice or obedience to law assumes special significance when one remembers that our Western conception of law is essentially Roman. While the common law of England and America is not formally based upon the Justinian code, the same individualistic bias is also definitely present. One of the great advantages of such a system is that it admirably protects the individual from what has been styled the "tyranny of the majority." The cost, however, is a relative weakness in the functional operation of justice, namely, the obligation of obedience.

A Simplified Model: Job versus Hobbes

It is patently impossible to catch the nuances that each society in different epochs gave to the content of justice. Yet an overly simplified model of two extreme ways of viewing justice analytically may help to develop perspectives for measuring the implications of our own institutions and practices. The conflict of views may be presented in terms of the biblical Job and the secular Hobbes.[24]

Despite literary controversy between those who argue that Job never existed—that he was a storybook figure borrowed from a Greek tragedy—and those who assert his real identity, the Book of Job remains one of the most revered books of the Bible.[25] What is the real significance of the book of Job? It is the story of justice and injustice.

The tyrant on the throne, the thief who robs his fellow, the murderer who mounts over the prostrate body of his victim, the dishonest dealer who defrauds his customer by false scales, the brutal employer who grinds the faces of the poor—are they not all around us, happy and prosperous while the weak and these defenseless perish? Such is the terrible indictment that we encounter in the utterances put into the mouth of Job. Here is a problem indeed well worthy of discussion. Where is God while innocents suffer and terrible injustice is going on in this world. Is a solution possible?[26]

How did Judeo-Christian theology render its answer? The reply was given in terms of God-given rights, which Job could assert through a covenant with his Maker. Lowly man had rights even in the presence of the Almighty. Certain things were owed to man simply because he existed, and our political traditions interpret these to mean life, liberty, and the right to seek happiness.

Hobbes resurrected Job, not in the traditional manner, but as the original, embittered God-fighting Job who seeks to arraign Divinity before an earthly court. Hobbes created a dichotomy between an immortal God and a mortal god, the state, which he called the Leviathan. The omnipotent Leviathan was the center of both spirit-

---

[24] The idea was suggested in Max M. Laserson's essay "Power and Justice: Hobbes versus Job," *Judaism*, Vol. II (January, 1953) , pp. 50–59.

[25] Morris Jastrow, *The Book of Job: Its Origin, Growth and Interpretation* (Philadelphia: J. B. Lippincott Co., 1920). Jastrow points out that the Talmud contains only one daring denial of the existence of an important biblical personality—Job. At the same time, the Rabbis ascribed authorship to Moses himself.

[26] *Ibid.*, p. 33. For a contemporary handling of Job's meaning by a major American dramatist see Archibald MacLeish, *J.B.*, which had a successful Broadway run in 1958.

ual and secular power. Out goes the old doctrine of man's right and in comes the new doctrine of man's subservience! The Leviathan creates and confers rights, and when it takes away what it freely bestows it cannot be called unjust. How have these respective traditions been articulated throughout history? The model of Job has been reflected in the pagan Aristotle, the Jewish commentator Ibn-Pakada, and Christian theorists like Aquinas, Suarez, and Grotius. The Hobbesian tradition has attracted men like John Austin and Sir Robert Filmer in England, Bossuet in France, Burckhardt in Switzerland, Trietschke in Germany, and perhaps José Ortega y Gasset in Spain.

Let us take two representatives of the Hobbesian school to underscore the differences. Ortega held to the belief that historical development has no ultimate goal but is simply the development of a peculiar kind of life according to its own laws of evolution. Since the new culture is hammered out by the creators of history, these man are not subject to any moral considerations; indeed, the rules they impose must be viewed as just in themselves.[27] Jacob Burckhardt argued that the great man was exempt from ordinary moral codes. "The crimes of the man, therefore, who bestows on a community greatness, power and glory are condoned. . . . Here everything depends on success."[28] And Napoleon could cry out on Elba: "My name will live as long as God's."

The contrary view asserts simply that justice is achieved not through rule by men but through rule of law, and the law appeals for its ultimate rationale to the norms of justice that, society has been taught, have validity. Under the Hobbesian view, therefore, justice is that which is meted out by the powerful. Under Job, justice is that which exists by right. The implications are poles apart!

LAW

From Roman times onward there has been a close nexus between the concept of law and the concept of justice. As Max Radin has observed: "Law is directed to justice. It aims at justice, knowing that its aim can be only imperfectly realized."[29] Its coverage may um-

---

[27] See C. Cepelcha, *Historical Thought of José Ortega y Gasset* (Washington: Catholic University Press, 1960).

[28] Jacob Burckhardt, *Force and Freedom: Reflections on History* (New York: Pantheon Books, 1943), pp. 339–40.

[29] Max Radin, *The Law and You* (New York: New American Library [Mentor Book], 1948), p. 156.

brella activities that are intrinsically good and bad and "indifferent" activities that seem preferable or more reasonable to a particular society. Adjusting to the nature of the times, man-made law is not inflexible. It is slow to change, for one of the values inherent in the idea of law is stability and predictability. The ideal of justice is indispensable to a society built on freedom under law, for it does not admit of rights without duties or of duties without rights.

In analyzing the concept of law, let us examine first the major differences between the natural-law theorists and the positivists and then move on to draw a line between the two major legal traditions in Western society: common law and civil law.

NATURAL AND POSITIVE LAW

Until comparatively recent times it was taken for granted that there existed a natural law, over and above the man-made laws of the judge of the statutes of the legislator, that was superior to the positive laws of men. Wrongly made human edicts therefore did not compel obedience. "An unjust law," Aristotle tells us "is not a law."[30]

The origin of natural law rests in religion and philosophy. Sophocles' *Antigone* appeals to the "unwritten and unalterable laws of God and heaven."[31] And, when Christianity replaced the pagan forms, it received the old doctrine of divinely sanctioned law with ease. The appeal to fundamental rights beyond the power of the existing authorities to alter or negate has generally given strong support to those who struggled for freedom against tyranny. One noted scholar has shown that the American federal Constitution is founded largely on natural-law ideas.[32] The framers' principles were derived, via Locke, from the Fathers of the Church and originated with the Stoic thinkers. Back of the political theory upon which our free society rests is a theory of God-sanctioned, eternal justice—a theory, moreover, with a long, useful, and eminently respectable history.

Toward the end of the 16th century a new development in jurisprudence became evident. The creative job of the medieval canonist was to make the Justinian Code useful for the needs of early Europe. With the late Renaissance, however, attempts were

---

[30] *Rhetoric* I. 15. 1375.

[31] *Antigone*, trans. E. F. Watling (Baltimore: Penguin Books, 1953).

[32] E. S. Corwin, *The "Higher Law" Background of American Constitutional Law* (New York: Great Seal Books, 1928).

made to explain the Roman codes philologically and to capture the sense of the original by comparing ancient law to other social products of the ancient world. As a result, the humanist concluded that codification of the Justinian laws was far from complete and that many of the rules were designed for the special needs of Roman citizens. There was, therefore, an inadvertent break with the authority of Rome, which was conceptualized in the ideas of comparative jurisprudence developed by Jean Bodin. A new way of looking at law and a new era of historical interpretation was ushered in by Bodin. His insistence on absolute sovereignty was extended by later writers to an extreme that, in fact, denied a higher law.

The formal attack on natural law began in the realm of philosophy. The Scottish skeptic, David Hume, published in the 18th century a book drily entitled *A Treatise on Human Nature,* which argued that natural law had no claim to universal validity, since men and nations usually disagreed about its content. From Hume's relativistic position it was easy to draw the conclusion that the only law that could certainly be shown to exist is the body of rules laid down by authority. In the years that have followed, this positive-law school has gradually become the dominant influence. But it has not escaped certain dilemmas. If one authority, operating within a fixed boundary, imposes an obligation that is totally rejected by another authority, with control over a different territory, are both just? Which of the two authorities shall prevail in case of conflict?

THE MAJOR SYSTEMS

Within Western civilization two major systems of law developed that were called the "civil-law" and the "common-law" traditions, respectively. Civil law, though it includes the noncriminal law of all systems, has come to suggest the extension of the Roman system. Most of our modern codes flow from the Justinian patterns, and the most famous examples are the French Civil Code of 1804, the German Code of 1900, and the Swiss Code of 1907–11. When corporations operate in Latin American countries, they operate under derivatives of the Napoleonic system of law.

The other system comes from England and is called the "common law." This body grew out of the feudal law of medieval England and was refined by great legalists like Coke and Blackstone. Perhaps the most distinctive functional feature is the jury system, which became part of the European pattern only after the French

Revolution and then only in criminal cases. Under the civil law, codes become the final determinant of legality, whereas in common-law countries there is more of a pragmatic tendency to await developments, to rule on facts rather than a priori theories. Specialists argue the relative merits of the two major systems, but the really important point is that each system has served rather admirably the needs of the society that adopted it.

On our own continent, Canada presents superb opportunities for comparative studies of the operations and fruits of the civil- and common-law traditions, respectively. The initial suspicion that proximity between the French-speaking people of Quebec and the English groups elsewhere would encourage mutual interchanges of concepts and practices has not been borne out by the evidence. Except for the Civil Code of 1866, when Quebec jurists adopted several English business concepts, there is little evidence of borrowing and exchange.[33]

The evolution of common law is erratic and often accommodates itself to demands that are already in the process of dissolution as the new law rises to explain and meet them. Looking at the way judges had made laws, Bentham was moved to declare:

Do you know how they (the judges) make it? Just as a man makes laws for his dog. When your dog does anything you want to break him of, you wait till he does it, and then beat him for it. This is the way you make laws for your dog and this is the way the judges make law for you and me. They won't tell a man beforehand what it is he should not do— they won't so much as allow of his being told: they lie by till he has done something which they say he should not have done, and then they hang him for it. What way, then, has any man of coming at this dog-law? Only by watching their proceedings: by observing in what cases they have hanged a man, in what cases they have sent him to jail, in what cases they have seized his goods, and so forth.[34]

SCHOOLS OF AMERICAN JURISPRUDENCE

If law is what the judges say it is, then, in the American context, the legal philosophy entertained by nine men in a Supreme Court becomes crucial to any understanding of how law can be used to

---

[33] See the excellent treatment on this phase by Edward McWhinney (ed.), *Canadian Jurisprudence: The Civil Law and Common Law* (Toronto: Carswell Co., 1958).

[34] Jeremy Bentham, *Works* (2nd ed.; London: Simpkin Marshall & Co., 1843), p. 235.

enlarge or restrain the spheres of human freedom and justice. Recent legal theory in this country has been dominated by three major schools, which can be identified, respectively, as (1) sociological jurisprudence, (2) economic determinism, and (3) legal realism. Benjamin Cardozo, an outstanding proponent of the sociological approach, insisted that the judge as legislator "must heed the mores of his day," even though mores do not automatically fashion legal systems. His insistence that "law is not found, but made" constituted a sharp attack on the principle of *stare decisis* and on a restriction on the natural-law approach. He once categorized his own position as "midway between the extremes that are represented at one end by Coke and Blackstone and at the other by Austin and Holland and Gray and Jethro Brown."[35]

Economic determinists include among their members such distinguished thinkers as Brooks Adams, Francis Bohlen, and possibly Charles Beard. Here, law is viewed as the expression of the will of the economically dominant class. The Constitution itself is the result of the interplay between economic forces. Law may reflect the interests of an agrarian group at one time, an industrial elite at another, or a labor force at still another. "Far from being the governor it is the governed, a formal recapitulation of the underlying economic realities, shifting as they shift"—so observed Abram Chayes in his analysis of the rule of law in the modern corporation.[36] Often, and not always accurately, economic realists have been called neo-Marxists; actually, their view more nearly approximates that of Engels, who argued that law, viewed as an unadulterated expression of the ruling class, offends the very idea of justice.

And, finally, there are the legal realists. In its ranks are such names as Edward Robinson, Karl Llewellyn, Thurman Arnold, and Jerome Frank. Much of their inspiration was drawn from Oliver Wendell Holmes. The realists believe that law has neglected the psychological basis of human behavior itself and that theories advanced by such men as Sigmund Freud and J. B. Watson have much to teach us, particularly in the handling of criminals. Perhaps the most distinguishing feature of the realist is his skepticism toward accepted propositions of traditional law and of moral codes.

---

[35] Benjamin N. Cardozo, *The Nature of the Judicial Process* (New Haven: Yale University Press, 1921 [reissued as a Yale Paperback]), pp. 104, 115, and 124. See his Lecture III, "The Method of Sociology: The Judge as Legislator."

[36] In Edward S. Mason (ed.), *The Corporation in Modern Society* (Cambridge: Harvard University Press, 1959), p. 29.

The net gains flowing from the influences of the foregoing legal schools have been primarily in bringing greater resilience and flexibility into American legal patterns and in making the courts an active arm of the legislatures through their more liberal reading of statutes and of the Constitution. In a sense, it may not be too much to say that the doctrine of implied powers has been powerfully expanded by and to the judiciary itself. But there have been real losses in the process. One of the essential elements of law is its predictability. Ordinary citizens and business executives must be able to anticipate the legal effect of certain contemplated actions. The normal way is to look to precedent and to read the law. When *stare decisis* is weakened and when courts sometimes read their own meanings into statutory provisions, a certain amount of confusion becomes inevitable.

Thus the business community was shocked during the spring of 1960 by a decision that refused a federal court injunction against a strike called to enforce a union demand that no jobs be abolished by management without union consent. And in the Parke, Davis case the five-four decision to restrict the manufacturer's right to enforce established retail prices in non-fair-trade conditions upset normal expectancies. Both cases have very important implications for business, labor, and the customer, and both represent sharp departures from existing practices. In the tax field, delay and the very complexity of the issues add to the burden of a business community, which chafes under this climate of judicial uncertainty. Really, our concern is to get the courts to do quickly what ought to be done, but to exercise great self-restraint in the process.[37]

The development thus far suggests that the cherished American ideal of "rule of law"—itself a repudiation of the Hobbesian version of justice—is meaningful only in terms of court interpretations. While this may have been true at the time John Commons was doing his significant researches into the changing content of property and contract, it is no longer the full story today. Techniques for the legal control of business, initiated primarily with the Interstate Commerce Commission, have been steadily expanded, so that administrative law is a highly important element of our legal system for the businessman. The National Labor Relations Board and the Securities and Exchange Commission, for example, can issue orders and render judgments that have the effect of law on labor practices,

---

[37] Charles L. Black, Jr., *The People and the Court: Judicial Review in a Democracy* (New York: Macmillan Co., 1960) .

on financial policies, and on accounting procedures. This corpus of regulations is only in its infancy, and there is conflicting evidence as to whether the agencies are the rulers or the ruled in their relations with business.[38] In addition, decisions by arbitrators vitally affect business. The recent denial of a New York garment manufacturer's effort to move South is a case in point.

LAW AND THE CORPORATION

A constant concern in this analysis has been to test the abstract meanings of freedom and justice in the context of large organization. The wisdom of simple mandates, such as "Thou shalt not kill," is readily perceived. But prescription is less characteristic of modern law than are efforts to create a climate and to provide facilities through which the work of society can be done efficiently and equitably. The importance of this function of the law is underscored in the following observation:

> To illustrate: it is possible to look at the law of contract as a command of the state not to break certain classes of promises. This is not, however, a very useful point of view if the object is to understand the role of contract law in the development of our society. For this purpose, contract must be seen as a way in which men dealing with each other can insure that their promises will outlast their transitory states of mind.
>
> The law does not prescribe contract. It attaches no immediate normative value to the act of promising. It says only that if you wish to act, and more important, if you wish to make your action binding, in some sense, on the future, act in such and such a way. If you do not follow the approved path, the promise made to you may nevertheless be kept. But the law will lend you no aid to see that it is kept.
>
> It will be seen that what the law of contract has provided is a device by which private persons are enabled to some extent to stabilize and make predictable—to control—the future. That is, they are enabled to make their own law to govern their own affairs. The state lends its judicial machinery to enforce this personal law, if necessary. The law appears to exhaust itself in defining the conditions on which the public force will be enlisted to effectuate the private end. And it is true that these conditions, in our system at least, are elastic enough to permit a wide range of autonomously directed private activity. The ideal of the rule of law dictates, however, that these conditions be not arbitrary, but must be ration-

---

[38] Walton Hamilton argued that the regulatory bodies had been captured by the very business groups that they had been set up to police. *The Politics of Industry* (New York: Alfred A. Knopf, 1957), pp. 54–93.

ally related to legitimate social purpose. By providing useful facilities on such condition, the legal system mobilizes powerful inducements to action in support of those purposes.

The rule of law, as here conceived, then, is concerned with regularizing and rationalizing the use of power. But it is concerned with power in both its faces—not only as an evil, to be restrained, but as a resource to be harnessed in the service of society. The creation of legal institutions which enlist the energies of men in the service of legitimate social purposes is the most important mode by which this dual end of the rule of law is approached.[39]

The corporation is the major facility provided by the American legal system for handling the business phases of a democratic society. It grew logically out of the theory of contract, and efforts to refine the idea of the corporation are duplicating in substantial measure the earlier efforts to modernize the law of contract. Questions of law are becoming increasingly concerned with the nature of the real constituency of the corporation. Is it only the stockholders? The law is fairly clear on stockholders' legal rights, but practical efforts to rally the share owner constituency as a disciplinarian of management have produced more histrionics than constructive history. If the workers are viewed as a major constituency, the law has yet to determine whether in fact they constitute an effective opposition and whether the opposition can be legitimized. Are suppliers an integral part of the corporate society? And if so, how is the law developing to accommodate this relationship? Finally, one should observe that in a real sense corporation law is advanced by management itself, sometimes independent of statutory prescription, when it makes the rules for internal governance more explicit. An example of this would be a definition of rights of a worker who, for example, faces dismissal not for inefficiency but for security reasons.[40]

CONCLUSION

Every generation is challenged to understand the primary ideas that give inspiration and meaning to the society of which it is the

---

[39] Abram Chayes, "The Rule of Law," in E. S. Mason (ed.), *op. cit.*, pp. 31-32.

[40] See e.g., Alan F. Westin, *Civil Liberties in the Big Corporation* (New York: Macmillan Co., 1960); and Melville Dalton, *Men Who Manage* (New York: John Wiley & Sons, 1959). The corporation's imperative to make advances in this area, is discussed by Richard Eells, *The Government of Corporations* (New York: The Free Press, 1962).

heir. Freedom and justice, touchstones of every democratic creed, require never-ending refinement and application. What freedom consists of and what justice really means depend in substantial measure on the interpretation given to human nature itself and to society's understanding of the common good. In somewhat truncated form we have suggested restudy of the following propositions:

1. Freedom is a limited quality conditioned by man's own nature, but, within this framework, freedom is the most impelling force in Western society. Denial of freedom to men or any groups of men because of race or of occupation is the surest way to rend the seamless garment of the republic.

2. Justice does not flow from the Leviathan—the mortal-state-god of Hobbes—but its production and enhancement depend primarily upon the civil government.

3. In terms of positive law we may be witnessing a drift toward codification practices that reflect Continental law as it emanated from early Roman practices. If this becomes pronounced, we may give greater legal orderliness to our business procedures but we run the risk of stifling innovation and creativity by our regulatory commissions.

4. Certainly there is a movement away from *stare decisis,* from the natural-rights philosophy, toward bolder judicial interpretation, which seeks in sociological, psychological, and economic facets the real inspirations for lawmaking.

5. During the stress-and-strain period of adapting notions of freedom, justice, and law to a rapidly changing economy, there will develop a strong desire to keep the discourse at the lower level of technique rather than on the higher plane of substantial meaning. Every man may subscribe to freedom, for example, not because it imposes a discipline of costs but because (by infusing it with the content of his own biases) he can create a satisfactory basis for rationalizing his own behavior.

The job, essentially, is to civilize: to build the edifice on pillars of freedom, justice, and law that have internal strength. With his customary incisiveness Alfred North Whitehead defined the task in these terms:

There is a great function which awaits the American universities, and that is to civilize business: or better, to get businessmen to civilize themselves by using their power over the practical processes of life to civilize their sociological functions. It is not enough that they should amass for-

tunes in this way or that and then endow a college or a hospital. . . .
What I mean is, law has been civilized—that was done by the Greeks and
the Romans, Justinian and that lot;—medicine has been taken out of
magic; education has been getting rid of its humbug; and next it is time
to teach business its sociological function; for if America is to be civilized,
it must be done (at least for the present) by the business class, who are in
possession of the power and the economic processes. . . . If the American
universities were up to their job they would be taking business in hand
and teaching it ethics and professional standards.[41]

RECOMMENDED READING

ADLER, MORTIMER J. *The Idea of Freedom: A Dialectical Examination
of the Concept of Freedom.* Garden City, N.Y.: Doubleday & Co., 1958.

CLARK, J. M. *Economic Institutions and Human Welfare,* chaps. i–ix.
New York: Alfred A. Knopf, 1957.

Crime and Justice and *Revolution in Civil Rights.* Washington, D.C.:
Congressional Quarterly Service, 1967.

DOBZHANSKY, T. *The Biological Basis of Human Freedom.* New York:
Columbia University Press, 1956.

DOUGLAS, WILLIAM O. *The Anatomy of Liberty: The Rights of Man
without Force.* New York: Pocket Books, Inc., 1964.

FRIEDRICH, CARL J., and CHAPMAN, JOHN W. (eds.). *NOMOS VI: Justice,* chaps. 1, 2, 9, 14, and 15. New York: Atherton Press, 1963.

MASON, EDWARD S. (ed.). *The Corporation in Modern Society,* chap. ii.
Cambridge: Harvard University Press, 1959.

MILLER, ARTHUR (ed.). "The Ethics of Business Enterprise," *The Annals* of The American Academy of Political and Social Science, Vol.
343, September, 1962.

MURRAY, JOHN COURTNEY. *We Hold These Truths: Catholic Reflections
on the American Proposition,* Introduction and chap. ix. New York:
Sheed and Ward, 1960.

POUND, ROSCOE. *Justice According to Law,* Parts I and III. New Haven:
Yale University Press, 1951.

PROSSER, WILLIAM L. *Handbook of the Law of Torts,* sec. 3, p. 12; and
sec. 31. 2d ed. Los Angeles: Institute of Industrial Relations, University
of California at Los Angeles, 1955.

SABINE, GEORGE H. *A History of Political Theory,* 3d ed., chaps. 31 and
32. New York: Holt, Rinehart & Winston, Inc., 1961.

---

[41] Lucien Price (ed.), *The Dialogues of Alfred North Whitehead* (New York:
Little, Brown & Co., The Atlantic Press, 1956), pp. 56–57.

SAMUELSON, PAUL A. "Personal Freedoms and Economic Freedoms," in Earl F. Cheit (ed.), *The Business Establishment,* pp. 193–227. New York: John Wiley & Sons, Inc., 1964.

WALLICH, HENRY. *The Cost of Freedom.* New York: Harper & Bros., 1960.

FURTHER READING

ABRAHAM, HENRY J. *Freedom and the Court: Civil Rights and Liberties in the United States.* New York: Oxford University Press, 1967.

ALLEN, SIR CARLETON KEMP. *Aspects of Justice,* chap. v. London: Stevens & Sons, 1958.

BRYSON, LYMAN, et al. *Freedom and Authority in Our Time.* New York: Harper & Bros., 1953.

CARDOZO, BENJAMIN. *The Nature of the Judicial Process,* chap. iii. New Haven: Yale University Press, 1921.

Coppage v. *The State of Kansas,* 236 U.S. 1 (1914).

CROCE, BENEDETTO. *History as the Story of Liberty.* New York: W. W. Norton & Co., 1941.

FRIEDMAN, MILTON. *Capitalism and Freedom,* chaps. 1, 2, and 13. Chicago: University of Chicago Press, 1962.

FRIEDRICH, CARL J. (ed.). *NOMOS IV: Liberty,* chaps. 1, 5 and 13. New York: Atherton Press, 1962.

Giboney v. *Empire Storage and Ice Co.,* 336 U.S. 490 (1949).

KAUFMAN, ARNOLD S. *The Radical Liberal: New Man in American Politics.* New York: Atherton Press, 1967.

KELSO, LOUIS, and ADLER, MORTIMER J. *The Capitalist Manifesto.* New York: Random House, 1958.

Lincoln Federal Labor Union v. *Northwestern Iron and Metal Co.,* 335 U.S. 525 (1949).

Lochner v. *The State of New York,* 198 U.S. 45 (1905).

MARELLA, PAOLO CARDINAL. "Religious Postulates of the Economic-Social Order," in *The Future of Capitalism,* a Symposium on the Fiftieth Anniversary of the National Industrial Conference Board. New York: The Macmillan Co., 1967.

MILL, JOHN STUART. *On Liberty.* Everyman ed. London: J. M. Dent Co., 1948.

MULLER, H. J. *Issues of Freedom: Paradoxes and Promises.* New York: Harper & Bros., 1959.

National Labor Relations Board v. *Jones and Laughlin Steel Corporation,* 301 U.S. 1 (1937).

PATTERSON, E. W. *Jurisprudence,* chaps. iv, xii, and xviii. Brooklyn: Foundation Press, 1953.

POUND, ROSCOE. *New Paths of the Law,* chap. i. Lincoln: University of Nebraska Press, 1950.

————. *The Task of the Law,* chap. i (strongly recommended). Lancaster: Franklin and Marshall College, 1944.

RADIN, MAX. *The Law and You.* New York: New American Library, 1948.

REYNARD, CHARLES A. (ed.) . *Readings on Labor Law,* Part IV. Boston: Little, Brown & Co., 1955.

SALVADORI, MASSIMO. *Economics of Freedom: American Capitalism Today,* chap. i. New York: Doubleday & Co., 1959.

SHUSTER, GEORGE N., (ed.) . *Freedom and Authority in the West.* New York: The Ronald Press, 1967.

"Trade Rules and Trade Conferences: The FTC and Business Attack Deceptive Practices, Unfair Competition and Antitrust Violators," *Yale Law Journal,* Vol. LXII (May, 1953) , pp. 912–53.

United States v. *Darby,* 312 U.S. 100 (1941) .

VEBLEN, THORSTEIN. *The Theory of Business Enterprise.* New York: Charles Scribner's Sons, 1927. (Sections as excerpted in Jerome Hall, *Readings in Jurisprudence,* pp. 306–15. Indianapolis: Bobbs-Merrill Co., 1938) .

WESTIN, ALAN F. *Privacy and Freedom,* chap. 14, "Restoring the Balance of Privacy in America." New York: Atheneum, 1967.

WU, JOHN C. H. *Fountain of Justice,* chaps. xix and xxii. New York: Sheed and Ward, 1955.

17. *Authority and Power*

OUTLINE

To TALK of authority and power is to raise questions regarding their nature, how they are acquired and legitimized, who should wield them, and under what safeguards. These questions deal with what has been called the *vocatio regis*—the calling and functioning of administrators—and have inspired classic observations in Plato's *Republic* and Aristotle's *Politics,* in Aquinas' *Governance of Rulers* and Suarez' *De legibus.* Perhaps the educational legacy impressed most vividly on the Western mind is Machiavelli's *The Prince* and those portions dealing with authority in John Locke's *Essay in Human Understanding.* Indeed, Machiavelli and Locke were used, along with Sir Thomas Elyot's *The Book Named the Governour,* as basic reading for the training of colonial officers by the British East India Company.

In our nation's agrarian period Jefferson paid eloquent testimony to the need for an aristocracy of virtue and talent as prerequisite to a successful democracy, whereas in this country's atomic era the alleged vesting of vast influence in an interlocking directorate of a few politicians, businessmen, and generals has led to a variety of denunciations of the new power elite. For those of C. Wright Mills' persuasion this new aristocracy represents neither virtue nor talent; it manipulates rather than leads, coerces rather than convinces, pressures rather than persuades.

Guglielmo Ferrero, the distinguished Italian philosopher, said the central problem of our times was how to end with a principle of legitimacy the disorder generated by power in this troubled century. History offers examples of many kinds of techniques through which legitimacy may be recognized: hereditary, democratic, aristocratic, economic, or a blending of several types. "Of all human inequalities," Ferrero wrote, "none is so important in its effects or has greater need of logical justification than that established by power."[1] In a society like ours, the ideal of equality runs into a head-on collision with obvious inequalities. Yet the dilemma may contain the seeds of its own resolution by suggesting a formula which correlates equality with opportunity. Right of access to positions of influence in America is based increasingly on demonstrated abilities. And functions exercised on the basis of a new kind of ownership— possession of wide knowledge and skills—may provide some meaningful measure of legitimacy.

After their study of big business leaders in America, Warner and Abegglen concluded:

> The ordered process of occupational succession in Big Business demonstrates that at least in this prestigeful and highly valued part of economic life, our society is more fluid and flexible than it was yesterday. There is more circulation in and out of higher and lower statuses; more men from different family backgrounds enter, hold and leave powerful positions. The fathers of the elite, and the ambitious striving men at the bottom, both have greater awareness that the precedent of birth alone is insufficient for maintaining high status today. Values of achieved status and social mobility are expressed more fully, and those of inherited positions less so than a generation ago.[2]

---

[1] Guglielmo Ferrero, *The Principles of Power* (trans. T. R. Jaeckel) (New York: G. P. Putnam, 1942), p. 32.

[2] W. L. Warner and J. C. Abegglen, *Big Business Leaders in America* (New York: Harper & Bros., 1955), p. 220. The same point is tellingly made by Andrew Hacker in "Liberal Democracy and Social Control," *American Political Science Review*, Vol. LI (December, 1957), pp. 1009–26. Hacker attributes the rise of "the new men" to two factors: Americanization of the immigrant and expansion of the economy.

America's experience bears some general relevance to Pareto's doctrine of "the circulation of elites" (which occurs because the dominant class eventually dissolves, to be replaced by a new dominant class) and to Henri Pirenne's analogous theory that each major change in history generates a new class of leaders.[3]

AUTHORITY AND POWER

A turbine or a rocket involves power—but not authority. When the distinguished British novelist-scientist C. P. Snow[4] reproaches humanists for their appalling ignorance of such basic scientific facts as the second law of thermodynamics, the humanist winces because the arrow hits home so unerringly. Yet he can remind the scientist that power is a fact of the physical universe, whereas the humanist's major concern—and properly so—is with the power exercised by men over other men and with the authorization that accords or denies legitimacy to that specific kind of human activity.

DISTINCTION BETWEEN AUTHORITY AND POWER

First, we must attempt to draw some important distinctions between authority and power. After having examined the manner in which scholars have used the terms "authority" and "power" interchangeably in the theoretical order and the way tyrants and dictators have always claimed that their authority is necessary to assure freedom in the practical order, Hannah Arendt goes on to say that the time has come to consider

the importance of making distinctions. To stress such a conviction seems to be a gratuitous truism in view of the fact that, at least as far as I know, nobody has yet openly stated that distinctions are nonsense. There exists, however, a silent agreement in most discussions among political and social scientists that we can ignore distinctions and proceed on the assumption that everything can eventually be called anything else, and that distinctions are meaningful only to the extent that each of us has the right "to define his terms." Yet does not this curious right, which we have come to grant as soon as we deal with matters of importance—as though it were actually the same as the right to one's own opinion—already indicate that such terms as tyranny, authority, totalitarianism have simply lost their

---

[3] Cf. "Business in Historical Context" herein.

[4] C. P. Snow, *The Two Cultures and the Scientific Revolution* (New York: Cambridge University Press, 1959) , p. 16.

common meaning, or that we have ceased to live in a common world where the words we have in common possess an unquestionable meaningfulness, so that short of being condemned to live verbally in an altogether meaningless world we grant each other the right to retreat into our own worlds of meaning and demand only that each of us remain consistent within his own private termonology? If, under these circumstances, we assure ourselves that we still understand each other, we do not mean that together we understand a world common to us all, but that we understand the consistency of arguing and reasoning, of the process of argumentation in its sheer formality.[5]

What, then, shall we point to as a primary distinction? Jacques Maritain, the great contemporary French philosopher, observed that

authority and power are two different things. Power is the force by means of which you can oblige others to obey you. Authority is the *right* to direct and command, to be listened to or obeyed by others. Authority requests power. Power without authority is tyranny. Thus authority means right . . . [and] since it means right, it has to be obeyed by force of conscience, that is in the manner in which free men obey and for the sake of the common good.[6]

Even a hasty consideration of the proposition Maritain offers for consideration quickly reveals the crucial importance of such terms as "right," "conscience," and "common good" to a total comprehension of authority's dimension. In the entire universe of living matter, only man is presumed to have rights; in this same vast universe, only man is presumed to have a power of reflection and introspection that leads him to approve or disapprove an already committed act, and, finally, only man is charged by himself and by his fellow men to view a contemplated course of action in the light of its possible effects on the rights of others and on the existence of the social organization of which he is a part. Clearly, authority can be the possession of a community peopled by rational beings—not perfectly rational beings, as the Freudians or the behaviorists would be quick to point out, but beings rational in those human acts that so affect themselves or others that they require deliberation and conscious assent.

Authority therefore stresses that reasonableness in man that per-

---

[5] Hannah Arendt, "Authority in the Twentieth Century," *Review of Politics*, Vol. XVIII (October, 1956) , pp. 413–14.

[6] Jacques Maritain, in the *Social and Political Philosophy of Jacques Maritain* (London: G. Bles, 1956) , pp. 89–90.

mits his assent to mandates and propositions whose basic sanction is their own internal logic. Since authority is a faculty that induces assent, to follow authority is to be involved in a voluntary act. De Jouvenel adds the telling note that

authority ends where voluntary assent ends. There is in every state a margin of obedience which is won only by the use of force or the threat of force: it is this margin which breaches liberty and demonstrates the failure of authority. Among free people it is a very small margin because there authority is very great.[7]

Yet, legitimate authority often fails because men themselves fail, and the failures can come equally from the side of governors or governed. A man who obeys a policeman's order to leave a disturbance is assenting to a reasonable injunction; if he refuses the officer's order, the nightstick becomes the instrument of violence.

Extending the concept to the business world, we become aware that in a factory system managerial authority asks of workers three responses: subordination, loyalty, and productivity. Subordination may be achieved through fear and coercion, but what Bendix calls "the internalized ethic of work performance" cannot be realized by these means. Authority must itself be reasonable and must appeal to the reason of those subjected to it.

Authority is a partly legal, partly philosophical, concept, which, though it must be vested in persons, is of necessity impersonal and is relative not to the nature of the individual in whom it is vested but to the nature of the office he holds. One of our proudest boasts in the United States is that ours is an authority of laws and not of men. As a result, men in whom rests the authority to declare how the general welfare shall be served are expected to exert power only in the extreme and as an instrument of flouted authority. Whereas authority tends to reflect the common will, power all too frequently interposes the personal will, for power is resident in men themselves rather than in the offices they hold.

Thus power, unlike authority (which we think of as restricted to

---

[7] Bertrand de Jouvenel, *On Power: Its Nature and the History of Its Growth* (New York: Viking Press, 1949), p. 33. Hannah Arendt stresses the same note: "Authority always demands obedience; it is commonly mistaken for some form of power or violence. Yet, authority precludes the use of external means of coercion; where force is used authority itself has failed." And she adds that we have too readily succumbed to the specious notion that "since violence fulfills the same function as authority, namely, makes people obey, then violence is authority." See "Authority in the Twentieth Century," *op. cit.*, p. 416.

an assigned area) appears to be illimitable, since it is an implement of, as well as a complement to, authority. Its tendency to overflow the natural bounds of authority is what causes alarm and resistance. And it is power exercised without authority that constitutes a threat to freedom, for power is a human capacity before it functions in a social or political capacity. These distinctions become clearer as one considers the need for, sources of, and use of authority in human organization.

Need for Authority

When theorists get down to a discussion of authority, they usually become involved in attempts to answer this question: Why is authority everywhere, and at all times, a persistent feature of all societies? Even among primitive tribes the apparent presence of anarchy veils the subtle ways in which simple people often translate their vision of authority into practical processes. Taboos, dances, and orgies may constitute the outward manifestations of codes that flow from a recognition and acceptance of authority. Nor is it too surprising to note that sanctions against violating authority may be self-imposed.

Answers to the question why authority is always found in society usually take two forms. One asserts, in the Hobbesian tradition, that man are rapacious, reckless, and combative; hence, authority armed with power is a necessary evil, lest unrestrained man bring about his own destruction. The second view asserts that man's nature is a compound of virtue and of vice but that—and this is the interesting point to observe—even if he were as wise as the gods and as gentle as the angels, he would still need authority.

One of the most articulate contemporary exponents of the first point of view is Bertrand de Jouvenel, who proffers the opinion that there is no real difference between authority and power.

Power is authority and makes for more authority. It is force and makes for more force. Or, if a less metaphysical terminology is preferred, ambitious wills, drawn by the lure of Power, expend unceasingly their energies in its behalf that they may bind society in an even tighter grip and extract from it more of its resources.

The process is not uninterrupted, but the checks and recoils which it receives have not prevented the advance of the state through the centuries, as is sufficiently proved by the history of taxation, the history of armies, the history of legislation, and the history of police forces. It is clear enough that the fraction of society's wealth appropriated by public authority is a growing one, as is the fraction of the population which it mobilizes. It regulates private activities more and more closely, and watches more and more narrowly those who are its subjects.[8]

Authority and power flow out of conquest because conquest can give birth to large social formations. De Jouvenel underscores this point by saying that "the state is in essence the result of the successes achieved by a band of brigands who superimpose themselves on small, distinct societies; this band, which is itself organized in a fraternal society, behaves towards the vanquished and the subjected as Power in the pure state."[9] Thus the need for authority, de Jouvenel holds, is largely the result of ambitious wills seeking dominance over others.

A persuasive exponent of the contrary view—that authority and power are distinct and that the former would be a necessary adjunct to human society even if that society were one of saints and sages—is Yves Simon.

Let us now inquire into the reasons why it may be good that a person be regulated in his conduct by some other person rather than by his own reason. To be ruled by another may be expedient or even necessary on the ground of one's inability to rule one's self. This is the case with children. . . .

Thus, it is not only in the theoretical order, which is in no way its proper sphere, but also in the practical order, that authority enjoys substitutional functions. The question is now whether authority has any essential function; whether the necessity of authority always results from some deficiency; whether authority, when necessary, is necessary solely on the ground of some defect in the one who is subjected to it. The idea that authority has no essential function but only substitutional ones, is in fact very widespread. It is current among anarchists and liberal theorists. Let us mention, as particularly representative, Proudhon and J. S. Mill. . . .

The assumption that authority has but substitutional functions has far-reaching consequences, for if authority is made necessary by deficiencies alone, it will be destined to disappear insofar as the deficiencies which make it necessary disappear. This assumption does not mean that authority will ever vanish completely: it is clear that the child will never be able to accomplish self-government, that there will always be feeble-

---

8 De Jouvenel, *op. cit.*, p. 157.

9 *Ibid.*, p. 100.

minded and wicked people. It means that the amount of authority necessary in a society is inversely proportional to the perfection reached by
that society and by the persons and the elementary groups which compose
it. At the ideal term of human progress, the field of authority would be
limited to the government of the youngest children. Thus, the law of
progress would take the form of an asymptotic curve at whose unattainable term there would be a complete elimination of authority.

The best method of ascertaining whether there is such a thing as an
essential function of authority is to consider a community of adults, intelligent and of perfect good will, and to inquire into the requirements of
the common life of that community. (A community composed only of intelligent and good-willed persons is no utopian fiction, provided that we
have in view a very small group, for instance, one formed by a husband
and his wife.) This community, however small it may be, must be regulated in its common action by decisions which bind all its members. How
will these decisions be made? They can be made unanimously, but the
unanimity is not guaranteed. There is no steady principle which could
indefectibly assure this unanimity. Any member of the community under
consideration can disagree with the others as to the best course to take in
the common action. In case of a persistent disagreement, either the unity
of action of the community will be broken, or one judgment will prevail,
which means that some person or some group of persons will be recognized as having authority. I say: *a person or a group of persons,* because
the decision which is to prevail can be issued by a single individual or by
a majority vote of the whole community, or by a majority vote of a selected group within the community as well: as far as the principle of authority is concerned, it makes no difference.

And thus we have pointed out the essential function of authority: to
assure the unity of action of a united multitude. A multitude aiming at a
common good which can be attained only through a common action,
must be united in its action by some steady principle. This principle is
precisely what we call authority.[10]

Of these two views, we find the latter more persuasive. De Jouvenel's position may reflect in large measure the actual manner by
which authority was seized by men in the exercise of their power,
but it fails significantly to point up the real meaning of authority
and why men voluntarily submit to it. Every society must summon
authority for its own maintenance, and what often appears as the
master is in reality the servant of man.

---

[10] Yves Simon, *Nature and Functions of Authority* (Milwaukee: Marquette University Press, 1940) , pp. 7–18 *passim.*

SOURCES OF AUTHORITY

In considering how authority is translated from concept to working mechanism, the inquiry turns from theory to the practical question whether authority is to be viewed as flowing from top to bottom or vice versa. The model that provides the premise for the view that authority must move upward is adopted and adapted from the American political tradition based on consent-of-the-governed theories. Unlike aristocratic societies of other times and other places, the American experiment was launched in 1787 in a highly egalitarian atmosphere. But it is equally true that the Framers were, by present standards, a highly conservative lot. They were firmly convinced that property should determine the suffrage, and they entrusted the task of setting up precise standards to conservative states. They removed control over membership in the most exclusive club in the world, the Senate, from direct taint of popular touch. By all standards, the evidence suggests that these men at Philadelphia desired to perpetuate the genteel tradition in government.

Yet there were sharp breaks with the historic view of government by aristocracy. Ultimate power was believed to reside in the people, and the authority inherent in public office was regarded as a public trust. Regular elections were provided for, to make certain that the authority granted was adequately restrained. The relationship between equality and equality of opportunity was clearly understood. In this sense, therefore, the Framers constituted a forward-looking group. Comparison with other traditions can go a long way toward pointing out where our strengths and weaknesses lie. Incidentally, such comparison can provide a historical backdrop for considering the issue of authority and power from the standpoint of the business organization. Basic differences in managerial ideology may be shown to have relation even to structural differences in bureaucratization.

ANGLO-AMERICAN AND RUSSIAN ATTITUDES

In this respect the history of changes in ideology that have occurred in Anglo-American and in Russian history over the last two centuries offers some valuable clues.[11] During the early stages of industrialization England was dominated by what John Stuart Mill

---

[11] Reinhard Bendix, "Industrialization, Ideologies, and Social Structure," *American Sociological Review*, Vol. XXIV (October, 1959), pp. 613–23. Bendix's challenging propositions provide the focus for our approach.

called the "theory of dependence," which held that the laboring poor are children incapable of thinking for themselves and, therefore, are obliged to render instant obedience to their master-employers. The late 18th century adhered to a creed whose first article of faith was that all authority was at the top. The ruling class was as fore-ordained as was the laboring mass; since the latter was not actually responsible for its sad lot, leadership must attend carefully to its needs. It was a *quid pro quo* concept of trusteeship based on a reciprocal restraint: the obligation of the worker to obey imposed a corresponding obligation on the employer to help.

The 19th century repudiated this doctrine and replaced it with the concept of personal, individual responsibility: everyone was captain of his own ship, and if the vessel went aground one had only oneself to blame. Two aspects of this doctrine deserve note. On the one hand, it clearly represented a step in the direction of democracy, for it encouraged men to rise above the lowly station to which they were born; it was an open invitation to seize opportunity, and opportunity was golden only if a man had sufficient training and skill to take it. Indirectly, then, the doctrine also encouraged the doctrine of equality of opportunity and the spread of free public education. On the other hand, the new dogma of individualism also involved some harsh paradoxes. In the milieu in which it was cast (the dog-eat-dog ethic of social Darwinism), the new look provided a rationale whereby the employer could attribute his own success to ability and effort and the singular lack of fortune among the masses to the latter's inability, shiftlessness, and refusal to work. The excesses that this thinking produced led to a wholesome reaction. "Thus, over the past two hundred years," remarked Bendix, "managerial ideologies in Anglo-American civilization have changed from the 'theory of dependence' to laissez-faire, to Social Darwinism, and finally to the human relations approach."[12]

Interestingly enough, in its assertion of paternal authority and worker dependence, the pattern in Russia offers striking similarities to that of the West. But voluntary associations in England were presumed to have some measure of autonomy, whereas in Russia all authority flowed directly from the tsar. It was the tsar, as the creator and center of all control, who had responsibility for *his* people. The struggle between employers and workers in tsarist Russia was never

---

[12] *Ibid.,* p. 614.

allowed to work itself out in any kind of orderly transition. The tsar kept tight control over both segments by curbing employers' exercise of authority and workers' efforts to organize.

What is interesting from our viewpoint is that when the Russian revolutions of 1905 and 1917 destroyed autocracy, its managerial ideology lived on. While Lenin preached the equality of workers as participants in management, the hard fact was that both supervisor and worker had to give loyal and undeviating submission to the Communist Party.[13] All wisdom is still presumed to reside in a tight group or in the executive secretary of the party, who, like the tsar, knows what is good for *his* people much better than they understand their own good.

The great difference between democratic and totalitarian attitudes toward authority consists in this: free, liberal tradition has encouraged managements to presuppose the possibilities for reasonable discourse between superiors and subordinates, whereas this conviction is lacking in dictatorships. Good faith, good sense, and rule of law are taken for granted by a liberal society in its development of organizations to implement authority. Totalitarian regimes, on the other hand, assume their opposites—worker evasion, irrationality, and disobedience. That is why, in large measure, Joseph Berliner was able to document the systematic subversion of authority by the most successful Soviet managers in their effort to realize business goals.[14] And that was why every Russian factory, office, army unit, and educational association had its work planned, co-ordinated, supervised by some agency of government—as Margaret Mead's study of the Stalinist uses of authority demonstrates. The responsibilities of the party functionary, the secretary, were described by *Pravda* (February 19, 1941) as follows:

As Stalin, and the central organization in whose name Stalin's decisions are phrased, are to the whole of the Soviet Union, so also is each smaller leader to those he leads. The functions of the Party Secretary at the provincial level are there described as follows: ". . . to know the plants exactly, to visit them regularly, to be directly in contact with the plant managers and the corresponding People's Commissariat, to support them in fulfilling the Party's plans and decisions concerning industry and

---

[13] See Margaret Mead, *Soviet Attitudes toward Authority* (New York: McGraw-Hill Book Co., 1956).

[14] Joseph Berliner, *Factory and Manager in the USSR* (Cambridge: Harvard University Press, 1957).

transportation, to control systematically the fulfillment of these decisions, to reveal the defects in the work of the plants and to aim at their removal."[15]

But, as productive efficiency became impaired by the Stalinist Soviet System, the changes demanded for improvements had important influence in mitigating some of the harsher rules and in altering party attitudes toward the dispersal of authority.

The historical contrast between the Anglo-American and Russian traditions was never more effectively demonstrated than in the decision of the Mayflower group over three centuries ago. Here was a band of Pilgrims who had elected to abandon a hostile native political environment and who, perhaps also as a result of the vicissitudes of the voyage,

simply refused to land on strange soil without first having taken the precaution of establishing a constitution of government. The party "solemnly and mutually" bound themselves "together into a civil body politic" for their "better ordering and preservation"; and they agreed to "enact, constitute, and frame" laws for the common welfare to which they promised "all due submission and obedience." It should be remarked that submission and obedience were to be granted only to the *laws duly enacted, constituted* and *framed*. No person or class of persons was empowered by the instruments to assume authority in the new community. And there was no mention of any special knowledge or skills appropriate to the exercise of political authority. The Mayflower Compact became the model for all future agreements of government in America. It is the only form of social contract of which Americans were to have any experience at all.[16]

What is the significance of the Compact? Principally, that it assumed the possibility of dialogue between ruler and ruled and therefore sought to make explicit some basic ground rules for making such a necessary dialogue effective. The history of labor-management relationships in the West during the 19th century reveals an almost complete rupture with the Mayflower precedent, but realignments of power in the 20th century have restored at least the desire to continue the dialogue. Current efforts to maintain and improve

---

[15] Quoted in Mead, *op. cit.*, pp. 54–55.

[16] Norman Jacobson, "Knowledge, Tradition, and Authority: A Note on the American Experience," in Carl Friedrich (ed.), *NOMOS I: Authority* (Cambridge, Mass., 1958), pp. 117–18. Reprinted by permission of The Bobbs-Merrill Co., Inc. Cf. George H. Sabine, *A History of Political Theory* (3d ed.; New York: Holt, Rinehart and Winston, Inc., 1961), pp. 429–33, 440, 531–34, 602–3.

this dialogue are often frustrated by what former Secretary of Labor James Mitchell described as the "gap in the communications process," but the conviction that managers and workers can hammer out the answers to their own problems remains stronger than ever.

TYPES OF AUTHORITY IN BUSINESS

That there are different kinds of management within industry, as there are kinds of government among nations, is obvious. The "ideal" types of business management might be divided into *patriarchal* or patrimonial, *political,* and *professional.*[17]

In the *patriarchal* form the manager runs the enterprise as a virtual dictatorship. The experiences of Henry Ford and Sewell Avery illustrate this type of management in the United States. While this tradition has been somewhat eclipsed within large American corporations, it persists in many newly industrialized nations— for example, in the great majority of Egyptian-owned private concerns—and in some highly developed industrial nations like today's Germany, where owner-managers often appear to believe in a kind of divine-right kingship. French and Italian *(padrone)* management partake of similar views. This managerial philosophy recalls Louis XIV's classic identification of public and private interests in his statement *"l'état, c'est moi."* In such patrimonial enterprises the goals of the firm are family goals, and major decision making usually remains within the narrow circle of kinship.

Political management, which corresponds most closely to the Russian experiences, involves the assignment of key positions primarily on the basis of civic affiliation and loyalties. For many years the Egyptian National Railways had this kind of management. If supranational authorities should ever become more interested in the political than the business affairs of the European Common Market, it could also become more pronounced in western Europe.

Professional management implies that key decision-making positions are held by those who have demonstrated competence. When corporation executives talk, it is usually within the framework of attempts to solve current management and operating problems.

---

[17] The designations of typologies of management are numerous, but these given above appear most useful to our analysis. Cf. Frederick Harbison and Charles Myers, *Management in the Industrial World: An International Analysis* (New York: McGraw-Hill Book Co., 1959) , pp. 68–69.

Thus Harold Smiddy's statement of the management philosophy of General Electric, with its explicit concern for the concept of authority and its emphasis on individual responsibility as a reflection of man as a moral agent, constitutes an interesting exception.[18] At a meeting of business executives held at Indiana University, Mr. Smiddy quoted approvingly the late Dr. Harry A. Hopf's statement that managerial success comes "not through authority of position but through authority of knowledge" and that this authority must be widely shared through a deliberate policy of "decentralized sources of authority."[19]

A pragmatic concern for results rather than dedication to the democratic ideal may well be the motivation for such business practices. Yet may it not be equally true that democracy itself survives because it has met the pragmatic demand for effective results over the long haul?

THE INVESTITURE OF AUTHORITY: THE USERS OF AUTHORITY

What is the process whereby authority falls on certain officers as a consequence of demands for performance of certain functions? How this comes about is difficult to trace, but it might be illustrated by the English jury system. Here was a device that thrust men, as Sir John Fortescue observed, "into the very arcana of the judiciary, and forced them to become finders of fact, and judges in the most important crises of one another's affairs. For better or for worse, the lives, the limbs, the property, the prosperity or adversity, the happiness or sorrow of the bulk of the English people in most of the crises of their lives depended on the knowledge, discretion, good will or judgment of their neighbors."[20] These, it might be recalled, are the essential characteristics of British and American attitudes toward sharing authority that mark their sharp differences from the Russian experience. The forms of investiture develop out of a particular

---

[18] Harold Smiddy, *General Electric's Philosophy and Approach for Management Development* (New York: American Management Association, 1955). See also Roger Blough, *Free Man and the Corporation* (New York: McGraw-Hill Book Co., 1959), pp. 56–79.

[19] "Are Profits and Social Responsibilities Compatible? A Consultation," *Business Horizons*, Vol. II (Summer, 1959), p. 58.

[20] Quoted from Richard O'Sullivan, *The Inheritance of the Common Law* (London: Stevens & Sons, 1950), p. 77.

effort by particular men to meet the exigencies of a particular time. If the process shows consistent and effective results, it becomes a built-in and accepted feature of organization and thus makes the behavior of men in society more predictable.

The history of the English jury system illustrates another interesting feature of authority. The authority of jurors arose because of a specific and difficult task that had to be done—the ascertaining of facts and the making of a judgment thereon. Authority may be said, therefore, to be related to the character of the work for which it is invoked.

From this point flows another corollary. Americans are accustomed to regarding authority and liberty as being in fundamental conflict: to be authoritarian is to be undemocratic. But, if authority assumes a particular form or shape and if this form is related to the kind of work to be done, then progression of freedom corresponds to the progression of authority. Plato's famous example of the authority relationships that existed between the helmsman and his crew is apposite. When the helmsman, during a violent storm, changed course, ordered passengers below, or worked the crew beyond their normal watch, he in no sense violated their freedoms. The more involved and demanding the task, the more intelligence and integrity are required and the greater the measure of authority required to fulfill the need. If the function is legitimate, then the corresponding authority is legitimate; if the authority is legitimate, then the means appropriate to achieving the purpose for which authority exists is legitimate. This is not the same as saying that the end justifies the means. A father's authority does not deny freedom to the child; a manager's authority does not deny freedom to the worker; a president's authority does not deny freedom to the citizen. As a matter of hard fact, the citizen's freedom is greater than the child's, even as the president's authority is greater than the father's, because the adult citizen comprehends more fully the reasonableness of the authority relationship. Does there seem to exist in the foregoing account an uncritical assumption that, since authority creates its own legitimacy, all who acquire it have done so legitimately? Nothing is more extraneous to the thesis. Men may kill, cajole, bribe, and intimidate to acquire functions and with them authority. Those who so act break the pattern of authority itself, which insists as much on reasonable means *to* authority as on reasonable use *of* it.

The upshot of this presentation of the relation of human freedom to authority is that there must be authority in social groups, that it must be exercised in the name of reason, that it is possible to get to an objective code of morality by reason, and that when the state imposes its authority on the individual in the name of this objective code . . . it does not violate his liberty because this code is not against reason, and freedom should be used according to reason.[21]

And investiture follows the performance of legitimate and necessary function. Legitimate need calls authority into being, and, as needs change, the kinds of authority change with them. In a free society there is an almost automatic working-out of the authority relationship and purpose; there is no impressive liturgy, no formal consecrations to mark the conferral of authority as such. Some minor ceremony, however, often accompanies the bestowal of the office that represents the authority on a particular person. Elections and installations of college presidents or corporation chairmen or union executives can approach regal proportions even in a democratic society. But the creation of the office, not the appointment to it, represents the real investiture. Again, we are reminded that authority goes with the office, is impersonal, and is essentially independent of the person who exercises it, even though the degree of acceptance can be mightily influenced by the personality of the officeholder. Weber called this kind of authority "legal-rational."[22]

Since authority involves the imposition of rule by one man over another, it involves necessarily some kind of organization—an insight that has led Drucker to conclude that in an industrialized society it is the "organization rather than the individual who is productive. . . ."[23] Without committing ourselves on the merits of this observation, we may agree that Drucker's recognition of the organization as a reflection of authority and as a productive mechanism for getting things done is surely correct. In labor-management relations, for example, the question of what organization should be invested with what kind of powers touches such issues as nationaliza-

---

[21] Louis J. A. Mercier, "The Problem of Authority and Freedom," in Lyman Bryson *et al.*, *Freedom and Authority in Our Time* (New York: Harper & Bros., 1953) , p. 616. Cf. Richard Peters, *Authority, Responsibility, and Education* (New York: Atherton Press, 1966) .

[22] Max Weber, *The Theory of Social and Economic Organization* (trans. A. M. Henderson and Talcott Parsons) (New York: Oxford University Press, 1947) , p. 328.

[23] Peter F. Drucker, *The New Society* (New York: Harper & Bros., 1950) . p. 6.

tion of industry in Britain, codetermination in Germany, work rules in the United States.

Authority has, in addition to a *who* element, a *what* factor. The substance of authority includes values and their significance to those who have been invested with authority. What are these values? And how do we sense that various authorities are promoting or inhibiting such values?

As to the first question, the following identification of essential values (made by Lasswell and Kaplan) may be reviewed here. They are wealth, well-being, skill, enlightenment, affection, respect, rectitude, and power.[24]

The second question—the promotion or the hindrance of values in a free society—involves dilemmas facing all leaders. It calls for the balancing of relationships between one function and other functions, between one set of values and others. A businessman prizes efficiency and profits, but a grinding efficiency and handsome profits can stultify both human creativity and free market operations. Or how should government authority be limited? Ordinarily, the answer is that political powers should be limited to promoting the common good, which, in practice, means the prosperity and peace of all the citizens. "Prosperity means an equitable access to the available resources required for human activity and evolution. Peace . . . means an environment that permits the citizen to act freely, provided that he does not so intrude on his neighbor that the latter loses his prosperity and liberty."[25] If peace and prosperity are possible without a given restriction by government, the restriction becomes an unwarranted "intrusion" into the lives of the citizens, and no theory can whitewash such action. Extended to the business environment, it means that both managers and workers operate best in an atmosphere of freedom appropriate to their functions.

POWER AND LEADERSHIP

How do we sense the proper limits to the authority exercised by the top executives of a great corporation? Historically, we have railed against bigness per se without ever defining a criterion for

[24] See Harold Lasswell and Abraham Kaplan, *Power and Society* (New Haven: Yale University Press, 1950) , chap v.

[25] Gustav Weigel, "Authority: Intellectual and Political," in Lyman Bryson *et al.*, *op. cit.*, p. 664.

size. We have been sharply critical of monopoly over markets, autocracy in administration, and interference with the political or civic affairs of employees. Yet our attitudes (which often emerge from values alien to the business world) become institutionalized through pragmatic reactions to specific issues or conflicts.

The interplay here between belief and behavior is hard to disentangle. Mary Parker Follett's emphasis on group dynamics is relevant. She asserts that, since power inheres not in one person but

in the combined capacities of a group, we are beginning to think of the leader not as the man who is able to assert his individual will and get others to follow him, but as the one who knows how to relate the different wills in a group so that they will have driving force. It is recognized by many that the most successful president of a business is not usually the one who can force his ideas on his executives, but the one who can make them do the best kind of teamwork.[26]

This view in no way modifies the prudential nature of authority's use where suggestion and persuasion go hand in hand and where a decision is "made and carried out even when [full] agreement cannot be reached."[27]

Honest, capable leadership involves a talent for implementing the static nature of authority with the dynamism of power. This power can be described, in a neutral way, as competence or ability. Such leadership is the best expression of that impulse which prompts free men to agree to live by rules that some few administer but that all obey.

Leadership is the temporary acquisition of a specified amount of authority granted by a group or enterprise to an individual who is considered by the group or enterprise as being most capable of satisfying immediate needs. This authority is withdrawn and transferred to other individuals if the primary source of authority does not perceive observable progress toward goal attainment.[28]

Authority confers on an individual the power to assert the will of the group. There is, in short, power *to,* which is necessary to any leadership backed by authority. It is the illegitimate extension of

---

[26] M. P. Follett, *Dynamic Administration* (New York: Harper & Bros., 1942), pp. 282–83.

[27] Herbert Simon, *Administrative Behavior* (New York: Macmillan Co., 1957), p. 152.

[28] Michael A. Mescon, "The Dynamics of Industrial Leadership," *Journal of the Academy of Management,* Vol. I (August, 1958), p. 13.

power *to* into power *over* that disturbs the free citizen. For the drive to power is a natural human drive and not an abstract, rational-legal convention like authority. It can overreach the bounds of any job orientation and thus change from the acceptable civic level of power *to* into the social pathology of power *over*.

With the rise of large-scale organization in the 20th century, this potential of power has caused considerable dismay, especially with regard to the power inherent in economic organization. More lately, as the authority of government undertakes to control the power of economic organization, many are additionally dismayed at the prospect of a developing government power.

In the series of values cited by Lasswell and Kaplan, we have noted that power occupies a significant place. Power is valued as the ultimate instrument of control. It can be exercised legitimately when it is employed by the officeholder to discharge efficiently the functions of that office. But if it exceeds means that are appropriate to the function, it can quickly become illegitimate.

Of course, power can exist without authority. The robber who holds a man at gunpoint will just as surely achieve compliance as a policeman armed with the same kind of weapon. Yet authority frequently provokes a reaction very like the response to such naked power. Numerous examples within industry itself show that this is the case. The job of getting people to accept authority by persuasion rather than coercion has always been a persistent challenge to leadership.

RESOURCES FOR POWER

For our purposes, we are content to define power as a drive to affect the values and/or behavior of others, even when there is unwillingness to conform, and ability to employ force to assure desired behavior.[29] It need not be exercised by one having title to office, and it may not be intended for the common weal. Power is

---

[29] Power can be approached from many angles: (1) its location in kinds of elites (Daniel Lerner and Harold Lasswell, *The Policy Sciences* [Stanford: Stanford University Press, 1951]); (2) access or avenues to power (David Truman, *The Governmental Process* [New York: Alfred A. Knopf, 1951]); (3) as a reflection of social structure (R. A. Brady, *Business as a System of Power* [New York: Columbia University Press, 1943]). For general treatments see R. H. Tawney, *Equality* (New York: Macmillan Co., 1931); Bertrand Russell, *Power: A New Social Analysis*, chaps. i and ii (New York: W. W. Norton & Co., 1938); Albert Mueller-Deham, *Human Relations and Power*, Part II (New York: Philosophical Library, 1957); and Will Herberg, *Judaism and Modern Man* (New York: Farrar, Strauss and Young, 1951), pp. 175–83.

the capacity to get things done either in a certain manner or for a certain purpose or both. It has its own instruments, and the arsenal includes propaganda, influence, violence, threat, flattery—and the list is by no means exhausted.

Every major organization possesses certain assets that permit it to employ with greater or less effect whatever power it has acquired. For a nation, these would include food and raw materials, the size, age level, and education of its population, the quantity and quality of the armed forces, the "national morale," the vitality and resiliency of its government, the skills of its diplomacy, and its position vis-à-vis potential friends or enemies.[30]

Corporate resources include large amounts of capital or access to it; specialized knowledge and skills; ability to hire, fire, and lay off the work force; power to affect wide markets; funds to sustain political pressure groups; and the like. The inner dynamics of these resources for power have led to contrasting conclusions. Adolf Berle, for example, sees hope that the corporate conscience will restrain any lust for power, whereas Robert Brady concludes that business management is a predatory, self-seeking, self-serving, and power-hungry elite checked only by the countervailing of power of government.[31]

What of labor's resources for power? John L. Lewis could count a labor movement that numbered a little over 2 million workers, or less than 6 percent of the labor force. Today unions enroll 17 million workers, or a quarter of the labor force. Yet it is hard to assert that the power of the Reuthers, MacDonalds, or Currans is greater than that of their business contemporaries, the Fords, Bloughs, or Humphries, because steel workers can shut down 88 percent of steel-making capacity in a 1959 strike or the Transport Workers Union can grind the gigantic Pennsylvania Railroad to a halt.[32] The situation defies precise measurement and precise judgment. The loss of union membership in the past decade, when the labor force itself

---

[30] See Hans J. Morgenthau, *Politics among Nations: The Struggle for Power and Peace* (New York: Alfred A. Knopf, 1960), chap. ix.

[31] See Adolf A. Berle, Jr., *The 20th Century Capitalist Revolution* (New York: Harcourt Brace & Co., 1954), and Brady, *Business as a System of Power* (New York: Columbia University Press, 1953), Cf. also Alpheus Mason, "Business Organized as Power: The New *Imperium in Imperio*," *American Political Science Review*, Vol. XLIV (June, 1950), pp. 323–42.

[32] James Kuhn, "The Myths of Labor's Power," *The New Leader*, Vol. XLIII (September 19, 1960), pp. 18–21.

was growing, imposes a sharp restriction on generalization. Numbers alone do not tell the story, and, so long as unions can exercise ability to withhold essential workers in essential industries, their power must be reckoned with as considerable.

Beyond this, there is the question how the union power represented by the vast funds accumulated in union treasuries and in pension and welfare funds is to be used and safeguarded. And, internally, there is concern over growing centralization within the union, which could result in a denial of workers' rights. Benjamin Selekman has remarked that "with union security clauses so widespread, the opportunity to work depends a great deal on how a man stands in his unions."[33]

THE AUTHORITY DILEMMA

It sometimes appears that both corporations and labor unions have, like Topsy, "just growed." Lacking any conscious polity, they are forced in times of stalemate to turn to governmental authority for arbitration of grievances. It is not strange that under the duress of conducting "business as usual" they have not had time to consider what the sheer size of their "citizenry" might need in the way of government. What is curious is that, though the numbers they represent are really legion, the problem of polity that follows upon the organization of any society goes largely unheeded among them. As a result, government must adjudicate.

Yet, whenever one or the other of these power centers loses a round, there are loud cries of "statism," "privilege," "republicanism," and even "communism," depending on how the decision goes. The public is reminded that there is a worse fate than domination of its affairs by either business or labor, namely the planned society, which dominates everything and everybody. Government control means the triumph of bureaucracy, it is said, and the average citizen has had too much of that already to be willing to encourage more.

But, until some internal control is developed over those economic decisions that have wide public impact, it seems inevitable that government as the representative of the public will have to make itself felt and heard. The will of the people asserted through elected representatives is not necessarily a symptom either of tyranny or of public power's minding something other than its political

---

[33] Benjamin M. Selekman, *A Moral Philosophy for Management* (New York: McGraw-Hill Book Co., 1959), pp. 202–3.

business. It would seem to imply, rather, that there is an authority vacuum and that the substitute for lack of firm and formulated internal governance within corporations and unions is some kind of external control.

Corporate power is now so influential that it is possible to imagine that the corporation might continue to function after the revocation of its charter (independent not only of public sanction but also of the traditional restraint of competition), an institution to be reckoned with because it is there, first on the list of those vital institutions that must survive if men are to preserve their lives. And labor power, born as it was of freedom to associate and the individual drive for justice and equality, may ultimately, as it appears to hope, be influential enough, in spite of constitutional guarantees, to unionize everyone.

We may conclude that two dynamic and influential private governments exist within the borders of this republic, the corporation and the union. They hold a power they perhaps never planned for, since they seem to have little internal discipline that might contain it. When their power to do what they were organized to do has begun to overflow into power over other sectors of society, it has, thus far, been controlled only by external public restraint. What must be decided sometime soon is whether a situation that necessitates public intervention in private governments is as much a threat to freedom as those decisions, whether of business or labor, that come between the individual citizen and his right to life, liberty, and the pursuit of happiness. For it is part of the nature of freedom that it exists for all only where every man's right to it is respected.

RECOMMENDED READING

BALL, GEORGE W. *The Discipline of Power: Essentials of a Modern World Structure*. Boston: Atlantic–Little, Brown, 1968.

BERLE, ADOLF A. *The American Economic Republic*. New York: Harcourt, Brace & World, Inc., Harvest Book Edition, 1965.

DAHL, ROBERT A., and LINDBLOM, CHARLES E. *Politics, Economics, and Welfare*, Part IV: "Four Central Sociopolitical Processes." New York: Harper & Bros., 1953.

DEUTSCH, KARL W. *The Nerves of Government: Models of Political Communication and Control* (with a new Introduction). New York: The Free Press, 1966.

EELLS, RICHARD. *The Government of Corporations.* New York: The Free Press, 1962.

FRIEDRICH, CARL J. *Man and His Government,* Part II: "The Dimensions of Power and Justice." New York: McGraw-Hill Book Co., 1963.

McDOUGAL, MYRES S. and Associates. *Studies in World Public Order,* esp. Chapter 1, "The Identification and Appraisal of Diverse Systems of Public Order"; Chapter 5, "The Rights of Man in the World Community"; and Chapter 12, "Perspectives for an International Law of Human Dignity." New Haven: Yale University Press, 1960.

SILVER, ISADORE. "The Corporate Ombudsman," *Harvard Business Review,* June, 1967, pp. 77–87.

FURTHER READING

BACHRACH, PETER. *Corporate Authority and Democratic Theory,"* in SPITZ, DAVID (ed.), *Political Theory and Social Change.* New York: Atherton Press, 1967.

BARNARD, CHESTER I. *The Functions of the Executive,* chap. xii. Cambridge: Harvard University Press, 1938.

BENDIX, REINHARD, and LIPSET, SEYMOUR MARTIN (eds.). *Class, Status, and Power: A Reader in Social Stratification.* New York: The Free Press, 1953.

CARTWRIGHT, DORWIN. (ed.) *Studies in Social Power.* Ann Arbor: Research Center for Group Dynamics, Institute for Social Research, University of Michigan, 1959.

FRIEDRICH, CARL J. (ed.). *NOMOS I: Authority.* Cambridge: Harvard University Press, 1958.

HALE, ROBERT L. *Freedom through Law: Public Control of Private Governing Power.* New York: Columbia University Press, 1952.

KERR, CLARK, et al. *Industrialism and Industrial Man,* Chapter 6, "Managers of Enterprises: Their Power, Position, and Policies." Cambridge, Mass.: Harvard University Press, 1960.

LINDBLOM, CHARLES E. "Democracy and Economic Structure," in William N. Chambers *et al.* (eds.), *Democracy in the Mid-Twentieth Century: Problems and Prospects.* St. Louis: The Washington University Press, 1960.

LIPSET, SEYMOUR M. *Political Man: The Social Basis of Politics,* Part IV: "The Politics of Private Government: A Case Study." Garden City, N.Y.: Doubleday & Co., 1960.

LYFORD, JOSEPH. *The Agreeable Autocracies.* New York: Oceana Publications, 1961.

MASON, EDWARD S. "The Apologetics of 'Managerialism'," *The Journal of Business,* Vol. XXXI (January, 1958), pp. 1–11.

MILLER, ARTHUR S. *Private Governments and the Constitution.* Santa Barbara, Cal.: Center for the Study of Democratic Institutions, 1959.

OSGOOD, ROBERT E., and TUCKER, ROBERT W. *Force, Order, and Justice,* Part II: "The Rationale of Force." Baltimore: The Johns Hopkins Press, 1967.

18. Pluralism

OUTLINE

PLURALISM always implies multiplicity, frequently diversity, and sometimes conflict. It is as much the generator as the result of freedom. Pluralism is intimately associated with toleration as opposed to bigotry, with voluntarism as opposed to coercion, and with a happy blending of individualism and associationism. A pluralistic society reflects those differences of interests that characterize the large, modern nation-state. In a pluralistic society the existence of many autonomous groups makes tyranny by the majority less likely.

Pluralism is concerned with the roles that these autonomous associations can play as a result of the power they enjoy, with the interplay of forces among these various groups as they enhance or

464

diminish a specific group's power, and with the effect of power blocs on individual freedom and creativity.

SOME RELATED PHILOSOPHICAL PRESUPPOSITIONS

Pluralism encompasses an aim (wide diffusion of power) and a structure (voluntary groups operating between the national government and the citizen in a manner that neither subordinates nor dominates the individual), but it also involves a method for evaluating results. This method does not seek to construct broad social programs on the basis of prior fixed dogma but relies on the consequences flowing from various groups' actions for the emergence of policy. Pluralism is less concerned with the lack among Americans of a "public philosophy"—to use Lippmann's apt phrasing—than it is with the loss of a "sharp perception of consequence" by the leaders of these various private sectors in American society.[1] This emphasis on the weighing of consequences of actions already consummated is a major strand in the peculiarly American philosophy of pragmatism as expounded by William James and John Dewey.

Even so, pluralism also rests on certain natural-law tenets. It draws inspiration from the essentially medieval "two-swords" concept of a division of authority between lay and secular governments and from a recognition that ultimate sanctions for the exercise of secular powers spring—as Aquinas argued in his *Governance of Rulers*[2]—from the people themselves. This notion has been resurrected in modern times under the guise of the "principle of subsidiarity," which holds that the state should restrict its functions to those areas that, while essential to the common good, cannot be effectively discharged by private associations. Indeed, this is a theme that appears as frequently in papal encyclicals on the social order as it does in the writings of liberal, secular theorists.

From a political standpoint, pluralism seeks to build a bridge connecting the traditions of liberalism and conservatism in American history. In the liberal tradition, pluralism is marked by references to problems rather than solutions, by faith in change rather

---

[1] For contrast see Walter Lippmann, *Essays in the Public Philosophy* (Boston: Little, Brown & Co., 1955); and David Truman, "The American System in Crisis," *Political Science Quarterly*, Vol. LXXIV (December, 1959), pp. 481–93.

[2] Thomas Aquinas, *Governance of Rulers*. For the gist of these ideas see Dino Bigongiari, *The Political Ideas of St. Thomas Aquinas* (New York: Hafner Publishing Co., 1957).

than a change of faith. This liberalism insists that transformation and reformation are the natural products of a pluralistic and creative society. Pluralism's conservative lineaments show in its skepticism of state power and centralized state planning, on the one hand, and in its esteem of local responsibility and states' rights, on the other. The conservative tradition, conscious of Lord Acton's dictum that "power tends to corrupt, and absolute power corrupts absolutely," seeks to interpose as many viable voluntary associations between the nation-state and the citizen as possible.

The objectives of the following analysis are twofold: to provide a conceptual foundation for treating a phenomenon that has been, almost uniquely, a major characteristic of our society and to relate the concept of pluralism to the contemporary business system in a meaningful fashion. On this latter point, it should be observed that pluralism affects the institution of business in two very direct and relevant ways. In the first instance, there is the task of defining what powers are appropriate to the business and the nonbusiness sectors of society. Second, there is the problem of understanding the widely variegated patterns of organizations that have sprung up to assume powers that are open to the business sector as a whole. Why, for example, has the large corporation become the major instrument for the conduct of our business affairs? How is this giant related to the numerous small businesses on its periphery? Here the clash between the goal of efficiency, on the one hand, and the kind of pluralism typified by small, locally controlled and operated business firms, on the other, neatly illustrates the relationship of theory to fact. And there are the further ramifications of power centers in business (represented by government corporations like TVA, the New York Port Authority, and various turnpike commissions, not to mention the better known examples of partnerships and trade associations) that influence and have influenced our historic understanding of the concept of pluralism.

WORKING DEFINITIONS AND DISTINCTIONS

Pluralism seeks to diffuse power into many organizations and groupings and thus to prevent the development of imbalances of power and to assure the freedom of the individual from the tyranny of the one, the few, or the many. It constitutes a continuing challenge to totalitarianism of every kind, whether the rule be held by a political dictator, by a business or labor oligarchy, or by the masses themselves. It is suspicious of claims to omniscience, and omnipotence and is therefore as much opposed to the ambitious pretenses of a James Stuart (the king can do no wrong), as it is to the Rousseauian version of democracy (the collectivity can do no wrong).

Pluralism takes many forms. It can be seen in the American doctrine of the separation of church and state, which recognizes the right of sects to exist and to preach their various creeds but denies any one of them the powerful support of the civil arm. Spurred by memories of the unfortunate consequences of a state religion—of Torquemada in the Spanish Inquisition, of Luther and his entente with the German princes, of Calvin's stern domination of the Geneva theocracy, and of Henry VIII's exploitation of the Anglican clergy—Americans have become firmly convinced that religious pluralism represents the best formula for preserving the religious group's autonomy and the integrity of the individual conscience.

The manifestations of pluralism in the political community are also apparent. The debates of Hamilton and Jefferson, of Webster and Hayne, of Lincoln and Douglas, offer practical illustration of a common effort to refine the doctrine of pluralism on specific matters of great national import. In the business community the manful struggle, since the days of the Sherman antitrust laws, to define the limits of autonomy and monopoly of the giant combines offers another illustration of the pervasive quality of pluralism.

Since pluralism encourages the growth of new forms of association to meet hitherto unprecedented needs, it is constantly enmeshed in certain unavoidable forms of ambiguity. The Port of New York Authority, for example, has emerged as a form of political-economic association designed to meet the transportation problems of a metropolitan area that spills over state boundaries. Its charter flows from the powers of New York and New Jersey, but its heavy immersion in problems of interstate commerce has created vexations as to control and definition. Yet the nation as a whole tolerates with good humor the political maneuverings and legal skirmishes that are inherent in pluralistic politics, confident that pluralism is a constitutional device of such immeasurable value in encouraging ingenuity that temporary dislocations are a small price to pay.

PLURALISM AND CONSTITUTIONALISM

The basic concern of pluralism, as a constitutional device, is with the distribution of authority and functions, first among various major sectors of the national life (political, economic, religious, and cultural) and then among the various kinds of associations within each of these major sectors. Pluralism and constitutionalism share a common skepticism toward concentrations of power.

An important element of constitutionalism is to be found in the perennial search by the individual man for an inner fortress of the soul that cannot be taken by the very institution to which he gives allegiance. It is an attempt to ward off what appears to be the irresistible urge of every organization to demand eventually the complete loyalties of its members. As Frank Tannenbaum has observed:

These perennial institutions, structured about the incommensurable experiences of man, all in their turn claim him as their own. He is a member of each of them and cannot escape them. The very content of life is found within their framework, and their claim upon it is in each case a total claim. Quite without deliberate intent, these institutions, in turn, in the unplanned insistence to fulfill the need represented by the unique experience around which they are structured, tend to embrace all of the life of man. They compete not merely for his loyalty, but also for the exercise of the innumerable responsibilities and functions, and the satisfaction of the innumerable needs and aspirations that the life of man generates in a living world. The difficulty lies in the fact that the field, though it be complex, is limited, and that whatever one institution performs, and takes upon itself to perform, is at the expense of the other.[3]

Elliott and McDonald have viewed the problem in this light:

Pluralism, as a political philosophy which attacked the whole basis of the State as a sovereign community exercising control over its members and over internal groups, with moral validity drew most of its inspiration from the idea that many other types of groups had wills as real as the State's. Indeed, if one allows to the State itself a true general will in the manner of Rousseau or of Hegel or of Dr. Bosanquet, there can be little ground for denying real wills to other types of associations such as the

_____

[3] Frank Tannenbaum, "Institutional Rivalry in Society," in R. C. Synder and H. H. Wilson (eds.), *Roots of Political Behavior: Introduction to Government and Politics* (New York: American Book Co., 1949), p. 169.

Church and, perhaps, professional associations and labor unions. . . .

Actually, the use of the term "will" in the same sense that it is applied to the will of an individual person is inappropriate to describe what is more properly an organization of wills that make up the State or, for that matter, other associations governed by a shared general purpose. That the character of the purpose of the democratic and constitutional state is different both in kind and in degree from those of other associations within it, must be a cardinal point for any modern democratic political theory.[4]

From the viewpoint of the individual's reactions and needs, Walter Lippmann has offered this rationale for pluralism:

Each man finds himself the center of a complex of loyalties. He is loyal to his government, he is loyal to his state, he is loyal to his village, he is loyal to his neighborhood. He has his own family. He has his wife's family. He has his church. . . . He may be an employer. . . . He may be an employee. . . . He is a buyer in many markets. . . . He is a seller. . . . He owns shares in many businesses. . . . He belongs to a political party, to clubs, to a social set. The multiplicity of his interests make it impossible for him to give his whole allegiance to any person or to any institution.

The statement that modern society is pluralistic cannot, then, be dismissed as a newfangled notion invented by theorists. It is a sober description of the actual facts. Each man has countless interests through which he is attached to a very complex social situation. The complexity of his allegiance cannot fail to be reflected in his political conduct.[5]

Since the widest latitude for individual freedom is the ultimate objective of a pluralist society, such a society always approves of any device or process that disperses the decision-making power. On this point Hayek adds a very valid insight when he observes:

The reason why a division of powers between different authorities always reduces the power that anybody can exercise is not always understood. It is not merely that the authorities will, through mutual jealousy, prevent one another from exceeding their authority. More important is the fact that certain kinds of coercion require the joint and coordinated use of different powers or the employment of several means, and, if these

---

[4] William Y. Elliott and Neil A. McDonald, *Western Political Heritage* (New York: Prentice-Hall, 1949), pp. 871–72.

[5] Walter Lippmann, *A Preface to Morals* (New York: Macmillan Co., 1929), pp. 268–69.

means are in separate hands, nobody can exercise those kinds of coercion.[6]

Yet there is another side to this question. Carried to extreme lengths, this division of power and responsibility can lead to chaos. If power becomes so fragmented that no individual or group can act in behalf of the common weal, with ensuing incentives for creativity, society becomes frustrated. Responsibility for the performance of *specific* function does not guarantee that any group will bear responsibility for the functioning of the *whole*. Society is not simply the sum of its individual parts.

PLURALISM AND MARXISM

There is one further distinction to be noted. We have seen that implicit in the notion of pluralism is acceptance of the reality of inevitable competition among group interests. Karl Marx made the same assumptions in developing his dialectic for communism. Yet the varying emphases given these notions by Marxist and Western noncommunist theorists have led them to startlingly different conclusions. Marx was himself persuaded that pluralism consists only in terms of *classes,* such as peasants, feudal landlords, bourgeoisie, and the like, whereas liberals have insisted that the groupings of a pluralist society transcend simple class distinctions. Marx also concluded that the political behavior of men was determined by their economic interests, whereas Western pluralism recognizes that men often act to further the interests of their church, their country, their province, or their leader.

There is one other area in which the Communist and Western variants of pluralism are startlingly dissimilar. The West believes that negotiation and compromise are the appropriate methods for resolving differences among various groups, whereas Marx's insistence on violent conflict is too well known to need detailed elaboration. The ultimate difference, of course, is that, before the withering of the state into the classless society envisioned by Marx, it was the government that would reserve to itself all monopoly of power. Other groups, existing only by sufferance of the state, are allowed to function only to the degree that they sustain and further the state's purposes. To claim a pluralism for a Marxist society is—as Djilas in *The New Class* so convincingly showed—to embrace a fable.

---

[6] Friedrich A. Hayek, *The Constitution of Liberty* (Chicago: University of Chicago Press, 1960), pp. 184–85.

PLURALISM IN THEORY AND IN PRACTICE

EARLY PATTERNS

Since pluralism is so vitally concerned with human freedom, there is a tendency to conclude that the history of pluralism coincides with the history of freedom. But this is not so. Unlike the ideal of freedom, the concept of pluralism was alien to Roman thought and practice, which conceived of a social order based on a universal state, a universal language, and a universal law. For accelerated growth, pluralism requires, paradoxically enough, a period of disorder. Only when the dominion of the Roman scepter waned, and men were forced to shift for themselves in creating and adapting new associations to meet needs once carefully tended and superintended by a powerful central authority, did pluralism begin to flourish. It is not too much to suggest that certain power vacuums must develop before private associations receive enough impetus to move forward vigorously.

Thus it was not until the medieval period that conditions conducive to pluralism existed. This was the time when authority everywhere was dispersed and challenged.

Church and state, pope and emperor, emperor and king, king and baron, lord and vassal are in continual opposition. Society is divided into estates which are often in a high degree class-conscious, but nowhere is there a national consciousness. Decrees of emperor, pope, and king, which frequently conflict with one another, are opposed and checked by local law and custom.[7]

It should be observed, parenthetically, that divided authority meant neither efficiency, productivity, nor public order for the medieval citizen.

The assertion of absolute sovereigty by the newly emerging nation-states of the 16th century implied the rejection of this division of authority. From that point forward it became the heroic endeavor of humane political philosophers in the West to formulate a theory that would mitigate the harsh rigors of a political system inhospitable to private, intermediary organizations. The intellectual assignment these philosophers set themselves was, among other

---

[7] H. Krabbe, *The Modern Idea of the State* (trans. with Introduction by George H. Sabine and Walter J. Shepard) (New York: Appleton & Co., 1922), p. xvi.

things, to enunciate a philosophically tenable defense of pluralism. They fashioned a concept that, in its internal logic, in its simplicity, and in its appeal to the instincts of free men, would eventually excite and rally sufficient support to challenge concentrated power.

The modern notion of sovereignty, as Hocking has noted, was "a sixteenth century artifact" that represented "a complete misreading of the historical situation, the futile attempt of the state to concentrate and usurp an authority which had in reality become dispersed, fluid, and widely humane."[8] The state at length had to pass for what it was worth, and its yield in terms of human welfare and effective liberty tended to dissipate its traditional aura. Nor was this the less true in the resurgence of nationalism after World War I. Not only the excesses of Fascism and Nazism, both extremely nationalistic movements, but also the disruptive nationalism of liberal regimes, tended to bring the state into disrepute among many political theorists. Within all states, again to quote Hocking, who wrote in the twenties, "all hierarchies become suspect; authorities are in a safer position when they assume a preliminary equality and fraternity among themselves, and adopt federal relations rather than relations of subjection to a political overlordship"; and in the world arena, "nationalistic exaltation of political entities is felt to be the storing of an international powder mine, and as a matter of theory the survival of a superstition which it is now time to cast off."[9]

ENGLISH AND AMERICAN PLURALISTS

Political pluralism—a tendency in many writers and social movements at the turn of the century and after—can be traced back at least to Otto Gierke's insistence that from medieval times other groups than the state have had lives of their own which the state is bound to respect and to Maitland's translation of a part of Gierke's historical work into the highly influential *Political Theories of the Middle Age* (1900). Thereafter, writers in England, on the Continent, and in the United States, have pursued the subject into many aspects of authority in what we now term the "private sector." In an extreme form, political pluralism once took the form of complete denial of sovereignty to the state. Even in the less extreme forms, pluralism has insisted that the state must share fortunes of ascend-

---

[8] William Ernest Hocking, *Man and the State* (New Haven, Conn.: Yale University Press, 1926), p. 85.

[9] *Ibid.*, pp. 86–87.

ancy with other aspirants, and that good political doctrine requires that we follow the natural lines of authority in the social order; at times the state, at other times and places the church, and even ethnic and economic groupings will justifiably determine the dominant authority centers of society. But in its more usual form, political pluralism backs down from any radical revision of traditional constitutional authority in the state, with its force-using power in reserve to assert dominance when necessary. Unlike the anarchists, the pluralists do not challenge the whole apparatus of state-force. Hocking saw them asserting hardly more than the importance of group authority and of its migrations, and an appeal for modest deference to these and other authorities on the part of governments.

In the United States, the major effect of political pluralism as theory has been to spur the study of the governmental process as a process that involves an intricate complex of group interrelationships. On the descriptive and analytical side of political theory, the result has been a vast literature on pressure groups and political dynamics since the trail-blazing work of A. F. Bentley in 1908, *The Process of Government*. On the normative side, the basic position of the English pluralists has appealed to many Americans; this position, as stated by Frederic M. Watkins, is that:

Politics in a proper constitutional democracy is a game in which all who so wish are invited to compete as fully and freely as possible. This is the essential difference, indeed, between democracy and totalitarianism. But games need rules to define the permissible strategies of competition, and to permit a clearcut decision as to who has rightfully won. The democratic state is a neutral empire which enforces the rules of the game, as laid down by the law and usages of the constitution. It is also an impartial executive, which rewards the rightful winner, in the interval between matches, by carrying out the political decisions for which the winning team has fought. For the proper performance of its functions, both as empire and as executive, the state is vested with sovereign authority, and may apply coercive measures against anyone who tries to step out of line. By preference it ought not, however, to be an active contestant in the game itself. Its function is to supervise, and to validate the outcome of, a never-ending series of contests and negotiations between rival pressure groups. Such is the nature of the decision-making process in any well-ordered constitutional democracy.[10]

---

[10] F. M. Watkins, "The English Pluralists Reconsidered," a paper prepared for delivery at the 1961 annual meeting of the American Political Science Association.

The Critique of Pluralism

The assumptions on which the English pluralists based their work were never fully realistic, as Watkins has pointed out, and they were daily becoming more incompatible with the realities of contemporary politics. The English pluralists had been worried about the dangers of excessive authority. Contemplating a political system so deeply entrenched and so widely accepted that few would think of challenging its decisions, they had sought, in the interests of social justice, to weaken its hold on the minds of men, and to encourage a wider diffusion of political responsibilities. This made some sense, granting their assumptions. But for Watkins the most spectacular feature of contemporary politics was the unprecedentedly rapid and widespread disintegration of political authority. He saw colonial regimes collapsing in droves, leaving behind them native governments whose authority was, in most cases, either precarious or nonexistent. Vast areas of Europe and Asia were held down by Communist regimes that had to rely, in large though varying measure, on coercion rather than consent. In the noncommunist world, he saw large and growing numbers of people transferring their allegiance to Communist movements which believed, in principle, in the illegitimacy of all noncommunist governments. Pretorianism, once a Latin-American specialty, was turning up everywhere, and even in France the army could no longer be relied upon to obey its legitimate rulers. Now, the survival of constitutional democracy was going to depend, for a long and unpredictable future, on the development of effective leadership, and on an increasingly widespread and enlightened sense of the values and responsibilities of democratic citizenship. It would no longer be possible, if indeed it ever had been, to rely on a decision-making process that asks the government to stand idly by while pressure groups fight it out between themselves, expecting the spontaneous generation of public goods through the balancing of private interests.

This view of pluralism has been increasingly reflected in criticism of the group interpretation of politics. It is said that too many academic studies of this kind are "derived from the premise of pluralism" and then "proceed compulsively to vindicate it."[11] Early

---

[11] Henry S. Kariel, *The Decline of American Pluralism* (New York: The Free Press, 1961), p. 3. His study, *The Promise of Politics* (Englewood Cliffs, N.J.: Prentice-Hall, Inc., 1966), Parts I and IV, further develops this critique.

theorists of pluralism are said to have relied too much on certain organizations to sustain the individual against the oppression of a unified government, while these very organizations have now become oligarchically governed hierarchies that dangerously threaten democracy. In Kariel's terms, "the theory of pluralism under conditions of large-scale technology conflicts with the principles of constitutional democracy."[12]

The critique of pluralism emphasizes the dangers of social disruption by many kinds of groups, including racist elements, but for the student of business institutions the most important critics are those who assert the necessity of stronger governmental controls of economic life, as against the older view of a self-regulating market with private-sector countervailing controls operating automatically in the public interest. Andrew Shonfield, an English economist, states the case clearly:

Increasingly the realization is forced upon us that the market, which purports to be the reflection of the way in which people spontaneously value their individual wants and efforts, is a poor guide to the best means of satisfying the real wishes of consumers. That is because market prices generally fail to measure either social costs or social benefits. . . . Unless the state actively intervenes, and on an increasing scale, to compel private enterprise to adapt its investment decisions to considerations such as these, the process of economic growth may positively impede the attainment of things that people most deeply want.[13]

The thrust of science, we are told, is toward a rational control of resources and a rational solution of social problems through planning, a viewpoint at odds with the capitalist creed of the self-regulating market economy that "abdicates as much decision-making as possible to the rule of profits."[14]

THE AMERICAN EXPERIENCE

How to make central government control in nation-states compatible with democracy is a problem that pluralists must face, and it involves both politics and economics. One answer in political terms

---

[12] *Ibid.*

[13] Andrew Shonfield, *Modern Capitalism: The Changing Balance of Public and Private Power* (New York & London: Oxford University Press, 1965) , p. 22. Cf. the views of Robert L. Heilbroner, *The Limits of American Capitalism* (New York: Harper & Row, 1966) .

[14] Robert L. Heilbroner, "The Future of Capitalism," *Commentary*, April, 1966, p. 28.

is that the public interest is best served not by small competing political constituencies but by large ones nationally based, such as the party system, the Presidency, and the national government. One critic of the pluralists' faith that liberty and equality are best served by grass-roots voters, dispersed political power, and the deference of government to private groups with concrete, narrow interests, declares that the public interest becomes lost in the contentions of private interest groups, and that these groups more often than not continue to work their will with the collaboration of the new regulative agencies, such as the FCC, the CAB, and the ICC.[15] American democracy, according to this view, can succeed only if we recognize that while political power cannot be abolished and we must get over a traditional fear and distrust of the state, we must also make sure that the state speaks for the entire nation as its constituency and not for pressure and special-interest groups in the guise of national interest.

On the other side of this argument about pluralist theory and practice is the more conservative position, well expressed by Robert Strausz-Hupé:

I believe what has kept the flavor of American Democracy sweet has been the citizenry's abiding distrust of authority and the vigor and variety of associations, from family and church to corporation and trade union, flourishing in the private sector of life. The excellence of the Constitution, devised as a safeguard against the despotism of the one and the many, monarch and mob, would have stood for little had the American people allowed politics to encroach on the profusion of their private associations and on the idiosyncrasies and the very disorderliness of their everyday lives.[16]

EQUILIBRIUM AND PUBLIC INTEREST

GOVERNMENT

When it is remembered that constitutionalism was historically viewed as a device for curbing the power only of public governments and that private associations were presumed to be free from such restraints, we can begin to appreciate the dilemma posed by our

---

[15] Grant McConnell, *Private Power and American Democracy* (New York: Alfred A. Knopf, 1966) .

[16] Robert Strausz-Hupé, *In My Time* (New York: W. W. Norton & Co., 1965) , pp. 127–28.

growing awareness that major policies today are often made outside the government. This raises the question how such decisions can be made in what Lippmann calls the "public interest." Peter Drucker formulates the question in this way: "Should government be the representative of major interest groups, the arbiter between them, or the guardian of the common weal against them all?"[17] This problem seems certain to rise again and again when decisions must be made about labor-management relations and the pricing policies of business.

Taking a hard look at both business and labor organizations, Wolfgang Friedmann has concluded that

the corporate organizations of business *and* labor have long ceased to be private phenomena. That they have a direct and decisive impact on the social, economic, and political life of the nation is no longer a matter of argument. It is an undeniable fact of daily experience. The challenge to the contemporary lawyer is to translate the social transformation of these organizations from private associations to public organisms into legal terms.[18]

Labor reporter A. H. Raskin testified to the same basic concern as Friedmann, when he wrote:

The clear need is for a more fundamental acceptance by all the forces in our interrelated economy of the extent to which their private interests must be subordinated to the larger needs of the community. Up to now each has been much too preoccupied with explaining why what is good for it is good for everybody.[19]

WITHIN THE BUSINESS COMMUNITY

The very power that each of three major components of our society—government, business, and labor—can mount in dealing with one another has led leadership in government, in business, and in unions to concentrate naturally enough on the interplay among the rivals. Yet within the business community itself there are additional autonomous or semiautonomous groups that demand attention. Two excellent examples of neglected groups within the business world are the vocational groups that contain the skilled professional

---

[17] Peter F. Drucker, "Politics for a New Generation, Part II: Three Unforeseen Jobs for the Coming Administration," *Harper's*, Vol. 221 (July, 1960), p. 46.

[18] Wolfgang Friedmann, "Corporate Power, Government by Private Groups, and the Law," *Columbia Law Review*, Vol. LVII (1957), p. 155.

[19] *New York Times Magazine*, September 4, 1960.

workers in the employ of the business and the trade association, made up of groups of companies banded together for some mutual purpose. The central problem of these two types of organization has been, although to a lesser degree, the same as the problem of the union.

In a sense, the professional association resembles the union, in that it is an organization whose existence is completely outside the confines of the business firm itself. But the similarity ends threre. The professional organization is not set up primarily to represent members in their relationship with the employer. Its main objective is to set and maintain professional standards, to disseminate knowledge among its members, and, finally, to give recognition for professional achievement by individuals.

The business manager has not always understood these functions, and as a result his relations with these organizations has not always been ideal. There is evidence that this situation is changing, particularly as the ranks of managers become more and more filled with men who themselves have come from professional backgrounds.

The potential of the professional association as an aid and reinforcement to business is largely untapped. The standards of professional work, while not necessarily within the province of the businessman, should certainly be of prime interest to him. In this respect, much could be done on a cooperative basis to help define and maintain such standards.

The trade association offers a different set of problems and opportunities. While there are many examples of effective and worthwhile trade associations, the history of most of them does not offer a very pretty picture. The objectives typically include some such statement as "the interchange of mutual information; the cooperative undertaking of programs that will redound to the benefit of the industry as a whole." While these aims are worthy of pursuit, their realization is often rendered difficult by distrust and jealousy among member companies and inability to find men of a caliber to carry out the job. The trade association could help police the industry against individual members who transgress and thereby injure the industry as a whole. In many industries this is a necessary function —a corollary of any pluralist society. For pluralism applies *within* any broad sector of human study just as surely as it applies to these areas viewed in the aggregate. Pluralism is as dynamic within business itself as within other major groupings—encouraging new ventures and new business forms lest monopoly assume a stultifying primacy.

To sum up, it must be reemphasized that, in any organization in which the individuals or member groups are autonomous or semiautonomous, the necessity for maintaining the authority and responsibility for the welfare of the whole is critical. In the case of the trade association, for example, we have, depending upon the size and influence of the member organizations, a society of unequal equals. If it happens that the largest and most influential members are concerned with the welfare of the industry, then the association is likely to be effective. But when the most influential members use their power for their own selfish ends, the organization will prove largely ineffective. Pluralism then becomes petty politics.

DECENTRALIZATION IN BUSINESS

The corporate drive to achieve both efficiency and independence has led business leadership to reexamine its own operation with increasing care. At the moment, two alternatives are open: either the business community will police its own use of power (even as it refrains from too many new additions to its structure) or the government will be asked to provide the blueprints. Architects of the business organization, therefore, sense the need for keeping alive the value of pluralism to a free society, even as they rebel against the economic costs that its practice sometimes entails. At the same time, they are aware of fantastic changes within the large enterprise itself. Shipping lines with South American ports of call recognize a need to help in the development of local economies if they are to turn in a profit. Electrical manufacturing companies have moved from the production of washing machines, toasters, and radios for private consumption to the production of atomic submarines and giant turbines. Oil companies have dramatically enlarged their interests from liquid fuels to petrochemistry. Multimarket, multiproduct, multiprocess—and often multinational—companies defy traditional organizational treatment. Thus desire for efficiency and profits reinforces the determination of business firms to remain autonomous and consequently to arrive at formulas that will enable them to use judiciously what powers they do possess.

Since organization has so often resulted from the allocation of responsibility and authority on a functional basis, the conclusion has been drawn that any such organizations represent effective pluralism in operation. But history affords ample evidence that concern for the part does not necessarily result in attention to the whole. Various devices are evidently being urged to get around this difficulty. One of the most popular of these involves the application of the principle of decentralization.

Sociologists designate the approach of corporate decentralization with such terminology as "federalism," "extended autonomy," or "integrated divisionalization," but the aim is clear—to diffuse authority outward and downward so that the decision-making process occurs at the point at which there is a convergence of action with required knowledge. Some corporations are still tightly controlled from the center, while others are in various stages of transition. As late as 1956 the United States Steel Corporation described itself as "two-thirds centralized and one-third decentralized."[20] At the other extreme are companies like the pharmaceutical firm of Johnson and Johnson at New Brunswick, New Jersey. General Robert Wood Johnson, when its chief executive, presided over the division of the firm into "a number of autonomous subsidiaries which are actually legal entities of their own.[21] Intermediate patterns have been followed by the General Electric Company and the General Motors Corporation, whose chief executive operates through a cabinet, so to speak, which coordinates at the highest level the activities of decentralized components.

The intimate connection between decentralized corporate organization and the much older concept of pluralism has been recognized in some corporations. Speaking at the University of California in Los Angeles in the spring of 1960, the then chairman of the board of the General Electric Company made the following statement:

We in the United States have a political and economic system that, in spite of its imperfections, is the most productive and admired system in the world. It not only preserves, but utilizes human freedom as the key to social and economic progress. We want to maintain this free society in a world where many factors are pushing the nations toward statist systems.

One of the basic principles of the American system is the principle of decentralized power. This country has what is known as a "pluralistic society." There is not just one basic source of initiative and decision here,

---

[20] John Chamberlain, "Industrial Firms Explore Diverse Forms of Organization," *Wall Street Journal*, December 17, 1956.

[21] *Ibid.*

as in the government-controlled societies. Rather, in the United States, there are many competing points of initiative, risk, and decision—and that is the secret of this nation's drive and creativity. . . . This decentralization of power is the strength of the free society, and it must be preserved.[22]

CONCLUSION

As in the past, power relations will tend to be worked out on an *ad hoc* basis that sometimes defies the concept of pluralism and always suggests indifference to it. Yet so embedded in the thinking and structure of American life is pluralism that its importance is greater than is realized by many empirical researchers.

Whatever the pattern and whatever the semantics, the long history of pluralism will have growing significance in the business life of the United States. As private power centers grow and threaten pluralism, the emphasis may shift to a consideration of the possible relevance of the principle of constitutionalism in industrial organization. Pluralism, as has been indicated, rests its superstructure on four major premises: the right of men voluntarily to associate for their own ends; the right of such associations to operate as autonomous units under the rule of law; the conviction that a pluralistic society provides the greatest incentive toward freedom and creativity; and the notion that society at large will hold each autonomous association responsible for performance. Beyond these premises exists a triple challenge that pluralism poses for businessmen in every free society. These are the translating of accountability to practical operating practices, the fostering of a milieu in which existing associations cannot prevent entry by vigorous newcomers, and the assurance that concern for the parts does not blind them to the needs of the whole society within which they flourish.

The facts of life of those ages when pluralism was in the ascendancy were facts flowing from small, family-owned business operations, small political entities or large ones with traditions of strong local responsibility, and thriving associations of various kinds (church, guilds, towns) catering to human needs. In a society of business oligarchy, of suprapaternal political associations, of unitary

---

[22] Ralph J. Cordiner, "Competitive Private Enterprise in Space" (Lecture V in the series "Peacetime Uses of Space," sponsored by the University of Caifornia Extension at Los Angeles, May 4, 1960).

power centers, pluralism seems somewhow out out of date. Shall it remain so or must new vigor be breathed into the vanishing ideal?

RECOMMENDED READING

COKER, FRANCIS W. "Pluralism." *Encyclopedia of the Social Sciences.*

DAHL, ROBERT A. *Pluralistic Democracy in the United States: Conflict and Consent.* Chicago: Rand McNally & Co., Inc., 1967.

DILL, WILLIAM R. "Business Organizations and Society," in JAMES G. MARCH (ed.). *Handbook of Organizations,* pp. 1101–6. Chicago: Rand McNally & Co., 1965.

GALBRAITH, JOHN K. *American Capitalism: The Concept of Countervailing Power.* Boston: Houghton Mifflin Co., 1952.

KARIEL, HENRY S. *The Decline of American Pluralism.* Stanford, Cal.: Stanford University Press, 1961.

MAYO, ELTON. *The Social Problems of an Industrial Civilization.* Cambridge: Harvard University Press, 1945.

STINCHCOMBE, ARTHUR L. "Social Structure and Organizations," in JAMES G. MARCH (ed.), *Handbook of Organizations,* pp. 142–93. Chicago: Rand McNally & Co., 1965.

FURTHER READING

BERLE, ADOLF A., JR. *The 20th Century Capitalist Revolution.* New York: Harcourt, Brace & Co., 1954.

BOULDING, KENNETH E. *The Organizational Revolution.* New York: Harper & Bros., 1953.

HSIAO, K. C. *Political Pluralism.* London: Kegan Paul, Trench, Trubner & Co., 1927.

KERR, CLARK. *Industrial Relations and the Liberal Pluralist.* Reprint No. 80 from *Proceedings of the Seventh Annual Meeting of Industrial Relations Research Associations.* Berkeley: Institute of Industrial Relations, University of California, 1955.

POLANYI, KARL. *The Great Transformation.* New York: Farrar and Rinehart, 1944.

TRUMAN, DAVID B. *The Governmental Process: Political Interests and Public Opinion.* New York: Alfred A. Knopf, 1951.

19. Constitutionalism

OUTLINE

CONSTITUTIONAL GOVERNMENT is generally regarded as a basic condition for the conduct of business as we know it in the United States and in all countries of the modern world in which there is a high degree of freedom from arbitrary rule. Freedom from arbitrary invasions by public officials of the rights of persons and property is a necessary condition for personal initiative and creativeness in all its many forms—economic, educational, scientific, religious, artistic,

483

cultural.[1] But aside from this, liberty is a human imperative, and liberty means, negatively stated, protection against the abuse of organized power wielded by all governments, public and private.

There is an eternal clash between the individual's assertion of independence and the obligation of those who govern to exercise control. Constitutional governments are characterized by specific restraints, established by law and custom and imposed on the wielders of power in order to insure that human rights will not be unduly transgressed. The qualifying word, "unduly," is crucial. For, in any organized community, a certain amount of power has to be mobilized in order to get those things done that need to be done through common effort. The right to use this power must therefore be lodged in the hands of those comparatively few who alone can make the decisions for directing the common effort. Some encroachments by the organized community on the "rights of man" are therefore inevitable, whether a society be governed constitutionally or despotically. This, in essence, is the underlying assumption of the legal concept of "due process of law." That some men, under any government, will at times be deprived of their life, liberty, and property by official action is certain. But that they cannot be so deprived "without due process of law" is an ancient principle of our jurisprudence dating at least from Magna Carta and stated explicitly in the Fifth and Fourteenth Amendments to the Constitution.

In every constitutional regime today, there are similar legal restraints on government officials. As McIlwain has said:

> Constitutionalism has one essential quality: it is a legal limitation on government; it is the antithesis of arbitrary rule; its opposite is despotic government, the government of will instead of law. In modern times the growth of political responsibility has been added to this through the winning of the initiative in the discretionary matters of national policy by the people's representatives . . . ; but the most lasting of the essentials of true constitutionalism still remains what it has been almost from the beginning, the limitation of government by law.[2]

---

[1] F. C. S. Northrop in *The Meeting of East and West* (New York: Macmillan Co., 1946) points to a certain consensus among the cultures of the world on human rights. Cf. A. N. Holcombe, *Human Rights in the Modern World* (New York: The New York University Press, 1948) ; H. Lauterpacht, *International Law and Human Rights* (New York: Frederick A. Praeger, 1950) ; and commentary on the "Universal Declaration of Human Rights" (U.N. Assembly, 1948) , by H. W. Briggs, *The Law of Nations* (2d. ed.; New York: Appleton-Century-Crofts, 1952) .

[2] Charles H. McIlwain, *Constitutionalism Ancient and Modern* (rev. ed.; Ithaca: Cornell University Press, 1940) , p. 24.

As the term is used today, constitutionalism takes many forms. In this chapter we shall consider the basic principles of constitutionalism as a major strand in the development of Western political thought. Then we shall turn to the more specific application of these principles, in modern times, to the problem of government in both the public and the private sectors of society.

BASIC PRINCIPLES OF CONSTITUTIONALISM

SOME DEFINITIONS

In addition to McIlwain's definition of constitutionalism, here are some other noteworthy views:

Constitutionalism embodies the simple proposition that the government is a set of activities organized by and operated on behalf of the people, but subject to a series of restraints which attempt to ensure that the power which goes with such governance is not abused by those who are called upon to do the governing. . . . Constitutionalism by dividing power provides a system of effective restraints upon governmental action.[3]

. . . the idea of *constitutional* government [emphasizes] the rights of individuals and the moral responsibility of the citizen as a person. . . . the basic underlying conception of constitutional restraints . . . rests upon the idea of a law higher than that of government and limiting the operation of the state.[4]

Absolute arbitrary power, or governing without settled standing laws, can neither of them consist with the ends of society or government which men would not quit the freedom of the state of Nature for, and tie themselves up under, were it not to preserve their lives, liberties, and fortunes, and by stated rules of right and property to secure their peace and quiet.[5]

If men were angels, no government would be necessary. If angels were to govern men, neither external nor internal controls on government would be necessary. In framing a government which is to be administered by men, the great difficulty lies in this: you must first enable the government to control the governed; and in the next place oblige it to control itself. A dependence on the people is, no doubt, the primary control on the government; but experience has taught mankind the necessity of aux-

---

[3] Carl J. Friedrich, *Constitutional Government and Democracy* (rev. ed.; Boston: Ginn & Co., 1950), pp. 35, 587, and 26.

[4] William Y. Elliott and Neil A. MacDonald, *Western Political Heritage* (New York: Prentice-Hall, 1949), pp. 18 and 251.

[5] John Locke, *Of Civil Government* (1690), Book II, par. 137.

iliary precautions. This policy of supplying, by opposite and rival interests, the defect of better motives, might be traced through the whole system of human affairs, private as well as public. We see it particularly displayed in all the subordinate distributions of power, where the constant aim is to divide and arrange the several offices in such a manner as that each may be a check on the other—that the private interest of every individual may be a sentinel over the public rights.[6]

. . . all states have constitutions. But that does not mean that all states observe constitutionalism. Constitutional government is government whose exercise and functions are limited.

. . . a state in which the plenitude of power is concentrated in a few hands, or in the hands of one, where constitutional provisions and institutional arrangements are merely tools to be used as the leadership sees fit and to be discarded at will when they are no longer of service—such a state may have a constitution, but it does not have a constitutional government.[7]

. . . Devices for the containment of power do not exist or operate automatically; they must be created deliberately and built consciously into the power process. It took political man many centuries to realize that the good of society, in which he possessed rights, and in which these rights were secure, was conditioned on the containment of the power holders, whatever the legitimation—factual, religious, or legal—of their social control. In time this purpose appeared to be served best by articulating the restraints society wished to place on the power holders in the form of a set of fixed rules—the "constitution"—limiting their exercise of political power. The constitution, thus, became the basic instrumentality for the control of the power process.[8]

The Dual Objective of Constitutionalism

It has been said that the United States Constitution is both an "instrument" and a "symbol." As an *instrument* of the American people to achieve its national purpose through a strong and effective national government, the Constitution is a grant of powers. But the Constitution is also "a limitation upon the powers of government in the hands of agents" of the American people,[9] and in this respect it is a *symbol* of their reserved rights.

---

[6] *The Federalist*, No. 51 (1788).

[7] Robert G. Neumann, *European and Comparative Government* (3d ed.; New York: McGraw-Hill Book Co., 1960), p. 671.

[8] Karl Loewenstein, *Political Power and the Governmental Process* (Chicago: University of Chicago Press, 1957), p. 123.

[9] Thomas M. Cooley, *A Treatise on the Constitutional Limitations* (Boston: Little, Brown & Co., 1871), p. 38.

The dual objective of American constitutionalism was well expressed by Corwin during the great debate over the New Deal, when the positive aspect of governmental power was being vigorously asserted by the legislative and executive branches of the federal government, and as vigorously—and at first successfully—attacked in the federal courts:

> While . . . the constitutional instrument exists to energize and canalize *public power*, it is the function of the constitutional symbol to protect and tranquilize *private interest or advantage as against public power*, which is envisaged as inherently suspect, however necessary it may be.[10]

Corwin observed that the Constitution had become "a symbol of distrust of the political process—a symbol of democracy's fear of democracy,"[11] with heavy reliance on judicial review of legislation to check the use of governmental powers, mainly by invoking the Tenth Amendment against Congress. Historically, the Constitution had passed through three phases: from " (1) an instrument of national government, a source of powers," under Chief Justice Marshall's long tenure, to " (2) an object of popular worship, finally valued chiefly for the obstacles it interposed to the national power, to (3) a protection of certain minority interests seeking escape from national power."[12]

Corwin traced this growth of "constitutional negativism" in part to "the fundamental premise of economic individualism . . . the assumption that economic power is *natural* and political power *artificial,* from which the conclusion is drawn that 'arbitrary' power is characteristically *governmental* power." The then approaching "constitutional crisis of unpredictable gravity . . . due chiefly to the [Supreme] Court's endeavor to put 'Big Business' and its methods," amounting in fact to the use of private power, "out of the reach of effective government" had raised the question whether the entire system of constitutional limitations, judicially implemented, was compatible with popular government.

Corwin was not convinced of the incompatibility, but if the dilemma were to be resolved within a constitutional framework the Court would "have to enlarge some of its conceptions, and especially . . . its conception of public power *to include economic power.*"

---

10 Edward S. Corwin, "The Constitution as Instrument and as Symbol," *American Political Science Review,* Vol. XXX (December, 1936) , p. 1072.

11 *Ibid.,* p. 1076.

12 *Ibid.,* p 1082.

For when this is done certain other important truths will emerge. It will be seen that most people have to take orders from some source or other, and that therefore the problem of human liberty is not to be completely solved by the purely negative device of setting acts of Congress aside as contrary to the Constitution. Also recognition will dawn that there is no reason underlying the nature of things why acts or procedures which are regarded as unjust when they are resorted to by government are necessarily more defensible when resorted to by business management. Lastly, it will appear that unless we are to resign ourselves to economic autocracy, governmental power must be as little embarrassed by boundary lines as is economic power.[13]

In the sequel,[14] the Court did reinterpret the Constitution far more broadly as an "instrument" of positive government, thereby, in the opinion of many in the business community, weakening the Constitution as a "symbol" of limitations on government.

Judicial review is but one of many devices by which limitations on governmental power are made effective. But, as Corwin's comments indicate, whether we are considering the public government of a nation or the private government of a voluntary association, the *symbolic* aspect of constitutionalism has clearly to be balanced against its *instrumental* side. The heated debates in our constitutional history over the proper balance between these two imperatives of power and restraint have their counterparts in the debates within every private polity. Restraint on power is a constitutional necessity, but adequate power there must be. This principle applies within any well-governed organization.

The need for restraint applies to the state, above all, because of the immensity of its enterprise, the extreme sanctions it can use, and the lengths to which it can and does go in tampering with men's goods, their families, and their lives.[15] But we know that it is not the state alone that threatens liberty, for the organized power that man requires to do the things he wants done is by no means limited to states or to "sovereign" entities.

Constitutionalism, in short, has throughout the history of West-

---

[13] *Ibid.*, pp. 1083–85.

[14] Notably in a series of decisions from 1937 on expanding the areas of control over the economic life of the country by both federal and state governments. See Carl B. Swisher, *American Constitutional Development* (2nd ed.; Boston: Houghton Mifflin Co., 1954), chaps. xxxvi and xxxvii, and Bernard Schwartz, *The Supreme Court: Constitutional Revolution in Retrospect* (New York: Ronald Press Co., 1957), *passim*.

[15] Ernest W. Hocking, *Man and the State* (New Haven: Yale University Press, 1926), p. ix.

ern civilization raised both the basis issues of adequate authority in officialdom and the circumscription of that authority. Both aspects have a venerable tradition in political thought, but it is the emphasis on *limitations* that has come to be more closely identified with the concept of constitutionalism in the Western world.

CONSTITUTIONALISM IN PERSPECTIVE

HISTORIC ROOTS OF THE IDEA OF RESTRAINT ON POWER

One of the deeper historic roots of constitutional restraints is the natural-law concept of antiquity, the idea that there is a universal right and justice that binds even the gods and "that Nature herself, the mother of all things animate and inanimate dictated principles of human dignity and the fundamental decencies of human behavior."[16] The Stoics had contrasted natural law, based on reason and justice, with man's laws. Their conception of nature as a great rational process[17] profoundly influenced Roman law and through it the development of constitutional theory in modern Europe and America. The commands of any human lawgiver were to be tested against rules of law emanating from a higher source. Thus the Stoics and Roman jurists regarded civil rule and the rule of masters over slaves as "conventional," demanding justification, and not natural —a point of view that stands in sharp contrast to the political theories of Plato and Aristotle.

This belief in the conventionality of human rule was strongly reinforced by the political theory of the Roman republic, which regarded the state as founded on the consent of the whole people and welded together by a bond of law (*juris vinculum,* in Cicero's phrase) into a corporate body with supreme legal authority. The later Roman jurists perpetuated this idea—with far-reaching results for modern constitutionalism—in the famous text from Justinian's *Institutes:* "Whatever has pleased the prince has the force of law, *inasmuch as . . . the Roman people have vested in him all their power and authority.*"[18] And while there was much debate through-

---

[16] Samuel Eliot Morison, *Freedom in Contemporary Society* (Boston: Little, Brown & Co., 1956) , p. 10.

[17] John Herman Randall, Jr., *The Making of the Modern Mind* (rev. ed.; Boston: Houghton Mifflin Co., 1940) , pp. 198, 244 ff.

[18] Ulpian, *Digest,* Vol. I, No. 4, p. 1. (The italicized clause was often omitted by those who cited Roman law as a justification of unlimited princely rule.)

out the Middle Ages on whether the power thus ceded by the people in the *lex regia* could ever be recovered, champions of popular sovereignty, like Suarez and Bellarmine, Locke and Jefferson, over the centuries have urged public—if not always democratic—limitations on governmental power[19] and even, in extremity, the ultimate remedy of tyrannicide.[20]

Western constitutionalism has also been strongly influenced by religious doctrine. Judeo-Christian teachings on the ultimate moral worth of persons as possessors of souls, equal in the sight of God; on the right of resistance to immoral and therefore unlawful authority; and on the Gelasian theory of the "two swords" representing power wielded by bishops and kings, respectively—these and other aspects of religious doctrine have contributed significantly to modern constitutionalism as a principle of restraint on power.[21]

The system of restraints on royal power inherent in feudal conceptions of property and the law of franchises or "liberties," privilege, and personal status also contributed to the evolution of constitutionalism. Magna Carta, an essentially conservative thirteenth-century affirmation of medieval rights, was not only

. . . a redress of grievances of the great landowners, imposing limits of order and reason upon the king's exactions as feudal overlord . . . (but) also a redress of grievances of the church, imposing respect for the then fundamental division of powers between the spiritual and the temporal . . . (and) a redress of the grievances of the merchants and traders, providing for uniform-weights and measures, freedom of travel, and freedom from unjust taxation. Most of all . . . a redress of common grievances for all (calling) for reasonable fines, proportioned to the offense of the offender . . . for justice as something of right, not to be sold, denied, or delayed . . . for security of property, which is not to be taken for the king's purposes without the old customary payment . . . for security of the person. The free man is not to be banished or outlawed or diseised or deprived of his established privileges without a lawful judgment or otherwise than according to law.[22]

---

[19] Otto von Gierke, *Political Theories of the Middle Age* (trans. with Introduction by F. W. Maitland) (Boston: Beacon Press, 1958) , p. 150, nn. 158, 159.

[20] John Dickinson (trans.) , *The Statesman's Book of John Salisbury* (New York: Alfred A. Knopf, 1927) , pp. lxvi ff. "It is not only kings who practice tyranny," wrote John of Salisbury, "but among private men there are a host of tyrants, since the power they have, they turn to some forbidden object."

[21] See Elliott and MacDonald, *op. cit.*, pp. 250–52 and 288–99.

[22] Roscoe Pound, *The Development of Constitutional Guarantees of Liberty* (New Haven: Yale University Press, 1957) , p. 21.

The principle that legitimate governments always rest on the consent of the governed is undoubtedly the most pervasive element in modern constitutionalist doctrine and is frequently encountered throughout the long history of Western political thought. But it was not until relatively modern times that it was translated into practical measures. Although significant, independent, and indigenous constitutional developments are to be found in other countries—especially in Switzerland, Sweden, and Holland—and in the churches, the most decisive and influential first steps toward translating "government by consent" into constitutional practice took place in England.[23]

Despite the ringing phrases of Magna Carta, it was not until 1688 that England—after undergoing three revolutions and five authoritarian regimes in the seventeenth century alone—successfully asserted parliamentary sovereignty. In the pithy words of Samuel Eliot Morison,

By the time the eighteenth century dawned, Englishmen had thoroughly, once and for all, learned the lesson that authoritarian regimes *stink*. They wanted no more of them; they wanted liberty—security against absolutism. And so strong and universal was this conviction in all classes of English society that the need of a written constitution, headed by a formal bill of rights, was never felt. Magna Carta, the Petition of Right, the Habeas Corpus Act of 1679 and the Bill of Rights of 1689 were enough. The last three were merely Parliamentary statutes, yet they acquired a status equal to that of fundamental law.[24]

In the American colonies, however, the principle of consent was expressed in written constitutions as basic guarantees of government under law. For the colonists and, later, for the founders of the republic, a constitution was not mere rhetoric but fundamental law binding on the highest officials of government and enforceable upon them by the courts. A constitution was, in the Lockeian tradition, a compact between the people and their representatives. Under the terms of this agreement the "legislative" was bound to protect "property," which in Locke's definition was equated with the "life,

---

[23] Friedrich, *op. cit.*, p. 30; Ernst Troeltsch, *The Social Teaching of the Christian Churches* (New York: Macmillan Co., 1931), Vol. I, pp. 323 ff., and Vol. II, pp. 810 ff.; and George H. Sabine, *A History of Political Theory* (3d ed.; New York: Holt, Rinehart & Winston, 1961), chap. xvi.

[24] Morison, *op. cit.*, pp. 13–14.

liberty, and estate" of citizens. Governance was thus conceived as an essentially "fiduciary" function.

According to Locke, "force without authority" by government amounted to "rebellion," for "those who set up force again in opposition to the laws, do *rebellare*—that is, bring back again the state of war." Such "rebels" act only under the mere pretext of authority, and it is therefore justifiable to unseat them. But "such revolutions happen not upon every little mismanagement of public affairs" but only following "a long train of abuses, prevarications, and artifices." In this way, Locke provided the rationale for revolution.

. . . This power in the people of providing for their safety anew by a new legislative when their legislators have acted contrary to their trust by invading their property, is the best fence against rebellion and the probablest means to hinder it.[25]

The principle of consent as the basis for legitimacy thus led Locke after the Glorious Revolution, and the signers of the Declaration of Independence less than a century later, to insist upon political action—and not just the invocation alone of abstract doctrine—as a practical method for realizing constitutional objectives.

But the revolutionary remedy for abuse of power has always been too extreme to stand by itself as the sole means of restraining officialdom. Like the medieval remedy of tyrannicide outlined by John of Salisbury, revolution does not provide that system of *regularized* and *institutionalized* restraints on power that now characterizes modern constitutional systems. It is to such restraints that we now turn. But, in doing so, it is well again to emphasize the antiquity of the philosophical foundations of constitutionalism. The idea of restraint is not new, even though it has taken Western civilization many centuries to translate the idea into practical measures.

THE DEVELOPMENT OF CONSTITUTIONAL TECHNIQUES

The translation of constitutionalist theory into practice is a modern achievement that involves widely differing methods and techniques for establishing and maintaining effective restraints on governmental action. The historical origin[26] of these techniques can in part be traced to the medieval heritage of "estates"—the barons, the

---

[25] John Locke, *op. cit.*, para. 225 and 226.

[26] Friedrich, *op. cit.*, chap. i. The brief historical résumé at this point follows Friedrich's account.

free cities, the Church—which resisted the rise of royal absolutism and laid the groundwork for modern representative assemblies. At the start, the mercantile middle class provided most effective support, and they were joined later—not always in friendly embrace—by the rising working classes. While there were representative assemblies in various parts of Europe in the late Middle Ages, the English-speaking peoples were undoubtedly the leaders in developing viable institutions that could restrain absolute power. It was mainly from England that constitutionalism spread to the American colonies.

The steady spread of constitutionalism during the 19th century was a concomitant of the rise of industrialization; as the prime mover in the Industrial Revolution, the commercial and professional middle class also led the movement toward constitutional government. They did not keep the leadership in their own hands indefinitely, however, for during the early 19th century constitutionalism was transformed in country after country from a limited to a more or less democratic form. Nor did the transition stop with the recognition of popular majorities; after the revolution of 1848 in Europe, socialism became an issue, raising the question whether constitutional democracy requires "capitalism" or "free enterprise" for its successful operation.

Constitutionalism seems to require a certain equipoise among the various classes and economic interests of a society. The dominance of any one class, whether under simple majority democracy or the "dictatorship of the proletariat," clearly runs contrary to constitutionalism. Yet the enfranchisement of most of the adult population, on the one hand, and the nationalization of considerable parts of the economy, on the other, have not necessarily resulted in the demise of constitutional government. Jacksonian democracy and universal suffrage in the United States did not sweep away our basic pattern of constitutional limitations. Nor has some degree of socialization in New Zealand, Great Britain, and the Scandinavian countries undermined the basic patterns of constitutional restraints in their governments.

The social balance necessary for the survival of constitutionalism, however, may be endangered by certain social trends observable in the world today. Unchecked majoritarian "mass" democracy[27]

---

[27] Cf. Carl J. Friedrich and Z. B. Brzezinski, *Totalitarian Dictatorship and Autocracy* (2d ed.) (Cambridge: Harvard University Press, 1965); José Ortega y Gasset, *The Revolt of the Masses* (New York: W. W. Norton & Co., 1932); William

and total nationalization of the economy are two of these. But perhaps the most insidious threat to the survival of constitutionalism is the centralization of bureaucractic power in national states for the purpose of defense and warfare. When nations must gird themselves for the task of "deterrence" in the age of missiles and nuclear warfare, they unavoidably take on increasingly the character of garrison states, in which the whole economy—and indeed the entire social fabric—is gradually subordinated to the overwhelming demands of military preparedness.

GLOBAL AND LOCAL ASPECTS OF CONSTITUTIONALISM

Constitutionalism *within* nation-states may thus be jeopardized unless ways and means are found to provide some minimal requirements of law and order on a global scale—an order secured by adequate supranational authority and a regime of world law commensurate with the rapidly developing international economy and a world-wide community.[28] It is increasingly said that "the political frontier is an anachronism" and "a heritage from a former age, not a creature of the march of technology and commerce."[29] Thus the development of constitutional devices in future decades will necessarily include those applicable to international as well as national governments.[30]

At the other end of the organizational scale there is a concurrent development of constitutionalist techniques for organizations within nations. Voluntary and private associations of all kinds also tend to be increasingly influenced by the ubiquitous demand for responsible government. Polities on international, national, local, and private levels may all, sooner or later, be required to adopt systems of governance in which power and authority are matched by workable devices to assure accountability to constituencies.

Kornhauser, *The Politics of Mass Society* (New York: The Free Press, 1959) ; Robert A. Dahl, *A Preface to Democratic Theory* (Chicago: University of Chicago Press, 1956) ; and Anthony Downs, *An Economic Theory of Democracy* (New York: Harper & Row, 1957) .

[28] Cf. Bruce M. Russett, *Trends in World Politics* (New York: Macmillan Co., 1965) ; Harry G. Johnson, *The World Economy at the Crossroads* (Oxford: Clarendon Press, 1965) ; and Joseph Frankel, *International Relations* (New York: Oxford University Press, 1964) .

[29] Walton Hamilton, *The Politics of Industry* (New York: Alfred A. Knopf, Inc. 1957) , p. 109.

[30] See Herbert J. Spiro, *Government by Constitution* (New York: Random House, 1959) , chap. xxvi.

These devices of accountability have been worked out most elaborately within the constitutional regimes of certain nation-states, so that it is to their long experience in the creative development of constitutionalism in practice that one must turn for clues to the emerging patterns of constitutional government in other spheres.

CONSTITUTIONALISM IN PRACTICE

The translation of ancient constitutionalist theory into modern practice can be summarized under two general headings: the distribution of power and the techniques of "responsible government." In this brief review we shall focus primarily upon the American pattern of constitutional devices. But it should be borne in mind that constitutionalism takes many other forms than those with which we are familiar. Moreover, the devices we have adopted for our *public* polity in the American political system are not always and necessarily those that would be applicable to the *private* polities of religious, educational, and business institutions. Nevertheless, the constitutional devices established in our public polity are important points of departure, since it is probable that the spread of constitutionalism to the private sectors here will be strongly influenced by these established patterns.

This latter assumption can be questioned, to be sure. It is by no means a foregone conclusion that if new techniques of constitutional government should be devised, leadership will always remain in the hands of those who direct public affairs or even in the hands of Western political leadership. It is at least arguable that the future of constitutionalism will be molded mainly by functional entities and not by nation-states. Among those entities worthy of careful observation are such special organs of government as the recent economic "communities" and customs unions, as well as the great public and private corporations that already carry forward a considerable part of the world's work in every free country. The patterns of government now under development in these and other non-state organizations could conceivably influence the future of constitutional government in emergent political entities.

THE DISTRIBUTION OF POWER

Assuming that there is adequate power and authority in our national and state governments to achieve national purpose at public governmental levels—a matter that we shall not pursue here —the problem of constitutionalism is first of all one of distributing that power. For in our political tradition the concentration of power in too few hands has always been regarded as the forerunner of despotism. In our constitutional system the distribution of power takes three main forms: (*a*) territorial—the federal structure; (*b*) functional—the separation of powers; and (*c*) chronological—periodic elections and limited tenure of office.

Territorial Distribution of Power. The geographic distribution of power between national and state governments should not be confused with systems in which power is devolved or delegated from the center to peripheral decision centers. Many constitutional systems have a unitary and not a federal system; their provinces and local units have only delegated powers, which can be altered by national law. "Decentralized" companies, to take another example, are not truly federal in structure, nor are states of the union in which municipalities have been granted "home rule," which could be abolished by state action.

"A federal system distributes power between a common and constituent government under an arrangement that cannot be changed by the ordinary process of central legislation."[31] The basic charter under which the arrangement is laid down may be quite difficult to amend, as in the case of the United States Constitution. The constituent units of a federal system are not entrusted with trivial matters only. In our system these units are often referred to as "sovereign states," and, while this designation is inaccurate, since their autonomy is to some extent limited by the basic charter, they do claim extensive and important residual powers that are nowhere defined in that charter.[32]

Federations, as distinguished from looser forms of union, have central organs that exercise authority directly over individuals within the constituent units; to an extent, the central officialdom represents these individuals, is elected by them, and can tax and regulate them directly. In a federation the constituency of the central government is to some extent at the grass roots and not alone at the federal unit (state) level. Member states, on the other hand, also

---

[31] Arthur W. Macmahon (ed.), *Federalism, Mature and Emergent* (Garden City, N.Y.: Doubleday & Co., 1955), p. 4.

[32] In the Canadian federation it is the other way round: provincial powers are delegated, while those of the central government at Ottawa are residual.

draw their authority in large part from the same grass-roots level and they may, within certain limits, devise and change their forms of government as they will. Equality of the constituent states as to legal status in the federation is a further essential in a true federation.

In unitary, as distinguished from federal, states these conditions do not prevail. Since many modern constitutional regimes flourish in unitary states (England, France, the Scandinavian countries, for example), federalism is clearly not a prerequisite for constitutional government. The case for federal as against unitary government has been summarized by Arthur W. Macmahon under five heads. He concedes that, as to the first four, the results they contemplate could be approximated in a decentralized unitary state:

First, when diversities are pronounced and located with reasonable compactness, the geographical concentration of important powers secures greater correspondence between public policies and local majority senti-ment on matters entrusted to the constituent governments. Second, by multiplying the independent legislative arenas, the system gives scope for experimentation, followed by imitation. Third, the multiplication of the bodies of elected officials who bear considerable responsibility in their own right broadens the opportunity for political participation. Fourth, the system is suitable for government over large or scattered areas. . . . Fifth, federalism lessens the risk of monopoly of political power by pro-viding a number of independent points where the party that is nationally in the minority at the time can maintain itself while it formulates and partly demonstrates its policies and capabilities and develops new leader-ship.[33]

But, while unitary governments, properly decentralized, could theo-retically achieve these results "a federal constitution helps by guar-anteeing and stabilizing the institutions of regional self-government and by subtly galvanizing them through a heightened awareness of re-sponsibility," and in certain unitary systems "seemingly strong man-dates for devolution in provinces and communes are largely disre-garded."[34]

The role of federal systems in the development of modern consti-tutionalism is that they provide an ingenious device for preventing undue concentration of power *territorially,* while at the same time assuring that the constituent states will not encroach unduly upon the powers of the central government or upon rights of persons

---

[33] Macmahon (ed.) , *op. cit.,* pp. 10–11.
[34] *Ibid.,* p. 11.

which that government is bound to protect. The need for authoritative interpretation of the basic federal charter in order to preserve this territorial distribution of power was well put by Justice Holmes:

> I do not think the United States would come to an end if we (the Supreme Court) lost our power to declare an Act of Congress void. I do think the Union would be imperilled if we could not make that declaration as to the laws of the several States.[35]

The American federal system, with its equipoise of national and state powers, is a constitutional device of particular significance to business: it provides a useful national framework, but it also poses special problems, for business corporations. A strong federal *union* with adequate national powers was undoubtedly a precondition for a truly continental market. On the other hand, corporations are almost all state created, and the preservation of adeqaute authority in the individual *states* was a necessary condition for the preservation of government adapted to local conditions. For more than 70 years, from the end of the Civil War to 1937, the playing-off of state and national power claims against each other was used by constitutional lawyers to create a kind of no-man's-land in which neither federal nor state governments were able, in fact, to exert effective regulatory power over business.[36] More recently, the Court's reinterpretation of the Constitution has permitted a considerable extension of regulatory and taxing powers, as these affect business, at both national and state levels.

Thus, from the standpoint of businessmen, federalism alone is not necessarily the most effective means of limiting governmental power; on the contrary, in the face of economic crises and the threats of total war the pendulum has swung strongly in the direction of public power rather than in the other direction.

Functional Distribution of Power. A second method of dividing power is along *functional* rather than geographic lines (as in federalism). Montesquieu's classic 18th-century argument for this

---

[35] Oliver Wendell Holmes, Jr., *Collected Legal Papers* (New York: Harcourt, Brace & Co., 1920), pp. 295–96.

[36] For the rise and demise of "dual federalism" and its relations to business regulation see E. S. Corwin, *The Commerce Power versus States Rights'* (Princeton: Princeton University Press, 1936) ; *The Constitution and What It Means Today* (12th rev. ed.; Princeton: Princeton University Press, 1958) , pp. 32–54; and *The Twilight of the Supreme Court* (New Haven: Yale University Press, 1934) , chap. i.

method—the "separation of powers"—proposed two theses: that there are different *kinds* of governmental powers and that, to safeguard liberty, these powers must not be concentrated in one and the same body of government officials.[37] "Constant experience shows us," wrote Montesquieu, "that every man invested with power is apt to abuse it, and to carry his authority until he is confronted with limits."[38] These limits, he thought, could be defined in terms of the functions appropriate to an official's authority.

The traditional American doctrine of separation of powers envisages three sorts of power: legislative, executive, and judicial. This triadic division has been criticized as unscientific and unworkable— unworkable because powers hermetically sealed and separated would render effective government impossible and, in any case, unrealistic because governmental functions cannot be so neatly classified under these three or any other headings.

The critique is valuable, but the basic emphasis on the necessity of modifying the concentration of power has not been successfully challenged. Dictatorial regimes have always insisted upon a complete fusion of power, and their theorists have bitterly attacked the fundamental assumptions of separation of powers.[39] The classical view of a triadic division may not be the final answer to the other requirements of constitutionalism—limitation and restraint—but what can we put in its place? It is a doctrine that "has ever been made to defend certain spiritual and material values from the control of government," but, "since all government is a single process, its division into parts, and their relative power, depends upon the purpose of the government and the relative technical capacity of the various bodies of men and women who are employed in its realization."[40]

Is there a golden mean between a system of power distribution so intricately checked and balanced that rights are protected to the point of governmental paralysis and a fused, efficient, and quick-acting system that offers no protection at all? The answer lies in

---

[37] See Herman Finer, *The Theory and Practice of Modern Government* (rev. ed.; New York: Henry Holt & Co., 1949), chaps. vi and vii.

[38] Charles de Secondat, Baron de Montesquieu, *De l'esprit des lois* (1748), Book XI, 4. Montesquieu's doctrine to some extent influenced American constitutional theory. Madison, in *The Federalist*, No. 47, wrote that Montesquieu is "the oracle who is always consulted and cited on this subject."

[39] See Robert G. Neumann, *op. cit.*, chap. iv.

[40] Herman Finer, *op. cit.*, p. 115.

conceiving governance broadly to embrace not only the official governments of nations but also those nonstate sectors of private government, including corporate governments, that constitute in effect integral parts of a functional separation of powers in any truly constitutional system. We turn later in this chapter to the constitutionalizing process within the corporation; but here we must note the essential role of all so-called private-sector organizations in society's total functional distribution of powers.

A pluralistic structure of society in itself provides structural restraint on power by preserving many power centers. But in addition to a multiplicity of power centers, pluralism provides a functional distribution of authority over the entire social structure. The business system as a "private sector" is but one example of this. The press, under the protection of the First Amendment of the U.S Constitution, is an integral part of this wider functional distribution of power. Other specialized institutional centers, such as autonomous educational and scientific institutions, churches, and organizations in the arts, contribute to this important structural device in modern constitutionalism.

Chronological Distribution of Power. A third form of power division is along the time axis, especially in the limitation of tenure of office.[41] Periodic and frequent election of chief executives and legislative representatives is regarded as a basic necessity in all constitutional systems. Life tenure, even for judges, is precluded in many states of the union, although the Founding Fathers regarded it as essential to federalism and to the protection of liberty under the United States Constitution. A distinction is ordinarily made between nonpolitical career personnel, with indefinite tenure, and "political" though appointive officers, whose tenure depends on the discretion of elected officials.

As a general rule, tenure of office is limited in order to secure the *representative* character of officialdom—that is to say, its responsive-

---

[41] The limitation of appropriations to fixed periods, as in annual budgets, is another example of the chronological distribution of power. The periodicity of official tenure and of budgeting and planning is a subject of much debate in both public and private organizations. Are short terms of office and "fiscal years" too limiting for "long-range" planning? The same principle applies to corporate planning; see George A. Steiner, "The Nature and Significance of Multinational Corporate Planning," in George A. Steiner and Warren M. Cannon, *Multinational Corporate Planning* (New York: Macmillan Co., 1966) , pp. 8–16.

ness to the constituency on whose behalf it is expected to act and its continuing accountability for the exercise of the powers entrusted to it. While the chronological distribution of power is obviously an incomplete solution to this problem of responsibility, constitution makers have always put much emphasis upon it.

The periodic election of directors of a corporation by its stockholders, as distinguished from the indefinite tenure of executive managers and subordinate employees, is an example of the chronological distribution of powers drawn from the business world. On the other hand, corporate governments have no such complex bicameral legislative system as is found in the national government and in all states except Nebraska. The two houses presumably "check and balance" each other (an example of functional division of power) ; in addition, members of the lower house are usually elected for shorter terms and thereby forced to seek their mandates from the people at relatively short intervals. Similarly, in the national Congress, representatives must face popular check every two years, as opposed to the six-year term for senators. It is no coincidence that the members of the House, which originates all appropriations bills, should be held more closely accountable to their constituents.

The longer tenure of nonrepresentative officials, such as appointive civil servants, military officers, and judges, is justified under constitutionalist theory on the ground that their accountability is provided for otherwise than through periodic elections. The removal power, in their case, is vested in "political" (elected and representative) bodies. They carry out functions that are more clearly professional and are governed, to a degree, by the canons of their professions. In this sense, the development in business of a corps of professional managers presents a parallel to nonelective officialdom in constitutional governments. The counterparts in corporations of the "political" branches of public government are the board of directors and the chief executive officer.

RESPONSIBLE GOVERNMENT

James I believed that he ruled England by divine right. He always insisted that he was responsible in the highest degree, but responsible to God and not at all to his own subjects. Modern constitutionalism requires a more mundane kind of responsibility: first, through representative government, in which officials are held responsible to a democratic electorate based on nearly universal suffrage, and second, by "limited government" or government under due process of law.

Representative Government. The nexus between "the people" and a responsible government is maintained by various systems of representation:

The invention or discovery of the representative technique was as decisive for the political evolution of the West and, through it, of the world as the mechanical invention—steam, electricity, the combustion engine, atomic power—have been for man's technological evolution. Government is indispensable for the organized state of society. Only the representative technique permitted the institutionalization of the parliament as a power holder separate and independent from the government. . . . Without the introduction of the representative principle, political power in the western world would have remained monolithic indefinitely, as it remained in the non-western realm until it was undermined by the fertilization of liberal constitutionalism of the West.[42]

The "general will" does not operate automatically; it has to be exercised by leaders. Leaders are held accountable in modern constitutional regimes by an elaborate electoral process designed or evolved for the purpose of keeping officials responsible to their constituencies, not only through periodic elections but through continuous publicity of their acts and deliberations and through the exercise of the rights of association and petition by the citizenry at large.

Representative government, then, is achieved not merely by formal systems of representation but quite as importantly by many "pressures"[43] on officialdom. The art of politics, it is said, is the art of the possible, and what might be possible in an autocracy becomes so difficult in a constitutional regime that, as President Truman once remarked, "if you can't stand the heat, you'd better stay out of the

---

[42] Loewenstein, *op. cit.*, pp. 40–41. By "government," as distinguished from "parliament" (and representative assemblies generally), Loewenstein refers to what Friedrich calls "the core of modern government: bureaucracy." Friedrich, *op. cit.*, chap ii.

[43] Pendleton Herring, *Group Representation before Congress* (Baltimore: Johns Hopkins Press, 1929); David B. Truman, *The Governmental Process* (New York: Alfred A. Knopf, 1951); V. O. Key, *Politics, Parties and Pressure Groups* (4th ed.; New York: Thomas Y. Crowell, 1958); Abraham Holtzman, *Interest Groups and Lobbying* (New York: Macmillan Co., 1966); Raymond A. Bauer, Ithiel de Sola Pool, and Lewis A. Dexter, *American Business and Public Policy: The Politics of Foreign Trade* (New York: The Atherton Press, 1963); and Henry W. Ehrmann (ed.), *Pressure Groups on Four Continents* (Pittsburgh: University of Pittsburgh Press, 1958).

kitchen." The practical result is an intricately interrelated functional as well as territorial representation[44] and the pervasive participation in the governmental process of a great variety of informal groups.

In private governments, which are essentially based on functionally defined groups, this kind of representation is the rule rather than the exception. A corporation, for example, is from the governmental point of view a polity based on a stockholder constituency that is not territorially defined. The same is true of polities based on communities of religious, scholars, professionals, and so on, whose voluntary associations are based on voting constituencies that are only incidentally divided into geographical groups.

In public governments far more than in these private governmental systems, the nexus of accountability is strengthened by the party system. Without competing parties, modern constitutional government could not function at all, and their role in representative government is now generally established by law and custom. The "loyal Opposition" in England has official status, as have minority parties in other countries. With the aid of the "fourth estate" —a free press—and together with the multiplicity of voluntary associations in the private sector, popular government grounded on the party system provides one of the most powerful means of implementing those ancient ideas of limited government that we reviewed earlier.

Authoritarian and dictatorial regimes reject this complex of techniques for assuring the accountability of representatives to their public. Nor is the principle of authoritarianism confined today to those regimes abroad that we regard as antithetical to responsible and constitutional government. Our own society, with its general frame-work of public constitutionalism, contains many private polities that are essentially nonconstitutional in theory and in practice.

This diversity of governmental forms is not necessarily inconsistent with the American system of government. A pluralistic society has room for many sorts of polities, each patterned after the desires and needs of its own constituent group. Some churches, for example, are extremely democratic in theory and practice; others are aristo-

---

[44] Functional representation has been formally adopted in some constitutional systems; see Finer, *op. cit.*, chap. xxii. In our own, "lobbying" is a case of the informal use of it, but the "lobby" includes only those functional groups that impinge directly on official agencies. Unofficial groups of other kinds are obviously vital forces in restraining official governments in every free society.

cratic and authoritarian. Few would maintain that business organizations should be converted forthwith into private democracies. It
would not be easy to get agreement today as to the basic constituent
group in a business corporation: is it the stockholders, the employees, the state that creates the corporation, or some other group, such
as the consumers it serves? Is a university the instrument of its
faculty, its student body, its alumni, its board of trustees, or of the
creating authority that established its board of governors?

These questions indicate that there is no universally applicable
or "responsible government" in a constitutional regime. Careful
students of politics understand that we are only at the beginning
and not at the end of a solution of the problem of accountability,
even in the public sector. Representative government as we know it
today is a relatively recent phenomenon is constantly undergoing
change.[45]

"Due Process of Law." The "symbolic" aspect of constitutionalism as a complex of restraints on power is expressed in the phrases
"limited government," "government under law," and, especially,
"due process of law." In the United States, where judicial review has
become "the cornerstone of American constitutionalism,"[46] it is the
courts that stand between the people and the political branches of
government as the special guardian of liberties.[47] Their power to set
aside acts of legislative and administrative officials that, they judge,
violate the basic charter is probably more thoroughly established
here than in any other modern government.

Fairness in judicial and quasi-judicial administrative proceedings as to due notice, hearing both sides of a case before a decision is

---

[45] Compare John Stuart Mill, *Considerations on Representative Government*
(1861), a classic statement of the problem a century ago, with the more complex
formulation of it today in, e.g., Robert A. Dahl and Charles E. Lindblom, *Politics,
Economics and Welfare* (New York: Harper & Bros., 1953).

[46] *The Constitution of the United States Annotated: Analysis and Interpretation*
(prepared by the Legislative Reference Service, Library of Congress, and edited by E. S.
Corwin) (Washington, 1953), p. 559. See pp. 553 ff. for a succinct summary of the
development of judicial review. The "due process" clauses of the Fifth and the
Fourteenth Amendment have received judicial interpretation far more frequently than
have any other of the limiting clauses in the Constitution.

[47] Corwin, in the work cited in n. 46, observed that the immunization of these
branches from judicial restraint under the doctrine of "political questions" not subject
to judical review indicated the necessity for increasing reliance on other kinds of
constitutional restraints, such as the electoral process and a free press. The "political"
branches of government have on occasion insisted that they are quite as much the
guardians of the Constitution as the courts. Recent cases, such as those on reapportion-
ment, indicate some narrowing of the doctrine of political questions.

taken, the right of counsel, and so on is the older procedural meaning of due process of law. Today the very substance of federal and
state legislation also falls under judicial scrutiny. Unreasonable and
arbitrary encroachments on life, liberty, and property are subject to
challenge in the courts.

Over the years, the critics of judicial review have been found in
various camps, depending on whose ox was gored. "Judicial supremacy" is an evil or a virtue, depending upon the point of view. When
one wants strong governmental action, either to advance the "public
interest" or to protect certain rights, a resistant Court may seem to
be a bar to progress, but, when one simply wants to prevent any
action by legislators and administrators, judicial review may seem to
be the last resort against tyranny.

Supreme Court justices have themselves disagreed about the
proper scope of their power to disallow legislative or administrative
acts. Yet the doctrine of judicial review has never been abandoned
since its firm establishment in Chief Justice John Marshall's time,
and it is not likely to be. This judicial power is not a universal and
indispensable element of constitutionalism. Judicial review is unknown to English constitutionalism, for example, and as Holmes
remarked, its function as a control over state law under federalism is
probably more important than its check on coordinate branches of
government. Judicially enforced constitutional limitations are to be
found in several contemporary federal systems. Judicial review thus
survives as an institutional arrangement, not only because of tradition and inertia, but for reasons of prudence, and partly because it is
never pushed too far and never inhibits too gravely the "instrumental" and positive action of government.

Many hope, on the other hand, that through its use government
as an instrument of the popular will, or of the arbitrary will of some
officials, can be successfully checked. The hope has not always been
vain. Justice Holmes protested in 1905, is his dissenting opinion in
the bakery case,[48] that "the Constitution is not intended to embody a
particular economic theory, whether of paternalism and the organic
relation of the citizen to the state or of laissez-faire." In fact, however, the Court until about 1937 continued "to frown upon legisla-

---

[48] *Lochner* v. *New York*, 198 U.S. 45, in which the Court, in a five to four decision,
held that a state law limiting work in bakeshops to 10 hours a day and 60 hours a week
was unconstitutional because it "interferes with the right of contract between the
employer and the employees," that right being "part of the liberty of the individual
protected by the Fourteenth Amendment."

tive projects, whether state or national, which were calculated to curtail freedom of business judgment."[49] Since then, and in the wake of the economic crisis of 1933, the Court has in general sustained the federal policy and responsibility to improve the economic health of the country.[50]

A notable statement of that federal policy is the Employment Act of 1946, in which Congress declared that the federal government was to use all practical means "to coordinate and utilize all its plans, functions and resources for the purpose of creating and maintaining, in a manner calculated to foster and promote free competitive enterprise and the general welfare, conditions under which there will be offered useful employment opportunities, including self-employment, for those able, willing and seeking to work and to promote maximum employment, production and purchasing power." Due process of law, once read only as a *procedural* bar to federal and state action, had become in the late thirties a bar to much *substantive* legislation in the economic field as well. Now, the way is open again, through more permissive judicial action, to more affirmative legislation. Nor is this affirmative trend limited to economic policy. If the Court in recent years has strongly asserted its authority on behalf of civil liberties, under the Bill of Rights and the Fourteenth Amendment, in striking down state action in violation of religious freedom, freedom of speech and press, and the right to "equal protection of the laws," it has also strongly upheld federal legislative and executive power to sustain these rights.[51]

CORPORATE CONSTITUTIONALISM

Judicial review, in general, has played such a major role in American constitutionalism that it hardly comes as a surprise that the current movement among lawyers for the "constitutionalizing" of corporations takes the form primarily of a demand for "due

---

[49] E. S. Corwin, *The Constitution and What It Means Today* (12th rev. ed.; Princeton: Princeton University Press, 1958), p. 253.

[50] The basic constitutional and statutory law undergirding the more positive governmental action in the economy is succinctly described in Adolf A. Berle, *The American Economic Republic* (New York: Harcourt, Brace & World, Inc., Harvest Book Edition, 1965), Part II.

[51] See George W. Spicer, *The Supreme Court and Fundamental Freedoms* (2nd ed.; New York: Appleton-Century-Crofts, Inc., 1967); S. Krislov, *The Supreme Court in the Political Process* (New York: Macmillan Co., 1965); M. R. Konvitz, *Expanding Liberties; Freedom's Gains in Postwar America* (New York: The Viking Press, 1966).

process" in business organizations. Berle compares an economic system with a political government:

> If it denies rights of men to life as they understand life, or to liberty as they understand that, or to property, whatever modern property shall turn out to be, the community gathers itself for a kind of revolt whose results are unforeseeable.[52]

But, as he sees it, the long tradition of the common law and of the American Constitution offers ways and means to meet the problem.

> Corporate action . . . may in the not distant future be held to be controlled by the provisions of the Fourteenth Amendment. . . . Where the corporation is actually working under state regulation, as in the case of a public utility, or enjoys some specific state privilege, the tie-up between corporate and state authority becomes clear.[53]

When a corporation has the power to affect a great many lives, Berle insists, it differs in this respect from the small enterprise whose power can be balanced out by the operation of market forces. Therefore, "it should be subject to the same restraints under the Constitution that apply to an agency of the Federal or state government."[54]

In summing up the significant role of constitutionalism as a force affecting modern business it appears that the long tradition of a higher law that demands restraint on arbitrary power has passed through several stages. At the beginning, for many centuries, this tradition was passed on from generation to generation as a corpus of ideas that, though forcibly expressed, remained nonetheless in the realm of aspiration rather than realization. Only within the past few centuries has modern constitutionalism emerged with effective measures for regularizing and institutionalizing restraint on government while recognizing the authority to govern. The trend today is toward the extension of constitutionalist doctrine not only to *public* governments but to powers exercised by *private* organizations, and more particularly to such economic associations as labor unions and business corporations.

Corporate constitutionalism has thus become one of the major

---

[52] Adolf A. Berle, *The 20th Century Capitalist Revolution* (New York: Harcourt, Brace & Co., 1954) , p. 114.

[53] *Ibid.*, p. 104. See also Adolf A. Berle, "The Developing Law of Corporate Concentration," *University of Chicago Law Review*, Vol. XIX (Summer, 1942) , pp. 639–61.

[54] Adolf A. Berle, *Economic Power and the Free Society* (New York: Fund for the Republic, 1957) , pp. 17–18.

issues confronting corporate executives and public policy-makers. To ask about the influence of boards, stockholders, customers, the public, and, not least, the unions in the shaping of a company's objectives and even in the day-by-day running of the business, is to get into problems of authority and responsibility. When they occur *within* the organization structure below the board level, these problems are usually discussed in terms of "scientific management," business administration, and so on. But beyond these considerations there exists also the question of adapting and assimilating the corporation as a private government into the general social picture.

Who really controls a company? What power does it exercise? To whom should the power wielders be accountable, and how? What is the role of the large corporation in the total power structure of the nation? Is it an important element in the balance of social powers?

The corporation is a decision-making center with an impact on the larger society where many authority centers exist. But it is also a complex of forces seeking places at the table of power within the corporation itself. The corporation is an instrument of power and authority, an institution with its own constitutional structure, maintaining a system of organization, discipline, and morale within its own ranks as well as influential external relations with other authority centers public and private. A corporation, like any other organization, exhibits certain more or less well-defined patterns of leadership, subordination, superordination, and coordination within the boundaries of the firm, and patterns of authority relationships with other organizations and persons beyond its corporate frontiers.

One of the most important problems confronting the managers of the modern corporation is whether the basic pattern of authority relationships—internal and external to the organization—is functionally appropriate in view of contemporary corporate objectives and the organizational requirements for achieving these objectives. The tensions that are building up in economic organization are traceable to external as well as internal forces. Inside the company the stockholder-manager-employee complex reveals the tug and pull of certain easily definable forces. But outside, in the immediate neighborhood, there are the forces of labor unionism and plant-community interests; and in the farther reaches of the environment, the rising fiscal and other demands of public governmental agencies, the still quiescent but looming power of pension and investment trusts, the ever changing market picture at home and abroad, and epoch-making changes in the global patterns of political authority.

The resulting constitutional crisis in the corporation derives from the extension of the authority relationships both within and beyond the firm. The major issues in corporate constitutionalism center on the scope and legitimacy of power and the means of controlling it. Of these two major problems, the emphasis in contemporary writing on the corporation is given to the problem of control. There are two major possibilities for the control of corporate power: controls of managerial power by external agencies and internal controls through institutionalized devices within the firm, designed to secure responsible corporate government. What likelihood is there that such institutionalization will resolve the problem of corporate constitutionalism? The fact is that the trend in this direction is already well started, though the evidence is not to be found in too narrowly defined organizational terms within the formal structure of the firm. The evidence is to be gathered rather in such peripheral developments as collective bargaining and the attendant growth of the idea of the work force as a corporate constituency; the newer relations between franchised dealers and manufacturing companies; the rise of pension trusts with their yet unrealized potential as corporate policy-determiners; the gradual internalizing of cultural mores in the form of "social responsibility of the businessman"; and the shift of internal authority from the upper reaches of traditionally hierarchical management to what Galbraith calls the "technostructure"[55] made up of amorphous und changing combinations of specialized talent, grouped within a company at all levels and with motivations and goals of their own that profoundly affect corporate goals.

The issue of control of power is logically subordinate to (though not necessarily of less practical importance than) the question of legitimate power. The standards of justice to be applied in corporate constitutionalism will depend upon what we expect corporate power

---

[55] John Kenneth Galbraith, *The New Industrial State* (Boston: Houghton Mifflin Co., 1967). Raymond J. Saulnier, former chairman of the Council of Economic Advisers, has taken exception to this further extension of the "now-conventional wisdom" concerning the separation of ownership and control: "It misses entirely the hawkeye surveillance of corporate management by institutional investors and security analysts, all surrogates of the individual shareholder"; *The New York Times Book Review,* June 25, 1967.

to accomplish. The scope of social functions and the standards of performance we expect of a business corporation supply the key to the scope of its powers. The production of goods for profit is undoubtedly the major business of the corporation, but this is hardly the *sole* concern of its members, who are, after all, bound by ties to societies other than the corporate institution.

This multiplicity of ties alone is certain to modify the otherwise clear-cut purpose of a business corporation, and the modification is in the direction not of a narrowing but rather a widening of the scope of corporate authority. Quite aside from the powers of officials in any organization, arising logically from its specialized purpose, there are always other powers growing out of organizational necessities of a more general kind. There are at least minimal disciplines to be enforced to build up and maintain an *esprit de corps* and to preserve unity of effort in the face of internal disintegrating forces as well as external threats to the common enterprise.

The pluralism of our relatively competitive economy is in itself an immeasurable source of strength for the nation as a whole. The dispersal of power in this way is a necessary protection of liberty. But a corollary of constitutionalism is the adequacy of decisional authority in the dispersed centers of privately organized power. If authority is to be widely dispersed in the interests of liberty and freer choice, it must not be forgotten that choice in itself means decision making, and decision is the most important component of power. The decision centers, in other words, are *power* centers; and in an increasingly organizational economy these power centers are found not entirely or even mainly in the individual human units of a completely atomized society but increasingly in the artificial units of capital aggregates. This means that, under the impact of the organizational revolution, a pluralistic society is not a society of individual free men who release bits of their primitive freedom of choice to public government alone, retaining all other decision-making power to themselves as private persons. Rather it is a society in which decision making is transferred to a variety of public and private governments.

In this process of transfer, the accretions of power by these governments are responses to the need for collective action. The debate about shrinkage of individual freedom of choice, as this transfer proceeds apace, is not mainly a debate about the individual *versus* the state; it is a debate about the *kinds* of organization that ought to have the power to govern men, and about the distribution of powers among these public and private organizations. It is from this point of view that one has to approach the normative question of power mustering (that is, decisional authority) in the business corporation. What power has to be transferred to the private government of the corporation if it is to perform the tasks assigned to it? And how can one define those tasks in such a way as to make a rational distribution of decisional authority between this particular kind of private government and other kinds of public and private government? The political economies of countries throughout the free world provide various answers to these questions, as they do the question of control over power within public and private sectors. The student of comparative government in both sectors does well to examine the differences, and to note the modalities in constitutionalist patterns that result from technological change and a growing insistence upon human rights and "the revolution of rising expectations."

CONCLUSION

Constitutionalism is an ancient concept. The modern expression of its essential elements—legitimate power and institutionalized restraints on power—takes many forms. The form in which constitutionalism is most familiar is the constitutional theory and law of one's own country. Yet we know that that theory and practice is subject to change in order to meet changing conditions of life, and that when we look abroad there are many approaches to the two central problems of constitutionalism. And in one's own country, where organizational power grows to meet the demands of modern life, it is likewise possible to discern diverse solutions to these problems. Corporate constitutionalism, then, is but one aspect of the more universal search for the balance between the rights of men and the powers they concede to their organizations to get done the things that they believe ought to be done.

RECOMMENDED READING

BERLE, ADOLF, A. *The American Economic Republic*, pp. vii–xi and 95–116. New York: Harcourt, Brace & World, Inc., Harvest Book Edition, 1965.

BREWSTER, KINGMAN, JR. "The Corporation and Economic Federalism," in E. S. MASON (ed.), *The Corporation in Modern Society*, pp. 72–84. Cambridge: Harvard University Press, 1959.

CHAYES, ABRAM. "The Modern Corporation and the Rule of the Law," pp. 25–45, in E. S. MASON (ed.), *ibid.*

CORWIN, EDWARD S. *Liberty against Government: The Rise, Flowering and Decline of a Famous Juridical Concept,* esp. chap. i, pp. 1–9, and chap. v, pp. 169–83. Baton Rouge: Louisiana State University Press, 1948.

EELLS, RICHARD. *The Government of Corporations*, pp. 31–88, 125–38, and 184–212. New York: The Free Press, 1962.

FRIEDRICH, CARL J. "Constitutions and Constitutionalism," *International Encyclopedia of the Social Sciences,* Vol. III, pp. 318–26.

LOEWENSTEIN, KARL. *Political Power and the Governmental Process*, pp. 70–120. Chicago: University of Chicago Press, 1957.

FURTHER READING

DEUTSCH, KARL W. "Strategies of Freedom: The Widening of Choices and the Change of Goals," in C. J. FRIEDRICH (ed.), *NOMOS IV: Liberty,* pp. 301–7. New York: Atherton Press, 1962.

KNIGHT, FRANK H. "Authority and the Free Society," in *NOMOS I: Authority,* pp. 67–77. Cambridge: Harvard University Press, 1958.

LIPSET, SEYMOUR M. "The Political Process in Trade Unions: A Theoretical Statement," in BERGER, MONROE; ABEL, THEODORE; and PAGE, CHARLES H. (eds.), *Freedom and Control in Modern Society,* pp. 82–124. Princeton: D. Van Nostrand Co., 1954.

MCILWAIN, CHARLES H. *Constitutionalism: Ancient and Modern.* Rev. ed. Ithaca: Cornell University Press, 1940.

MASON, ALPHEUS T. "Business Organized as Power: The New *Imperium in Imperio,*" *American Political Science Review,* Vol. XLIV (June, 1950), pp. 323–42.

POUND, ROSCOE. *The Development of Constitutional Guarantees of Liberty.* New Haven: Yale University Press, 1957.

SPIRO, HERBERT J. *Government by Constitution: The Political Systems of Democracy,* esp. chaps. iii, xxv, and xxvi. New York: Random House, 1959.

SUTHERLAND, ARTHUR E. *Constitutionalism in America: Origins and Evolution of Its Fundamental Ideas.* Waltham, Mass.: Blaisdell Publishing Co., 1965.

WALTON, CLARENCE, and EELLS, RICHARD (eds.). *The Business System,* Vol. III, pp. 1677–1783. New York: Macmillan Co., Arkville Press Series, 1967.

VI. CHANGING PERSPECTIVES

THROUGHOUT this volume has run a consistent theme which may be expressed in terms of the interplay between forces encouraging stability and forces inducing change. Increasingly challenged is the idea that "changing times" can be identified with change itself as we know it today.

Except perhaps in the universe of the mathematical physicist, the idea of time appears to be relative rather than absolute. Yet, though most of us are tentative when dealing with abstruse ideas, we feel fairly authoritative on the subject of time. We tend to speak of it as if it grew around us like grass and had to be trimmed and controlled accordingly. Even men who claim that they cannot believe in anything they do not see, feel, or understand accept time in somewhat the same fashion that older societies accepted myth. For time accounts for much in life that would otherwise be inexplicable. It is presumed to control biochemistry, in animal and plant life even more obviously than in man, and to determine the seasons, and thereby the elements.

These manifestations are the strongest evidence of time as a factor in the natural condition, though we rarely advert to them as such. From its most intrusive aspect, death, we turn our faces away. The tribal conventions that have grown up around the disguise and easement of burial are sufficient example of this.

How then do we understand time, beyond the mere acknowledgment of it as a part of the nature of life? Is it the climate of biology? Is it a dynamic inevitability of this planet, or is it a fact only of life? Is time a kind of weight that disappears with gravity? Can we describe it by analogy as like the yeast in bread, or should we compare it to a vehicle in motion? Perhaps we lean toward the latter. Consider the aphorism "time and tide wait for no man" and the poetic metaphor that calls time a winged chariot, an old gypsy man, a river flowing. Time is passing, we say. The calendar and the clock are metric measures of its speed.

On the other hand, we also manage to think of time as a static thing, a commodity or medium of exchange. In our everyday vocabulary, time is wasted, saved, well or ill spent. The idea of time as capital, high in purchasing power and limited in supply, seems, paradoxically, to flourish beside the idea of time as a jostling and crowding element, moving us toward an unknown destination at its own pace, not at ours. All we can say of time with any measure of certainty is that its impact differs for each of us in duration, reward, or transmutation. But there are indications today that time as the arbiter of change may someday be displaced by human initiative and that, as our technological culture develops, time may be displaced as a major factor of change and may become a mere statistic.

The writers and thinkers of the West have tended to speak of time and change as if the two were synonymous. But, in an era in which the term "accelerating change" has become a cliché, we are beginning to feel that change need no longer be time-conditioned, that the two may be, to some extent, made independent of each other. Some may account for the rapid change that a man living in our century witnesses in his own lifetime by concluding that time has speeded up.

The trouble today is that time is so short. Five years could be wasted a century ago, or even two decades ago, without losing the chance to recoup mistakes and negligence. The acceleration of technology has made the pace much too swift for such leisure trial and error.[1]

What is implied here is that time as a condition of change is not the dominant factor that it was even two decades ago. While time may still be a condition of nature, it does not have the same impact

---

[1] Harry Howe Ransome, "Review of Central Intelligence and National Security," *American Political Science Review*, Vol. LIV (June, 1960), p. 508.

it once had on the production of the human intellect. In short, technological progress may be separating change from time.

A look at the cultural history of traditional societies, or at what we now call underdeveloped countries, would emphasize this conclusion. Where time is accepted as a state of endlessly recurring repetitions, change is very little and very slow, and, as a result, there is little progress as we understand it. This may explain why, among the Indians of the forest and the plain, the travois was never outmoded by the wheel through all those centuries before the white man. When time is an "eternal now," as it tends to be in oriental civilizations, there is no "then" or "when," save to describe the past, and apparently no desire for historical evolution but only for preservation of the status quo.

Though this conception also influences the West, we tend to exploit time intellectually at the level of movement and change. It is perhaps this difference in awareness that has inspired us to try to escape the domination of time by embracing change, not in any revolutionary sense, because we regard what *is* as totally unsatisfactory, but in an evolutionary sense that presupposes a certain dynamic potential for change in any time situation.

It has already been reported how—in the research laboratories of industry—the word "time" is qualified to read "*lead* time," and lead time is the basis of innovation. Strictly speaking, it means time for a spurt ahead of time. Implicit in this qualification is the awareness that innovation can occur simultaneously in widely separated geographical locations. Creativity in any one line is not the property of any one culture. It is rather a potential in human nature that is fed by imagination and fostered by circumstance. The Russians may legitimately claim to have been the inventors of the telegraph, nuclear fission, or satellites. By a similar process of reasoning, Daedalus, of ancient myth, may be said to have invented aviation many years before Leonardo or the Wright Brothers. In each case there was an idea with more lead time than technology behind it. Mere precedence of innovating ideas is irrelevant. It is the possibility of realizing such ideas on their technological level that makes the difference in the significance of time as it relates to material progress.

But no one would deny that time is still a delaying element in the development of technology, however much the modern speed-up in knowledge may alter its ultimate influence as a restraining factor. At present it is assumed that it will take at least 10 years for atomic power to replace other power sources, even at the pace with which we are moving from research to development. New ideas for material progress, though conceived in a society whose external nature, at least, is scientific and technological, are therefore still, to some extent, time-bound.

In 1700 the time sequence from the facts of nature, through the ivory tower to the fund of human knowledge, to the attic inventor, and then to marketable goods or ideas, an entrepreneur, and a customer, was 200 years. In 1900 it was 50 years. In 1950 it was 25 years. This improvement was the result of the 20th-century organizational or coordinated approach: from the facts of nature, through research, engineering, manufacturing, and marketing and on to the customer. By now the lag is said to be 10 years from laboratory to customer.

In addition, innovational ideas may be further delayed by what has been described as "lag" between technical feasibility and social receptivity. Lag results from failure to appreciate the altering impact of manipulated change upon time as stasis. When we conceive of time as a commodity rather than as an impetus, then we see change as subtracting from the total sum of time. It cancels some of our conditioning and much of our experience. Anyone who has changed one career, one domicile, one community, or one school for another has had experience of this. In these situations we appear to have lost some time invested elsewhere. On the other hand, if we think of change in terms of impetus, we are aware that the time drag has been lightened by rapid and successive changes.

Yet neither technologically nor socially do we ever manage completely to leave what *was* behind us, whether it be artifacts or a frame of reference. The computer is an instrument for information conversion, but so is the thermostat on the household furnace. And that most ancient tool, the shovel, leans on the bulldozer when it is quiet for the night. Daily the oldest devices are employed along with the new. Each serves its purpose, and, since these are largely practical purposes, lag here is a negligible factor. On this level it is possible to defend such a concept as planned obsolescence, which is built into many modern technological products, not merely to force the consumer to renew his level of living periodically without improving it, but to give him time to adjust to radical change. Radiation techniques, for instance, now make it possible to preserve perishable food so that it can be kept fresh on the pantry shelf. But how long will it take for the housewife to be persuaded to store it outside her refrigerator?

Even in a society as receptive to change as ours, progress must be tempered in the interests of stability. But it is a fact that quite apart from time lag, or social lag, progress is frequently delayed by periods of growth and development. Today's telephone, for instance, is not dramatically different from what it was when one turned a crank to call central; in some ways, perhaps, it is not as efficient. The numerous companies that have developed it have for some time been promising drastic innovation—the possibility of talking from anywhere in a room equipped with an instrument and of a picture as well as sound reception. Meantime, we are encouraged to have, not one phone, but one in every room, with suitable colors, night lights, code service, and similar reemphases. Ideas for innovation in this field are apparently still ahead of the technology to realize them.

What one may conclude from an examination of this child of modern technology—and other examples exist—is that progress appears to be of three kinds. There is the initial surge forward—the concept of the thing or the system hitherto unachieved. Then occurs the lag during which the inevitable problems of developing and improving are ironed out. This is horizontal growth, which involves time not only for trial and error but for financing and promotion. Finally, there is a kind of innovation that is at once vertical and lateral and results from a creative combination of tested technological and scientific knowledge to create something new. Both the automobile and the computer are examples. Advertising, another child of progress, undertakes to convince man to buy what technology has created.

Advertising is not a new concept, but its 20th-century techniques are as innovative as they are competitive. Like the programing for modern communications media, the ability of advertising copy to influence the mass of men has unfortunately been exploited rather than developed. Many of the points made against modern advertising are, therefore, well taken. But there are points to be made for it. First, it has grown so rapidly that it is still unaware of its potential or of what its duty to society may be. Second, advertising's potential is as much for good as for its widely deplored superficiality and crass expediency. It can be said to its credit that advertising has forced progress by consciously setting human assiduity to speed the slow course of time, and in this way it has helped to bring about speedier change. It discounts time drag, not with logic, certainly, but with determination and repetition. Whatever its ends, its means are most effective. Science and technology can compound wonders, but they cannot always popularize them; advertising can.

Material progress, therefore, may be said to result from the composite effort of these three: science, technology, and advertising. At the consumer-goods level, at least, they have outmoded the old, time-bound rate of change and speeded it up considerably. But, if inventors and researchers cannot make change immediately palatable, as advertising often succeeds in doing, they can foresee and control its impact and in this way foster the stability of the society they tend so radically to alter. Much of the current talk about long-range planning is a direct result of this effort at control. For it has become as important to foresee the implications of radical change, and to channel it accordingly, as to effect change itself. One of the curious features of change and progress is that it is often the product not of demand but of the knowledge and curiosity of a very few men. Teamwork is the talisman of research today, but a team has to be led. And, in spite of the modern emphasis on group-think and brain-storming, it takes no more than one singularly gifted man to foresee and plan for the potential altering force of one good idea out of many, though it need not have been his to begin with.

Thus far we have talked in terms of material change. It is important not to lose sight of the fact that there have been ideological changes in this hemisphere related ultimately to the change from bondage to freedom, from status to contract, from nation-oriented economy to the supranational economic community. How have we been able to move so fast and so far without becoming disoriented by the adjustments we are called upon to make? In providing a comfortable, if complicated, existence for our people, have we undermined their integrity and self-reliance?

There is much to be read on that subject. One reference may suffice:

The discovery of the new world exercised a sort of selection among the inhabitants of Europe. All the colonists, except the Negroes, were voluntary exiles. The fortunate, the deeply rooted, and the lazy remained at home; the wilder instincts or dissatisfaction of others tempted them beyond the horizon. The American is accordingly the most adventurous, or the descendant of the most adventurous of Europeans. It is in his blood to be socially a radical, though perhaps not intellectually. What has existed in the past, especially in the remote past, seems to him not only not authoritative, but irrelevant, inferior, and outworn. He finds it rather a sorry waste of time to think about the past at all. But his enthusiasm for the future is profound; he can conceive of no more decisive way of recommending an opinion or a practice than to say that it is what everybody is coming to adopt. This expectation of what he approves, or approval of what he expects, makes up his optimism. It is the necessary faith of the pioneer.[2]

The fact seems to be that the natural adaptability of a pioneer citizenry not only made accelerated progress possible but even strained at the limits of improvising. And, with it all, our society has thus far managed to remain on an even keel, even though the massive organization that makes technological production feasible seems at times to have attenuated much of the rugged individualism that brought men here in the first place.

It is probably true that group activity in a modern organization defeats the individual sense of accomplishment in much the same way as does the assembly line. Here, again, the whole man has too much of himself left over, unspent, at the end of a day's work. Human energy and ability need to have effort demanded of them, otherwise there is no sense of achievement or fulfillment. Production equipment, because it exists in space, can be developed by technology to the point of eliminating deadening, repetitious, endless man effort, but if this deprives a man of his livelihood it is hardly a positive improvement in his lot. Organization, which has no existence in space, but only in time, must think this problem through before it acts. Time is the dynamics of organizational existence. When time becomes an endless "now," organization becomes bureaucracy.

It is not necessary to point to the Chinese to prove that the ethos of bureaucracy is far older than modern organization. Where our present economic organizations differ conspicuously from the older types is in their phenomenal productivity. This has sometimes been regarded as evidence of the fact that the American is an imaginative man, whose heritage has left him with a tendency to turn this faculty to the practical solution of problems attendant upon moving goods, people, and political idealism over a vast terrain. As a result of his

---

[2] George Santayana. *Character and Opinion in the United States* (New York: Charles Scribner's Sons, 1920) , p. 168–69.

efforts, this terrain is no longer as unlimited as it once appeared to
be. Hence, despite the rising volume of complaints about the collec-
tivized nature of what was once a relatively untrammeled way of
life, it would appear that the focus of the American pioneering
mentality, having shifted from exploring and mastering the earth to
mastering that more elusive factor, time, in the last five years has
undertaken to conquer and explore outer space.

Science and technology have led the way there also. Communications media opened up the world geographically as no amount of
colonizing had been able to do. Men conversed over thousands of
miles via telegraph and telephone. They entertained and informed
each other further by radio. Then they became spectators, seeing as
well as hearing each other on TV. Once units of distance became
mere minutes or seconds, our attention turned to the new frontier,
space. Now, in Sugar Grove, West Virginia, we have built a new
kind of ear to listen in on the universe. Whether we can tune in at
last to that music of the spheres that the ancients claimed is made by
the stars in their eternal orbits, or whether we will at last hear other
voices, is part of the new hope of progress. The satellites and missiles, products of ambitious and enlightened enterprise, roar up
from their launching pads or topple over to become a laboratory for
new research and redevelopment.

Characteristically, we think of space as a kind of new route to the
Indies. But the potential of change inherent in its exploration is far
more challenging than the mere novelty of voyaging across oceans
not of water but of ether. Those things that we now, literally, see
through a glass darkly, and probe with delicate instruments, we
aspire to have investigated by trained and curious men.

When this happens, we may perhaps come to grips at last with
the mystery of time. For if it is true that the biochemistry of the
astronaut can be sufficiently slowed so that he returns to his earth
younger than men who were his age when he left, then we should at
last be able to know, rather than to speculate, about that detaining,
disintegrative force we call time. The effort to anticipate time, to
lead it rather than to be dragged along by it, may be perfected by a
society dedicated to progress and so completely in control of change
that time will have small significance. The dream of progress with
stability would at that point be realized, for, once time has no
dimensions, death, indeed, should have no dominion.

Finally, one can only allude to the fantastic possibilities that are being unearthed by molecular biologists and others for creating a new science of "human engineering." Yet with each new unveiling of an old mystery we become aware of the necessity for adapting existing social mechanisms—like the corporation and the union—to serve new purposes in a restless and creative society.

20. The Changing Functions of Business: The Economic Performance

OUTLINE

ORIGINALLY the word "business" appears to have been used to make a distinction between the life of action and the life of contemplation.

According to Toynbee, "The English word 'business' is a literal translation of the Latin word *negotium*. *Negotium* means 'the opposite of leisure,' and the Latin word for 'businessman' is *negotiator*—which means, of course, not a negotiator in our English sense of the word, but a man who denies himself leisure in order to get business done."[1]

Now "leisure," according to the dictionary, means "freedom or opportunity to do something," and as a denotation this contains a certain amount of ambiguity. But the connotation of the word seems always to have been freedom to pursue some course of one's own choice, on one's own terms, and for the sake of whatever imponderable satisfaction it gives the spirit. Business, by contrast, presupposes profit, money profit, as its end—otherwise not only is it not good business, it is not business at all. Many people make money on a hobby or on sports participation, but this is incidental to excellence in what they have chosen to develop as interests. The income from sport, which sets up a tax problem as to when a sport is not a sport but a business, is a modern dilemma. In the past, then, business was for profit, and leisure was for personal advantage.

Aristotle distinguished three ways of life which men might choose in freedom, that is, in full independence of the necessities of life and the relationships they originated. The prerequisite of freedom ruled out all ways of life chiefly devoted to keeping one's self alive—not only labor, which was the way of life of the slave, who was coerced by the necessity to stay alive and by the rule of his master, but also *the working life of the free craftsman and the acquisitive life of the merchant*. In short, it excluded everybody who involuntarily or voluntarily, for his whole life or temporarily, had lost the free disposition of his movements and activities.[2]

But Aristotle also believed that the good, free life depended upon having a certain amount of goods to begin with. Wherefore we may concede that property or income of some kind inevitably precedes leisure in the evolution of human society. And, using this thesis as a first premise, we can better understand the changes that have occurred in the functioning of modern business.

With mass production, the idea of mass consumption had to be

---

[1] Arnold Toynbee, "Thinking Ahead," *Harvard Business Review*, Vol. XXXVI (September–October, 1958) , p. 30.

[2] Hannah Arendt, *The Human Condition* (Chicago: University of Chicago Press, 1958) , p. 12 (Italics added.)

fostered, and, once this was accomplished in terms of a wage that provided not merely for human needs but left a margin of surplus for the satisfaction of human wants, our way of life was born. This, in itself, was a radical change, which brought in its train other changes both in the attitude and function of business.

Society's attitude toward the businessman is also changing. He is expected to think of the significance of his enterprise to society in larger terms, to think less of money and more of the common good, to think of men less in terms of cost-of-living raises and more in terms of their human hopes and human fears. Though often confused by those who still insist that its only real responsibility is to produce goods and services for profit, business knows that it is not what it was, that it has somehow become a social institution. But it is not at all certain how it should cope with the duties of a new environment. Every effort by business to meet society on its own terms has received the mixed reception that a tame bear might get at a fund-raising banquet. One would assume that its presence was necessarily a publicity stunt and that, however clean it might keep its napkin and the tablecloth, there was no real assurance that it might not at any point revert to nature and devour a few of its table companions. And there are several ancient reasons for this mistrust.

SOCIAL AND RELIGIOUS ATTITUDES
TOWARD BUSINESS

Since very early times the man of business has been regarded as a creature apart. Walter Lippmann recalls that "the early Christian writers looked upon business as a peril to the soul"; and Bishop Porteus once wrote that "It seldom happens that men of a studious turn of mind acquire any degree of reputation for their knowledge of business."[3] This distinction sees the businessman as crafty rather than intelligent, conniving rather than wise. Perhaps it is also responsible for the distinction we make between *profession* and *trade,* though it is quite obvious that many professional men today are better than average at coping with the business side of their occupation.

Upper-class British and European theories of what constitutes a suitable life of action for a gentleman have also left us with a heritage that tends to distinguish between trade and business, the

---

[3] *Webster's Unabridged Dictionary,* 2d ed., under "business."

latter having been regarded as highly respectable only when it involved administering one's estate, the former having been held somewhat in contempt. Trade was the occupation of a merchant, especially a retail merchant. It was the "act or business of exchanging commodities by barter, or of buying and selling for money."[4] However prosperous a merchant might become, he was still held at arm's length by the landed gentry, the land-grant aristocracy of a predominantly agricultural society. To be in trade was to be a member of the middle class and consequently "not a gentleman."

Despite the fact that today's aristocracy is backed by stocks and bonds rather than by real property, the convention that the typical businessman is a loud, tasteless parvenu, neither well bred nor well educated, still persists in many circles. The banker or financier, however, is somewhat better thought of, perhaps because, in a society that worships material values, there is a mystique about his occupation. He makes money make money and so assumes something of the role of the shaman or medicine man of the more archaic cults.

But it should be remembered that the most ancient prejudice against "making money" as a way of life was not social but religious. The Bible had stated flatly that the love of money was the root of all evil, and the early Christian writers therefore looked upon business as a peril to the soul. The more a man prospered in this world as a result of getting and spending, the more his well-being in the next was jeopardized. There was an inverse ratio between material and spiritual welfare. "It is harder for the rich man to enter heaven than for a camel to pass through a needle's eye," was the biblical summing-up. In biblical times, barter was the traditional, acceptable medium for exchange of both goods and services. Once money entered into the transaction, it was assumed to have brought with it its inherent evil—avarice. Today we are all but unable to comprehend the theological conviction that money is a sterile thing. The myth of Midas is the pagan analogy of the theological argument. Because he loved gold, Midas begged the gods to grant him the power to create it at his touch. Yet the gift proved fatal, for, while it transformed the food he ate into further riches for him, it deprived him of sustenance, and his embrace froze his living child to a golden image.

The notion that money, an inanimate metal counter, could generate more money was therefore anathema to the Christian dispensa-

---

4 *Ibid.*

tion. Throughout the Middle Ages, money earned by money, or interest, was condemned as usury, a mortal sin for which Christians risked eternal damnation. The Jews, outside the fold, ran no such risk, and as a result they became the great loan agencies of the Middle Ages and among the first to engage in the practice of investing money at interest as an occupation. Thus business gradually became not merely a matter of administering the affairs of an estate, or a way of earning a living with the exchange of particular goods or craft services, but an objective kind of practice, which dealt in any and all kinds of goods and services, including banking and finance.

THE NATURE OF BUSINESS TODAY

The word "business" is today used as a blanket term that covers a number of varied occupations—manufacturing, commerce, and trade, as well as such special aspects of these functions as marketing, merchandising, and advertising. The term includes the operations of banks, stock exchanges, insurance companies, public services, communications, transportation, and even the accounting divisions of large noneconomic organizations. Indeed, it has become difficult to say what is not a business. As a general rule, it is probably safe to conclude that any individual or group whose working career is dedicated to making a day-to-day profit is in business. Strictly speaking, therefore, the salaried organizational employee is not a businessman unless his business is dedicated to making a profit. We may thus make a distinction between making a living and profit making.

The other major distinction we make in speaking of business is with respect to size.[5] There is "small business," which appears to be allied in most people's minds with the connotations surrounding the old idea of trade, and "big business," a 20th-century innovation that has so many ramifications that all its social functions are not yet clearly understood. It is significant enough socially, however, to be a focus of respect, of fear, and of demand for financial contributions. The one denominator that all businesses, both large and small, have in common as their reason for being is profit.

THE SINGLE-FUNCTION ENTERPRISE

These classifications of business as large and small, while intelligible to everybody, are too elementary to describe the unique nature

---

5 See Chapter 5 above on Erpf's "Spectrum of Companies."

of much of 20th-century business. The category "small" is intended to include the single-function enterprise characteristic of an agrarian society—the enterprise offering a single product or service and managed directly by its owner or owners. But this describes not only the family-run grocery store but also the early steps in the development of banking, manufacturing, mining, and transportation services. Of these, the railroads were the most complex, right from the beginning. The geographical dispersion of lines and stations, the need for coordinated planning and scheduling, for a system of rates, and for communication demanded the kind of know-how for supervising a network of operational activities that is the hallmark of modern management.

The rise of management brought another dimension—the organizational—to business. A single-function company, as does any business, offers a product or a service in order to make a profit. This is the entrepreneurial or static reason for the venture of capital. The dynamics, or organizational aspect, is personified by a central-office staff, whose function is to plan, communicate, coordinate, and evaluate the total enterprise and to anticipate new entrepreneurial opportunities.

THE MULTIFUNCTION ENTERPRISE

The multifunction enterprise is the more modern version of the single-function enterprise. On the frontier, the only multifunctional enterprise was probably the medicine show, which manufactured its own product, bottled it, promoted it with handbills, drew the customers with costumed entertainers as part of its advertising, and then peddled its product, creating a market on which it could depend for the years to follow. Today's multifunctional enterprise is the type of industrial firm that, in addition to manufacturing, handles its own financing, does its own mining, transporting, research, engineering, and marketing.

THE MULTIPRODUCT ENTERPRISE

Another new type of entprerise is the multiproduct firm, a diversified enterprise that handles not only a variety of products but a variety of single-enterprise functions within each product line. As a rule, these have developed out of merger and consolidation.

Competition produced consolidation among businesses that had heavy fixed costs and could derive economics of scale through merger. Such consolidation was vertical as well as horizontal. Vertical integration meant greater size, as an individual business unit took over a number of related operations for economy of operation, and more readily available facilities.

The creation of the corporation as a business unit stimulated the drive toward greater size. The corporation provided an outlet for accumulated capital, and it met the need for an economic entity at once impersonal and flexible enough to serve the material needs of a prosperous and growing population.

The single-function firm became, through the corporate device, better able to finance its developing and increasingly dispersed enterprises and to consolidate them under hired management, which in pursuit of efficiency and growth created massive organization for mass production.

The Multinational Enterprise

Although companies doing transnational business on a large scale are not new, American multinational corporations in the number and scope of their operations in the world arena today do present new issues concerning the changing functions of business. The nature of these issues will be considered in a special section of this chapter. Here we will indicate some tentative definitions of the truly multinational company as distinguished from an enterprise that merely engages in trade across international frontiers or has some financial stake abroad.

The multinational corporation has its home and headquarters in one country but bases also in other "host" countries where manufacturing or other business activities are carried on through direct investment and managerial staffs that give the company roots abroad. This multiple rootedness is the key to such a company's opportunities—and its more extensive managerial responsibilities. It lives and operates in other countries, their laws and their customs, as well as those at home. This brings in train problems of political as well as economic dimensions.

Unlike the managers of domestically confined companies, those of multinational companies have to make fundamental decisions on marketing, production, and research in terms of the alternatives open to them anywhere in the world. To do this most advantageously they should make such decisions on the basis of a genuinely global perspective that embraces the social and economic forces in a world arena of more than one hundred and twenty sovereign states. The indicated task of managers in these transnational enterprises is thus a highly professional one.

THE APPEARANCE OF THE PROFESSIONAL IN MANAGEMENT

HIS PRESENT STATUS

The nature of the change in the functioning of business brought about by the rise of the corporation can be summed up as follows:

Before the wide-spread application of the corporate device, a business career was envisaged as one in which the owner of property, whether in the form of money, material, or equipment, put it to use for profit-making under personal direction, and personally pocketed the gains or bore the losses . . . The dominant type of business organization at present is the corporation, to which owners commit their property by contracts of limited liability, to be used by hired workers ranging from unskilled manual laborers to highly trained specialists.[6]

Many of these highly skilled specialists specialize in management, and their lot, though remunerative for the most part, is at present an uneasy one. The question of precisely what management is or may become—an art, a science, or a profession—is still being debated. The fact that a man can move from one business to another and handle a totally different type of responsibility of merchandise may be interpreted as indicating that there is professional skill involved. Within management itself, these days, a distinction is made between top, middle, and lower management. According to this classification, it is perhaps safe to say that management is a practice in the lower echelons and a profession in the higher.

But, regardless of his training, intention, or assignment, today's manager finds himself assailed alternately, by labor as the man whose ambitions for his firm and for himself are destroying the immemorial opportunity of the laborer to be worthy of his hire, and by society, which accuses him of exerting arbitrary power over the lives of too many men. Management power, say these critics, is illegitimate power. With its profit-seeking gambits, it can destroy a man's chance for livelihood. And yet who is the manager himself but a hireling who does not own what he administers? As a mere salaried

---

[6] Dexter M. Keezer, "Business," *Encyclopaedia of the Social Sciences*, Vol. III, p. 85.

employee, how can he presume to reorganize the working lives and investment returns of thousands of individuals?

Who, indeed, is the manager? Today he is a man, hired at a salary to be all things to the business enterprise, which today consists of all kinds of men. If he appears to have failed to measure up, it may be the fault of his approach to his duties or it may be owing to the very breadth of his task.

THE TECHNICIST APPROACH

The cultural climate of the last hundred years has infected management, as it has everyone, with a scientific or technicist approach to living. Economics and technology have not developed independent of human nature and should never have been separated from it even theoretically. But this is precisely what has occurred.

The typical technicist, a familiar figure in our society, has been defined thus:

A man who considers all the problems of his daily activity (including the human ones), from an exclusively technical point of view is a technicist. One of the usual characteristics of the technicist in offices and factories is that, when faced with a problem, he begins by making a draft, writing down figures, and if possible, formulating an equation.[7]

Unfortunately, the scientific-management movement was begun on this basis. Time-and-motion study may have contributed greatly toward efficiency, but it tended to make men the tools of mass production. Finding the efficient way to do a job did, of course, provide a satisfaction for some men—and yearly we have better tools for competent men to tend. But "soldiering" is still an aspect of much human nature, and only the elimination of human nature in the workshop will remove it altogether.

The technicist's "scientific" approach to modern business ignored the whole question .of natural environment, an environment in which the whole man could participate. By creating, first, semi-independent machines and then automated machines, the technicist mentality has reduced further the element of artisanship that gave many a man a conscientious pride in work well done. Not only has the importance of human skill diminished, but the traditional knowledge of materials that was part of the stock in trade of the skilled

---

[7] Georges Friedmann, "Technological Change and Human Relations," *Cross Currents*, Vol. X (Winter, 1960), p. 35.

craftsman is vanishing also and now depends on research and engineering. But, however humiliating to the artisan, this is inevitable in an era that has the resources and the knowledge for creating synthetic materials. A critique of management should establish first which of these developments is the responsibility of the technicist mentality and which is the natural result of advancing research and technology. Today's automation may be relieving the worker of an opportunity to earn a living, or it may be relieving him of the kind of inhuman drudgery that was the lot of Taylor's "first-class man," the pig-iron handler, Schmidt.

The "Balanced Best Interests" Approach

To the extent that it now demands of the men who administer it that they "balance the best interests" of stockholders, employees, customers, suppliers, distributors, and the general public, business has already outgrown the technicist approach. This is an incredibly difficult assignment for the manager, who is frequently a specialist in engineering, accounting, or marketing. History has produced few men who can balance the best interests even of a nation—and a nation is frequently smaller than the far-flung interests of a really large modern enterprise. The manager, moreover, can look for no guidance from the owners of his enterprise, who sometimes number in the hundred thousands, for they have made it plain that what they want from him is principally a return on invested capital. Although he often does not own more than a few shares of the enterprise he helps to govern, he has considerable control of its destinies. Some of his obligations have been summed up as follows:

Since World War I professional managers made nearly all the entrepreneurial and operational decisions without interference of family or financial owners and these decisions were primarily concerned with markets and technology.

Since the 1930's, decisions as to personnel, and to a less extent to competition and capital allocation, have been somewhat influenced by labor unions, government regulations including taxes and the needs of the continuing national emergency.

So in the 1950's and 60's major managerial challenges may have been or will be more concerned with the requirements and needs of personnel at all levels and the external social and political conditions rather than with the markets and technology.[8]

---

[8] A. D. Chandler, "The History of Managing in the United States" (talk given at General Electric's Advanced Management Course, Crotonville, N.Y., May 26, 1960).

It is perhaps safe to infer that the larger the organization engaged in the production and sale of goods and services for profit, the more impact it has on its social environment. As government and unions circumscribe its vast entrepreneurial activities by making demands on its wealth and setting limits to the powers of that wealth, the management of an economic organization must move out of the ethical vacuum of pure economic theory and into the main stream of human existence. For the rise of large business organizations, and the need for men to manage them, has inevitably led to a demand that the holders of economic power employ it for other than exclusively economic ends.

THE ORGANIZATIONAL REVOLUTION

But, before business evolved to its present stage, there were drastic changes in its organization that should be considered in any discussion of management. For it was the destiny of the manager, in holding together and developing the interests of a multifunctional enterprise, to atomize the total task for its better accomplishment.

THE SEPARATION OF PLANNING FROM DOING

Perhaps the most inevitable dichotomy was the separation of planning from doing. Essentially, the function of a manager is to determine what needs to be done and to allocate these tasks to competent specialists who can best handle them.

Planning and organizing became an occupation in itself and was the prerogative of the managers. The labor force followed through with the activity, the doing of the task. Once the task had been planned and allotted to craft or trade, the managerial force measured its results with a critical eye to see whether there were better and faster ways of doing it than the traditional ways. Time-and-motion study gave rise to "task management," the better way of doing a familiar job. It also probably fostered the idea of the assembly line and of mass production in general.

THE DIVISION OF THE TOTAL PRODUCTION TASK

The assembly line revolutionized production techniques. It destroyed once and for all the guild-born notion that a craft had to be learned by hard apprenticeship. By specializing tasks, it could put together complicated technological products with a minimum of training and thus substitute speed and specialization for technique. It also separated men from the totality of their effort, from any exhaustive knowledge of materials or tensile strengths, and asked of them merely assiduity at a mindless kind of task that was never finished and had to be endlessly repeated. This partitioning of skills followed very naturally upon the separation of planning and doing. Other technological developments pointed in the same direction. Before the introduction of the assembly belt, factories had already introduced semi-independent tools, like the lathe and the loom, which did a more consistent and faster job than the skilled workman might but which still needed his hand to guide them. The semi-independent tool was followed by automated tools, like the analogue computer, which, guided by tape, reproduces an endless number of identical artifacts, monitored not by skilled craftsmen but by trouble shooters, whose job is to keep the automated mechanism running and to repair it when it flags. These changes affected both product and labor markets. The impact of these developments on labor was profound. With the decline in demand for their skills, or for the participation of the whole man in the specialized task, a restlessness developed among hourly workers. In his pursuit of the "scientific" study of human potential, Taylor had ignored the fact that the man went with the job. Taylor's willingness to pay a "first-class man" a first-class wage was not enough. The size and strength of the labor movement today may be the result of an effort on the part of labor to meet business organization on its own terms, or it may result from the fact that the workingman must participate in something, and modern conditions make this virtually impossible in the work place.

THE SEPARATION OF OWNERSHIP AND CONTROL

The modern economic organization goes a step further in dividing responsibility, and this extends to the corporate owners of the business. Much has been said lately about the fact that investment-ownership precludes control of holdings, since financial assets fare better in the hands of the experts at finance, accounting, and managing.

Anyone can buy a piece of a corporation, most of the time, but only those who manage the enterprise, whatever its nature, administer this ownership. Not only is the individual stockowner dependent on the judgment of the management of the company in which he invests, but today's most substantial investors are the trustee banks, mutual funds, pension funds, and insurance companies, who vote the stock for their stockholders. The crucial point is that the right has been transferred from the actual ownership to the investing institution.[9]

THE SEPARATION OF BUSINESS FROM EXCLUSIVELY ECONOMIC GOALS

The most modern dichotomy is a subtle one that indicates a new potential for change in the nature of business functions. As it is, it is perfectly possible today for a firm to have only one customer, the government. Are firms that fill government orders, work to government specifications and on a cost-plus basis, any longer private enterprises, in the strict sense?

In the making of the atom bomb, the most important single project government has undertaken in our lifetime, it was quickly decided that operations could not proceed at Hanford, one of the two basic projects involved in that operation, without Du Pont, that Du Pont alone had the size and the personnel, the human resources and the knowhow to produce the uranium or plutonium out of which the bomb was to be made.

The entire Hanford operation was taken over by Du Pont on a cost plus one dollar basis because the government recognized that there was no other way to get the work done. No one even thought of socialism, nor of competition. The way to do it was to take a going concern with experience and resource allocation and give it the task.[10]

Are there today public as well as private businessmen, as suggested by Khrushchev's remark at the Leipzig fair: "I represent the Soviet business interests here"? Or is it a misuse of the term "business" to classify operations undertaken for the good of a country rather than exclusively for profit as business?

THE FUNCTIONS OF BUSINESS IN CONTEMPORARY SOCIETY

This state of affairs throws some doubt on the nature and extent of the duties and ends of today's business. If we are to judge them by the old criterion of production and service for consumption and a

---

[9] Lois Shepherd Headings, "Sanctity or Sanctions: Explorations of Power," *Business Horizons*, Vol. II (Winter, 1959), p. 99 n.

[10] John M. Blum, "Corporate Size in a World of Accelerating Technology" (talk given at General Electric's Advanced Management Course, Crotonville, N.Y., June 9, 1960).

final profit, they certainly seem to be mixed. Consider Drucker's statement:

There is only one valid definition of business purpose: *to create a consumer* . . . [Therefore] any business enterprise has two—and only these two—basic functions: marketing and innovation. They are the entrepreneurial functions.

Marketing is the distinguishing, the unique function of the business. A business is set apart from all other human organizations by the fact that it markets a product or a service. Neither Church, nor Army, nor School, nor State does that. Any organization that fulfills itself through marketing a product or a service, is a business.[11]

PROFIT MAKING

Of all human organizations, a business is still the only one whose existence depends on profit. The government can tax for its survival and support basic institutions like the Army and the School with the proceeds. The Church can likewise call upon its members to provide for it so that it can continue to act as agency for them. The family can continue to survive if it can provide for its day-to-day needs. But an economic organization has no chance for survival if it cannot make a profit. Breaking even, in business, may be a necessary part of becoming established and recognized at all, but beyond a certain point it is senseless. In fact, we do not regard a business as a business unless it makes a profit. The so-called nonprofit institution is, strictly speaking, a service organization and not a business. Profit is a condition of the existence of business, which could not come into being without the promise of it, nor could it hope to survive without it. Other types of organizations can and do exist without profits— largely because they can depend on individual or corporate profit making for contributions.

But today the goal of profit-making is complicated by the tax situation, by the need for foresight in its investment for the firm's growth and survival, and by considerations of social as well as economic responsibility in the distribution of the fruits of enterprise.

SERVICE

The idea of service as part of business objectives is familar enough in this country. A good man in business will not cheat his

---

[11] Peter F. Drucker, *The Practice of Management* (New York: Harper & Bros., 1954), pp. 37–38.

customers any more than he would cheat himself. He regards this not as virtue but as a kind of prudence. If he does not give good service, he knows his customers will not come back, while the goods he has sold them will. This is not good for business.

Yet today the preoccupation of "balancing the best interests" of the contributor claimants on business is such that, conscious as he is of the old idea of service and the even older concern with profits, a man like Yntema can say: "The fundamental test of any business is whether it serves our society well—whether it provides good, well-paying jobs for employees, and whether it yields a profit to owners commensurate wth the risks involved."[12]

Social Responsibility

It has been noted previously that the question of serving society well, over and above the production of goods and the rendering of service, might never have arisen had not the multifunctional or multiproduct organization reached such a gigantic size. Corporate growth has thus helped to create "social responsibility."

An organization employing over 200,000 men and women (and we have several of those) tends, unless it is widely dispersed, to become the economic mainstay of whole cities. Under such circumstances its decision to withdraw from an area becomes fraught with social implications. If an economic decision to move elsewhere to save taxes or labor costs creates a social disaster for the community, then some second thoughts are in order. The large business enterprise today is owned in part by its own customers and employees who have, therefore, more than a one-sided interest in its survival. A corporation's decision to abandon plant facilities in one locale may throw some of its employee-stockholders out of work. Should these insist that it stay and lose money for them as stockholders and perhaps eventually cease to exist by putting "social responsibility" before economic necessity? This is a 20th-century dilemma, not easily resolved either by management or by labor.

Survival

Once it achieves such size and influence, business can be regarded as an institution with a duty to survive, since the social and economic security of so many has come to depend on it. The survival

---

[12] Statement of Theodore O. Yntema before the Subcommittee on Antitrust and Monopoly of the Committee on the Judiciary, U.S. Senate, February 4–5, 1958.

goal is furthered by the professional managerial organization loyalty. This loyalty is perhaps tacit rather than explicit, but it exists nevertheless.

The problem of survival has created a change in attitude toward expansion on the part of executives in a large corporation concerning the problem of how big is "too big" for efficiency. There are numerous opinions. Apparently the old economic law of diminishing returns begins to operate, once a corporation is too big. There comes a point at which its identity as an organization begins to militate against its profit position, and the specters of bureaucracy and bankruptcy loom. Unfortunately, no one yet knows quite at what point this occurs.

TRANSNATIONAL BUSINESS

The changing functions of business today are nowhere more dramatically exposed than in transnational business carried on by multinational corporations. Nor is the operation of such companies a special and exceptional case of business management. As business expands everywhere into the world arena, more companies will be multinational, seeking to surmount the nationalistic barriers of frontiers. Most managers of the future will have to be prepared for strategic action in this more expansive arena.

It is an arena in which international relations among sovereign states dominate the scene, as they have done for 300 years since the Peace of Westphalia. They still dominate the scene; but transnational forces of many kinds are at work in the world of affairs and some of these forces may at length work profound changes in the Westphalian system. These transnational forces are forces that move across political frontiers and often transcend them. The technology of modern communications; the flow of scientific discourse; the universal concern for human rights; the growing interest in transnational law to facilitate the interchange of goods, services, and personnel; and the reach of corporate business into hitherto unexplored markets—all indicate the cosmopolitan nature of these forces. They indicate, too, an expanded environment in which the multinational corporation may become an instrument of change as well as a skillful adaptor to a new ecosystem.

The wisdom of business strategy for the transnational operations ahead will depend upon a realistic appraisal of this larger business environment—the world arena—as well as a mastery of the instruments of multinational corporate policy. We turn first to the character of the world arena.

THE WORLD ARENA

The orderly marketplace for domestically oriented enterprise secured by national law stands in sharp contrast to the nearly anarchic world arena of transnational business. A somber view of this arena is that we all teeter on the edge of an abyss, faced with a balance of terror between nuclear giants who seem unable to create a viable structure of world peace. It seems unlikely that the proliferation of nuclear power among the more than 126 sovereign states can be stopped. It seems more probable that they will all continue to brook no superior authority in this arena that has no supranational law. The drive toward national independence is not yet complete among the irredenta and in the Third World of less developed and uncommitted parts of the globe; nor is there much evidence that the older sovereign entities are prepared to surrender enough power to supranational authorities so that the dangers of a new world war can be forestalled. So fraught with peril is the nationalistic element in the present states system that one writer insists that "the peace of the world must in the end rest on an institutional base that is indifferent to the idea of national security" since "in a world of nationalism . . . the state, great or small, can no longer protect its own from annihilation"; and this writer argues that while political entities rise and fall over the centuries, trade and commerce always continue. If today's nation-states go the way of their feudal predecessors, "the extra-national corporation may well take over, illustrating Darwin's law of the survival of the fittest."[13]

The question arises whether ours is "a civilization whose roots have rotted until they will no longer sustain the great weight of its trunk and the vast spread of its branches," or only a transitional one that "still contains much sound timber."[14] And is the corporate system in transnational business a part of that sound timber? The "international system"[15] we have managed to live with up to now is but a few

---

[13] Frank Tannenbaum, "The Survival of the Fittest," *Columbia Journal of World Business*, Vol. III (March–April, 1968), pp. 13–20.

[14] J. M. Clark, *Alternative to Freedom* (New York: Vintage Books, 1960), p. 126.

[15] Charles A. McClelland, *Theory and the International System* (New York: Macmillan Co., 1966); Klaus Knorr and Sidney Verba (eds.), "The International System: Theoretical Essays," a special issue of *World Politics*, Vol. 14, No. 1 (October,

centuries old; it is not necessarily a permanent solution to the problem of government. But it seems doubtful that its basis in sovereign states—although faulty in its pluralistic excesses—ought to be, or will be, displaced by some other kind of worldwide pluralism. Yet somehow a legitimate authority must be found for the nonstate and nonsovereign entities that mankind cannot do without in the world arena.

Business corporations and other nonstate entities are not the major participants in the so-called international system, and are in fact generally regarded as mere "objects" of the law of nations[16] and not as "subjects," that is to say, neither sovereign states nor internal public organizations that make the law and the strategic power decisions. In a legal sense only the "national systems"[17] of power constitute the major "actors" in the world arena. In addition to these major actors, however, there are in fact literally thousands of nonstate power centers in the so-called private sector, some of which actually at times become the prime movers in diplomacy. And there are emergent "national subsystems" as well as functional organizations[18] that do much of the world's work while the sovereigns' diplomats and warriors carry the more public roles. Seen realistically the world arena is a vastly complicated pattern and movement of intercommunicating decision processes that involve both public- and private-sector entities.

Yet the fact must be faced that the international system of today is run from relatively few of these decision centers. In the public sector, the realities of this concentration of power in the world arena is well described in *The Discipline of Power*,[19] written by George W. Ball, a former Undersecretary of State under two Administrations. Brushing aside the ideas that an organization of 120-odd sovereign states, on the one hand, could govern this arena, or, on the other, that the United States should attempt the "lonely, dangerous role of global policeman," Ball bluntly declared that the core of a future

---

1961) ; also, Richard A. Falk and Saul H. Mendlovitz (eds.) , *International Law*, Vol. II of *The Strategy of World Order* (New York: The World Law Fund, 1966) .

[16] Wolfgang Friedmann, "The Changing Dimensions of International Law," *Columbia Law Review*, Vol. 62 (November, 1962) , pp. 1147–65.

[17] McClelland, *op. cit.*, p. 21.

[18] E. B. Haas, *Beyond the Nation-State: Functionalism and International Organization* (Stanford, Cal.: Stanford University Press, 1964) .

[19] George W. Ball, *The Discipline of Power: Essentials of a Modern World Structure* (Boston: Atlantic-Little, Brown, 1968) .

modern world structure would be found in four centers: the U.S.A., the U.S.S.R., a united Europe, and Japan. As for the United States, he wrote that

A sense of priority dictates that we regard our vital interests—things that touch our very life and existence—as most heavily concentrated in the world's north temperate zone. That is where our strongest competitors and all of our most deadly enemies in this century have been located. That is the heartland of industrial might. That is the sensitive terrain where a major political change or military upset could tilt a fragile polar balance of power and bring a war of mass death in the blink of an eye.[20]

From this point of view every effort should be made to establish a United Europe that would include a united Germany and possess the potential of a third power that will be friendly but not subservient to the United States. Europe in the West would thus become a full-fledged superpower.[21] On the other side of the globe, in the Pacific arena, Japan would emerge as the only large modern industrial state in Asia with the capacity to play a major role. For a long time to come, however, neither Europe nor Japan could be expected to approach the scope and authority of America and the U.S.S.R.; so Ball thought it realistic to look toward a new age not of four superpowers but "in the terms that matter of something equivalent to three and one half." In the Far East, however, Japan (the only large modern state in Asia) would properly become the solid base of some durable system of power; therefore it would be a primary aim of U.S. foreign policy to "encourage Japan to take a greater and greater degree of responsibility for the defense and economic development of the Far East."[22]

Whether this or some other strategy of world order will turn out to be the path of the future cannot now be foreseen. On this basic issue the managers of multinational companies will be faced increasingly with the need for corporate intelligence[23] to guide them safely through turbulent times ahead. They cannot rely, for intelligence concerning the dynamics of the world arena, solely upon their national governments. They must develop independent sources of

---

[20] *Ibid.*, p. 345.

[21] Ball, *op. cit.*, pp. 356–57: "Only when Europe builds an adequate political structure can there be anything resembling a political partnership that fully reflects the common interests of a common civilization." Cf. J.-J. Servan-Schreiber, *The American Challenge* (New York: Atheneum Publishers, 1968).

[22] Ball, *op. cit.*, p. 354.

[23] John J. Beauvois, "International Intelligence for the International Enterprise," *California Management Review*, Vol. III, No. 4 (Winter, 1961), pp. 39–46.

knowledge in this difficult field of the policy sciences. It is a field of promising, but still immature, scientific knowledge about international society and prescriptions for its management.[24]

It is possible that an orderly global marketplace is only a distant and nearly unattainable goal. Who knows whether George Liska was correct in calling the war in Vietnam merely "the first imperial war the United States has been called upon to fight in the newly emerging constellation of world power and order," and in declaring that America has become "the manifestly preponderant world power" with the consequence that until it is dislodged from this position it must plan on such "policing" being "repeated in comparable situations?"[25] Liska's thesis is that because the world is one of conflicting and successive local and regional "imperialisms" the United States must work toward "the plateau of maturity" in a "true empire," becoming a strong and salient power able to maintain minimum order: "a task exceeding its national limits but not its national resources."[26] For him, an "empire" is like Ball's superpower: "a state exceeding other states in size, scope, salience, and sense of task," and not a traditionally exploitative colonial aggregation. Liska's analysis of the multistate and imperial orders of today and of the interempire and interstate relations of tomorrow is useful as a provocative hypothesis concerning the future of the world arena, a hypothesis to be fed into the processes of corporate intelligence. Other hypotheses along a spectrum of possible international systems, all the way from extremely nationalistic and isolationist pluralism to a world order under law, must also be considered.

The essence of corporate intelligence for transnational operations lies not in accepting some favored design for world order, but rather in the *methods* used to arrive at an operative understanding of the forces at work in the world arena and in the *goals* sought both for the multinational corporation itself and for a world order.

THE ROLE OF MULTINATIONAL COMPANIES

The pursuit of profitable enterprise will doubtless continue to be the major goal of multinational as well as domestic business corpora-

---

[24] Richard A. Falk and S. H. Mendlovitz (eds.), *The Strategy of World Order.* 4 vols. (New York: World Law Fund, 1966).

[25] George Liska, *Imperial America: The International Politics of Primacy* (Baltimore: Johns Hopkins University Press, 1967). See "Author's Preface."

[26] *Ibid.,* p. 108. Cf. Ernest Lee Tuveson, *Redeemer Nation: The Idea of America's Millenial Role* (Chicago: University of Chicago Press, 1968); and Thomas R. Adam, *Western Interests in the Pacific Realm* (New York: Random House, 1967).

tions. Yet there are other functions that transnational businesses can and probably must perform deliberately. It may be too much to expect that an obsolescent system of sovereign states will be succeeded by a new era of extranational corporations and other functional entities under some global, or at least regional, authority or authorities. Corporate managers can justifiably decline to assume joint responsibility for the preservation of public order and the definition and defense of the public interest tasks that are now generally assigned to states and public international organizations. But on a less ambitious plane they can assume responsibility for urgently needed functions in the world arena: "Whether economic rationality on a world scale is inevitable or not, most men would agree that it is desirable, and the multinational corporation, with its almost limitless possibilities as a disseminator of products, capital, and technology does seem an ideal mechanisms for increasing it."[27]

In this and other respects there is a creative role for transnational business. It is said that "the global businessman is ahead of his time and far ahead of the politicians and diplomats who still think in terms of national interests" alone, and that the global businessman's command of technology gives him a power that can be subversive of the status quo, leading to a better future for the global arena.

But the purposes and methods of multinational managers have to be directed toward rather specific tasks. These tasks tend to polarize about the special relationships of multinational companies. There are parent-subsidiary relationships within a company in which conflicts between global and national interests arise. The host and home countries may make conflicting demands on a multinational company and these demands in turn may conflict with the more universal requirements of an orderly global marketplace. Far from running an independent course as a business enterprise pure and simple, the multinational company often is met by demands that it be the instrument of national policy,[28] for example, to control international capital flows, to strengthen a country's security position, or to hasten its "modernization."[29]

---

[27] Charles F. Stewart, "The Business of America Abroad," in Ivar Berg (ed.) , *The Business of America* (New York: Harcourt, Brace & World, Inc., 1968) , p. 144.

[28] Thomas Aitken, Jr., "Can Business Carry the Flag?," *Business Horizons*, Vol. V (Winter, 1962) , pp. 101–7.

[29] Charles E. Black, *The Dynamics of Modernization* (New York: Harper & Row, 1966) .

These external demands and pressures may or may not be legitimate claims that corporate managers must acknowledge and work into their companies' objectives. On the whole subject of development—for example, in the Third World—what should be the corporate social goals consistent with profitable enterprise? Intensive industrialization? Literacy and education? A more intensive agriculture? Population control? A hastening of a genuine social revolution or its arrest? On all these points there is much room for doubt due to the immature present state of the art of social analysis applicable to developmental problems.[30] Before a multinational company ventures into new and untried fields abroad, the assessment of its costs, including those under the heading of social responsibilities to the host countries, will depend upon rational answers to the questions posed above. And these answers depend, in turn, upon perspectives of the world arena as a whole as well as perspectives of the domestic economies and polities of the host countries.

In both cases perspectives are subject to change among the experts and at the political decision centers in home and host countries. At one time and among some experts, for example, social and economic development for the less developed countries is said to depend mainly on capital movements toward these areas; others may stress improvement in the quality of local manpower through education and health; and still others may urge plans for balanced growth. The very concepts of growth and development have been questioned in influential quarters. The questions of foreign aid from the home countries of multinational companies and balance-of-payments problems in these home states further complicate the picture. Multinational corporate managers are certain to be caught in the currents of these changing perspectives.

The wider and deeper functions of the multinational corporation and of transnational business in general, thus vary with time and place. There are few fixed norms beyond the goal of profitability; and because of the complexities of doing business in the Third World it would seem that most American multinational companies stick to the globe's northern industrial zone indicated by Ball. At length, however, transnational business may extend heavily into other zones; as this occurs, the multinational company's managers

---

[30] Gunnar Myrdal, assisted by William J. Barber *et al., Asian Drama: An Inquiry Into the Poverty of Nations* 3 vols. (New York: Twentieth Century Fund, 1968) , is a basic source for the whole field of economic development.

will be drawn more directly into the general problem of a world order.

CONCLUSION

These developments give some idea of the changed nature of business conducted on a large scale. Dependent initially on social and political conventions for its existence, the large business finds itself today in a position of power in social and civic situations, along with, and as a result of, its economic activity.

"Economic activity" is a much broader term than "business" and includes all physical, mental, and mechanical processes by which human and material resources are converted into commodities and services for human use. But in a capitalist society the economic process is mainly entrusted to the private businessman.

If today's business is too doctrinally regarded as the instrument of a single function—such as the entrepreneurial—there remain many phenomena in the whole picture of modern business that cannot be accounted for.

Rather, the multifunction or multiproduct business so characteristic of our time has two tasks in a private-enterprise economy: first, to keep operating as a profitable private enterprise and, second, to perform adequately the regulatory functions of private and decentralized decision centers in a "mixed economy." This is a heterogeneous economy, of which a part is "small business" operating to some extent under conditions described in classical economic theory, another part operated by government or under its control, and the remainder, perhaps two thirds, under the conditions of mass production within the ambit of corporate decision making.

The goals of corporate policy are primarily economic. But the economic and social functions of the modern corporation cannot be stated with anything like the comparative simplicity of principle that one encounters in earlier theories about the role of the entrepreneur. The corporation as we know it today is not simply a larger model of the owner-entrepreneur. The attainment of maximum profits is no longer the sole motivation for business. For the corporation, policy aims can be expected to include, beyond the accumulation of wealth and the distribution of earnings, status for the company, influence in the industry and in the community generally, good corporate citizenship, and other qualities associated with rectitude, solidarity, or a sense of belonging and of being favorably regarded by others. All this is a part of the new institutional intention in business, the will to carry on indefinitely and, wherever necessary, to adapt as it can to the demands of its environment.

RECOMMENDED READING

ALLEN, FREDERICK LEWIS. *The Big Change.* New York: Harper & Bros., 1952.

ARON, RAYMOND. "The Social Context of Corporate Planning," in STEINER, GEORGE A., and CANNON, WARREN M. (eds.), *Multinational Corporate Planning,* pp. 183–202. New York: Macmillan Co., 1966.

BEARD, CHARLES A. "Individualism and Capitalism," *Encyclopaedia of the Social Sciences* (1930), Vol. I, pp. 145–63, esp. Secs. II–IV.

BERG, IVAR. (ed.). *The Business of America,* Chap. 1, 4, 5, and 7. New York: Harcourt, Brace & World, Inc., 1968.

CARR-SAUNDERS, A. M., and WILSON, P. A. "Professions," in *Encyclopaedia of the Social Sciences,* Vol. XII, pp. 476–80.

DONHAM, WALLACE B. *Administration and Blind Spots: The Biography of an Adventurous Idea,* pp. 11–16 and 90. Boston: Graduate School of Business Administration, Harvard University, 1952.

ROBINSON, RICHARD D. *International Business Policy,* Chap. 1 and 6. New York: Holt, Rinehart & Winston, 1964.

SCHUMPETER, JOSEPH A. "Capitalism," in *Encyclopaedia Britannica* (1958 ed.), Vol. 4, pp. 801–4.

FURTHER READING

BEARD, MIRIAM. *A History of the Business Man.* New York: Macmillan Co., 1938.

BLOUGH, ROY. *International Business: Environment and Adaptation.* New York: McGraw-Hill Book Co., 1966.

BOWEN, HOWARD R. "Business Management: A Profession," *Annals of the American Academy of Political and Social Science,* Vol. 297 (January, 1955), pp. 112–17.

COCHRAN, THOMAS C. *Basic History of American Business.* Princeton: D. Van Nostrand Co., 1959.

COYLE, JOHN J., and MOCK, EDWARD J. (eds.). *Readings in International Business.* Scranton, Pa.: International Textbook Co., 1965.

DAHL, ROBERT A., and LINDBLOM, CHARLES, E. *Politics, Economics and Welfare,* pp. 129–68 and 456–58. New York: Harper & Bros., 1953.

DRUCKER, PETER F. *The Practice of Management,* chap. v. New York: Harper & Bros., 1954.

FARMER, RICHARD N., and RICHMAN, BARRY M. *Comparative Management and Economic Progress.* Homewood, Ill.: Richard D. Irwin, Inc., 1965.

FAYERWEATHER, JOHN. *Facts and Fallacies of International Business.* New York: Holt, Rinehart & Winston, 1962.

———. *The Executive Overseas: Administrative Attitudes and Relationships in a Foreign Culture.* Syracuse, N.Y.: Syracuse University Press, 1959.

GRAS, N. S. B. *Industrial Development,* pp. 1 and 7. Cambridge: Harvard University Press, 1930.

KAPLAN, MORTIMER A. "International Systems" in *International Encyclopedia of the Social Sciences,* Vol. XV, pp. 479–86.

LILIENTHAL, DAVID. "The Multinational Corporation," in M. ANSHEN and G. L. BACH (eds.), *Management and Corporations 1985,* pp. 119–58. New York: McGraw-Hill Book Co., 1960.

LLERAS CAMARGO, ALBERTO, and MOORE, GEORGE S. "The Future of Capitalism in the Developing Countries," in the National Industrial Conference Board's *The Future of Capitalism,* pp. 63–78.

MARTYN, HOWE. *International Business: Principles and Problems,* chap. 1. New York: The Free Press, 1964.

METCALF, HENRY C. (ed.). *Business Management as a Profession.* Chicago: A. W. Shaw Co., 1927.

PARSONS, TALCOTT, and SMELSER, NEIL J. *Economy and Society: A Study in the Integration of Economic and Social Theory,* chap. ii. New York: Free Press, 1956.

PIRENNE, HENRI. "The Stages in the Social History of Capitalism," *American Historical Review,* Vol. XIX (April, 1914), pp. 494–515.

SLICHTER, SUMNER. *The American Economy,* pp. 5–7. New York: Alfred A. Knopf, 1948.

VERNON, RAYMOND. "Multinational Enterprise and National Sovereignty," *Harvard Business Review,* Vol. XL (March–April, 1967), pp. 156–72.

WARD, BARBARA. "The Western Corporation and the Undeveloped Economies," in M. ANSHEN and G. L. BACH (eds.), *Management and Corporations 1985,* pp. 159–82. New York: McGraw-Hill Book Co., 1960.

21. Business and the Creative Society: The Cultural Dimension

OUTLINE

WE HAVE BEEN LOOKING at ethical values in business, seen in its larger social context. We turn now to other values, and especially to those appropriate to "a great society . . . in which the men of business think greatly of their functions." Alfred North Whitehead's famous aphorism calls for more than appears on the surface. It calls, in the first place, for an operative definition of greatness in a society; and in the second place, for the indexes of greatness in businessmen's thinking about business functions. It calls, finally, for great common purposes among leaders of business and of society generally, and for the arresting idea that businessmen will identify themselves as men of *business* with these elevated purposes. It calls, in short, for the daily pursuit of goals that are not ordinarily thought of as business objectives.

547

THE CREATIVITY OF HIGH CULTURE

Greatness in a society must refer to more than wealth and power. It has something to do with the creative capabilities of a people and with the fruits of their efforts beyond production, growth, and similar measures of economic performance in businesses and nations. It has to do with his achievements in science and technology, but not only these. It has to do with aspiration, with man's hopes and dreams, with his works of art as cognition of feeling—as Susanne Langer has used that term to cover the widest range of perception by heart and mind. Greatness will be sought in a people's standards of its education in the humanities, the arts, the sciences, the professions.

CHARACTERISTICS OF A HIGH CULTURE

A major characteristic of greatness in a society, and one of special significance here, is the encouragement of innovation and creativity. But here we must note the place of creativity in closely related qualities of a "high culture." This term, which is not necessarily the opposite of "popular culture,"[1] was used by Edward Shils[2] in an illuminating examination of the cultural level of civilization in our age as compared with previous civilizations. Creative minds always were and are now major elements in civilizations of high culture. But the life of the intellect has always been carried on by very few until recently. In the England of 1688, for example, there were probably fewer than 70,000 persons engaged in broadly intellectual pursuits, counting not only the core of creative spirits in the universities, the churches, the medical and legal professions, and in the dramatic and other arts, but also their various audiences and the ranks of the less creative engaged in instructing and entertaining these audiences. Yet England at the time was what must be regarded as one of the great societies of world history.

In terms of numbers of creative people our modern high cultures would appear to have outstripped the Elizabethan Age. The great

---

[1] Robert N. Wilson, "High Culture and Popular Culture in a Business Society" in Ivar Berg (ed.), *The Business of America* New York: Harcourt, Brace & World, Inc., 1968), pp. 390–406, esp. p. 404.

[2] Edward Shils, "The High Culture of the Age," in Robert N. Wilson (ed.), *The Arts in Society* (Englewood Cliffs, N.J.: Prentice-Hall, Inc., 1964), pp. 317–62.

contemporary societies in Europe and America exhibit an "oceanic outpouring" of production in the intellectual domain (here Shils includes the humanities and the arts) that is incomparably greater in sheer volume and diversity than in any previous epoch. Nor does he discount unduly the quality of this output merely because of its volume. Our present high culture might, from some objective viewpoint, be judged poorer than that of any of its predecessors in a comparable span of years. But he dismisses most conceptions of "mass society" as "the latest form of this unexamined devil whose mere existence degrades the culture of his betters." He could find no impressive evidence for a general cultural decline, though admitting that the map is variegated. On the contrary, he thought that this century has seen an extended horizon of intellectual life and "a fertilization of its sympatheies" of the sort never before seen in any great civilization, and not least in the United States.

How is the quality of a high culture to be measured? Shils suggests a criterion of direct concern to us here: the degree of responsibility shown by the custodians and the practioners of culture in carrying out a threefold task. This task includes *discovery and creation*—adding to the stock of culture of the human race; the *conserving and reinterpreting* of the inheritance; finally, *maintaining and extending* the influence of high culture in other sectors of society.

CRITIQUES OF AMERICAN HIGH CULTURE

The shortcomings of American society in getting these things done is sharp and detailed. He notes, for example, "the predominant tone of unfriendliness toward high culture which appears to emanate from the economic, political, and technological elites, however brilliant and important the exceptions."[3] He indicts the crudities and vulgarities that appear too often in our society, even though he sees these as defects at the periphery of our cultural creativity while "the center is very much alive" and "its vitality, its curiosity, its openness are its virtues."[4]

Of special interest is Shils's comment on the impact of the vast growth of applied science on the quality of creative intellectual life. Here, "the considerations of national power, private profitability,

---

[3] *Ibid.*, p. 353.
[4] *Ibid.*, p. 345.

and public welfare have taken a place alongside and even superior to scientific curiosity and in the internal direction of science itself."[5] Still, he does not seem to think that the scientific culture of the universities will be swamped by bureaucratically conducted research institutions in business and government.

A far more sombre note is struck by John K. Galbraith[6] on this point; because the "mature corporation" of today, as distinguished from the entrepreneurial corporation of yesterday, depends upon the supply of qualified talent in its "technostructure" as the decisivie factor in production, and because this technostructure is absorbed by its own values and priorities in the industrial system, it greatly influences the quality of scientific work in the universities. The "single-minded preoccupation" of our culture with the production of goods, writes Galbraith, is a commitment induced by the industrial system, with a resultant emphasis on the value of technology out of all proper proportion to the needed support of independent and unbiased scientific work. The deleterious effect on the arts and the humanities would be even greater, in Galbraith's opinion, were it not for the fact that the artistic and intellectual community has been nurtured by rising income in our industrial system and enjoys some independence as a community that lives mainly to itself outside the system.

For both these commentators on American culture there is clearly an important role for creativity as a necessity to the business system. But scientific and technological creativity seem to be valued more highly because they make a direct contribution to, and are an indispensable element in, the mature corporation. Does business have no need for creative genius in the arts and the humanities? Innovation, which is essential to business enterprise, has long been thought of as related to mainly science and technology rather than the arts and the humanities. But innovation in the future may take radically new directions and open up novel opportunities for the ingenious businessman of tomorrow. This may be the case in the space industries, for example, in oceanic developments, and in the new industries arising from combining the arts and advanced communications technology as well as information systems. It is not unlikely that the innovative requirements of successful business in

---

[5] *Ibid.*, p. 338.

[6] John K. Galbraith, *The New Industrial State* (Boston: Houghton Mifflin Co., 1967).

these and other relatively unexplored fields will call upon the creative talents of the artist as well as the scientist and the technologist. The technostructure, already so heavily dependent upon the academy in the latter two areas of creative work, would then call more and more upon the humanities and upon the art world outside the academy. At this point it would be well to examine the relationship of creativity in this wider sense to innovation as that term has been understood in the history of business.

CREATIVITY AND INNOVATION

Entrepreneurial activity which still characterizes much of the business system (even though the "entrepreneurial corporation" of Galbraith's analysis has been succeeded in the more narrowly defined *industrial* system by the "mature corporation"), involves the making of "new combinations" or the "putting together" of a new enterprise, to use Schumpeter's phrases.[7]

INNOVATION AS A CREATIVE ACT

Schumpeter regarded this innovative element the distinguishing characteristic of the entrepreneurial task, as distinguished from routine management, the current administration of a going concern, or even risk taking and profit seeking. But this innovative function of enterprisers is not confined to the creation of new business organizations. It includes innovations in commercial combinations. The introduction of large-scale manufacturing businesses into an economic system where they were not known before is a familiar creative process, and it has led at length to the now prevalent institution of the modern corporation in all of the world's highly industrialized zones. This has been a difficult task, first of creating the organizational form and then of conserving the institution, of interpreting it, and of assuring its survival not only in domestic national habitats but now in the world arena. The task is difficult because of numerous social and political resistances that work against it. The will and the action required for such a task applies equally to the task of commercial combinations, as for example, "the choice of a new and

---

[7] Joseph A. Schumpeter, *Capitalism, Socialism, and Democracy* (New York: Harper & Brothers, 1942), chap. XII. See the critique of Schumpter's "institutionalized innovation" in Andrew Shonfield, *Modern Capitalism* (New York: Oxford University Press, 1965), pp. 52–55.

cheaper source of supply for a means of production, perhaps a raw material,"[8] a choice of new trade routes or communications media, a replacement of one production or consumption good by another to serve the same or nearly the same purpose more cheaply, and the creation of a new good (Schumpeter cites improved musical instruments) which more adequately satisfies existing and previously satisfied needs.

In all of these cases the entrepreneurial profit, under capitalism, stimulates the will and the action of the enterpriser; but his creativity appears in the innovation and not the pursuit of profit. Schumpeter's analysis of "the obsolescence of the entrepreneurial function" pursued to its logical conclusion led him to the prospect of capitalism's "crumbling walls" because, by its very achievements capitalism presumably would automatize progress and make itself superfluous. Capitalism in its advanced stages, characterized by depersonalization, bureaucratization, and automatization of the productive process, would tend to make sheer personality and willpower count for less and less. Managers would find it progressively easier to do things that lie outside the familiar routine. The innovator, he thought, would run up against less resistance to the new only because it is new, and the environment would become completely accustomed to, and even expectant of, economic change. Technological progress, he wrote, would increasingly become the business of teams of trained specialists who turn out what is required and make it in predictable ways. The romance of earlier commercial adventure seemed to him to be rapidly wearing away, because so many more things could not be strictly calculated that had of old been visualized in a flash of genius.

But are these observations valid today? In the quarter century since that was written the innovative possibilities of the space age have loomed, and who knows what lies beyond the year 2001? New combinations will be needed, and the creativity of the entrepreneur will be there to meet the needs and to take business advantage of new opportunities. The wonders of the space age, indeed, have already served to inspire the creativity of both artist and enterpriser. Both insist upon that "unrestrainedness" on the use of their talents

---

[8] Joseph A. Schumpeter, *The Theory of Economic Development* (Cambridge: Harvard University Press, 1934), p. 133.

that a free society offers.[9] The innovator of business enterprise and the creative artist have this negative stand in common: the desire to exclude from their innovative work external intruders, conformists, and hidebound traditionalists. But there is a positive common ground that is more important and little explored either by men of business or by those in the arts and the humanities.

INNOVATION IN THE ARTS AND IN INDUSTRY

Both the creative artist and the innovating enterpriser do their creative work essentially as individuals. They have, therefore, a common interest not only in warding off the interference with their work but also in efforts toward a cultural environment that encourages and rewards individual creative effort. On this point there are a number of comments that seem to be in order.

There is the observation of John Steinbeck, who declared that there is but one creative instrument: "the individual mind and the spirit of a man, whether in music, in art, in poetry, in mathematics, or in philosophy." It is "the free, exploring mind of the individual human" that "separates us from the uncreative beasts"; so we must fight for "the freedom of the mind to take any direction it wishes, undirected."[10] There is also the observation of Whitehead about the importance to civilization of the mind free to wander:

Mankind has wandered from the trees to the plains, from the plains to the seacoast, from climate to climate and from habit of life to habit of life. When man ceases to wander, he will cease to ascend in the scale of being. Physical wandering is still important, but greater still is the power of man's spiritual adventures—adventures of thought, adventures of passionate feeling, adventures of esthetic experience.[11]

This freedom to wander is a demand of the scientist, too, and in fact a general requirement of intellectual effort of the creative and innovative kind. It is interesting that Schumpeter insisted upon the individualistic element in the innovative entrepreneurial function, rejecting any notion that it could be done effectively by teamwork

[9] Karl W. Deutsch, "Strategies of Freedom: The Widening of Choices and the Change of Goals," in Carl W. Friedrich (ed.), *NOMOS IV: Liberty* (New York: Atherton Press, 1962), pp. 110–18.

[10] John Steinbeck, *East of Eden* (New York: Bantam Books, 1962), pp. 113–14.

[11] Alfred North Whitehead, *Science and the Modern World* (New York: Macmillan Co., 1925), p. 298.

(which, he pointed out, was quite appropriate for management of large organizations). Yet there are two views on this matter, as Donald Schon has indicated in discussing the American reaction to sputnik.[12] Scientific activity would have to be undertaken on a larger scale than ever before to keep up with and exceed the Russians; research and development would have to become permanent independent functions of Government and corporations; and there was a conviction that about any technological goal could be achieved if it were well enough organized and backed up by sufficient investment.

But as the articles and the talk on this subject proliferated opposing views of ways and means began to appear. One view was that you hire a good man and leave him alone, since the scientific function is unique, and corporate peering over a man's shoulder would retard progress. Schon calls this a theory of scientific laissez-faire coupled with a theory of the "Great Man." The other view emphasized rational management of the innovative process in exactly the same way that a firm carries out any other business function. In the late 1950's, however, a wave of skepticism overtook American companies that had been committed to faith in growth through central research divisions. This questioning, buttressed by well-known resistance to new departures that threaten established patterns, offices and products, led to a wave of reaction against research and development because of uncertainty about payoff.

This resistance to innovation is in Schon's view central to the working of the corporation despite verbal approval in official releases. For the corporation is a society,[13] a setting in which people live, with its own values, style of conduct for its members, its own system of rewards and punishments, its highly functional system of division of labor, and a highly rationalized way of getting work done, especially by reducing tasks to series of simple, uniform, repeatable and predictable steps. In the investment game played by top management and in the war games played out in the competitive arena of affairs, the corporate society "is built to function on the model of the production process—that is to say, in a manner that is rational, orderly, uniform, and predictable."[14] But internal resistance to this orderliness appears in this society when invention and

---

[12] Donald A. Schon, *Technology and Change: The New Heraclitus* (New York: Dell Publishing Co., 1967), pp. 53 ff.

[13] *Ibid.*, p. 56.

[14] *Ibid.*, p. 62.

innovation—essentially nonrational processes that resist control—enter to defy harnessing.

Thus invention, defined as the process of bringing new technology into being or new technology created in the process, together with innovation, defined as the process of bringing invention into use, both run afoul of the managerial mind. They do so, because "corporate behavior is based on regular, orderly, linear, predictable processes."[15] The inventive and innovative processes, requiring change that is often quite unpredictable, can disturb marketing, finance, engineering and other functions so as to bring negative response. And while Schon's picture would not apply throughout Erpf's spectrum of companies,[16] especially the aggressive ventures and the wildcatters, it probably does apply far too uncomfortably to the larger and more established ones at the other end of the scale.

Creativity, in other words, is not necessarily an unquestionable virtue everywhere and in all forms in American industry. One cannot assume that businessmen will universally encourage either the industrial innovator or the artistic and humanistic creative mind. The creative mind can be a disturber. But for the country as a whole, and for an industry in general, there needs to be a national climate for both technological innovation and creativity in all disciplines. A favorable climate depends upon a complex of institutions that include governments, universities, foundations, professional societies, research institutes and art centers, industry associations, and companies themselves. Our concern here is how business can be expected to make its own contribution.

THE BUSINESS SYSTEM AND THE CREATIVE SOCIETY

The contributions of business to the creative arts, to invention, and to the innovative function of society generally, are often thought of solely in terms of corporate giving. But donations, although substantial, are a relatively small part of this complex subject. There are in fact reciprocal relationships between business and nonbusiness sectors of the creative society that must be considered with some care before one attempts to formulate a proper role for

---

[15] *Ibid.*, p. 65.
[16] See chap. 5, above.

corporation giving itself, to say nothing of the more widely ranging efforts of the business community on behalf of the realm of value we have been considering here. The business system is now so intimately tied in with society's reach for the values of a high culture that we are seeing today a complete reorientation of thought about the social function of business. This reorientation appears clearly in the development of theory and practice concerning corporate giving, which we shall consider first; and less clearly, perhaps, but more significantly in developing relationships between business and the arts and sciences.

CORPORATE GIVING—A REORIENTATION

Business giving was once regarded simply as a philanthropic activity. Philanthropy means literally the love of mankind, and alms have nothing to do with the profit seeking of the business world. Nevertheless there has been, in the United States, a steady growth of business giving during the past few decades. It began to rise to significant proportions with health and welfare types of contributions to local community chests; to the "war chests" of World War I; to Red Cross and other fund-raising drives; and to hospitals and private agencies in aid of the ill, the aged, the poor, and the youth of the land. The philanthropies of the very rich and of the millions of individual givers came to be supplemented by the philanthropies of business.

Business giving had become, in fact, so important a part of the support of nonprofit health and welfare agencies that a decline in business giving after World War I brought to Washington some outstanding community seeking changes in the federal tax laws. Tax exemption on charitable gifts, so effective in building up wartime contributions, was at length extended as a permanent national policy to corporate contributions. The "5 percent" clause of the Federal Revenue Act of 1935 offered "charitable bargains" to corporate donors; for example, when the corporation income tax rate stood a 52 percent or higher the federal tax collector would forego $5.20 for each $10 of corporate contributions for authorized charitable and educational purposes, so that a company's actual cost was only $4.80. In the higher tax brackets the cost would drop to 18 cents on the contribution dollar. Even with lower tax rates there are real economic advantages to be gained by the corporate contributor under the clause of the revenue code that permits tax deductions up to 5 percent of corporate net income for corporate support of nonprofit institutions.

Encouragement of corporate giving under federal revenue policy has been followed by favorable legislation in the states. Most of the states have now adopted permissive legislation that authorizes—it does not direct—corporations to make gifts for broad categories of charitable, educational, and cultural institutions and activities. This legislation is significant because of the earlier prevalent doctrine of the common law that corporate boards were powerless to give away corporation funds. The common-law rule of "direct benefit" appeared to preclude corporate charity since any allowable gifts could be sustained only on the ground of some *quid pro quo*. The rule was consistent with the idea that a business has nothing whatever to *give* away and that at least some benefit, direct or indirect, must accrue to corporate properties as a result of every expenditure. Whatever may be the wisdom of this position on corporate giving, the fact is that both federal and state enactments, together with judicial reinterpretation of corporate powers, have cleared the way for a substantial *corporate donative power*[17] that has far-reaching implications for corporate support of a creative society of high culture.

As one lawyer has put the matter succinctly: "The corporation may now love mankind," and indeed the figures on giving would seem to sustain the case for philanthropic action on a large scale by business corporations. If business giving is a part of total *philanthropic* donations, which ran in 1965 to well over $11 billion, it is a substantial part—nearly $800 million in that year. The greater part, to be sure, came from individual giving ($8.7 billion in 1965) and foundations ($1.1 billion); but the nearly 7 percent of the total coming from corporate coffers was a very important part of the nation's giving for good causes. What are these causes? In 1965 almost half the nation's total giving was for religion, a little less than a fifth for education, around one tenth each for welfare and health, and the rest for foundations, civic, cultural, and other purposes. Corporation giving, as shown in a sample survey by the National Industrial Conference Board, indicated a very different breakdown:

---

[17] Richard Eells, *Corporation Giving in a Free Society* (New York: Harper & Bros., 1956), chap. 2, and *The Corporation and the Arts* (New York: Macmillan Co., 1967), chap. 8.

almost 42 percent for health and welfare (the traditional incidence of corporation giving), over 38 percent for education, and the rest for cultural, civic, and other causes.

Whether this corporation giving can properly be regarded as philanthropy, in the etymological sense of that term, is questionable. In the first place, look at the above-mentioned breakdown. Health and welfare giving, the largest part of the total, grew out of mixed motivations and has always been justified by diversified rationales. At the local level of plant communities companies can hardly escape heavy canvassing for contributions for community drives; "charity," yes, but perhaps a special kind of hard-headed philanthropy not always thought appropriate for a business corporation, even after the general establishment of the donative power. It may be just good business to go along with the drives for corporate contributons. With the rise of educational contributions, due mainly to aggressive leadership by businessmen who saw grave threats to the whole business system in the serious financial situation of higher educational institutions in the fifties and sixties, corporate giving certainly strengthened the high culture of the nation; yet the argument made for this use of the donative power in the leading cases[18] stressed not so much the love of mankind in true philanthropy as it did the pragmatics of corporate efforts in this field of corporate support work. The rationale is essentially one of showing the indirect benefits to be derived from corporate contributions to education, and even of showing the necessity of such contributions if the business system is to survive. That boards and managers accept this necessary relationship is now generally enough to uphold the donative power and its use in educational support.

The conception of "corporate support work" as a proper function of those who manage American business corporations has come to be widely accepted. The problem facing those who undertake this specialized work is no longer one of corporate power to engage in corporate giving; it is rather a task of corporate ecology, namely, of discovering the vital ties of a company to its natural and social environment, and then seeking ways in which these vital ties can be strengthened through corporate support in one field or another.

-----

[18] Especially *A. P. Smith Manufacturing Co.* v. *Barlow et al.*, 26 N.J. Super. 106 (1953); affirmed 98 Atl. (2nd) 581; appeal to the U.S. Supreme Court dismissed for want of a substantial federal question, 346 U.S. 861 (1953); and *Union Pacific R.R. Co.* v. *Trustees, Inc. et al.*, 8 Utah (2nd) 101, 329 Pac. (2) 398 (1958).

The scope of inquiry into this problem of corporate ecology, as it affects contributions in money or in kind (managerial assistance to outside nonprofit institutions figures here), has broadened during the past three decades to include education as well as health and welfare. Now it is broadening still further to include cultural institutions and activities generally. Corporate concern for civic affairs is on the rise, especially as to urban problems and improved governmental institutions at federal, state, and local levels. There is also growing concern in the business community about the state of the arts and the humanities, and NICB's survey indicates growing, though still small, corporate support in this field.

Corporate giving is still far smaller in volume than it could be and ought to be. If corporations actually were to contribute all that the law allows for tax-exemption purposes, and assuming that pretax corporate profits reach the probable annual figure of $100 billion, corporate giving could come to approximately $5 billion a year. In practice, corporate tax-deductible contributions have seldom exceeded one fifth of the 5 percent allowed by the revenue code. This may indicate a reluctance to undertake the cost of what many businessmen still regard as essentially philanthropic and charitable activities. But there is another possible meaning to be drawn from trends in corporate giving, and especially from the thinking of those who direct corporate support work. It seems probable that corporate support policy, both in theory and in practice, has failed in general to measure up to the most advanced thinking about corporate ecology, with special reference to the ecological factors that ought to govern corporate giving.

By this is meant the understanding of cause-and-effect relationships between specific types of corporate business and their social environments, and particularly the nonprofit institutions in the private sector that are vital to the successful operation and survival of a company. These relationships are certainly well understood under some headings, chiefly legal and economic. They are less well understood, or hardly understood at all by most of us, when it comes to the problem of business in a creative society with all this implies for the institutions of a high culture. In the relationships of cause-and-effect between cultural institutions and the business system (using that term to embrace more than Galbraith's "industrial system") there are complexities that still elude us when it comes to formulating business policy.

Even the remarkable reorientation of thought about corporate giving, mind-expanding as it is, does not reach nearly far enough for the purpose of comprehending these reciprocal relationships. For, after all, when one speaks of corporate support of the creative society it is necessary at the same time to consider the dependence of the business system on that society.

THE RECIPROCAL RELATIONSHIP

This reciprocal relationship will be clearer if it is accepted that interrelationships among major social institutions are involved, the modern corporation being regarded as one of these institutions. Acceptance of this proposition meets resistance, curiously enough, nowhere more remarkable than in the discipline of economics where the layman would have expected the corporation to be the subject of exhaustive study and illumination for its role in the economy and in society generally. Yet this is not the case. Even within the economy there is reluctance boldly to examine the modern corporation as "an instrument of planning that transcends the market," and to look at the real goals of its "technostructure" and how these goals are actually pursued.[19] And its institutional role from the standpoint of the political sociologist and political scientist is only now beginning to be explored in depth.

So far as the creative society is concerned, the corporation's role is best seen in terms of the converging interests of institutions in the arts, the sciences, and the humanities, on the one hand, and business institutions on the other. The corporate-arts relationship, for example, turns out, on examination, to be highly instructive. One by no means exhausts the meaning of this relationship by pursuing *ad infinitum* the question of "corporate support of the arts," as though this were the essence of the matter. The basic tie is not to be found in corporate charity but rather in common interests and common goals of artist and executive. On the surface, the worlds of art and business seem disparate. At the deeper levels of understanding on both sides, however, one sees both uniting and antagonistic forces that are indicative of interdependence, but hardly of mutual indifference.

The creative and the innovative faculties of man are of deep concern to both the man of business and the man of art. What

---

[19] Galbraith, *op cit.*, chap. 7, 11, and 13.

Gilson has called the "factivity" of art, the artist as a maker of things, is related to the "new combinations" of the enterpriser. Nor are the goals of beauty and utility to be set up as opposites here, with the artist unconcerned about the latter and the businessman indifferent to the former. There is increasing pressure on the world of business to respect esthetic as well as ethical canons in the design and content of industrial and commercial products and advertising, in the architecture of business structures, and in the effect of industry on urban design. As makers of things and doers in the world of affairs, the businessman of today encounters esthetic imperatives that were seldom heard before but now demand more than a veneer showing of social responsibility. But there are deeper satisfactions for the businessman who meets the artist more than halfway, for aside from the fact that beauty has salable value, active participation in the cultural efforts of a community brings rewards of a different order. Direct association of the business world with the essential activities of a high culture yields satisfactions that are not often enough attached to the term "corporate citizenship."

On the side of the artist, there are practical as well as esthetic goals and activities that draw him toward the business system. The larger market, due to mass consumption, for the artist's talents and the things he makes is no small part of this; nor can one discount the contributions that good management, as it has developed in business institutions, can make to cultural institutions. More interesting are the parallel goals of artist, educator, and the industrial maker and doer in the search for knowledge. The truths about man and his world are only partly discoverable by science and philosophy; the artist has an indispensable role to play here, too. For, despite dissenters among artists and estheticians, art is a way of knowing as well as an expressive way; and without the insights provided by the arts and the humanities the rest of us, including the world of business, will find it that much harder to find our way out of the crises that beset our contemporary civilization.

CONCLUSION

The business world and the creative society, then, are organically interrelated in the most intimate way. And the interrelationship demands attention by those who manage business institutions—notably the executives of the modern corporation—as well as those who are responsible for leadership in the institutions of "high culture." A creative society leans heavily on both and contributes to both. Creativity in arts and letters is basically related to the inventive and innovative talents on which business depends. In both the worlds of business and art there are resistant forces opposed to the new, the nontraditional, the revolutionary; these forces are useful, too, and in previous chapters—especially those on ownership and governance—we have tried to show the role of conservatism as one of the conceptual foundations of business. In these last chapters other concepts have been introduced in order to show how, in the wide realm of value, there are both conserving and renewing efforts of man without which the business system would have little meaning and could not, in fact, long survive.

RECOMMENDED READING

EELLS, RICHARD. *The Corporation and the Arts,* chaps. 2, 3, 4, 8, 9, and 10. New York: Macmillan Co., 1967.

———. "Executive Suite and Artist's Garret," *Columbia Journal of World Business,* Vol. 1 (Inaugural Issue, Fall, 1965), pp. 37–44.

———. "Business for Art's Sake: The Case for Corporate Support of the Arts," in IVAR BERG (ed.), *The Business of America,* pp. 407–23. New York: Harcourt, Brace & World, Inc., 1968.

FREEDMAN, MARCIA. "Business and Education," in IVAR BERG (ed.), *ibid.,* pp. 363–87.

GALBRAITH, JOHN KENNETH. *The New Industrial State,* chaps. 6, 15, 25, 32, 33, 35. Boston: Houghton Mifflin Co., 1967.

SCHON, DONALD A. *Technology and Change: The New Heraclitus.* New York: Dell Publishing Co., 1967.

SHILS, EDWARD. "The High Culture of the Age," in ROBERT N. WILSON (ed.), *The Arts in Society,* pp. 315–62. Englewood Cliffs, N.J.: Prentice-Hall, Inc., 1964.

The Performing Arts, Rockefeller Panel Report on the Future of Theatre, Dance, Music in America: Problems and Prospects, pp. 81–93. New York: McGraw-Hill Book Co., 1965.

WILSON, ROBERT N. "High Culture and Popular Culture in a Business Society," in IVAR BERG (ed.), *op cit.,* pp. 388–406.

FURTHER READING

BARZUN, JACQUES. *The House of Intellect.* New York: Harper & Bros., 1959.

BAUMOL, WILLIAM J., and BOWEN, WILLIAM G. *Performing Arts: The Economic Dilemma.* New York: The Twentieth Century Fund, 1966.

DORIAN, FREDERICK. *Commitment to Culture: Art Patronage in Europe, Its Significance for America,* pp. 457–83. Pittsburgh: University of Pittsburgh Press, 1964.

EELLS, RICHARD. *Corporation Giving in a Free Society.* New York: Harper & Bros., 1956.

GHISELIN, BREWSTER (ed.). *The Creative Process: A Symposium.* Berkeley: University of California Press, 1952.

LANGER, SUSANNE K. *Mind: An Essay on Human Feeling.* Baltimore: The Johns Hopkins Press, 1967.

22. Business and Value-Forming Institutions

OUTLINE

IT IS AXIOMATIC that historic values are in convulsion today and that any destruction of value-forming institutions in America means the destruction of our free society. A conviction that certain precapitalist institutions had provided pillars for a nineteenth-century order led Schumpeter two decades ago to intensive studies of these precapitalist institutions. Incidentally, Schumpeter concluded that the very institutions that provided energy and direction for capitalism were doomed eventually by the success of the economic system they had encouraged.

What, then, are some of the major precapitalist institutions that

564

provide values for the American society? Clearly, one can identify at least four such basic instruments: family, church, school, and state. Because the family is such a small, closely knit kind of social unit, its contributions will not be discussed, even though its role as a value determinant is primary for its various members. Each of the other institutions, however, has a distinctive dogma, a set of identifiable objectives, a corpus of law, and a recognizable ruling group and therefore offers greater opportunity for fruitful analysis. Moreover, since each represents large aggregates of human beings working in a very durable relationship, there is a greater need for such analysis.

MAJOR VALUE-FORMING INSTITUTIONS

THE CHURCH

On April 9, 1960, *The Wall Street Journal* editorialized:

The country would do better . . . to face the fact honestly that religion is, and always has been, a political issue and that it is not improper for it to be so.

Men's religious beliefs embrace not only man's relation to God but also man's relations to man. They thus touch the forms of society around him and are inevitably deeply political in the truest sense of that word.

If the "truest sense of that word" means the Aristotelian context, which equates political man with social man, who is necessarily involved in organization, then it follows that religion has impact upon all other pivotal human associations. Yet the assessment is complicated by inconsistencies. Religion has long provided a unifying role among primitives by strengthening the sense of reality of common values among believers—as Professor William Goode demonstrated in *Religion among the Primitives.* It has also been a disruptive force, as religious wars of the 16th century have so dramatically illustrated. Religions have produced real-life characters like Jobs and Judas Iscariots and fictional ones like Kristin Lavransdatters and Elmer Gantrys.

American business has been peopled with men like Daniel Drew ("thin as a dried herring," in Parrington's acid description, "yet a builder of churches and founder of Drew Theological Seminary, who pilfered and cheated his way to wealth with tobacco juice drooling from his mouth."[1]) ; and business has had the opposites of

---

[1] Vernon Louis Parrington, *Main Currents in American Thought* (New York: Harcourt, Brace & Co., 1930) , Vol. III, p. 13.

Drew: men like Peter Cooper, founder of Cooper Union, whose behavior reflected high norms of religious and moral idealism. Finally, the task is complicated by the particular symbolism employed by each religion, which suggests a form of magic to the uninitiated, even as it elicits the deepest kind of meanings for the elect.

Yet religion calls to holiness, and holiness harbors the values of soul or personality of society, which culminates in the community of man, and of God as the power that makes for man's salvation. Mysticism has often succeeded when religions of reason have failed. What, then, has the church, generically speaking, contributed to American value constructs? Have these values been effective in influencing the growth of business institutions or the day-by-day operation of business affairs?

In pursuing this inquiry, a working model for analysis developed by Troeltsch in *Die Sozialphilosophie des Christentums* proves singularly useful.[2] After calling attention to the tension that must necessarily exist between an "other-worldly" system of values and the secular society in which religion operates, Troeltsch then expressed the view that every major religion has reacted to the worldly order in one of two ways: either it has behaved as a *church* by seeking to adapt creatively to the historic environment, or it has assumed a posture of withdrawal (often coupled with strong opposition to secular institutions) and behaved as a *sect*. Something of the same point is suggested in Kant's last mature publication, *Religion within the Limits of Reason Alone,* in which the German philosopher argued that a moral commonwealth could never be realized except within an existing political commonwealth; hence the need for creative adaptation by the church.

The Church and Society. While we are conscious of the risks of oversimplification, it seems fair to say that Judaism, Catholicism, and some denominations of Protestantism have behaved in ways described by Troeltsch as sectarian. This is not to understate the vast contribution that Judaism has made in its insistence—especially marked in the Talmudic writings—on the importance of a philosophy of history. Much of our sense of mission is directly related to this concept. Nor do we want to overlook the importance of the Mosaic code on our legislation, or the constant dialogue between love of God (school of Hillel) versus fear of God (school of Shammai), which became so embedded in much Christian thought.

---

[2] Ernst Troeltsch, *The Social Teaching of the Christian Churches* (trans. Olive Wyon) (New York: Macmillan Co., 1931) .

Similarly, the restrictions placed on Catholic contributions are not intended to denigrate the importance of the Maryland prototype of religious toleration and its lessons for church-state relations; nor do we ignore the assistance rendered to an infant nation by the Barrys, Fitzsimons, and Carrolls. Yet, not only have Catholics been a minority in America but this minority has been composed to a large extent of the lowest strata of the social classes. The legacy of the urbane and cultivated Carrolls of Carrollton literally vanished in the surge of mid-19th-century immigrant invasions. Catholics developed what Monsignor John Tracy Ellis called the "ghetto mentality": they built their own schools and hospitals; they operated their own Scout and youth movements; they sponsored their own associations for scholars. With the exception of the trade-union movement, Catholic influence has not been a decisive factor in major policy formulations. Clearly since Pope John XXIII and Vatican II, historic changes have been initiated, but it is too early to perceive their full implications.

Thus, by a process of elimination, we are left with Protestantism. In 1930, when André Siegfried observed that Protestantism was the "national religion" of America, few were disposed to challenge the assertion. While the subsequent four decades have considerably modified this earlier judgment, it remains true that Protestantism has been the most important religious influence in America. Historian Ralph Henry Gabriel of Yale who has isolated three types of "constructive" Protestantism, merits extensive quotation.

The first was Pietism, the name for the social outlook for Lutheranism. Luther, militant mystic, emphasized the inner life: only God can rule the human spirit; only the spirit is important. Pietism led its followers to focus their attention upon reforming the world's sinful institutions.

The second type of constructive Protestantism was Calvinism. The brilliant Genevan, although often represented as a pessimist, was optimist enough to believe that all areas of human life, all institutions of society, could be redeemed. He was unwilling to abandon to Satan even politics and economics. As he looked out upon his sixteenth century European world, a sense of crisis filled him. Calvin saw the hearts of the sons of Adam full of sin, the institutions which they had created to make life possible hastening them to destruction, and evil triumphant and threatening the world. Evil in 1536, when young Calvin hurried his *Institutes of the Christian Religion* to the press of Thomas Platter and Balthasar Lasius at Basle, was personified by France's political rulers who had compelled the prophet of reform to flee his native land to save his life. The purpose of God and the duty of man, thought Calvin, is to restrain Satan, ranging over the earth like a beast seeking his prey. Both Church and State must share in the all-important task of checking the corrupt passions of men. American constitutionalism, which seeks by means of a written document to restrain from wrong-doing individuals, majorities, and even governments, owes a heavy debt to that young Frenchman who, in the summer of 1536, made his home in Geneva and began to expound the epistles of St. Paul.

The Separatists formulated the third approach to the problem of constructive Protestantism. Like some disillusioned citizens of the twentieth century, the Separatists were convinced that politicians as a breed are beyond the possibility of saving. Because of the close alliance of Church and State in their day, these radicals grouped bishops and ministers of state in that company of human rebels whom a despairing God had marked for destruction. The Separatists urged the faithful to withdraw themselves from a corrupt world. They were the anarchists of their day. They felt that the time was near at hand when the present sinful order would pass away and when the kingdom of God would take on its final perfection. Of all the early Protestants the Separatists, alone, emphasized the millennial hope.

The uncompromising Genevan system was well adapted to pioneers struggling against a wilderness. Beginning at the edge of the clearings beyond the village palisade, the untamed forest stretched endlessly westward into the unknown. The hard conditions of life required labor; the system of John Calvin sanctified work. It urged men to be prodigal in the expenditure of constructive effort, but saving of the gains they won. When the tension of the frontier struggle relaxed and life became easier, certain defects of Calvinism became increasingly evident. Its theology was as harsh as the social conditions in the sixteenth-century European cities in which it had had its origin. The doctrine of an avenging deity who flings multitudes of his creatures into the eternal torment of the burning lake was out of harmony with the warm sympathies expressing themselves in the humanitarian movements of the nineteenth century. The time came when Calvin's portrait of God seemed an immoral caricature. The dour determinism essential in the Calvinist doctrine of foreordination fitted ill with the mood of post-Yorktown Americans, jubilant over their successful defiance of the world's most powerful empire. The generation which created the American Republic was not pleased to be told from the pulpit that man could do nothing to save himself and that his every act was ordained from the alpha of time. . . .

The first form of the American rebellion against Calvinism was evangelical Protestantism. Evangelicism came to New England in Calvinist guise when Jonathan Edwards in the eighteenth century lighted the fire of the Great Awakening in the Connecticut Valley. It swept the back country of the southern colonies when the magic words of George Whit-field, Methodist evangelist, called thousands of simple frontiersmen into the fold. Then, at the close of the eighteenth century the frontier, which for a century and a half had been inching westward from the Atlantic shoreline toward the Appalachians, suddenly began an advance that, in scarcely more than fifty years, carried it across the continent to distant Oregon and to the Golden Gate. Organized Puritanism and Quakerism stood helpless before the unchurched west. Beyond the wooded Appalachians the prophets of a new evangelicalism, hard-riding Methodist circuit riders and vehement Baptist preachers, deployed on the thin battle lines of the Lord. The camp meeting, that unique American contribution of Christianity, evolved as the only practicable solution of the problem of carrying the Gospel to the cabin population of a sparsely settled border.

The central appeal of evangelicism was the winning by the individual of freedom from bondage. . . . Its emphasis upon the individual and his emotions, its central vision of the perfect man in remote antiquity, its gospel of love which cleanses the world—all reflected that romantic mood so important in Europe and in America in the first half of the nineteenth century. . . . Its view of civilization was that of the progress of men away from the necessity of external restraint by man-made laws and toward individual liberty founded upon self-control. So great is the similarity that the doctrine of liberty seems but a secular version of its counterpart in evangelical Protestantism.[3]

This long quotation from Gabriel catches the sweep of the Protestant movement in America and identifies many specific values that have been transferred to the business community: the gospel of work, the virtues of thrift and industry, responsible individualism, skepticism of concentrated power, the philosophy of progress, and the sense of mission. Even when Emerson, in the celebrated Phi Beta Kappa address to Harvard College in 1838, called upon Americans to proclaim their intellectual independence from the "courtly muses of Europe" by fashioning their own democratic faith, the foundations remained frankly supernatural and derived from the Judeo-Christian tradition. Unlike the Indic-Brahmanic and the Buddhistic systems, which recede into a purer kind of inwardness, Christianity maintained everywhere and almost uniquely a close nexus between organization and theory, between practice and principle. Later nineteenth-century developments leading to social Darwinism, and the chaos of the post-Versailles days have dealt shattering blows to the

---

[3] Ralph Henry Gabriel, *The Course of American Democratic Thought* (New York: Ronald Press Co., 1940) , pp. 30–32. See also D. W. Brogan, *The American Character* (New York: Alfred A. Knopf, Inc., 1944) , pp. 95–107.

older tenets of the democratic faith, but the religious roots remain tenaciously implanted in America's intellectual soil.

The Church and Business. What shall we say of the relevance of religious values to the evolution and operation of the business community? From the business world itself come two contradictory points of view. The first was asserted vigorously by K. W. Underwood at the 75th anniversary of the Harvard Business School, who said that consciousness of the incarnate God "brings new meanings to the present and opens new hopes for the future." He went on to state:

As a Christian, I try to reason, by analogy, about the events of my life, my business, and my world, knowing that the Incarnation reveals the nature of power that truly rules this world. . . .
Men in business are never given the moral choice between personal values and the treat to these from circumstances without value or principle. Rather, they must choose between various proposals and demands by men and organizations, all of which combine principle and data, value and facts. The choice is not between some 100% "right world" known by the man of principle, in business or labor, that needs to be defended against the demands of others who could compromise this ideal. The choice is between demands of men who argue for shifts in past arrangements of power and goods in terms of mutual and differing value and factual perspectives on the present and future.[4]

Other business theorists have also insisted on the direct relevance of religious ideals to business. Harold L. Johnson, associate professor of economics at Emory University, believes that "if the business manager will rid himself of the notion that the doctrines of the church . . . offer him nothing but vague ideas about human relationships, and sit down with the theologian to explore the teachings of his faith, he will find vast quantities of material out of which he can construct a map for his business life."[5] James Worthy, a vice president of Sears, Roebuck, holds that "modern business enterprise has evolved within a matrix of Judaeo-Christian ethics" and that ideas of "fair play and self-restraint are essentially religious."[6]

One of the most eloquent and widely quoted statements in sup-

---

[4] In Dan H. Fenn, Jr., *Management's Mission in a New Society* (New York: McGraw-Hill Book Co., 1959) , pp. 188–89.

[5] Harold L. Johnson, "Can the Businessman Apply Christianity?" *Harvard Business Review*, Vol. XXXV (September–October, 1957) , p. 76.

[6] James Worthy, "Religion and Its Role in the World of Business," *Journal of Business*, Vol. XXXI (October, 1958) , pp. 293–303.

port of religion as the provider of essential "skyhooks" for business was made by O. A. Ohmann, an executive of the Standard Oil Company of Ohio. Ohmann says that religion must be a primary concern of the manager and that the way the administrator answers the question "Is God a myth, or is He the final and absolute judge to whom we are ultimately responsible?"[7] is reflected in the entire enterprise.

Several Quaker firms have, with characteristic vigor, joined hands with Walter Lamb, president of Robert E. Lamb, Inc., in an attempt to "think of moral-ethical ideals and profit goals as consistent parts of the same effort."[8]

Yet there is a strong and articulate opposition view which asserts that "business by admonition" is so much pious but impractical day-dreaming, that reliance on a corporate conscience thus formed is pure hogwash.

Consider the wage, investment, and price decisions to be made by corporate managements, and ask what contributions consciences can make to the solutions of the problems they pose. These decisions affect all of society, not just the persons in the immediate family. . . . This is quite an assignment to impose on innocent, artless consciences. I am not at all sure that they can stand the strain. Ponder the plight of the management of a giant firm producing a basic commodity, employing thousands of workers at good wages, making splendid profits, and presently facing a crippling strike unless it accedes to a demand for a wage increase. The increase can easily be passed along in higher prices. Workers want higher wages and no interruption in employment; consumers want continued output at an increasing rate and so do stockholders. The public does not want further inflation and larger numbers of small firms do not want further increase in wages. The White House, which wants high production, full employment, healthy wages, abundant profits and low prices, now admonishes industrial statesmen to recognize their public responsibility and to adopt measures appropriate to the maintenance of equity, full employment, stability, and progress. The management—as allocator, distributor, stabilizer, trustee, consecrator, prophet, and chaplain, as well as manager— consults its conscience. The diagnosis of the attending psychiatrist will be "multiple schizophrenia": The management's personality will not be split. It will be shredded and powdered![9]

---

[7] O. A. Ohmann, "Skyhooks: With Special Implications for Monday through Friday," *Harvard Business Review*, Vol. XXXIII (May–June, 1955), pp. 1–9.

[8] F. H. Blum, "Social Audit of the Enterprise," *Harvard Business Review*, Vol. XXXVI (March–April, 1958), p. 77.

[9] Ben W. Lewis, "Power Blocs and the Operation of Economic Forces," *American Economic Review*, Vol. XLIX (May, 1959), pp. 396–97.

And the author goes on to state that the time is not yet ripe for systematic identification, let alone defense, of the present business system—giant firms are "sitting like fat, delectable ducks, virtually inviting the government to open fire with something more effective than antitrust. The invitation will be accepted."

The essence of much of the argument is that the personal ethics of love, sacrifice, self-abnegation are irrelevant to a gigantic business machine, which generates moral problems of a distinctly extrapersonal kind as rapidly as it generates the production of goods. Chester Barnard, businessman, foundation executive, public servant, and author, insisted that the perfectionist standards of the Protestant ethic for personal behavior do not constitute a "valid criterion of moral behavior" in business. Such ideals are general and unrelated to concrete situations; they do not account for the fact that business behavior is *representative* rather than *personal,* that things are done in behalf of others and not for the self.[10]

In the face of such diverse and cogently reasoned positions regarding the relevance of religion to business, what practical guides remain? Clearly, there is need for theologians themselves to bring to ritual and symbol a greater relevance for modern social needs, to effect a more satisfying reconciliation between faith and reason. This was the great achievement of Augustine and Aquinas in Christianity, of Averroes and Alghazali in Islam, of Judah Ha-Levi and Maimonides in Judaism. And there are signs on many fronts that efforts are being undertaken to achieve such syntheses, among which might be mentioned the Danforth seminars, the studies and symposiums of the Federal Council of Churches of Christ in America, the Institute for Religious and Social Studies of the Jewish Theological Seminary of America, and the labor schools for unionists sponsored by the Jesuits. On the side of business there is need for a rather humble admission that in a complex industrial society their special functions are heavily tinged with a teleology closely allied to theology; consequently, professional competence may be helped by theological insights. Hortatory as this is, in the absence of clearer evidence that more sophisticated syntheses are available, this is about the length to which any immediately practical conclusion dare go. By way of caveat, we should like to emphasize that nothing would be worse for the cause of religion or business than to assume, as

---

[10] Chester Barnard, "Elementary Conditions of Business Morals," *California Management Review*, Vol. I (Fall, 1958), pp. 1–13.

some do, that God can be spelled Get, that piety and profits are reverse sides of the same coin, or that the mansion of the spirit has the same dimensions as the countinghouse.

THE SCHOOL

Education in America has traditionally been the way through which the ideal of equality could be translated into the reality of opportunity. Education has represented a treasured value for the American community, and its accomplishments are many. It has given us one of the highest literacy rates in the world, and its varied curricula support a vast army of technical and professional men. Americans are passionately dedicated to the open, free, public school system, whatever its weaknesses.

But there is another way of viewing the school that involves analysis of education as a value-forming agent in higher, professional education, whence comes the bulk of today's American business managers. Historically, religion and education operated as allies.

The first six institutions of higher learning in this country were launched under religious auspices, and two others (Brown and Pennsylvania), although interdenominational, provided for moral instruction in their curricula. The close working partnership between pulpit and classroom resulted in an educational philosophy frequently dominated, and always influenced, by men of the cloth. It is not without point to note that some of our most distinguished early economists were practicing ministers or students of moral philosophy. George Tucker (1775–1861) was professor of morals at Virginia, Francis Wayland (1796–1865) was a leading Baptist minister of Boston, and Francis Bowen (1811–90) occupied the chair of "natural religion, moral philosophy, and civil polity" at Harvard.

New Intellectual Currents. The shift from the sacred to the secular was rather dramatically illustrated in 1885 when the founders of the American Economic Association declared in their statement of principles that, while they appreciated the work of former economists, they looked not so much to speculation as to the historical and statistical study of the actual conditions of economic life for satisfactory accomplishment. Faith was required to yield to reason, and speculation to empirical science.

Like other professional men, most American business leaders are the product of an intellectual tradition that has been eddying con-

vulsively around internal contradictions. On the one hand, there are
the remains of the old faith in a Maker, a Providence, a human soul,
and an afterlife; on the other, there are new wines blended from the
fruits of religious agnosticism, a kind of Cartesian skepticism, and a
reverence for the man-made theology of progress. Symptomatic of
the times was Illinois Governor Frank Lowden's apostrophe at the
dedication of Northwestern University's new campus in 1927 to the
new social sciences as the "best hope for the future progress of our
civilization. . . . For speculation of the scholastics we are substitut-
ing the more prosaic methods which Bacon indicated in his *No-
vanum organum*. The science of economics affords us an excellent
illustration."[11]

There are now evidences that the intellectual waters are backing
up. Economics has been indicted by some for its overemphasis on
quantifications and for its indifference to the qualitative aspects of
human society. Professor Meyer, of M.I.T., spoke to this point in the
following terms:

> Western economics has . . . a chance to weave into its doctrine ideas
> and ethical concepts which will signify that it is at least aware that mate-
> rial advance is not all of life. Advance in net per capita income, the basis
> of value judgment of most Western economic writings, denotes a materi-
> alism which oddly enough is often more Marxist than Capitalist. If the
> Western world has anything to export, it is the set of concepts, freedoms,
> and ideas which have shaped it. The production of goods and services has
> been at best a by-product of these, and material advance cannot forever
> have primacy as a goal in the literature.[12]

On the credit side, it must be noted that education in America
has never been exploited exclusively for state purposes. Government
qua government has not claimed the right to determine the content
or truth of the intellectual discipline. The Nazi government prohibited the teaching of Einstein's theory of relativity on grounds that it
was "Jewish physics"; the Soviets have had their party line in biology and genetics. In the Western tradition the right to pursue truth
is still cherished, and, if the pursuit does not necessarily result in
happiness, it does result in a continuing enlargement of the frontiers
of human knowledge.

---

[11] *Proceedings of the Northwestern University Conference on Business Education*
(Chicago: Northwestern University Press, 1927) , p. 143.

[12] Albert J. Meyer, *Middle Eastern Capitalism* (Cambridge, Mass.: Harvard University Press, 1959) , p. 122.

Curricula and National Growth. Above all else, the ability of American schools to stay close to the demands of American society has been nothing short of remarkable. Americans believed with evangelical fervor the gospel of Adam Smith that "the education of the common people requires in a civilized and commercial society the attention of the public more than that of people of the same rank and fortune."[13] The present upsurge of population and the growing concern over the intellectual content of the school curricula strongly suggest that the patterns, whether of traditionalism or faddism, will eventually subserve a more carefully developed national manpower policy program. The mistakes of the past have been primarily in trying to do, too quickly, too much for too many. The mistakes of the present may stem from a policy of "too little too late."

THE STATE

The state may be viewed either as an abstraction to designate a form of human association or as a concrete organization characterized by particular governors and governed and occupying a defined territory. Generally speaking, the former approach has involved philosophers and jurists in long debate over whether the state is necessary because of man's nature (Aristotle, Aquinas, and Marshall) or whether the state evolves, through voluntary agreement, the social compact to prevent the evils of anarchy (Hobbes, Rousseau, Holmes).

Our present concern is less with a general philosophy of the state than with the values fostered by the American Commonwealth. In this connection, it is appropriate to distinguish between statements of political creed embodied in the Declaration of Independence, the Gettysburg Address, and portions of *The Federalist,* and the work rules spelled out in the Constitution and in court decisions. The Declaration of Independence explicitly recognizes a divine lawmaker who accords to his creatures certain inalienable rights—life, liberty, and pursuit of happiness—and it implicitly accepts a law higher than man-made statute. But no *deus ex machina* lurks in the wings to solve human dilemmas, even though the American creed posits a beneficent Providence, which has made available all neces-

---

[13] This theme is developed by Eli Ginsberg, *Human Resources: The Wealth of a Nation* (New York: Simon and Schuster, 1958), p. 15.

sary ingredients for transcendent success if only men would employ them properly.

Legal Values. From the theory that permeates our democratic system there emerge legal values that can be classified under four main headings[14]: (1) *The legal rights of the individual* (freedom of contract, association, labor, property rights, enterprise, and the person); (2) *Equality before the law* (as the only effective device for assuring justice); (3) *Control of government by the people* (representative government, minority rights, universal suffrage); and (4) *The rule of law* (administration of rules without distinction as to persons, and acceptance of the legal rule that everyone counts for one).

Unlike the postwar constitutions of France, Germany, and Italy, which contain explicit references to the inviolability of basic human dignities, the original American constitution is extraordinarily reticent. Even the Bill of Rights addresses itself less to theory and more to definition of what these dignities actually mean under the positive law. What does the document reveal in terms of attitudes?

1. *Skepticism of concentrated power.* Power is divided spatially between the central government and the various states and functionally, according to the separation-of-power theory, among the executive, legislative, and judiciary. The check and balance system was designed to promote harmony even as it restricted any one branch of government from achieving a monopoly on power. Finally, certain powers were specifically denied to both federal and state governments.

2. *Skepticism of the masses in the short run.* Illustrations of this are such various devices as indirect election of senators and of the President, the rather cumbersome amending process, appointment rather than election of federal judges, and so on.

3. *Confidence in compromise and bargaining.* Calhoun's doctrine of the "concurrent minority" set the tone of democratic morality by insisting that the minority be treated as if "you belonged to it." Except for the Civil War, the doctrine of compromise and bargaining has worked efficaciously.

4. *Recognition of the importance of business and of government-business interdependence.*

This last item is worthy of particular comment in view of the orientation of this inquiry. In *The Economic Basis of the Constitution,* Charles Beard so successfully persuaded a generation of stu-

---

[14] Wolfgang Friedman, *Legal Theory* (London: Stevens & Sons, 1953), pp. 477–510.

dents that narrow business interests determined the outcome of the American constitutional drama that business has tended to adopt a Pilate-like attitude toward its own contribution to government— and with unfortunate results. It is well to recall that James Bryce, in *The American Commonwealth,* showed how the Founding Fathers shaped the new Constitution on a structure already developed by business enterprise. All the original colonies were started, chartered, and governed as British trading companies; therefore, public organizations owed much to the private ones which provided the models.

Bryce traced these contributions by recalling that within the period of ten years, under the last of the Tudors and the first of the Stuarts, two trading charters were issued to two companies of English adventurers. One charter became the root of English title to the East and the other to the West. One of these Companies has grown into the Empire of India; the other into the United States of America. If England had done nothing else in history, she might trust her fame to the work which these charters began. And the foundations of both dominions were laid in an age which was adorned by the greatest of her creative minds, and gave birth to the men who set on a solid basis a frame of representative government which all free nations of the modern world have copied.[15]

A bill of particulars underscores the rightness of Bryce's conclusion. In a continuous historical development, the Massachusetts Bay Trading Company had become the Commonwealth of Massachusetts as the Virginia Company at Jamestown had become the Commonwealth of Virginia. The story of Maryland is the story of businessman Calvert's shrewd bargaining for a franchise to a profitable business operation. Penn took land in lieu of moneys owed by the Crown. Indeed, much of the theoretical work regarding representative government was accomplished by persons, like John Locke, in their capacities as directors or consultants to various stock companies.

Interdependence of Business and Government. That the nation's founders were aware of the interdependence of business and government comes out forcefully (as noted in Chapter 2) in the 15th paper of *The Federalist* by Hamilton. Alluding to reasons why a strong central government was necessary, Hamilton wrote:

We may indeed, with propriety, be said to have reached almost the last stage of national humiliation. There is scarcely any thing that can

---

[15] James Bryce, as quoted in Scott Buchanan, *Essay in Politics* (New York: Philosophical Library, 1953), p. 28.

wound the pride, or degrade the character, of an independent people, which we do not experience. Are there engagements, to the performance of which we are held by every tie respectable among men? These are the subjects of constant and unblushing violation. Do we owe debts to foreigners, and to our own citizens, contracted in a time of imminent peril, for the preservation of our political existence? These remain without any proper or satisfactory provision for their discharge. Have we valuable territories and important posts in the possession of a foreign power, which, by express stipulations, ought long since to have been surrendered? These are still retained, to the prejudice of our interests not less than of our rights. Are we in a condition to resent or to repel the aggression? We have neither troops, nor treasury, nor government. (I mean for the union.) Are we even in a condition to remonstrate with dignity? The just imputations on our own faith, in respect to the same treaty, ought first to be removed. Are we entitled, by nature and compact, to a free participation in the navigation of the Mississippi? Spain excludes us from it. Is public credit an indispensable resource in time of public danger? We seem to have abandoned its cause as desperate and irretrievable. Is commerce of importance to national wealth? Ours is at the lowest point of declension. Is respectability in the eyes of foreign powers, a safeguard against foreign encroachments? The imbecility of our government even forbids them to treat with us: our ambassadors abroad are the mere pageants of mimic sovereignty. Is a violent and unnatural decrease in the value of land, a symptom of national distress? The price of improved land, in most parts of the country, is much lower than can be accounted for by the quantity of waste land at market, and can only be fully explained by that want of private and public confidence, which are so alarmingly prevalent among all ranks, and which have a direct tendency to depreciate property of every kind. Is private credit the friend and patron of industry? That most useful kind which relates to borrowing and lending, is reduced within the narrowest limits, and this still more from an opinion of insecurity than from a scarcity of money. . . .

This is the melancholy situation to which we have been brought by those very maxims and counsels, which would now deter us from adopting the proposed constitution; and which, not content with having conducted us to the brink of a precipice, seem resolved to plunge us into the abyss that awaits us below. Here, my countrymen, impelled by every motive that ought to influence an enlightened people, let us make a firm stand for our safety, our tranquility, our dignity, our reputation. *Let us at last break the fatal charm which has too long seduced us from the paths of felicity and prosperity.*[16]

---

[16] *The Federalist*, No. 15.

In a more specific fashion, Section 8 of Article 1 of the Constitution introduces us to business-oriented values esteemed by the American government: uniform duties, imposts, excises; stable coinage and weight systems; encouragement of post roads; and prohibition of import duties on goods moving in interstate commerce to promote trade; denial to states of the right to impair the obligation of contracts. The bare enumeration does not include the Fourteenth Amendment and the uses to which due process was put in the interest of the business community—sometimes at the expense of other basic values.

Since the New Deal, the government has taken a more positive hand in the economic affairs of the country. The Jones and Laughlin Steel Corporation case interpreted Congress' interest in interstate commerce to comprehend legislative control over "activities intrastate which have a substantial effect on the commerce or the exercise of Congressional power over it. . . ."[17] In a nation dominated by giant corporations and giant unions, whose activities inevitably spill over state boundaries, the net effect of the Supreme Court's decision was to reverse the historic and more cautious application of congressional control over intrastate business activities.

Allusion to the Jones and Laughlin case is intended primarily to serve as a logical preface to values implicit in current debate over this question: Should governments do much more than they are already doing in aid to distressed areas or on behalf of such public goods as educational and hospital services? Or should the state maintain a neutral policy and rely on the business community itself to generate satisfactory rates of growth, equitable distribution of incomes, and general efficiency of operations? In the debate, the values and capabilities of business as an institution are being increasingly called into question. But each of the institutions discussed here—church, school, and state—has in its turn been exposed to similar challenges.

CHALLENGES TO CHURCH, SCHOOL, AND STATE

The impact of the church is indirect and oftentimes secondary. Church influence comes through admonition, and this has been criticized by men like Professor Ben Lewis and Chester Barnard as

---

[17] *National Labor Relations Board* v. *Jones and Laughlin Steel Corp.*, 301 U.S. 1 (1937) .

irrelevant to actual business operations. Despite church attempts to adjust to an industrial society—in the eyes of the critics—no theology has yet produced meaningful guidelines for business activity. As Boulding remarked:

There is an anti-economic strain in the teaching of almost all the prophets and poetics. The careful, calculating, economizing way of life is neither prophetic nor poetic. It counts the cost; it asks for reward; it has no fine frenzies; it is humdrum, commonplace, even a little sordid. The stimulation to economic progress is not in the ethic of the New Testament itself; rather it is in the Puritan substitute-ethic, the product of the impact of the ethic of love on the iron laws of the world.[18]

Despite these strictures, Boulding feels that religion may well become more important as an "autonomous force in the development of the technical revolution."

To concede to business the right to develop an ethic independent of religious ideals on grounds that modern organization involves its own mystiques, its own ritual, its own behavioral codes, its own rewards and sanctions is to risk creating hopeless dichotomies between the church and the market place.[19] Realism suggests that business has a firm and modest claim on the church to establish value constructs; it cannot ask the church to substitute religious panacea for business policy or theological formula for decision making.

Of all agencies in libertarian and secular America, the school exercises the most profound influence. What the schools have done has often determined what the professions have become. By transforming the curriculum in medical schools, the Flexner Report brought new advances to the healing professions. In business education, the Carnegie and Ford studies of a decade ago led to curricula reappraisals that have had beneficial results for the business profession. And how universities react to the demands for continuing adult education will have additional impact on the new society.

More relevant at this point than appraisals of trends and needs is appraisal of the values esteemed by the school itself. Truth is still the mistress of the educational kingdom, and the state has happily

---

[18] Kenneth E. Boulding, "Religious Foundations of Economic Progress," *Harvard Business Review*, Vol. XXX (May–June, 1952), pp. 33–40.

[19] See Richard Kerschagl, *Einfuhrung in die Methodenlehre der Nationalökonomie* (Wien: Hölder-Pichler-Tempsky, 1948), and Walter Goerlitz, *History of the German General Staff*, trans. Brian Battershaw (New York: Frederick A. Praeger, 1953).

never tampered with this dominion. Yet truth has many guises. We have seen the overthrow of the speculative by the empirical methods, and this change fitted the mood of a pragmatic nation. Yet if a value judgment is now in order, it appears that great wisdom attaches to Whitehead's observations that

. . . until the last hundred and fifty years, the speculative Reason produced singularly little effect upon technology and upon art. It is arguable that on the whole within the modern period art made no progress, and in some respects declined. Having regard to the rise of modern music, we may reject the theory of a general decline in art. But, on the whole, as artists we certainly have not surpassed the men of a thousand years before Christ, and it is doubtful whether we reach their level. We seem to care less about art. Perhaps we have more to think about, and so neglect to cultivate our esthetic impulses.

Technology has certainly improved during the last three thousand years. But it would be difficult to discern any influence of the speculative Reason upon this progress, until the most recent period. There does not seem to have been much quickening of the process. For example, the technology of Europe in the eighteenth century had made a very moderate advance over that of the Roman Empire in its prime. The advance does not seem to be much greater than that made in the two thousand years preceding this culmination of the classical civilization.

The enormous advance in the technology of the last hundred and fifty years arises from the fact that the speculative and the practical Reason have at last made contact. The speculative Reason has lent its theoretic activity, and the practical Reason has lent its methodologies for dealing with the various types of facts. Both functions of Reason have gained power. The speculative Reason has acquired content, that is to say, material for its theoretic activity to work upon, and the methodic Reason has acquired theoretic insight transcending its immediate limits. We should be on the threshold of an advance in all the values of human life.[20]

As far as the state is concerned, it is important to remember that this nation was conceived as much in the prosaic practices of the colonial trading companies as in the dedication to liberty majestically recalled by Lincoln.

While not identical with the *casas* (business firms) of medieval Italy (which assumed government functions to the point that the line between government and business was lost until after Colum-

---

[20] Alfred North Whitehead, *The Function of Reason* (Princeton: Princeton University Press, 1929) , pp. 33–34.

bus' time), the rapport between politics and business demonstrated great sustaining power, which was reflected in both British and American practices during the 17th and 18th centuries. The American founders desired a harmony of interest between government and business. This has not always been true of other nations, and the biography of mercantilism is often the story of the state's determination to subordinate business to the state's objectives. As with its relationship to the school, the American republic moved initially toward support of business divorced from control; more recently the government has moved beyond the control stage reflected in the Sherman Antitrust Laws to a direct involvement in business activity along the lines of the TVA enterprise.

Have the objectives outlined in the Constitution's preamble been realized? A more perfect union formed on both the political and economic fronts has been achieved; the larger ends of justice are being more adequately served; domestic tranquillity has been attended to and the general welfare promoted; the defenses have always proved adequate to the needs of the past, even as there remain large and vexatious questions regarding the atomic present. And, in spite of aberrations, liberty still holds a treasured place in the ideals and practices of our courts and legislatures. The audit, therefore, is one of large accomplishment. Indeed, the state's performance has been so substantial that a growing number of scholars are urging the application of political instruments and political criteria (federal organization, due process toward employees, and even separation of powers) to the corporate structure.

It may be expected that this line of inquiry will grow in importance as long as observers see profits flowing less from efficient operations and more from built-in power positions. Power is—and has been for centuries—the domain of special interest to the political scientist. And, indeed, it is the political scientist who will have much to contribute to our understanding of the American business system.

A BUSINESS APPROACH TO VALUE

Yet even as it is recognized that business has historically tended to mirror the value constructs of nonbusiness institutions, it is clear today that business as an institution is trying to build values of its own. If honest men can and do reflect on the realities of modern business and pronounce them good or evil—as they manifestly have done—then, patently, their visions of a good society are predicated on certain values and value systems.

While there is concern in some quarters that these ideals are no longer being converted into social levers, that interest in coldly abstract inquiry no longer is matched by a passion to act—as Daniel Bell movingly showed in *The End of Ideology*[21]—there seems little doubt that, in a period of accelerating change both here and abroad, ideology, like the young girl of the Bible, is not dead but sleeping. The construction of a theory of business value includes many things, not the least of which is a definition of value and a differentiation among the hierarchies of values that business is called upon to sustain. And this leads into areas wherein imprecision and bias create booby traps.

RESPONSIBILITY THROUGH PHILOSOPHY

This present inquiry is not a didactic on responsibility but rather a tentative probe into the meaning of certain philosophical tenets that provide a reference point to the problem of responsibility. Nor will there be any pretense at any serious philosophical inquiry into the meaning of value as such. As "profits" and "markets" are the careful words of the businessman, so "value" is the careful word of the philosopher. When business leaders study or speak of values, three avenues are open to them. They can devote large portions of an active life to the unaccustomed role of a contemplative dedicated to the serious study of the very notion of value; they can speak only of "business" values, like rate of return or efficiency, and thus restrict the dialogue to members of their own fraternity;[22] or they can borrow unshamedly the distilled knowledge of the professional philosopher. Since the first of these alternatives is unlikely, and the second unpalatable, business is literally driven toward the third prospect.

Now this involves some serious risks. Borrowing from a vocabulary in which common words have uncommon meanings, in which precisions are refined and given shifting emphasis, the businessman may misinterpret meanings. Again, it is not the appropriate func-

---

21 New York: The Free Press, 1960. Also Bell's précis, "The End of Ideology in the West," *Columbia University Forum*, Winter, 1960, pp. 4–7.

22 See, e.g., Theodore Houser, *Big Business and Human Values* (New York: McGraw-Hill Book Co., 1957).

tion of the businessman to explore methodological problems involved in the determination of values and in the making of value judgments; it is his function to understand the kind of definition he accepts and the likely applications to business practices that such acceptance implies.

To arrive at a working definition of value as developed by competent philosophers and to relate this definition to the values cherished by American society, American business, and the American businessman, involves raising the following questions:

1. What is an acceptable definition of value that may be learned from philosophy?
2. Thus defined, what are the major values of American society?
3. What organizations have contributed what values to this society?
4. What expectations are placed on business by the American people because of the values they espouse?
5. What values does business hold for itself?
6. How is the businessman judged in terms of the personal values he accepts for himself?

When business turns to philosophy for help in understanding its own values, it invites questions such as these:[23]

1. By what right do you hold such values?
2. By what process and on what basis (faith, reason, instinct) do you determine your principles?
3. How do you establish relevance of your principles to the world of action?
4. What is your appraisal of the factual situation?

Beyond these are more difficult questions involved in analyzing how values complement or collide within the same organization and among different organizations and what priorities determine the resolution of issues when conflicts do arise. A dramatic illustration of the last issue is revealed in challenging what business today assumes as an almost natural right, namely, the ability to enlarge its spheres of influence, with consequent power to mold and move men.

---

[23] John F. A. Taylor, "The Marks of Society: The Grounds of Obligation in a Scientific Enterprise," *Journal of Philosophy*, Vol. LV (June 5, 1958), pp. 485–502, esp. pp. 485–92.

Should such power be curtailed and transferred to the determination of other institutions, such as church or state?

Thus business is reminded of the enormous difficulties that stand in the way of a satisfactory explanation of values. The lack of a common basis of knowledge between scientist and philosopher, the inadequate sharing of a common and stable tradition despite the Judeo-Christian religious legacy, and the common insistence on a monolithic approach to values (whether through mathematics, scientific experiment, or religious mysticism) constitute the three most common obstacles.[24]

And the manner in which traditional words like "morals" and "soul" are being used interchangeably with terms like "mores" and "psyche" suggest an important development. As Thucydides observed in his story of the revolution of Corcyra, the first sign of revolution is that old words lose their old meanings. And the American intellectual revolution has been no less upsetting than the technological and ecological revolutions that impress themselves more directly upon us.

While business may be excused for a certain impatience when confronted with a statement of difficulties and no statement of clarification, the growing awareness and fear of the complexities in the realm of value may well be the first step toward practical wisdom. What then do we learn from philosophy? We learn to make important distinctions. If "good" is defined as "that which is appropriate to the nature of him who desires it," then the terms "good" and "value" may be used interchangeably; indeed, metaphysically there may be no distinction. The problem then shifts to the determination of what is appropriate to man's nature, and here the intellectual cart has been pulled in a variety of directions by a variety of men.

SOME REPRESENTATIVE VIEWS OF VALUE

Thomas Hobbes (1588–1679) said that power was a basic human drive and was, therefore, appropriate to man: "The value or worth of a man is his Price; that is to say, so much as would be given

---

[24] Cf. C. P. Snow, *The Two Cultures and the Scientific Revolution* (New York: Cambridge University Press, 1959), pp. 2–7; J. Robert Oppenheimer, "In the Keeping of Unreason," *Bulletin of the Atomic Scientists,* Vol. XVI (January, 1960), *passim;* and Jacques Maritain, *Distinguish to Unite:* or *The Degrees of Knowledge,* trans. G. E. Phelan (New York: Charles Scribner's Sons, 1959), *passim.*

for the use of his Power; and therefore not absolute; but a thing dependent on the need and judgment of another. . . . And as in other things, so in men, not the seller but the buyer determines Price."[25]

Thomas Aquinas (1225–74), on the other hand, found value to be rooted in the perfection of man's intellect, will, and body. Unlike Hobbes, Aquinas stressed virtue as opposed to power and asserted an intrinsic worth for the human person as opposed to Hobbes's emphasis on the market as the determinant of value. Since the incorruptible soul is destined for union with God, spiritual needs are of a higher order of value than are physical needs. The natural-law position holds that, since human nature is intrinsically changeless, the basic laws governing it and the fundamental values cherished by it are also essentially changeless.[26]

Bentham (1748–1832) found the clue to what is appropriate and good for man in a single principle: "Seek pleasure and avoid pain." On this bedrock he constructed an elaborate philosophical edifice called "utilitarianism," which offers as the measure of value the calculus revealed in the dictum "the greatest good of the greatest number." The challenge to weigh decisions always in terms of consequences has had strong appeal to the fashioners of a philosophy for business.[27]

John Dewey (1859–1952) offered a home-grown philosophy in his system of instrumentalism. Violently opposed to armchair philosophizing, Dewey urged men to concentrate on solving specific and concrete problems out of which could emerge value systems for a democratic society. While Dewey has been criticized on the grounds that instrumentalism "throws rocks after the event but can lay no cornerstones," it has held a virtual monopoly on higher education in America for over a quarter-century, and the case method employed at both Harvard's Law and Business schools also owes much to Dewey's influence.[28]

Each of the foregoing philosophies posits a certain kind of value

---

[25] Michael Oakeshott (ed.), *The Leviathan* (Oxford: Basil Blackwell, n.d.), Part I, chap. x, p. 57.

[26] Some of the best studies of natural law as applied to modern conditions are currently being done at the Natural Law Institute of the University of Notre Dame, South Bend, Ind.

[27] Jeremy Bentham, *Introduction to the Principles of Morals and Legislation* (New York: Hafner Publishing Co., 1948).

[28] John Dewey, *Individualism, Old and New* (New York: G. P. Putnam, 1930).

with meaning for American business. In our earlier history the natural-law adherents (Hamilton and Jefferson, who reflected John Locke) held a dominant position. This is no longer true today, and, because of the lack of a public philosophy, bemoaned by essayists like Walter Lippmann, we have turned more and more toward the employment of techniques of countervailing powers to maintain a mechanical equilibrium in our social values.[29]

Ralph Barton Perry has said that value is that "which is the object of interest—any interest," and "interest is a train of events determined by the expectation of its outcome," and that meaning of value is in the ascendant position today.[30] This notion approximates the position taken by the distinguished economist John Bates Clark (1847–1938), who found that "utility and value are inseparably bound in thought" and that utility represents "a capacity to serve, a power to satisfy wants. To satisfy wants is to change the condition of the person served, to bring him from a lower degree of happiness to a higher one. Without the useful object, man for the time being is in one condition; with it he is in another. The power thus to modify subjective conditions is utility. . . ."[31]

CONCLUSION

The relationship of value to utility and to interest—indeed, even to Hobbes's "power" or to Bentham's "pleasure"—has a distinct place in the scheme and operation of business in that it provides discernible goals, relationships, and, in the market place and the election booth, valid mechanisms for translating these interests and these utilities into meaningful results. Yet, whenever business has responded only to economic interest, it has become involved with government regulations, such as the pure food acts or the SEC regulations. In a vague way, therefore, business as an institution is aware that a concern with intrinsic values—with good in its most essential sense—has to have a place in its scheme of things. And this recognition leads to an interesting conclusion.

---

[29] Walter Lippmann, *Essays in the Public Philosophy* (New York: New American Library, 1956).

[30] Ralph Barton Perry, *Realms of Value* (Cambridge, Mass.: Harvard University Press, 1954). Also A. H. Maslow, *New Knowledge in Human Values* (New York: Harper & Bros., 1959).

[31] John Bates Clark, *Philosophy of Wealth* (Boston: Ginn & Co., 1894), pp. 72–73 and 76–81.

When business is not in a position to make a valid judgment on value, it must accept the value judgments of other institutions. And, in an affluent society in which basic material needs are being satisfactorily met, the challenge to business to understand and apply noneconomic values mounts, and the relevance of other value-giving institutions becomes critical.

The fact is that there is no need for business to invent "value"— if such a term can be used to describe what is essentially a manifestation of experience. Values exist in the experience and the consciousness of the thousands of people who, together, make up the corporation. The major problem for business is to apply these individual values, because the *level* of application is different for the individual from that of the level for the total organization.

On the individual level values are interpreted in terms of what is called "charity," the identification of men with each other and the consideration of the problems of other men as if they were one's own. "Do as you would be done by," as the folkways put it. But the other level of application is more difficult because it makes its demand not on the will but on the intellect. This is the level of justice. For, along with the obligation of charity toward each other, men have an obligation of justice to the larger social or organizational group.

Within the business organization, an employer must consider the welfare and even some of the peculiarly personal problems of his employees, but not to the point at which charity runs counter to the welfare of the organization. If it is to further the ends of the organization that the community of workers exists, then their successes or failures as persons in pursuing their own ends cannot, in justice, be put before the achievement of the ends of the business. As a result, the employee not only has an obligation of charity toward the men among whom he works but also an obligation toward the organization that employs him to put in the number of hours he has agreed upon and to do the best job he can during those hours.

The concept of justice, basic though it is to our society, has never been an easy one to implement. The manager, in his effort to "balance the best interests" of the numerous claimants on the corporation is thinking in terms of justice, whether he is aware of it or not, because he is thinking in terms of the good of the organization. The labor-union leader, representing groups of employees, pursues justice also, for the good of *his* organization.

It is plain that the effort toward the proper application of values is launched in the economic sector. It is now the lot of economic organization, given its power and pervasiveness in the lives of all of us, not to seek so much to form new values as to be conscientious and rational in the application, in new circumstances, of those that have been preached and taught and legislated in this country for the last 300 years.

RECOMMENDED READING

BARNARD, CHESTER. "Elementary Conditions of Business Morals," *California Management Review,* Vol. I (Fall, 1958), pp. 1–13.

BENNETT, JOHN. *Christian Ethics and Social Policy.* New York: Charles Scribner's Sons, 1946.

BOULDING, KENNETH E. "Religious Foundations of Economic Progress," *Harvard Business Review,* Vol. XXX (May–June, 1952), pp. 33–40.

———. *The Organizational Revolution.* New York: Harper & Bros., 1953.

BOWEN, HOWARD. *The Social Responsibilities of the Business Man.* New York: Harper & Bros., 1953.

BRYSON, LYMAN, *et al.* (eds.). *Symbols and Values: An Initial Study,* pp. 1–13, 87–109, 121–48, and 477–84. New York: Harper & Bros., 1954.

CAHN, E. N. *Moral Decision.* Bloomington: Indiana University Press, 1955.

CHILDS, MARQUIS, and CATER, D. E. *Ethics in a Business Society.* New York: Harper & Bros., 1954.

DUFF, EDWARD, S.J. *The Social Thought of the World Council of Churches.* New York: Association Press, 1956.

ELLIS, JOHN TRACY. *History of American Catholicism.* Chicago: University of Chicago Press, 1956.

FANFANI, AMINTORE. *Catholicism, Protestantism and Capitalism.* New York: Sheed and Ward, 1935.

FINKELSTEIN, RABBI LOUIS. "The Businessman's Moral Failure," *Fortune,* Vol. LVIII (September, 1958).

HERBERG, WILL. *Judaism and Modern Man.* New York: Farrar, Strauss and Young, 1951.

LEYS, WAYNE A. R. *Ethics for Policy Decision.* Englewood Cliffs, N.J.: Prentice-Hall, Inc., 1952.

MASON, EDWARD S. "The Apologetics of 'Managerialism,'" *Journal of Business,* Vol. XXXI (January, 1958), pp. 1–11.

MESSNER, J. *Social Ethics.* St. Louis: B. Herder Book Co., 1949.

MOODY, JOSEPH (ed.). *Church and Society: Catholic Social and Political Thought and Movements, 1789–1950*, Part VIII. New York: Arts, Inc., 1953.

MUDELDER, WALTER. *Religion and Economic Responsibility*. New York: Charles Scribner's Sons, 1953.

MURRAY, JOHN COURTNEY. *We Hold These Truths*. New York: Sheed and Ward, 1960.

OHMANN, O. A. "Skyhooks: With Special Implications for Monday through Friday," *Harvard Business Review*, Vol. XXXIII (May–June, 1955), pp. 1–9.

PERRY, RALPH BARTON. *Realms of Value*. Cambridge: Harvard University Press, 1954.

SALVADORI, MASSIMO. *The Economics of Freedom*. New York: Doubleday & Co., 1959.

SUTTON, F. X.; HARRIS, S.; KAYSEN, C.; and TOBIN, J. *The American Business Creed*. Cambridge: Harvard University Press, 1956.

TAWNEY, R. H. *The Acquisitive Society*. New York: Harcourt, Brace & Co., 1948.

————. *Religion and the Rise of Capitalism*. New York: Harcourt, Brace & Co., 1954.

TILLICH, PAUL. *The Protestant Era*. Chicago: University of Chicago Press, 1948.

WEBER, MAX. *The Protestant Ethic and the Spirit of Capitalism*. London: G. Allen and Unwin, 1930.

WEISS, PAUL. *Our Public Life*. Bloomington: Indiana University Press, 1958.

WORTHY, JAMES. "Religion and Its Role in the World of Business," *Journal of Business*, Vol. XXX (October, 1958), pp. 293–303. See rejoinder by H. B. ARTHUR, *Journal of Business*, Vol. XXXII (April, 1959), pp. 183–84.

FURTHER READING

BELLOC, HILAIRE. *The Servile State*. London: Foolis Ltd., 1912.

BERDYAEV, N. *The Destiny of Man*. London: Geoffrey Bles, 1954.

CULLITON, JAMES. "Business and Religion," *Harvard Business Review*, Vol. XXVII (May–June, 1949), pp. 265–71.

DANIEL, JOHN. *Labor, Industry and the Church*. St. Louis: Concordia Publishing Co., 1957.

DEMANT, V. A. *Religion and the Decline of Capitalism*. New York: Charles Scribner's Sons, 1952.

DEVAUX, LOUIS. "Les Rélations Humaines: Clef de la Société Moderne," *Chefs d'Enterprise,* Vol. XIX (August, 1959), pp. 33–48.

Evanston Report, World Council of Churches, 1954.

GABRIEL, RALPH. *The Course of American Democratic Thought.* New York: Ronald Press Co., 1940.

HEILBRONER, ROBERT. *The Worldly Philosophers.* New York: Simon and Schuster, 1953.

HOUSER, T. V. *Big Business and Human Values.* New York: McGraw-Hill Book Co., 1957.

HUGHES, R. S. *Consciousness and Society: The Revolution of European Social Thought, 1890–1930.* New York: Alfred A. Knopf, 1959.

KNIGHT, FRANK. "Economists and Economic Ethics," *Ethics,* Vol. XLVIII (October, 1957).

LAZARUS, M. *The Ethics of Judaism.* 2 vols. Philadelphia: Jewish Publication Society, 1900.

MASLOW, A. H. (ed.). *New Knowledge in Human Values.* New York: Harper & Bros., 1959.

MORA, JOSÉ FERRATER. *Philosophy Today: Conflicting Tendencies in Contemporary Thought.* New York: Columbia University Press, 1960.

NELL-BRUENING, O. VON. *Reorganization of Social Economy.* Milwaukee: Bruce Publishing Co., 1936.

OXFORD CONFERENCE. *The Economic Report,* 1949.

Papal Encyclicals: Five Great Encyclicals, esp. Leo XIII, "On the Condition of Labor," and Pius XI, "Reconstructing the Social Order." New York: Paulist Press, 1939.

PERRY, RALPH BARTON. *The Moral Economy.* New York: Charles Scribner's Sons, 1909.

SELEKMAN, SYLVIA and BENJAMIN. *Power and Morality in a Business Society.* New York: McGraw-Hill Book Co., 1959.

TEILHARD DE CHARDIN, PIERRE. *The Phenomenon of Man.* New York: Harper & Bros., 1959.

TROELTSCH, ERNST. *Christian Thought: Its History and Application.* London: University of London Press, 1923.

WARD, BARBARA. *Faith and Freedom.* New York: W. W. Norton Co., 1954.

WARD, JOHN WILLIAM. "The Organization Society," *Princeton University Magazine,* Summer, 1960, pp. 8–10.

WEISSKOPF, W., and THAIN, R. "Value Research in Business, Economics Long Overdue," *Business and Society,* Vol. I (Autumn, 1960), pp. 3–9.

VII. APPENDIX

Appendix. The Institution of Business in Pre-Columbian Mexico: A Case Study

OUTLINE

SCHOLARS interested in delineating the conceptual foundations of business obviously cannot approach such study in an a priori fashion. But empirical research in this field presupposes considerable knowledge of the origin and evolution of various concrete forms of business in their own historical context. To determine better the various social, juridical, and, in a word, cultural, conditions that have made business possible, it is necessary to study the development of this institution not only in a particular civilization, important as that is, but also as it appeared in other places and times. This could

595

offer the Western-minded student new and unexpected perspectives.

Such an opportunity is provided by the study of the institution of business in pre-Columbian Mexico. Here, certainly, is a unique opportunity to contemplate a human society, isolated from the old civilizations of Asia and Europe, creating a superior culture in which business as an institution also came into existence.

What makes this study possible is the not-so-well-known fact that the ancient Mexicans had developed various forms of ideographic and partially phonetic writing at least 1,500 years before the arrival of the Spaniards. Some of their pre-Columbian books and other ancient transcriptions are still preserved in museums and libraries. In these pre-Columbian sources and in some chronicles and histories written by Spanish missionaries soon after the Conquest, there is, among other things, information about several hundred years of recorded business in ancient Mexico.

It is important to remember that pre-Columbian business encompassed a quite large territory. Ancient Mexican merchants had established markets and permanent trade routes from the Pacific to the Gulf Coast and from what is today Central Mexico to distant centers in Yucatan, Guatemala, El Salvador, Nicaragua, and occasionally to Costa Rica and Panama. And so prominent was the status of the pre-Columbian merchants that by the time of the Spanish Conquest they were probably the most powerful social group. The description given by Bernal Diaz, one of the conquistadors who in 1519 visited the large market of Tlatelolco, close to the city of Mexico, represents an initial and superficial reaction, but it offers vivid testimony nonetheless to the development and significance of pre-Columbian business:

When we arrived at the great market place, called Tlatelolco, we were astounded at the number of people and the quantity of merchandise that it contained, for we had never seen such a thing before. The chieftains who accompanied us acted as guides. Each kind of merchandise was kept by itself and had its fixed place marked out. Let us begin with the dealers in gold, silver, and precious stones, feathers, mantles and embroidered goods. Then there were other wares consisting of Indian slaves both men and women. . . . Next there were other traders who sold great pieces of cloth and cotton, and articles of twisted thread, and there were those who sold cacao. In this way one could see every sort of merchandise that is to be found in the whole of New Spain. . . .

There are also buildings where three magistrates sit in judgment, and there are executive officers who inspect merchandise. . . . I could wish that I had finished telling of all the things which are sold there, but they are so numerous and of such different quality and the great market place with its surrounding arcades was so crowded with people, that one would not have been able to see and inquire about it all in two days. . . .

Before leaving the market place itself, there were many more merchants, who, as I was told, brought gold for sale in grains, just as it is taken from the mines. The gold is placed in thin quills of the geese of the country, white quills, so that the gold can be seen through, and according to the length and thickness of the quills they arrange their accounts with one another, how much so many mantles or so many gourds full of cacao were worth. . . .[1]

The organization of a market place like this—which was by no means unique—presupposes, among other things, the existence of various guilds of traders busy with the exportation and importation of goods from distant places. But, above all, it presupposes the existence of a vigorous socioeconomic structure that made commerce and business possible.

THE HISTORICAL CONTEXT

The Land and the People

In spite of numerous ethnic and linguistic differences, almost all the peoples who, before the arrival of the Spaniards, inhabited the area from the central section of present-day Mexico to the distant regions of El Salvador and Nicaragua shared numerous cultural institutions in common. At the beginning of the Christian Era two principal cultural nuclei existed that were later to influence many other peoples. There was the great center of Teotihuacan, located some 28 miles to the north of the present city of Mexico, and then there were the various centers of the classical Maya culture, which flourished in the lowlands of the state of Chiapas, the Guatemalan Peten, Yucatan, and Northern Honduras.

The existence of such highly developed culture centers implies the prior existence of other peoples who discovered, among other things, agriculture and pottery-making. Archeological discoveries indicate that these so-called pre-Classical peoples, who lived at least

---

[1] Bernal Díaz del Castillo, *The Discovery and Conquest of Mexico* (ed. and trans. from the only exact copy of the original MS, by A. P. Maudslay) (New York: Grove Press, Inc., 1956), pp. 215–17.

1500 years B.C., were the first to engage in various forms of commerce and even in some elementary business transactions. Nevertheless, we have more reliable information about the Teotihuacans and the Mayas, creators of superior types of culture, and we shall therefore consider them as the starting point for this discussion of the development of business in ancient Mexico.

Thanks to archeology, it is known that at least from the fourth century A.D. organized commerce was carried on by Maya traders, who transported their products (principally ceramics, cacao, cotton, skins, and quetzal feathers) to distant regions along the coast of the Gulf of Mexico, and thence by boat to the Caribbean Islands. With respect to the Teotihuacan traders, even pictorial representations have been preserved. The discovery of archeological objects of Teotihuacan origin or artistic influence in distant regions of Southern Mexico and even as far as Guatemala give evidence of how far afield Teotihuacan traders managed to penetrate.

When, for reasons still unknown, the Teotihuacan and the principal Mayan cities collapsed almost simultaneously around the ninth century A.D., new centers of culture appeared in the central region of Mexico as well as in the north of Yucatan and in the highlands of Guatemala. Historical evidence, such as inscriptions and other forms of ancient texts, becomes much more abundant and precise around the ninth century A.D. Thus we have fairly detailed knowledge of the various cultural institutions of these peoples.

Specifically, we know that in the new city of Tula, the Toltec metropolis, located 40 miles to the north of present-day Mexico City, a great market and ancient merchant guilds already flourished in the ninth century A.D. The same is true of such centers as Cholula in the Valley of Puebla, Chichen Itza, Uxmal, and the other cities of the Maya world. Cultural contacts through both war and commerce brought the towns of Central Mexico and those of the Maya of Yucatan more closely together. A good proof of this is the new architecture of Chichen Itza, inspired in the Toltec metropolis of Tula. But around the 11th century A.D., probably because of the pressure of numerous barbarian hordes arriving from the North, the cultural metropolis, this time Tula, had once again to be abandoned.

Various Nahuatl-speaking groups now made their appearance in Central Mexico and, influenced by the ancient culture creators, organized new cities and states. Of these states, the best known are the kingdoms of Azcapotzalco and Culhuacan and, most recent of all, that of the Aztecs. The latter, who inherited the ancient cultural institutions of the Teotihuacans, began to build, around 1325, the city of Mexico-Tenochtitlan, which came to be the center of a powerful empire.

With the Aztecs and their neighbors, the ancient cultural institution of commerce achieved enormous development and importance. Thanks to their ancient books of paintings, and to various other pre-Hispanic texts, it is possible to study the organization of their merchant and artisan guilds, the legal statutes and principles that governed them, their trade routes, and the various markets they established, not only in Central Mexico, but even in distant regions of Guatemala and others close to the Maya region.

Such, in a few words, is the cultural sequence and the geographic framework in which the institution of business developed in the pre-Columbian world.

The Historical Sources

Historical evidence during the periods before the Christian era consists first of archeological pieces, principally pottery, taken from one place to another, which indicate trade and contact between the peoples of various regions. With the appearance of the great ritual centers of Teotihuacan and of the Maya Zone, there are other evidences, such as murals and stone inscriptions, the latter among the Maya. Written evidence also becomes more abundant for the periods after the ninth century A.D.

Some codices of pre-Columbian origin, Mayan as well as from the central zone of Mexico, have been preserved. Executed on Indian paper made from the bark of a tree called *amate* (*Ficus petiolaris*), these codices, some of them quite extensive, are really long strips, folded up like a screen, containing inscriptions concerning historic, religious, astronomic, and commercial subjects.

All these codices contain abundant information on the cultural development of these peoples and their various institutions, among them, business. The existence of abundant historical sources of pre-Hispanic origin is precisely what makes it possible to study the cultural institution of pre-Columbian business on a factual basis.

It must not be forgotten that, of all the peoples of America, only the ancient Mexicans (including Toltecs and Aztecs, Mayas and Mixtecs, and others) had a truly genuine form of writing and a historiography. In view of the impossibility of supplying a complete list of these historical sources, a few of the works that describe and analyze some of the documents related to the history of ancient Mexico are mentioned in a footnote.[2] In addition to the pre-Hispanic sources, there exist other chronicles and histories by Spanish missionaries of the 16th century that are a valuable complement to the study of the pre-Columbian institution of commerce.

STATUS OF THE AZTEC MERCHANTS AT THE TIME OF THE SPANISH CONQUEST (1519)

Thanks to the aforementioned sources, it is possible to study the origin and development of business over a period of several centuries in pre-Columbian Mexico. But, since in this study an attempt is made not only to describe the outward aspects of pre-Hispanic business but also to provide an analysis of the social, legal, and cultural conditions that made it possible, it seems best to limit ourselves to the last period, or that of the Aztecs, about which the greatest information exists.

The student of pre-Hispanic business discovers within the Aztec social organization two sectors or groups of great importance: the organization of the *pochtecas,* or merchants, and that of the various groups of artists and artisans, like the gold and silver workers, the feather artists, and so on. To understand their social status requires a brief description of the general sociopolitical organization of the Aztecs.

The stratification of what had been an ancient tribe of nomads into social classes had its origin in a somewhat singular fact. As the Aztecs, during the middle of the 13th century, came into contact with the peoples of a more advanced culture, the descendants of the Toltecs, they experienced a tremendous admiration for these peoples and as a result wished to be linked with the Toltec world through kinship. To achieve this, they succeeded in having as their first king or *tlatoani* a Culhuacan noble of Toltec descent, called Acamapichtli. He had many children by Aztec women, and his

---

[2] See, among others, the following works: Paul Radin, *The Sources and Authenticity of the History of the Ancient Mexicans* (Berkeley: University of California Publications in American Archaeology and Ethnology, 1920); Angel Ma. Garibay K., *Historia de la Literatura Náhuatl* (2 vols.; Mexico: Porrúa Publishers, 1953–54); Donald Robertson, *Mexican Manuscript Painting of the Early Colonial Period* (New Haven: Yale University Press, 1959); Miguel León-Portilla, *The Mind of Ancient Mexico* (Norman: University of Oklahoma Press, 1961).

descendants came to form the nucleus of the Aztec nobility (*pipil-tin*). The *pipiltin* usually received the best possible education and were owners of land held in individual title. They came to occupy the highest posts in the government and only from among them could the king or *tlatoani* be elected.

In contrast to the social class of the *pipiltin*, a clearly defined class of the common people, the *macehualtin* existed. These formed part of the geographic clans, that is, groups of interrelated kinsmen, living in one area and owning lands in common. It is true, at least among the Aztecs, that both the *pipiltin* and the *macehualtin* were required to attend the communal schools, although more attention was paid to the education of the *pipiltin*. The common people engaged in agriculture, provided the soldiery, and, what is very important, provided the men who formed the organizations or guilds of merchants, artisans, and artists. Together with these social classes, there were also such groups as the *mayeques,* who worked the land for others, as well as various categories of slaves, whose period of bondage was usually limited. Nevertheless, it must be emphasized that neither the *mayeques* nor the slaves formed social classes that could be clearly distinguished from the *macehualtin,* or common people.

According to the opinion of some authors, the groups of guilds of merchants and artisans originated from groups of distinct ethnic origin. Nevertheless, by the 15th century, merchants and artisans were fully integrated into the Aztec world.

Although they had sprung from the masses, both these groups, but especially the merchants, or *pochtecas,* had acquired extraordinary social importance. This is clearly shown by the fact that they possessed what could be called their own legal and economic code and the virtually exclusive right to perform various functions. The merchants had their own religious rites and ceremonies and their own courts. They organized the various systems of commercial exchange, and they frequently performed the duties of ambassadors, emissaries, and spies. At the time of the Spanish Conquest, merchants played such an important role in the social structure, both through their wealth and through the important functions they performed, that they often exerted more influence on public life than did the nobles, or *pipiltin*. In a sense, the *pochtecas,* or merchants, of the Aztec world played a role similar to that of the bourgeoisie in the modern history of European states. Among other

things, the *pochtecas* had obtained for themselves individual possession of land as well as exemption from personal tribute, thus placing
themselves in some aspects in a position almost equal to that of the
nobility.

A study of the way these Aztec merchants carried on their various
business functions within the prevailing legal and social framework
presupposes an understanding of the basic concepts that made this
cultural institution possible. An analysis of their concept of law,
justice, property, association, contract, and exchange should give us
a clearer understanding of what the institution of business meant
among a people who, in spite of a clear social class structure, still
exhibited elements of their ancient tribal organization.

THE PRE-COLUMBIAN INSTITUTION OF BUSINESS

LAW AND JUSTICE IN ANCIENT MEXICO

The various special guilds or associations of merchants and artisans in ancient Mexico had their origin within an ancient legal
framework. From numerous sources it is clear that two forms of law
existed among the Aztecs: common and written.

The common law stemmed, above all, from an ancient juridical
tradition, deriving probably from Teotihuacan and Toltec times.
Thus the following text, literally translated from the Nahuatl or
Aztec language, declared:

> The ancient way of life
> that of the Chichimecs,
> that of the Toltecs,
> that of the Acolhuas,
> that of the Tepanecs. . . .
>
> They spread their power
> throughout the entire world,
> they furnished
> authority, power,
> glory, fame.[3]

When they established themselves in Mexico-Tenochtitlan
around 1325, the Aztecs patterned their social and political structure

---

[3] *Libro de los Coloquios* (published by Walter Lehmann in *Sterbende Gotter und
Christliche Heilsbotschaft*) (Stuttgart: Quellenwerke zum alten Geschichte Amerikas,
1949) , p. 105.

after this ancient way of life. But they very soon abandoned the tribal form of government and elected a king, or *tlatoani*, of Toltec lineage and a supreme council of government, called *tlatocan*. In this council the various functions of the state appear as differentiated and distinct. They were vested in a chief charged with the administration of justice, a chief of the army, a head priest, and a royal treasurer. Each member of the council had the power to appoint his collaborators and subordinates. Through them, justice, the worship of the gods, education, and the organization of the army and of the economy were attended to.

One hundred more years passed before the Aztecs emerged as a strong and fully independent state. Then, in 1428, a permanent alliance was concluded with two other centers having the same language and culture: Texcoco and Tlacopan. In this alliance the Aztec king, or *tlatoani*, had the principal role in the religious, economic, and military fields, pursuing the conquests of peoples in the most distant regions. It was precisely this design of conquest, originating from religious motives, that led not only to an increased flow of tribute to the Aztec capital but also to the emergence of great commercial organizations dedicated to the importation and exportation of the most varied products.

The principle that governed legal relationships within Aztec society requires special consideration. As far as the obligations of each person to himself, to his fellow beings, and to the state were concerned, the supreme principle was stated in the following idiomatic Nahuatl expression: "what is desirable, what is right" (*in qualli, in yectli*). That is to say, the rule was to look for what was best suited to the interests of the person involved but at the same time to seek that which was proper in itself and which, if put into practice, would not harm the interests of the other members of the community.

This rule of "what is desirable, what is right" was the guiding principle for commercial relations in ancient Mexico. It was on the basis of this principle that justice was administered in the markets. The scale of tributes was established, rules and regulations were fixed, the unalterability of the means of exchange and the various forms of contract were executed. Finally, the principle of "what is desirable, what is right" came to form the basis of another concept, that of property. Property played a fundamental role within the economic life of the Aztec world, which, already divided into social classes, fixed new legal forms for possession and use of the goods of production.

PROPERTY

To understand the concept of property that prevailed in the pre-Hispanic world and that also conditioned its various forms of business relations, we must first consider ownership of land, a factor of the greatest importance in a basically agricultural society such as the Aztec. When they arrived in the Valley of Mexico, the nomad Aztecs lacked lands. When, after much persecution within the valley, the Aztecs established themselves on the island in the great lake to build their capital, they obtained lands, but only on loan. More than a century passed after the time Mexico-Tenochtitlan was founded before they achieved full independence, around 1428, and, with it, ownership of the lands.

When the original Aztec clans were first established on the island, the distribution of land was made on a communal basis. Applying the principle of "what is desirable, what is right," the concept of landownership found its justification in the need of each clan for a piece of land to cultivate so that it could feed itself. This principle is stated most expressively in an ancient text in the Aztec language:

> "What is desirable, what is right":
> take care with the things of the earth,
> do something, cut wood, work the land,
> plant *nopales*, plant *magueyes*,
> and so you will have drink, food and clothing.
> With this you will be on your feet,
> with this you will be able to walk.[4]

This communal right to land was linked, in the Aztec mentality, with the concept that it was obligatory for those who possessed the land to work it. Those who did not work the land lost their right to possess it. In this way, property came to be conceived of as a dynamic relation between persons and things, based on two factors: the necessity to live from it and the need for its uninterrupted exploitation through the work of its possessors.

The Aztec expressed this through a phrase that, taking as a symbol of the human person his own face, stated that something is

---

[4] "Huehuetlatolli," collected by Fray Andrés de Olmos (unpublished Nahuatl manuscript preserved in the Library of Congress, Washington, D.C.), fol. 116 r.

the property of someone if "it is linked with his face," and "if the face has drawn itself near to it." The double concept "linking, approximation" (*teixcoyan, teaxca*) implies a dynamic and constant relationship through work.

In accordance with the tribal and clan structure, which still partially survived among the Aztecs, the relationship of things with "human faces" at first existed in a collective form. But as the nobility grew more powerful, thanks particularly to the military triumphs of the Aztecs, a clearly individual relationship between persons and things appeared among the social class of the nobles. This was considered just, because theirs were the human faces that had distinguished themselves and had thus acquired the right to individual ownership of lands. In this way, first the nobility and later the merchants (by virtue of their merits and riches) obtained private ownership of great areas of land.

Thus, by the time the Spaniards arrived, the two forms of ownership, private and communal, coexisted in Ancient Mexico. The general population possessed their land in communal form. The various clans were supplied with land parcels, known as *calpulalli*. These lands were divided among the various members of each clan who, at least in the beginning, lived together in one certain neighborhood. Each family held one parcel, not as owners, but only to enjoy its use. Applying to this form of possession the criterion of "what is desirable, what is right," it was established that a family that did not work the land lost its right to use it, and therefore it was turned over to others who would make it produce.

The king, or *tlatoani,* like the nobles and also the merchants, had his own lands, with vassals who paid a fixed tribute to work them. The state also possessed other lands: the *tecpantlalli,* "palace lands," for the purpose of paying the expenses of public administration. The *milchimalli,* or "lands of the shield," were used to cover other expenses related to war. Finally, there were the *teopantlalli,* or "lands of the temples," the products of which were destined for the maintenance of the priests and the practice of the cult.

The evolution of the Aztec society, especially of a class of nobles and priests and the emergence of a state apparatus, was to make possible the appearance among the common people of various forms of clearly defined work and activity. In particular, there arose groups who traded and sold, no longer just the products of the land, but also innumerable manufactured products.

It is true that for a set number of years the entire population had to perform certain services, such as military. But it is also true that those who began to dedicate themselves to trade soon found a way to organize guilds or associations that permitted them to perform their functions better until, as a consequence, they achieved an extraordinary social importance.

The appearance of these forms of association, given the prevailing concept of ownership in the pre-Hispanic world, doubtless posed numerous problems. It seems, however, that the Aztec guilds of merchants and artisans knew how to resolve these difficulties adequately, since they succeeded in obtaining for themselves the same privileges as the nobles insofar as the possession of land and exemption from personal tribute were concerned.

THE BEGINNING OF LARGE BUSINESS ENTERPRISES AMONG THE AZTECS

A rapid look at the way of life of the Aztecs shortly after they established themselves on the island of Mexico-Tenochtitlan will help to show how business enterprises began among them. Although the majority of the people were engaged in agriculture and fishing, they had found the way to satisfy their own necessities. They themselves built their houses of adobe and straw. The women made the clothing—at that time from thread of the maguey fiber. Almost all people were capable of supplying themselves with their own work equipment: nets for fishing; the *coa,* or piece of curved wood for planting corn; and their principal domestic utensils, such as clay dishes and straw baskets.

Their food came mainly from the products of the lake and the land. The latter supplied them with corn, beans, and chile. The domestic breeding of turkeys and small dogs, as well as occasional hunts, allowed them to supplement their diet with the meat of these animals, eaten usually during fiestas.

Those who enjoyed a surplus over and above their necessities— for example, of corn—frequently bartered for another product, which in some cases could have been maguey-fiber thread or a few pieces of pottery or some baskets. Thus was born, freely and spontaneously, the most ancient form of commerce. As barter became a more usual practice, the rulers began to organize centers or markets *(tianquiztli)* , where these transactions were carried on.

But from the moment that the Aztec nation achieved its independence and began to enlarge its domains by conquest, the solemnity of the religious celebrations and the desires of the nobles, or *pipiltin,* for greater pomp and prestige created new necessities. The native documents show that in response to these demands the members of some clans began, from the early years of the 15th century, to bring products like jade, cotton, cacao, and precious metals from distant regions, while the inhabitants of certain districts began to abandon agriculture in order to dedicate themselves to arts and crafts related to these products. Little by little, the demand of the nobility and priests for these manufactured products made possible the development of groups that, linked together by ties of kinship, adopted the profession of merchant or artisan.

There is proof that by the first third of the 15th century there were various distinct guilds that lived in special areas. It is known that the feather artists, for example, were established in the neighborhood of Amantlan, while there were groups of merchants on the neighboring island of Tlatelolco to the north of Mexico-Tenochtitlan and in other quarters of the Aztec capital itself and in neighboring towns. Thus, what had started as a sporadic activity, carried on by persons who, because of a trip or for some similar reason, brought products from other regions, grew to acquire a special character of its own. The institution of business was also strengthened by the continual wars of the Aztecs, which stimulated contacts with other people and permitted them to discover other goods from distant regions. The following text, translated from the Aztec language, describes the beginning of organized commerce:

> In the times of Cuacuauhpitzaua [1375–1418]
> the merchant chiefs
> Itxcohuatzin and Tziuhtecatzin
> started the art of trade.
>
> That which they bartered,
> that which they sold
> were only red feathers
> and the green feathers of rare birds
> and feathers from red birds.
>
> Only these three things
> were used in their business.
> Then Tlacatéotl came to govern,
> and in his time there were installed
> the merchant chiefs:
> Cozmatzin and Tzompantzin.

> In their time,
> the quetzal feathers
> began to be known,
> although not the very long ones
> and those of the bird of gilded plumage,
> and the turquoises and the jades
> and the soft mantles and the cloths,
> since up to that time the people
> had only worn clothing
> made of maguey fibers. . . .[5]

So it was owing to the merchants that the nobles and priests began to acquire these costly things. And it was precisely in satisfying these needs of the nobility and the religious cult that the merchant organization was able to achieve growth. The merchants themselves were aware, from the beginning, of the importance of their functions. Conscious of their role, and formulating a new application of their concept of ownership, they declared in one Indian text:

> This is what we have acquired,
> what we have achieved,
> the price of our breasts,
> of our heads.
>
> With this we will show
> with this we will give Mexico:
> amber lip rings,
> ear plugs with quetzal feathers,
> staffs with color mosaics,
> fans made of pheasant feathers.
>
> Our capes,
> mantles of twisted thread,
> cloths of twisted thread.
> All this will be ours,
> our attainment,
> our fame as men. . . .
> For this we tire ourselves,
> it will be ours alone. . . .[6]

Those who thus show themselves to be conscious of their func-

---

[5] Texts of the Informants of Sahagún, *Códice Matritense de la Academia de la Historia* (facsimile ed.; Madrid: Francisco del Paso y Troncoso, 1907) , fol. 26 r.

[6] *Ibid.*

tions and importance had already managed to give their merchant guilds a structure of their own.

AZTEC MERCHANT GUILDS

The first guild of merchants, known by the ancient title of *pochtecas,* appeared among the Aztecs at the beginning of the fifteenth century on the neighboring island of Tlatelolco, to the north of the city of Mexico-Tenochtitlan. Some years later, seven other such groups of *pochtecas,* or merchants, appeared within the city of Mexico itself. There the *pochtecas* lived in the districts of Acxotlan, Atlauhco, Amaxtlan, Itzolco, Pochtlan, Tepetitlan, and Tzomolco.

In each case the members of the guild belonged to the same clan, and only exceptionally was a person admitted as a member if he were not related to those of the clan. In this way, at least in the beginning, elements of the ancient Aztec tribal organization managed to survive in the field of commerce, in spite of the gradual diversification of this group into a society with classes.

Each of the merchant guilds had its chief and various categories of members. The directors of the guilds received the title of "chiefs of the *pochtecas*" (*pochtecatlatoque*). In the case of the merchants of the districts of Pochtlan and Acxotlan, within the city of Mexico, the guild leaders were known as *Tlailotlac* and *Acxotecatl,* respectively. Among the various subordinate types of merchants, mention should be made of the *Oztomecas,* who were experts on far-off regions and spoke their languages, since they had lived there posing as natives of the region. According to a text of the native informants of Sahagún, there were 69 different categories of traders. Among these were traders in slaves, precious metals, tobacco, cacao, animals, *amate* paper, and loans of corn.

The following generic description of the *pochteca,* or merchant, will permit a better understanding of the aims and functions of the ancient traders' guilds:

> The *Pochteca:* trader, merchant,
> he makes loans, makes contracts,
> he accumulates wealth, makes it grow,
> is a traveler, a walker,
> he makes profits,
> finds what he seeks,
> he is honorable.[7]

---

[7] *Ibid.,* fol. 124.

In addition to trading, buying, and selling products, the merchants also had to do with various types of contracts and loans, in order to make their business possible. It is definitely known that the state, as well as some of the aged merchants (including some women), made loan contracts with those who traveled to distant regions. Thus, the native informants of Sahagún mention an occasion when King Ahuítzotl granted 1,600 mantles as a loan to the merchants on their way to the Pacific Coast:

> When the merchants went
> to the house of King Ahuítzotl,
> he gave them his property:
> 1600 small mantles,
> he gave them with which to trade. . . .
>
> With these mantles, clothing
> was bought for the nobles,
> with adornments of feathers,
> mantles with eagle paintings,
> with borders and trim of feathers,
> garments for the nobles,
> embroidered blouses and skirts for the women.
> These things were the property of and belonged
> to King Ahuítzotl.
> They carried them as their commission,
> the traders of the coast.[8]

The mention of the small mantles called *quachtli*, as will be shown later,[9] refers to a particular form of monetary symbol that existed among the Aztecs and that anticipated modern bills of exchange. There were also various forms of loans, consisting of small tubes full of gold, as well as sacks of cacao of various sizes.

With respect to the internal organization of the merchant guilds, it is clear that they had created their own legal code as well as their own tribunals. Their legal code was transmitted, usually by word of mouth, to the neophyte merchants on various occasions. Some speeches, preserved in the native documents, offer an explanation of the fundamental principles governing their activity. Thus, for example, the young merchants were inculcated with the following ideas:

---

[8] *Ibid.*, fol. 28 r.

[9] See section on contracts and monetary symbols below.

Your profession is to travel,
you will leave the city,
your home in Mexico,
you will have to go away. . . .

You will find yourself on plains
in the middle of immense lands. . . .
Lift up your spirits,
you have to make your life a true one. . . .
Follow the example of your predecessors,
those who ruled and governed,
those who took over
the rule and government
of the merchants. . . .
You will be going into,
entering and leaving,
foreign places.
It may be that nothing is achieved anywhere,
it may be that nowhere
will your merchandise,
your trade items be accepted. . . .
Do not retreat, stand firm. . . .
You will achieve something. . . .
Something will be granted you
by the Lord of the Universe.[10]

In this way they made the young merchant conscious at once of the difficulties inherent in his undertaking and of its grandeur and the possibility of success. It is worth mentioning that one of the principles most emphasized among the merchants was that of "what is desirable, what is just," by which they had established units of measurement and thus the utmost honesty in all their contracts and negotiations.

According to their legal code, the administration of markets and the establishment of standards of exchange were a function of the merchants. The importance of the merchant class led to another event of great import. The native chronicler, Ixtlilxochitl, details the activities of one of the four supreme councils of government under the famous ruler Nezahualcóyotl: "The fourth council was that of the Treasury, wherein all the stewards of the King and some

---

[10] Texts of the Informants of Sahagún, *op. cit.,* fol. 38 v.

of the most important merchants of the city met to discuss the Treasury matters of the King and royal tributes."[11]

With the merchants participating as economic advisers to the state, it is not strange that they acquired numerous privileges that made them almost equal to members of the nobility. Besides having their own tribunals, they collected tributes, frequently traded on behalf of the king, and acted as spies in distant regions.

A last element, perhaps one of the most important in the structure of the merchant guilds, is to be found in their own religious ritual. It is known that the principal patron of merchants was the god Quetzalcóatl, also a culture hero since ancient Toltec times. The merchants worshipped him as Yacatecuhtli, "Lord Guide" of the traders. When a group of merchants set forth or returned from a journey, the guilds held their own celebrations, including sumptuous banquets attended by the most prominent personages as well as by the populace of Mexico-Tenochtitlan. Food was distributed freely at these banquets, which demonstrated the desire of merchant guilds to ingratiate themselves with both state and people by assuming a kind of social responsibility. This was the way they attempted to avoid friction, which would hinder the activities and development of the ever-more-powerful guilds.

In addition to the merchant guilds in Mexico-Tenochtitlan, there were also the artisan guilds, dedicated to the manufacture of objects made of precious metals, jade, fine feathers, *amate* paper, and so on. Their function was of prime importance, since they worked with many of the raw materials brought by the merchants. Their art and techniques enabled the members of the nobility to acquire these prestige products, which were also employed in great quantities in the religious cults. The close relationship between these artisan guilds and those of the merchants allowed them to achieve an equally privileged status. It is difficult to calculate the number of members in each guild of merchants and artisans. Nevertheless, from the data offered by various native sources, it can be stated that there were a considerable number in each guild, sometimes as many as several hundred.

Thanks to the merchants and artisans, who gave new strength to various forms of contract and exchange standards, the ancient institution of the market acquired a new meaning. The import and

---

[11] Fernando de Alva Ixtlilxochitl, *Obras Historicas* (Mexico, 1891–92), Vol. I, p. 326.

export trade, in which those who today would be called "specialists" participated, both transformed the life of the nobility and the religious cults and consolidated and widened the frontiers of Aztec domination.

MARKETS AND BUSINESS ROUTES

The words of Bernal Diaz del Castillo, quoted at the beginning of this study, offer a vivid image of the main market of Tlatelolco in the north quarter of the city of Mexico-Tenochtitlan. But many other markets existed—some, like that of Tlatelolco, dating from Toltec times. Such is the case of the famous Cholula market in the Valley of Puebla and of others, like that of Azcopotzalco near the city of Mexico, dedicated principally to the buying and selling of slaves.

To give an idea of the extraordinary diffusion achieved by these markets, thanks to the routes established by the *pochtecas,* or merchants, it is sufficient to mention those of distant places like Xalapan in the present capital of the state of Veracruz, and Coaixtlahuacan, Nochiztlan, Puctla, and others in the state of Oaxaca. But, of all the places visited by the merchants, two are worthy of special mention. One was Xicalanco, near the Laguna de Terminos, on the Gulf of Mexico. From ancient times, Xicalanco had been a commercial center. Merchants from the Maya region also arrived there in their boats. Products could be acquired in Xicalanco from such widely separated regions as Yucatan, Honduras, and the Caribbean islands. The other Aztec commercial center was on the Pacific Coast in the rich Xoconusco zone, close to present-day Guatemala, from whence came cacao, quetzal feathers, jade, and precious metals.

The merchant groups departed on set dates considered propitious for protection by their gods. Since there were no beasts of burden in ancient Mexico, they were accompanied by numerous bearers or *tamemes* in their trek toward the Gulf Coast or toward the south and the Pacific Coast. Two extremely eloquent accounts in Aztec concerning these commercial routes have been preserved.

> When they had begun the trip,
> the traders who go to the coasts,
> they divided up there in Tochtepec (Oaxaca) :
> Half went toward the coast of Ayotla (the Pacific) ,
> the other half directed themselves
> to the coast of Xicalanco (Gulf of Mexico) . . . .

Those who entered Xicalanco
carried merchandise
of King Ahuízotl
to trade with it,
that already mentioned:
mantles for the nobles,
fine skirts,
embroidered or fringed,
half skirts and embroidered blouses.

Golden bands for the forehead,
intricate necklaces,
necklaces of gold with figures of fruit
made by the goldsmiths of Mexico. . . .
For the people in general,
what they needed was
obsidian earplugs,
earplugs of cheap metal,
obsidian razors,
bodkins and needles,
cochineal, wire,
rabbit skin with its hair,
drugs and medicines. . . .

When the traders had arrived
on the coast of Xicalanco. . . .
The lords from there brought forth
huge pieces of jade,
round, very green,
and size of green tomatoes,
and grooved jades. . . .

Precious jades, emeralds
turquoise shields,
tortoise shells,
parrot feathers,
and feathers of the black sea bird. . . .
Red tiger skins. . . .

When they returned to Mexico
they presented all this to King Ahuítzotl,
all that the traders had gone to bring.
They had gone on a royal commission,
in this way the city prospered,
and the Aztec people too. . . .

> For this reason King Ahuítzotl
> held the businessmen in great esteem,
> he considered them equal to the nobles,
> he made them equal,
> as if they were knights of war,
> the traders had this reputation,
> so they were considered.[12]

The description of the merchants who marched to the coast of the Gulf tells us something of their functions. Above all, they traded on commission for King Ahuítzotl. To Xicalanco, they carried products manufactured by artisans of Mexico-Tenochtitlan. They also brought other products for the nobles, with which, as the text says, "the city was enriched, and the Aztec people." It is repeated at the end that because of the services they rendered, King Ahuítzotl regarded them as the equals of nobles.

The second native account, translated from the Aztec language, speaks of the traders who marched to the Pacific Coast:

> When the traders
> entered Tzinacantan (Chiapas),
> this place had still not been conquered,
> (the merchants) who were Aztecs, were not discovered,
> they were disguised. . . .
> They learned the way of speaking
> (of the people of Tzinacantan),
> they entered incognito,
> so that no one knew they were Aztecs. . . .
> There in *Tzinacantan* is found
> amber and the long quetzal feathers. . . .
> Also the red tiger skins. . . .
> The merchants in disguise
> found out for the first time
> all that the region produces. . . .[13]

Upon their return to Mexico-Tenochtitlan the merchants were the ones who reported to the nobles and rulers on how these rich lands could be conquered. Thus their role as spies made it possible for the Aztec armies to march south and take over these regions. The merchants were also the ones who suggested the form of government

---

[12] Texts of the Informants of Sahagún, *op. cit.,* fol. 31 r. and v.
[13] *Ibid.,* fol. 32 r.

organization necessary to assure full economic control of Xoconusco and other provinces.

On certain days the merchants held great fairs to display products from the Pacific Coast, from the Gulf, and from many other intermediate regions. There they fixed the price of the products, established the units of exchange, and prevented any disturbance. As is noted in another text of the Florentine Codex:

> They had charge of the market,
> of all the merchandise,
> for the good of the people in general,
> of the people from many villages,
> of the orphans, of the poor,
> so they would not be cheated,
> so they would not have difficulties,
> so they would not be slighted.
> That which was bought and sold
> was put into order,
> the various things were sold separately,
> merchandise was not mixed together.
> They elected their market supervisors,
> they took much care in ruling the market,
> the various merchandise which was there.
> The supervisors took care of everything,
> they saw that no one deceived anyone else,
> the way in which prices were given,
> the way in which merchandise was sold.[14]

CONTRACTS AND MONETARY SYMBOLS

We have already mentioned some of the forms of contract that existed in ancient Mexico. With respect to organized business, the formation of the guilds obviously implies an early type of organizational contract. We know from the native texts that before undertaking their business expeditions the merchants pooled their efforts and capital in pursuit of their common commercial objective. According to one Aztec account, the old merchants and even some women frequently had the traders act as commission agents for them, giving them articles to barter or some of the existing monetary symbols with which to acquire products from other regions.

The small mantles that King Ahuítzotl delivered for trading

---

[14] Charles E. Dibble and Arthur J. O. Anderson (eds.), *Florentine Codex* (Santa Fe, N.M., 1958), Book VIII, p. 67.

purposes were called *coachtli* in Aztec. There were, in fact, mantles of varying sizes, and their value was symbolic, since they were considered to be backed by the wealth and authority of the supreme Aztec ruler. Frequent mention is made in the texts of the price of some articles in terms of a certain number of mantles, or *coachtlis*. Thus, for example, it is said that "the price for a canoe of water was a *tencoachtli*"—a small mantle, approximately the size of a handkerchief.

The same account, transmitted by the native informants of Fray Bernardino de Sahagún, gives the equivalent of these small mantles in relation to the other monetary symbol, cacao beans: ". . . each *tencoachtli* had as a price 100 cacao beans. . . . There was another *tencoachtli* which was valued at 80 cacao beans. The series was completed by a *tencoachtli* (smaller) which was worth 65 cacao beans."[15] As is pointed out by Dr. Angel Ma. Garibay K., in his book *Economic Life of Tenochtitlan*, "a basis for calculating cost of living is given to us in the price paid for a canoe full of drinking water, taken to the buyer's door, which was generally 100 cacao beans or one *tencoachtli*, equivalent to this many beans."[16]

The cacao beans used as a monetary symbol were different from those used in the preparation of drinks. Ordinarily, they were defective seeds, which had no other use than that of serving as a symbol. According to the native documents, small packages of seeds were equal to a certain number of *coachtlis*, or mantles. There were two other monetary symbols in ancient Mexico: gold nuggets or dust contained in small tubes made of goose quills, which, since they were transparent, allowed the metal to be seen. The other form, which is perhaps closer to metallic coins, consisted of small T-shaped copper pieces used to acquire objects of little value.

Of all these monetary symbols, the one that shows the greatest economic development is without doubt the *coachtli*, or small mantle, a true forerunner of the modern bill. By making use of these monetary symbols, the ancient Mexicans could execute forms of contract other than the commission contracts previously described.

The simplest form of sales contract was always executed in the markets, in accordance with the fixed prices, and guaranteed the

---

15 Texts of the Informants of Sahagún, *op. cit.*, fol. 32 r. and v.

16 Angel Ma. Garibay K., *Vida Económica de Tenochtitlán, Los Pochtecas* (Mexico: Seminario de Cultura Náhautl de la Universidad Nacional de México, 1961) , Appendix I.

quality of the products that were being sold. In fact, there were very severe penalties for those who sold a defective product or altered the quality or the price of it.

There were also trust contracts to guarantee fulfillment of some obligation or pledge, particularly those used as a complement to certain sales contracts. Finally, the native text that describes the appearance and functions of the *pochtecas,* or merchants, shows that loan contracts also existed, including in some cases an interest charge, since the debtor had to pay a sum somewhat greater than that which he had received as a loan.

Since such contract forms necessarily required monetary symbols, they made possible the development of commerce as a cultural institution on a grand scale. Thanks to this, the merchant guilds could develop their most obvious function of making a profit and cooperating in the general prosperity. But they were also able to assume true social responsibility and participate directly in the political life of the Aztec nation.

FUNCTIONS OF PRE-HISPANIC BUSINESS

PERSONAL PROFITS

The pre-Columbian merchant is always characterized in the texts as a rich man, who accumulated and husbanded the fruits of his labor. It was precisely for this reason that the merchants were able to achieve a status equal to that of the nobles and win a form of prestige until then unknown. Their wealth enabled them to acquire production goods, such as land in individual ownership. Above all, it permitted them to increase constantly their mercantile activities.

Nevertheless, this enriching of the guilds and of their merchant members raised various problems. Some of the nobles began to envy the merchants' position and to fear their possible domination. The texts refer to several occasions on which merchants were accused of some lack of honor or of disloyalty to rulers so that they could be deprived of their fortunes, which then reverted to the state.

But the merchants of ancient Mexico found an answer to such threats to their survival. To counteract the image of greed provoked by their riches, they used to declare that their property really belonged to the union and that they personally were poor. Thus, when a merchant arriving from Xoconusco was questioned concerning his riches, he said:

> In reality I have no property,
> what I have brought is the property
> of our mothers and fathers,
> of the merchants of Pochtlan and Oztoman.[17]

And later on in the same text we find the following comment on the merchant's words: "In this way they tried not to make themselves appear important, but rather to humiliate themselves, bowing heads and shoulders. They made no show of their possessions nor of their wealth. They always tried to wear the same clothing as the rest of the people."[18]

This attitude, common to the merchants of every era, sought to diminish the envy of the rest of the people. It is one more proof of the caution with which the merchants of ancient Mexico acted. Interested in accumulating large fortunes, they felt that, instead of making a great show of their wealth, their role should be that of servants of the people and of the nobility. The same feeling prompted them to undertake what we would today call various forms of social responsibility.

SOCIAL RESPONSIBILITY

Three principal forms of social responsibility were assumed by the pre-Hispanic merchants. First, they acted as promoters of culture. Because of them, as was stated in the afore-mentioned text, "the city was enriched, and the Aztec people," principally by such products as cotton, quetzal feathers, and precious metals, which permitted a better way of life. The tributes they paid to the state in the form of merchandise permitted more impressive religious and public celebrations.

The merchants also furthered cultural development by disseminating many of the techniques of the artisans of various regions. It was owing to the merchants of Toltec times (10th century A.D.) that the art of working metals, among other things, was introduced to the central region of Mexico.

The second responsibility assumed by the merchants was directly related to the state. As was seen in the case of King Ahuítzotl, merchants were in charge of the royal trade, which they carried out on direct commission from the rulers of Mexico-Tenochtitlan. Bet-

---

[17] Texts of the Informants of Sahagún, *op. cit.*, fol. 35 r.
[18] *Ibid.*

ter acquainted with the distant regions than any others, they were also charged with the duty of accompanying the armies and reporting on the possibilities of enlarging the domains of the Aztec nation. Such was the case of the Pacific Coast merchants, who, learning the language of that region and serving as spies, made possible the conquest of Xoconusco, with its abundance of cacao and other products.

The third form of social responsibility was linked with the Aztec population in general. The solemn banquets that the merchants organized for religious purposes were designed principally to entertain the members of the nobility and the general populace.

> The merchants prepared
> all they needed
> for the banquet. . . .
>
> They gathered everyone together there,
> their close relatives,
> the merchants' women,
> the slave merchants.
> Water was offered to them
> to wash their hands and mouth. . . .
> After having washed,
>
> the people were served food.
> Once the banquet was over,
> everyone washed
> their hands and mouth.
> Cacao was passed around
> in the form of a drink.
> Finally, everyone was given tobacco.[19]

The nobles and the people as a whole enjoyed themselves hugely at these banquets. They were, of course, grateful to the merchants for what they considered their generosity. By thus periodically sharing their prosperity with everyone, the traders established rapport with the rest of the community.

These forms of social responsibility contributed greatly to the prestige of the merchant guilds. It is worth repeating that just before the Conquest the merchants had become the most powerful social sector. One might even speculate that, if the Conquest had not occurred, they might have taken over the government of Mexico-Tenochtitlan. Certainly, there is no doubt that they had managed to

---

[19] *Ibid.,* fol. 28 r.

create an authentic cultural institution, an exceedingly important factor in the economic, social, political, and religious life of the Aztec world.

This brief discussion of the fundamental characteristics of the cultural institution of business in ancient Mexico will probably suggest similarities to business forms in other societies. But it should be emphasized that business in ancient Mexico reached its maximum development before the appearance of social classes had completely eradicated some elements of their ancient tribal organization.

Thus several of the characteristic traits of the pre-Hispanic merchant and artisan guilds can be understood only by remembering that their members joined together not so much by free association as by kinship ties. Even so, the gradual transformation of the Aztec nation can be seen in the fact that, in very special cases, new merchants who were not members of the same clan were admitted through a contract of association. To observe the emergence in ancient Mexico of the principles of law, justice, property, contracts, and monetary symbols should provide the student with some historical perspective on the conceptual foundations of business.

RECOMMENDED READING

CASO, ALFONSO. *The Aztecs: People of the Sun.* Norman: University of Oklahoma Press, 1958.

FLORENTINE CODEX, BOOK 9. *The Merchants,* Part X. Trans. from the Aztec into English by C. E. DIBBLE and A. J. O. ANDERSON. Santa Fe, N.M.: School of American Research and the University of Utah, 1959.

LEÓN-PORTILLA, MIGUEL. "The Concept of the State among the Aztecs," in *Alpha Kappa Deltan: A Sociological Journal,* Vol. XXX (Winter, 1960), pp. 7–13.

POLANYI, KARL; ARENSBERG, CONRAD M.; and PEARSON, HARRY W. (eds.). *Trade and Market in the Early Empires.* New York: The Free Press, 1957.

VAILLANT, GEORGE C. *The Aztecs of Mexico.* New York: Doubleday, Doran & Co., 1944. Republished by Pelican Books, 1950.

FURTHER READING

ACOSTA SAIGNES, MIGUEL. "Los Pochtecas," *Acta Antropológica,* Vol. I, No. 1 (1945).

BARLOW, ROBERT H. *The Extent of the Empire of the Culhua Mexica,* Vol. 28. Berkeley and Los Angeles: Ibero-Americana, 1949.

DÍAZ DEL CASTILLO, BERNAL. *The Discovery and Conquest of Mexico.* New York: Grove Press, Inc., 1958.

GARIBAY K., ANGEL MA. *Historia de la Literatura Náhuatl.* 2 vols. México: Editorial Porrúa, 1953–54.

————. *Vida Económica de Tenochtitlán, Los Pochtecas.* México: Seminario de Cultura Náhuatl de la Universidad Nacional, 1961.

KATZ, FRIEDRICH. *Die Sozialökonomischen Verhältnisse bei den Azteken im 15. und 16. Jahrhundert.* Berlin: Ethnographisch-Archäologische Forschungen, 3, 1956 teil 2.

LEÓN-PORTILLA, MIGUEL. *The Mind of Ancient Mexico.* Norman: University of Oklahoma Press, 1961.

MONZÓN, ARTURO. *El Calpulli en la Organización Social de los Tenochca.* México: Instituto de Historia, 1949.

SÉJOURNÉ, LAURETTE. *Burning Water: Thought and Religion in Ancient Mexico.* London: Thames and Hudson, 1956.

SOUSTELLE, JACQUES. *La Vie quotidienne des Aztèques.* Paris: Librairie Hachette, 1955.

INDEX

Index

*This book has been set in 11 and 10 point
Baskerville, leaded 2 points. Part numbers
and titles are in 16 point Bulmer italic;
chapter numbers and titles in 18 point
Bulmer italic. The size of the type page is
27 x 45 picas.*